HUMAN GEOGRAPHY

Places and Regions in Global Context

FOURTH CANADIAN EDITION

PAUL L. KNOX
VIRGINIA TECH

SALLIE A. MARSTON
UNIVERSITY OF ARIZONA

MICHAEL IMORT
WILFRID LAURIER UNIVERSITY

ALAN E. NASH
CONCORDIA UNIVERSITY

PEARSON

Toronto

Vice-President, Editorial Director: Gary Bennett
Executive Acquisitions Editor: Cathleen Sullivan
Sponsoring Editor: Kathleen McGill
Senior Marketing Manager: Kim Ukrainec
Developmental Editor: Paul Donnelly
Project Managers: Sarah Lukaweski,
  Rachel Thompson
Manufacturing Coordinator: Susan Johnson
Production Editor: Jared Sterzer

Copy Editor: Nicole Schlutt
Proofreader: PreMediaGlobal
Compositor: PreMediaGlobal
Photo & Permissions Researcher: Debbie Henderson
Art Director: Julia Hall
Cover Designer: Julia Hall
Interior Designer: Julia Hall
Cover Image: Getty Images

Environmental Statement
This book is carefully crafted to minimize environmental impact. Pearson Canada is proud to report that the materials used to manufacture this book originated from sources committed to sustainable forestry practices, tree harvesting, and associated land management. The binding, cover, and paper come from facilities that minimize waste, energy usage, and the use of harmful chemicals.

Equally important, Pearson Canada closes the loop by recycling every out-of-date text returned to our warehouse. We pulp the books, and the pulp is used to produce other items such as paper coffee cups or shopping bags.

The future holds great promise for reducing our impact on Earth's environment, and Pearson Canada is proud to be leading the way in this initiative. From production of the book to putting a copy in your hands, we strive to publish the best books with the most up-to-date and accurate content, and to do so in ways that minimize our impact on Earth.

Library and Archives Canada Cataloguing in Publication
     Human geography : places and regions in global context / Paul L.
Knox ... [et al.]. — 4th Canadian ed.

Includes index.
ISBN 978-0-321-74729-7

     1. Human geography—Textbooks.   I. Knox, Paul L.

GF41.K56 2012   304.2   C2011-905484-1

ISBN-13 978-0-321-74729-7

Brief Contents

Contents

CHAPTER 3   Geographies of Population   96

CHAPTER 11   City Spaces: Urban Structure   480

CHAPTER 12   Future Geographies   524

Preface

With this fourth Canadian Edition, the book you are holding in your hands is passing into the care of a new author. Material is changed, statistics are updated, and emphasis is placed on new aspects, but the message of the book remains the same: you and I are living in a world that is changing faster than ever before, and much of that change is driven by (and in turn drives) a process called globalization. How will your future job be affected by globalization? What role will your country play in the global competition for power, wealth, and security? Will we have enough resources for a growing global population? Are we living in the 'Chinese Century'? To answer these and similar questions, you can do no better than to start with a solid understanding of the tools and concepts geographers use to discuss, research, and ultimately affect the world.

This book introduces you to human geography: the study of how people and places interact. The idea for this book evolved from conversations between the authors and colleagues about how to teach human geography in colleges and universities. Our intent was to find a way not only to capture the exciting and troubling changes that are rewriting the world's landscapes and reorganizing the spatial relationships between people, but also to convincingly demonstrate why the study of geography matters. Our aim was to show why a geographical imagination is important, how it can lead to an understanding of the world and its constituent places and regions, and how it has practical relevance in many realms of life.

The fourth edition interprets these aims from a Canadian perspective by showing the relevance of a geographical imagination constituted in Canadian terms, and how a clearer understanding of geography is essential to comprehend not only the effects of global change on Canada but also this country's role in the world.

Objective and Approach

The objective of the book is to introduce the study of human geography by presenting not only a body of knowledge about the creation of places and regions but also fostering an understanding of the interdependence of places and regions in a globalizing world. More precisely, we hope that you recognize the daily interconnections between your own life and the lives of people in other parts of the world.

The book takes a fresh approach to human geography, reflecting the major changes that have recently been impressed on global, regional, and local landscapes. These changes include the globalization of industry, the rise of China and India, the upwelling of ethnic regionalisms on the heels of decolonization and the formation of new states, the rapid urbanization of the periphery and the physical restructuring of cities, the transformation of traditional agricultural practices, the trend toward transnational political and economic organizations, and the dramatic advances in information and communication technologies. *Human Geography: Places and Regions in Global Context* introduces the many new ideas, concepts, and theories that address these changes while also teaching the fundamentals of human geography: the principles, concepts, theoretical frameworks, and basic knowledge that are necessary to more specialized studies.

The most distinctive feature of this approach is that it emphasizes the interdependence of places and processes at different geographical scales. In overall terms, this approach is designed to provide an understanding of relationships between the global and the local and the outcomes of these relationships. It follows that one of the chief organizing principles is how globalization frames the social and cultural construction of particular places and regions at various scales.

This approach has several advantages:

- It captures aspects of human geography that are among the most compelling in the contemporary world—the geographical bases of cultural diversity and their impacts on everyday life, for example.

- It encompasses the salient aspects of new emphases in academic human geography—geography's new focus on the social construction of spaces and places, for example.

- It makes for an easier connection between topical and regional material by emphasizing how processes link them—technological innovation and the varying ways in which technology is adopted and modified by people in particular places, for example.

- It facilitates meaningful comparisons between places in different parts of the world—how the core-generated industrialization of agriculture shapes gender relations in households both in the core and the periphery, for example.

In short, this textbook is designed to focus on geographical processes and to provide an understanding of the interdependence among places and regions without losing sight of their individuality and uniqueness.

Several important themes are woven into each chapter, integrating them into the overall approach:

- The relationships between global processes and their local manifestations

- The interdependence of people and places, especially the interactive relationships between core regions and peripheral regions

- The continuing transformation of the political economy of the world-system, and of nations, regions, cities, and localities

- The social and cultural differences that are embedded in human geographies (especially the differences that relate to ethnicity, gender, age, and class)

The Development of the Text

Adapting *Human Geography: Places and Regions in Global Context* for the Canadian audience provided, in his own words, "both an exciting opportunity and a formidable challenge" for the first Canadian author, Alan Nash from Concordia University. As the new Canadian author, I am honoured to continue Alan's outstanding work and I am thankful for the foundation he built. While I have been involved in the Canadian adaptation from the very beginning in various capacities, taking over the sole responsibility for the book has taught me how true those words were and continue to be. To quote Alan once again: "The opportunity was to make the book's exposition of the major themes of modern human geography more relevant to the Canadian reader. The challenge was to do this without sacrificing the general approach, insight, and clarity of the original American text."

From the outset, it was clear that any worthwhile adaptation involved more than simply replacing a number of American examples with Canadian illustrations (for example, replacing Denver with Winnipeg, or Seattle with Vancouver). The reasons for this are obvious enough, but two can be highlighted here. First, since European contact, the country that we now call Canada has been developed according to a very different geographical set of principles than our neighbour to the south. This country's spatial economy, articulated to facilitate the export of staple commodities, has produced a geography of heartland–hinterland dependencies that contrast with ones developed in the United States on the basis of local manufacture for a large domestic market. Second, because Canada's population is made up of a far greater proportion of recent immigrants from a wider range of countries than is the population of the United States, it can be argued that Canada's interest in world affairs is of a far different nature. Many Canadians, for example, view the geographic processes of globalization through the prism of their local connections with other parts of the world—and not, as in an American case, from the geopolitical perspective of a superpower.

Therefore, to make the book truly relevant for Canadians, it was felt that an adaptation must also address the major themes that are of importance

- in understanding this country's geography
- in looking at the world from a Canadian perspective
- in interpreting this country's role in global affairs

Thus, for the first Canadian edition, the entire text of *Human Geography: Places and Regions in Global Context* was extensively revised to meet the goals of adaptation. Subsequent editions built on that foundation, adding new topics and updating examples where necessary.

Under the new authorship, the fourth Canadian edition has been substantially revised. At the same time, material has been cut or condensed to allow for the integration of the following new or expanded topics without increasing the overall length of the book:

- The importance of a geographic education for future employment (Chapter 1)
- Geographical scales from the body to the world region (Chapter 1)
- Perspectives on globalization and interdependence: hyperglobalists, sceptics, and transformationalists (Chapter 1)
- Worlds Apart: comparing life in Switzerland and Ethiopia (Chapter 1)
- Key issues in a globalizing world: environment, health, security, and the production of risk (Chapter 1)
- Absolute, relative, and cognitive space (Chapter 1)
- Understanding the world as a system (Chapter 2)
- BRIC(S) countries (Chapter 2)
- Long distance trade and its effect on the English language (Chapter 2)
- Technology systems and geographic change (Chapter 2)
- Geography and exploration (Chapter 2)
- Technology and the early integration of the global periphery (Chapter 2)
- Colonization and decolonization in Africa (Chapter 2)
- Neocolonialism, transnational corporations, and early globalization (Chapter 2)
- Contemporary globalization (Chapter 2)
- The homogenization of consumer markets (Chapter 2)
- Opposition to globalization (Chapter 2)
- Administrative record linkage (Chapter 3)
- Environmental refugees (Chapter 3)
- Environmentalism and surges in resource consumption since 1970 (Chapter 4)
- Differences in affluence within China (Chapter 4)
- The rise of renewable energy sources (Chapter 4)
- The culture of hip-hop (Chapter 5)
- The effect of Facebook and social media on culture (Chapter 5)
- Cultural systems (Chapter 5)
- Landscapes of suburbia (Chapter 6)
- Cell phones and personal space (Chapter 6)
- Place marketing: Niagara Falls (Chapter 6)
- Postindustrial and lifestyle redevelopments (Chapter 6)
- The cultural geography of cyberspace (Chapter 6)

- Restaurants as places and objects of consumption (Chapter 6)
- Women and children as victims of uneven development (Chapter 7)
- China's economic development (Chapter 7)
- Technological change and key resources: cultivable land, energy, and minerals (Chapter 7)
- Globalization and the shift in economic activities (Chapter 7)
- Critiques of development (Chapter 7)
- Dependency theory (Chapter 7)
- International trade, debt, and aid (Chapter 7)
- Commodity chains (Chapter 7)
- Flexible production and neo-Fordism (Chapter 7)
- Big-box retailing, chains, and global sourcing (Chapter 7)
- Walmart's economic landscape (Chapter 7)
- The global office (Chapter 7)
- Globalization of the tourist industry (Chapter 7)
- The Green Revolution (Chapter 8)
- Biotechnology and agriculture (Chapter 8)
- The new geography of food and agriculture in New Zealand (Chapter 8)
- Food regimes and alternative food movements (Chapter 8)
- The new world order and the increase in terrorism (Chapter 9)
- Afghanistan: from the cold war to the new world order (Chapter 9)
- State terrorism in Chechnya (Chapter 9)
- Globalization and transnational governance: the end of the state? (Chapter 9)
- The Palestinian-Israeli conflict (Chapter 9)
- The Pearl River delta: an extended metropolis (Chapter 10)
- Globalization and splintering urbanism (Chapter 10)
- European cities (Chapter 11)
- Islamic cities (Chapter 11)
- Shock city of the semiperiphery: Dubai (Chapter 11)
- Shock city of the periphery: Lagos, Nigeria (Chapter 11)
- The informal sector in peripheral cities (Chapter 11)
- Life in a Mega-Slum (Chapter 11)
- The 2020 global landscape: relative certainties and key uncertainties (Chapter 12)
- Uneven development: the elites, the embattled, and the marginalized (Chapter 12)
- China as a contender for global hegemony (Chapter 12)
- Security and sustainability (Chapter 12)
- The Asian brown cloud (Chapter 12)

The fourth Canadian edition also introduces a new feature called "Geography in the Information Age," which highlights the many effects of the new information and communications technologies on geography at all scales.

I am grateful to Dr. K. Bruce Newbold, professor of geography at the School of Geographical and Environmental Sciences at McMaster University in Hamilton, Ontario, and director of the McMaster Institute of Environment and Health (MIEH), for updating his six short essays on "Human Geography and Climate Change." First introduced in the third edition, these essays examine various aspects of climate change and may be read as "stand-alone" pieces, or as integral parts of the chapters in which they are located:

- Human Geography and Climate Change: Population Displacement (Chapter 3)
- Human Geography and Climate Change: Population and Health (Chapter 3)
- Human Geography and Climate Change: Energy (Chapter 4)
- Human Geography and Climate Change: Legislating for Climate Change: Kyoto, Cancun, and Onward (Chapter 4)
- Human Geography and Climate Change: Agriculture (Chapter 8)
- Human Geography and Climate Change: Climate Change and Social Action (Chapter 12)

The pedagogical structure of the text is unchanged since experience with previous editions has been very positive. The beginning of each chapter features a section on the main points, including those of relevance to a Canadian audience, that will be covered in the chapters. These main points are revisited and enlarged at the end of each chapter to reinforce the most important points and themes from each chapter. All of the end-of-chapter exercises have been designed for Canadian students, and the website has been specially created for a Canadian audience. Lastly, each chapter includes Canadian material in its list of suggested further readings.

Chapter Organization

The organization of the book is innovative in several ways. First, the chapters are organized in such a way that the conceptual framework—why geography matters in a globalizing world—is laid out in Chapters 1 and 2 and then deployed in thematic chapters (Chapters 3 through 11). The concluding chapter, Chapter 12, provides a coherent summary of the main points of the text by showing how future geographies may unfold, given what is known about present geographical processes and trends. Second, the conceptual framework of the book builds on two introductory chapters rather than the usual one. The first describes the basics of a geographic perspective; the second explains the value of the globalization approach.

Third, the distinctive chapter ordering within the book follows the logic of moving from less complex to more complex systems of human social and economic organization, always highlighting the interaction between people and the world around them. The first thematic chapter (Chapter 3) focuses on human population. Its early placement in the book reflects the central importance of people in understanding geography. Chapter 4 deals with the relationship between people and the environment as it is mediated by technology. This chapter capitalizes on the growing interest in environmental problems and develops a central theme: all human geographical issues are about how people negotiate their environment—whether the natural or the built environment.

The six boxes by Dr. Newbold that examine the theme of climate change are interspersed throughout the volume in order to emphasize the fact that this issue intersects with all other concerns discussed in this textbook.

The chapter on nature, society, and technology is followed by Chapter 5 on cultural geography. The intention in positioning the cultural chapter here is to signal that culture is the primary medium through which people operate and understand their place in the world. In Chapter 6, the impact of cultural processes on the landscape is explored, together with the ways in which landscape shapes cultural processes.

In Chapter 7, the book begins to move toward more complex concepts and systems of human organization by concentrating on economic development. The focus of Chapter 8 is agriculture. The placement of agriculture after economic development reflects the overall emphasis on globalization. This chapter shows how processes of globalization and economic development have led to the industrialization of agriculture at the expense of more traditional agricultural systems and practices.

The final three thematic chapters cover political geography (Chapter 9), urbanization (Chapter 10), and city structure (Chapter 11). Devoting two chapters to urban geography, rather than a more conventional single chapter, is an important indication of how globalization increasingly leads to the rapid urbanization of the world's people and places. The final chapter, on future geographies (Chapter 12), gives a sense of how a geographic perspective might be applied to the problems and opportunities to be faced in the twenty-first century.

Features

The book employs four different boxed features, as well as more familiar pedagogical devices such as chapter overviews and end-of-chapter exercises:

"Geography Matters" boxes examine one of the key concepts of the chapter, providing an extended example of its meaning and implications through both visual illustration and text. The Geography Matters features demonstrate to students that the focus of human geography is on real-world problems.

"Visualizing Geography" boxes highlight key concepts of the chapter with a photographic essay. This feature helps students recognize that the visual landscape contains readily accessible evidence about the impact of globalization on people and places.

"Human Geography and Climate Change" boxes focus on different aspects of the general challenge of climate change and relate them to the specific concerns of the chapter. These features help students realize that environmental change connects with almost all of the topics discussed in the chapters of the textbook, that issues of environmental concern affect various aspects of our daily lives, and that individual actions can indeed shape the global environment.

The new **"Geography in the Information Age"** boxes are brief vignettes that highlight how the new information and communications technologies are changing geography at all scales.

Also new to this edition is **Study on the Go**. This free, downloadable app enables students to link to Pearson Canada's unique Study on the Go content directly from their smartphones, allowing them to study whenever and wherever they wish. Upon scanning the QR code, students can follow the online instructions to search the rich study tools, including Glossary Flashcards and Quizzes.

Pedagogical Structure within Chapters: Each chapter opens with a brief real-life vignette that introduces the theme of the chapter and illustrates why a geographical approach is important. A list of the Main Points that will be covered in the chapter follows this vignette. Throughout each chapter, key terms are printed in boldface as they are introduced, with capsule definitions of the term in the margin of the same page. These key terms are listed alphabetically, together with their location in the text, at the end of the chapter, and are compiled in the Glossary at the end of the text. Figures with extensive captions are provided to integrate illustration with text.

At the end of each chapter, there are five useful devices to help students review. First comes a chapter Conclusion that summarizes the overarching themes and concepts of the chapter. Next the Main Points of the chapter are listed again, but this time they are expanded to include a summary of the text discussion of each Main Point. Then there is a comprehensive list of Key Terms for the chapter, followed by a number of suggested Additional Readings on the topic of the chapter. Each chapter concludes with a set of Discussion Questions and Research Activities that require students to put into practice several of the key concepts of a chapter. Finally, students are referred to the premium website at **www.mygeoscienceplace.ca** to find chapter review quizzes, videos, maps, and much more.

On the premium website, students will find two exciting media features. Five thought-provoking CBC video segments with accompanying cases offer students an opportunity to engage more deeply with certain aspects of Chapters 2, 3, 5, 8, and 11. Students will also be able to listen to audio interviews Alan Nash has conducted with four prominent Canadian human geographers. Interviews accompany Chapters 1, 4, 7, 10, and 12.

Supplements

The book includes a complete supplements program for both students and instructors.

For the Student

NEW MYGEOSCIENCEPLACE with Pearson eText prepared by Cherie Mongeon of Wilfrid Laurier University. Each new copy of *Human Geography*, fourth Canadian edition, comes with a Student Access Code for MyGeosciencePlace. This new premium website has been designed to provide students with useful tools needed for online study and review.

Features include:

- Self-study quizzes, tests, and exercises: These will help students expand their understanding of human geography.
- CBC videos
- Audio interviews with human geographers
- MapMaster Interactive Maps
- Pearson eText
- And more!

Pearson eText gives students access to the text whenever and wherever they have access to the Internet. eText pages look exactly like the printed text, offering powerful new functionality for students and instructors. Users can create notes, highlight text in different colours, create bookmarks, zoom, click hyperlinked words and phrases to view definitions, and view in single-page or two-page view. Pearson eText allows for quick navigation to key parts of the eText using a table of contents and provides full-text search. The eText may also offer links to associated media files, enabling users to access videos, animations, or other activities as they read the text.

CBC Videos: For Chapter 2, watch the CBC video, *India: Myth and Might*, which highlights aspects of the world-system theory by illustrating how India is struggling to transform itself from a peripheral to a semiperipheral country—and, in certain respects, even a core country.

For Chapter 3, watch the CBC video, *Dying for Doctors—South African Doctors*, which highlights some of the cultural and economic issues of emigration and immigration.

For Chapter 5, watch the CBC video, *Inuktitut Survival*, which highlights some of the cultural and political issues of language use, decline, and retention.

For Chapter 8, watch the CBC video, *Made in Canada*, which highlights some of the issues around the production, safety, and environmental impact of food.

For Chapter 11, watch the CBC video, *Big Thirst*, which highlights some of the challenges of environmental change for cities discussed in this chapter, particularly how the predicted decline of water supplies in the Prairies will affect both the urban and rural inhabitants of that region within the next 20 years.

You can access our premium website by visiting us at **www.mygeoscienceplace. ca**—a 24/7 personal study portal. Our site provides an excellent platform from which to start using the Internet for the study of human geography. You will need the access code that has been packaged with your copy of the text to register and log on.

For the Instructor

All the supplements that instructors need to teach and test their students can be downloaded from Pearson Canada's Instructor Resources Centre. They are also available in one easy-to-access Instructor's Resource CD-ROM (IRCD). Instructors can view the supplement on their computers or print them out.

The following resources are available:

Instructor's Resource Manual: Prepared by Lisa Sonnenburg of McMaster University, the Instructor's Resource Manual, intended as a resource for both new and experienced teachers, includes a variety of lecture outlines, additional source materials, teaching tips, advice on how to integrate visual supplements, answers to the end-of-chapter exercises, and various other ideas for the classroom.

Activities Manual: Prepared by Cherie Mongeon of Wilfrid Laurier University, this manual contains 20 different activities, tailored to the needs of individual chapters. Each activity identifies concepts to be learned and includes instructor's notes and assessment options.

Computerized Test Item File: Prepared by Mark Troy Burnett of Mount Royal University, this test bank contains approximately 1,400 questions of different types (multiple choice, short-answer, graphing, and scenario-based). Available in both MS Word and TestGen formats. We identify a suggested answer, an associated learning objective, and a difficulty level of easy, moderate, or difficult for all questions. The Pearson TestGen is compatible with IBM or MacIntosh systems.

PowerPoint® Lecture Slides: Prepared by Michele Wiens of the University of British Columbia, the PowerPoint lecture slides include selected illustrations, maps, figures, and tables from the text.

Image Library: The Image Library includes many of the illustrations, maps, figures, and tables from the text.

CBC Videos: A one-hour and forty minute video has been prepared to support this textbook. It features extracts from five CBC programs that examine the emergence of India as a superpower, the emigration of South African doctors to northern British Columbia, the future of Inuktitut as a living language, the real source of foods labelled "Made in Canada," and the problems of future water shortages in the cities and farms of the Prairies. Of relevance to Chapters 2, 3, 5, 8, 11, respectively, each video extract is supported by a video summary, study questions, and list of further resources, available on MyGeosciencPlace.

Study on the Go

Featured at the end of each chapter, you will find a unique barcode providing access to Study on the Go, an unprecedented mobile integration between text and online content. Students link to Pearson's unique Study on the Go content directly from their smartphones, allowing them to study whenever and wherever they wish! Go to one of the sites below to see how you can download an app to your smartphone for free. Once the app is installed, your phone will scan the code and link to a website containing Pearson's Study on the Go content, including the popular study tools Glossary Flashcards, and Quizzes, which can be accessed anytime.

ScanLife
http://getscanlife.com/

NeoReader
http://get.neoreader.com/

QuickMark
http://www.quickmark.com.tw/

CourseSmart

CourseSmart goes beyond traditional expectations–providing instant, online access to the textbooks and course materials you need at a lower cost for students. And even as students save money, you can save time and hassle with a digital eTextbook that allows you to search for the most relevant content at the very moment you need it. Whether it's evaluating textbooks or creating lecture notes to help students with difficult concepts, CourseSmart can make life a little easier. For more information, visit www.coursesmart.com.

Technology Specialists

Pearson's Technology Specialists work with faculty and campus course designers to ensure that Pearson technology products, assessment tools, and online course materials are tailored to meet your specific needs. This highly qualified team is dedicated to helping colleges and universities take full advantage of a wide range of educational resources, by assisting in the integration of a variety of instructional materials and media formats. Your local Pearson Education sales representative can provide you with more details on this service program.

Pearson Custom Library

For enrollments of at least 25 students, you can create your own textbook by choosing the chapters that best suit your own course needs. *To begin building your custom text, visit www.pearsoncustomlibrary.com.* You may also work with a dedicated Pearson Custom editor to create your ideal text—publishing your own original content or mixing and matching Pearson content. *Contact your local Pearson Representative to get started.*

Acknowledgments

I am indebted to the following professors for their assistance, advice, and constructive criticism in the course of preparing this adaptation:

James Abbott
Nipissing University

Ken Brooks
Conestoga College

William Carlyle
University of Winnipeg

Conny Davidsen
University of Calgary

Bernard Momer
UBC Okanagan

Mark Troy Burnett
Mount Royal University

Brent Doberstein
University of Waterloo

Kim Naqvi
Thompson Rivers University

Sasha Kebo
University of Ottawa

Raj Navaratnam
Red Deer College

Katrina Erdos
Langara College

Michele Wiens
University of British Columbia

Similarly, I am grateful to the thousands of undergraduate students who unknowingly tested the materials included in this adaptation.

I would like to thank Pearson Canada for its continuing commitment to this project, and especially the Toronto office team of Cathleen Sullivan (Executive Acquisitions Editor), Paul Donnelly (Developmental Editor), Sarah Lukaweski (Project Manager), and Nicole Schutt (Copy Editor), as well as Jared Sterzer (PMG Production Editor) for all of their help and support. A special Thank-you goes to Paul McInnis, who was the first to see the potential; and to Kathleen McGill (Sponsoring Editor), who trusted me to realize it.

It is a privilege to record here my indebtedness to the many people who have helped me with advice, information, understanding, and support. In particular, I thank my colleagues in the Department of Geography and Environmental Studies at Wilfrid Laurier University: Mary-Louise Byrne, Doreen Dassen, Jim Hamilton, Jo-Anne Horton, Cherie Mongeon, and Bob Sharpe. The team in the Dean of Arts Office and especially the indomitable Julie Pong made sure that every day was filled with camaraderie and laughter—they did not know it, but in their own way they were writing this book, too.

Many able minds have tried to polish the rough diamond of my own geographical imagination. It all started in high school with Werner Wallert, who made me realize that everything is geography; and that geography is everything. At Brock University, Alun Hughes introduced me to the joys of methodical learning by doing. At Queen's University, I found magnificent role models that sustain me to this day: Peter Goheen, Brian Osborne, and most of all Anne Godlewska. Thank you for your trust, your patience, and your challenges. If I am a geographer at all, you have made me one.

This fourth Canadian edition is dedicated to Maggie, who keeps me smiling; my mother, who keeps dancing; and Cathie, who keeps me in her heart. It is from her that I stole many of the hours it took to conceive and produce what you are now holding in your hands. Thank you.

Michael Imort

About the Authors

Paul L. Knox

Paul Knox received his Ph.D. in Geography from the University of Sheffield, England. In 1985, after teaching in the United Kingdom for several years, he moved to the United States to take up a position as professor of urban affairs and planning at Virginia Tech. His teaching centres on urban and regional development, with an emphasis on comparative study. In 1989, he received a university award for teaching excellence. He has written several books on aspects of economic geography, social geography, and urbanization. He serves on the editorial board of several scientific journals and is co-editor on a series of books on World Cities. In 1996, he was appointed to the position of University Distinguished Professor at Virginia Tech, where he currently serves as dean of the College of Architecture and Urban Studies.

Sallie A. Marston

Sallie Marston received her Ph.D. in Geography from the University of Colorado, Boulder. She has been a faculty member at the University of Arizona since 1986. Her teaching focuses on the historical, social, and cultural aspects of American urbanization, with particular emphasis on race, class, gender, and ethnicity issues. She received the College of Social and Behavioral Sciences Outstanding Teaching Award in 1989. She is the author of numerous journal articles and book chapters and serves on the editorial board of several scientific journals. In 1994 and 1995, she served as Interim Director of Women's Studies and the Southwest Institute for Research on Women. She is currently a professor in, and serves as head of, the Department of Geography and Regional Development.

Michael Imort

Michael Imort received his PhD from Queen's University in Kingston, Ontario. Ever the geographer, he took the long way to get there, studying at Brock, York, Waterloo and Freiburg, Germany, with stints in the Arctic, Hawaii, Mali, and Zaire (now DRC), and a teaching appointment in an English castle—not to mention the days when he worked as a lumberjack or ran a bookstore. When the time came to get serious, he joined the Department of Geography and Environmental Studies at Wilfrid Laurier University, where he currently is the Associate Dean of Arts. Originally trained as a forest scientist with an interest in fire ecology, he soon became interested in the human side of environmental problems. Today his research interests include environmental thought and the many ways in which representations of landscape are used and abused for political purposes.

Alan E. Nash

Alan Nash received his Ph.D. in Geography from the University of Cambridge in England, and began his teaching career at the University of Sheffield. After moving to Canada in 1981, he taught at Queen's University, before becoming a research associate at the University of Western Ontario's Centre for Canadian Population Studies. From 1986 to 1989, he was a research associate at the Institute for Research on Public Policy in Ottawa. Since then, he has been a member of the Geography Department at Concordia University in Montreal, where he has served as Chair. His teaching focuses on human geography; his recent research activities and academic publications deal with the cultural geography of restaurants. From 2002 to 2005, he was Secretary-Treasurer of the Canadian Association of Geographers.

List of Maps

List of Special Elements

Geography Matters

Visualizing Geography

Human Geography and Climate Change

Geography in the Information Age

HUMAN GEOGRAPHY

Places and Regions in Global Context

1

Geography Matters

Protest over the soaring cost of food, Jakarta, Indonesia, 2008.

In today's world, where places are increasingly interdependent, it is important to know something about human geography and to understand how places affect, and are affected by, one another. Consider, for example, some of the prominent news stories of recent years. In 2008, a major crisis shook banking and financial institutions around the world, accompanied by precipitous drops in stock markets. There were food riots in Burkina Faso, Cameroon, Mexico, Mozambique, Pakistan, and 25 other countries as soaring food prices squeezed almost half a billion people. The price of oil fluctuated sharply, reaching almost US$150 a barrel at one time. Meanwhile, Tata Group, India's biggest industrial conglomerate, acquired Jaguar and Land Rover from Ford and launched the world's cheapest car, the Tata Nano, for the burgeoning domestic market in India. While the wars in Iraq and Afghanistan were grinding on, they had long been bumped from the front pages by reports about the startling economic growth of China and India, concerns over the effects of global warming, and the threat of unemployment, bankruptcy, and foreclosures Canadian homeowners might face right here at home.

At first glance, these events are a mixture of achievements, disputes, and disasters that might seem to have little to do with geography, apart from their international scope. Look a little closer, though, and we find that they have geographical dimensions and that they are linked. The problem of food shortages in many countries, for example, was partly the result of increasing food consumption in other parts of the world, especially in booming China and India, where many have stopped growing their own food and now have the cash to buy a lot more of it. Increasing meat consumption helped drive up demand for feed grain, and this in turn drove up the price of bread everywhere. Sensing an opportunity for easy profit, speculators in international commodity markets hoarded grain, further accelerating price hikes.

Energy prices are another key linkage: the increase in oil prices (itself the result of the aftermath of Hurricane Katrina, China's ballooning hunger for energy, and fears over diminishing global oil reserves) pushed up fertilizer prices, as well as the cost of trucking food from farms to local markets and shipping it abroad. Meanwhile, in an attempt to reduce their dependence on oil and become more environmentally friendly, many industrialized countries started to pay subsidies for the production of biofuels from grain, soybeans, etc. As these subsidies lured farmers away from growing crops for food, the food supply was further strained: the grain needed to fill the tank of a car once could feed a person for an entire year!

Then there is climate change. In 2007–2008, harvests in many countries were seriously disrupted by extreme weather, including prolonged droughts in

Australia and southern Africa, floods in West Africa, an exceptionally deep and widespread frost in China, and record-breaking warmth in northern Europe. In short, we begin to see that food shortages are not just local events, but the result of the interaction of environmental, economic, and political factors in far-flung parts of the world.

Fast-forward to 2010. Different events are occurring in different places, but the mechanisms and interconnections remain the same: floods in Australia and drought in Russia cause wheat prices to double. At the same time, the EU pushes the use of more (plant-based) ethanol in its gasoline, lifting corn prices to new heights. By the end of the year, the UN food price index has risen by one-third, leaving many poor people unable to pay for bread and other staples. In early 2011, so-called bread revolts erupt across Northern Africa and the Middle East, quickly turning into regime-changing revolutions organized via Facebook and cell phones. With the oil-rich region in turmoil, concerns over the supply of oil push its price well above the US$100 mark again—making food even more expensive and starting yet another feedback loop.

Human geography can help us make sense of all of this. As we learn about the world by finding out *where* things are, *why* they are there, and *how* they affect things elsewhere, we begin to recognize and understand the many interconnections among places and regions. In this book, we will explore the tools and methods geographers use to study these interconnections and ultimately understand and explain the world. By the time you read this book, the events described above will be history already, but with the help of these tools and methods, you will be able to make sense of *your* world and the events and processes that are shaping it right now.

MAIN POINTS

- Geography matters because specific places provide the settings for people's daily lives. It is in these settings that important events happen, and it is from them that significant changes spread and diffuse.

- Places and regions are highly *interdependent,* each filling specialized roles in complex and ever-changing networks of interaction and change.

- Some of the most important aspects of the interdependence between geographical scales are provided by the relationships between the *global* and the *local.*

- Human geography provides ways of understanding places, regions, and spatial relationships as the products of a series of interrelated forces that stem from nature, culture, and individual human action.

- The first law of geography is that "everything is related to everything else, but near things are more related than are distant things."

- Distance is one aspect of this law, but connectivity is also important, because contact and interaction are dependent on channels of communication and transportation.

WHY PLACES MATTER

An appreciation of the diversity and variety of peoples and places is a theme that runs through the entire span of **human geography**, the study of the spatial organization of human activity and of people's relationships with their environments. This theme is inherently interesting to nearly all of us. Canadian magazines, such as *Canadian Geographic* or *Harrowsmith Country Life*, are popular because they draw on the wonder and endless fascination that Canadians have for this country (**Figure 1.1**). Yet, at the same time, many surveys show how little we really know about Canada or the world in general. In fact, a 2005 survey conducted by the Royal Canadian Geographic Society found that "about one-third of Canadian adults can be considered geographically illiterate"—and that the rate is even higher among Canadians aged 18 to 24.[1] How does this compare internationally? In a nine-country survey conducted by the National Geographic Society in 2002, Canada had the third-lowest level of geographic literacy, with only the United States and Mexico faring worse.[2]

So, although most people are fascinated by different places, relatively few have a systematic knowledge of them. Fewer still have an understanding of how different places came to be the way they are or why places matter in the broader scheme of things. This lack of understanding is problematic because geographic knowledge is more than a glimpse of the inherently interesting variety of peoples and places—it is quickly becoming an indispensable qualification for success in a globalizing world. Employers value employees with expertise in geographical analysis and an understanding of the uniqueness, influence, and interdependence of places (see **Geography Matters 1.1—The Importance of a Geographic Education**).

The importance of geography as a subject of study is thus becoming more widely recognized as people everywhere struggle to understand a world that is increasingly characterized by instant global communications, rapidly changing international relationships, unexpected local changes, and growing evidence of environmental degradation. As we try to negotiate our increasingly globalized lives, we face the task of learning about the world, and interpreting it for ourselves: each of us needs to be a geographer. The first step on this journey is to understand the basic geographic concept of "places."

human geography: the study of the spatial organization of human activity and of people's relationships with their environments

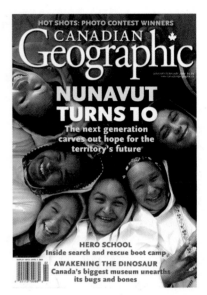

Figure 1.1 Geography's popularity *Canadian Geographic* magazine is available on newsstands across this country and is sent out across the world to many subscribers. Focusing on Canada, it deals with many geographical issues that affect Canada. Its popularity reflects Canadians' interest in the variety of landscapes and communities across this country.

1.1 | Geography in the Information Age

Geographical knowledge and technology are present (if not always visibly so) in almost every aspect of your life. Watch the trailer for the Geospatial Revolution Project launched by Penn State University to learn, in the words of one interviewee, how "ordinary" geography has become: **http://geospatialrevolution.psu .edu/trailer.php**.

[1] See the results at **www.ccge.org/programs/geoliteracy/docs/geoliteracy_survey_presentation.ppt**. You can take the 20-question survey yourself at **www.ccge.org/programs/geoliteracy/survey/q1.asp**.

[2] **www.nationalgeographic.com/geosurvey2002/index.html**.

The Importance of a Geographic Education

In Canada, a decade-long debate over the value of geographic education in a globalizing world has resulted in the realization that being literate in geography is essential in equipping Canadians to be competitive in the labour market, to appreciate the richness of life, and to participate responsibly in public affairs. The Canadian Council for Geographic Education has compiled the following "Top 10 Reasons to Study Geography."[3]

1. To understand basic physical systems that affect everyday life (e.g., earth–sun relationships, water cycles, wind, and ocean currents).
2. To learn the location of places and the physical and cultural characteristics of those places in order to function more effectively in our increasingly interdependent world.
3. To understand the geography of past times and how geography has played important roles in the evolution of people, their ideas, places, and environments.
4. To develop a mental map of your community, province or territory, country, and the world so that you can understand the "where" of places and events.
5. To explain how the processes of human and physical systems have arranged and sometimes changed the surface of the Earth.
6. To understand the spatial organization of society and see order in what often appears to be random scattering of people and places.
7. To recognize spatial distributions at all scales—local and worldwide—in order to understand the complex connectivity of people and places.
8. To be able to make sensible judgements about matters involving relationships between the physical environment and society.
9. To appreciate Earth as the homeland of humankind and provide insight for wise management decisions about how the planet's resources should be used.
10. To understand global interdependence and to become a better global citizen.

These reasons indicate that geography can help us understand the intrinsic nature of the world in which we live so that we can take better care of it. Geography also helps us understand each other by overcoming ignorance and prejudices about the way people live in other parts of the world. Finally, knowing one's geography simply means having an advantage over others in an increasingly competitive labour market.

Making a Difference: Geographers at Work

Geography, then, is very much an applied discipline as well as a means of understanding the world. Geographers employed in business, industry, and government are able to use geographic theories and techniques to understand and solve a wide variety of specific problems. A great deal of the research undertaken by geography professors also has an applied focus. As a result, geography is able to make a direct and significant contribution to society. Because of the broad nature of the field, these contributions cover every aspect of human activity and every scale from the local to the global. A number of examples reflect this:

- **International Affairs.** Geographers' knowledge and understanding of regional histories and geographies, along with their ability to analyze the interdependence of places and regions, enables them to effectively contribute to discussions of international policy. Geographers' work within governmental agencies, corporations, and nonprofit organizations in shaping international strategies is especially important in view of the accelerating process of globalization.
- **Location of Public Facilities.** Geographers use specialized techniques to analyze the location patterns of particular population groups, to analyze transportation networks, and to analyze patterns of geographic accessibility to alternative sites. Such analysis enables geographers to determine the most effective locations for new public facilities, such as transit terminals, public libraries, or emergency shelters.
- **Marketing and Location of Industry.** Similar techniques are used in determining the most efficient, or most profitable, location for new factories, stores, and offices. Geographical research is also used to analyze the changing geography of supply and demand, allowing industry to determine whether, and where, to relocate. Basic techniques of geographic analysis are also used in **geodemographic research**, an important aspect of marketing that targets specific groups.
- **Geography and the Law.** Geographical analysis can help resolve complex social and environmental issues. One important example is the issue of property development and the implications of environmental hazards such as flooding, coastal erosion, toxic waste dumps, and earthquake fault zones for policies, codes, and regulations affecting development. Another example is the task of maintaining geographical boundaries for electoral ridings to ensure equal representation as the population distribution changes. Finally, **Geographic Information Systems (GIS)** in particular have been successfully used in law enforcement, for example in identifying and predicting the mobility patterns of criminal offenders.

---

[3] www.ccge.org/.

- **Disease Ecology.** By analyzing social and environmental aspects of diseases, geographers are able to shed light on the causes of disease, to predict the spread of particular outbreaks, and to suggest ways in which the incidence of disease might be controlled.
- **Urban and Regional Planning.** Urban and regional planning adopts a systematic, creative approach to address and resolve physical, social, and economic problems of neighbourhoods, cities, suburbs, metropolitan areas, and larger regions. Planners work directly on preserving and enhancing the quality of life in communities, protecting the environment, promoting equitable economic opportunity, and managing growth and change of all kinds. Planning has roots in engineering, law, architecture, social welfare, and government, but geography, because of its focus on the interdependence of peoples and places, offers the best preparation for specialized professional training in urban and regional planning.
- **Economic Development.** Geographers' ability to understand the interdependence of places and to analyze the unique economic, environmental, cultural, and political attributes of specific regions enables them to contribute effectively to strategies and policies aimed at economic development. Geographers are involved in applied research and policy formulation concerning economic development all over the world, addressing the problems not only of individual places and regions but also of the entire world economy.
- **Security.** Geographers' knowledge and understanding of geopolitics, political geography, demographics, medical geography, and cultural geography, together with an appreciation of the interdependent relationships among local, regional, and global systems, provide a sound basis for work in many areas of security. Knowing how places and regions "work" also means knowing about their vulnerability to potential security risks. A regional specialization may also be very relevant to certain intelligence occupations, while proficiency in using and interpreting GIS applications is fundamental to most aspects of security.

These are just a few examples of how geographers make a difference in today's world. Canadian geography graduates are employed in a wide range of occupations.[4] Many enter professions such as planning, teaching, or public administration. Geographers also find employment in marketing (using geodemographic research) or evaluating the most profitable location for stores, businesses, or factories. Increasingly, geographers work in the environmental field (as industry consultants, researchers for non-governmental organizations, environmental impact analysts, or government scientists and field workers). Finally, since 2001, geography graduates have increasingly been sought out by the defence and intelligence sectors.

The skills that uniquely qualify geographers for these varied careers include the ability to integrate data from both the physical and the social sciences, to use **geographic information systems (GIS)** (see **Geography Matters 1.5— Geographic Information Systems on p. 27**) as well as statistics, to create and interpret maps, and to write. In addition, they are familiar with laboratory analysis, project management, urban and regional planning, and international development.

Through this wide range of skills, combined with an appreciation of the diversity and variety of the world's peoples and places, geography provides real opportunities not only for contributing to local, national, and global development but also for understanding and promoting multicultural, international, and feminist perspectives on the world. In other words, geography graduates have the opportunity to make a positive contribution to the world in many ways and at many levels.

geodemographic research: investigation using census data and commercial data (such as sales data and property records) about the populations of small districts to create profiles of those populations for market research

geographic information system (GIS): an organized collection of computer hardware, software, and geographical data that is designed to capture, store, update, manipulate, and display spatially referenced information

[4] The Geography Department at St. Mary's University in Halifax has published an analysis of the employment of its graduates: **www.smu.ca/academic/arts/geography/documents/gradsurvey.pdf.**

1.2 Geography in the Information Age

For a very candid peek at how UPS uses geographic knowledge and technology to optimize its operations and keep tabs on every single one of their delivery trucks, you can watch this five-minute video at **http://geospatialrevolution.psu.edu/episode2/chapter2.**

The Influence and Meaning of Places

Places are dynamic, with changing properties and fluid boundaries that are the product of the interplay of a wide variety of environmental and human factors. Places provide the settings for people's daily lives and their social relations (patterns of interaction among family members, between genders, at work, in social life, in leisure activities, or in political activity). In these settings, people thus learn who and what they are and how they should think and behave. Obviously, places are important in shaping people's lives and in influencing the pace and direction of change. Moreover, because different places can foster rather different values, attitudes, and behaviours, they can also make it difficult for people raised in different settings to understand and appreciate one another.

Places thus exert a strong influence, for better or worse, on people's physical well-being, their opportunities, and their lifestyle choices. Living in a small town dominated by petrochemical industries, for example, means a higher probability than elsewhere of being exposed to air and water pollution, having only a limited range of job opportunities, and having a relatively narrow range of lifestyle options because of a lack of amenities, such as theatres, specialized stores and restaurants, and recreational facilities. Living in the central neighbourhood of a large metropolitan area, however, usually means having a wider range of job opportunities and a greater choice of lifestyle options because of the variety of amenities accessible within a short distance.

Places also contribute to people's collective memory and become powerful emotional and cultural symbols (**Figure 1.2**). And for many people, ordinary places have special meaning: a childhood neighbourhood, a university campus, a hockey arena, or a family vacation spot. This layering of meanings reflects the way that places are *socially constructed*—given different meanings by different groups for different purposes. Places exist, and are constructed by their inhabitants, from a subjective point of view. In fact, the meanings given to a place may be so strong that they become a central part of the identity of the people experiencing them. Your own neighbourhood, for example, centred

Figure 1.2 The power of place   Some places acquire a strong symbolic value because of the buildings, events, people, histories or myths, and images with which they are associated. For example, for many Canadians, the Peace Tower on Parliament Hill in Ottawa is a place that draws its meaning from its associations with important events in this country's political life. Other places in Canada evoke more general, but no less powerful, symbolic associations. For example, this picture of a canoe trip (on the Bloodvein River in Manitoba) has a much wider symbolic meaning because of its connotations with our images of a vast northern landscape and all the cultural values we associate with such a landscape. Indeed, for many people, especially those outside this country, such pictures are iconic of Canada and serve as a shorthand for tourist and other promotional literature.

on yourself and your home, is probably heavily laden with personal meaning and sentiment. However, your neighbourhood may well be viewed very differently, and perhaps unsympathetically, from an outsider's perspective (including geographers).

Finally, places are the sites of innovation and change, of resistance and conflict. The unique characteristics of specific places can provide the preconditions for new modes of economic organization (for example, the Industrial Revolution that began in England in the late eighteenth century); new cultural practices (the punk movement that began in disadvantaged British housing projects); and new lifestyles (the "hippie" lifestyle that began in San Francisco in the late 1960s). It is in specific locales that important events happen, and it is from them that significant changes spread.

The influence of places is by no means limited to the occasional innovative change. Because of their distinctive characteristics, places always modify and sometimes resist the imprint of economic, cultural, and political trends (**Figure 1.3**). Consider, for example, the way that Indian communities in London developed Bhangra—a "world beat" composite of traditional Punjabi music, Mumbai (Bombay) movie scores, and Western disco. Further cross-fertilization with local music cultures in New York and Los Angeles has produced Bhangra rap. As another illustration of the influence of place, even in a globalized world, think of the way that some communities have declared themselves as nuclear-free zones. They are, to use the slogan, thinking globally and acting locally. In doing so, they may influence thinking in other communities so that eventually their challenge could result in a reversal of established trends (**Figure 1.4**).

In summary, places are settings for social interaction that, among other things,

- structure the daily routines of people's economic and social life
- provide both opportunities and constraints in terms of people's long-term social well-being
- provide a context in which everyday, commonsense knowledge and experience are gathered
- provide a setting for processes of socialization
- provide an arena for contesting social norms

Figure 1.3 Argentine dance spreads to China Popular trends are easily spread around the world. Here, tango dancers dance in front of the North Gate to the Forbidden City in Beijing during a tango marathon popularizing South America's most famous dance. Tango originated in Argentina at the end of the nineteenth century as a mixture of Argentine, Cuban, and African music played on European folk instruments.

Figure 1.4 Acting locally The town of Überlingen, Germany, has established itself as a "GM-free" zone. Shown here is Cornelia Wiethaler, who initiated the movement to ban genetically modified crops and food from the town. The example shows how individual action in one place can cause local change and, through the very fact that you are reading this, foster global awareness.

The Interdependence of Places

Places, then, have an importance of their own. Yet, at the same time, most places are *interdependent*, each filling specialized roles in complex, far-reaching, and ever-changing geographies. Consider, for example, the way that Manhattan, New York, operates as a specialized global centre of corporate management, business, and financial services while relying on thousands of other places to satisfy its needs. For labour, it draws on analysts and managers from business schools all over the United States, blue- and pink-collar workers from neighbouring boroughs, and skilled professional immigrants from around the world. For food, it draws on fruits and vegetables from Florida; dairy products from Pennsylvania; and specialty foods from Europe, the Caribbean, and Asia. For energy, it draws on coal from southwest Virginia to fuel its power stations, and it pumps drinking water down from upstate New York. Finally, for consumer goods, it draws on specialized manufacturing settings all over the world.

This interdependence means that individual places are tied into wider processes of change that are reflected in broader geographical patterns. New York's attraction for business-school graduates, for example, affects labour markets elsewhere: New York's gain is somewhere else's loss. An important issue for human geographers—and a central theme of this book—is to recognize these wider processes and broad geographical patterns without losing sight of the individuality and uniqueness of specific places. This means that we have to recognize another kind of interdependence: the interdependence that exists *between different geographical scales*.

The Interdependence of Geographical Scales

In a globalizing world, it is increasingly important to understand the many interrelationships between the *global* and the *local* scales. The study of human geography shows not only how global trends influence local outcomes but also how events in particular localities can come to influence patterns and trends elsewhere—remember Figure 1.4!

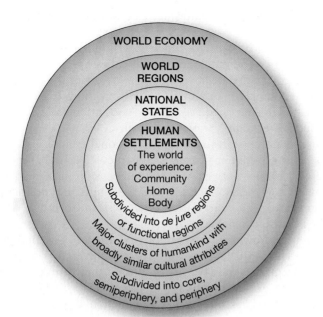

Figure 1.5 Spatial levels
Geographic phenomena may be identified, analyzed, and understood at different levels. This diagram shows some of the principal levels or scales used in geographic research. (Adapted from S. Marston, P. Knox, and D. Liverman, *World Regions in Global Context.* Upper Saddle River, NJ: Prentice Hall, 2002, p. 18.)

We can illustrate this by taking the example of Canada's pulp and paper industry. *Global* effects, such as the European environmental movement's protests against clear-cutting in British Columbia's forests, adversely affect the industry *locally* by reducing demand for Canadian products. Tree planters, forest managers, lumberjacks, and pulp and paper mill workers are all affected by the contraction of the industry in the wake of these boycotts halfway around the globe. The economy of the small towns in which the mills are located will also feel the effects of such changes. Conversely, *locally induced* factors such as tree planting efforts can have *global* environmental effects by helping absorb carbon dioxide.

Between the global and the local, there are many intervening levels or scales (**Figure 1.5**). Geographers use all of these scales because different aspects of human geography are understood best, and analyzed most effectively, at different spatial levels. At the same time, these different scales are interrelated and interdependent, which means that geographers must learn to relate things at one level to things at another.

World regions are large-scale geographic divisions based on continental and physiographic settings that contain major groupings of peoples with broadly similar cultural attributes. Examples include Europe, Latin America, and South Asia. These regions are constantly evolving as natural resources and technologies create opportunities and constraints to which particular cultures and societies respond.

Superimposed on these regions, sometimes with only approximate fit, is the mosaic of the *de jure* territories of national states. States are independent political units with territorial boundaries that are recognized by other states (see the discussion of states, nations, and national states in Chapter 9). *De jure* simply means legally recognized. Below the level of the state, there are other *de jure* spaces, such as provinces, counties, municipalities, and so on. However, national states are seen as the most important geographic scale because they have the power to enact laws that regulate the flows of people, goods, money, and information. However, when political or economic circumstances change, national states may feel the need to join supranational organizations.

Supranational organizations are collections of individual states with a common goal that may be economic and/or political in nature and that diminish, to some extent, individual state sovereignty in favour of the group interests of the membership. Examples of supranational organizations include the European Union (EU), the North American Free Trade Association (NAFTA), and the Association of South East Asian Nations (ASEAN).

Within most national states and all international regions are smaller, functional regions. This geographical scale is constructed around specific resources and industries, with their networks of producers, suppliers, distributors, and ancillary activities and their associated social, cultural, and political identities. Examples include the Canadian Prairies, the American Corn Belt, the Argentine pampas, or the Scottish coalfields.

For most people, however, the realm of experience is encompassed by human settlements. This is the level at which people's lives are organized through their work, consumption, and recreation. Within the realm of experience, we find sublevels ranging from community and the home to the body. The community is the loosely defined location of social interaction, of personal relationships, and daily routine, all of which depend a great deal on the economic, social, and cultural attributes of local populations. Much more sharply defined is the home, which is an important geographic site insofar as it constitutes the physical setting for the structure and dynamics of family and household. It also reflects, in its spatial organization, the differential status accorded to men and women and to the young and the elderly.

Next, the body is of interest to geographers because it represents the intimate location where differences are ultimately defined—not only through physical attributes (hair, skin, facial features) but also through the socially constructed attributes of the body, such as norms of personal space, preferred bodily styles, and acceptable uses of bodies. Particularly important is the way that, in many cultures, the body is seen as the "natural" justification for the differential treatment of men and women. The result is that differential geographies are created and experienced: "women's worlds" and "men's worlds." Finally, the self is of interest to geographers because it represents the operational scale for cognition, perception, imagination, free will, and behaviour. It is at this level that geographers try to understand the interrelationships between nature, culture, and individual human agency in shaping places and regions.

Perhaps the most important conclusion that we can draw from this discussion is that although certain phenomena can be identified and understood best at specific spatial scales or levels, the reality of geography is that social, cultural, political, and economic phenomena are very fluid, constantly being constructed, reinforced, undermined, and rebuilt. The real world has to be understood, ultimately, as the product of interdependent phenomena at a variety of spatial scales.

Interdependence as a Two-Way Process

One of the most important tenets of human geography is that places are not just distinctive outcomes of geographical processes: places are part of the processes themselves. Think of any city neighbourhood, with its distinctive mix of buildings and people. This mix is the product of a combination of processes, including real estate development, the dynamics of the city's housing market, the successive occupancy of residential and commercial buildings by particular groups who move in and then out of the community, the services and upkeep provided by the city, and so on. Over time, these processes result in a distinctive physical environment with an equally distinctive population profile, social atmosphere,

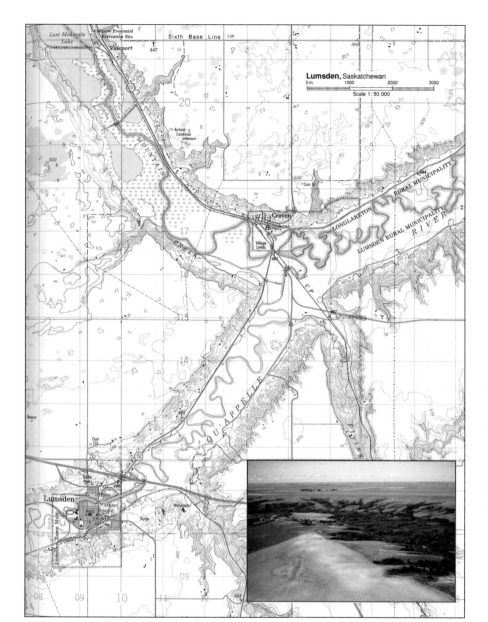

Figure 1.6   Place making   People develop patterns of living that are attuned to the opportunities and constraints of the local physical environment. When this happens, distinctive landscapes are produced. This section of a topographic map and photo show part of the Qu'Appelle Valley, near Lumsden, Saskatchewan. As you can see, this prairie landscape is not flat. Largely the result of the most recent glaciations, it is made up of an undulating succession of low hills and shallow depressions. Low rainfall, caused by the rain-shadow effect of the Rockies, originally supported a grassland ecology, perhaps maintained by local fires set by Aboriginal peoples. Encouraged by a landscape that appeared so easy to clear for farming, thousands of nineteenth-century immigrants were drawn to Saskatchewan, establishing a regular pattern of farms and rectangular property divisions and road networks. As the different place names and names for natural features show, these settlers had various origins (Qu'Appelle—French; Longlaketon—English; Lumsden—the name of the Scottish-born CPR chief engineer). Occasionally, rivers meander sluggishly through wide valleys (originally carved out by glacial meltwaters). Attracted to water, human settlement has focused on these rivers but generally avoids the valley bottoms with their risk of annual flooding following snow melt. Some settlements, because they are bridging points, have grown into larger centres.

image, and reputation. Yet, these neighbourhood characteristics exert a strong influence, in turn, on the continuing processes of real estate redevelopment, housing market dynamics, and migration in and out of the neighbourhood. Places, then, are *dynamic* phenomena. They are created by people responding to the opportunities and constraints presented by their environments. As people live and work in places, they gradually impose themselves on their environment, modifying and adjusting it to suit their needs and express their values. At the same time, people gradually accommodate both to their physical environment and to the people around them. This is a *continuous two-way process* in which people create and modify places while being influenced by the settings in which they live and work (**Figure 1.6**).

Place making is always incomplete and ongoing, and it occurs simultaneously at different scales. Processes of geographic change are constantly modifying and reshaping places, and places are constantly coping with change. It is important for geographers to be sensitive to this kind of interdependence without falling into the trap of overgeneralization, or losing sight of the diversity and variety that constitute the heart of human geography.

The Development of Geographic Thought

Although elementary geographical knowledge has existed since prehistoric times, the ancient Greeks were probably the first to demonstrate in detail the practical utility of geographic knowledge, particularly in politics, business, and trade. As Greek civilization expanded, descriptive geographical writing became an essential tool for recording information about sea and land routes and for preparing colonists and merchants for the challenges and opportunities they would encounter in faraway places. The word *geography*, in fact, is derived from the Greek language and means "Earth writing" or "Earth describing" (**Figure 1.2.1** and **1.2.2**).

The Greeks were also the first to understand the intellectual importance of geography as they recognized that places embody fundamental relationships between people and the natural environment. With the decline and fall of the ancient empires of the Greeks and Romans, however, geography and geographical knowledge were neglected. In medieval Europe, from around A.D. 500 until after A.D. 1400, Church dogma discouraged the use of science or philosophy of any kind.

During this period, the base of geographical knowledge was preserved and expanded by Chinese and Islamic scholars. Chinese maps of the world were more accurate than those of European cartographers because they were based on information brought back by imperial China's admirals, who are widely believed to have successfully navigated parts of the Pacific and Indian oceans. They showed, for example, that Africa was a southward-pointing triangle, whereas European and Arabic maps of the time always represented Africa as pointing eastward.

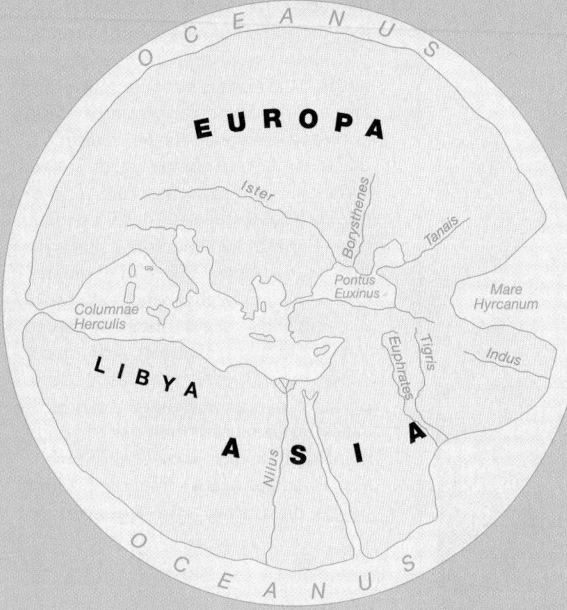

Figure 1.2.1   A reconstruction of one of the earliest maps of the world, by Anaximander of Miletus   Around 500 B.C., his student Pythagoras speculated that Earth was spherical rather than flat. Some 300 years later, Eratosthenes (273–192 B.C.), who is supposed to have coined the term *geography*, was the first person to calculate accurately the circumference of Earth. He also developed a system of latitude and longitude, which allowed the exact location of places to be plotted on the world's spherical surface.   (*Source:* J.B. Harley and D. Woodward [eds.], *The History of Cartography*, vol. 1. Chicago: University of Chicago Press, fig. 8.5, p. 135.)

Figure 1.2.2   Ptolemy's map of the world   Ptolemy began his *Guide to Geography* with an explanation of how to construct a globe, together with its parallels and meridians, and then showed how to project the world onto a plane surface. His map of the world stood for centuries as the basis for cartography. This example, published in 1482 by Leinhart Holle in Ulm, Germany, was typical of the basic map of the world in use at the time that Christopher Columbus was trying to reach China by sailing west.

With the rise of Islamic power in the Middle East and the Mediterranean in the seventh and eighth centuries A.D., centres of scholarship emerged throughout these regions, including Baghdad, Damascus, Cairo, and Granada, Spain. Here, surviving Greek and Roman texts were translated by Arabic scholars, who were also able to draw on Chinese geographical writing and cartography brought back by traders. The requirement that the Islamic religious faith-ful should undertake at least one pilgrimage to Mecca created a demand for travel guides. It also brought scholars from all over the Arab world into contact with one another, stimulating considerable debate over different philosophical views of the world and people's relationship with nature.

Despite such progress in the non-Christian realm, geographical knowledge during the Middle Ages throughout Western Europe was dictated by the views of the Church, which taught that the world literally embodied Christian theology. This view, conveyed for example, in the form of what are known today as "T-O maps," stated that the holy city of Jerusalem lay at the centre of the world and outwards from it radiated three continents (Europe, Africa, and Asia), separated by the waters of the Nile and Mediterranean (**Figure 1.2.3**). This view was finally proven false by the European voyages of discovery of the fifteenth century (see Chapter 2: **Geography Matters 2.2—Geography and Exploration**). These voyages produced an enormous amount of new geographical information about the world that necessitated a new physical representation of the globe—provided to the next generation of explorers in 1569 by the Mercator projection (**Figure 1.2.4**).

Not as easy, however, was the task of developing a new set of theories that would make sense of all of this new information. Consequently, the history of geographical thought over the succeeding centuries is marked by the search for just such a framework—one that would not just record but also interpret and explain the world again.

Notable efforts in this search were made by Immanuel Kant (1724–1804), who argued that all knowledge could be divided into two general fields of knowledge: geography, which classified things according to space; and history, which classified things according to time. Kant was an influential philosopher, and his insistence

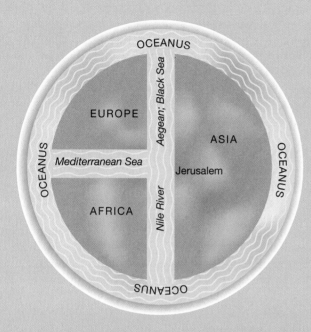

Figure 1.2.3 The medieval T-O map Maps such as these both reflected (and shaped) Western Europe's view of the world during the Middle Ages. Traditionally these maps were oriented with Asia at the top (a direction we now associate with "north") and Jerusalem in the centre. (*Source:* This diagram is a simplified version of a T-O map prepared by the author to highlight basic generic features.)

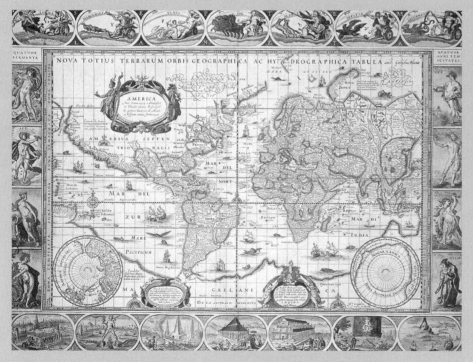

Figure 1.2.4 Mercator's world map Accurate mapping was important to the Europeans' ability to open up the world for commerce. The historical period in Europe known as the *Renaissance* (from the mid-fourteenth to the mid-seventeenth centuries) saw an explosion of systematic mapmaking and the development of new *map projections*. Gerardus Mercator's world map was specially devised, in 1569, as a navigational chart of the world on which mariners could plot the exact compass distance between any two points as a straight line. The Mercator projection became very popular as a general-purpose map of the world. This example is from an atlas created by Willem Blau, published in 1635. The use of the term *atlas* for a collection of maps also originated with Mercator, who decorated one of his books of maps with an illustration of the Greek mythological figure Atlas carrying the world on his shoulders.

on the intellectual importance of geography marked an important step toward establishing it as a formal discipline and developing an analytical basis for its practice.

The next significant steps were taken by German geographer Alexander von Humboldt (1769–1859), who showed how people, like other species, have to adapt to their environment. He also demonstrated how humans' behaviour affects the environment that surrounds them—in other words, he emphasized the mutual causality that exists between species and their environment.

By the mid-nineteenth century, thriving geographical societies had been established in a number of cities, including Berlin, London, Frankfurt, Moscow, New York, and Paris. By 1899, there were 62 geographical societies worldwide, and university chairs of geography had been created in many of the most prestigious universities around the world. It must be said, however, that geography was seen at first in narrow terms, as the discipline of discovery and exploration. Because the importance of geography was linked so clearly to European commercial and political ambitions, places and regions tended to be portrayed from a distinctly European point of view and from the perspective of particular national, commercial, and religious interests. Geography mattered, but mainly as an instrument of colonialism.

One result of geography's involvement with colonialism and **imperialism** was that the discipline fostered ethnocentrism and masculinism. **Ethnocentrism** is the attitude that one's own race and culture are superior to those of others. **Masculinism** is the assumption that the world is, and should be, shaped mainly by men for men. These trends became more and more explicit as European dominance increased, reaching a peak in the late nineteenth century at the height of European geopolitical influence.

We should also note that most of the geographic writing in the nineteenth century was strongly influenced by environmental determinism. **Environmental determinism** is a doctrine holding that human activities are controlled by the environment. It rests on a belief that the physical attributes of geographical settings are the root not only of people's physical differences (skin colour, stature, and facial features, for example) but also of differences in people's economic vitality, cultural activities, and social structures.

One of the most influential geographers who propagated this belief was Friedrich Ratzel (1844–1904), who was strongly influenced by Charles Darwin's theories about species' adaptation to environmental conditions and competition for living space. (Darwin's *On the Origin of Species* was published in 1859.) Ratzel argued that civilization and successful economic development are largely the result of invigorating climates, which he defined as temperate climates with marked seasonal variations. Followers of Ratzel's idea later used this assertion to justify what they saw as the "natural" domination of northwestern Europe and the northeastern United States within the world economy.

Environmental determinists thus tend to think in terms of the influence of the physical environment on people rather than the other way around. The idea that people's social and economic development and behaviour are fundamentally shaped by their physical environment lasted well into the twentieth century, though geographers now regard it as simplistic and even racist.

A decisive development away from environmental determinism and toward modern geographical thought came in 1925 with a paper written by Carl Sauer, a professor of geography at the University of California, Berkeley. Sauer argued that landscapes should provide the focus for the scientific study of geography because they reflect the outcome, over time, of the interdependence of physical and human factors in the creation of distinctive places and regions. Sauer stressed that although everything in a particular landscape is interrelated, the physical elements do not necessarily determine the nature of the human elements. Sometimes they do, sometimes it is the other way around, and sometimes it is a bit of both.

imperialism: the extension of the power of a nation through direct or indirect control of the economic and political life of other territories

ethnocentrism: the attitude that a person's own race and culture are superior to those of others

masculinism: the assumption that the world is, and should be, shaped mainly by men for men

environmental determinism: a doctrine holding that human activities are controlled by the environment

INTERDEPENDENCE IN A GLOBALIZING WORLD

As a subject of scientific observation and study, geography has made important contributions both to the understanding of the world and to its development. As we move further into the Information Age, geography continues to contribute to the understanding of a world that is more complex and fast-changing than ever before. In fact, as our fortunes and ideas become increasingly bound up with those of other people in other places, the study of geography provides an ever-more important understanding of the crucial interdependencies that underpin all people's lives. Consequently, the *interdependence* of people and places is one of the central themes throughout this book.

Geography in Canada

Early Geographical Knowledge

Geography has been practised by both women and men in Canada since people first came to this land. The ways in which that geographical knowledge has been enlarged and passed on to other generations has changed over time: We now emphasize the university and college classroom, but we should not overlook the contributions made by earlier people to our understanding of this country's geography.

Given its importance, it is hardly surprising that we find an appreciation of what we would now call "geography" among the men, women, and children of all societies, whether from past eras or the present day, from Western or Eastern traditions, or from the developed or developing world. For instance, the ancient Chinese practice of *feng shui* paid close attention to the location of sites in the landscape and of "energy lines" across its surface. For thousands of years, Australia's Aborigines have celebrated their landscape in songs that record its sacredness and show how its mythological meanings can best be understood if places are visited in a particular order. Using simple star navigation, Polynesians were able to travel around the Pacific Ocean: as early as A.D. 300, settlers from the Marquesas Islands reached Hawaii, more than 3,000 kilometres to the north.

In Canada, the high latitudes of the Arctic make star navigation impractical because stars are invisible during five months of continuous daylight. Moreover, the sun rises and sets at all points of the compass (rather than only in the east, as in lower latitudes). So how did the Inuit navigate? According to John MacDonald of the Nunavut Research Institute at Igloolik:

> When navigating, Inuit bring all their knowledge, experience, and senses to bear on every available environmental sign and circumstance including wind direction, the set of snowdrifts, landmarks, vegetation, sea currents, clouds, and various astronomical bodies [such as the Aurora Borealis]; clues are even derived from the behaviour of sled-dogs and other animals.[5]

Directional information is then readily interpreted within the context of the Inuit's overall geographical knowledge of the local area to provide an exact location. Indeed, scholars have long recognized the Inuit people's ability to construct "cognitive maps," a skill aided by the detailed names given to landscape features and by the ability of the Inuit language, Inuktitut, to describe locations precisely by the use of certain word categories known as "localizers."

It is important to note here that this sophisticated grasp of location and navigation was not historically the preserve of Inuit men. A large amount of evidence attests to the importance of Inuit women's knowledge. For example, Sir William Parry was rescued on his second voyage of Arctic exploration (1821–1823) by a sketch map drawn for him by an Inuit woman called Iligliuk. "To her alone," John Barrow (secretary of the British admiralty) later said, "is the merit due to the discovery of the extreme northern boundary of America." Geographical knowledge in most early societies, as we might expect, is not the exclusive domain of either sex.

Pre-Confederation

A profound interest in geography considerably pre-dates the creation of Canada as a country in 1867. This country's Aboriginal peoples, European explorers, and immigrant settlers all had particular interests in acquiring geographical knowledge about the land they inhabited.

- Canada's Aboriginal peoples built a considerable store of information about this country's environments—knowledge necessary to hunt, track food resources, find shelter, and interpret their world. Aboriginal peoples also drew maps on paper or animal skins to help the first Europeans find their way across Native lands (**Figure 1.3.1**).

- European explorers, keen to open up Canada as quickly as possible, sought the best routes into the country, recorded that information following Western cartographic practice, and described the new lands. The French explorer Samuel de Champlain (1570–1635), for instance, illustrated his accounts of travels along the St. Lawrence River with his own paintings and maps. Two centuries later, David Thompson (1770–1857), an employee of the Hudson's Bay Company, mapped the company's vast western lands before they were transferred to Canada in 1869.

- The Arctic and its exploration occupy an important place in the development of Canadian geography. For example, many expeditions were launched to find the fabled "shortcut" to the Pacific, the Northwest Passage (**Figure 1.3.2**). When the expedition party of Sir John Franklin disappeared in 1847, numerous rescue expeditions were mounted: in 1850 alone, ten British and two American ships were searching for Franklin. Over the next few decades, dozens more tried to find the remains of the expedition. The knowledge accumulated on these voyages resulted in a redrawing of the map of Canada's north, and many of its places were named after the captains involved. In 2008, the Canadian government launched a three-year effort to locate Franklin's two ships in the High Arctic—an opportunity to stake Canada's claim to sovereignty over this area at a time when rising oil prices and global warming have turned the attention of other nations toward the Northwest Passage once again.

---

[5] John MacDonald, *The Arctic Sky: Inuit Astronomy, Star Lore and Legend*. Toronto: Royal Ontario Museum/Iqaluit: Nunavut Research Institute, 2000, p. 161.

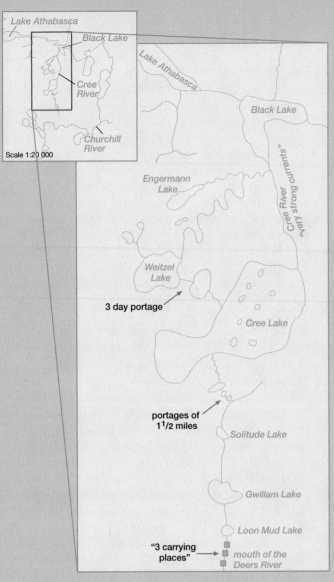

This map was drawn in 1810 by a Chipewyan Indian named Cot aw ney yaz zah. It provides essential information on canoe travel between Churchill River and Lake Athabasca. The map exaggerates scale to clarify important features, such as portages. It also conveys information on route choice: the original map indicated that those travelling north should take the fast-flowing Cree River and those travelling south should travel via Weitzel Lake to avoid struggling against the river's fast currents. The map was drawn for Peter Fidler of the Hudson's Bay Company, who (like all fur traders) depended on the local knowledge of Aboriginal peoples.

Note: The outline of the map preserves that of the original. Place names, however, have been modernized to aid in interpretation, and annotations by Peter Fidler have been omitted.

Figure 1.3.1   Early Aboriginal maps
Canada's Aboriginal peoples possessed a well-developed sense of their surroundings. Evidence of this knowledge is preserved in the maps that they drew to guide Europeans on their voyages of "discovery" into this country. (*Source: D. Wayne Moodie, "Indian Maps." The Historical Atlas of Canada, Volume 1: From the Beginning to 1800. Toronto: University of Toronto Press, 1987, plate 59. Reprinted with permission of the University of Toronto Press.*)

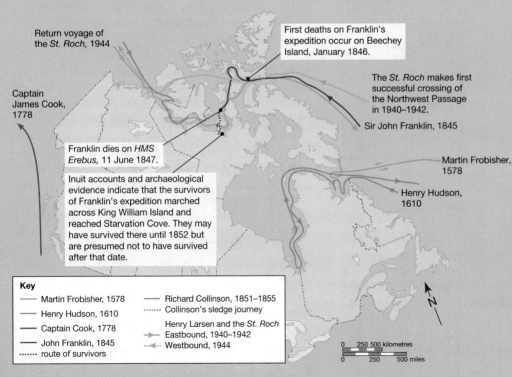

First deaths on Franklin's expedition occur on Beechey Island, January 1846.

Return voyage of the *St. Roch,* 1944

The *St. Roch* makes first successful crossing of the Northwest Passage in 1940–1942.

Sir John Franklin, 1845

Captain James Cook, 1778

Franklin dies on *HMS Erebus,* 11 June 1847.

Inuit accounts and archaeological evidence indicate that the survivors of Franklin's expedition marched across King William Island and reached Starvation Cove. They may have survived there until 1852 but are presumed not to have survived after that date.

Martin Frobisher, 1578

Henry Hudson, 1610

Key
— Martin Frobisher, 1578
— Henry Hudson, 1610
— Captain Cook, 1778
— John Franklin, 1845
······ route of survivors
— Richard Collinson, 1851–1855
······ Collinson's sledge journey
Henry Larsen and the *St. Roch*
▶ Eastbound, 1940–1942
◀ Westbound, 1944

0   250 500 kilometres
0   250   500 miles

Figure 1.3.2   The Northwest Passage   More important for its place in legend than as a practical route, the search for the Northwest Passage was a spur to the exploration of Canada's Arctic region throughout the nineteenth century.   (*Source: Compiled by author from maps in James P. Delgado, Across the Top of the World: The Quest for the Northwest Passage. Toronto: Douglas and MacIntyre, 2000.*)

- Next was the less daring but equally demanding work of detailed land surveying as the country was divided into and settled as farms and townsites and lines of communications were opened up. Accurate work was essential but often difficult and time consuming, given the dense cover of forest across much of the country. One account of survey work along the Rideau Canal (completed in 1831) describes how surveyors would set fire to a distant tree to have an unambiguous point of reference for their sightlines.
- Once they arrived, settlers expressed their own keen interest in knowing more about the resource potential and economic future of their farm, province, and country—interest that prompted government action. No less important was that these settlers, in their paintings and letters, began to record descriptions of the world they had made (see Chapter 3).

1870s to 1930s: An Immense Task

"Despite these promising beginnings," John Warkentin and Paul Simpson-Housley write in their account of the history of Canadian geography, "the task of geography remained immense in the 1870s. Knowledge of most parts of the country was thin and sketchy."[6] For the next 60 years or so, that immense task was in the hands of three main groups: the federal government, individual writers and artists, and interested citizens.

- Beginning in 1892, the federal government prepared Canada's first extensive topographic map series—a survey of the Prairies. In 1906, the first *National Atlas of Canada* was published, under the direction of James White, the government's chief geographer. White's office also had the responsibility of systematically recording all new place names, elevations, and natural features—of "cataloguing" Canada.
- Among the Canadian writers of travel and adventure books in this period were some who had great insights regarding the geographical development of Canada. Many of the themes they discussed are ones that remain important to this day, for example:
  - Canada's relations with the United States
  - the regional character of Canada
  - the European settlement of Canada
  - French-speaking Canada's relations with English-speaking Canada

University economists and historians with an interest in geographical issues, such as Harold Innis and Donald Creighton, added the following themes:
  - the role of the St. Lawrence and the lower Great Lakes as an organizing axis of Canadian development

  - the importance of the **ecumene**, or total amount of habitable land, as a limit on agricultural settlement
  - the role of the frontier as a catalyst for development

In some circumstances, a novel or poem described people's worlds more succinctly or captured underlying geographical truths not amenable to conscious analysis. Painters, such as the Group of Seven (1910–1930s), enabled Canadians to reinterpret and appreciate the rugged landscape of the Canadian Shield by developing a new aesthetic for landscape painting. Emily Carr's paintings of Haida landscapes had a similarly profound effect on the way British Columbia's coastal forests and Aboriginal peoples were viewed.

- Individuals also grouped together to advance the cause of geographical research. In 1877, *La Société de géographie de Québec* was established, at that date only the third geographical society to be founded in all of North America. In 1905, the Champlain Society was founded to publish historical documents relating to Canada. The Canadian Geographical Society was founded in Ottawa in 1929 (becoming the Royal Canadian Geographical Society in 1957) and began to publish the *Canadian Geographical Journal* (**Figure 1.3.3**) in 1930 (now *Canadian Geographic*).

1930s to Present: A Canadian Geography

Geography had been taught since the late nineteenth century as a school subject in many parts of Canada. But it was not until the early part of the twentieth century that the discipline was taught at the university and college levels. The Geology Department at the University of British Columbia was renamed in 1923 to include "Geography" in its title, and by the mid-1920s, geographers trained by the eminent French regional geographer Paul Vidal de la Blache lectured at the Université de Montréal. It was only in 1935 that the first fully fledged geography department in this country was established at the University of Toronto by Griffith Taylor, a geographer who had survived Scott's ill-fated Antarctic expedition from 1910 to 1912.

In 1951, the Canadian Association of Geographers (CAG) was founded with 65 members, and its journal, *The Canadian Geographer,* was established (**Figure 1.3.4**). Fifty years later, there were departments or programs in geography in 48 Canadian universities and a nationwide membership of 750 professors. The subject's growth between these years was fuelled by two factors. First, there was a steady demand for geography graduates from the federal and provincial or territorial public services, which were eager to map Canada's resources and plan the post-war world. The development, by 1966, of the innovative technology needed for the Canadian Geographic Information System (CGIS) to inventory this country in detail is but one example of how government needs drew on university training and research. Second, Canadian geography benefited from the rapid increase in the number of universities in this country and the

[6] John Warkentin and Paul Simpson-Housley, "The Development of Geographical Study in Canada, 1870-2000." In Gary S. Dunbar (ed.), *Geography: Discipline, Profession and Subject since 1870.* Dordrecht: Kluwer, 2001, p. 282. This section draws substantially on their work.

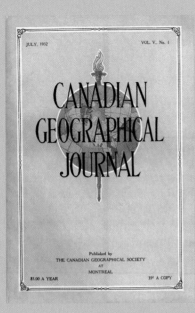

Figure 1.3.3 **The *Canadian Geographical Journal*** This issue of the journal was published in July 1932 and cost 35 cents a copy. It is clear that the publishers saw Canada, although an independent country, as still very much a part of the British Empire (shown by the red shading of British possessions on the globe behind the title lettering).

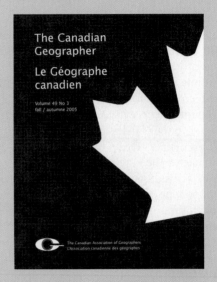

Figure 1.3.4 **The *Canadian Geographer*** Published since 1951, this journal is one of the leading outlets for the academic work of Canadian geographers and for geographers based elsewhere who write about this country.

post-war desire to adapt university curricula to the challenges of the modern world.

Today, Canadian geography is a more vibrant and absorbing discipline than ever for three main reasons:

1. Technological developments, such as GIS and remote sensing, have enabled geographers to deal with growing amounts of spatial data in an increasingly sophisticated manner.
2. Growing public concerns about environmental change have given heightened relevancy to many aspects of geographical research.
3. The addition of a number of new research themes in recent years has significantly increased Canadian geography's purchase on real-world issues. Examples include the introduction of feminist analysis and ideas of gendered place, the development of rural geography, and the growth of research into sustainable urban transportation.

ecumene: the total habitable area of a country. Because it depends on the prevailing technology, the available ecumene varies over time. It is an important concept in Canada's case, because the ecumene is so much smaller than the country's total area.

globalization: the increasing interconnectedness of different parts of the world through common processes of economic, environmental, political, and cultural change

Another central theme is globalization. **Globalization** is a process and a condition that involves the increasing interconnectedness of different parts of the world through common processes of economic, environmental, political, and cultural change. A world economy has been in existence for several centuries, and with it a comprehensive framework of sovereign nation-states and an international system of production and exchange have developed. This system has been reorganized several times. Each time it has been reorganized, however, major changes have resulted, not only in world geography but also in the character and fortunes of individual places.

In the last two decades, both the pace and the nature of globalization have changed dramatically, leading to a highly interdependent world. New information technologies have helped create a frenetic international financial system, while transnational corporations are now able to transfer their production activities from one part of the world to another in response to changing wage rates, market conditions, and transportation and communications technologies (see Chapter 7).

This locational flexibility has meant that a high degree of functional integration now exists between economic activities that are increasingly dispersed. In turn, this means that resources, components, final products, and even wastes are transported around the globe, while markets and organizations are both spread and linked across continents. National governments, finding themselves increasingly ineffective at regulating and controlling the new transnational economy, have sought new ways of dealing with the consequences of globalization, including new international political and economic alliances such as NAFTA and the European Union (see Chapter 9).

The interdependence associated with globalization operates in a multitude of ways. In many cases, interdependence seems very unequal in nature—as in the example of a transnational firm based in a rich country taking advantage of low-cost labour in a poor country. In other cases, interdependence can work to mutual advantage—as in Canada and the United States sharing the costs and responsibilities of managing the Great Lakes as a transborder resource. In almost every case, however, the outcomes of the increased geographic interdependence associated with globalization are very much open to interpretation. Who "wins" and who "loses" depends very much on one's perspective and the geographic scale. Understanding what the experts believe about globalization will help us gain a better understanding of the complex interdependence between the global and the local.

Perspectives on Globalization and Interdependence

Check out the shelves in any good bookstore and you will find hundreds of books on globalization and its impact on the world's regions. It is possible to group the main participants in the contemporary debates about globalization into three general camps: the hyperglobalists, the sceptics, and the transformationalists.

The Hyperglobalist View At one extreme is the view that open markets and free trade and investment across global markets allow more and more people to share in the prosperity of a growing world economy. Economic and political interdependence, meanwhile, creates shared interests that help prevent conflict and foster support for common values. Democracy and human rights, it is asserted, will spread to billions of people in the wake of neoliberal policies that promote open markets and free trade.

Neoliberal policies see free markets as the ideal condition not only for economic organization but also for political and social life. Consequently, they allow only a minimal role for the state. Hyperglobalists believe that the current phase of globalization signals the beginning of the end for the nation-state and the "denationalization" of economies, meaning that national boundaries will become irrelevant with respect to economic processes. Instead, global governance will increasingly rest with global institutions like the International Monetary Fund (IMF) and the World Trade Organization (WTO).

The Sceptical View The sceptics believe that contemporary levels of global economic integration represent nothing particularly new and that much of the talk about globalization is exaggerated. Drawing on statistical evidence of world flows of trade, labour, and investment, they argue that contemporary economic integration is actually much less significant than it was in the late nineteenth century, when nearly all countries shared a common monetary system known as the gold standard.

The sceptics assert that we are today witnessing not globalization, but rather "regionalization," as the three major regional financial and trading blocs of Europe, North America, and East Asia (effectively, Japan) control the world economy and limit the participation of other regions in that economy. The sceptics are also dismissive of the idea that the nation-state is in decline.

The Transformationalist View   According to the transformationalist view, contemporary processes of globalization are historically unprecedented, as governments and peoples across the globe confront the absence of any clear distinction between the global and the local, between domestic affairs and international affairs. Like the hyperglobalists, this group understands globalization as a profound transformative force that is changing societies, economies, and institutions of government—in short, the world order. In contrast to the hyperglobalists and the sceptics, however, the transformationalists make no claims about the future trajectory of globalization, nor do they see present globalization as a pale version of a more "globalized" nineteenth century. Instead, they see globalization as a long-term historical process that is underlain by crises and contradictions that are likely to shape it in all sorts of unpredictable ways. Moreover, they believe that the historically unprecedented contemporary patterns of economic, military, technological, ecological, migratory, political, and cultural flows have functionally linked all parts of the world into a larger global system in which countries and regions are increasingly interdependent.

In this book we adhere generally to the transformationalist position. We suggest that we are all heading toward a world where places and regions will experience a wide range of internal changes at the same time that the strength of their connections with other parts of the world will increase. The complex interdependence of the contemporary world was dramatically underscored by the global financial crisis of October 2008, though it remains to be seen just how its continuing ripple effects will change individual places and regions.

What is perhaps most unsettling about the transformationalist view of globalization is the anticipated increase in inequality. Transformationalists believe that globalization is leading to increasing social stratification, in which some states and societies are more tightly connected to the global order while others are becoming increasingly marginalized. They contend that the world will increasingly consist of a three-tiered system—comprising the elites, the embattled, and the marginalized—that cuts across national, regional, and local boundaries (see Chapter 12). Within nations, disparities of wealth—already striking in many countries—will increase, just as they will between nations (see **Geography Matters 1.4—Worlds Apart**). Meanwhile, the increasing interdependence among places and regions raises some key issues in relation to the environment, health, and security.

Key Issues in a Globalizing World

Environmental Issues   The sheer scale and capacity of the world economy means that humans are now capable of altering the environment at the global scale: already the "footprint" of humankind extends to more than four-fifths of Earth's surface (**Figure 1.7 on page 25**). Humans have altered nature in ways that have brought economic prosperity to some areas and created environmental dilemmas and crises in others. For example, clearing land for settlement, mining, and agriculture provides livelihoods and homes for some but alters physical systems and transforms human populations, wildlife, and vegetation. The inevitable by-products—waste, air and water pollution, hazardous substances, and so forth—place enormous demands on the capacity of physical systems to absorb them. Apart from the increasingly menacing spectre of global warming, we also face the reality of serious global environmental degradation through deforestation; desertification; acid rain; loss of genetic diversity; smog; soil erosion; groundwater decline; and the pollution of rivers, lakes, and oceans (see Chapter 4).

Worlds Apart

Meet Paul Rust and his family, who live and enjoy life in Zug, Switzerland, the richest canton in the world's richest country. And meet Hussein Sormolo and his family, who live in Addis Ababa, capital of the world's poorest country, Ethiopia.

Hussein Sormolo left the village where he was born for the big city in 1978. He left his eight brothers and seven sisters behind, as the land that the family farmed was being forcibly collectivized by a new regime. Hussein, aged 16, travelled the 160 kilometres north to the city in the back of a truck. A kinsman from the same village took him in until he found a job in a bakery. Paul Rust left his village when he was 17 and also ended up in a bakery. The two men are similar in other ways. Both are friendly, hospitable, generous, and love their families. Both work hard. Both like to watch the news. Both are active worshippers, without being religious dogmatists.

Yet their lives are different. Hussein lives with his wife, sons, and daughters in a leaky shack of corrugated asbestos and steel in the Nefas Silk district of Addis Ababa (**Figure 1.4.1**). Paul lives with his wife in a six-room house (not counting the ground-floor apartment where his son Martin lives with his girlfriend) overlooking the lustrous green waters and steep wooded slopes of Lake Aegeri in Zug (**Figure 1.4.2**).

The income difference is huge, of course. Hussein supports his wife and three younger children on wages of about US$280 a year (more than twice the average income in Ethiopia). Paul and his wife, Hedi, draw about US$68,000 between them each year from their bakery, though the Rusts are not affluent by Swiss standards (the average income per head in Zug is about US$50,000).

It is the rainy season in Addis. Fat raindrops drum against, and often through, the rusting grooves of the corrugated roofs of the houses in Nefas Silk. Nights can be chilly and dank. From Debre Zeit road, the busy main north–south street lined with small businesses including the bakery where Hussein works, it's a 10-minute walk to the alley where he lives. Inside the Hussein shack, a single bare light bulb always burns. There is little natural light: There are no glass windows, and the openings punched in the asbestos walls are covered to keep out drafts. Hussein pays his neighbour 18 birr (about US$2) a month, almost a tenth of his 200-birr salary, to sublet his electricity supply for the bulb in the shack. The family has no other electrical appliances, apart from a battery-operated radio. Neither Hussein, his wife Rukia, nor his eldest daughter, Fate, 17, who is lucky enough to be at school, has ever used a computer, taken a photograph, or made a phone call. Hussein and Rukia have a pair of

Figure 1.4.1   Hussein Sormolo and his family in Addis Ababa, Ethiopia

Jane

Figure 1.4.2 Paul Rust and his family in Zug, Switzerland

shoes each. They buy new ones every two years. They have no savings, and the family doesn't take holidays.

Except for feast days, the family eats the same dish every meal—a grey, spongy, limp bread called injera, spread out like a cloth, and a spicy vegetable stew. Meat, fish, cheese, and eggs are luxuries. They only buy fruit when one of the children is sick. Just under a quarter of the family income is spent on cooking charcoal and cans of water. In a country where only a quarter of the people in the countryside have access to safe drinking water, Hussein's family is lucky. A standpipe is around the corner with reasonably clean water. That's about where their luck ends. With their neighbours, they used to have a toilet for 26 people. Now they have no toilet at all.

The Rust house, not counting the apartment, has three toilets, one each in the bathroom and two shower rooms of the four-story building. On the balconies under its broad, dark, solid eaves are cascades of red flowers. The well-used furnishings inside are not ostentatious, but the building is roomy and comfortable. From the top, there is a loft, four bedrooms, two living rooms, a kitchen, an office, a small wine cellar, a work room, and a garage parking three cars (Paul, Hedi, and Martin Rust have one each) with room for another five on the forecourt. The house has its own elevator.

Paul and Hedi are going on vacation for two weeks in Austria this month, and usually take a week at Easter. Each has a mobile phone. The home office has computers and Internet access. They have a TV, a VCR, and a dishwasher. They eat what they want, although their tastes are plain—meat with several vegetables, salad, sometimes a little wine.

Switzerland is a rich country landlocked by other rich countries. Ethiopia is a poor country landlocked by other poor countries. Unlike other African nations, Ethiopia was not a European colony, but its people have endured regular European military incursions, proxy superpower duels, and local wars that have exacerbated the ravages of famine and disease. Famines in the 1970s, 1980s, and 1990s killed 1.3 million people. Through the 1970s and 1980s, the country was embroiled in ideological and ethnic civil war. HIV/AIDS has infected 3 million Ethiopians and kills 300,000 a year.

Hussein knows little about Switzerland. "I heard about Switzerland on the radio but I don't know. I heard it was a rich country, they help poor countries," he said.

Paul thought he could find Ethiopia on the map. Switzerland is not as aloof from the world as it was, he points out: They joined the boycott of apartheid South Africa. He said his brother helped build a dairy in Nepal 20 years ago. His church had adopted a village in Romania, giving it money for a new church and a school. The talk turned to immigration. "The really poor people, they can't come to Switzerland, they need money to get here," said the Rusts' daughter, Andrea. "We work, and have our life, we have our own problems," said Andrea. "So we don't think very often of other people's problems. It's a little bit selfish."

Based on an article by James Meek. *The Guardian*, 22 August 2002.

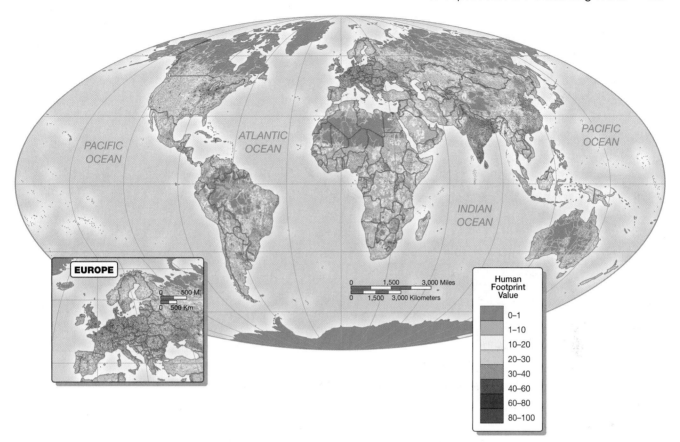

Figure 1.7 The human footprint This map, prepared by a team of scientists from the New York–based Wildlife Conservation Society and Columbia University's Center for International Earth Science Information Network (CIESIN), shows the extent and intensity of human influence on the land, reflecting population density, agricultural use, access from roads and waterways, electrical power infrastructure, and urbanization. The lower the number, the lesser the overall degree of human influence. *Source:* Sanderson, E.W., Jaiteh, M., Levy, M.A., Redford, K.H., Wannebo, A.V., and Woolmer, G. 2002. The human footprint and the last of the wild. BioScience 52(10): 891–904. (www.wcs.org/humanfootprint)

Health Issues The increased intensity of international trade and travel has also heightened the risk and speed of the spread of disease. Take the example of Severe Acute Respiratory Syndrome (SARS) in China in November 2002, which quickly spread and within four months had killed people as far afield as Brazil, Canada, Ireland, Romania, Spain, South Africa, Switzerland, the United Kingdom, and the United States. Similarly, there is serious concern about the possibility of epidemics resulting from zoonotic diseases (diseases originating with other species, e.g., anthrax, avian flu, Ebola, West Nile virus). The most significant international health issue so far, however, has been the spread of HIV/AIDS.

Over the past quarter century, HIV/AIDS quickly spread around the world from a single hearth area in Central Africa (**Figure 1.8**). Although it is now a disease of worldwide dimensions, it is Africa that suffers most from its effects: more than 15 million Africans have lost their lives to HIV/AIDS—it has become the main cause of death in Africa, killing more people than malaria and warfare combined.

Security Issues The increasing concern over international security can also be attributed in part to globalization. The attack on the World Trade Center in New York in September 2001 was an attempt to tear down a potent symbol not merely of the economic might of the United States but also of the values of capitalism and Western materialism that are threatening to displace the values of traditional Islamic societies.

More generally, as sociologist Ulrich Beck has pointed out, the high degree of interdependence that is now embedded in a globalizing and highly interconnected world has brought about all sorts of security issues. Beck argues that the contemporary world is characterized by the global—or at least transnational—*production* of risk. In traditional societies the risks faced by individuals and groups were associated mostly with hazards arising from nature (disease, flood, and famine), along with socially determined hazards such as invasion and conquest. The industrial societies of the nineteenth and twentieth centuries, with

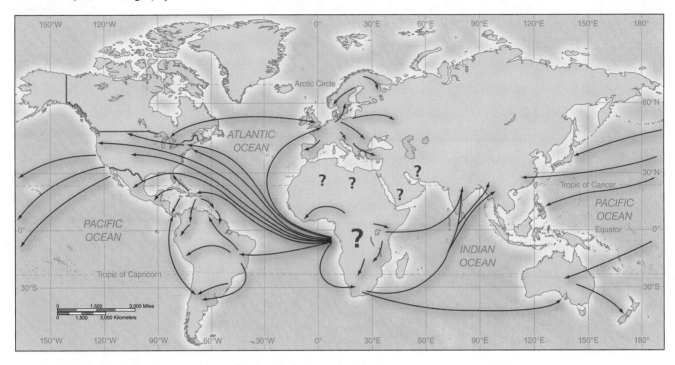

Figure 1.8 Diffusion of the HIV virus The probable early diffusion of HIV/AIDS. (Adapted from M. Smallman-Raynor, A. Cliff, and P. Haggett, *London International Atlas of AIDS*. Oxford: Blackwell Reference, 1992, Fig. 4.1(c), p. 146.)

more powerful technologies and weaponry, faced still more hazards, but these were mostly local and regional in nature.

Contemporary society, Beck points out, is characterized by the endemic production of potentially catastrophic risks, so that we now face another set of hazards, many of them uncontrollable and with a global reach. Examples include climate change as a result of human activity; the spread of weapons of mass destruction (i.e., nuclear and biological warfare); and the risk of accidents involving radioactivity from nuclear fuel and waste.

Overall, Beck argues, we are moving toward a *risk society*, in which the significance of wealth distribution is being eclipsed by the distribution of risk and in which politics is increasingly about avoiding hazards. As a result, knowledge—especially scientific knowledge—becomes increasingly important as a source of power, while science itself becomes increasingly politicized—as, for example, in the case of global climate change.

Geography in a Globalizing World

All this adds up to an intensification of global connectedness and the beginnings of the world as one interdependent system. Or, to be more precise, this is how it adds up for the 800 million or so of the world's population who are directly tied to global systems of production and consumption and who have access to global networks of communication and knowledge. All of us who are in this privileged position (and the fact that you are reading this book identifies you as one) are in the middle of a major reorganization of the world economy and a radical change in our relationships to other people and other places.

At first glance, it might seem that globalization will render geography obsolete—especially in the more developed parts of the world. High-tech communications and the global marketing of standardized products seem as if they might soon wash away the distinctiveness of people and places, permanently diminishing the importance of differences between places. Far from it. The new

Geographic Information Systems (GIS)

Geographic information systems (GIS) have rapidly grown to become one of the most important methods of geographical analysis. A *geographic information system* is an organized collection of computer hardware, software, and geographical data that is designed to capture, store, update, manipulate, and display geographically referenced information. The software in GIS incorporates programs to store and access spatial data, to manipulate those data, and to draw maps.

The most important aspect of GIS, from an analytical point of view, is that they allow data from several different sources on different topics and at different scales to be merged. This allows analysts to emphasize the spatial relationships between the objects being mapped. A GIS makes it possible to link, or integrate, information that is difficult to associate through any other means. For example, using GIS technology and water-company billing information, it is possible to simulate the discharge of materials into the septic systems in a neighbourhood upstream from a wetland.

The primary requirement for data to be used in GIS is that the locations for the variables are known. Location may be annotated by x, y, and z coordinates of longitude, latitude, and elevation or by such systems as postal codes. Any variable that can be located spatially can be fed into a GIS.

Data capture—putting the information into the system—is the time-consuming and expensive component of GIS work. Currently, for every dollar spent on GIS hardware, $10 must be spent on software and training and $100 on acquiring and updating data. As a result, it is only the more developed nations and the larger and more prosperous organizations that can take full advantage of GIS technologies.

Applications of GIS Technology

GIS technology can render visible many aspects of geography that were previously unseen. GIS can, for example, produce incredibly detailed maps based on millions of pieces of information—maps that could never be drawn by human hands. One example of such a map is the satellite image reconstruction of the land cover of part of Essex County in Ontario, shown in **Figure 1.5.1**. At the other extreme of spatial scale, GIS can put places under the microscope, creating detailed new insights using huge databases and effortlessly browsable media.

One frequent application of GIS is the weighing of different scenarios: What is the shortest route for emergency response vehicles? What is the best location for a new business, and where are its likely customers located? How can the spread of infectious diseases be blocked? What is the best option for a new road, power line, or sewer?

Critiques of GIS Technology

Within the past decade, GIS technology has resulted in the creation of more maps than were created in all of previous human history. One result is that as maps have become more commonplace, more people and more businesses have become more spatially aware. Nevertheless, some critics have argued that GIS technology represents no real advances in geographers' understanding of places and regions. The results of GIS, they argue, may be useful but are essentially mundane. This misses the point that however routine their subject may be, all maps constitute powerful and influential ways of representing the world. A more telling critique, perhaps, is that the real

© CNES 1988

Figure 1.5.1   Image of land cover   This image shows part of the intensive farming area of Essex County, south of Windsor, Ontario. GIS technology allows the interpretation of the satellite data to identify different types of land use. For example, Band 3 of the spectrum (near infrared) is displayed as red and indicates healthy, vigorous crops. In contrast, bare fields are shown as blue-white, water appears blue to black (depending on its depth), and the towns of Harrow and Kingsville are distinguished by their lack of colour.

impact of GIS technology has been to increase the level of surveillance of the population by those who already possess power and control. The fear is that GIS may be helping to create a world in which people are not treated and judged by who they are and what they do but more by where they live. People's credit ratings, their ability to buy insurance, and their ability to secure a mortgage, for example, are all routinely judged, in part, by GIS-based analyses that take into account the attributes and characteristics of their neighbours.

Sources: This feature draws from the GIS page of the United States Geological Service (www.usgs.gov/research/gis/title.html) and from Chapter 7 in D. Dorling and D. Fairbairn, *Mapping: Ways of Representing the World.* London: Addison Wesley Longman, 1997.

1.3   Geography in the Information Age

GIS is one of the ten "hottest" fields in terms of job creation. Penn State University has produced a four-minute video showing the astounding technological development and capabilities of GIS technology. You can watch it here: **http://geospatialrevolution.psu.edu/episode1/chapter3.**

GIS is a tool that can be used for different purposes. In military applications, GIS can allow cruise missiles to fly below enemy radar, supply target information for air strikes, and provide a comprehensive basis for military intelligence. GIS can also be used to make peace. The Geospatial Revolution Project at Penn State provides video examples of both applications of GIS: **http://geospatialrevolution .psu.edu/episode3/chapter1.**

In recent years, geospatial technology and GIS have also revolutionized police work and security surveillance. Learn more in this short video from Penn State University: **http://geospatialrevolution.psu.edu/episode3/chapter3.**

Environics Analytics, a Canadian GIS company, uses information from consumer surveys and censuses to develop likely behaviour profiles of postal code areas, which can then be used to target future marketing campaigns. You can enter your own postal code at **www.environicsanalytics.ca** and see what type of profile your neighbourhood has been assigned: Are you tagged as Blue-Collar Comfort, Electric Avenues, Les Chics, or Lunch at Tim's?

mobility of money, labour, products, and ideas actually increases the significance of place in the following very real and important ways:

- The more universal the diffusion of material culture and lifestyles, the more cherished regional and ethnic identities become. One example of this is the way in which the Quebec government is legislating against the Anglicization of the Quebecois language and culture.

- The faster the information highway takes people into cyberspace, the more they feel the need for a subjective setting—a specific place or community—they can call home. Examples are residential developments that have been carefully designed to create (or fake) a sense of community, identity, and heritage.

- The greater the reach of transnational corporations, the more easily they are able to respond to place-to-place variations in labour markets and consumer markets and the more often and more radically that economic geography has to be reorganized. Athletic shoe and apparel manufacturers, for example, frequently move production from one developing country to another in response to the changing international geography of wage rates and currencies.

- The greater the integration of transnational governments and institutions, the more sensitive people have become to localized cleavages of race, ethnicity, religion, or other markers of identity. Examples include the resurgence of Quebec nationalism and the rise of regionalist movements in Alberta.

In summary, there is no one experience of globalization. Although some places and regions have become more closely interconnected and interdependent as a result of globalization, others have been bypassed or excluded. All in all, the reality is that globalization is variously embraced, resisted, subverted, and exploited as it makes contact with specific cultures and settings. In the process, places are modified or reconstructed rather than destroyed or homogenized. Geography is the discipline that helps us understand exactly how globalization and places interact.

STUDYING HUMAN GEOGRAPHY

The study of geography involves the study of Earth as created by natural forces and as modified by human action. Accordingly, there are two main branches of geography—physical and human. *Physical geography* deals with Earth's natural processes and their outcomes. It is concerned, for example, with climate, weather patterns, landforms, soil formation, and plant and animal ecology. *Human geography* deals with the spatial organization of human activity and with people's relationships with their environments. This focus necessarily involves looking at natural physical environments insofar as they influence, and are influenced by, human activity. This means that the study of human geography must cover a wide variety of phenomena. These phenomena include, for example, agricultural production and food security, population change, the ecology of human diseases, resource management, environmental pollution, regional planning, and the symbolism of places and landscapes.

What is distinctive about the study of human geography is not so much the phenomena that are studied as the *way* in which they are approached. The contribution of human geography is to reveal, in relation to a wide spectrum of natural, social, economic, political, and cultural phenomena, *how and why geographical relationships are important*. Thus, for example, human geographers are interested not only in patterns of agricultural production but also in the geographical relationships and interdependencies that are both the cause and effect of such patterns. To put it in concrete terms, geographers are interested not only in what a specialized agricultural subregion is like (e.g., how the dairy farming area of Quebec produces its agricultural output, what makes its landscapes and culture distinctive, and so on) but also in its role in national and international agro-food systems (e.g., its interdependence with producers, distributors, and consumers in other places and regions—see Chapter 8).

Basic Tools

In general terms, the basic tools employed by geographers are similar to those in other disciplines. Like other social scientists, human geographers usually begin with *observation*. Information must be collected and data recorded. This can involve many different methods and tools. Fieldwork (surveying, asking questions, using scientific instruments to measure and record things), laboratory experiments, and archival searches are all used by human geographers to gather information about geographical relationships. Geographers also use **remote sensing** (**Figure 1.9**) to obtain information about parts of Earth's surface by means of aerial photography or satellite imagery designed to collect data on visible, infrared, and microwave sensor systems. For example, agricultural productivity can be monitored by remotely sensed images of crops, and energy efficiency can be monitored by remotely sensed levels of heat loss from buildings.

Once data have been obtained through some form of observation, the next important step is to portray and describe them through *visualization* or *representation*. This can involve a variety of tools, including written descriptions, charts, diagrams, tables, mathematical formulas, and maps. Visualization and representation are important activities because they allow large amounts of information

remote sensing: the collection of information about parts of Earth's surface by means of aerial photography or satellite imagery designed to record data on visible, infrared, and microwave sensor systems

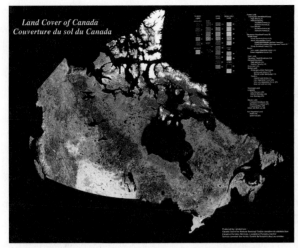

This image is based on data obtained from the SPOT 4 satellite. Prepared by the Canadian Centre for Remote Sensing, it shows the distribution of 31 different land cover types across Canada.

This Radarsat image shows the extent of the Red River flood on 27 April 1997. Areas of standing water are shown in blue. As can be seen, the floodway successfully diverted water around Winnipeg. Further south, toward Morris, localized flooding is evident. The interpretation of such images has enabled the Canadian Space Agency and the Manitoba Remote Sensing Agency to aid in flood preparedness.

Figure 1.9 Remotely sensed images Remotely sensed images can provide new ways of seeing the world, as well as unique sources of data on all sorts of environmental conditions. Remotely sensed images can be helpful in explaining problems and processes that would otherwise require expensive surveys and detailed cartography. (*Source:* Photos courtesy of Canada Centre for Remote Sensing, Natural Resources, Canada.)

model: often described as a theory or concept, a model is best thought of as "a simplification of reality" designed to help generalize our understanding of a particular process or set of phenomena; it can take the form of a diagram, equation, or simple verbal statement (such as a law) and may be used as a summary of past and present behaviour or to predict future events

to be explored, summarized, and presented to others. They are nearly always a first step in the analysis of geographical relationships, and they are important in conveying the findings and conclusions of geographical research.

At the heart of geographical research, as with other kinds of research, is the *analysis* of data. The objective of analysis, whether of quantitative or qualitative data, is to discover patterns and establish relationships so that hypotheses can be established and models can be built. **Models**, in this sense, are simplifications of reality that help explain the real world. Such models require tools that allow us to generalize about things. Once again we find that geographers are like other social scientists in that they use a wide range of analytical tools, including conceptual and linguistic devices, maps, charts, and mathematical equations.

In many ways, therefore, the tools and methods of human geographers are parallel to those used in other sciences, especially the social sciences. In addition, geographers increasingly use some of the tools and methods of the humanities—interpretive analysis and inductive reasoning, for example—together with ethnographic research and textual analysis. The most distinctive tools in the geographer's kit bag are, of course, maps and GIS (see **Geography Matters 1.5—GIS** and **Geography Matters 1.6—Understanding Maps**). As we have seen, maps (many of which are now generated with the help of GIS) can be used not only to describe data but also to serve as important sources of data and tools for analysis. Because of their central importance to geographers, maps can also be objects of study in their own right.

Fundamental Concepts of Geography

Region, location, distance, space, place, accessibility, spatial interaction, and *scale* are eight important concepts that geographers have developed in their approach to the world. Although these concepts may be familiar from everyday language, they do require some elaboration.

region: a larger-sized territory that encompasses many places, all or most of which share similar attributes that are distinct from the attributes of places elsewhere

Region The concept of the **region** is applied by geographers to larger-sized territories that encompass many places, all or most of which share similar attributes that are distinct from the attributes of places elsewhere. The concept of the region is thus used to distinguish one area from another. In everyday speech, we

Understanding Maps

All maps are simplifications of the world because they cannot show everything and therefore must select what they do show. They also distort what they show because maps are usually two-dimensional, graphic representations that use lines and symbols to convey information or ideas about spatial relationships that in reality occur in three dimensions. Maps that are designed to represent the *form* of Earth's surface and to show permanent (or at least long-standing) features, such as buildings, highways, field boundaries, and political boundaries, are called *topographic maps* (**Figure 1.6.1**). The usual device for representing the form of Earth's surface is the *contour*, a line that connects points of equal elevation. Maps that are designed to represent the spatial dimensions of particular conditions, processes, or events are called *thematic maps*. These can be based on any one of a number of devices that allow cartographers or mapmakers to portray spatial variations or spatial relationships.

One of these is the *isoline,* a line (similar to a contour) that connects places of equal data value (for example, air pollution, as in **Figure 1.6.2**). Maps based on isolines are known as *isopleth maps*. Another common device used in thematic maps is the *proportional symbol*. Circles, squares, spheres, cubes, or another shape can be drawn in proportion to the frequency of occurrence of some particular phenomenon at a given location. Linear symbols, such as arrows or lines, can also be drawn proportionally, to portray flows of things between particular places. **Figure 1.6.3** shows two examples of proportional symbols: flow lines and proportional circles. Simple distributions can be effectively portrayed through *dot maps*, in which a single dot or other symbol represents a specified number of occurrences of some particular phenomenon (an example used later in this book is Figure 4.19). Thematic maps can also be based on *located charts*, in which graphs or charts

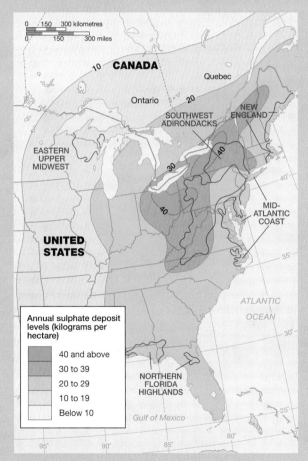

Figure 1.6.1 Topographic maps Topographic maps are maps that represent the form of Earth's surface in both horizontal and vertical dimensions. This extract is from a British Ordnance Survey map of the area just to the south of Edinburgh, Scotland. The height of landforms is represented by contours (lines that connect points of equal elevation), which on this map are drawn every 50 feet (15 metres), with contour values shown to the nearest metre. Features, such as roads, power lines, built-up areas, and so on, are shown by stylized symbols. Note how the closely spaced contours of the hill slopes are able to represent the shape and form of the land. (*Source:* Extract from Sheet 66, 1:50,000 Series, Ordnance Survey of the United Kingdom. Copyright © Crown copyright [87375M].)

Figure 1.6.2 Isoline maps Isoline maps portray spatial information by connecting points of equal data value. Contours on topographic maps (see Figure 1.6.1) are isolines. This map shows equal levels of air pollution in eastern North America. (*Source:* Reprinted with permission of Prentice Hall, from J.M. Rubenstein, *The Cultural Landscape: An Introduction to Human Geography,* 1996, p. 584. Adapted from William K. Stevens, "Study of Acid Rain Uncovers Threat to Far Wider Area." *New York Times,* 16 January 1990, p. 21, map.)

Figure 1.6.3 Two examples of proportional symbols in thematic mapping (a) *Flow lines.* In such maps, the magnitude of movement (or flow) to individual places or regions is expressed as a proportion of the total movement. This particular map shows the 1942 forced movement of 20,881 Japanese Canadians from their homes in coastal British Columbia to detention camps in the province's interior and to sugar beet farms in Alberta and Manitoba.
(b) *Proportional circles.* In these types of maps, the size of the circles is proportional to the phenomenon being mapped. This particular map shows the percentage of people across the country who curled in 1975.   *(Sources:* (a) Map prepared by Sean Dougherty, Vanier College, Montreal. (b) Douglas J. Dudycha, Stephen L.J. Smith, Terry O. Stewart, and Barry D. McPherson, *The Canadian Atlas of Recreation and Exercise.* Department of Geography, University of Waterloo, 1983: Department of Geography Publication Series No. 21, p. 37.)

(a) Flow lines

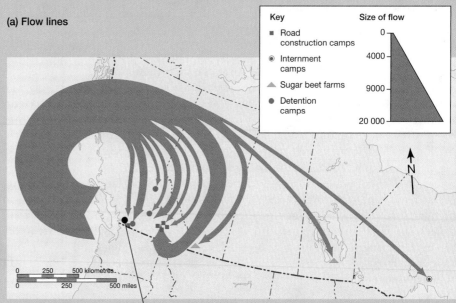

Vancouver: All 20 881 people removed were processed through a temporary camp at the Pacific National Exhibition grounds.

(b) Proportional circles

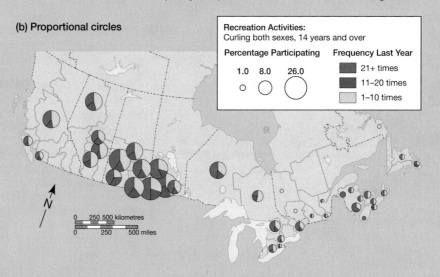

are located by place or region. In this way, a tremendous amount of information can be conveyed in one single map.

Yet another device is the *choropleth map*, in which tonal shadings are graduated to reflect area variations in numbers, frequencies, or densities (an example used later in this book is Figure 3.12). Choropleth maps use data that relate to the specific areas, or spatial units of measurement, that compose the map and from which the relevant information has been collected or recorded. Known more generally by geographers as **areal units**, these units may comprise areas as small as a city block or as large as a province or territory. Most large areal units of measurement are built up from smaller component units. For example, Statistics Canada data for *Census Metropolitan Areas* (or CMAs, which are defined as having an urban core population of at least 100,000 people) are built up (or *spatially aggregated*) from small component areal units, known as *census tracts*, which individually comprise between 2,500 and 8,000 people.

Map Scales

A *map scale* is the ratio between linear distance on a map and linear distance on Earth's surface. It is usually expressed in terms of corresponding lengths, as in "one centimetre equals one kilometre," or as a *representative fraction* (in this case, 1/100,000) or ratio (1:100,000). *Small-scale* maps are maps based on small representative fractions (for example, 1/1,000,000 or 1/10,000,000). Small-scale maps cover a large part of Earth's surface on the printed page. A map drawn on this page to the scale of 1:10,000,000 would easily cover a third of Canada; a map drawn to the scale of 1:16,000,000 would cover the whole of Europe. *Large-scale* maps are maps based on larger representative fractions (e.g., 1/25,000 or 1/10,000). A map drawn on this page to the scale of 1:10,000 would cover a typical suburban subdivision; a map drawn to the scale of 1:1,000 would cover just a block or two of it.

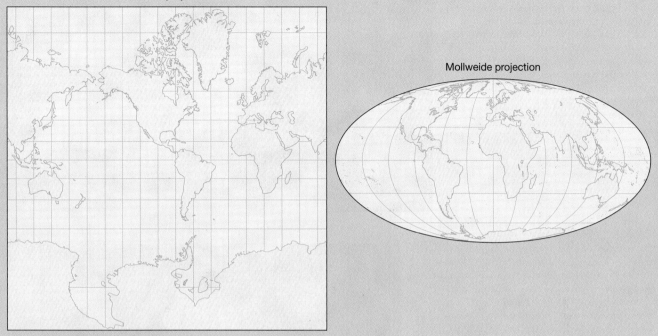

Mercator projection

Mollweide projection

Figure 1.6.4 Comparison of map projections Different map projections have different properties. On the Mercator projection, compass directions between any two points are true, and the shapes of land masses are true, but their relative sizes are distorted. On the Mollweide projection, relative sizes are true, but shapes are distorted. Note how vastly different in size Greenland appears!

Map Projections

A **map projection** is a systematic rendering on a flat surface of the geographical coordinates of the features found on Earth's surface. Because Earth is not a perfect sphere and its surface is curved, it is impossible to represent on a flat sheet of paper or monitor screen without some distortion. Cartographers have devised a number of different techniques of projecting latitude and longitude onto a plane surface, and the resulting representations of Earth have both advantages and disadvantages. None of them can represent distance correctly in all directions, though many can represent compass bearings or area without distortion. The choice of map projection depends largely on the purpose of the map.

Projections on which compass directions are rendered accurately are known as **conformal projections**. Another property of conformal projections is that the scale of the map is the same in any direction. The Mercator projection (**Figure 1.6.4**), for example, preserves directional relationships between places, and so the exact compass distance between any two points can be plotted as a straight line. As a result, it has been widely used in navigation. As Figure 1.6.4 shows, however, the Mercator projection distorts and exaggerates area more and more toward the poles—so much so that the poles cannot be shown as single points.

Projections that portray areas on Earth's surface in their true proportions are known as **equal-area** or **equivalent projections**. Such projections are used where the cartographer wants to compare and contrast distributions on

Earth's surface (for example, the relative area of different types of land use). Equal-area projections, such as the Mollweide projection (Figure 1.6.4), are especially useful for thematic maps showing economic, demographic, or cultural data. Unfortunately, preserving accuracy in terms of the *size* of areas means distorting the *shape* of areas.

For some applications, aesthetic appearance is more important than conformality or equivalence, and so cartographers have devised a number of other projections. Examples include the Times projection, which is used in many world atlases, and the Robinson projection, which is used by the National Geographic Society in many of its publications. The Robinson projection (**Figure 1.6.5**) is a compromise projection that distorts both area and directional relationships but provides a general-purpose world map.

There are also political considerations. Countries may appear larger and therefore more important on one projection rather than on another. The Gall-Peters projection, for example (**Figure 1.6.6**), is a deliberate attempt to give prominence to the poorer countries of the equatorial regions and the Southern Hemisphere. As such, it was officially adopted by the World Council of Churches, numerous agencies of the United Nations, and other international institutions. Its unusual shapes cause people to look at the world from a fresh perspective and so discover new insights.

In this book, we sometimes use another striking projection, the Dymaxion projection devised by Buckminster Fuller (**Figure 1.6.7**). Fuller was a modernist architect and industrial designer who wanted to produce a map of the

Figure 1.6.5   The Robinson projection
On the Robinson projection, distance, direction, area, and shape are all distorted in an attempt to balance the properties of the map. It is designed purely for appearance and is best used for thematic and reference maps at the world scale.   (*Source:* Reprinted with permission of Prentice Hall from E.F. Bergman, *Human Geography: Cultures, Connections, and Landscapes,* © 1995, p. 12.)

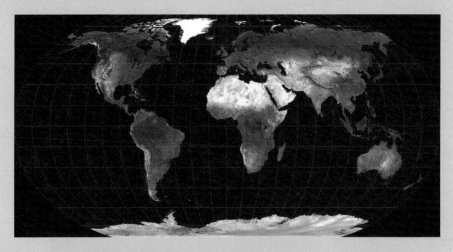

Figure 1.6.6 The Gall-Peters projection This equal-area projection is an attempt to offer an alternative to traditional projections, most of which exaggerate the size and apparent importance of the higher latitudes—that is, the world's core regions—and so promote the "Europeanization" of Earth. Although it has been adopted by the World Council of Churches, various agencies of the United Nations, and other international institutions, it has been criticized by cartographers on the grounds of aesthetics: one of the consequences of equal-area projections is that they distort the shape of land masses. (*Source:* Reprinted with permission of Prentice Hall from E.F. Bergman, *Human Geography: Cultures, Connections, and Landscapes,* © 1995, p. 13.)

Figure 1.6.7   Fuller's Dymaxion projection This striking map projection was designed by Buckminster Fuller (1895–1983). As this figure shows, Fuller achieved his objective of creating a map with the minimum of distortion to the shape of the world's major land masses by dividing the globe into triangular areas. Those areas not encompassing major land masses were cut away, allowing the remainder of the globe to be "unfolded" into a flat surface.   (*Source:* Buckminster Fuller Institute and Dymaxion Map Design, Santa Barbara, CA. The word *Dymaxion* and the Fuller Projection Dymaxion™ Map design are trademarks of the Buckminster Fuller Institute, Santa Barbara, California, © 1938, 1967 & 1992. All rights reserved.)

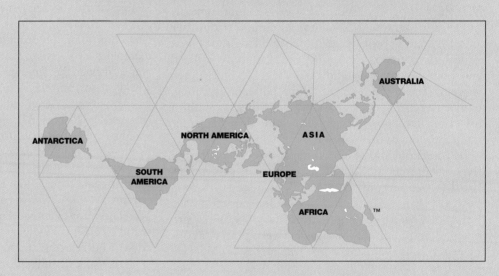

world with no significant distortion to any of the major land masses. The Dymaxion projection does this, though it produces a world that at first may seem disorienting. This is not necessarily such a bad thing: just like the Gall-Peters projection, it can force us to take a fresh look at the world and at the relationships between places. Because Europe, North America, and Japan are all located toward the centre of this map projection, it is particularly useful for illustrating two of the central themes of this book: the relationships among these prosperous regions and the relationships between this prosperous core group and the less prosperous, peripheral countries of the world. Fuller's projection shows the economically peripheral countries of the world as being cartographically peripheral, too.

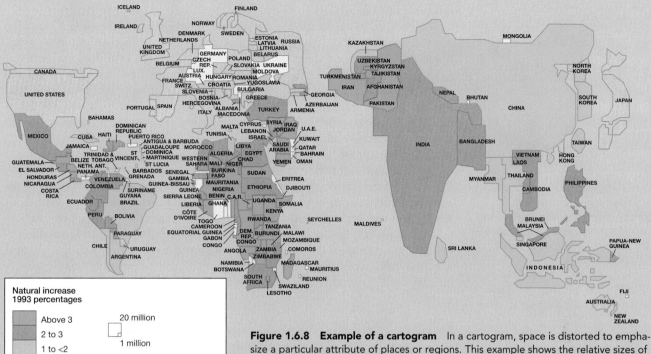

Natural increase 1993 percentages

- Above 3
- 2 to 3
- 1 to <2
- <1
- Decrease
- Not applicable

20 million
1 million

The size of each nation is proportional to its population.

Figure 1.6.8   Example of a cartogram   In a cartogram, space is distorted to emphasize a particular attribute of places or regions. This example shows the relative sizes of countries based on their populations rather than their areas; the cartographers have maintained the shape of each country as closely as possible to make the map easier to read. As you can see, population-based cartograms are very effective in demonstrating spatial inequality. Notice how Canada has all but disappeared.   (*Source:* M. Kidron and R. Segal [eds.], *The State of the World Atlas,* rev. 5th ed. London: Penguin Reference, 1995, pp. 28–29.)

One particular kind of map projection that is sometimes used in small-scale thematic maps is the *cartogram*. In this kind of projection, the size of a given area is rendered proportional to the statistical value of the phenomenon that is found in that area: the larger the area, the greater the value. **Figure 1.6.8** shows a cartogram of the world in which countries are represented as proportional to their population. This sort of projection is particularly effective in helping to visualize relative inequalities among the countries of the world.

Finally, the advent of computer graphics has made it possible for cartographers to move beyond the use of maps as two-dimensional representations of Earth's surface. Computer software that renders three-dimensional statistical data onto the flat surface of a monitor screen or a piece of paper facilitates the **visualization** of many aspects of human geography in innovative and provocative ways (**Figure 1.6.9**).

areal units: spatial units of measurement, such as a city block or province, used for recording statistics

map projection: a systematic rendering on a flat surface of the geographic coordinates of the features found on Earth's surface

conformal projections: map projections on which compass bearings are rendered accurately

equal-area (equivalent) projections: map projections that portray areas on Earth's surface in their true proportions

visualization: a computer-assisted representation of spatial data, often involving three-dimensional images and innovative perspectives, that reveals spatial patterns and relationships more effectively

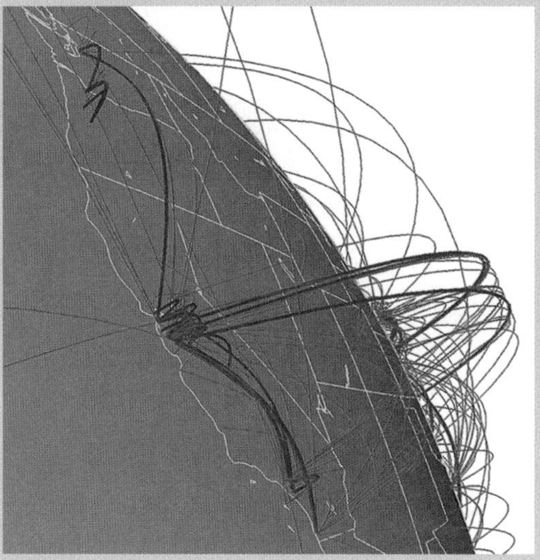

Figure 1.6.9   Visualization   This example shows the spatial structure of the Internet's multicast backbone that is the most popular way of transmitting real-time video and audio streams. (*Source:* T. Munzner, E. Hoffman, K. Claffy, and B. Fenner, "Visualizing the Global Topology of the MBone," *Proceedings of the 1996 IEEE Symposium on Information Visualization,* pp. 85–92, 1996, San Francisco, CA.)

talk very imprecisely about regions. To be useful to a geographer, however, a region must be based on specific definitions to have any real meaning.

Geographers have traditionally divided regions into three types: *formal, functional,* and *vernacular.* A *formal region* is one that is uniform in terms of specific criteria—the Canadian Shield is an example if we consider geological characteristics. A *functional region* is an area that literally functions as a unit, economically or administratively, and is usually organized by transport routes focused on a dominant city. A *vernacular region* is the local region as identified by the region's own inhabitants.

The concept of the region underlies the subdiscipline of *regional geography,* which combines elements of both physical and human geography. **Regional geography** is concerned with the ways in which unique combinations of environmental and human factors produce territories with distinctive landscapes and cultural attributes. Indeed, some of the most famous geographers (such as Vidal de la Blache and Carl Sauer) have believed that regional geography *is* geography. Vidal de la Blache compared the way in which the physical and human aspects of a region mould each other to that of a "snail growing into its shell" so that the region becomes "a medal struck in the likeness of a people."

Location   In everyday speech, location is often *nominal,* or expressed solely in terms of the names given to regions and places. We speak, for example, of Vancouver, or of Stanley Park, a location within Vancouver. Location can be used also as an *absolute* concept, whereby locations are fixed mathematically through coordinates of latitude and longitude (**Figure 1.10**). **Latitude** refers to the angular distance of a point on Earth's surface, measured in degrees, minutes, and seconds north or south of the equator, which is assigned a value of 0°. Lines of latitude around the globe run parallel to the equator, which is why they are sometimes referred to as *parallels.* **Longitude** refers to the angular distance of a point on Earth's surface, measured in degrees, minutes, and seconds east or west from the *prime meridian* (the line that passes through both poles and through Greenwich, England, which is assigned a value of 0°). Lines of longitude, called *meridians,* always run from the North Pole (latitude 90° north) to the South Pole (latitude 90° south). Vancouver's coordinates are precisely 49°20′N, 123°10′W.

Thanks to the **Global Positioning System (GPS)**, it is now very easy to determine the latitude, longitude, and elevation of any given point. The GPS consists of approximately 30 satellites that orbit Earth on precisely predictable paths, broadcasting highly accurate time and locational information. Using those signals, GPS receivers in cars and even cell phones can calculate their precise position day or night, in all weather conditions, in any part of the world. The GPS

regional geography: the study of the ways in which unique combinations of environmental and human factors produce territories with distinctive landscapes and cultural attributes

latitude: the angular distance of a point on Earth's surface, *measured north or south* from the equator, which is 0°

longitude: the angular distance of a point on Earth's surface, *measured east or west* from the prime meridian (the line that passes through both poles and through Greenwich, England, and that has the value of 0°)

Global Positioning System (GPS): a system of satellites that orbit Earth on precisely predictable paths, broadcasting highly accurate time and locational information

1.4   Geography in the Information Age

The Geospatial Revolution Project at Penn State features a two-minute video describing how GPS works: **http://geospatialrevolution.psu.edu/episode1/chapter2.**

The GPS capabilities of smartphones make it possible to locate the positions of their users—for better or for worse: GPS locators have helped find people buried under rubble or washed out to sea by the 2011 earthquake and tsunami in Japan; but they can also be used to track the movements of people without their knowledge and so reveal whether homes are unattended or where victims of abusive spouses have fled to. To learn why you should be aware of the locator settings on *your* smartphone, go to **http://geospatialrevolution.psu.edu/episode3/chapter4.**

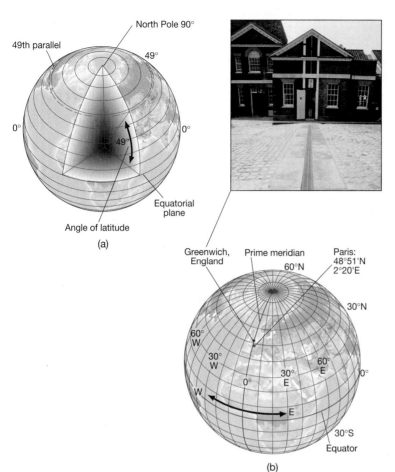

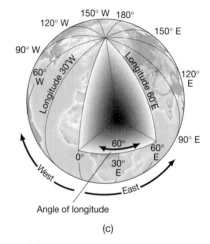

The prime meridian at the Royal Observatory in Greenwich, England—The observatory was founded by Charles II in 1675 with the task of setting standards for time, distance, latitude, and longitude—the key components of navigation.

Figure 1.10   Latitude and longitude   Lines of latitude and longitude provide a grid that covers Earth, allowing any point on Earth's surface to be accurately referenced. Latitude is measured in angular distance (that is, degrees and minutes) north or south of the equator, as shown in (a). Longitude is measured in the same way, but east and west from the prime meridian, a line around Earth's surface that passes through both poles (North and South) and the Royal Observatory in Greenwich, just to the east of central London, in England. Locations are always stated with latitudinal measurements first. The location of Paris, France, for example, is 48°51′N and 2°20′E, as shown in (b). (*Sources:* (a) and (c), adapted from R.W. Christopherson, *Geosystems: An Introduction to Physical Geography,* 2nd ed., © 1994, pp. 13, 15. (b), adapted from E.F. Bergman, *Human Geography: Cultures, Connections, and Landscapes,* © 1995, Figs. 1–10 and 1–13.)

has drastically increased the accuracy and efficiency of collecting spatial data. In combination with GIS technology and remote sensing, the GPS has revolutionized mapmaking and spatial analysis.

Location can also be *relative,* fixed in terms of site or situation (**Figure 1.11**). **Site** refers to the physical attributes of a location: its terrain, soil, vegetation, and water sources, for example. **Situation** refers to the location of a place relative to other places and human activities: its accessibility to routes, for example, or its nearness to population centres. For example, Stanley Park has a coastal site and is situated northwest of downtown Vancouver.

Finally, location also has a *cognitive* dimension, in that people have mental images of places and regions. These "**mental maps**" can be compiled from people's own knowledge and experience of places, their imaginations, hearsay, or a combination of these sources. Location in these mental maps is fluid, depending on people's changing information and perceptions of the principal landmarks in their environment. **Figure 1.12** shows one person's cognitive image of Montreal. As the drawing shows, the relative importance of places affects our mental maps.

Distance   Distance is also useful as an *absolute* physical measure, whose units we may count in kilometres, and as a *relative* measure, expressed in terms of time, effort, or cost. For instance, it can take more time to travel 10 kilometres

site: the physical attributes of a location—its terrain, soil, vegetation, and water sources, for example

situation: the location of a place relative to other places and human activities

cognitive images (mental maps): psychological representations of locations that are created from people's individual ideas and impressions of these locations

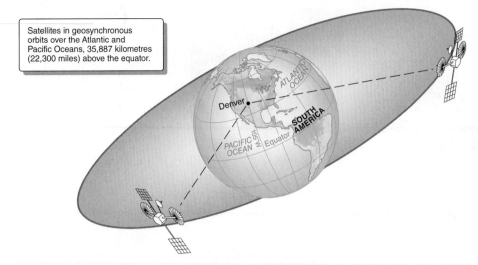

Satellites in geosynchronous orbits over the Atlantic and Pacific Oceans, 35,887 kilometres (22,300 miles) above the equator.

Figure 1.11 The importance of site and situation The location of telecommunications activities in Denver, Colorado, provides a good example of the significance of the geographic concepts of site (the physical attributes of a location) and situation (the location of a place relative to other places and human activities). Denver houses the headquarters of large U.S. cable companies, an industry-wide research lab, and a cluster of specialized support companies that employ thousands of people. Denver's high elevation *site* (1,600 metres above sea level) is important because it gives transmitter and receiver dishes a better "view" of communications satellites. Its *situation*, on the 105th meridian and equidistant between the telecommunications satellites that are in geostationary orbit over the Pacific and Atlantic Oceans, allows it to send cable programming directly, not just to the whole of the Americas, but to every continent except Antarctica. This is important because it avoids "double-hop" transmission (in which a signal goes up to a satellite, then down, then up and down again), which increases costs and decreases picture quality. Before the location of telecommunications facilities in Denver, places east or west of the 105th meridian would have to double-hop some of their transmissions because satellite dishes would not have a clear "view" of both the Pacific and Atlantic telecommunications satellites.

Figure 1.12 One person's cognitive image of Montreal This mental map was drawn by a geography student at Concordia University in Montreal as part of a class exercise. The student has included some (but not all) of Montreal's prominent landmarks, particularly "the mountain" in the city's centre. In addition, the shape of Montreal's island is distorted, emphasizing areas most familiar to the student. Canadian architectural scholar Witold Rybczynski observes of his own years as a student at McGill University in Montreal that "the gym marked the northernmost edge of my campus world, just as Joe's Steak House circumscribed it to the south. The latter does not appear on the official map of the university, but each of us carries mental place maps within us—maps that often bear little resemblance to reality." Yet, for us, he concludes, "they are truer depictions than those of cartographers." (*Source:* Witold Rybczynski, *Looking Around: A Journey through Architecture.* Toronto: HarperCollins, 1992, p. 116.)

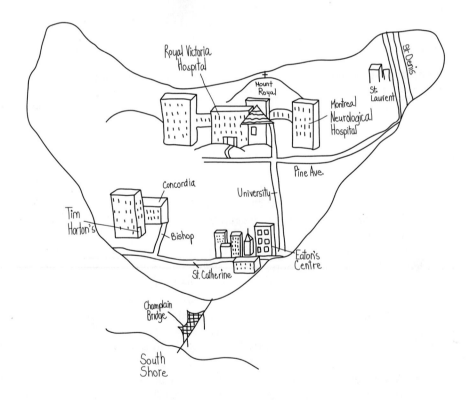

from point A to point B than it does to travel 10 kilometres from point A to point C. Similarly, it can cost more (or less).

The distance (in social space) between social groups is known as *social distance* and has, for example, been used in explanations of how social areas within cities develop (see Chapter 11). Groups that are close together in terms of social distance will interact more frequently than groups that are socially very distant from each other—irrespective of the actual physical distance between them. In this way, social processes of assimilation and discrimination can also become powerful spatial processes shaping a city.

Geographers also have to recognize that distance can sometimes be in the eye of the beholder: it can *seem* longer or more pleasant going from A to B than from A to C. This is **cognitive distance**, the distance that people *perceive* to exist in a given situation. Cognitive distance is based on people's personal judgments about the degree of spatial separation between points. It is precisely this cognitive distance that is reflected in mental maps.

The importance of distance as a fundamental factor in determining real-world relationships is a central theme in geography. It was once described as the "first law" of geography: "Everything is related to everything else, but near things are more related than distant things." Waldo Tobler, a geographer from the University of California, Santa Barbara, who put it this way, is one of many who have investigated the **friction of distance**, the deterrent or inhibiting effect of distance on human activity.

These geographers established that these effects are not uniform; that is, not directly proportional to distance itself. This is true whether distance is measured in absolute terms (kilometres, for example) or in relative terms (time or cost, for example). The deterrent effects of extra distance tend to lessen as greater distances are involved. Thus, for example, although there is a big deterrent effect in having to travel 2 kilometres rather than 1 to get to a grocery store, the deterrent effect of the same extra distance (1 kilometre) after already travelling 10 kilometres is relatively small.

This sort of relationship creates what geographers call a distance-decay function. A **distance-decay function** describes the rate at which a particular activity or phenomenon diminishes with increasing distance. A typical distance-decay function is described by the graph in **Figure 1.13**, which shows how the measure of almost any aspect of human behaviour diminishes with increasing distance.

Distance-decay functions reflect people's behavioural response to opportunities and constraints in time and space. As such, they are a reflection of the utility of particular locations to people. The **utility** of a specific place or location refers to its usefulness to a particular person or group. In practice, utility is thought of in different ways by different people in different situations. The business manager of a supermarket chain, for example, will decide on the utility of potential new store locations by weighing the projected costs and revenues for each potential site. When deciding where to retire, however, that same manager will be weighing a wide range of quality-of-life aspects such as prestige, convenience, or feelings of personal safety that may well modify or override financial aspects as the dominant measure of utility.

The common unifying theme here is that in most circumstances, regardless of how people think of place utility, they tend to *seek to maximize the net utility of location*. The supermarket chain's business manager, for example, will seek the new store location that is most likely to yield the greatest profit. Seeking to maximize the net utility of location means that a great deal of human activity is influenced by what University of Washington geographer Richard Morrill once called the "nearness principle." According to this principle—a more explicit version of Tobler's first law—people will seek to

- maximize the overall utility of places at minimum effort
- maximize connections among places at minimum cost
- locate related activities as close together as possible

As a result, behaviours, locational decisions, and interrelations between people and places come to take on fairly predictable, organized patterns. One of the tasks of geographers is to identify, describe, map, and analyze these patterns, thus making them intelligible to non-geographers.

cognitive distance: the distance that people perceive to exist in a given situation

friction of distance: the deterrent or inhibiting effect of distance on human activity

distance-decay function: the rate at which a particular activity or process diminishes with increasing distance

utility: the usefulness of a specific place or location to a particular person or group

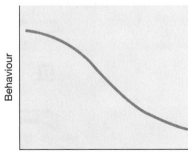

Figure 1.13   The friction of distance   The effects of distance on people's behaviour can be charted on graphs like this one. The friction of distance is a reflection of the time and cost of overcoming distance: the farther people have to travel, the less likely they are to do so.

TABLE 1.1 Different Kinds of Spaces Analyzed by Human Geographers

Absolute Space: Mathematical Space	Relative Space: Socioeconomic Space	Relative Space: Experiential/ Cultural Space	Cognitive Space: Behavioural Space
Points	Sites	Places	Landmarks
Lines	Situations	Ways	Paths
Areas	Routes	Territories	Districts
Planes	Regions	Domains	Environments
Configurations	Distributions	Worlds	Spatial Layouts

Source: Based on H. Couclelis, "Location, Place, Region and Space," in R. Abler et al., *Geography's Inner Worlds*. New Brunswick, NJ: Rutgers University Press, 1992, Table 10.1, p. 461.

Space   Like distance, space can be measured in absolute, relative, and cognitive terms. **Table 1.1** lists the concepts human geographers use in talking about space in these various terms. Absolute space is a mathematical space, described through points, lines, areas, and planes whose relationships can be fixed precisely through mathematical reasoning. Several ways of analyzing space mathematically are useful to geographers. The conventional way is to view space as a container, defined by rectangular coordinates and measured in absolute units of distance (kilometres, for example). Geographers also use other mathematical conceptions of space, however. One example is **topological space**, defined as the connections between, or connectivity of, particular points in space (**Figure 1.14**). Topological

topological space: the connections between, or connectivity of, particular points in space

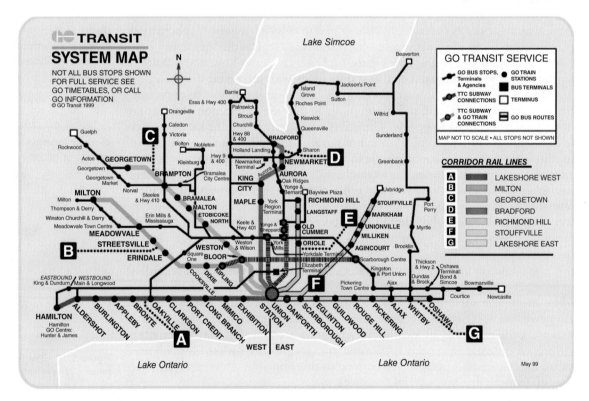

Figure 1.14 Topological space   This map of the GO Transit system in Toronto is a topological map, showing how specific points are joined within a particular network. The most important aspects of networks of any kind, from the geographer's viewpoint, are their connectivity attributes. These attributes determine the flow of people and things (goods, information) and the centrality of places. For example, the GO system gives Brampton a very high degree of connectivity because several lines intersect there. Brampton is therefore relatively central within the "space of flows" of passenger traffic in the Greater Toronto Area. Bramalea—nearby in absolute terms—is much less central, however, and much less of a nexus of passenger flows. Note that, in a topological map, distances are not necessarily drawn to scale.   (*Source*: Transit Toronto http://transit.toronto.on.ca/archives/maps/go99.gif)

space is measured not in terms of conventional measures of distance but rather by the nature and degree of connectivity between locations.

Relative measurements of space can also take the form of socioeconomic space or of experiential or cultural space. *Socioeconomic space* can be described in terms of sites and situations, routes, regions, and distribution patterns. In these terms, spatial relationships have to be fixed through measures of time, cost, profit, and production, as well as through physical distance. Dividing the world into economic blocks, such as the West, or according to gross national product (GNP) are examples: an economic scale replaces simple distance as a measure. *Experiential or cultural space* is the space of groups of people with common ties, and it is described through the places, territories, and settings whose attributes carry special meaning for these particular groups. Finally, **cognitive space** is defined and measured in terms of people's values, feelings, beliefs, and perceptions about locations, districts, and regions. Cognitive space can be described, therefore, in terms of behavioural space—landmarks, paths, environments, and spatial layouts.

cognitive space: space defined and measured in terms of the nature and degree of people's values, feelings, beliefs, and perceptions about locations, districts, and regions

When we begin to think about space in these relative terms, we can understand that space is much more than an objective "container" in which activity occurs; in many ways, space is itself *created* or called into being by that activity. This is not an easy point to grasp and is the focus of some of the latest research in geography. However, a simple example can illustrate the idea. Consider the history of settlement of the Prairies, and imagine being one of the first immigrants to establish a farm there. In the first phase of settlement, distance has no effect on us because we are isolated and self-sufficient. But once a town is established in that landscape, a "centre" is created and the location of our farm is now redefined in terms of its distance from that centre. This is extremely important if we begin to transport our grain to the grain elevator in that newly created town, from where it will be transported to a distant market by rail. In other words, *distance* and all of the effects of the friction of distance are *created*—in this case, by the form of economic exploitation being used to settle the Prairies—and *space is itself produced*. (This process is one of the reasons why the exact route of the Canadian Pacific Railway across the country was so hotly contested, and many speculators lost money gambling on the sites to be chosen for settlements.)

Contemporary geographical thinking about the concept of space owes a great deal to the work of the French scholar Henri Lefebvre (1901–1991) and, in particular, his 1974 book *The Production of Space*.[8] In this work, Lefebvre explores how society constantly produces space, for example by assigning economic value to distance: in communist economies, common ownership of land prevented the creation of a land market and the creation of rich and poor economic zones found in Western capitalist societies. Lefebvre's finding that space is a cultural and social creation holds the promise that many geographical problems are not, ultimately, rooted in physical space as much as they are in more abstract social spaces—spaces in which it might be possible to effect change for the better.

Place   Throughout this chapter, we have been considering the concept of **place**. As we have seen, places are objective locations that have both uniqueness and interdependent relations with other places. It is appropriate now to consider how to define this concept because its full meaning can only be understood in contrast to that of *space*.

Canadian author Mordecai Richler once described Canada as "justifiably better known for its spaces rather than its places."[9] At first sight, this seems a

place: a concept with two levels of meaning: (1) an objective location that has both uniqueness and interdependence with other places; (2) a subjective social and cultural construct—somewhere that has personal meaning for individuals or groups

[8] Alison Blunt and Jane Wills, *Dissident Geographies: An Introduction to Radical Ideas and Practice*. Harlow: Prentice Hall, 2000, pp. 75–79.

[9] Mordecai Richler, "Quebec City's Prime Time." In A.M. Rosenthal and A. Gelb (eds.), *The Sophisticated Traveler. Winter: Love It or Leave It*. New York: Villard Books, 1984, p. 89.

reasonable enough statement. But, in some respects, Richler may be quite wrong. If we follow the geographer Yi-Fu Tuan's memorable remark that "place is space filled with meaning," we will see that the concept of place draws its real meaning from us. Our lives in the world inevitably make certain small parts of that world unique and meaningful to us as individuals. We are also influenced in these assessments by our wider social and cultural frames of reference. Place, in this sense, is therefore defined subjectively as somewhere that has personal meaning to individuals or groups. In a more formal way, we can define it as a social and cultural *construct*. On the basis of this discussion, we can see that the term **place making** describes any activity, deliberate or unintentional, that enables space to develop meaning.

place making: any activity, deliberate or unintentional, that enables space to acquire meaning

In this sense, Canada is full of places, for it is a land that embodies the lives and memories of Aboriginal peoples, of immigrants and their descendants who settled the land with farms and cities, and of tourists enraptured by our landscape. As Wallace Stegner, an American writer raised on the Saskatchewan–Montana border, has written:

> The geologist who surveyed southern Saskatchewan in the 1870s called it one of the most desolate and forbidding regions on earth. . . . Desolate? Forbidding? There was never a country that in its good moments was more beautiful. Even in drouth [drought] or dust storm or blizzard it is the reverse of monotonous, once you have submitted to it with all the senses.[10]

Accessibility Given that people tend to pursue the nearness principle, the concept of accessibility is very important. **Accessibility** is generally defined by geographers in terms of relative location: the opportunity for contact or interaction from a given point or location in relation to other locations. It implies *proximity*, or nearness, to something. Because it is a fundamental influence on the utility of locations, distance is an important influence on people's behaviour—but it is by no means the only important aspect.

accessibility: the opportunity for contact or interaction from a given point or location in relation to other locations

Connectivity is also an important aspect of accessibility because contact and interaction are dependent on channels of communication and transportation: streets, highways, railways, telephone lines, cell phone coverage, and broadband connections, for example. Effective accessibility is thus a function not only of distance but also of the configuration of networks of communication and transportation.

Accessibility is often a function of economic, cultural, and social factors. In other words, relative concepts and measures of distance are often as important as absolute distance. A nearby facility, such as a health care clinic, is accessible to us only if we can actually afford the cost of getting there; if it seems close according to our own standards of distance; if we can afford to use the facility; if we feel that it is socially and culturally acceptable for us to use it; and so on. To take another example, a daycare centre may be located just a few blocks from a single-parent family, but the centre is not truly accessible if it opens after the parent has to be at work or if the parent feels that the staff, children, or other parents at the centre are from an incompatible social or cultural group.

Spatial Interaction Interdependence between places and regions can be sustained only through movement and flows. Geographers use the term *spatial interaction* as shorthand for all kinds of movement and flows involving human activity. Freight shipments, commuting, shopping trips, telecommunications, electronic cash transfers, migration, and vacation travel are all examples of spatial interaction. The fundamental principles of spatial interaction can be reduced

---

[10] W. Stegner, *Wolf Willow*. New York: Ballantine, 1973 [first published 1955], pp. 6, 8.

to four basic concepts: complementarity, transferability, intervening opportunities, and—most importantly—spatial diffusion.

■ *Complementarity.* A precondition for interdependence between places is complementarity. For any kind of spatial interaction to occur between two places, there must be a demand in one place and a supply that matches, or complements, it in the other. This complementarity can be the result of several factors. One important factor is the variation in physical environments and resource endowments from place to place. For example, the flow of sun-starved Canadian visitors to Florida, Mexico, and Cuba during the winter is the result of climatic complementarity. To take another example, the flow of crude oil from Saudi Arabia (with vast oil reserves) to Japan (with none) is a function of complementarity in natural resource endowments.

A second factor is the international division of labour that derives from the evolution of the world's economic systems. In a nutshell, the more developed countries specialize in more profitable manufacturing and knowledge-based industries, whereas the less developed countries are left with the less profitable function of supplying foodstuffs, raw materials, and exotic produce (see Chapter 2). This uneven division of labour was brought about through a combination of colonialism, imperialism, and sheer economic dominance on the part of the more developed countries. Among the many flows resulting from this complementarity are shipments of sugar from Barbados to the United Kingdom, bananas from Costa Rica and Honduras to Canada, palm oil from Cameroon to France, automobiles from France to Algeria, school textbooks from the United Kingdom to Kenya, and investment capital from Canada to mining projects in many less developed countries.

A third contributory factor to complementarity is the operation of principles of specialization and economies of scale. Places, regions, and countries can derive economic advantages from the efficiencies created through specialization, which allows for larger-scale operations. **Economies of scale** are cost advantages to manufacturers that accrue from high-volume production, since the average cost of production per unit falls with increasing output (**Figure 1.15**). Economic specialization results in complementarities, which in turn contribute to patterns of spatial interaction. One example is the specialization of Israeli farmers in high-value fruit and vegetable crops for export to the European Union, which in return exports grains and root crops to Israel.

■ *Transferability.* In addition to complementarity, another precondition for interdependence between places is *transferability,* which depends on the frictional or deterrent effects of distance. Transferability is a function of two things: the costs of moving a particular item, measured in real money or time, and the ability of the item to bear these costs. If, for example, the costs of moving a product from one place to another make it too expensive to sell successfully at its destination, then that product does not have transferability between those places.

Transferability varies between places, between kinds of items, and between modes of transportation and communication. The transferability of coal, for example, is much greater between places that are connected by rail or by navigable waterways than between places connected only by highways. This is because it is much cheaper to move heavy, bulky materials by rail, barge, or ship. The transferability of fruit and salad crops, on the other hand, depends more on the speed of transportation and the availability of specialized refrigerated vehicles. Finally, the degree of transferability of money, information, and other virtual goods has been greatly altered through recent advances in communications technologies.

economies of scale: cost advantages to manufacturers that accrue from high-volume production, since the average cost of production falls with increasing output

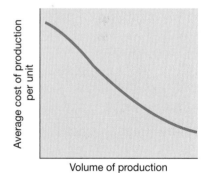

Figure 1.15 Economies of scale In many manufacturing enterprises, the higher the volume of production, the lower the average cost of producing each unit. This relationship occurs partly because high-volume production allows for specialization and division of labour, which can increase efficiency and hence lower costs. It also occurs partly because most manufacturing activities have significant fixed costs (such as product design and the cost of renting or buying factory space) that must be paid for irrespective of the volume of production, and so the larger the output, the lower the fixed cost per unit. These savings are known as *economies of scale.*

1.5   Geography in the Information Age

What is most significant about the latest developments in transport and communication infrastructure is that they are not only global in scope but also are able to penetrate to local scales. As this penetration occurs, some places that are distant in kilometres are "moving" closer together, whereas some that are close in terms of absolute space are becoming more distant in terms of their ability to reach one another electronically. Much depends on the mode of communication—the extent to which people in different places are "plugged in" to new technologies: microwave channels are good for person-to-person communication but depend on line of sight; telecommunications satellites are excellent for reaching remote areas but involve significant capital costs for users, whereas fibre-optic cable is excellent for areas of high-population density but not feasible for more remote, rural areas.

Transferability also varies over time, as successive innovations in transport and communications technologies and successive waves of infrastructure development (canals, railways, harbour installations, roads, bridges, and so on) alter the geography of transport costs. As a result, the spatial organization of many different activities is continually changing and readjusting. Overall, infrastructure improvements have the effect that the world appears to be "shrinking": places move closer together in travel time or cost, or ease of communication. Geographers use the concept of *time-space convergence* to express how, in general, such space-adjusting technologies have brought places closer together over time. Overland travel between New York and Boston, for example, has been reduced from 3.5 days (in 1800) to 5 hours (in 2000) as the railroad displaced stagecoaches and was in turn displaced by automobile travel. Other important space-adjusting innovations include air travel and air cargo; telegraphic, telephonic, and satellite communications systems; national postal services and package delivery services; and fax machines, cell phones, fibre-optic networks, and email.

- *Intervening opportunities.* Although complementarity and transferability are preconditions for spatial interaction, intervening opportunities are important in determining the *volume* and *pattern* of movements and flows. Intervening opportunities are simply alternative origins or destinations. Such opportunities are not necessarily situated directly between two points. Thus, for Scottish families considering a Mediterranean vacation in southern France, resorts in Spain, Italy, or Greece that are physically more distant may nonetheless represent intervening opportunities if they can be reached more quickly and more cheaply than resorts in France.

  The size and relative importance of alternative destinations are also important aspects of the concept of intervening opportunity. For our Scottish families, Spanish resorts may offer the greatest intervening opportunity because they contain the largest number of hotel rooms. We can state the principle of intervening opportunity as follows: spatial interaction between an origin and a destination will be proportional to the number of opportunities at that destination and inversely proportional to the number of opportunities at alternative destinations.

- *Spatial diffusion.* Disease outbreaks, technological innovations, political movements, and new musical fads all originate in specific places and subsequently spread to other places and regions. The way in which things spread through space and over time—**spatial diffusion**—is one of the most important aspects of spatial interaction and is crucial to an understanding

spatial diffusion: the way in which things spread through space and over time

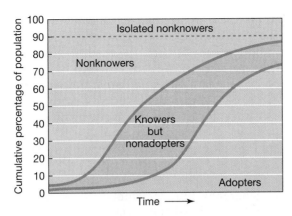

Figure 1.16   Spatial diffusion   The spatial diffusion of many phenomena (such as diseases or ideas) tends to follow an S-curve of slow build-up, rapid spread, and levelling off. In the case of the spread of a disease, such as measles, or the adoption of an innovation, for example, it usually takes a while for enough people to become exposed to the disease or for sufficient potential adopters to get to know about the innovation, and even longer for a critical mass of them to adopt it. After that, the disease or innovation spreads quite rapidly, until most of the susceptible population or potential adopters have been exposed to the disease or innovation. (*Source:* D.J. Walmsley and G.J. Lewis, *Human Geography: Behavioural Approaches.* London: Longman, 1984, fig. 5.3, p. 52. Reprinted by permission of Addison Wesley Longman Ltd.)

of geographical change. Diffusion seldom occurs in an apparently random way, jumping unpredictably all over the map. Rather, it occurs as a function of statistical probability, which is often based on fundamental geographical principles of distance and movement. The diffusion of a contagious disease, for example, is a function of the probability of physical contact, modified by variations in individual resistance to the disease. The result is typically a "wave" of diffusion that describes an S-curve, with a slow build-up, rapid spread, and final levelling off (**Figure 1.16**).

It is possible to recognize several different spatial tendencies in patterns of diffusion. In *expansion diffusion* (also called *contagious diffusion*—**Figure 1.17a**), a phenomenon spreads due to the proximity of carriers, or agents of change, who are fixed in their location. A good example is the spread of a contagious disease across a region. With *hierarchical diffusion*, a phenomenon (e.g., a fashion trend) can be diffused from one location to another without necessarily spreading to places in between (**Figure 1.17b**). This is because such phenomena first only spread *between* centres of equal rank in an urban hierarchy (between major world cities, for example), before spreading *down* the urban hierarchy (from city to town to village, for example). A third type of diffusion that involves the actual movement of people is called *relocation diffusion* (not shown in Figure 1.17). The spread of European religions and languages to the new world we will discuss in Chapter 5 are examples of relocation diffusion.

Hierarchical diffusion has two important consequences. First, it can spread phenomena much more quickly around the world than expansion diffusion, and the opportunities for hierarchical diffusion are greatly enhanced by the processes of globalization. Second, although hierarchical diffusion can be faster than expansion diffusion, it is not always as thorough in reaching everywhere quickly, illustrating our earlier observation that phenomena close together in one type of space may be far apart in another type of space.

One example of hierarchical diffusion would be the initial spread of the HIV-1 virus from a hearth area in Central Africa to other parts of the world (see Figure 1.8 on p. 26). The virus initially appeared almost simultaneously in the major metropolitan areas of North and South America, the Caribbean, and Europe. From these areas it then spread to major metropolitan areas in Asia and Oceania and to larger provincial cities in North and South America, the

Caribbean, and Europe. Next in this cascading pattern of diffusion were provincial cities in Asia and Oceania and small towns in North and South America, the Caribbean, and Europe.

Actual diffusion processes often occur in mixed forms as different aspects of human interaction come into play at different times in different geographic settings (**Figure 1.17c**). The diffusion of cholera outbreaks in North America in the nineteenth century, for example, suggests a combination of hierarchical and expansion diffusion (**Figure 1.18**). It also reflects the way that changing networks of transportation resulted in different patterns and sequences of contagion.

Scale The last of geography's fundamental concepts we need to examine is **scale**. So far, we have considered this term in its cartographical context of *map scale*. However, geographers also use this term more generally when they refer to the different levels at which processes occur or where explanation is

scale: the general concept that there are various scales or levels of analysis (local, regional, national, global), that they are linked, and that processes operating at one scale can have significance at other scales

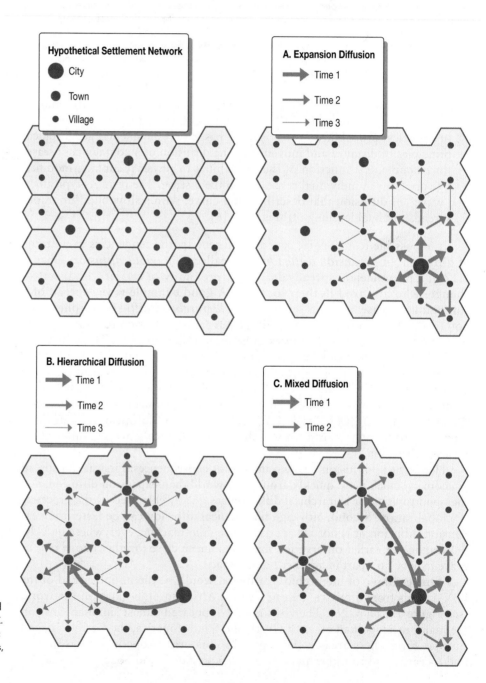

Figure 1.17 Patterns of spatial diffusion (a) Expansion diffusion (for example, the spread of an innovative agricultural practice, such as the use of hybrid seed stock, across a rural region); (b) hierarchical diffusion (the spread of a fashion trend from large metropolitan areas to smaller cities and towns); (c) mixed diffusion. (*Source:* E.K. Cromley and S. L. McLafferty, GIS and Public Health 2nd edition, New York; Guilford Press, p. 239.)

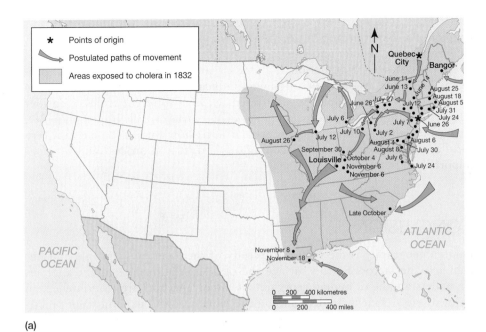

(a)

(b)

Figure 1.18   Diffusion of cholera in 1832 from Gross Île (Quebec) and New York
(a) Nineteenth-century cholera epidemics followed a combination of hierarchical and expansion diffusion. The 1832 epidemic occurred when the urban system was loosely linked together by water transport, and the epidemic spread relatively slowly from its sources in Grosse Île (northeast of Quebec City, in the St. Lawrence) and New York. Both were important ports of entry for immigrants to Canada and to the United States, respectively. (b) Grosse Île, Quebec, served as a quarantine point for those afflicted with cholera in 1832. Sadly, however, the disease was able to spread from this point and diffused along the St. Lawrence to Montreal and its surroundings.   (*Source for map:* "The Diffusion of Cholera in the United States in the Nineteenth Century," by G.F. Pyle, *Geographical Analysis*, vol. 1, no. 1. Reprinted by permission. Copyright © 1969 by the Ohio State University Press. All rights reserved.)

undertaken. The most obvious example is one we have already seen in this chapter and is summed up in the well-known slogan "think global, act local." Geographers have long understood that there are various scales (or levels) of analysis (local, regional, national, global), that they are linked, and that processes operating at one scale can have significance at other scales. Indeed, in some cases, processes operate in different ways at different scales. Consider again the example of the diffusion of the HIV-1 virus (see Figure 1.8 on p. 26). At a *global scale*, a hierarchical process of diffusion dominates, but at a very *local scale,* the expansion (or "contagious") diffusion process will be more important.

CONCLUSION

Human geography is the systematic study of the location of people and human activities across Earth's surface and of their relationships to one another. An understanding of human geography is important, both from an intellectual point of view (that is, understanding the world around us) and from practical points of view (for example, contributing to environmental quality, human rights, social justice, business efficiency, political analysis, and government policy-making).

Although modern ideas about the study of human geography developed from intellectual roots going back to the classical scholarship of ancient Greece, as the world itself has changed, our ways of thinking about it have also changed. What is distinctive about the study of human geography today is not so much the phenomena that are studied as the way in which they are approached. The contribution of human geography is to reveal, in relation to economic, social, cultural, and political phenomena, how and why spatial relationships matter in terms of cause and effect.

Geography matters because it is in specific places that people learn who and what they are and how they should think and behave. Places are a strong influence, for better or worse, on people's physical well-being, their opportunities, and their lifestyle choices. Places contribute to people's collective memory and become powerful emotional and cultural symbols. Places are the sites of innovation and change, of resistance and conflict.

To investigate specific places, however, we must be able to frame our studies of them within the context of the entire globe. This is important for two reasons. First, the world consists of a complex mosaic of places and regions that are interrelated and interdependent in many ways. Second, place-making forces—especially economic, cultural, and political forces that influence the distribution of human activities and the character of places—are increasingly operating at global and international scales. The interdependence of places and regions means that individual places are tied into wider processes of change that are reflected in broader geographical patterns. An important issue for human geographers is to recognize these wider processes and broad geographical patterns without losing sight of the individuality and uniqueness of specific places.

This global perspective leads to the following principles:

- Each place and each region is largely the product of forces that are both local and global in origin.
- Ultimately, each place and region is linked to many other places and regions through these same forces.
- The individual character of places and regions cannot be accounted for by general processes alone. Some local outcomes are the product of unusual circumstances or special local factors.

MAIN POINTS REVISITED

- Geography matters because specific places provide the settings for people's daily lives. It is in these settings that important events happen, and it is from them that significant changes spread and diffuse.

  Places are settings for social interaction that, among other things, structure the daily routines of people's economic and social lives; provide both opportunities for and constraints to people's long-term social well-being; establish a context in which everyday, commonsense knowledge and experience are gathered; provide a setting for processes of socialization; and provide an arena for contesting social norms.

- Places and regions are highly *interdependent,* each filling specialized roles in complex and ever-changing networks of interaction and change.

  Individual places are tied into wider processes of change that are reflected in broader geographical patterns. An important issue for human geographers is to recognize these wider processes and broad geographical patterns without losing sight of the individuality and uniqueness of specific places. Processes of geographical change are constantly modifying and reshaping places, and places are constantly coping with change.

- Some of the most important aspects of the interdependence between geographic scales are provided by the relationships between the *global* and the *local*.

  The study of human geography shows not only how global trends influence local outcomes but also how events in particular localities can come to influence patterns and trends elsewhere. With an understanding of these trends and outcomes, it is possible not only to appreciate the diversity and variety of the world's peoples and places but also to be aware of their relationships to one another and be able to make positive contributions to local, national, and global development.

- Human geography provides ways of understanding places, regions, and spatial relationships as the products of a series of interrelated forces that stem from nature, culture, and individual human action.

  Places are dynamic phenomena. They are created by people responding to the opportunities and constraints presented by their environments. As people live and work in places, they gradually impose themselves on their environment, modifying and adjusting it to suit their needs and express their values. At the same time, people gradually accommodate both to their physical environment and to the people around them. A continuous two-way process exists in which people create and modify places while being influenced by the settings in which they live and work. Places are not just distinctive outcomes of geographical processes; they are part of the processes themselves.

- The first law of geography is that "everything is related to everything else, but near things are more related than are distant things."

  A great deal of human activity is influenced by the "nearness principle," according to which people seek to maximize the overall utility of places at minimum effort, to maximize connections between places at minimum cost, and to locate related activities as close together as possible. In doing so, people are responding to the friction of distance, the deterrent or inhibiting effect of distance on human activity. A distance-decay function describes the rate at which a particular activity or phenomenon diminishes with increasing distance from a given point.

- Distance is one aspect of this law, but connectivity is also important because contact and interaction are dependent on channels of communication and transportation.

  Interdependence among places and regions can be sustained only through movement and flows. Accessibility and spatial interaction are two of the fundamental concepts that distinguish the study of human geography.

Key Terms

accessibility (p. 42)
areal units (p. 35)
cognitive distance (p. 39)
cognitive images (p. 37)
cognitive space (p. 41)
conformal projections (p. 35)
distance-decay function (p. 39)
economies of scale (p. 43)
ecumene (p. 20)
environmental determinism (p. 16)
equal-area (equivalent)
  projections (p. 35)
ethnocentrism (p. 16)

friction of distance (p. 39)
geodemographic research (p. 7)
geographic information system
  (GIS) (p. 7)
globalization (p. 20)
Global Positioning System (GPS) (p. 36)
human geography (p. 5)
imperialism (p. 16)
latitude (p. 36)
longitude (p. 36)
map projection (p. 35)
masculinism (p. 16)
mental maps (p. 37)

model (p. 30)
place (p. 41)
place making (p. 42)
region (p. 30)
regional geography (p. 36)
remote sensing (p. 29)
scale (p. 46)
site (p. 37)
situation (p. 37)
spatial diffusion (p. 44)
topological space (p. 40)
utility (p. 39)
visualization (p. 35)

Additional Reading

Agnew, J., D. Livingstone, and A. Rogers (eds.). *Human Geography: An Essential Anthology.* Cambridge, MA: Blackwell, 1996.

Andrey, J., and J. Gordon (eds.). *Public Issues: A Geographical Perspective.* Waterloo: Department of Geography, University of Waterloo, 1994.

Buttimer, A. *Geography and the Human Spirit.* Baltimore: Johns Hopkins University Press, 1993.

Cloke, P., C. Philo, and D. Sadler. *Approaching Human Geography: An Introduction to Contemporary Debates.* London: Chapman, 1991.

Davis, N.Z. *Trickster Tales: A Sixteenth-Century Muslim between Worlds.* New York: Hill and Wang, 2006.

Dear, M., and J. Wolch. "How Territory Shapes Social Life." In J. Wolch and M. Dear (eds.), *The Power of Geography.* Boston: Unwin Hyman, 1989, 3–18.

Delgado, J.P. *Across the Top of the World: The Quest for the Northwest Passage.* Toronto: Douglas and McIntyre, 2000.

Dorling, D., and D. Fairbairn. *Mapping: Ways of Seeing the World.* London: Addison Wesley Longman, 1997.

Frye, R. *Ibn Fadlun's Journey to Russia: A Tenth-Century Traveler from Baghdad to the Volga River.* Princeton, NJ: Marcus Wiener, 2005.

Gaile, G., and C. Willmott (eds.). *Geography in America.* Columbus, OH: Merrill, 1989.

Gordon, S. *When Asia Was the World: Traveling Merchants, Scholars, Warriors and Monks Who Created the "Riches of the East."* Philadephia: Da Capo Press, 2008.

Gould, P. *The Geographer at Work.* Boston: Routledge & Kegan Paul, 1985.

Gregory, D. *Power, Knowledge, and Geography: An Introduction to Geographic Thought and Practice.* Oxford: Blackwell, 1999.

Hamelin, L. *Canadian Nordicity: It's Your North.* Montreal: Harvest House, 1979.

Harley, J.B., and D. Woodward. *The History of Cartography.* Chicago: University of Chicago Press, 1987.

Harris, R.C., and G.J. Matthews (eds.). *Historical Atlas of Canada. Volume 1: From the Beginning to 1800.* Toronto: University of Toronto Press, 1987.

Harvey, D.W. *Explanation in Geography.* London: Edward Arnold, 1969.

Helferich, G. *Humboldt's Cosmos: Alexander von Humboldt and the Latin American Journey That Changes the Way We See the World.* New York: Gotham Books, 2004.

Johnston, R.J. "The World Is Our Oyster," *Transactions, Institute of British Geographers* 9, 1984, 443–459.

Johnston, R.J., and J.D. Sidaway. *Geography and Geographers: Anglo-American Human Geography Since 1945,* 6th ed. London: Edward Arnold, 2004.

Kobayashi, A. "Truly Our Own: Canadian Geography 50 Years After," *Canadian Geographer* 45, 2001, 3–13.

Litalien, R., J.F. Palomino, and D. Vaugeois. *Mapping a Continent: Historical Atlas of North America, 1492–1814.* Montreal and Kingston: McGill-Queen's University Press, 2007.

Livingstone, D.N. *The Geographical Tradition: Episodes in the History of a Contested Enterprise.* Oxford: Blackwell, 1993.

MacEachern, A.M., and D. Taylor (eds.). *Visualization in Modern Cartography.* Oxford: Pergamon, 1994.

Mackintosh-Smith, T. *Travels with a Tangerine: A Journey in the Footsteps of Ibn Battutah.* London: John Murray, 2001.

Mackintosh-Smith, T. (ed.). *The Travels of Ibn Battutah.* London: Picador, 2002.

Massey, D., and J. Allen (eds.). *Geography Matters!* New York: Cambridge University Press, 1984.

Peet, R. *Modern Geographic Thought.* New York: Blackwell, 1998.

Pickles, J. (ed.). *Ground Truth: The Social Implications of Geographic Information Systems.* London: Longman, 1995.

Robinson, J.L. "Geography," *The Canadian Encyclopedia.* Edmonton: Hurtig, 1985, Volume 2, 725–726. [A revised online version by Lewis Robinson and Larry Bourne is now available at **www.thecanadianencyclopedia.com**, Historica Foundation of Canada: 2002.]

Royal Geographical Society. *Atlas of Exploration.* New York: Oxford University Press, 1997.

Sachs, A. *The Humboldt Current: Nineteenth-Century Exploration and the Roots of American Environmentalism.* New York: Viking Penguin, 2006.

Sack, R.D. *Place, Modernity, and the Consumer's World.* Baltimore: Johns Hopkins University Press, 1992.

Sanderson, M. *Griffith Taylor: Antarctic Scientist and Pioneer Geographer.* Ottawa: Carleton University Press, 1988.

Sauer, C.O. "Morphology of Landscape," *University of California Publications in Geography* 2, 1925, 19–54.

Unwin, T. *The Place of Geography.* London: Longman, 1992.

Walmsley, D.J., and G.J. Lewis. *People and Environment: Behavioural Approaches in Human Geography.* London: Longman, 1984.

Warkentin, J. *A Regional Geography of Canada: Life, Land, and Space.* Scarborough, ON: Prentice Hall, 2000.

Warkentin, J., and P. Simpson-Housley. "The Development of Geographical Study in Canada, 1870–2000." In G.S. Dunbar (ed.), *Geography: Discipline, Profession and Subject Since 1870.* Dordrecht: Kluwer, 2001, 281–315.

Withers, C.W.J. *Placing the Enlightenment: Thinking Geographically about the Age of Reason.* Chicago: University of Chicago Press, 2007.

Wood, D. *The Power of Maps.* New York: Guilford Press, 1992.

Discussion Questions and Research Activities

1. List five geographic settings that have strong symbolic value for you, and state in 25 words or less why each setting has acquired such value.

2. Consider geographical interdependence from the point of view of your own life. Take an inventory of your clothes, noting where each garment was manufactured. Where did you buy the garments? Was the store part of a regional, national, or international chain? What can you find out about the materials used in the garments? Where were they made? Why do you think they were made in those places?

3. The food we consume provides a good illustration of globalization and geographical interdependence. Try to establish all of the places involved in the ingredients of your next meal. Start with the regions or countries where the crops were grown (or animals reared). Next, find out where the ingredients were processed, warehoused, distributed, and so on. Finally, think about how and where you got them. Geographers call the various steps involved in a foodstuff's journey a *commodity chain.* Think about how commodity chains might be different in shape or size depending on what part of the world or what time period we examine.

4. Describe, as exactly and concisely as possible, the *site* (see p. 37) of your campus. Then describe its *situation* (see p. 37). Can you think of any reasons why the campus is sited and situated just where it is? Would there be a better location; and, if so, why?

5. Choose a local landscape, one with which you are familiar, and write a short essay (500 words or two double-spaced, typed pages) on how you consider the landscape has evolved over time. Note especially any evidence that physical, environmental conditions have shaped any of the human elements in the landscape, together with any evidence of people having modified the physical landscape.

MyGeosciencePlace
Visit www.mygeoscienceplace.ca to find chapter review quizzes, videos, maps, and much more.

2

The Changing Global Context

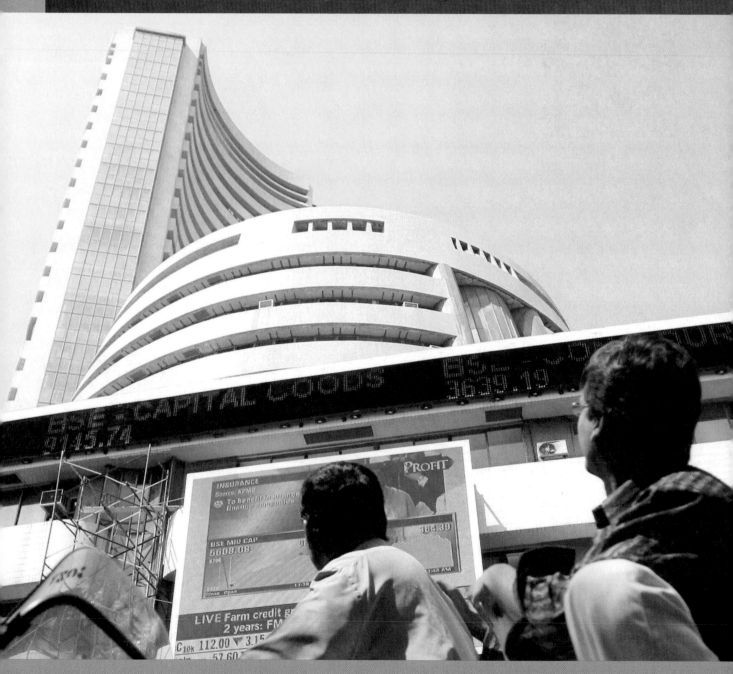

Men looking at Indian Stock Exchange Ticker

It has become a cliché about the twenty-first century that everywhere will come to look like everywhere else: the same McDonald's, Pizza Huts, and Starbucks; the same television programming with Hollywood movies and TV series; and the same malls selling the same Nike shoes, Sony electronics, and GAP clothing. Instantaneous global telecommunications, satellite television, and the Internet will melt away all but the last vestiges of geographical differentiation in human affairs. Large corporations will no longer be headquartered in a "home country" but disperse their activities across the entire globe in search of the lowest taxes, the cheapest labour, and the laxest environmental laws. Employees will work as effectively from home, car, or cottage as they could in offices that need no longer exist. Events halfway across the world will be seen, heard, and felt with the same immediacy and intensity as events across town. National differences and regional cultures will disappear as a global marketplace brings a uniform dispersion of people, tastes, and ideas.

Although many of these processes are already well underway, they will not lead to the complete erosion of geographical differences. Even in the Information Age, geography still matters, and it may well become more important than ever. Places and regions will undoubtedly change as a result of the new global context of the Information Age. But geography *still matters* because of several factors: transport costs, differences in resource endowments, fundamental principles of spatial organization, people's territorial impulses, the resilience of local cultures, and the legacy of the past. An editorial in the *Economist* magazine, debunking the cliché of a spaceless information economy and pointing out that place and space *do* matter, explained, "The main reason is that history counts: where you are depends very much on where you started from."[1]

In this chapter we take a long-term, big-picture perspective on changing human geographies, emphasizing the continuing interdependence among places and regions. We show how geographical divisions of labour have evolved with the growth of a worldwide system of trade and politics and with the changing opportunities provided by successive technology systems. As a result of this evolution, the world is now structured around a series of core regions, semiperipheral regions, and peripheral regions; and globalization seems to be both diminishing *and* intensifying many of the differences among places and regions.

MAIN POINTS

- Places and regions are part of a "world-system" that has been created as a result of processes of private economic competition and political competition among states.
- Today, the world-system is highly structured and is characterized by three tiers: *core regions*, *semiperipheral regions*, and *peripheral regions*.

---

[1] "Does It Matter Where You Are?" *Economist*, 30 July 1994, 13–14.

- The world system is made up of a nested set of cores and peripheries.
- Canada is simultaneously part of the global core and semiperiphery.
- The evolution of the modern world-system has exhibited distinctive stages, each of which has left its legacy in different ways on particular places, depending on their changing role within the world system.
- At the end of the eighteenth century, the new technologies of the Industrial Revolution brought about the emergence of a global economic system that reached into almost every part of the world and into virtually every aspect of people's lives.
- The growth and internal colonization of the core regions could take place only with the foodstuffs, raw materials, and markets provided by the colonization of the periphery.
- Within each of the world's major regions, successive technological innovations have transformed regional geographies.
- Globalization has intensified the differences between the core and the periphery and has contributed to the emergence of a digital divide and an increasing division between a fast world and a slow world with contrasting lifestyles and levels of living.

UNDERSTANDING THE WORLD AS A SYSTEM

Why are places different, and how did they evolve into what they are today? More precisely, why are certain countries rich or poor, ethnic groups dominant or oppressed, regions stable or crisis-ridden? These seemingly simple questions are difficult to answer without a good understanding of geography *and* history. In other words, human geography requires an ability to understand places and regions as components of a constantly changing global system with deep historical roots: built into every place and each region is the legacy of a long sequence of major changes in world geography. We can best understand these changes and their consequences for different places and regions by thinking of the world as an evolving, competitive, political-economic system that we can call the *world-system*. The hyphenation in the term *world-system*, which was coined by historian Immanuel Wallerstein in the 1970s, is meant to emphasize the interdependence of places and regions around the world: they are all part of a system in which every place or region reacts to changes occurring in another.

A **world-system** is an *interdependent* system of countries linked by political and economic competition. Over time, the effects of this competition lead to uneven development: some countries benefit more than others from the interactions and thus rise to dominance over those countries that benefit less. In fact, the disadvantaged countries fuel the further development of the already advantaged countries: a colonized country may be forced to supply raw materials to the colonizing country, or a non-industrialized country may be forced to sell its natural resources below fair value because it has little else to sell and thus disproportionately depends on these exports for hard currency revenues. How did such a system come about?

The modern world-system had its origins in fifteenth-century Europe, when exploration beyond European shores began to be seen as an important way of opening up new opportunities for trade and economic expansion. By the sixteenth century, new techniques of shipbuilding and navigation had begun to bind more and more places and regions together through trade and political competition. At the same time, the decline of feudalism and its replacement by merchant capitalism also profoundly changed Europe's economy. As increasingly more peoples around the world became exposed to one another's technologies and

dynamic

world-system: an interdependent system of countries linked by economic and political competition

revolution in transport technology

ideas, their different resources, social structures, and cultural systems resulted in different competitive potentials and ultimately quite different pathways of development. Some societies were incorporated into the new, European-dominated international economic system faster than others; some resisted incorporation; and some sought alternative systems of economic and political organization. Some parts of the world were barely penetrated, if at all, by the European world-system. Australia and New Zealand, for example, were not discovered by Europeans until the late eighteenth century. Such regions not yet absorbed into the world-system are called **external arenas** (**Figure 2.1**).

Since the seventeenth century, the world-system has been consolidating into a capitalist system of global reach in which all of the world's countries are now involved to some extent: there are few external arenas left. There have, however, been many instances of resistance and adaptation, with some countries (Tanzania, for example) attempting to become self-sufficient and others (for example, China and Cuba) seeking to opt out of the system altogether to pursue a different path to development—that of communism. The result is a highly structured yet dynamic relationship between places and regions that is organized around three tiers: *core, semiperipheral,* and *peripheral* regions. These tiers have been created through a combination of processes of private economic competition and competition among states.

The **core regions** of the world-system are those that dominate trade, control the most advanced technologies, and have high levels of productivity within diversified economies. As a result, they enjoy relatively high *per capita* incomes. The first core regions of the world-system were the trading hubs of Holland and England. Later, these were joined by manufacturing and exporting regions in other parts of Western Europe and in North America and, later still, by Japan and the Pacific Rim.

As we said above, the success of these core regions depends on their dominance and exploitation of weaker regions. This dominance, in turn, depends on the participation of these weaker regions in the world-system. Initially, such participation was achieved by military enforcement; then by European colonialism; and finally by the sheer economic, political, and even cultural might of the core regions. **Colonialism** involves the establishment and maintenance of political and legal domination by a state over a separate society. This domination usually involves some colonization (that is, the physical settlement of people from the colonizing state) and always results in economic exploitation by the colonizing state.

Weaker regions that have remained economically and politically unsuccessful throughout this process of incorporation into the world-system are called *peripheral.* **Peripheral regions** are characterized by dependent and disadvantageous trading relationships, obsolete technologies, and undeveloped or narrowly specialized economies with low levels of productivity. As a result, their *per capita* incomes are low.

In between core regions and peripheral regions are semiperipheral regions. **Semiperipheral regions** are able to exploit peripheral regions but are themselves exploited and dominated by core regions. They consist mostly of countries that were once peripheral. This semiperipheral category underlines the dynamic nature of the world-system: neither peripheral status nor core status is necessarily permanent. Canada, the United States, and Japan all achieved core status after having been peripheral; Spain and Portugal, both part of the original core in the sixteenth century, became semiperipheral in the nineteenth century but are now once more part of the core. Quite a few countries, including Brazil, India, Mexico, South Korea, and Taiwan, have become semiperipheral after first having been incorporated into the periphery of the world-system and then developing a successful manufacturing sector that moved them into semiperipheral status.

So far, we have talked about core regions as if they are uniform, homogeneous areas. However, they are not. The same types of economic, political, social, and cultural processes that have created and that sustain core regions at a global

external arenas: regions of the world not yet absorbed into the modern world-system

core regions: regions that dominate trade, control the most advanced technologies, and have high levels of productivity within diversified economies

colonialism: the establishment and maintenance of political and legal domination by a state over a separate society

peripheral regions: regions with dependent and disadvantageous trading relationships, obsolete technologies, and undeveloped or narrowly specialized economies with low levels of productivity

semiperipheral regions: regions that are able to exploit peripheral regions but are themselves exploited and dominated by core regions

Figure 2.1 The world-system core, semiperiphery, and periphery in 1800, 1900, and 2000 Note how the Dymaxion projection (see Chapter 1) used in these maps emphasizes the geographic centrality and proximity of core regions: their clustered location in the centre reflects the notion of a core in the "centre" of the world that looks "outward" to an isolated, marginalized periphery. (*Source:* Map projection, Buckminster Fuller Institute and Dymaxion Map Design, Santa Barbara, CA. The word *Dymaxion* and the Fuller Projection Dymaxion™ Map design are trademarks of the Buckminster Fuller Institute, Santa Barbara, California, © 1938, 1967, & 1992. All rights reserved.)

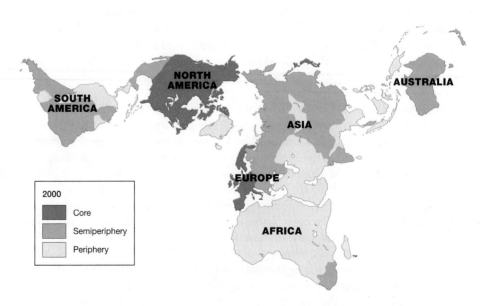

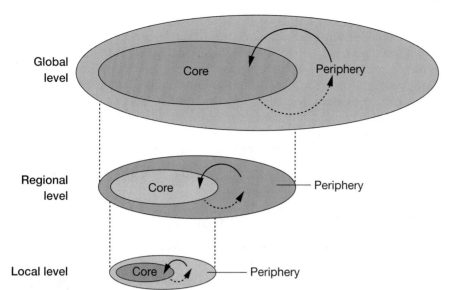

Figure 2.2 A simplified model of the world-system The arrows indicate the various economic, political, military, and cultural means used by cores to dominate their peripheries. The diagram illustrates how the world-system is made up of a nested set of cores and peripheries.

level also operate at regional and local scales (**Figure 2.2**). The "global core," if we look at it more closely, is itself made up of a number of *regional cores, semiperipheries,* and *peripheries.* For example, Canada, a rich industrialized country, is undoubtedly part of the global core. However, we know that not all of Canada's provinces and territories share uniformly in this prosperity. In fact, this country could be divided into the "heartland" and "hinterlands," as many Canadian geographers have come to call the regional cores and peripheries within this country.

Similarly, regional cores are made up of *local cores* and *peripheries,* the result of more local processes of development. The city of Toronto, for example, as a whole represents a highly developed region, but there are relatively wealthier and poorer sections: in 2003, more than half a million Toronto households had incomes below the poverty line, and 31,985 homeless individuals (including 4,779 children) stayed in a Toronto shelter at least once during 2002.[2] We will be considering these regional and local levels in greater detail in later chapters (especially in Chapters 7 and 10). The important point to understand here is that the world-system is not made up of a few homogeneous regions. It is much more geographically varied than that. In fact, it is made up of a nested set of cores, semiperipheries, and peripheries at different scales of analysis.

We also need to understand that in certain cases—and Canada is one of them—a region can be simultaneously part of the global core and semiperiphery.

2.1 Geography in the Information Age

Recently, the acronym BRICS has been used to denote a grouping of countries that is similar to the semiperipheral category we use in this book. The letters stand for Brazil, Russia, India, China, and (since 2010) South Africa, some of the largest emerging economies, which are expected to surpass the economies of the current core countries by 2050. Its leaders now meet at annual summits to discuss common strategies for economic development that foster their own interests, rather than those of the core countries. The BRIC category shows the power of the written word to *create* reality, rather than merely describe it: the term BRIC was first used as a theoretical construct in a paper written by an economist in 2001, years before the group actually constituted itself in 2009.

---

[2] *Toronto Housing and Homelessness Report Card 2003,* http://www.toronto.ca/homelessness/ index.htm. Regrettably, this is the most recent official investigation of homelessness in Toronto.

Canada has a GNP and standard of living that places it in the global core. Canadian-owned businesses and banks make substantial profits from investments overseas, especially in the Caribbean periphery. Yet, at the same time, we recognize characteristics of the semiperiphery: large parts of the Canadian economy are American-owned, and Canada's political and economic influence over the behemoth to its south is negligible. Canada's dual position helps us understand the difficulties a middle power faces on the world scene.

Because the world-system model is so useful in understanding the human geography of the world, it is well worth summarizing its most important features here.

- The world-system model states that the world can be divided into a series of cores, semiperipheries, and peripheries.

- In dividing the world in this way, we are using a relative concept of space, based on a socioeconomic measure of distance (see Chapter 1).

- The global core maintains its dominance through the exercise of the economic, political, military, and cultural forces at its disposal.

- The core also maintains its dominance through environmental and ecological means. For example, the introduction of European crops and animals overseas itself became an instrument of imperialism, and genetic modification is increasingly enabling Western agribusiness corporations to control the seed supply of cash crops grown in the periphery.

- The global periphery is kept in a dependent position by the global core. Some experts have even suggested that the core actively "undevelops" the periphery; others point out how space is, in at least an economic or social sense, *created* in the first place by these interplays between the core and the periphery.

- The global core and periphery have changed their locations over time.

- The world-system is made up of a nested series of cores and peripheries. In this, we see another of the concepts that we examined in Chapter 1, the concept of scale. In this way, local developments are transmitted to the regional and global levels, and the forces of globalization manifest themselves at the local level.

For the rest of this chapter, we will consider in more detail the evolution and operation of the world-system at the global scale.

GEOGRAPHIC EXPANSION, INTEGRATION, AND CHANGE

The world-system evolved in successive stages of geographic expansion and integration. This evolution has affected the roles of individual places and the nature of the interdependence among places. It also explains why places and regions have become distinctive and how this distinctiveness has formed the basis of geographic variability.

Mini-Systems

Systematically differentiated human geographies began with mini-systems. A **mini-system** is a society with a single cultural base and a *reciprocal* social economy. That is, individuals specialize in particular tasks and share the surplus of their activities with others, who reciprocate by doing the same. In prehistoric times, mini-systems were based on hunting and gathering societies that were finely tuned to local physical environments. They were all very small in geographical extent and very vulnerable to environmental change (**Figure 2.3**).

After the first agricultural revolution between 9000 and 7000 B.C., mini-systems were able to grow food, thus becoming both more stable and more extensive. These qualities eventually contributed to new forms of spatial organization, including urbanization and long-distance trading.

mini-system: a society with a single cultural base and a reciprocal social economy

Figure 2.3   A remnant mini-system
An Amazon tribal group, photographed in May 2008. Mini-systems were rooted in subsistence-based social economies that were organized around reciprocity. Today, few of the world's remnant mini-systems are "pure," unaffected by contact with the rest of the world. This group is believed to be related to the Tano and Aruak tribes of the Peru-Brazil border region. Brazil's National Indian Foundation believes there may be as many as 68 "uncontacted" groups around Brazil, although only 24 have been officially confirmed. Anthropologists say almost all of these tribes know about Western civilization and have sporadic contact with prospectors, rubber tappers, and loggers, but choose to turn their backs on civilization, usually because they have been attacked.

The transition to food-producing mini-systems had several important implications for the long-term evolution of the world's geographies. First, as we will see in Chapter 8, it allowed much higher population densities and encouraged the proliferation of permanent settlements. Second, it brought about a change in social organization, from loose communal systems to systems that were more highly organized on the basis of kinship. Kin groups provided a natural way of assigning ownership rights over land and resources and of organizing patterns of land use. Third, it allowed some specialization in non-agricultural crafts, such as pottery, woven textiles, jewellery, and weaponry. This specialization led to a fourth development: the beginnings of barter and trade between communities, sometimes over substantial distances.

Most mini-systems vanished a long time ago, although some remnants of mini-systems have survived, providing a stark counterpoint to the landscapes and practices of the contemporary world-system. Examples of these residual and fast-disappearing mini-systems are the bush people of the Kalahari, the hill tribes of Papua New Guinea, and the tribes of the Amazon rain forest.

The Growth of Early World-Empires

The higher population densities, changes in social organization, craft production, and trade brought about by the first agricultural revolution provided the preconditions for the emergence of several world-empires. A **world-empire** is a group of mini-systems that have been absorbed into a common political system while retaining their fundamental cultural differences. The social economy of world-empires can be characterized as redistributive-tributary; that is, a powerful elite class appropriates wealth from less powerful producer classes in the form of tribute or taxes. This redistribution of wealth is most often achieved through military coercion, religious persuasion, or a combination of the two. The best-known world-empires are the largest and longest lasting of the ancient civilizations—Egypt, Greece, China, Byzantium, and Rome. World-empires brought two important new elements to the evolution of the world's geographies. The first was the emergence of *urbanization* (see Chapter 10). Towns and cities became essential as centres of administration, military garrisons, and theological centres for the ruling classes, who were able to use a combination of military and theological authority to hold their empires together. As long as these early world-empires

world-empire: mini-systems that have been absorbed into a common political system while retaining their fundamental cultural differences

Figure 2.4 Terraced landscapes This photo shows rice cultivation in Sikkim, formerly a kingdom but now an Indian state. This landscape is the legacy of a hydraulic society—a world-empire in which despotic rulers once organized labour-intensive irrigation schemes that allowed for significant increases in agricultural productivity.

law of diminishing returns: the tendency for productivity to decline, after a certain point, with the continued application of capital or labour or both to a given resource base

were successful, they gave rise not only to monumental capital cities but also to a whole series of secondary settlements, which acted as intermediate centres in the flow of tribute and taxes from colonized territories.

The second important contribution of world-empires to evolving world geographies was *colonization*. In part, this was an indirect consequence of the **law of diminishing returns**. This law refers to the tendency for productivity to decline, after a certain point, with the continued addition of capital, labour, or both to a given resource base. In other words: for each additional person working the land, the gain in output per worker becomes smaller. Because of the law of diminishing returns, world-empires could support growing populations only by colonizing nearby land and thus enlarging their resource base. Such colonization immediately established uneven power relationships between dominant original areas of settlement and subordinate colonies. Other spatial consequences were the creation of settlement hierarchies and improved transportation networks. The military underpinnings of colonization also meant that new towns and cities now became carefully sited for strategic and defensive reasons.

The legacy of these important changes is still apparent in many of today's landscapes (see **Visualizing Geography 2.1—The Legacy of World-Empires**).

Some world-empires were exceptional in that they were based on a particularly strong central state, with totalitarian rulers who used forced labour to organize large-scale, communal irrigation and drainage schemes to increase agricultural productivity. Such states have been called *hydraulic societies*. Today, their legacy is seen in the landscapes of terraced fields that have been maintained for generations in such places as Sikkim, India, and East Java, Indonesia (**Figure 2.4**).

The Geography of the Pre-Modern World

Figure 2.5 shows the generalized framework of human geographies in the Old World as they existed around A.D. 1400. The following characteristics of this period are important. First, harsher environments in continental interiors were still sparsely peopled by isolated, subsistence-level, kin-ordered hunting and gathering mini-systems. Second, the dry belt of steppes and desert margins stretching across the Old World from the western Sahara to Mongolia was a continuous zone of kin-ordered pastoral mini-systems. Third, areas with various forms of

The Legacy of World-Empires

Long after they have collapsed, the physical remains of imperial systems survive in today's landscape. Ruined defensive systems, cities, walls, and aqueducts provide some of the tangible signs that these places were once part of a previous economic and political system.

Known as the "abandoned city of the Mughals," Fatephur Sikr was built in the 1540s to serve a Muslim kingdom after the invasion of Central India. It was abandoned after only 14 years because of a lack of nearby water.

The Maori peoples of New Zealand built defensive works known as *pa* to defend their territory. Usually built on hilltops, these earthworks required the excavation of massive ditches and banks (still visible as grooves and ridges on the land surface) to provide a secure refuge from attack.

This spectacular aqueduct was built in the time of Augustus (63 B.C. to A.D. 14) to supply the city of Nîmes, a thriving Roman provincial capital in southern France, with water from Uzès, 50 kilometres away. The water dropped only 17 metres over the whole distance.

Hadrian's Wall, a Roman defensive barrier built during the reign of emperor Hadrian to guard the northern frontier of the province of Britain. Completed in A.D. 136, it extended almost 120 kilometres from the eastern coast to the western coast of northern England with an original height of 6 metres, a thickness of 2.5 metres, and a parallel ditch. The wall was protected by a series of small forts, but it was abandoned in A.D. 383 after several incursions by northern tribes.

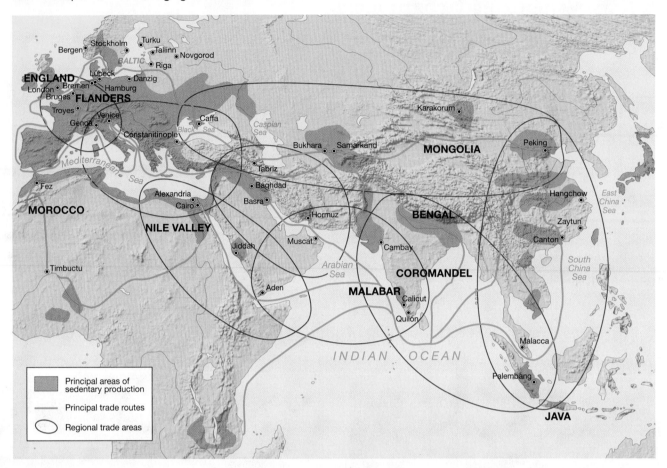

Figure 2.5   The precapitalist Old World, circa A.D. 1400   Principal areas of sedentary agricultural production are shaded. Some high-value goods were traded over long distances from one region to another, but for the most part, exchange was limited to a series of overlapping regional circuits of trade.   (*Sources*: R. Peet, *Global Capitalism: Theories of Societal Development.* New York: Routledge, 1991; J. Abu-Lughod, *Before European Hegemony: The World-System A.D. 1200–1350.* New York: Oxford University Press, 1989; and E.R. Wolf, *Europe and the People without History.* Berkeley: University of California Press, 1983.)

sedentary agricultural production formed a discontinuous arc from Morocco to China, with two main outliers: in the central Andes and in Mesoamerica. The dominant centres of global civilization were China, northern India (both of them hydraulic societies), and the Ottoman Empire of the eastern Mediterranean. Other important world-empires were based in Southeast Asia, in Muslim city-states of coastal North Africa, in the grasslands of West Africa, around the gold and copper mines of East Africa, and in the feudal kingdoms and merchant towns of Europe.

These more-developed realms were interconnected through trade, which meant that several emerging centres of capitalism existed. Port cities were particularly important, and among the leading centres were the city-state of Venice, the Hanseatic League of independent city-states in northwestern Europe, as well as Cairo, Calicut, Canton, Malacca, and Sofala. Traders in these port cities began to organize the production of agricultural specialties, textiles, and craft products in their respective hinterlands. The **hinterland** of a town or city is its sphere of economic influence—the tributary area from which it collects products for export and throughout which it distributes imports.

By the fifteenth century, several regions of budding capitalism existed: northern Italy, Flanders, southern England, the Baltic, the Nile Valley, Malabar, eastern coastal India (Coromandel), Bengal, northern Java, and southeast coastal China (**Figure 2.5**). Between those regions, high-value goods such as spices and textiles

hinterland: the sphere of economic influence of a town or city were traded over long distances. To this day, the English language reflects how geographically extensive the textile trade was:

> The word *satin* comes from the name of an unknown city in China that Arab traders called Zaitun. *Khaki* is the Hindi word for dusty. The word *calico* comes from India's southwestern coastal city of Calicut; *chintz*, from the Hindi name for a printed calico; *cashmere*, from the region of Kashmir. *Percale* comes from the Farsi word *pargalah*. Another Farsi derivative is *seersucker*, whose bands of alternating smooth and puckered fabric prompted a name that literally means milk and sugar. Still another Farsi borrowing is *taffeta*, which comes from the Farsi for "spun." The coarse cloth we call *muslin* is named for Mosul—the town in Iraq—whereas *damask* is a short form of Damascus. Finally, cotton takes its name from *qutun*, the Arabic name of the fiber.[3]

MAPPING A NEW WORLD GEOGRAPHY

With the emergence of the modern world-system at the beginning of the sixteenth century, a whole new geography began to emerge. Although several regions of budding capitalist production existed and although imperial China could boast of sophisticated achievements in science, technology, and navigation, it was European merchant capitalism that reshaped the world. Several factors motivated European overseas expansion. A relatively high population density and a limited amount of cultivable land meant that there was a continuous struggle to provide enough food: a consequence of the law of diminishing returns. Meanwhile, the desire for overseas expansion was intensified by both competition among a large number of small monarchies and inheritance laws that produced large numbers of impoverished aristocrats with little or no land of their own (because all land went to the firstborn son). Many of these landless aristocrats were eager to set out for adventure and profit.

Added to these motivating factors were the enabling factors of innovations in shipbuilding, navigation, and gunnery. In the mid-fifteenth century, for example, the Portuguese developed a cannon-armed ship—the caravel—that could sail anywhere, defend itself against pirates, pose a threat to those who were initially unwilling to trade, *and* carry enough goods to be profitable. The quadrant (1450) and the astrolabe (1480) enabled more accurate navigation and mapping of ocean currents, prevailing winds, and trade routes (**Figure 2.6**). Naval power enabled the Portuguese and the Spanish to enrich their economies with capital from gold and silver plundered from the Americas and so strengthen their position.

Europeans were able not only to send adventurers overseas for gold and silver but also to commandeer land and exploit coerced labour to produce high-value crops (such as sugar, cocoa, tobacco, cotton, and indigo) on **plantations**, large landholdings that usually specialized in the production of one particular crop for markets back in Europe. Some regions with high population densities, a good resource base, and strong states were able to keep Europeans at arm's length and permitted only coastal trading stations. For the most part, these regions were in South and East Asia.

Within Europe, innovations in business and finance (banking, loan systems, credit transfers, commercial insurance, and courier services, for example) helped increase savings, investment, and commercial activity. European merchants and manufacturers also became adept at **import substitution**—copying and making goods previously available only by trading. The result was the emergence of Western Europe as the core region of a world-system that was penetrating and incorporating significant portions of the rest of the world.

In Europe itself, this overseas expansion stimulated further improvements in marine technology, including nautical mapmaking, naval artillery, shipbuilding, and the use of sails. It also provided a great practical school for

Figure 2.6   Champlain's astrolabe
This astrolabe allowed French explorers to determine their latitude by measuring the noon altitude of the sun. Lost by Champlain soon after he set out through the Ottawa Valley, it was recovered in the nineteenth century and is now on exhibit in the Canadian Museum of Civilization in Gatineau, Quebec.

plantations: large landholdings that usually specialize in the production of one particular crop for market

import substitution: the process by which domestic producers provide goods or services that formerly were bought from foreign producers

---

[3] B. Wallach, *Understanding the Cultural Landscape*. New York: Guilford Press, 2005, p. 148.

Geography and Exploration

In the early fifteenth century, the Portuguese began to explore the Atlantic and the coast of Africa, at the same time improving methods of navigation and cartography. **Figure 2.2.1** shows the key European voyages of discovery. Portuguese explorer Bartholomeu Dias reached the Cape of Good Hope (the southern tip of Africa) in 1488. Six years later, Vasco da Gama reached India; two years after that, Pedro Cabral crossed the Atlantic from Portugal to Brazil. A small fleet of Portuguese ships reached China in 1513, and the first circumnavigation of the globe was completed in 1522 by Juan Sebastián del Cano, a survivor of the expedition originally led by Portuguese navigator Fernando de Magellan in 1519 (**Figure 2.2.2**). Portuguese successes inspired other countries to attempt their own voyages of discovery. For instance, in 1492, Christopher Columbus sailed to Hispaniola (the island that is now Haiti and the Dominican Republic) under the sponsorship of the Castilian (Spanish) monarchy. These explorations led to an invaluable body of knowledge about ocean currents, wind patterns, coastlines, peoples, and resources, which in turn helped Europeans establish dominance over the newly "discovered" parts of the world. Barred from access to more southerly parts of America by prior Portuguese and Spanish claims, French and British explorations focused instead on the land that became known as Canada and based their initial routes on earlier information about the rich fishing grounds known to lie off its shores (see Chapter 4).

Geographical knowledge acquired during this Age of Discovery was crucial to the expansion of European political and economic power in the sixteenth century. In European societies that were becoming more commercially oriented and profit conscious, geographical knowledge became a valuable commodity in itself. Information about regions and places was a first step toward controlling and influencing them, and this in turn was an important step toward amassing wealth and power. As the New World was being affected by European colonists, missionaries,

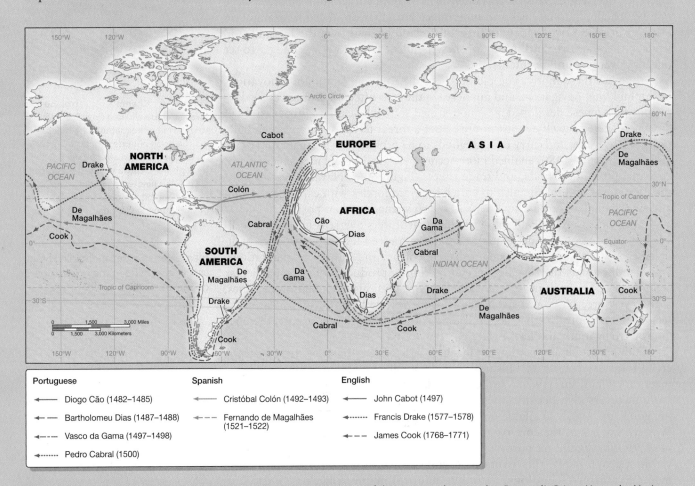

Portuguese
←— Diogo Cão (1482–1485)
←— Bartholomeu Dias (1487–1488)
←-— Vasco da Gama (1497–1498)
←······ Pedro Cabral (1500)

Spanish
←— Cristóbal Colón (1492–1493)
←--- Fernando de Magalhães (1521–1522)

English
←— John Cabot (1497)
←······ Francis Drake (1577–1578)
←-— James Cook (1768–1771)

Figure 2.2.1 The European Age of Discovery The European voyages of discovery can be traced to Portugal's Prince Henry the Navigator (1394–1460), who set up a school of navigation and financed numerous expeditions with the objective of circumnavigating Africa in order to establish a profitable sea route for spices from India. The knowledge of winds, ocean currents, natural harbours, and watering places built up by Henry's captains was an essential foundation for the subsequent voyages of Columbus, da Gama, de Magellan, and others. The end of the European Age of Discovery was marked by Captain James Cook's voyages to the Pacific in the 1770s.

and adventurers, the countries of the Old World found themselves pitched into competition with one another for overseas resources. Meanwhile, new crops, like corn and potatoes, introduced to Europe from the New World, profoundly affected local economies and ways of life.

The growth of a commercial world economy meant that cartography and geographical writing became essential for knowing about other places. Navigation, political boundaries, property rights, and rights of movement all depended on accuracy, impartiality, and reliable record keeping. Success in commerce depended on how clearly and reliably geographical writings described the opportunities and dangers presented by one region or another. International rivalries required sophisticated understandings of the relationships among nations, regions, and places. In short, geographical information became a key area of knowledge and a foundation of power. The historical period in Europe known as the Renaissance (from the mid-fourteenth to the mid-seventeenth centuries) saw an explosion of systematic mapmaking and the development of new **map projections** (see Chapter 1) and geographical

descriptions. Throughout the seventeenth and eighteenth centuries, the body of geographic knowledge increased steadily as Europeans explored and mapped more and more of the world, using increasingly sophisticated techniques of survey and measurement.

Figure 2.2.2   Departure from Lisbon for Brazil, the East Indies, and America   Illustration from "Americae Tertia Pars" (1592).

commercial entrepreneurship, investment, and long-distance trade. In this way, the self-propelling growth of European merchant capitalism was further intensified and consolidated.

For the periphery, European overseas expansion meant dependency (as it has ever since for many of the world's peripheral regions). At worst, territory was forcibly occupied and labour systematically exploited. At best, local traders were displaced by Europeans, who imposed their own terms of economic exchange. Europeans soon destroyed most of the Muslim shipping trade in the Indian Ocean, for example, and went on to capture a large share of the oceangoing trade *within* Asia, selling Japanese copper to China and India, Persian carpets to India, Indian cotton textiles to Japan, and so on.

As revolutionary as these changes were, however, they ultimately were constrained by a technology that rested on wind and water power, on wooden ships and structures, and on wood for fuel. Mills, for example, were built of wood and powered by water or wind. They could generate only modest amounts of power and only at sites determined by physical geography, not human choice. Within the relatively small European landmass, wood for construction and fuel competed with food, animal feed, and textile fibres for the available acreage. More important, however, was the size and strength of timber, which imposed structural limits on the size of buildings, the diameter of waterwheels, the span of bridges, and so on. In particular, it imposed limits on the size and design of ships (especially their masts), which in turn imposed limits on the volume and velocity of world trade. The expense and relative inefficiency of horse- or ox-drawn wagons for overland transportation also meant that for a long time the European world-system could penetrate into continental interiors only along waterways.

The Early Integration of Canada into the World-System

Canada provides a good illustration of this importance of waterways for early European access. Basque whalers from northeastern Spain were probably the first Europeans to exploit this country's natural resources on a regular basis. In their

Figure 2.7   Red Bay, Labrador
Archaeologists have found that this camp provided shelter for the production of whale oil and summer accommodation for the small Basque crews engaged in whaling in the 1540s.

Figure 2.8   Moose Factory   From its bases, such as this one at Moose Factory, the Hudson's Bay Company tapped the wealth of Rupert's Land and shipped furs to England.

whaling stations on the lower St. Lawrence (such as the one at Red Bay in Labrador, established in the 1540s and recently re-created in the Canadian Museum of Civilization in Ottawa-Gatineau), whales were rendered into lamp oil and candle wax for the European market (**Figure 2.7**). From the early sixteenth century onward, French, Portuguese, and Basque fishing ships took increasingly large quantities of cod from the Grand Banks off Newfoundland and Labrador. Initially only a summer undertaking from Europe, by the 1680s French and British fishing included overwintering on the coasts of Newfoundland and Labrador. Occasional exchanges of goods between sailors and Aboriginal groups led to the beginnings of the fur trade.

The subsequent development of an almost insatiable European market for Canadian furs drove itinerant French traders farther up the St. Lawrence and into the Great Lakes by the late seventeenth century to exploit the animal resources of those vast watersheds. An alternative method of fur trading was practised by the British. Using permanent bases (or "factories," such as Moose Factory), the Hudson's Bay Company was able to tap into the huge territory of Rupert's Land (covering the Hudson's Bay drainage basin), which it had been granted by the Crown in 1670, and to ship its furs out through northern waters (**Figure 2.8**).

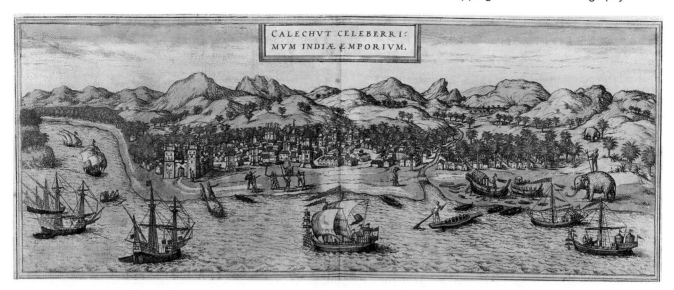

CALECHVT CELEBERRI:
MVM INDIÆ EMPORIVM.

In both cases, the real profits from the fur trade were realized in Europe, where furs were made into hats and garments. In addition, the Hudson's Bay Company was headquartered in London, where political and financial control over its Canadian resources was exercised. Only in the case of Montreal, where individual French traders based themselves and where the North West Company had its centre of operations from the 1780s to the 1820s, do we find any substantial profits from the fur trade being retained in Canada. Such merchant capital enabled the growth of Montreal's early business elite, which expressed itself in the mansions and built form of the city. That elite then invested in the early development of railroads in the Montreal region to profit from the encouragement of local trade and agriculture.

After 300 years of evolution, roughly between 1450 and 1750, the world-system had thus incorporated mainly those parts of the world that were relatively accessible by water: Mediterranean North Africa, Portuguese and Spanish colonies in the Americas, Indian ports and trading colonies (**Figure 2.9**), the East Indies, African and Chinese ports, the Greater Caribbean, and eastern North America. The rest of the world functioned more or less as before, with slow-changing geographies based around modified mini-systems and world-empires that were only partially and intermittently penetrated by market trading. This changed dramatically with the advent of industrialization in Europe and its associated technological advances, which gave Europe (and later the entire core) the power to rise to global dominance in both economic and political terms.

Figure 2.9   British, Portuguese, French, and Dutch ships in the harbour at Kolkata (Calcutta), India, around 1600   The expansion of European trade and the protection of trade routes required strong navies and a willingness to use them. English explorer Sir Walter Raleigh expressed the sentiment succinctly in 1608: "Whoso commands the sea commands the trade of the world; whoso commands the trade of the world commands the riches of the world."

Industrialization and Geographic Change

Beginning in the late eighteenth century, a series of technological innovations in power and energy, transportation, and manufacturing processes resulted in some crucial changes in patterns of economic development. Each of these major clusters of technological innovations—called **technology systems**—created new demands for natural resources as well as labour forces and markets. In turn, this favoured different regions and different kinds of places and so led to geographic change. Technology systems dominate economic activity for several decades at a time—until a new cluster of improved technologies evolves. Since the beginning of the Industrial Revolution, we can identify five of them:

technology systems: clusters of interrelated energy, transportation, and production technologies that dominate economic activity for several decades at a time

- 1790–1840: early mechanization based on water power and steam engines; development of cotton textiles and ironworking; development of river transport systems, canals, and turnpike roads.

- 1840–1890: exploitation of coal-powered steam engines; steel products; railroads; world shipping; and machine tools.

- 1890–1950: exploitation of the internal combustion engine, particularly in cars and trucks; oil and plastics; electrical and heavy engineering; aircraft; radio and telecommunications.

- 1950–1990: exploitation of nuclear power, aerospace, electronics, and petrochemicals; development of limited-access highways and global air routes.

- 1990 onward: exploitation of solar and wind energy, robotics, microelectronics, biotechnology, nanotechnology, advanced materials (fine chemicals and thermoplastics, for example), and ICT (information and communications technologies, such as the Internet, digital telecommunications, wireless and satellite communications, mobile and cloud computing, GPS and geographic information systems).

Each of these technology systems has rewritten the geography of economic development as it shifted the relative advantages of regions. Human geographies were recast again, this time with a more interdependent dynamic: new industrial production technologies, based on increasingly concentrated and mobile forms of energy, helped raise levels of productivity and create new and better products that stimulated demand, increased profits, and created a pool of capital for further investment: industrial capitalism truly became a global system that reached into virtually every part of the world and every aspect of people's lives. New transportation technologies triggered successive phases of geographic expansion, allowing for internal development as well as external colonization and *imperialism*, the deliberate exercise of military power and economic influence by core states to advance and secure their national interests (see Chapter 7).

The colonization and imperialism that accompanied the expansion of the world-system was closely tied to the evolution of world leadership cycles. **Leadership cycles** are periods of international dominance established by individual states through economic, political, and military competition. In the long term, success in the world-system depends on economic strength and competitiveness, which brings political influence and pays for military strength. With a combination of economic, political, and military power, individual states can dominate the world-system, setting the terms for many economic and cultural practices and imposing their particular ideology by virtue of their pre-eminence. This kind of dominance is known as *hegemony*. **Hegemony** refers to domination over the world economy exercised—through a combination of economic, military, financial, and cultural means—by one national state (the hegemon) in a particular historical epoch. Over the long run, the costs of maintaining this kind of power and influence tend to weaken the hegemon. This phase of the cycle is known as imperial overstretch. It is followed by another period of competitive struggle, which brings the possibility of a new dominant world power (see **Geography Matters 2.3—World Leadership Cycles**). The more far-flung the empire, the greater the challenges associated with the imperial overstretch—a clear example of the importance of the geographical concept of distance (see Chapter 1).

Industrialization, meanwhile, resulted not only in the complete reorganization of the human geography of the original European core of the world-system but also in an extension of the world-system core to the United States and Japan.

Europe   In Europe, three distinctive waves of industrialization occurred. The first, between 1790 and 1850, was based on the initial technology system (steam engines, cotton textiles, and ironworking) and was very localized in England and Scotland.

leadership cycles: periods of international power established by individual states through economic, political, and military competition

hegemony: domination over the world economy exercised by one national state in a particular historical epoch through a combination of economic, military, financial, and cultural means

World Leadership Cycles

The modern world-system has so far experienced the following five full leadership cycles.

Portuguese dominance was established through initial advantages derived from Atlantic exploration, trade, and plunder. The Treaty of Tordesillas, arbitrated by Pope Alexander VI in 1494, consolidated these advantages by limiting direct competition from Portugal's chief rival, Spain. The treaty allowed Portugal to lay claim to any territory to the east of approximately 48°W, which included the eastern coast of Brazil (**Figure 2.3.1**). Spain was allowed to claim the less accessible lands to the west of this line. Subsequently allied through royal marriage, Spain and Portugal sought to head off increasing competition from England and Holland, but their attempt to establish a global world-empire was thwarted by growing English naval superiority. Seizing the opportunity, however, it was the Dutch that used their superior merchant economy to become the next hegemon.

Dutch dominance began with the defeat of the Portuguese-backed Spanish Armada by the English in a decisive naval battle in 1588. Now Dutch ports and Dutch shipping dominated European overseas trade, and the Dutch government controlled trade through the Dutch East India Company and the Dutch West India Company (**Figure 2.3.2**). Dutch hegemony continued until the 1660s, when both the English and the French mounted a serious challenge. Three Anglo-Dutch wars between 1652 and 1678 were necessary to establish English supremacy, which was further solidified by the 1707 Act of Union with Scotland.

British dominance was sustained, in spite of a relatively poor domestic resource base, by overseas trade and colonization, backed by a powerful navy. In the 1770s, this dominance was shaken by an alliance between France and the American revolutionaries, and there followed a period of struggle between Britain and France that culminated in the Napoleonic Wars. This competitive phase of Britain's first leadership cycle was brought to a close by British victories at Trafalgar (1805) and Waterloo (1815). By then, the Industrial Revolution had given Britain an economic and military edge that allowed it to build and maintain a global empire, and to enjoy a leadership cycle of such unchallenged dominance that the following 100 years became known as the *Pax Britannica*.

The second cycle of British dominance was based on the economic advantages of early industrialization, which allowed for an unprecedented degree of incorporation of the world under British imperial and economic hegemony for almost the entire nineteenth century. But from the 1860s onward, imperial overstretch and increasing economic competition from the United States and Germany eroded British hegemony and marked the beginning of a period of struggle. The German challenge culminated

Figure 2.3.1 Portugal's claims to the New World The Treaty of Tordesillas (1494) gave Portugal control over what then were the more accessible parts of the New World. This map, drawn in 1502 by Alberto Contino, shows Portuguese territories (including the wooded island in the top centre representing Newfoundland) marked by flags with a blue interior and a red border. Spanish territories, farther west, are marked by the red, gold, and black flag of Spain.

Figure 2.3.2 Merchant vessels of the Dutch and English East India Companies The English East India Company was established in 1600 as a monopolistic trading company and agent of British imperialism in India. In response, the Dutch East India Company was founded in 1602 to protect Dutch trading interests in the Far East. It was granted a trade monopoly in the waters of the Indian and Pacific Oceans, together with the rights to conclude treaties with local rulers, to build forts and maintain armed forces, and to carry on administrative functions through officials who were required to take an oath of loyalty to the Dutch government. The company was almost a branch of the government and thus illustrates how interwoven political imperialism and economic expansionism were.

in the Great War of 1914–1918 (World War I), which left Germany defeated, Britain weakened, and the United States strengthened.

The *United States* was economically dominant within the world-system by 1920 but did not achieve hegemonic power because of a lack of political will to get involved in world affairs. It took a second world war, prompted by the resurgence of Germany and the sudden rise of Japan, to force the United States out of its isolationism. After World War II, the United States was unquestionably the hegemonic power, although its political and military superiority was contested during the cold war as the Soviet Union and its allies sought a non-capitalist path to modernization and power. This challenge disappeared in 1989, but by then, the economic foundation for U.S. hegemony had come under serious threat because of the resurgence of Japanese and European industries and the globalization of economic activity through transnational corporations.

Since 2000, China has been mounting an increasingly serious challenge to American financial and economic predominance, just when America's decade-long military engagement in Iraq and Afghanistan is causing what many analysts see as a prime example of imperial overstretch. Since 2010, China has been aggressively extending this challenge to the political and military arenas as well. Most analysts now predict that China will become the next hegemon by mid-century.

The second wave, between 1850 and 1870, involved the diffusion of industrialization to most of the rest of Britain and to parts of northwest Europe, particularly the coalfield areas of northern France, Belgium, and Germany (**Figure 2.10**). New opportunities were created as railroads and steamships made more places accessible, bringing their resources and their markets into the sphere of industrialization. The new materials and technologies of the second technology system (for example, steel and machine tools) created opportunities to manufacture and market new products. These new activities brought some significant changes in the logic of industrial location. The importance of railway networks, for example, attracted industry away from smaller towns on the canal systems toward larger towns with good rail connections. Similarly, the importance of steamships for coastal and international trade attracted industry to larger ports. The scale of industry increased as new technologies and improved transportation made larger markets accessible to firms. Local family firms became small companies that were regional in scope. Small companies grew to become powerful firms serving national markets, and specialized business, legal, and financial services emerged within larger cities to assist them. The growth of new occupations transformed the structure of social classes, and this transformation in turn became reflected in the politics and landscapes of industrial regions.

The third wave of industrialization, between 1870 and 1914, saw a further reorganization of the geography of Europe as the third technology system (including electricity, electrical engineering, and telecommunications) imposed different needs and created new opportunities. During this period, industrialization spread for the first time to more remote parts of Europe, as Figure 2.10 illustrates. The overall result was to create a core within a core. Within the world-system core, processes of industrialization, modernization, and urbanization had forged

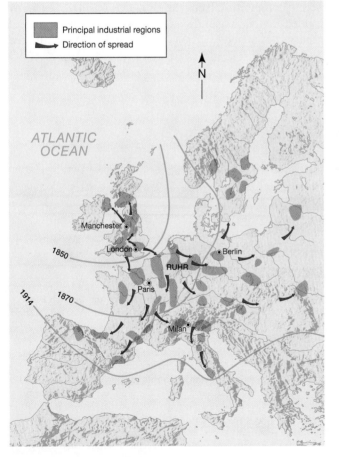

Figure 2.10   The spread of industrialization in Europe
European industrialization began with the emergence of small industrial regions in several different parts of Britain. As new technology systems emerged, industrialization spread to other regions with access to raw materials and energy sources, good communications, and large labour markets.

a core of prosperity centred on the "Golden Triangle" stretching between London, Paris, and Berlin.

The United States   By the end of the nineteenth century, the core of the world-system had extended itself to include the United States and Japan. The United States, politically independent just before the onset of the Industrial Revolution, was able to make the transition from the periphery to the core because of several favourable circumstances. Its vast natural resources of land and minerals provided the raw materials for a wide range of industries that could grow and organize without being hemmed in and fragmented by political boundaries. Its population, growing quickly through immigration, provided a large and expanding market and a cheap and flexible labour force. Its cultural and trading links with Europe provided business contacts, technological know-how, and access to capital for investment in a basic infrastructure of canals, railways, docks, warehouses, and factories.

As in Europe, industrialization developed around pre-existing centres of industrialization and population and was shaped by the resource needs and market opportunities of successive technology systems. America's industrial strength was established at the beginning of the twentieth century with the development of a new technology system that included the internal combustion engine, oil and plastics, electrical engineering, and radio and telecommunications (see Chapter 7). The outcome was a distinctive economic core (**Figure 2.11**)—another core within a core.

Canada   By 1900, Canada remained dependent on the global core, but it had become more integrated into the world-system. It had moved from peripheral to semiperipheral status on a world scale (see Figure 2.1 on p. 56). Politically, much had changed. The conquest of New France in 1760 by Britain and the loss of Britain's colonies in America (the Revolutionary War of 1775–1783) now meant that Canada became the focus of British colonial activity in North America. With Confederation in 1867, Canada became, nominally at least, in charge of its own affairs. Nevertheless, by the century's end, the increasing involvement of U.S. financial interests in Canada's economy was causing another change: Canada was shifting from being dependent on Britain to being dependent on the U.S. regional core. In 1900, for example, U.S. capital represented 15 percent of all foreign investment in Canada; by 1920, it totalled more than 50 percent.

Nineteenth-century developments were greatly aided by British and American investments in Canada's rail system and by the implementation of Canada's *National Policy* of 1879. This policy promoted the completion of a transcontinental rail link to tie the country together, encouraged immigration to the Prairies, and introduced tariffs to protect Canadian industry from cheaper American manufacturers. As a result, industrialization (which had begun by the 1850s) gathered pace, and by 1900, small manufacturing belts lay between Niagara (where hydropower was already in use) and Toronto, in the Montreal region, and around the Cape Breton coalfields of Nova Scotia.

To the existing Canadian exports of fish and furs, the nineteenth century added the development of a significant timber trade in Quebec and Ontario, the export of wheat from the Prairies to European markets, and, by the 1920s, the beginnings of pulp and paper production in British Columbia for American markets. After 1945, the development of northern mining sites and Alberta's substantial reserves of oil and gas meant that Canada's post-war economy remained heavily dependent on the exploitation of its natural resources, or *staples,* for sale abroad.

One danger of this was the **staples trap**, which left Canada vulnerable to fluctuations in world prices and without alternatives when resource depletion occurred. Another problem was the paradox of how such high levels of exports could result in such low levels of economic growth in Canada itself. This

staples trap: an over-reliance on the export of staples makes an economy (national or regional) vulnerable to fluctuations in world prices and without alternatives when resource depletion occurs

Figure 2.11   The North American core and periphery, 1911 (*Source:* L. McCann and A. Gunn, *Heartland and Hinterland: A Regional Geography of Canada.* Scarborough: Prentice-Hall, 1998.)

staples thesis: a proposition arguing that the export of Canada's natural resources, or staples, locked this country into dependency as a resource hinterland for more advanced economies and so delayed the maturing of its own economy

question prompted scholars, such as Harold Innis (1894–1952), to develop the staples thesis—50 years before Immanuel Wallerstein advanced his more general world-system model.

The **staples thesis** argues that the export of Canada's natural resources, or staples (such as fur, fish, timber, grain, and oil), to more advanced economies has delayed the development of this country's economic, political, and social systems: the value added in the subsequent manufacture of products derived from those staples (and the profits realized) accrued not to this country but to the manufacturers in Britain and the United States.

In this view, Canadian industry was stultified because it was cheaper and easier to export raw materials and to use that income to import manufactured items from Britain and the United States. Escape from this over-reliance on the export of basic commodities would have required the establishment of locally owned factories and a widely diversified industry. But finance capital was limited in Canada (because profits accrued elsewhere), and domestically produced products would be more expensive than British or American imports (because of the small production runs). What this means, if we focus on outcomes rather than on principles, is that Canadian economic growth could only be achieved, according to the staples thesis, by the continual discovery of new forms of staples to export. The staples thesis enables us to explain why many resource-producing activities in Canada (such as, for example, coal mining in Kimberley, British Columbia, or fishing along Newfoundland and Labrador's shores) have not produced sustained growth in other sectors of the local economy.

Internal Development of the Core Regions

Within the world's core regions, the transformation of regional geographies hinged on successive innovations in transport technology. These innovations opened up agrarian interiors and intensified interregional trading networks. Farmers were able to mechanize their equipment, whereas manufacturing companies were able to reach more resources and more markets.

Canals and the Growth of Industrial Regions   The first phase of this internal geographic expansion and regional integration was, in fact, based on an old technology, the canal. In the absence of surfaced roads, horse-drawn barges on rivers and canals were the most efficient method of transporting heavy and bulk goods. Extensive navigation systems that joined one river system to another underpinned merchant trade and the beginnings of industrialization: by 1790, France had more than 1,000 kilometres of canals and canalized rivers and Britain had nearly 3,600 kilometres. The Industrial Revolution provided both the need and the capital for a spate of additional canal building that began to integrate and extend emerging industrial regions.

In Canada, the main object of canal construction was to improve or protect navigation along the St. Lawrence–Great Lakes corridor, a project finally completed with the opening of the St. Lawrence Seaway in 1959. The Lachine Canal (1821–1825) and the small canals at Grenville and Carillon on the Ottawa River (1819–1834) bypassed rapids west of Montreal. The Rideau Canal (1826–1832) was designed to enable canal traffic to avoid possible American attacks on the St. Lawrence itself. The most ambitious project, the Welland Canal (built along four different routes in 1829, 1845, 1887, and 1913–1932, respectively), enabled vessels to climb 100 metres from Lake Ontario to Lake Erie. The Trent–Severn Waterway (1833–1920), now extremely popular for recreation, was never a commercial success because its hinterland was too thinly settled (**Figure 2.12**). Low population density was also the reason for the failure of Nova Scotia's Shubenacadie Canal (1826–1861), which connected Halifax to the Bay of Fundy.

Figure 2.12   The Trent–Severn Waterway's lift lock at Peterborough, Ontario   The Trent–Severn Waterway connects Trenton (on Lake Ontario) with Port Severn (on Georgian Bay, Lake Huron). Over a distance of 386 kilometres, 44 locks connect a series of lakes and rivers. Two of the locks, at Peterborough (illustrated here) and at Kirkfield, are hydraulic lift locks, which are unique in North America. Based on a design developed in Belgium and England, these were among the first structures built entirely of concrete in Canada. The waterway was built sporadically between 1833 and 1920 and was never a commercial success because of the low population density of its hinterland. It is now used almost exclusively by recreational boaters.

Figure 2.13   The S.S. Moyie   The last remaining sternwheeler on the Kootenay lakes is preserved at Kaslo, British Columbia. Before the construction of railroads or highways, these steamers (many of which transported trains on their decks) provided a vital link across many parts of Canada. Sternwheelers, for example, plied the Yukon, Mackenzie, and South Saskatchewan Rivers, and they were part of nineteenth-century transportation systems on Lake Winnipeg, the Great Lakes, and the St. Lawrence River.

Steamboats, Railroads, and Internal Development   The scale of North America was such that a network of canals was a viable proposition only in the more densely settled areas in the East. The effective colonization of the interior could not take place until the development of steam-powered transportation—first riverboats and then railroads. The heyday of the river steamboat was between 1830 and 1850. During this period, vast areas of the U.S. interior were opened up to commercial, industrialized agriculture—especially cotton production for export to British textile manufacturers. At the same time, river ports, such as New Orleans, St. Louis, Cincinnati, and Louisville, grew rapidly, extending the frontiers of industrialization and modernization.

In western Canada, the heyday of the riverboat lasted much longer. Steamers ferried thousands of people into British Columbia during gold rushes to the Fraser Valley (1858), the Cariboo region around Barkerville (1862), and Yukon in 1898. Stern paddle wheelers provided the only means of transport across the Kootenay lakes and continued in service into the 1950s (**Figure 2.13**).

By 1860, the railroads had taken over the task of internal development, further extending the frontier of settlement and industrialization and intensifying the use of previously developed regions. The railroad originated in Britain, where George Stephenson engineered the world's first commercial railroad in 1825. In other core countries, where sufficient capital existed to license (or copy) the locomotive technology and install the track, railroad systems led to the first full stage of economic and political integration.

In Canada, as we have already noted, railroad construction was one of the pillars of nation building. Indeed, a completed transcontinental railroad was a condition of British Columbia joining Confederation in 1871. By 1885, this was achieved with the completion of the Canadian Pacific Railroad. The construction of such lines enabled the export of British Columbia's timber and prairie agricultural products and the transportation of large numbers of immigrants to the frontiers of settlement (**Figure 2.14**). Cities that served as regional rail centres, such as Winnipeg, grew to substantial size during this period. Nevertheless, the Ontario–Quebec manufacturing region retained its primacy because it financed and controlled the rail network and because Montreal stood at the centre of Canada's rail and sea connections.

Although the railroads integrated the economies of entire countries and allowed colonization of vast territories, they also brought some important regional and local restructuring and differentiation. In the United States, for example, the railroads led to the consolidation of the Manufacturing Belt. They also

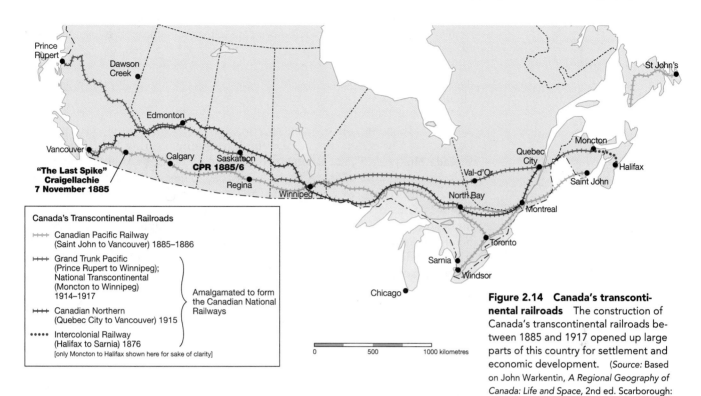

Canada's Transcontinental Railroads

├─┤─┤ Canadian Pacific Railway
(Saint John to Vancouver) 1885–1886

├─┤─┤ Grand Trunk Pacific
(Prince Rupert to Winnipeg);
National Transcontinental
(Moncton to Winnipeg)
1914–1917

├─┤─┤ Canadian Northern
(Quebec City to Vancouver) 1915

•••• Intercolonial Railway
(Halifax to Sarnia) 1876
[only Moncton to Halifax shown here for sake of clarity]

Amalgamated to form
the Canadian National
Railways

0   500   1000 kilometres

Figure 2.14 Canada's transcontinental railroads The construction of Canada's transcontinental railroads between 1885 and 1917 opened up large parts of this country for settlement and economic development. (*Source:* Based on John Warkentin, *A Regional Geography of Canada: Life and Space,* 2nd ed. Scarborough: Prentice Hall, 2000, p. 108, map 4–5.)

contributed to the mushrooming of Chicago as the focal point for railroads that extended the Manufacturing Belt's dominance over the West and South.

Tractors, Trucks, Road Building, and Spatial Reorganization In the twentieth century, the internal combustion engine powered further rounds of internal development, integration, and intensification (**Figure 2.15**). The spatial organization of all forms of land uses (agricultural, industrial, and residential) was radically reorganized, and a new round of geographical change took place. In rural areas, the replacement of horse-drawn farm implements with lightweight tractors, beginning in the 1910s, amounted to a major revolution in agriculture (see Chapter 8). Productivity was increased, the frontiers of cultivable land were extended, and vast numbers of agricultural labourers, now replaced by mechanization, became available for industrial work in cities. The result was a parallel revolution in the geographies of both rural and urban areas.

The development of trucks in the 1910s and 1920s suddenly released factories from locations tied to railroads, canals, and waterfronts. Trucking allowed movement of goods farther, faster, and cheaper than before. As a result, trucking

Figure 2.15 The geographical impacts of the internal combustion engine The internal combustion engine revolutionized the geography of the more affluent and developed parts of the world. Between 1946 and 1961, the total length of surfaced roads (concrete or bituminous) in Canada increased from 40,000 kilometres to 125,000 kilometres! By 2001, the total Canadian road network (excluding rural roads and roads within urban areas) was 215,000 kilometres. Within urban areas, private car ownership led to suburban sprawl (see Chapter 11).

made it feasible to locate factories on inexpensive land on city fringes and in smaller towns and peripheral regions where labour was cheaper. It also increased the market area of individual factories and reduced the need for large product inventories. This decentralization of industry, in conjunction with the availability of buses, private automobiles, and massive road-building programs, brought about another phase of spatial reorganization.

In Canada, construction began on the Queen Elizabeth Way in the 1930s. This four-lane controlled-access highway provided important links between Canada's economic heartland and the U.S. Manufacturing Belt. The Trans-Canada Highway (7,821 kilometres), opened in 1962, had the national goal of linking the entire country, this time by road. The outcomes of this phase in Canada and elsewhere were the specialized and highly integrated regions and urban systems of the modern core of the world-system. This integration was not simply a question of connecting places through highway systems; it also involved close economic linkages among manufacturers, suppliers, and distributors—linkages that enabled places and regions to specialize and develop economic advantages (see Chapter 7).

ORGANIZING THE PERIPHERY

Parallel with the internal development of core regions were changes in the geographies of the periphery of the world-system. Indeed, the growth and internal development of the core regions simply could not have taken place without the foodstuffs, raw materials, labour, and markets provided by the colonization of the periphery and the incorporation of more and more territory into the sphere of industrial capitalism.

As soon as the Industrial Revolution had gathered momentum in the early nineteenth century, the industrial core nations began to penetrate the interior of the world's midcontinental grassland zones for grain and livestock production. In the tropics, they established plantations that produced coffee, tea, cocoa, cotton, palm oil, rubber, or fibres. Most of the periphery came under the political and economic control—directly or indirectly—of one or another of the industrial core nations. In the second half of the nineteenth century, and especially after 1870, there was a vast increase in the number of colonies and the number of people under colonial rule.

The International Division of Labour

The fundamental logic behind all this colonization was economic: the need for an extended arena for trade, an arena that could supply foodstuffs and raw materials in return for the industrial goods of the core. The outcome was an international division of labour, driven by the needs of the core and imposed through its economic and military strength. This **division of labour** involved the specialization of different people, regions, and countries in certain kinds of economic activities.

The result was that colonial economies were founded on narrow specializations that were oriented to, and dependent on, the needs of core countries. Examples of these specializations include bananas in Central America; cotton in India; coffee in Brazil, Java, and Kenya; copper in Chile; cocoa in Ghana; rubber in Malaysia and Sumatra; sugar in the Caribbean; tea in Ceylon (now Sri Lanka); tin in Bolivia; and bauxite in Guyana and Surinam. Most of these specializations persist today. Thus, for example, 45 of the 55 countries in sub-Saharan Africa still depend on just three products—tea, cocoa, and coffee—for more than half of their export earnings.

The international division of labour brought about a substantial increase in trade and a huge surge in the overall size of the capitalist world economy. The peripheral regions of the world contributed a great deal to this growth; in fact,

division of labour: the specialization of different people, regions, or countries in particular kinds of economic activities

it would have been impossible without them. By 1913, Africa and Asia provided more *exports* to the world economy than either North America or the British Isles. Asia alone was *importing* almost as much, by value, as North America. The industrializing countries of the core bought increasing amounts of foodstuffs and raw materials from the periphery, financed by profits from the export of machinery and manufactured goods to the periphery. It should be noted that companies that produced these foodstuffs and raw materials in the periphery usually were owned by entrepreneurs in the core. In this sense, the core actually traded with itself but in the process used the resources and labour of the periphery.

Patterns of international trade and interdependence became increasingly complex. Britain, the hegemonic power of the nineteenth century, controlled a trading empire that was truly global (**Figure 2.16**), using its capital to invest not just in peripheral regions but also in profitable industries in other emerging core countries, especially the United States. At the same time, these other core countries were able to export cheap manufactured goods to Britain. Britain financed the purchase of these goods, together with imports of food from its dominion states (Canada, South Africa, Australia, and New Zealand) and colonies, through the export of its own especially manufactured goods to peripheral countries. India and China, with large domestic markets, were important. Thus, a widening circle of exchange and dependence developed, with constantly switching patterns of trade and investment.

This new global economic geography took some time to establish, and the details of its pattern and timing were heavily influenced by technological innovations. The incorporation of the temperate grasslands into the commercial orbit of the core countries, for example, involved successive changes in regional landscapes as critical innovations—such as barbed wire, the railroad, and refrigeration—were introduced. The single most important innovation stimulating the international division of labour, however, was the development of metal-hulled, oceangoing steamships. This development was cumulative, with improvements in engines, boilers, transmission systems, fuel systems, and construction materials adding up to produce dramatic improvements in carrying capacity, speed, range, and reliability. The construction of the Suez Canal (opened in 1869) and the Panama Canal (opened in 1914) was also critical, providing shorter and less hazardous routes between core countries and colonial ports of call. By the eve of World War I the world economy was effectively integrated by a system of regularly scheduled

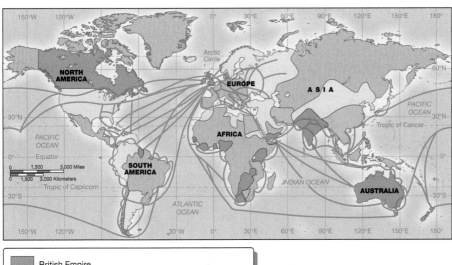

Figure 2.16   The British Empire in the late 1800s   Protected by the all-powerful Royal Navy, the British merchant navy established a web of commerce that collected food for British industrial workers and raw materials for its industries, much of it from colonies and dependencies appropriated by imperial might and developed by British capital. So successful was the trading empire that Britain also became the hub of trade for other states.   (*Source:* Adapted from P. Hugill, *World Trade since 1431.* Baltimore: Johns Hopkins University Press, 1993, p. 136.)

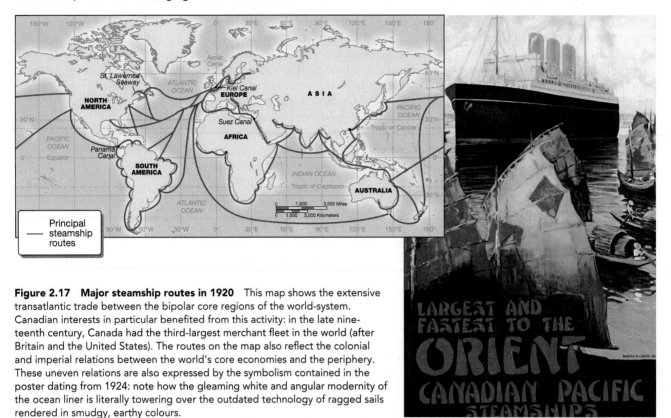

Figure 2.17 Major steamship routes in 1920 This map shows the extensive transatlantic trade between the bipolar core regions of the world-system. Canadian interests in particular benefited from this activity: in the late nineteenth century, Canada had the third-largest merchant fleet in the world (after Britain and the United States). The routes on the map also reflect the colonial and imperial relations between the world's core economies and the periphery. These uneven relations are also expressed by the symbolism contained in the poster dating from 1924: note how the gleaming white and angular modernity of the ocean liner is literally towering over the outdated technology of ragged sails rendered in smudgy, earthy colours.

steamship trading routes (**Figure 2.17**). This integration, in turn, was supported by the second most important innovation stimulating the international division of labour: a network of telegraph communications that enabled businesses to monitor and coordinate supply and demand across vast distances (**Figure 2.18**). Together, these improvements in transportation and communications technology both integrated and "shrunk" the world.

Imperialism: Imposing New Geographies on the World

The incorporation of the periphery was by no means only motivated by the basic logic of free trade and investment: the expansion of European influence was also seen as a question of power and even national pride. Although Britain was

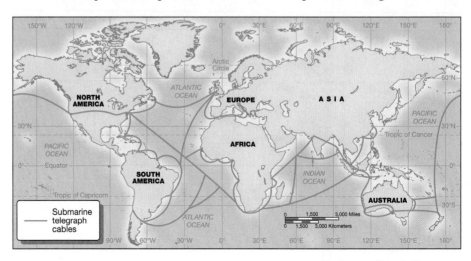

Figure 2.18 The international telegraph network in 1900 For Britain, submarine telegraph cables were the nervous system of its empire. Of the global network of 246,000 kilometres of submarine cable, Britain had laid 169,000 kilometres.

the hegemonic power in the late nineteenth century, several other European countries (notably Germany, France, and the Netherlands) together with the United States—and later Japan—were competing for global influence. The core countries engaged in pre-emptive geographical expansionism to protect their established interests and to limit the opportunities of others. Through a combination of military supervision, administrative control, and economic regulations they tried to ensure stable and profitable environments for their traders and investors. This competition escalated into a veritable scramble for territorial and commercial domination: between 1870 and 1900, European countries added more than 25 million square kilometres and 150 million people to their spheres of control—20 percent of Earth's land surface and 10 percent of its population.

Africa, more than any other peripheral region, was given an entirely new political geography. At the 1884 Berlin Conference, 14 core countries simply carved up the African continent into a patchwork of European colonies and protectorates—without any African representation and with little regard for physical geography, ethnic groups, or the pre-existing human geographies of mini-systems. This "arrangement" essentially continued until decolonization began in the 1950s. The only change was that, after losing World War I, Germany had to give control over its four colonies to the League of Nations—which promptly placed them under the mandate of other colonizing core states. Even after finally gaining their independence, many African nations retained the curiously straight and regular borders that the European powers had imposed on the map of Africa. They did so in an effort to avoid bloody border conflicts, but the price was that they continue to have to live with a political geography that was established to serve the interests of the core nations, rather than reflecting traditional affiliations. As a result, many African states are a patchwork of often quite disparate ethnicities and religions and thus are prone to civil unrest.

At the same time that the whole of Africa became incorporated into the modern world-system, the major powers jostled and squabbled over small Pacific islands that suddenly became valuable as strategic coaling stations for their roaming navies and merchant fleets. Resistance from indigenous peoples was quickly brushed aside by imperial navies with ironclad steamers, high-explosive guns, and troops with rifles and cannons. European weaponry was so superior that Otto von Bismarck, the founder and first chancellor (1871–1890) of the German empire, referred to these conflicts as "sporting wars." Quickly, all but one island (Tonga) came under the control of colonial powers.

As these examples show, the imprint of imperialism and colonization on the peoples and geographies of the newly incorporated peripheries of the world-system was immediate, profound, and lasting—often to this day. The periphery quickly became almost entirely dependent on European and North American capital, shipping, managerial expertise, financial services, and news and communications. Consequently, it also became dependent on European cultural products: language, education, science, religion, architecture, and planning. All of these influences were etched into the landscapes of the periphery in a variety of ways as new places were created, old places were remade, and regions were reorganized—including all the human suffering that came with such reorganization.

NEO-COLONIALISM AND EARLY GLOBALIZATION

The imperial world order began to disintegrate shortly after World War II. The United States emerged as the new hegemonic power, the dominant state within the world-system core. This core was called the "First World." The Soviet Union and China, opting for alternative paths of development for themselves and their satellite countries, were seen as a "Second World," withdrawn from the capitalist world economy. Their pursuit of alternative political economies was based on radically different values.

By the 1950s, many of the European colonies were seeking political independence. Some of the early independence struggles were very bloody because the colonial powers were initially reluctant to withdraw from colonies where strategic resources or large numbers of European settlers were involved. By the early 1960s, however, the process of peaceful decolonization had gained momentum and more and more colonies achieved independence (see Chapter 9). The periphery of the world-system now consisted of a "Third World" of politically independent states, some of which (India, for instance) chose not to align with the ideology of either the First or the Second World.

From the 1960s onward, the peripheral states struggled to achieve economic independence through industrialization, modernization, and trade, but at the same time the capitalist world-system changed yet again to adapt to the new global situation. The old imperial patterns of international trade were replaced by more complex patterns that resulted in more interdependence and integration. However, many of the old colonial links and legacies remained intact, and so the former colonial powers continued to influence the newly independent states. The result was a neo-colonial pattern of international development. **Neo-colonialism** refers to economic and political strategies by which powerful states in core economies indirectly maintain or extend their influence over other areas or people. Instead of formal, direct rule (colonialism), control is exerted through such strategies as international financial regulations, commercial relations, military aid and co-operation, and intelligence operations. Because of this neo-colonialism, the human geographies of peripheral countries are heavily shaped by the linguistic, cultural, political, and institutional influences of the former colonial powers and by the investment and trading activities of their firms.

Also around the middle of the twentieth century, a new form of imperialism was emerging: the commercial imperialism of giant corporations that had grown within the core countries through mergers and takeovers. Beginning in the 1960s, quite a few of them became *transnational* in scope. These **transnational corporations** (TNCs) have investments and activities that span continents, with subsidiary companies, factories, offices, or facilities in several countries. Their growth in recent years has been remarkable: according to the UN Conference on Trade and Development (UNCTAD), by 2002 more than 65,000 TNCs were operating (up from 40,000 in the mid-1990s), 90 percent of which had headquarters in core states. Together, these corporations control about 850,000 foreign subsidiaries (up from 180,000 in the mid-1990s) and account for 10 percent of the global GDP and 30 percent of world exports. As we will see in the next section, TNCs play a prominent role in fuelling the processes of contemporary globalization.

neo-colonialism: economic and political strategies by which powerful states in core economies indirectly maintain or extend their influence over other areas or people

transnational corporations: companies with investments and activities that span international boundaries and with subsidiary companies, factories, offices, or facilities in several countries

Contemporary Globalization

The basic framework for globalization has been in place since the nineteenth century, when the competitive system of states fostered the emergence of global networks of transportation and communication, international agencies and institutions, a standardized system of global time zones, international competitions and prizes, international law, and universal notions of citizenship and human rights. Global connections today, though, differ in at least five important ways from those in the past.

First, they function at much greater speed than ever before. Second, globalization operates on a much larger scale, leaving few people unaffected and making its influence felt in even the most remote places. Third, the scope of global connections is much broader and has multiple dimensions: economic, technological, political, legal, social, and cultural, among others. Fourth, the interactions and interdependencies among numerous global actors have created a new level of complexity for the relationships between places and regions.

Finally, the most distinctive feature of globalization over the past 30 years or so is a decisive increase in the proportion of the world's economic and cultural activities that are transnational in scope. This increase is linked to a significant shift in the *nature* of international economic activity: flows of goods, capital, and information that take place within and between transnational corporations are becoming more important than imports and exports between countries. TNCs organize these flows in the form of commodity chains that criss-cross global space. **Commodity chains** are networks of labour and production processes whose origin is in the extraction or production of raw materials and whose end result is the delivery and consumption of a finished commodity. As we will see in Chapter 7, these global assembly lines are increasingly important in shaping places and regions—not least because they directly affect people's lives at every stage.

commodity chains: networks of labour and production processes beginning with the extraction or production of raw materials and ending with the delivery of a finished commodity

Transnational flows and activities have also helped spread new values around the world. These new values range from superficial and resource-intensive consumer lifestyle preferences to deeper, altruistic concerns with global resources, global environmental changes, and famine relief. The ambiguities associated with globalization mean that the term is often controversial because it has different meanings for different people. Most broadly, globalization is the expansion and intensification of linkages and flows of capital, people, goods, ideas, and cultures across national borders. To some this process implies a serious decline in the importance of local communities and national governments. Globalization has produced a more complex system of interdependent states in which transnational rules and organizations have gained influence. States pursuing their national interests are still a major force, but corporations and international nongovernmental organizations (INGOs) can now critically influence world politics. World society therefore contains many centres of power and has no single power hierarchy. As power disperses and goals diverge, yet another new pattern of complex interdependence is emerging.

Globalization also has important cultural dimensions (see Chapters 5 and 6). One is quite simply the diffusion around the world of all sorts of cultural forms, practices, and artifacts that had previously been confined to specific places or regions. Examples include "ethnic" and regional cuisine, "world" music, and Caribbean carnivals. Another dimension of cultural globalization derives from consumer culture: everything that is sold in international markets, from sneakers, replica soccer shirts, and automobiles to movies and rock concert tours. This leads some observers to believe that globalization is producing a new set of universally shared images, practices, and values: literally, a global culture.

At the same time, a more integrated global system has also increased awareness of a set of common problems that many see as a consequence of globalization: climate change, transboundary pollution, drug trafficking, environmental diseases, crime, poverty, and inequality, to name but a few. This globalization of the contemporary world is a recurring theme through the rest of this book. Again and again, we will examine its causes and effects on specific aspects of human geographies at different spatial scales. For the remainder of this chapter, we will examine the principal causes and consequences of globalization.

2.2 Geography in the Information Age

Most observers regard the notion of globalization resulting in a single global culture as overly simplistic. They point to the fusion of different regional and international cultural elements that creates a *hybridization* of culture. Transgressions, adaptations, and subversions of "conventional" or "traditional" cultures originate in many different places and regions and then spread, resulting in a series of open-ended "global" cultures. Cultural anthropologist Arjun Appadurai has described five kinds of cultural flows that contribute to these global cultures:

- Ethnoscapes: produced by flows of people, including tourists, immigrants, refugees, exiles, and guest workers;

- Technoscapes: resulting from the diffusion of goods, technologies, and architectural styles;

- Finanscapes: produced by rapid flows of money in currency markets and stock exchanges;

- Mediascapes: images of the world produced by news agencies, magazines, television, and film;

- Ideoscapes: resulting from the diffusion of ideas and ideologies, concepts of human rights, democracy, welfare, and so on.

What Drives Globalization?

The globalization of the past quarter-century has been driven by four important and interrelated factors: a new international division of labour, an internationalization of finance, a new technology system, and a homogenization of international consumer markets.

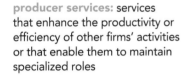

producer services: services that enhance the productivity or efficiency of other firms' activities or that enable them to maintain specialized roles

The New International Division of Labour   The new international division of labour has involved three main changes. First, beginning in the 1970s, the United States lost its pre-eminence in manufacturing to a rapidly growing Japan and a resurging Europe. Second, beginning in the 1980s, manufacturing production was increasingly decentralized from core regions to semiperipheral and peripheral countries, where wage costs are dramatically lower (**Figure 2.19**). Among other things, this wage differential has enabled China to attract much of the global mass manufacturing and become the "workbench of the world." Third, new specializations have emerged within the core regions of the world-system, specifically high-tech manufacturing and **producer services** (that is, such services as information services, insurance, and market research that enhance the productivity or efficiency of other firms' activities or that enable them to maintain specialized roles). One

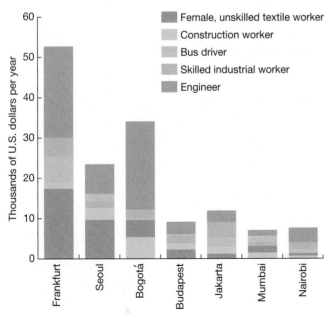

Figure 2.19   International differences in wage rates   Wages vary substantially across countries and regions, representing a substantial incentive for companies to locate their operations accordingly. The height of each bar segment in this chart indicates the range of salaries for several occupations in different cities. Adjusted for differences in purchasing power, the earnings of engineers in Frankfurt, Germany, are seven times those of engineers in Mumbai (formerly Bombay), India. International differences in the pay of unskilled workers are even greater—unskilled female textile workers in Frankfurt are paid 18 times as much as their counterparts in Nairobi, Kenya.   (*Source:* World Bank, *World Development Report 1995.* New York: Oxford University Press, 1996, p. 11.)

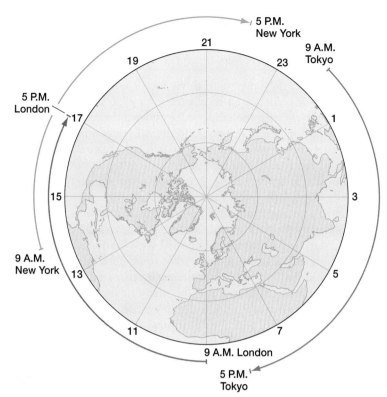

Figure 2.20 24-hour trading between major financial markets Office hours in the two most important financial centres—New York and London—overlap one another because the two cities are situated in broadly separated time zones. While these markets are both closed, Tokyo offices are open. This means that, among them, they span the globe with almost 24-hour trading in currencies, stocks, and other financial instruments.

significant result of this new international division of labour is that global trade between these specialized producers and service providers has grown much more rapidly over the past 30 years than global production—a clear indication of the increased economic integration of the world-system.

The Internationalization of Financial Markets The second factor intensifying globalization is the emergence of globally integrated financial markets. One indicator is the amount of money from one country being invested in the economy of another, also called *foreign direct investment,* or FDI. Between 1988 and 1998, the flow of investment capital from core to semiperipheral and peripheral countries increased more than twenty-fold, yet three-quarters of the total FDI still circulates between core countries, thus reinforcing their economic dominance. In 2007, total global FDI reached a record US$1.5 trillion.

The sheer volume and complexity of international investment and financial trading have created a need for banks and financial institutions that can handle investments on a large scale, across great distances, quickly and efficiently. This has led to the concentration of financial trading in a decreasing number of increasingly large financial institutions that are located in just a few places—London, New York, Frankfurt, and Tokyo, in particular. Their activities are interconnected around the clock (**Figure 2.20**), and their

2.3 Geography in the Information Age

The amount of FDI pales in comparison to another indicator of financial globalization: *every day* currencies worth several trillion U.S. dollars are traded by investors speculating on future exchange rate developments. This extremely high volume is made possible by recent advances in information and communications technologies (ICT): the capacity of computers and information networks to respond very quickly to changing international conditions makes it possible to trade "virtual money" almost instantaneously.

Figure 2.21 The impact of containerization on world trade Containerization revolutionized long-distance transport because it eliminated the need for slow, expensive, and unreliable loading and unloading of ships using manual labour. Before containerization, ships spent one day in port for every one day at sea; after containerization, they spent one day in port for every ten days at sea. By 1965, an international standard for containers was adopted, making it possible to transfer goods directly from ship to rail to road, and allowing for a highly integrated global transport infrastructure. The average container ship today holds 6,000 twenty-foot containers, but some are able to carry up to 14,000. Containerization requires a heavy investment in both vessels and dockside handling equipment, however. As a result, container traffic has quickly become concentrated in a few ports that handle high-volume transatlantic and transpacific trade.

networks penetrate into every corner of the globe. As noted in Chapter 1, it was this interconnectedness and complexity that contributed to the global financial crisis of October 2008.

The New Technology System The third factor contributing to globalization is the emergence of the most recent technology system that is based on a combination of innovations, including solar and wind energy, robotics, microelectronics, bio- and nanotechnology, and digital telecommunications and information systems. This new technology system has required the geographical reorganization of the core economies. It has also extended the global reach of finance and industry and permitted a more flexible approach to investment and trade. Especially important in this regard have been new and improved technologies in transport and communications—the integration of shipping, railroad, and highway systems through containerization (**Figure 2.21**); the introduction of wide-bodied cargo jets that can be loaded with standardized skids (**Figure 2.22**); the development of fax machines, fibre-optic networks, communications satellites, electronic mail and information retrieval systems, cloud computing, and the ubiquity of Internet access. Finally, many of these telecommunications technologies have also introduced a wider geographical scope and faster pace to many aspects of political, social, and cultural change, as we shall see in subsequent chapters.

The Homogenization of Consumer Markets A fourth factor in globalization is the growth and homogenization of consumer markets. Among the more affluent populations of the world, similar social processes create parallel trends

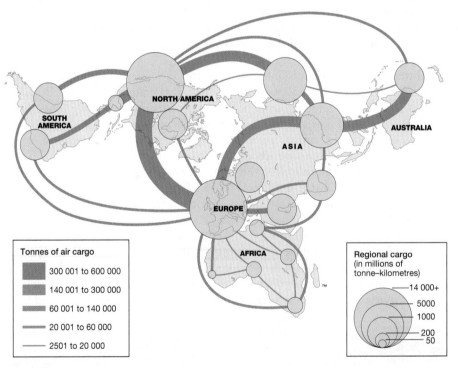

Figure 2.22 Global air cargo traffic in 1990 The introduction in the 1970s of wide-bodied cargo jets that could be loaded with standardized skids (such as the Boeing 747) was an important factor in contributing to the globalization of the world economy. Within a few years, specialized parcel services had established regular routes handling a high volume of documents and freight with a high value-to-weight ratio. This Dymaxion projection shows how the pattern of air freight reflects the tri-polar structure of the contemporary world economy, with the highest-volume flows between Western Europe, North America, and Japan. (*Source:* Map projection, Buckminster Fuller Institute and Dymaxion Map Design, Santa Barbara, CA. The word *Dymaxion* and the Fuller Projection Dymaxion™ Map design are trademarks of the Buckminster Fuller Institute, Santa Barbara, California, © 1938, 1967, & 1992. All rights reserved.)

in consumer taste. A new and materialistic international culture has taken root, in which people save less, borrow more, defer parenthood, and indulge in affordable luxuries that are marketed as symbols of style and distinctiveness. This culture is easily transmitted through the new telecommunications and social media, and it has been an important basis for transnational corporations' global branding and marketing of "world products" (German luxury automobiles, Swiss watches, British raincoats, French wines, American soft drinks, Italian shoes and designer clothes, and Japanese consumer electronics, for example). And it is not limited to core countries: nine of the ten most trusted brands in India in 2007, for example, were products of British or American transnational corporations.

This materialistic international culture is reinforced through other aspects of globalization, including the internationalization of television, especially CNN, MTV, Fox Broadcasting, Sky, Star Television, and the syndication of TV movies and light entertainment series. The number of television sets per 1,000 people worldwide doubled between 1980 and 2000, and multimedia industries are booming. The global market for popular cultural products carried by these media is becoming concentrated, however. At the core of the entertainment industry—film, music, and television—there is a growing dominance of U.S. products, and many countries have seen their homegrown industries wither. Hollywood obtains more than 50 percent of its revenues from overseas, up from just 30 percent in 1980. Movies made in the United States account for about 50 percent of the market in Japan, 70 percent in Europe, and 85 percent in Latin America. Similarly, U.S. television series have become increasingly prominent in the programming of other countries.

Canada has sought, with varying degrees of success, to protect its cultural industries from the effects of this Americanization. For instance, Canadian content rules require that 35 percent of music played on the radio and 60 percent of TV programming must be Canadian. On the production side, Canadian television and films are eligible for various federal and provincial or territorial subsidies. Until the Canadian dollar's recent increase in value, Vancouver, Montreal, and Toronto were frequent locations for Hollywood productions. However, it is interesting to note that in the majority of cases, the "Canadianness" of actors or locations is not acknowledged.

2.4   Geography in the Information Age

The current technology system has helped create a globalized economy in which smaller businesses usually find it hard to compete. However, the recently developed concept of the virtual "Logistics Mall" combines several ICT solutions in ways that allow small and medium-sized businesses to operate worldwide. The Logistics Mall is an online gateway to international logistics services ranging from export permits and international customer support services to customs clearing and shipping, services that are usually too complex or expensive for small businesses to cover in-house. Through a single interface, a business can purchase, combine, and pay for customized solutions from a variety of providers—and the integration of technologies goes even further: using cloud computing technology and an integrated web interface, the Logistics Mall frees the individual business from having to purchase any hardware or software beyond a simple personal computer. As geographers, we are thus reminded that the current technology system, depending on how it is employed, can work both up and down the scale, and can emphasize or minimize the importance of physical location.

Globalization and Core–Periphery Differences

The single most dramatic outcome of the globalization that has resulted from all these changes is the consolidation of the core of the world-system. The core is now a close-knit triad of the geographical centres of North America, the European Union, and Japan (**Figure 2.23**). These three geographical centres are connected through three main circuits, or flows, of investment, trade, and communication: between Europe and North America, between Europe and Asia, and among the regions of the Pacific Rim. **Figure 2.24**, for example, shows just how dominant North America has become in accounting for flows of international telephonic

Figure 2.23 The tri-polar core of the world economy In general terms, the world economy is now structured around a "core" with three centres: the United States, Japan, and the European Union. Most of the flows of goods, capital, and information are generated within and among these three centres. Together, they dominate the world's periphery, with each centre having particular influence in its own regional expansion zone—its nearest peripheral region. (*Source:* Map projection, Buckminster Fuller Institute and Dymaxion Map Design, Santa Barbara, CA. The word *Dymaxion* and the Fuller Projection Dymaxion™ Map design are trademarks of the Buckminster Fuller Institute, Santa Barbara, California, © 1938, 1967, & 1992. All rights reserved.)

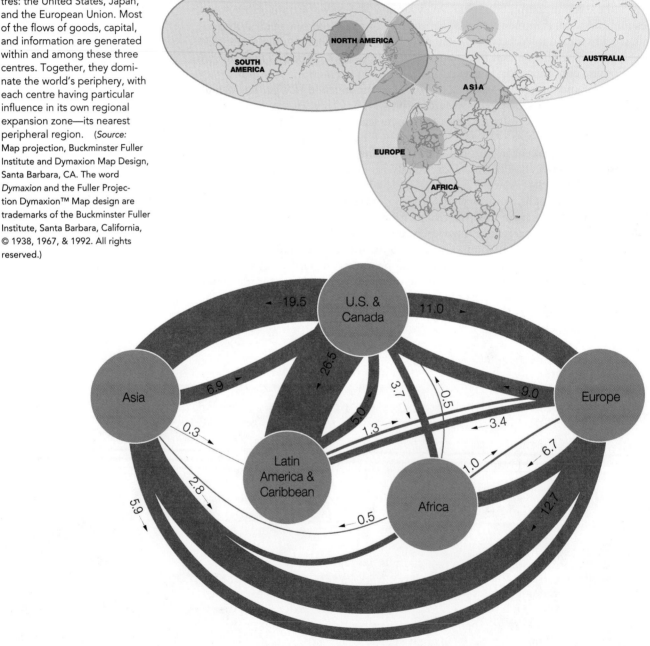

Figure 2.24 Communication flows among major world regions This diagram shows the flows, in billions of minutes of telecommunications traffic over public telephone networks, among major regions. The wider the band, the more flow is occurring. Note the virtual absence of Africa. (*Source:* G.C. Staple [ed.], *TeleGeography 1999.* Washington, DC: TeleGeography Inc., 1999, fig. 4, p. 255.)

communication. As we shall see in Chapter 7, this consolidation of the core of the world-system is having some profound effects on economic geography. Within the core regions, for example, a new hierarchy of regional economic specialization has been imposed by the locational strategies of transnational corporations and international financial institutions.

Globalization, although incorporating more of the world more completely into the capitalist world-system, has actually intensified the differences between the core and the periphery. According to the United Nations Development Programme (UNDP), the gap between the poorest fifth of the world's population and the wealthiest fifth increased more than threefold between 1965 and 2005. Per capita GDP in the world's 20 richest countries is now 40 times higher than in the world's poorest 20 countries. In 55 countries per capita incomes actually *fell* during the 1990s. Put bluntly: some parts of the periphery have almost slid off the economic map. In sub-Saharan Africa, economic output fell by one-third during the 1980s and stayed low during the 1990s; people's standard of living there is now, on average, lower than it was in the early 1960s. By 2007, the UNDP observed that the poorest 20 percent of the world's population accounted for only 1.5 percent of world income. To put it differently: in 1998, the wealth of the 200 richest *individuals* was greater than the combined annual income of 40 percent of the world's population.

Such enormous differences (many of which seem to be exacerbated, rather than evened out, by globalization) lead many people to question the equity, or fairness, of geographical variations in people's levels of affluence and well-being. The concept of **spatial justice** is important here because it requires us to consider the distribution of society's benefits and burdens at different spatial scales, taking into account variations in both people's needs and their contributions to the production of wealth and social well-being (see **Geography Matters 2.4—Opposition to Globalization**). Thinking about spatial justice is an important aspect of the "geographic imagination" described in Chapter 1, and it is a recurring theme in this book.

spatial justice: the fairness of the distribution of society's burdens and benefits, taking into account spatial variations in people's needs and in their contributions to the production of wealth and social well-being

The Fast World and the Slow World   The differences between the core and the periphery are now less easily captured by using the framework of states. Economic and cultural globalization have not been matched by political globalization or a system of governance that can cope with its powerful forces. Trade policy has been influenced by powerful transnational corporations, while national governments are unable to deal with large-scale environmental issues that transcend borders. Globalization has fuelled global economic expansion, but, in the process, it has widened the gap between rich and poor and made places and regions everywhere vulnerable to rapid and devastating change. As Ted Turner, then owner of CNN, observed in a 1999 United Nations report on international development, "It is as if globalization is in fast forward, and the world's ability to react to it is in slow motion."[4]

Ted Turner's observation points to a division that now exists between the "fast world" and the "slow world." The **fast world** consists of people, places, and regions directly involved, as producers and consumers, in transnational industry, modern telecommunications, materialistic consumption, and international news and entertainment. The **slow world** consists of people, places, and regions whose participation in transnational industry, modern telecommunications, materialistic consumption, and international news and entertainment is limited. Until recently, this slow world consisted chiefly of the impoverished periphery; now, however, it also includes many rural backwaters, declining manufacturing regions, and disadvantaged slums in core countries, all of them bypassed by this latest phase in the evolution of the modern world-system.

fast world: people, places, and regions directly involved, as producers and consumers, in transnational industry, modern telecommunications, materialistic consumption, and international news and entertainment

slow world: people, places, and regions whose participation in transnational industry, modern telecommunications, materialistic consumption, and international news and entertainment is limited

We can interpret this as another indication that the framework of the nation state is increasingly unable to capture the "messy" reality of a globalizing world. When looking at the map in **Figure 2.25** on p. 90 that tries to capture Internet

[4] United Nations, *Human Development Report 1999*. New York: United Nations Development Programme, 1999, p. 100.

Opposition to Globalization

At the global scale, a number of controversial issues are tied to globalization: the depletion of the ozone layer, for example, together with overfishing (see Chapter 4) and threats to biodiversity. At the regional scale, some areas disproportionately suffer the effects of resource depletion and environmental degradation, whereas others are able to "outsource" their environmental impacts and so protect their environment. But the effects of globalization also reach down to the very local scale of people's personal lives.

Many people, nations, and ethnic groups around the world feel marginalized, exploited, and neglected as the processes of globalization are transforming their lives at an ever-quickening pace. Across much of the peripheral world, the perception of a systematic injustice has been brewing for a long time. Longstanding resentment at past colonial and imperial exploitation is now being compounded as the more affluent places and regions of the world continue to exploit the periphery's labour and resources for their own wealth, rather than working toward a more equitable global division of opportunities and profits. In fact, from agriculture to education, transnational corporations from the core have moved in and displaced the traditional economic and social practices of peripheral and semiperipheral regions under the banner of modernization, often with severe consequences for the local population.

One particularly painful result of the increased integration brought about by globalization is the steep increase in food prices since 2008 (see Chapter 1). This increase is only partly the result of real changes in the supply of inputs (for example, the increased price of energy) or rising demand for food products (for example, by the growing middle class in the BRICS countries). Increasingly, it is also due to speculation on the financial markets, where foodstuffs are now being traded as a commodity. Poor people everywhere thus suffer the effects of an integrated and commodified global food system in very immediate ways.

Politically, globalization has reinforced disillusionment with the West, especially within traditional Islamic societies. Across much of the world, modernization now means Westernization and, more specifically, Americanization. Although many people in the core countries think of modernization as necessary and beneficial, many people in the periphery see it as resulting in their exploitation and humiliation (**Figure 2.4.1**). In most peripheral countries, only a minority can enjoy Western-style consumerism, and the impoverished majority is acutely aware of the affluence of the core countries and of their own elite that is disproportionately benefiting from the modernization. Meanwhile, the world's core countries, acting on the confident assumption that people everywhere want Western-style modernization, have until recently failed to recognize the cultural resentment, the sense of injustice, and the genuine rejection of modernization that exists in many parts of the world.

Globalization has brought a great deal of change to the economic, cultural, and political geography of places and regions throughout the world. Much of this change is progressive, bringing increased average levels of economic well-being, and an enriched flow of products, ideas, and culture among and between places and regions. It is also accompanied by increased international flows of pirated DVDs, brand-name knock-offs, counterfeit money, narcotics, weapons, stolen art, and laundered money, as well as a more extensive diffusion of diseases like tuberculosis and HIV/AIDS. These unwelcome consequences of globalization pose huge challenges to an international community more interconnected—and therefore more vulnerable—than ever before. At the same time, globalization has undercut the power of national and local governments to regulate their own affairs without interference as they find themselves competing against each other for investment monies: a race to the bottom in terms of taxation levels, environmental regulations, and labour laws is underway.

But globalization is not a one-way process, and it is not unresisted. Fundamental geographic differences—in climate, resources, culture, and so on—mean that economic globalization is variously embraced, modified, or resisted in different parts of the world. Indeed, a countermovement has emerged, a "mobilization against globalization," that could well affect the whole dynamic of economic globalization as it is played out over the next decade or two.

Figure 2.4.1 Westernization Turkish Muslims chat near an illuminated billboard advertising a Turkish Internet company at Istanbul airport.

One form of mobilization is old-fashioned popular protest (**Figure 2.4.2**). French farmers, for example, regularly employ tactics such as blocking streets with tractors, produce, manure, or animals to protest trade-liberalization policies that would affect their livelihood. Another form of mobilization is to counter the prevailing trend with alternatives, as in the case of Mecca Cola.

Third, and perhaps most significant in terms of future cultural struggles between local interests and transnational business interests, mobilization can be organized by coalitions of nongovernmental organizations (NGOs). This form of mobilization against globalization became much more powerful in the 1990s as a result of the Internet. Groups such as Kenya's Consumers' Information Network, Ecuador's Acción Ecologica, and Trinidad and Tobago's Caribbean Association for Feminist Research and Action are linked through scores of websites, listservs, and discussion groups to U.S., European, and Asian counterparts that support their causes.

The successes of networked NGOs are real: they set the agenda for the Earth Summit in Rio de Janeiro in 1992 and lobbied governments to attend; they publicized the Chiapas rebellion in Mexico in 1994, thereby preventing the Mexican government from suppressing it violently. In 1997, a loose alliance of 350 NGOs from 23 countries set out to ban land mines; they soon persuaded 122 nations to sign the so-called Ottawa Treaty (as of 2011, a total of 156 countries have signed the treaty—the United States and China are not among them).

In 1999, more than 775 NGOs registered with the World Trade Organization (WTO) and took more than 2,000 observers to the WTO summit in Seattle, Washington. They also helped organize some 70,000 protesters who took part in the most extensive teach-ins and demonstrations in the United States since the Vietnam War. The WTO meetings, delayed by the protests, ended in collapse. In 2001, a young man was killed by paramilitary police during antiglobalization riots in Genoa, Italy. Since then, economic summit meetings have been convening in hard-to-reach locations or under heavy police protection. In 2010, for example, Canada spent between $500 million and $1 billion (estimates vary and are hard to verify) to host the G8 and G20 meetings in Huntsville and Toronto. Newspaper reports put the cost of the perimeter fence alone at over $5 million.

These demonstrations highlight some of the central issues that surround globalization. Economic globalization depends on free trade, but should the abolition of economic protectionism be accompanied by the abolition of social and environmental protection? The WTO's mandate is the "harmonization" of safety and environmental standards among member nations as well as the removal of tariffs and other barriers to free trade. Most people support free trade, but not if it harms public health, and not if it is based on child labour.

There have been several examples of how the free trade principles embodied in the WTO can erode national environmental standards. In 1997, Venezuela and Brazil, on behalf of their gasoline producers, challenged U.S. Environmental Protection Agency (EPA) regulations on gasoline quality, which were designed to ensure minimal levels of pollution. The WTO ruled in favour of Venezuela. The EPA subsequently had to change its regulations, leaving it with a weakened ability to enforce U.S. air-quality standards. In a 2006 case, the WTO ruled against the European Union's intention to impose a regulatory system on genetically modified foods, thus setting a broad precedent that inhibits the ability of WTO member states to set food safety, public health, and environmental health measures related to genetic engineering. Other examples where WTO rulings placed free trade considerations above environmental concerns include the protection of dolphins and sea turtles, or the attempt by the European Union to ban U.S. beef raised with the assistance of hormone injections.

(a)

(b)

Figure 2.4.2 Antiglobalization demonstrations Globalization often leads to the downward convergence of wages and environmental standards, an undermining of democratic governance, and a general recoding of nearly all aspects of life to the language and logic of global markets. (a) Antiglobalization demonstration in the old town, Bern, Switzerland, prior to the 2008 meeting of the World Economic Forum (WEF) in the Swiss Alpine resort of Davos. (b) French farmers dump imported Chilean and Argentinean apples and melons on the streets of Marseille in 2005.

2.5 Geography in the Information Age

Recently, this rather crude distinction between a "fast core" and a "slow periphery" has been replaced with a much more nuanced view: although the centre of gravity of the fast world continues to be the tri-polar core of the world-system, the fast world also extends throughout the world to the more affluent regions, neighbourhoods, and households in the periphery that are "plugged in" to the contemporary world economy; the fast world now encompasses almost every*where* but not every*body*. This means that the differences found within a single country are often greater than the differences between different countries. For example, semiperipheral China now boasts more than twice the number of Internet users as the United States (note the jump from the 2008 numbers shown in Figure 2.25!) and three times the number of cell phone users, but the penetration rates of these technologies vary vastly between urban and rural regions and between wealthy and poor people.

Internet Users Worldwide

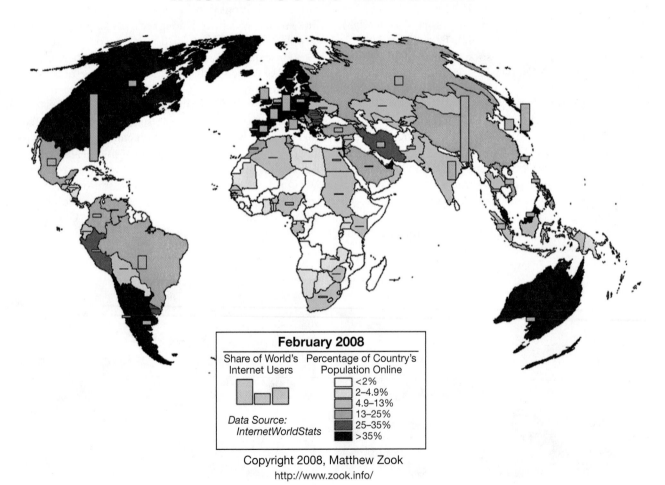

February 2008

Share of World's Internet Users   Percentage of Country's Population Online

- <2%
- 2–4.9%
- 4.9–13%
- 13–25%
- 25–35%
- >35%

Data Source: InternetWorldStats

Copyright 2008, Matthew Zook
http://www.zook.info/

Figure 2.25 Global Internet connectivity in 2008 Like all previous revolutions in transportation and communications, the Internet is effectively reorganizing space. This map shows the percentage of the total population in each country with access to the Internet (indicated by the density of shading) and the relative share of the world's Internet users accounted for by each country (indicated by the vertical bars). (*Source:* Zooknic, www.zooknic.com/.) Note the dramatic increase in Chinese Internet users in only two years: this 2008 map still shows China and the United States head-to-head; by 2010, China had already doubled its number of users.

2.6 Geography in the Information Age

As a result of the globalization of affordable technology, human geography now has to contend with the apparent paradox of people whose everyday lives are lived partly in one world and partly in another. Consider, for example, the shantytown residents of Mexico City. With extremely low incomes, only makeshift housing, and little or no formal education, they somehow are knowledgeable about international soccer, music, film, and fashion and are even able to copy fast-world consumption through cast-offs and knock-offs. Increasingly, the use of cell phones is enabling people to "leap frog" technologies and avoid costly land lines. With one cell phone sold for every four humans living on this planet in 2011, another substantial barrier to participation in the fast world is disappearing. In addition, the recent rise of smartphone technology is eliminating the need for an individual broadband Internet connection. Very few regions, therefore, remain largely untouched by globalization.

The differences between the fast and the slow worlds allow us to see what sociologist and planner Manuel Castells, in his monumental study *The Information Age*, has identified as spaces of social exclusion created by the uneven spatial development of "informational capitalism." Because access to networks and people is so crucial in the Information Age, Castells argues that denial of such access means exclusion from "the powerhouse of global capitalism" and instead means becoming part of the "Fourth World," a space he defines as "made up of multiple black holes of social exclusion throughout the planet." Castells uses the term "Fourth World" because he suggests that the Third World no longer has geopolitical relevance, that the Second World (of communism) has disintegrated, and that the First World of capitalism is not an all-encompassing world. He writes that the Fourth World "comprises large areas of the globe, such as much of sub-Saharan Africa, and impoverished rural areas of Latin America and Asia. But it is also present in literally every country, and city, in this new geography of social exclusion." It is, therefore, a space that includes the poor, the homeless, the sick, and the illiterate. And it is a world that will only get bigger if Castells is correct in his assertion that "the rise of the Fourth World is inseparable from the rise of international, global capitalism."[5]

---

[5] Manuel Castells, *The Information Age: Economy, Society and Culture. Volume 3, End of Millennium*, rev. ed. Oxford: Blackwell, 1999. The quotations are from pages 164 and 165.

connectivity at the national scale, we thus need to remind ourselves that great variations exist at the regional and local scales: inequalities between the fast world and the slow world are part of a **digital divide** that exists at *every* spatial scale.

This distinction between the fast world and the slow world brings us back to the themes of place, scale, and change that will recur throughout the rest of this book. At first glance, the emergence of the fast world—with its transnational architectural styles, dress codes, retail chains, and popular culture, and its ubiquitous immigrants, business`visitors, and tourists—seems as if it might have brought a sense of placelessness and dislocation, a loss of territorial identity, and an erosion of the distinctive sense of place associated with certain localities. Yet, the common experiences associated with globalization are still modified by local geographies. The structures and flows of the fast world are variously embraced, resisted, subverted, and exploited as they make contact with specific places and specific communities. *In the process, places and regions are reconstructed rather than effaced.* Often, this involves deliberate attempts by the residents of a particular area to create or re-create territorial identity and a sense of place. Inhabitants of the fast world, in other words, still feel the

digital divide: inequality of access to telecommunications and information technology, particularly the Internet

need for enclaves of familiarity, centredness, and identity. Human geographies change, but they don't disappear.

CONCLUSION

Places and regions everywhere carry the legacy of a sequence of major changes in world geography. The evolution of world geography can be traced from the prehistoric beginnings of human settlement, through the trading systems of the pre-capitalist, pre-industrial world, to the foundations of the geography of the modern world. These foundations were cast through industrialization, the colonization of the world, and the spread of an international market economy. As the *Economist* magazine pointed out, "History counts: where you are depends very much on where you started from." Today, these foundations can be seen in the geography of the Information Age, a geography that now provides a new, global context for places and regions.

Today's world is highly integrated. Places and regions have become increasingly interdependent, linked together through complex and rapidly changing commodity chains that are orchestrated by transnational corporations. Using new technology systems that allow for instantaneous global telecommunications and flexible patterns of investment and production, these corporations span the fast worlds and the slow worlds, whether they are in the core or the periphery. This integration does tend to blur some national and regional differences as the global marketplace brings a dispersion of people, tastes, and ideas. The overall result, though, has been an intensification of the differences between the core and the periphery.

Within this new global context, local differences in resource endowments remain, and people's territorial impulses endure. Many local cultures continue to be resilient or adaptive. Fundamental principles of spatial organization also continue to operate. All this ensures that even as the world-system becomes more and more integrated, places and regions continue to be made and remade. The new global context is filled with local variety that is constantly changing, just as the global context itself is constantly responding to local developments.

MAIN POINTS REVISITED

- **Places and regions are part of a "world-system" that is created as a result of processes of private economic competition and political competition among states.**
  Each place and region carries out its own particular role within the competitive world-system. Because of these different roles, places and regions are dependent on one another. The development of each place affects, and is affected by, the development of many other places.

- **Today, the world-system is highly structured and is characterized by three tiers: *core regions, semiperipheral regions,* and *peripheral regions*.**
  The core regions of the world-system are those that dominate trade, control the most advanced technologies, and have high levels of productivity within diversified economies. Peripheral regions are characterized by dependent and disadvantageous trading relationships, by primitive or obsolescent technologies, and by undeveloped or narrowly specialized economies with low levels of productivity. Semiperipheral regions are able to exploit peripheral regions but are exploited and dominated by the core regions. This three-tiered system is fluid, providing a continually changing framework for geographical transformation within individual places and regions.

- **The world-system is made up of a nested set of cores and peripheries.**
  In this way, local developments are transmitted to the regional and global levels, and the forces of globalization affect the local level.

- **Canada is simultaneously part of the global core and semiperiphery.**
  Possessing many core characteristics (such as high GNP), Canada nevertheless is still heavily interdependent with such countries as the United States.

- **The evolution of the modern world-system has exhibited distinctive stages, each of which has left its legacy in different ways on particular places, depending on their changing role within the world-system.**
  The modern world-system was first established over a long period that began in the late fifteenth century. More and more peoples around the world became exposed to one another's technologies and ideas over the next five centuries. Their different resources, social structures, and cultural systems resulted in quite different pathways of development, however. Some societies were incorporated into the new, European-based international economic system faster than

others; some resisted incorporation; and some sought alternative systems of economic and political organization.

- At the end of the eighteenth century, the new technologies of the Industrial Revolution brought about the emergence of a global economic system that reached into almost every part of the world and into virtually every aspect of people's lives. New transportation technologies triggered successive phases of European geographic expansion, allowing for an intensive period of external colonization and imperialism. The core of the world-system grew to include the United States and Japan, whereas most of the rest of the world was systematically incorporated into the capitalist world-system as a dependent periphery.

- The growth and internal colonization of the core regions could take place only with the foodstuffs, raw materials, and markets provided by the colonization of the periphery. In the eighteenth and nineteenth centuries, the industrial core nations embarked on the inland penetration of the world's midcontinental grassland zones to exploit them for grain and livestock production. At the same time, as the demand for tropical plantation products increased, most of the tropical world came under the political and economic control—directly or indirectly—of one or another of the industrial core nations. For these peripheral regions, European overseas expansion meant political and economic dependency.

- Within each of the world's major regions, successive technological innovations have transformed regional geographies. Each new system of production and transportation technologies has helped raise levels of productivity and create new and better products that have stimulated demand, increased profits, and created a pool of capital for further investment. This investment, however, has taken place in new or restructured geographical settings.

- Globalization has intensified the differences between the core and the periphery and has contributed to the emergence of a digital divide and an increasing division between a fast world and a slow world with contrasting lifestyles and levels of living.
The leading edge of the fast world is the Internet, which is now the world's single most important mechanism for the transmission of scientific and academic knowledge. Today, flows of goods, capital, and information that take place within and among transnational corporations are becoming more important than imports and exports among countries. At the same time, all these flows have helped spread new values—from consumer lifestyle preferences to altruistic concerns with global resources, global environmental changes, and famine relief—around the fast world.

Key Terms

colonialism (p. 55)
commodity chains (p. 81)
core regions (p. 55)
digital divide (p. 91)
division of labour (p. 76)
external arenas (p. 55)
fast world (p. 87)
hegemony (p. 68)
hinterland (p. 62)

import substitution (p. 63)
law of diminishing returns (p. 60)
leadership cycles (p. 68)
mini-system (p. 58)
neo-colonialism (p. 80)
peripheral regions (p. 55)
plantations (p. 63)
producer services (p. 82)
semiperipheral regions (p. 55)

slow world (p. 87)
spatial justice (p. 87)
staples thesis (p. 72)
staples trap (p. 71)
technology system (p. 67)
transnational corporations (p. 80)
world-empire (p. 59)
world-system (p. 54)

Additional Reading

Angus, J.T. *A Respectable Ditch: A History of the Trent–Severn Waterway 1833–1920*. Montreal and Toronto: McGill-Queen's University Press, 1988.

Baum, G. *Karl Polanyi on Ethics and Economics*. Montreal and Kingston: McGill-Queens University Press, 1996.

Blaut, J. *The Colonizer's Model of the World: Geographic Diffusionism and Eurocentric History*. New York: Guilford Press, 1993.

Britton, J. (ed.). *Canada and the Global Economy: The Geography of Structural and Technological Change*. Montreal and Kingston: McGill-Queen's University Press, 1996.

Castells, M. *The Information Age. Volume 1: The Rise of the Network Society*. Oxford: Blackwell, 1996.

Castells, M. *The Information Age: Economy, Society and Culture. Volume 3: End of Millennium*. Oxford: Blackwell, 1999.

Christopher, A.J. *The British Empire at Its Zenith*. New York: Croom Helm, 1988.

Daniels, P., and W.F. Lever (eds.). *The Global Economy in Transition*. New York: Addison Wesley Longman, 1996.

De Alcantara, C.H. *Social Futures, Global Visions*. New York: United Nations Research Institute for Social Development, 1996.

Dicken, P. *Global Shift*, 3rd ed. New York: Harper & Row, 1998.

Gentilcore, R.L., and G.J. Matthews (eds.). *Historical Atlas of Canada. Volume 2: The Land Transformed 1800–1891*. Toronto: University of Toronto Press, 1993.

Harris, R.C., and G.J. Matthews (eds.). *Historical Atlas of Canada. Volume 1: From the Beginning to 1800*. Toronto: University of Toronto Press, 1987.

Harris, R.C., and J. Warkentin. *Canada before Confederation: A Study in Historical Geography*. Toronto: Oxford University Press, 1974.

Hugill, P. *World Trade since 1431*. Baltimore: Johns Hopkins University Press, 1993.

Johnston, R.J., P.J. Taylor, and M. Watts (eds.). *Geographies of Global Change*. Cambridge, MA: Blackwell, 1995.

Kerr, D. *Historical Atlas of Canada*, 3rd ed. Don Mills, ON: Nelson, 1975.

Kerr, D., D. Holdsworth, and G.J. Matthews (eds.). *Historical Atlas of Canada. Volume 3: Addressing the Twentieth Century*. Toronto: University of Toronto Press, 1990.

Knox, P.L., and J. Agnew. *The Geography of the World Economy*, 3rd ed. New York: Routledge, 1998.

Leacy, F.H. (ed.). *Historical Statistics of Canada*, 2nd ed. Ottawa: Minister of Supply and Services, 1983.

McCann, L., and A. Gunn. *Heartland and Hinterland: A Regional Geography of Canada*, 3rd ed. Scarborough, ON: Prentice Hall Canada, 1998.

Norcliffe, G. *The Ride to Modernity: The Bicycle in Canada, 1869–1900*. Toronto: University of Toronto Press, 2001.

Peet, R. *Global Capitalism: Theories of Societal Development*. New York: Routledge, 1991.

Ruggles, R.I. *A Country So Interesting: The Hudson's Bay Company and Two Centuries of Mapping, 1670–1870*. Montreal and Kingston: McGill-Queen's University Press, 1991.

Said, E. *Orientalism*. New York: Pantheon, 1978.

Seitz, J.L. *Global Issues: An Introduction*. Cambridge, MA: Blackwell, 1995.

Terlouw, C.P. *The Regional Geography of the World-System*. Utrecht: Faculteit Ruimtelijke Wetenschappen Rijksuniversiteit Utrecht, 1994.

Unwin, T. (ed.). *Atlas of World Development*. New York: John Wiley and Sons, 1994.

Wallace, I. *The Global Economic System*. London: Unwin Hyman, 1990.

Wallace, I. *A Geography of the Canadian Economy*. Toronto: Oxford University Press, 2002.

Wolf, E.R. *Europe and the People without History*. Berkeley: University of California Press, 1983.

Discussion Questions and Research Activities

1. The present-day core regions of the world-system, shown in Figure 2.1 on p. 56, are those that dominate trade, control the most advanced technologies, have high levels of productivity within diversified economies, and enjoy relatively high *per capita* incomes. Looking at your own personal possessions or those of your family, what sort of products come from core countries? What are some of the products you use or own that were produced in the semiperipheral countries? Do you own or use *anything* that was made in the periphery? Reflecting on the international division of labour introduced in this chapter, why do you think that is?

2. We quoted the *Economist* magazine as saying that places and regions are important because "where you are depends very much on where you started from." Illustrate this point with reference to any two regions: one from the core and one from the periphery. Why did these two regions develop in different ways? Is there evidence that the core region benefits more from its position in the world-system than the peripheral region? What is holding back the peripheral region?

3. The idea of an international division of labour is based on the observation that different countries tend to specialize in the production or manufacture of particular commodities, goods, or services. In what product or products do the following countries specialize: Bolivia, Ghana, Guinea, Libya, Namibia, Peru, and Zambia? What led to those specializations? Are there any reasons that are not related to the resource endowment or physical geography of those countries? Can you find evidence of neo-colonial influences exerted by the core nations that had colonized them? What cultural legacies of those colonizing nations are still discernible in their former colonies?

MyGeosciencePlace

Visit www.mygeoscienceplace.ca to find chapter review quizzes, videos, maps, and much more.

3

Geographies of Population

Crowded downtown street, Toronto

Europe's population is declining. Every year, Germany is shrinking by the equivalent of the population of Halifax. Some Southern European countries such as Italy, Spain, and Greece are predicted to shrink by 25 percent by the year 2050, while some Eastern European countries such as Bulgaria, Estonia, and Latvia might lose up to a third of their current population. Meanwhile, the populations of the Palestinian Territories and Jordan are set to grow to more than twice their current size. Similarly, on a global scale, world population steadily increases, passing the 7 billion mark in late October of 2011, causing many to worry about a possible overpopulation of the planet and its environmental consequences. In August 2008, for example, Britain's *Guardian Weekly* newspaper summarized an editorial that had appeared in a recent issue of the *British Medical Journal* under the heading "Have fewer children and help save the planet." The editorial suggested that because every new person born in Britain would produce 160 times more greenhouse emissions than a person born in Ethiopia, a decline in Britain's birth rate would obviously have beneficial environmental consequences.

How can we reconcile these two very different views—one that is concerned about a decline in births, the other about their continued increase? Geographers, with their awareness of spatial differentiation, know that both are true: they are true for different places and for different reasons that are specific to those places. In most core countries, population growth has slowed or stopped altogether, while in most peripheral countries, population growth continues. Experts do agree that population growth is largely the result of the phenomenal decline of death rates in the twentieth century. Birth and death are the two variables that shape overall population growth and change. For geographers, however, knowing the fertility (or birth) figures or the mortality (or death) figures is not enough: they also want to know *where* births and deaths are occurring, and *why* they are occurring. In other words: geographers are interested in interconnections, even if they are not obvious at first sight.

Take the food supply for instance: in the spring of 2008, protests began erupting in dozens of peripheral countries in response to soaring food prices. In a period of two months, the global price of rice jumped 75 percent, and over a 12-month period, the price of wheat increased 120 percent. Tens of thousands of Mexicans protested against soaring tortilla prices, forcing the government to legislate price caps. Halfway around the world, rice farmers in Thailand stayed up in shifts at night to guard their fields against thieves. Though no riots have been reported in core countries, more and more poor families in Canada and other core countries are struggling to feed themselves as the price of food skyrockets. What caused food to become more expensive? Surging oil prices—which then boost related costs like fertilizer and transportation—combined with a drop in grain production due to droughts in Australia and the Ukraine, the falling U.S. dollar, and a growing global biofuels policy to promote ethanol (a corn-based product) in place of oil are the main factors in draining global foodstocks and stimulating the rising cost of food—not to mention financial markets that regard food staples as fair game for speculation. Ultimately, all of these factors are affecting the health, composition, dynamics, and distribution of populations around the globe.

The reason the price of grains is so important to population geography is that food shortages lead to malnutrition, specifically *undernutrition*. When individuals are undernourished, they can no longer maintain natural bodily capacities, such as growth, resisting infections and recovering from disease, learning and working, and pregnancy and lactation in women. Persistent undernutrition also ultimately leads to lowered life expectancy and higher mortality rates, as well as causing people to leave the affected area. Rising food prices, then, affect populations through changes in health status, mortality, fertility, and migration.

In this chapter we examine population distribution and structure as well as the dynamics of population growth and change, with a special focus on spatial variations and implications. In short, we look at the locations of population clusters, the numbers of men and women and old and young, and the different ways in which these dynamics combine to create overall population growth or decline. We examine as well population movements and the models and concepts that population experts have developed to better understand the potential problems posed by human populations.

MAIN POINTS

- Population geographers draw on a wide array of data sources to assess the geography of populations. Chief among these sources is the census, although other sources include vital records and public health statistics.

- Population geographers are largely concerned with the same sorts of questions as other population experts study, but they also investigate "the why of where": *why* do particular aspects of population growth and change (and problems) occur *where* they do, and what are the implications of these factors for the future of places?

- Two of the most important factors that make up population dynamics are birth and death. These variables may be examined in simple or complex ways, but in either case, the reasons for the behaviour of these variables are as important as the numbers themselves.

- A third crucial force in population change is the movement of populations. The forces that push populations from particular locations as well as those that pull them to move to new areas are key to understanding the resulting new settlement patterns. Population migration may not always be a matter of choice.

- As a generalization, world demographic patterns are easily described within a world-system framework. They are an important aspect of the very different economic and social "spaces" that this system produces. High birth rates and death rates are a feature of today's periphery; low birth rates and death rates are a feature of the core. The discrepancy in economic and political terms between them generates substantial flows of migrants and refugees.

- Perhaps the most pressing issue facing scholars, policy-makers, and other interested individuals is the one articulated at the International Conference on Population and Development, held in Cairo in 1994: how many people can the world adequately accommodate with food, water, clean air, and other basic necessities for the enjoyment of happy, healthy, and satisfying lives?

- Whether at the world, country, or local scale of analysis, the work of those geographers studying the interactions between population, health, and the environment shows us that the principal explanation for varying spatial patterns of health is variation in income distribution.

THE DEMOGRAPHER'S TOOLBOX

Demography, or the study of the characteristics of human populations, is an interdisciplinary undertaking. Geographers study population to understand the areal distribution of Earth's population. They are also interested in the reasons for, and the consequences of, the distribution of population from the international to the local level. Historians study the evolution of demographic patterns and sociologists the social dynamics of human populations, but it is geographers who focus special attention on the spatial patterns of human populations, the implications of such patterns, and the reasons for them. Using many of the same tools and methods of analysis as other population experts, geographers think of population in terms of the places that populations inhabit. They are also interested in how places are shaped by populations and, in turn, how places shape the populations that occupy them.

demography: the study of the characteristics of human populations

Sources of Information

Population experts rely on a wide array of instruments and institutions to carry out their work. Governments, for example, collect information on births, deaths, marriages, immigration, and other aspects of population change. The most widely known instrument for assessing the state of the population is the census. Essentially, a **census** is a count of the number of people in a country, region, or city, but most censuses also gather additional information about the population, such as previous residence, marital status, occupation, income, and other personal data.

census: the count of the number of people in a country, region, or city

In Canada, the earliest census dates from 1666 when the population of New France (Quebec) was recorded on the orders of Louis XIV. The first nationwide census dates from 1851. Since then, Canadian full censuses have been conducted every 10 years. In 1956, a shorter mid-decade census was added. The next censuses in this country will therefore be taken in 2016 (short) and 2021 (full).

Undertakings of this sort are hugely expensive (the 2006 census cost $567 million to conduct) and take several years to tabulate fully.[1] Even so, they are not completely error free. Estimates suggest an undercount of between

---

[1] It is because of this unavoidable delay that more detailed information from each census is not published until some years later. Check Statistics Canada's website for the latest releases of census data and related statistics at **www.statcan.gc.ca**.

1 percent and 2 percent in recent censuses, mainly because of enumerator error. We also know that some groups are more under-represented than others. The homeless are, almost by definition, going to be hard to survey, and some of Canada's Native reserves have declined to participate in recent surveys. Nevertheless, the impressive quantity and quality of data collected more than compensate for these disadvantages.

In addition to the census, population experts also employ other data sources to assess population characteristics. One such source is **vital records** (from the Latin word *vita*, meaning "life"), which report births, deaths, marriages, divorces, and the incidences of certain infectious diseases. These data are collected and recorded by provincial and territorial levels of government. Schools, hospitals and other public agencies, and international organizations such as the World Health Organization also collect demographic statistics that are useful to population experts.

In parts of New France, parish registers (a form of vital record) date from the beginning of the seventeenth century. Quebec historians who have analyzed these records have been able to reconstruct the demographic experiences of entire communities, using the techniques of **family reconstitution,** and have provided us with a fascinating glimpse of life along the St. Lawrence River nearly 400 years ago.

Not all information that population experts use is as straightforward as census or vital records data. Nor are such data always available. In many cases, it is necessary to utilize numerous other types of data to say something about a past population's size and structure. Consider, for example, the Aboriginal populations of British Columbia. To examine the terrible effects of European diseases, such as the 1792 smallpox epidemic, on the size of their populations, we need some way of estimating their numbers on the eve of contact with Europeans. However, turning Hudson's Bay Company head counts, archaeological evidence, or calculations of carrying capacities into population estimates with any degree of accuracy is virtually impossible. Still, the practical need to establish the validity of Aboriginal title to territory in British Columbia requires that we strive for the closest approximation possible. As Cole Harris, a historical geographer at the University of British Columbia, has observed, "as political debates about Native government and land claims intensify, and as appeals proceed through the courts, questions of disease and depopulation are explicitly repoliticized....For a society preoccupied with numbers, scale, and progress, more people imply fuller, more controlled occupation of land."[2]

Generally speaking, to get a full picture of what is happening, most contemporary population experts prefer to use a combination of both census and vital record information. This is because census data, although producing a wealth of data, can record only a snapshot view (or cross-section) of a population on the particular day the census was conducted. On the other hand, although vital records track changes over time, they can only do so for a limited number of variables.

At first sight, **administrative record linkage** looks like the ideal solution. By linking together a number of different databases, governments are able to not only build up a very detailed picture of individuals but also update this picture very regularly. Canada is a world leader in this respect and has, for the purposes of research, combined tax files with records of employment and immigration data to produce a very rich source of information on large samples of the population. Upon looking more closely, however, we can see that there are problems with this method: it holds much greater potential for data leakage, loss of privacy, and identity theft than the traditional census, and it collects fewer data points per person. Some Scandinavian countries, however, have already replaced the census by interlinking residential databases with business registers and tax records to track information about their population. In the United Kingdom, the government plans to cut the census for budget reasons after the 2011 survey and rely

vital records: information about births, deaths, marriages, divorces, and the incidences of certain infectious diseases

family reconstitution: the process of reconstructing individual and family life histories by linking together separately recorded birth, marriage, and death data

administrative record linkage: the linking together of a number of different government databases to build one database with much more detailed information on each individual

---

[2] Cole Harris, *The Resettlement of British Columbia: Essays on Colonialism and Geographical Change.* Vancouver: UBC Press, 1997, pp. 3–4.

on data sources such as credit card information and mail records. In Canada, an attempt by the federal government in 2010 to cut the so-called long-form census was abandoned after considerable protest—much of it from geographers, who depend on the rich census data for their research.

POPULATION DISTRIBUTION AND STRUCTURE

Because human geographers explore the interrelationships and interdependencies between people and places, they are interested in demography, or the systematic analysis of the numbers and distribution of human populations. Population geographers bring to demography a special perspective—the spatial perspective—that describes and explains the spatial differentiation of population distribution, patterns, and processes. Equally important are the implications and impacts of these differences. Thus, when geographers look at population numbers, they ask themselves two questions: Where are these populations concentrated, and what are the causes and consequences of such a population distribution?

Population Distribution

At a basic level, many geographical reasons exist for the distribution of populations around the globe. As the world population density map (**Figure 3.1**) demonstrates, some areas of the world are very densely inhabited; others only sparsely. Degree of accessibility, topography, soil fertility, climate and weather, water availability and quality, and type and availability of other natural resources are some of the important factors that shape population distribution. Other crucial factors include a country's political and economic experiences and characteristics. For example, the high population concentrations along Brazil's Atlantic coast date back to the trade patterns set up during Portuguese colonial control in the sixteenth and seventeenth centuries (see Chapter 2).

Figure 3.1 World population density, 2004 As this map shows, the world's population is not uniformly distributed across the globe. Such maps are useful in understanding the relationships between population distribution and the national contexts within which they occur. (*Source:* World Bank, *World Development Indicators, 2004.* Washington, DC: World Bank.)

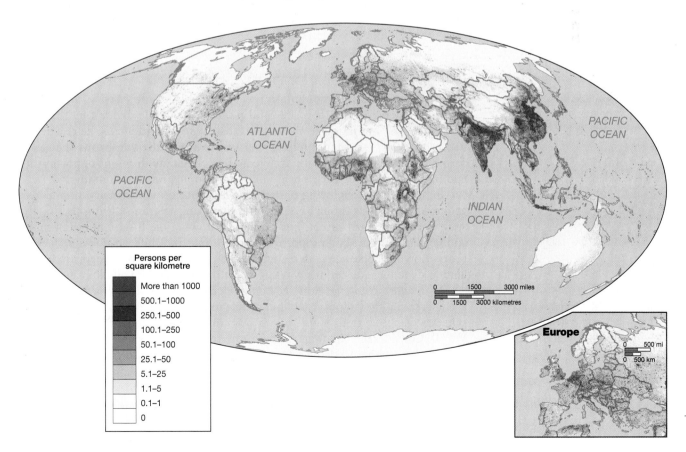

TABLE 3.1 World Population Estimates by Continents, 2009

Number of Inhabitants	Continent (in millions)	% of Total Population
Africa	999	14.7
Asia	4117	60.5
Australia, New Zealand, and the South Pacific Islands	36	0.5
Europe	738	10.8
North America	341	5.0
Latin America and the Caribbean	580	8.5
TOTAL	6810	100.0

Source: Population Reference Bureau website, **www.prb.org**, 2009 World Population Data Sheet.

Table 3.1 shows population estimates by continent. From the table, it is clear that Asia is by far the most populous continent, with 60.5 percent of the world's inhabitants in more than 40 countries. Running a distant second and third are Africa, with 14.7 percent of the world's population, and Europe, with 10.8 percent, respectively.

The population clusters we can identify have a number of physical similarities. Almost all of the world's inhabitants live on 10 percent of the land. Most live near the shores of oceans and seas or along rivers. Approximately 90 percent live north of the equator, where 63 percent of the total land area is located. Finally, most of the world's population lives in temperate, low-lying areas with fertile soils.

Population concentrations within countries, regions, and even metropolitan areas are also important for showing us where people are. For example, much of the population of Canada, which now exceeds 34 million, is concentrated along its southern boundary (**Figure 3.2**).

Population Density and Composition

crude density (arithmetic density): the total number of people divided by the total land area

Another way to explore population is in terms of **crude density**, also called **arithmetic density**, which is the total number of people divided by the total land area. The limitation of the crude density ratio—and hence the reason for its "crudeness"—is that it tells us very little about the variations that exist across the area, which in turn are created by the many different opportunities and obstacles that the relationship between people and land contains.

In addition to exploring patterns of distribution and density, population geographers also examine population in terms of its composition; that is, the subgroups that constitute it. For example, knowing the total number of males and females, number and proportion of old people and children, and number and proportion of people active in the workforce provides valuable insights into population dynamics; that is, the ways in which the population will likely develop.

baby boom: the increased number of births in the two decades following World War II

Many core countries now face unique challenges as their "baby boomers" age, increasing the proportion of old people in their populations. The **baby boom** generation includes those individuals born in the two decades following World War II. Considerable amounts of these countries' resources and energies are necessary to meet the needs of a large number of people who may no longer be contributing significantly to the creation of the wealth necessary for their support. There might also be a need to import workers to supplement the shrinking working-age population.

When trying to predict future population dynamics, governments rely on a number of indicators. One of the most important ones is the number of women

Population Distribution in Canada, 2006

According to Statistics Canada, a Census Metropolitan Area (CMA) is made up of a very large urban area (urban core) and those adjacent urban and rural areas that are highly integrated with that urban core. A CMA is defined as having an urban core population of at least 100 000 in the previous census.

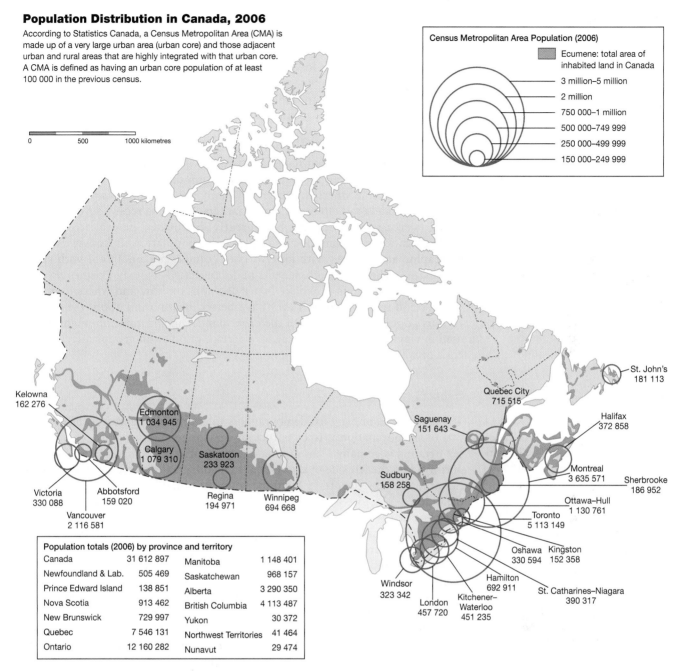

Census Metropolitan Area Population (2006)

Ecumene: total area of inhabited land in Canada

3 million–5 million
2 million
750 000–1 million
500 000–749 999
250 000–499 999
150 000–249 999

Kelowna 162 276
Edmonton 1 034 945
Calgary 1 079 310
Saskatoon 233 923
Victoria 330 088
Abbotsford 159 020
Vancouver 2 116 581
Regina 194 971
Winnipeg 694 668
Saguenay 151 643
Sudbury 158 258
Quebec City 715 515
St. John's 181 113
Halifax 372 858
Montreal 3 635 571
Sherbrooke 186 952
Ottawa–Hull 1 130 761
Toronto 5 113 149
Oshawa 330 594
Kingston 152 358
Windsor 323 342
London 457 720
Kitchener–Waterloo 451 235
Hamilton 692 911
St. Catharines–Niagara 390 317

Population totals (2006) by province and territory			
Canada	31 612 897	Manitoba	1 148 401
Newfoundland & Lab.	505 469	Saskatchewan	968 157
Prince Edward Island	138 851	Alberta	3 290 350
Nova Scotia	913 462	British Columbia	4 113 487
New Brunswick	729 997	Yukon	30 372
Quebec	7 546 131	Northwest Territories	41 464
Ontario	12 160 282	Nunavut	29 474

Figure 3.2   Population distribution in Canada, 2006   As shown by this map, Canada's population distribution has a number of major characteristics. First, population is extremely dispersed across the country (the area known as the *ecumene* shows the inhabited area of Canada). However, the population density of the ecumene is very low, and the bulk of the country's population is highly concentrated along Canada's southern border (more than 70 percent of the total population live within 150 kilometres of the U.S. border); in the three provinces of British Columbia, Ontario, and Quebec; and in the country's leading urban centres. In fact, despite its large size and relatively small population, Canada has become an urban (even metropolitan) country: almost 80 percent of the total population now lives in towns and cities of more than 1,000 people.   (*Sources:* The ecumene is from John Warkentin, *A Regional Geography of Canada,* 2nd ed. Scarborough: Prentice Hall, 2000, p. 71; 2006 Census figures are from Statistics Canada, "Population and Dwelling Counts for Canada, Provinces and Territories, Census Metropolitan Areas and Census Agglomerations, 2006 and 2001 Censuses—100% Data" [**www12.statcan.ca/English/census06**].)

of childbearing age in a population, along with other information about their status and opportunities. For example, populations in core countries, such as Denmark (which has a small number of women of childbearing age relative to the total population size), will generally grow very slowly, if at all. The reason is not only the small proportion of young women, but also their socioeconomic status: women with high levels of education, socioeconomic security, and wide opportunities for work outside the home tend to have fewer children. By contrast, peripheral countries, such as Kenya, will likely continue to experience relatively high rates of population growth because there a large number of women of childbearing age have low levels of education and socioeconomic security and relatively few employment opportunities. Evidently, the social and economic opportunities that are available to groups within a country's population very much shape the opportunities and challenges that the country faces on a national, regional, and local scale.

Understanding population composition not only can tell us much about the future demographics of regions but is also quite useful in the present. For example, businesses use population composition data to make marketing decisions and to decide where to locate. For many years, businesses used laborious computer models to help target their markets. With the recent development of GIS, however, this process has been greatly simplified. The practice of assessing the location and composition of particular populations is known as **geodemographic analysis**. As with all efforts to connect personal data with spatial information, there are both benefits and dangers. Obviously, businesses, planners, and governments can make better decisions on how and where to provide services and infrastructure if they have better information about the needs of various population groups. On the other hand, this information might also be used in ways that discriminate against certain population groups merely on the basis of where they live.

Age–Sex Pyramids

The most common way for demographers to graphically represent the composition of the population is to construct an **age–sex pyramid** (**Figure 3.3**). An age–sex pyramid is actually a bar graph displayed horizontally. Ordinarily, males are portrayed on the left side of the vertical axis and females to the right. Age categories are ordered sequentially from the youngest at the bottom of the pyramid to the oldest at the top. By moving up or down the pyramid, one can compare the opposing horizontal bars to assess differences in frequencies for each age group. Demographers call such population groups *cohorts*. A **cohort** is a group of individuals who share a common *temporal* demographic experience. A cohort is not necessarily based on age, but may also be defined by such criteria as time of marriage or year of graduation.

A critical aspect of the population pyramid is the **dependency ratio,** which is a measure of the economic impact of the young and old on the more economically productive members of the population. Traditionally, to assess this relation of dependency in a particular population, demographers divide the total population into three age cohorts. The **youth cohort** consists of members of the population who are less than 15 years of age and generally considered too young to be fully active in the labour force. The **middle cohort** consists of the population aged 15 to 64, who are considered economically active and productive. Finally, the **old-age cohort** consists of the population aged 65 and older, who are considered beyond their economically active and productive years. By dividing the population into these three groups, it is possible to obtain a measure of the dependency of the young and old on the economically active, and of the impact of the dependent population on the independent.

These various measures of dependency are a useful framework with which to consider Canada's age–sex pyramid (Figure 3.3). In common with many Western countries, Canada's post-war population has been almost entirely shaped by the rise of the birth rate during the baby boom years, followed by a decline since the mid-1960s. In fact, if we look back over a century of population change in this country, we see that there has been a long-run (or *secular*) decline in the

geodemographic analysis: the practice of assessing the location and composition of particular populations

age–sex pyramid: a representation of the population based on its composition according to age and sex

cohort: a group of individuals who share a common temporal demographic experience

dependency ratio: the measure of the economic impact of the young and old on the more economically productive members of the population

youth cohort: members of the population who are less than 15 years of age and generally considered too young to be fully active in the labour force

middle cohort: members of the population 15 to 64 years of age who are considered economically active and productive

old-age cohort: members of the population 65 years of age and older who are considered beyond their economically active and productive years

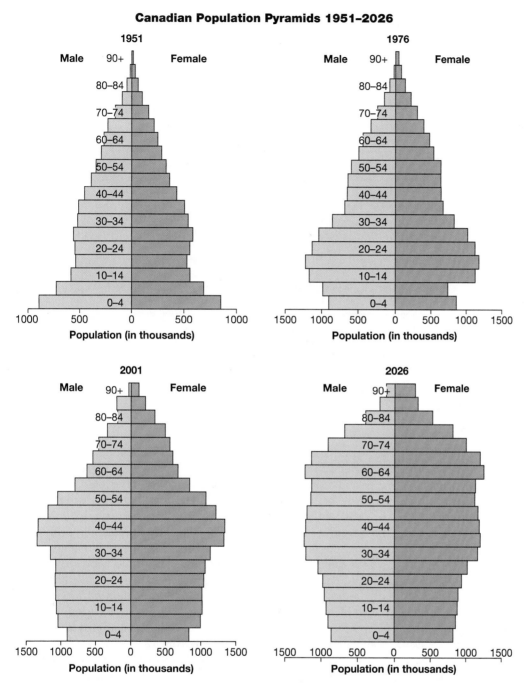

Canadian Population Pyramids 1951–2026

Figure 3.3 Population of Canada, by age and sex, 1951, 1976, 2001, and 2026 The profound effects of the baby boom (1947–1966) on Canada's population structure are seen in this series of age–sex pyramids. The four pyramids chart the baby boom's initial impact on a population shaped by low fertility rates of the Depression years and show how the baby boom has subsequently become a major factor in the aging of the Canadian population as the relative size of older age groups has increased over time. The decline in fertility rates since the end of the boom has accentuated the impact of aging on the population because, as the pyramids show, it has led to a relative decline in the size of younger age groups in the population. (*Sources:* "Canadian Population Pyramids," adapted from the Statistics Canada publication *The Daily*, Catalogue 11–001, 16 July 2002, available at **www12.statcan.ca/english/census01/products/Analytic**. A 30-second animated graphic showing how Canada's age–sex pyramids change over time can be seen at **www12.statcan.ca/english/census01/Products/Analytic/companion/age/cda01pymd.cfm**.)

birth rate since the 1870s (**Figure 3.4**). Before the onset of the decline, the crude birth rate was between 45 and 55 per 1,000; by 2001, it stood at 11 per 1,000, representing a total fertility rate of 1.4 births per woman. Fewer children being born means that the proportion of older age groups among the total population is growing. In other words, the population as a whole is **aging.** This effect is compounded by the fact that people, on average, now live longer than they did two or three generations ago as life expectancies have been increasing with improved nutrition and health care.

The effect of population aging was temporarily reversed by the baby boom. In Canada's case, the boom years were from 1947 to 1966 (the longest boom recorded in the developed world), and in these years, the crude birth rate increased to almost 30 per 1,000. Overall, birth rates have declined since those years, although two periods of increase have occurred. The first was from the

aging: a term used to describe the effects of an increasing proportion of older age groups on the population

Figure 3.4 The decline of the birth rate in Canada This graph shows the decline in the crude birth rate, measured as a rate per 1,000 population, for Canada and Quebec from 1801 to 1989. (*Sources:* Anatole Romaniuc, "Fertility in Canada: Retrospective and Prospective." *Canadian Studies in Population* 18(2), 1991, p. 59. See also Statistics Canada, "Births." *The Daily,* 21 September 2007 and 26 September 2008 [**http://www.statcan.gc.ca/dai-quo/index-eng.htm**]).

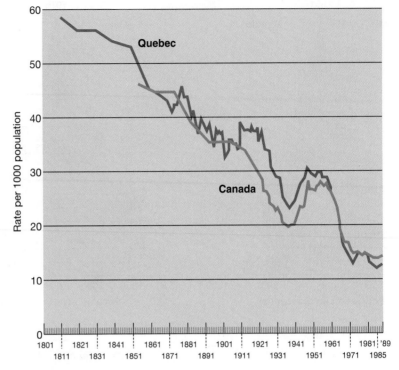

Crude Birth Rate per 1000 Population, Canada and Quebec,* 1801–1989

*Crude birth rates from 1801 through 1867 refer to the Catholic population of Quebec.

mid-1970s to 1990 and is sometimes known as the baby boom "echo" because it represents the children of the large baby boom cohort. We are currently experiencing a second period of increase (the "echo of the echo"): the total fertility rate in 2010 was 1.6 births per woman, the highest rate since 1996, but still far short of the 3.9 at the peak of the baby boom in 1959. And, as always, averages can hide considerable variations in the data: the value for Newfoundland is below 1.5, whereas Nunavut reaches almost 3 births per woman. In fact, only Nunavut and the NWT exceed the replacement fertility level of 2.1 births per woman.

There are many explanations for the secular decline of Canada's birth rate and for the baby boom. Most, however, are unable to explain *both*. How can we, for example, explain the increase in births (the baby boom) using the same explanations (such as social change, empowerment of women, improved hygiene) we are using to explain the longer-lasting decline from 1871? For this reason, we must recognize that there are likely to be several factors—perhaps working differently at different times. That said, nothing should obscure the basic finding of Canadian demography that the underlying cause involves the changing role of women as they have gained greater access to education and paid employment.

From their differing perspectives, such economists as David Foot, such sociologists as Roderic Beaujot, and such geographers as John Miron, Mark Rosenberg, and Eric Moore have analyzed the public-policy implications of Canada's aging population. Let us consider some of these implications as they now affect the three main age groups we used to define the concept of dependency ratios.

The Youth Cohort (0–15 years old) The relative and absolute decline of this group challenges the Canadian educational system with the problems of enrolment declines and, ultimately, school closures as the numbers of students shrink (especially when compared with the enormous expansion of the baby boom years). Meanwhile, colleges and universities are countering the projected declines by increasing the **participation rate;** that is, the proportion of a cohort attending such institutions.

participation rate: the proportion of a cohort or group that becomes involved in a specific activity, such as attending an educational institution

Indeed, the decline of this cohort affects all organizations that serve this age group. For example, in August 2004, Scouts Canada reported a decline from 300,000 members in the 1960s to 130,000 in 2004; Guides Canada noted a similar fall (from 235,000 guides in 1965 to 122,000 in 2004). Both organizations stated that because of such declines, a number of their camps across Canada would have to be closed.

At the sociocultural level, members of the youth cohort are faced with a country in which, sometime around 2017, there will be more people over 65 years than those under 16 years old. Consumer analysts have already begun to realize that the teenage demand for music, fashion, and recreation that drove the marketplace during the baby boom is being replaced by the consumer preferences of a much older demographic. An illustration of this trend is the recent format changes in the radio industry from contemporary rock to classic rock, retro, or talk radio.

The Middle Cohort (15–64 years old)   Demographically speaking, the major factor of change for this group is the baby boom cohort itself. Its oldest members, called "front-end boomers" by David Foot, were born in 1947 and begin to retire in 2012. Currently, the boomers occupy the upper ranks of many institutions and corporations and they also control most of Canada's personal wealth (as much as 50 percent by some estimates). Those born at the end of the boom, in the mid-1960s, are now entering mid-career and are set to take over the helm from the front-end boomers. Canada's workforce has had to expand enormously to accommodate the employment aspirations of the baby boomers and will only begin to free up space for younger cohorts when the boomers retire in large numbers, from about 2020 onward.

The 15–64 age group is the one whose behaviour most affects the housing market and, therefore, the form of our cities and towns. The demand for suburban nuclear family housing, small inner-city condos, and rural cottages can all be related to stages in the life cycle. Because of this, demographic analysis has had an important part to play in the real estate industry and in the halls of the Canada Mortgage and Housing Corporation. One prediction currently holds that as this country's population continues to age, the demand for cottages in rural areas will decline as people seek the lifestyle and health care amenities of urban centres.

The Old-Age Cohort (65 years and over)   The policy issues raised by this cohort are primarily those of health care and pension provision, both issues greatly affected by the increased relative and absolute numbers of Canada's elderly: over the last three decades, the number of Canadians older than 65 has doubled, and Statistics Canada projects that it will double again by 2036. Conversely, around 2017, Canada will for the first time have more senior citizens than children. In terms of average health care expenditures, because an individual over 65 years old costs between two and three times as much as someone under 15 years old, the impacts of an aging society on health care costs are magnified. The policy solutions are being hotly debated at the moment, with a number of provinces, such as Alberta, actively pursuing user fees and a private system to supplement what some see as a struggling universal health care system.

Public pensions are also under strain because one of the consequences of the aging of baby boomers has been that there will soon be more people receiving these pensions and fewer that are paying into the Canada Pension Plan and Quebec Pension Plan. To cover the shortfall, the federal government has already increased the premiums and will certainly have to do so again before long. Some countries, such as Germany and France, have also raised the age of retirement to cope with this problem. Finally, because this cohort is made up of larger numbers of women than men (because average female life expectancies are higher), policy problems are also gender-related ones.

Canadian geographers have examined the spatial distribution of Canada's population and have identified a number of areas that are likely affected by the aging of our society. Their work indicates that such cities as Victoria (British Columbia) and Kingston (Ontario) have a higher-than-average population of those aged over 65 because of the in-migration of the elderly to these communities. This obviously means increased financial strain as the demand for, among others, medical facilities, retirement homes, and wheelchair accessible public transit rises.

Other parts of Canada, such as rural Saskatchewan and Newfoundland and Labrador, have been aging not because of in-migration of the elderly but because of out-migration of the young. Meeting the needs of the elderly in isolated rural communities poses its own problems, especially at a time of rising costs. To what extent people have a right to expect to be cared for in their own communities where they have spent their lives, rather than elsewhere where services can be centrally provided, is a question that geographers have only begun to address. In general terms, we can conclude that the challenge of an aging society is likely to be felt much more in Canada's periphery. The metropolitan core of this country has far more resources to cope with the needs of our growing population of the elderly.

Policy-makers, including a number with geographical training, have put forward a variety of solutions to the problems we have outlined here. Broadly speaking, these can be divided into three types of response.

- *Pronatalism.* If declining birth rates lie at the heart of the problem, governments can try to reverse this trend by providing incentives for having children. For instance, in the 1990s, when Quebec had the lowest birth rate in Canada and concerns arose over a possible decline in the number of French speakers in the province, the government of Quebec issued "baby bonus" cheques. In reality, as international surveys have shown, no government scheme compensates for the true costs of raising children, and to pose the issue in only economic terms shows a basic misunderstanding of the causes of the decline in the birth rate.

- *Increased economic productivity.* Some economists have argued that the problems of an aging society could all be met by simply having a more productive economy. An economy that produces more can pay higher taxes and health insurance and pension premiums.

- *Immigration.* Canada's traditional "policy lever," the one used in the past to people the country and fuel economic growth, is now also promoted by the federal government as a solution to the problems of an aging population. The shortfall in births can be simply replaced by the recruitment of immigrants from overseas. Moreover, unlike many other core nations that have only just begun to contemplate this solution, Canada has the advantages of a trained bureaucracy already in place around the world and a public largely receptive to the policy. However, it should be added that estimates carried out for Health Canada's *Demographic Review* showed that because immigrants themselves age, annual immigration at the levels currently experienced in this country can only postpone the effects of aging by approximately seven years.

POPULATION DYNAMICS AND PROCESSES

To evaluate a different understanding of population growth and change, experts look at two significant factors: fertility and mortality. Birth and death rates, as they are also known, often are also indirect indicators of a region's level of development and its place within the world economy.

Birth, or Fertility, Rates

crude birth rate (CBR): the ratio of the number of live births in a single year for every thousand people in the population

The **crude birth rate (CBR)** is the ratio of the number of live births in a single year for every thousand people in the population. The crude birth rate is, indeed, crude because it measures the birth rate in terms of the total population and not with respect to a particular age-specific group or cohort. For example, Canada's crude birth rate in 2007 was 11 per thousand, which compares with 21 per thousand for Mexico in the same year.

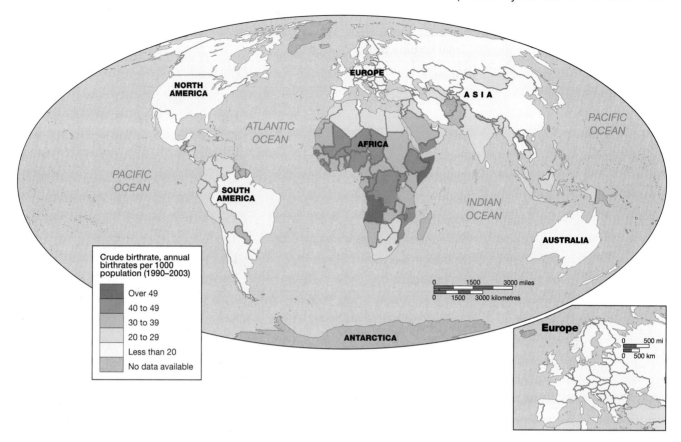

Figure 3.5 **World crude birth rates, 2004** Crude birth rates and crude death rates are often indicators of the levels of economic development in individual countries. Compare, for example, Australia, a core country, which offers a stark contrast to Ethiopia, a very poor peripheral country. (*Source:* World Bank, *World Development Indicators, 2004.* Washington, DC: World Bank.)

Although the level of economic development is a very important factor shaping the CBR, other, often equally important, influences also affect the CBR. In particular, it may be heavily affected by the demographic structure of the population, as graphically suggested by age–sex pyramids. In addition, an area's CBR is influenced by women's educational achievement, religion, social customs, diet, and health, as well as by politics, war, civil unrest, and, increasingly, environmental degradation. Most demographers believe that the availability of birth-control methods is also critically important to a country's or region's birth rate. **Figure 3.5** is a world map of the CBR showing high levels of fertility in most of the periphery and low levels of fertility in the core. The highest birth rates occur in Africa, the poorest region in the world.

Fertility is the childbearing performance of individuals, couples, groups, or populations. The crude birth rate is only one indicator of fertility and, in fact, is somewhat limited in its usefulness, telling very little about the potential for future fertility levels. Two other indicators formulated by population experts—the total fertility rate and the doubling time—provide more insight into the potential dynamics of a population. The **total fertility rate (TFR)** is a measure of the average number of children a woman will have throughout her childbearing years, approximately ages 15 through 49 (**Table 3.2**). Whereas the CBR indicates the number of births in a given year, the TFR is a more predictive measure that attempts to portray what birth rates will be among a particular cohort of women over time. A population with a TFR of slightly higher than 2.0 has achieved replacement-level fertility.

Closely related to the TFR is the doubling time of the population. The **doubling time,** as the name suggests, is a measure of how long it will take the population of an area to grow to twice its current size. For example, a country whose population increases at 1.8 percent per year will have doubled in about 40 years. In fact, world population is currently increasing at this rate. By contrast, a country whose population is increasing 3.18 percent annually will double in only 22 years—the doubling time for Kenya. Birth rates, and the population dynamics we can project from them, however, tell us only part of the story of the potential of the population for growth. We must also know the death, or mortality, rates.

fertility: the childbearing performance of individuals, couples, groups, or populations

total fertility rate (TFR): the average number of children a woman will have throughout the years that demographers have identified as her childbearing years, approximately ages 15 through 49

doubling time: the measure of how long it will take the population of an area to grow to twice its current size

TABLE 3.2   Total Fertility Rates for Selected Countries, 2009

Total Fertility Rate	
Country	**(TFR)**
Afghanistan	5.7
Canada	1.6
China	1.6
Germany	1.3
Haiti	4.0
India	2.7
Namibia	3.6
Palestinian Territories	4.6
Russia	1.5
United States	2.1

Source: Population Reference Bureau website, **www.prb.org**, 2009 World Population Data Sheet.

Death, or Mortality, Rates

crude death rate (CDR): the number of deaths in a single year for every thousand people in the population

Countering birth rates and also shaping overall population numbers and composition is the **crude death rate (CDR)**, the ratio of the number of deaths in one year for every thousand people in the population. As with crude birth rates, crude death rates often roughly reflect levels of economic development: countries with low birth rates generally have low death rates (**Figure 3.6**).

Although often associated with economic development, the CDR is also significantly influenced by other factors. A demographic structure with more men

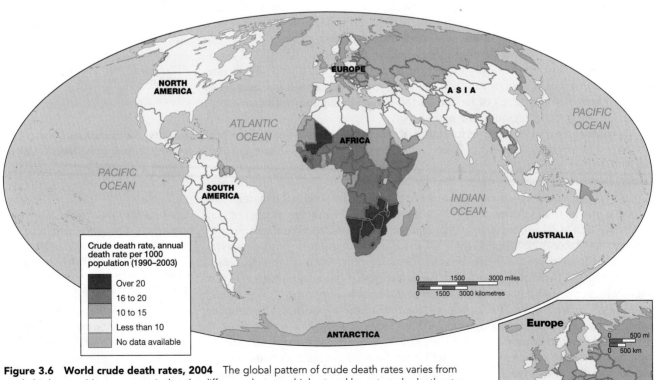

Figure 3.6   World crude death rates, 2004   The global pattern of crude death rates varies from crude birth rates. Most apparent is that the difference between highest and lowest crude death rates is relatively smaller than is the case for crude birth rates, reflecting the impact of factors related to the middle phases of the demographic transition.   (*Source:* World Bank, *World Development Indicators, 2004.* Washington, DC: World Bank.)

Some countries promote fertility with increased child benefits, maternal grants, child-care allowances, and special family allowances. Among these are France, Iraq, Israel, Singapore, and Malaysia, where more people are perceived as necessary for economic and strategic reasons.

In 1995, China's birthrate stood at 17.12 per thousand, with total births of 23.6 million and a mortality rate of 6.57 per thousand.

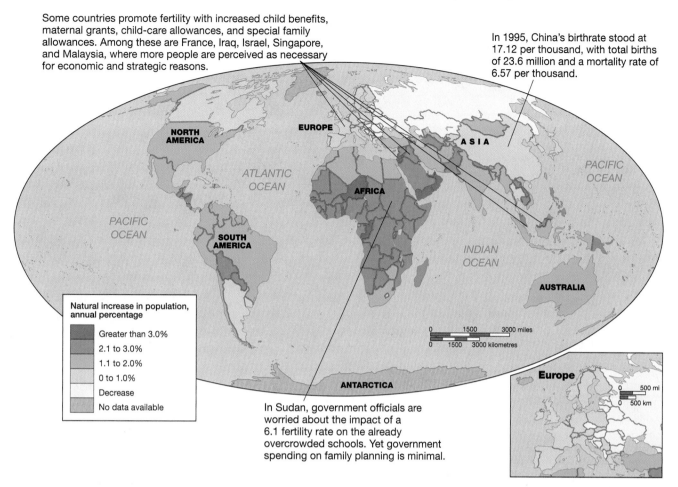

Natural increase in population, annual percentage

Greater than 3.0%
2.1 to 3.0%
1.1 to 2.0%
0 to 1.0%
Decrease
No data available

In Sudan, government officials are worried about the impact of a 6.1 fertility rate on the already overcrowded schools. Yet government spending on family planning is minimal.

Europe

Figure 3.7   World rates of natural increase, 2004   As the map shows, rates of natural increase are highest in sub-Saharan Africa, the Near East, and parts of Asia, as well as in parts of South and Central America. Europe and the United States and Canada, as well as Australia and parts of central Asia and Russia, have slow to stable rates of natural increase.   (*Source:* World Bank, *World Development Indicators, 2004.* Washington, DC: World Bank.)

and elderly people, for example, usually means higher death rates. Other important influences on mortality include health care availability, social class, occupation, and even place of residence. Poorer groups in the population have higher death rates than the middle class. The difference between the CBR and the CDR is the rate of **natural increase**—the surplus of births over deaths—or the rate of **natural decrease**—the deficit of births relative to deaths (**Figure 3.7**).

Death rates can be measured for both sex and age cohorts, and one of the most common measures is the **infant mortality rate.** This figure is the annual number of deaths of infants less than one year of age compared with the total number of live births for that same year. The figure is usually expressed as number of deaths during the first year of life per 1,000 live births.

The infant mortality rate is used by researchers as an important indicator both of a country's health care system and of the general population's access to health care. Global patterns show high infant mortality rates in the peripheral countries of Africa and Asia and low rates in the more developed countries of Europe and North America (**Figure 3.8**). Generally, these patterns reflect adequate maternal nutrition and the wider availability of health care resources and personnel in core regions. When patterns are examined at the level of countries, regions, and cities, infant mortality rates are not uniform. In east-central Europe, Bulgaria has a 9.7 per thousand infant mortality rate, whereas the Czech Republic has a rate of 3.3 per thousand. In Israel, the rate is 3.9; in the adjacent Palestinian Territories it is 25. The point is that global patterns often mask regional and local variations in mortality rates, both for infants and other population cohorts.

natural increase: the difference between the CBR and the CDR, which is the surplus of births over deaths

natural decrease: the difference between the CDR and the CBR, which is the deficit of births relative to deaths

infant mortality rate: the annual number of deaths of infants under one year of age compared with the total number of live births for that same year

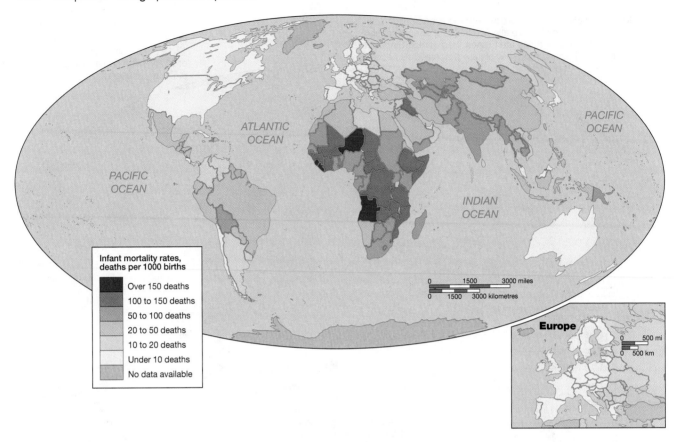

Figure 3.8 World infant mortality rates, 2004 The geography of poverty underlies the patterns shown in this map and allows us to analyze the linkages between population variables and social conditions. Infant mortality rates generally seem to parallel crude death rates, with sub-Saharan Africa generally reporting the highest rates. These rates reflect a number of factors, including inadequate or completely absent maternal health care as well as poor nutrition for infants. (*Source: After Hammond Atlas of the World.* New York: Oxford University Press, 1993. Update from the World Bank, *World Development Indicators, 2004.* Washington, DC: World Bank.)

A report from the United Nations Children's Fund (UNICEF) released in October 2004 makes use of a related measure, child mortality, to underline its concerns. Child mortality refers to the number of children who die before their fifth birthday and is measured in relation to every 1,000 live births. In 2002, according to UNICEF, industrialized countries had 7 deaths for every 1,000 births, whereas the poorest nations had an average of 158. (The highest rate, 284 per 1,000, was recorded for Sierra Leone.) Despite the goals adopted by world leaders at the U.N. Millennium Summit in 2000 to reduce child mortality by two-thirds by 2015, the UNICEF report notes "alarmingly slow progress on reducing child deaths." Indeed, in more than one-third of sub-Saharan African countries, child mortality rates had increased or stagnated.

Nevertheless, there is some reason for optimism. A 2005 report shows how advice from Canada's International Development Research Centre (IDRC) has helped reduce child mortality by more than 40 percent in the eastern parts of Tanzania since 2000.[3] Working with the Tanzania Ministry of Health, the IDRC discovered that redesigning the region's health care delivery to meet the needs of local clinics made it possible to properly diagnose illness and to make more efficient use of available financial resources. Given that Tanzania is only able to spend $8 per citizen per year on health care (Canada spends $2,700), the IDRC's recommendations should prove invaluable.

Related to infant mortality and the crude death rate is **life expectancy,** the average number of years an individual can expect to live. Not surprisingly,

life expectancy: the average number of years an individual can expect to live

---

[3] Stephanie Nolan, "Canadian Project Halves Tanzania's Child Deaths," *Globe and Mail,* 24 January 2005, A1, A8.

life expectancy varies considerably from country to country, region to region, and even place to place within cities and among different classes and racial and ethnic groups. Canada is no exception in this regard. There are considerable variations in life expectancies across the country and among groups. Aboriginal communities, for example, record some of the lowest average life expectancies in Canada (see "Population, Health, and the Environment" later in this chapter).

Another key factor influencing life expectancy is epidemics, which can quickly and radically alter population numbers and composition. In our times, epidemics can spread rapidly over great distances, largely because people and other disease carriers can now travel from one place to another very rapidly. Also, in countries with well-developed urban systems, diffusion will occur hierarchically, which (as we saw in Chapter 1) is much faster than simple spread, or contagious diffusion. Epidemics can have profound effects at various scales, from the international to the local, and reflect the increasing interdependence of a shrinking globe. They may affect different population groups in different ways and, depending on the quantity and quality of health and nutritional care available, may have a greater or lesser impact on different localities.

One of the most widespread epidemics of modern times is the spread of acquired immune deficiency syndrome (AIDS) and the human immunodeficiency virus (HIV) that is responsible for the disease. According to the *Report on the Global Aids Epidemic 2008* issued by the Joint United Nations Programme on HIV/AIDS (UNAIDS), there was a worldwide total of 33 million people living with HIV/AIDS in 2007, but signs of progress in the battle against the disease were shown by the fact that the number of new HIV infections had declined from 3.0 million in 2001 to 2.7 million in 2007. In other words, to quote the report itself, "the global epidemic is stabilizing, but at an unacceptably high level." By 2007, the annual death toll from the disease had declined from a peak of 2.5 million in 2004 to an estimated level of 2.0 million.

Since its beginnings in the early 1980s, probably in parts of Central Africa, HIV/AIDS has spread across most parts of the world and has usually been able to spread rapidly because it has been able to diffuse hierarchically (see Chapter 1)— especially in countries of the core, with their well-integrated urban systems. Regionally, however, sub-Saharan African nations (those south of the Sahara) have been the hardest affected (**Figure 3.9**). The 2008 UNAIDS report observes that 67 percent of all people living with HIV/AIDS in 2007 resided in this part of the world, and that this region accounted for 72 percent of all deaths caused by AIDS in 2007.

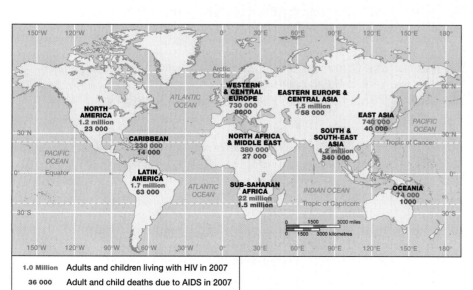

1.0 Million   Adults and children living with HIV in 2007

36 000   Adult and child deaths due to AIDS in 2007

Figure 3.9 Adults and children living with and dying from HIV/AIDS, 2007 HIV/AIDS infections are concentrated in the periphery and semiperiphery, with 86 percent of people with HIV/AIDS living in Asia and sub-Saharan Africa. Compare the number of adults and children living with HIV/AIDS in Africa with those in North America or Europe. Deaths from HIV/AIDS have also been highest in Africa. (*Source:* Joint United Nations Programme on HIV/AIDS [UNAIDS], "Annex 1," *Report on the Global Aids Epidemic 2008.* Geneva: UNAIDS, 2008, **www.unaids.org/en/dataanalysis/epidemiology/2008reportontheglobalaidsepidemic/**.)

Demographic Transition Theory

Many demographers believe that fertility and mortality rates are directly tied to the level of economic development of a country, region, or place. Pointing to the history of demographic change in core countries, they state that many of the economic, political, social, and technological transformations associated with industrialization and urbanization lead to a demographic transition. The **demographic transition** is a model of population change when high birth and death rates are replaced by low birth and death rates. Once a society moves from a pre-industrial economic base to an industrial one, population growth slows. According to the demographic transition model, the decrease in population growth is attributable to improved economic production and higher standards of living brought about by changes in medicine, education, and sanitation.

As **Figure 3.10** illustrates, the high birth and death rates of the pre-industrial phase (Phase 1) are replaced by the low birth and death rates of the industrial phase (Phase 4), but only after passing through a critical transitional stage (Phases 2 and 3). During this transitional stage, simple improvements in hygiene produce an early and steep decline in mortality, whereas fertility remains at levels characteristic of a place that has not yet industrialized. The resulting lag leads to rapid population growth.

What causes this lag? Essentially, the reason is that mortality rates react quickly to relatively simple improvements in hygiene (e.g., availability of clean water and basic sanitation), nutrition, and health care. On the other hand, fertility rates are mostly the result of social attitudes that are relatively slow to change. Historical trends in birth and death rates and natural increase are shown in **Table 3.3** for Scotland and England during their periods of demographic transition. Over a roughly 50-year period, both countries were able to reduce their rates of natural increase by nearly one-third. In the fourth phase (not shown in the table), birth and death rates have both stabilized at a low level, which means that population growth rates are very slow and birth rates are more likely to oscillate than death rates.

Whereas England and Scotland, early industrializers, passed through the demographic transition over a period of about 150 years beginning in the mid-eighteenth century, most peripheral and semiperipheral countries have yet to complete the transition. In fact, many peripheral and semiperipheral countries appear to be stalled in the transitional stage (Phases 2 and 3), which has been called a "demographic trap."

Although the demographic transition model is based on actual birth and death statistics of core countries during the period of industrialization, many population geographers and other experts increasingly question whether it is

demographic transition: the replacement of high birth and death rates by low birth and death rates

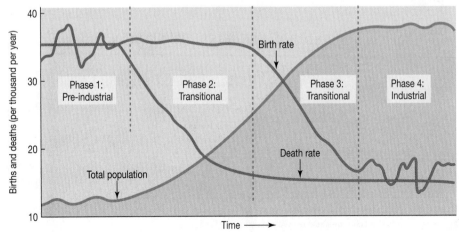

Figure 3.10 Demographic transition model The transition from a stable population based on high birth and death rates to one based on low birth and death rates progresses in clearly defined phases, as illustrated by this graph. With basic information about a country's birth and death rates and total population, it is possible to identify that country's position within the demographic transition process. Population experts disagree about the usefulness of the model, however. Many insist it is applicable only to the demographic history of core countries.

TABLE 3.3 Birth and Death Rates for England and Scotland, 1870–1920

The CBRs and CDRs for England and Scotland between 1870 and 1920 illustrate countries moving between Phase 2 and Phase 3 of the demographic transition, in which death rates are lower than birth rates. During the same 50-year period, both countries were completing their transformation into key industrial regions. England and Scotland are thus good examples of how the demographic transition has been theorized to operate in core countries.

	1870	1880	1890	1900	1910	1920
Crude Birth Rate						
England	35.2	35.4	32.5	29.9	27.3	22.7
Scotland	35.0	34.8	32.3	30.2	28.4	24.0
Crude Death Rate						
England	22.5	21.4	19.2	18.2	15.4	14.6
Scotland	22.1	21.6	19.2	18.5	16.6	15.3

Source: M. Anderson and D. Morse, *Scottish Demography* 42, 1993.

generalizable to the experience of countries and regions in the periphery today. Among other criticisms is that industrialization—which, according to the theory, is central to moving from Phase 2 to Phases 3 and 4—is seldom domestically generated in the peripheral countries. Instead, it is foreign investment from core countries and transnational corporations that seems to drive peripheral industrialization. As a result, the rise in living standards and other features of demographic change witnessed in core countries—where industrialization was largely a result of internal capital investment—have not occurred in many peripheral countries. Other critics of the demographic transition model point to several factors undermining a demographic transition fuelled by economic growth: the shortage of skilled labour, the absence of advanced educational opportunities for all members of the population (especially women), and limits on technological advances. In other words, the demographic transition model reflects how the core countries were able to take advantage of their privileged starting position as early industrializers, yet today's peripheral countries may find it impossible to repeat this development as they are in a much more difficult starting position (see Chapter 2).

POPULATION MOVEMENT AND MIGRATION

In addition to the population dynamics of death and reproduction, the third critical influence is the movement of people from place to place. Individuals may make far-reaching, international or intraregional moves, or they may simply move from one part of a city to another. Whatever the scale, mobility and migration reflect the interdependence of the world-system. For example, global shifts in industrial investment result in local adjustments to those shifts as populations move or remain in place in response to the creation or disappearance of employment opportunities.

Mobility and Migration

One way to describe such movement is with the broad term **mobility,** the ability to move from one place to another, either permanently or temporarily. Mobility may be used to describe a wide array of human movement ranging from a journey to work (for example, a daily commute from suburb to city or suburb to suburb) to an ocean-spanning, permanent move.

mobility: the ability to move, either permanently or temporarily

migration: a long-distance move to a new location

emigration: a movement in which a person *leaves* a country

immigration: a movement in which a person *arrives in* another country

international migration: a move from one country to another

internal migration: a move within a particular country or region

The second way to describe population movement is with the more narrowly defined term of **migration,** a long-distance move to a new location. Migration involves a permanent or temporary change of residence from one place to another. **Emigration** is a movement in which a person *leaves* one country to go to another. **Immigration** describes movement in which a person *arrives* in one country, having left another. Thus, a person from China who moves to Canada *emigrates* from China and *immigrates* to Canada. These types of movement from one country to another are types of **international migration.** Moves may also occur within a particular country or region, in which case they are called **internal migration.** Both permanent and temporary changes of residence may occur for many reasons but most often involve a desire for economic betterment; an escape from adverse political conditions, such as war or oppression; or, increasingly, a flight from environmental degradation.

Interprovincial migration in Canada is one example of the influence of economics on internal migration. Between the 2001 and 2006 censuses, only three provinces recorded net gains through internal migration according to data released by Statistics Canada in mid-2008. With its booming economy, it is no surprise that Alberta was the leading destination for those moving across Canada between 2001 and 2006, gaining a total of 88,180 people in this way. British Columbia (22,130) and Prince Edward Island (approximately 600) were the two other provinces benefiting from internal migration over this period, although, as can be seen from these totals, their relative attraction was no match for that of Alberta. On the other hand, the provinces of Newfoundland and Labrador (–6,245), New Brunswick (–10,615), and Saskatchewan (–25,385) lost people through internal migration. Local and regional economies change, of course, and Saskatchewan is an example of how quickly fortunes can reverse. Since early 2008, the substantial rise in prices for grain and potash (used for fertilizer) has boosted Saskatchewan's economy, leading to a population growth in 2010 that was second only to that of British Columbia.

Governments are concerned about keeping track of migration numbers, migration rates, and the characteristics of the migrant populations because these factors can have profound consequences for political, economic, and cultural conditions at national, regional, and local scales. For example, a peripheral country, such as Cuba, that has experienced substantial out-migration of highly trained professionals may find it difficult to provide needed services. On the other hand, such countries as Canada, the United States, Germany, and France have received large numbers of low-skilled in-migrants willing to work for low wages. Yet the situation is more complicated than that: Germany, for instance, in turn experiences a "brain drain" of highly qualified doctors and academics to the United Kingdom, Switzerland, and Scandinavia and has recently become a net exporter of population.

gross migration: the total number of migrants moving into and out of a place, region, or country

net migration: the gain or loss in the total population of a particular area as a result of migration

Demographers have developed several calculations of migration rates. Calculation of the in-migration and out-migration rates provides the foundation for discovering gross and net migration rates for an area of study. **Gross migration** refers to the total number of migrants moving into and out of a place, region, or country. **Net migration** refers to the gain or loss in the total population of that area as a result of the migration. Migration is a particularly important concept because the total population of a country, region, or locality is dependent on migration activity as well as on birth and death rates.

push factors: events and conditions that impel an individual to move away from a location

pull factors: forces of attraction that influence migrants to move to a particular location

Migration rates, however, provide only a small portion of the information needed to understand the dynamics of migration and its effects at all scales of resolution. In general terms, migrants make their decisions to move based on push factors and pull factors. **Push factors** are events and conditions that impel an individual to move away from a location. They include a wide variety of possible motives, from the idiosyncratic (such as an individual migrant's dissatisfaction with the amenities offered at home) to the dramatic (such as war, economic dislocation, or environmental degradation). **Pull factors** are forces of attraction that influence migrants to move to a particular location. Factors drawing individual migrants to chosen destinations, again, may range from the highly personal (such as a strong desire to live near the sea) to the very structural (such as strong economic growth and thus relatively lucrative job opportunities).

Usually, the decision to migrate is a combination of both push and pull factors, and many migrations are voluntary. In **voluntary migration,** an individual chooses to move. When migration occurs against the individual's will, push factors can produce **forced migration.** Forced migration (both internal and international) is a critical and growing problem in the contemporary world. In 2010, the Office of the United Nations High Commissioner for Refugees (UNHCR) reported that the total number of refugees and internally displaced people (IDP) worldwide had reached 43.3 million. The report noted that 15.2 million of this total were refugees (individuals who have crossed international boundaries, and also met criteria discussed below), and 27.1 million were IDPs.

According to the 1951 International Convention Related to the Status of Refugees, the term *refugee* has a formal definition. Sometimes known as "political" or "Convention" refugees to clarify their status, these are people who have fled their homelands because they have a well-founded fear of persecution on the grounds of race, religion, nationality, political belief, or social characteristic. People who meet these criteria are entitled to the right of non-return to their country of persecution and to the protection of UNHCR.

You will have noticed that this definition of refugee makes no reference to **environmental refugees:** people who have been physically displaced from their homes and livelihoods by the deterioration of the local environment. This is because in 1951 the United Nations was principally concerned with addressing the violations to people's political rights that had occurred during the upheaval of World War II. Today, however, forced **eco-migration**—population movement caused by the degradation of land and essential natural resources—is responsible for as many as 50 million refugees worldwide, thus more than doubling the total number of refugees! (See the discussions in the boxes **Human Geography and Climate Change 3.1—Population Displacement** and **Geography Matters 4.4—Disasters**).

For example, each year dams and irrigation projects are forcing between 1 million and 2 million people worldwide to move (by conservative estimates, the Three Gorges Dam in China alone displaced more than 1.3 million people). Droughts, floods, and other extreme weather events also push people off their homelands. In Bangladesh, for example, increasingly frequent and severe flooding of the floodplains (that were settled in the 1960s in response to growing population pressure) is routinely forcing huge numbers of people to temporarily relocate. Many other places are threatened by permanent sea-level increases because of global warming. Some low-lying island states such as Tuvalu, the Seychelles, and the Maldives may be permanently flooded by mid-century, prompting their governments to plan for a grim future in which leaving their islands may be the only option left. The Maldives, for example, began contacting Sri Lanka, India, and Australia in 2008 to buy a new homeland for their population. At the 2010 Climate Summit in Cancun, an "Alliance of Small Island States" (AOSIS) representing 43 countries (remember that there are only 195 states in the world!) urged global leaders to prevent further sea-level increases that would wipe their islands off the map.[4]

International Voluntary Migration

Not all migration is forced, however (**Figure 3.11**). Canada is a land made up entirely of successive waves of immigrants, adding their own contributions to the development of this country, progressively inhabiting its spaces, and constructing

voluntary migration: the movement by an individual based on choice

forced migration: the movement by an individual against his or her will

environmental refugees: people who have been physically displaced from their homes and livelihoods by the deterioration of the local environment

eco-migration: a population movement caused by the degradation of land and essential natural resources

---

[4] A Google Earth simulation of how rising sea levels would affect the coastlines and cities of Caribbean islands is available through the extensive Climate Change website of *The Guardian* (**www.guardian.co.uk/environment/video/2010/dec/01/cancun-climate-change-conference**). The site also features many other videos and reports on the effects of climate change around the world.

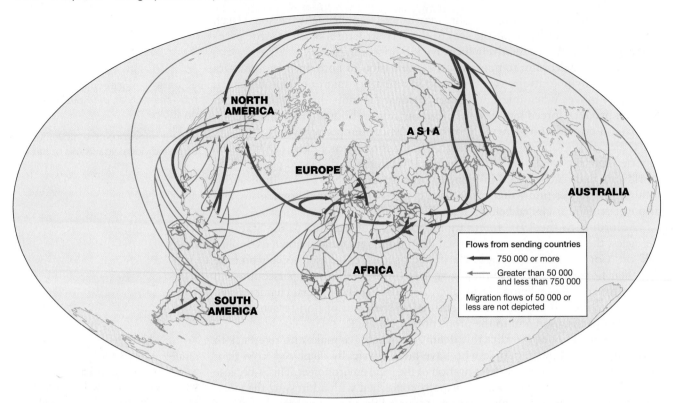

Figure 3.11   Global voluntary migration   This map illustrates very complex flows across borders of people who have migrated by choice. Although each of the flows represents a cluster of individual decisions, generally speaking, the flows emanate from the periphery and are moving toward the core. Intracontinental migration, such as that in South America and Africa, represents the apparent pull of economic opportunity for residents of relatively poorer countries.   (*Sources:* A. Segal, An Atlas of International Migration. New Providence, NJ: Hans Zell Publishers/Bowker-Saur, 1993, p. 23. Reproduced by permission of Hans Zell Publishing. © The estate of the late Aaron Segal; The Fuller Projection Map design is a trademark of the Buckminster Fuller Institute ©1938, 1967 & 1992. All rights reserved. **www.bfi.org**.)

their own places. Every year, Canada receives approximately 250,000 immigrants and refugees. Archaeological evidence suggests that Canada was first settled from the west by small bands of hunter-gatherer peoples migrating from Asia at least 11,500 years ago. More than 10,000 years later, the first known migration came from the east in the form of the short-lived Viking settlement in L'Anse aux Meadows in Newfoundland (about A.D. 1000). Another 500 to 600 years passed before permanent European immigration to Canada began, led by French ambitions to settle the gulf and lower valley of the St. Lawrence River. Only after the loss of its American colonies after 1783 and the flight of 100,000 Loyalists into Ontario, Quebec, and New Brunswick did Britain show any interest in settling Canada.

For the next century or so, the agricultural lands of Ontario and Quebec attracted a number of different migrant groups. It is estimated that from 1815 to 1865, over 1 million emigrants from the British Isles entered what was then known as British North America, many moving on to the United States. Approximately 60 percent of that flow was made up of migrants from Ireland, prompted to leave by disasters, such as the famine of 1846 to 1849. By the 1860s, little arable land remained to be colonized in the east, and Canada began to experience a net emigration. Many of those who stayed in this country chose to move internally, either to Canada's developing cities or to its agricultural frontiers. Indeed, it was in the west that Canada's policy-makers saw the solution to the loss of population growth. The purchase of Rupert's Land, in 1870, and treaty negotiations with the First Nations opened up the Prairies for European settlement. The eradication of the bison and the completion of the transcontinental Canadian Pacific Railroad made it feasible to establish in Canada an economy based on western agriculture.

There followed a 30- to 40-year period of substantial immigration from eastern and central Europe to Alberta, Saskatchewan, and Manitoba. The

Population Displacement

Scientists and policy-makers have largely reached consensus on the causes and certainty of climate change. However, the economic, demographic, and social consequences of this change are far less clear (**Figure 3.1.1**). Released in 2007, the Fourth Assessment Report of the Intergovernmental Panel on Climate Change (IPCC) discussed population displacement as a result of climate change,[5] predicting the displacement of hundreds of millions of people due to climate change by 2080.[6]

A concept that has recently emerged is that of the environmental refugee, or a person who has been physically displaced from their home and livelihood by the deterioration of the local environment. Although the term is widely used, governments and the office of the United Nations High Commissioner for Refugees (UNHCR) do not officially recognize these refugees, and their formal legal status remains undecided. Despite this, widespread recognition of these individuals exists, with the New Economics Foundation arguing that international law should "grant refugee status to people driven from [their] homes by a lost or ruined environment."[7]

So what might create environmental refugees? Long term, one of the most measurable outcomes associated with climate change is rising sea levels and the disappearance of coastal lands. The IPCC estimates that the average rate of sea level rise is 1 to 2 mm per year, with sea levels rising by an average of 60 cm by 2100.[8] For coastal communities and island nations, rising seas threaten their economic infrastructure by increasing erosion and flooding that destroy livelihoods and in many instances compromise fresh-water resources. Located in the South Pacific, the Cook Islands are mainly low-lying coral atolls. Rising sea levels have already meant the evacuation of 2,500 residents from the Carteret Islands of Papua New Guinea. With climate change, rising sea levels are likely to inundate the coastal areas of these islands where their populations concentrate. The loss of agricultural land means people will lose their way of life, and if local governments have limited economic capability to offset these environmental impacts, population displacement will be inevitable.

Climate change is also responsible for shifting precipitation patterns and desertification. Africa is extremely vulnerable to climate change and is expected to receive less precipitation than it currently does, a situation made worse by ineffective governments, weak economies, poverty, and an already fragile environment. Shifting precipitation patterns mean that almost half of Africa's land mass is at risk of desertification, where long-term declines in rainfall amounts have already resulted in the southward shift of the Sahelian, Sudanese, and Guinean deserts and resulted in a reduced growing season and decreased water flows on the Niger and Senegal Rivers. Africa's Sahel region, an area that includes Ethiopia, Eritrea, Djibouti, and Somalia, has experienced more intense and frequent droughts in the last 40 years, with rainfall approximately one-third less than the long-run average.[9]

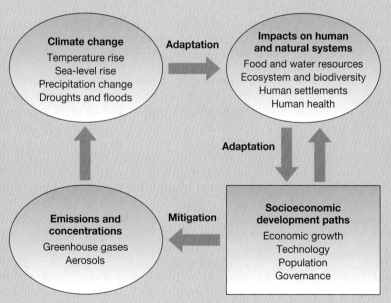

Figure 3.1.1 Climate change: an integrated framework The expected impacts of climate change are varied and widespread. It is widely expected that climate change will impact human and natural systems through such things as food and water resources, which in turn will affect economic development and personal livelihoods. (*Source:* IPCC, with permission.)

[5] IPPC 4th Assessment Report, 2007 (http://www.ipcc.ch/index.htm).

[6] Ibid.

[7] http://www.neweconomics.org/publications/environmental-refugees

[8] IPPC 4th Assessment Report, 2007.

[9] Ibid.

Further encroachment of deserts will force population displacement, with the U.N. Food and Agricultural Organization predicting that 135 million people are at risk of displacement due to desertification alone.[10] This influx of environmental refugees into neighbouring countries and regions will likely strain existing infrastructures and social relations.

Extreme weather events such as cyclones can also produce short-term displacement. Although we cannot definitively attribute particular storms to climate change, the IPCC notes evidence suggesting that cyclones have increased in average intensity, with further increases in their intensity and frequency expected.[11] The low-lying delta area of Bangladesh is particularly prone to flooding due to cyclones.[12] Cyclone Sidr, which struck Bangladesh in November 2007, resulted in the displacement of over 2 million people. Flooding in parts of Australia, including the states of Queensland and Victoria, affected over 200,000 people.

The contrast between Australia and Bangladesh, however, highlights differences in **vulnerability**, **adaptability**, and **resiliency**.[13] Australia, for instance, has greater resources to deal with flooding as compared to Bangladesh, given its higher income levels, better infrastructure such as roads and communication, and a larger economy that can better absorb the impacts of such events. Bangladesh, on the other hand, is characterized by weak economic infrastructure that is less able to adapt. More generally, climate change will likely have the greatest impact on populations in the developing world[14] where a lack of resources and/or a less stable political or economic infrastructure makes it more difficult to deal with its effects. According to a report distributed by the U.N. Food and Agriculture Organization, "the capacity to survive and recover from the effects of a natural disaster is the result of two factors: the physical magnitude of the disaster in a given area, and the socioeconomic conditions of individuals or social groups in that area. Altogether, it is estimated that 90 percent of victims and 75 percent of all economic damages accrue to developing countries."[15] National governments and the United Nations recognized these differences with the 2007 Bali Action Plan, which aimed to protect poor countries from climate change impacts by developing national and regional adaptation strategies and programs.

Although climate change is expected to cause massive population displacement, straining the coping ability of receiving countries and their governments, research has suggested that environmentally induced migration can be temporary and involve relatively short distances, as opposed to mass population movements across international borders.[16] In particular, responses to large-scale natural disasters such as tsunamis or cyclones do displace large numbers of people, but the displaced population quickly returns. The concern is that the number and frequency of these events is likely to rise with climate change, and the displaced need assistance with such necessities as shelter and food regardless of whether the displacement lasts one month or 10 years. The relationship between population displacement and the longer-term impacts of climate change on droughts and soil degradation is less clear, but research again indicates that they are also unlikely to lead to large-scale population displacement, although this may simply be masked as men migrate in search of jobs, leaving their families behind. In parts of the Sahel desert, 80 percent of the population is women and children, with the men working in Libya or Chad.[17] Regardless, research indicates that environmentally induced migration is real, but whether governments recognize this displacement remains open to debate.

—K.B.N.

vulnerability: a concept relating to the total exposure to risk brought on by climate change

adaptability: a broad-based term which encompasses all actions taken to address the changes that climate change produces

resiliency: a measure of how damaging an event will be and how quickly and efficiently an area or group of vulnerable people within an area will recover from such an event

---

[10] Elisabeth Rosenthal, "Water Is a New Battleground in Spain," *New York Times*, 3 June 2008, S1.

[11] Ibid.

[12] IPPC 4th Assessment Report, 2007.

[13] Phil Sivell, S.J. Reeves, L. Baldachin, and T.G. Brightman, "Climate Change Resilience Indicators," Transport Research Laboratory, September 2008.

[14] Ibid.

[15] Thouret and D'Ercole 1996: 409, noted in G. Martine and J.M. Guzman, "Population, Poverty and Vulnerability: Mitigating the Effects of Natural Disasters, Part 1." *SD Dimensions*, December 1999 (**www.fao.org/sd/wpdirect/wpan0042.htm**).

[16] Clark L. Gray, "Environmental Refugees or Economic Migrants?" Population Reference Bureau (**www.prb.org/Articles/2010/environmentalmigrants.aspx**).

[17] Geoffrey York, "On the Move in a Warming World: The Rise of Climate Refugees," *The Globe and Mail*, 17 December 2010, F1.

twentieth century, with the exception of the war years and the Depression, continued this trend (**Figure 3.12**). Two major changes in the patterns of immigration occurred as the century progressed. First, immigration increasingly focused on urban rather than rural areas as destinations. Second, once a nonracist selection policy was introduced in 1967, the main sources of Canada's immigrants

**Immigration to Canada
Destinations—1996 Census**

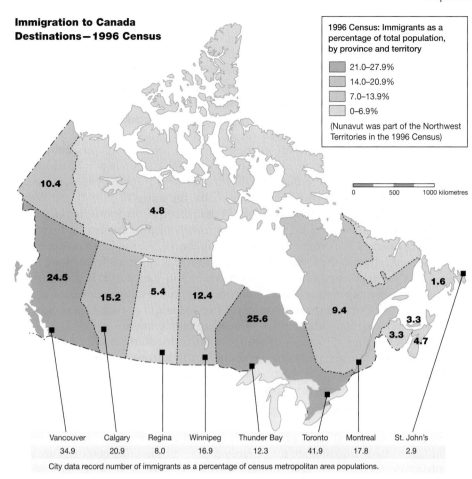

1996 Census: Immigrants as a
percentage of total population,
by province and territory

▨	21.0–27.9%
▨	14.0–20.9%
▨	7.0–13.9%
▨	0–6.9%

(Nunavut was part of the Northwest
Territories in the 1996 Census)

0   500   1000 kilometres

Vancouver	Calgary	Regina	Winnipeg	Thunder Bay	Toronto	Montreal	St. John's
34.9	20.9	8.0	16.9	12.3	41.9	17.8	2.9

City data record number of immigrants as a percentage of census metropolitan area populations.

Origins: Canada's immigrant population in 1996, divided into major world regions
and into two periods of arrival, to show changing origins over time.

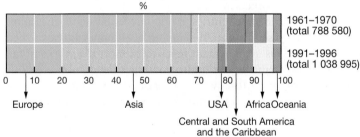

%

1961–1970
(total 788 580)

1991–1996
(total 1 038 995)

0   10   20   30   40   50   60   70   80   90   100

Europe   Asia   USA   Africa Oceania

Central and South America
and the Caribbean

**Immigration—Historical Perspective
(1860–2000)**

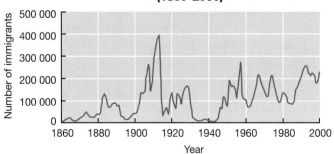

Number of immigrants

500 000
400 000
300 000
200 000
100 000
0

1860   1880   1900   1920   1940   1960   1980   2000

Year

**Figure 3.12   Immigration to
Canada, 1860–2000**   Since 1860,
annual immigration totals to Canada
have varied considerably, peak-
ing (as the graph shows) between
1910 and 1920, declining through
the Depression years until World
War II, and then rising in a series of
waves from 1950 to 2000. In general
terms, these changes have reflected
the changing requirements of the
Canadian economy. In the early
twentieth century, for example, the
demand for farm labour fuelled very
large annual immigration totals.
In more recent years, government
policy is to increase immigration
only when the economy is growing.
Considerable changes have also
occurred in the origins of Canada's
immigrants as Canada has altered its
immigration policies. If we compare
the years 1961–1970 with 1991–1996
(see bar graph), for example, we
see that the leading source region
has changed over this period from
Europe to Asia. A century ago, the
majority of Canada's immigrants
were headed to the Prairie provinces, but by 1996 (as the map
shows), the most important destinations were Canada's major metropolitan centres, especially Toronto,
Vancouver, and Montreal. Further
information on Canadian immigration is available from Citizenship and
Immigration Canada (**www.cic.gc.ca**)
and from the Metropolis Project,
an inter-university research group
on immigration (**http://canada.
metropolis.net**).   (*Sources:* Citizenship
and Immigration Canada, "Facts and
Figures 2000: Immigration Overview,"
available at **www.cic.gc.ca**; "Immigrant
Population by Place of Birth," Statistics
Canada, 1996 Census: Nation Tables,
available at **www.statcan.ca**.)

ceased to be European and became, by the century's end, predominantly Asian. In 12,000 years, then, Canada's immigration story has come full circle.

Of course, the full story of Canadian immigration lies buried beneath such statistics and generalizations. For many of us, the hopes and hardships, the memories of countries left behind, and the communities and cultures created in Canada form the real immigration experience. In places all across this country, we can see the indelible effects of that story. Contributions are evident from the Chinese workers brought in to build the railways; the Doukhobors who moved to Verigin in Saskatchewan from nineteenth-century Russia to flee religious persecution; the British gentlemen trying to plant apple orchards at Walkachin in pre–World War I British Columbia; the Czech and Yugoslav miners who, from the 1930s, extracted minerals from the mines of Flin Flon, Manitoba; the waves of post–World War II settlers from Europe who arrived at Pier 21 in Halifax, Nova Scotia, in the 1950s; the Chilean, Ugandan, and Vietnamese refugees who fled persecution in their own countries to settle in Toronto and Montreal in the 1970s; the Central Americans who sought refuge in the 1980s; and the latest wave of migrants from Hong Kong who have become a significant economic presence in Vancouver. It is impossible to sum up these experiences, but it is obvious that the resulting combined contribution has been to reshape this country. (Two examples of such experiences are provided in **Geography Matters 3.2—Canadian Immigration**.)

Of course, these processes of immigration and settlement are by no means unique to Canada: they are major themes of human history and have, to a greater or lesser extent, affected all parts of the globe. Recognizing that we share such common experiences with other countries enables us to understand other regions.

In some situations, migration does not involve a permanent change of residence. Temporary labour migration has long been an indispensable part of the world economic order and has at times been actively pursued by governments and companies alike. Individuals who migrate temporarily to take jobs in other countries are generally known as **guest workers** (although this is a somewhat incorrect term, since, strictly speaking, such migrants are not usually treated like "guests"). The temporary migration of Mexican and Caribbean farm labourers to Canada is a good example of this process (see **Geography Matters 3.3—Migrant Farm Workers in Canada** on pp. 129–130). Sending workers abroad is an important economic strategy for many peripheral and semiperipheral countries: it not only lessens local unemployment but also enables workers to send substantial amounts of money home to their families (called *remittances*). This arrangement helps to support the workers' families left behind in their home countries but it also continues the dominance of the core in global economic activities. Moreover, an economic downturn in the host country may result in a large decrease in remittances received by the home country, thus further aggravating that country's economic situation.

It is important to recognize the gender of temporary workers and the gender-based differences in the types of work performed. The Philippines, for example, has an Overseas Contract Worker (OCW) program that links foreign demand for workers to Philippine labour supply. The proportion of men and women OCWs is approximately equal, but the jobs they hold are gender biased. Men receive most of the higher-level positions, whereas women are largely confined to the service sector. Some interesting geographical variations exist as well. Although constituting a small percentage of the total number of women working abroad, a large proportion of the female OCWs who do have professional positions (such as doctors and nurses) work in the United States and Canada. More typical of Filipina OCW experience, however, are the patterns in Hong Kong, Singapore, and Japan. In Hong Kong and Singapore, Filipinas are almost exclusively employed as domestic servants; in Japan, most work in the so-called Entertainment Industry, a term often synonymous with prostitution. These women in many ways have been transformed from individuals to commodities—many are even chosen from catalogues. The OCW program has been criticized by feminist groups as well as human rights organizations. Many regard the OCW treatment of women as a contemporary form of slavery.

guest workers: individuals who migrate temporarily to take jobs in other countries

Canadian Immigration

It is impossible to convey a full impression of the myriad experiences of the immigrants to this country. However, we can see something of the measure of these experiences by taking as case studies the stories of two very different groups. Widely separated in time and circumstances, they illustrate the extraordinary range of backgrounds of Canada's immigrants and the resilience of the individuals and families.

The Petworth Emigration Committee, 1832–1837[18]

Our first example looks at an organized migration of people that occurred in the early part of the nineteenth century, when Canada was still part of the British Empire, and was part of a wider set of colonial policies that sought to encourage settlement overseas. Such policies argued that the increase of population in this way would lead not only to economic growth in the colonies but also to increased trade between Britain and its empire—both developments that would increase the value of the periphery to the core.

Surprising as it may at first seem, such early migrations to Canada are by no means forgotten today. They remain the focus of a small but active research community that consists of not just historians and geographers but also the many descendants of the original migrants interested in their own genealogy. Library and Archives Canada (LAC) now hosts a virtual exhibition called "Moving Here, Staying Here: The Canadian Immigrant Experience," which provides an introduction to Canada's migration history for the period 1800–1939 and to the documents, many of them now online, that facilitate individual research.[19] At a smaller scale, the Petworth Emigration Project investigates the history of one of the earliest organized efforts to send migrants to this country. We will now use this example to illustrate some of the experiences that surrounded early emigration to Canada.

Between 1832 and 1837, about 1,800 poor men, women, and children travelled from West Sussex in southern England to Upper Canada. They emigrated under the auspices of a body known as the Petworth Emigration Committee, one of a number of such bodies that existed in England at the time. The full costs of their passage were paid for by the Earl of Egremont, a wealthy landowner whose estates included Petworth House (see Figure 6.8). His reasons for helping such people, many of whom were paupers from his own estates, were not philanthropic. Rather, he (like many landowners of his day) thought that emigration would alleviate the pressure a growing population of poor farm labourers placed on local resources.

Once in Canada, the group of migrants sent by the Petworth Committee received further assistance from the colonial government. Most settled in southwest Ontario (particularly in Adelaide Township west of London and around Guelph), where they were given free or subsidized land on which to establish farms (**Figure 3.2.1**). From the letters these settlers wrote to their relatives back home in England, we are able to see how they coped with the experiences of migration and how many of these individuals subsequently prospered in their new surroundings.

The sea passage from Portsmouth to Quebec City took between five and a half and seven weeks. "When we came to the banks of Newfoundland," William Voice wrote to his sister in 1834, "we met with lumps of ice as large as your farm floating on the water on the 8th of May, and it was so cold we could not get on deck." Once docked in Quebec City, the dangers did not cease. In 1832, the city was gripped by cholera (see Figure 1.18) and immigrants were quarantined at Grosse Île before being allowed to continue their passage up the St. Lawrence. Describing this later to his father, James Rapson wrote that the disease "followed us all along the river, about a day behind us."

The trip from Quebec City to their destination in southwest Ontario could take another three or four weeks, because it involved negotiating the Lachine Rapids and a lengthy trip along wagon roads into the interior of southern Ontario. Once settled there, immigrants faced the arduous task of clearing the wild land that Edward Longley described in a letter in 1836 as "entirely covered with trees, from the huge spreading oak whose diameter is from four to five feet ... to the smallest sapling, all planted by the hand of nature and so thick that a squirrel may traverse thousands of acres without ever touching the ground."

However, for people who once earned 12 shillings a week as landless labourers, the backbreaking task of tree clearance was well worth the toil. John and Caroline Dearling wrote from Galt to her father in 1833 to tell him, "We have got 50 acres of land, at 3 dollars per acre; we have nothing to pay for 3 years. Our house will be

---

[18] This section is based on Wendy Cameron and Mary McDougall Maude, *Assisting Emigration to Upper Canada: The Petworth Project, 1832–1837*. Montreal and Kingston: McGill-Queen's University Press, 2000; and Wendy Cameron, Sheila Haines, and Mary McDougall Maude, *English Immigrant Voices: Labourers' Letters from Upper Canada in the 1830s*. Montreal and Kingston: McGill-Queen's University Press, 2000. From the latter, a highly informative volume of Petworth emigrants' letters, we include quotations from letters by William Voice (1834, p. 170), James Rapson (1832, p. 70), Edward Longley (1836, p. 203), John and Caroline Dearling (1833, p. 145; 1838, pp. 277 and 278), Harry Harwood (1834, p. 163), and Thomas Adsett (1832, p. 87). The Petworth Emigration Project website can be found at www.petworthemigrations.com.

[19] Library and Archives Canada, Moving Here, Staying Here: The Canadian Immigrant Experience, 2006 exhibition (www.collectionscanada.gc.ca/immigrants/index-e.html).

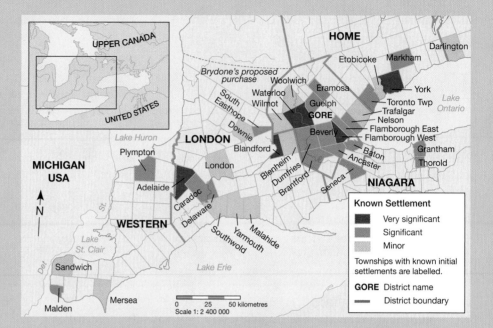

Figure 3.2.1 The lands settled by Petworth emigrants, 1832–1837

(*Source:* Wendy Cameron and Mary McDougall Maude, *Assisting Emigration to Upper Canada: The Petworth Project, 1832–1837.* Montreal and Kingston: McGill-Queen's University Press, 2000.)

done before long, then we are going to it." Five years later they wrote, "We have 3 acres rye, 3 of oats, 2 of peas, 1 acre of spring wheat, 1 acre of potatoes.... We have six hogs and I am hobbing [handrearing] a heifer calf. I have 34 chickens." An 1840 assessment for Waterloo Township recorded that by then the couple had 30 acres (12 hectares) cleared, 70 acres (almost 30 hectares) of wild land, two oxen, and three cows. By 1843, when John Dearling died, the farm was valued at 263 pounds sterling.

Other Petworth emigrants quickly found employment outside agriculture. For example, Harry Harwood wrote in 1834, "I have plenty of work at shoe-making, and can earn three shillings and my board a day." He relayed, concerning his three sons, that "Henry is working in a brick-yard at three pounds per month.... Alfred is in service with Mr Birch for six dollars per month.... Richard, I put apprentice to a blacksmith...."

Despite having to leave England and many of their relatives and friends behind, few emigrants would have disagreed with Thomas Adsett's general remark: "I can live better with working one day [in Canada], than in England in seven...." Certainly, Cameron and Maude conclude their recent study of this group by observing "that the bulk of Petworth immigrants were better off in Upper Canada than in England." Their success in southwestern Ontario was due not only to government assistance and the relatively easy access to land but also to their own readiness to embark on careers as farmers and craftspeople. "By contrast with more articulate middle-class immigrants, they integrated so successfully that their contribution to building the province has been largely ignored."[20]

---

[20] Wendy Cameron and Mary McDougall Maude, *Assisting Emigration to Upper Canada: The Petworth Project, 1832–1837.* Montreal and Kingston: McGill-Queen's University Press, 2000, pp. 194, 195.

Somali Refugees in Toronto, 1991–2005

Our second case study concerns a very different group of immigrants to Canada: Somali refugees. Settling in Toronto since 1991, this group has already been the focus of a number of studies by geographers and other researchers.[21]

Since the 1991 *coup d'état* that ousted its leader, General Mohamed Siad Barre, Somalia has been torn apart by civil war. Many hundreds of thousands of Somalis have been forced to leave their country for refugee camps in neighbouring countries. By 1996, for example, approximately 150,000 Somali refugees were living in Kenya where, according to Jennifer Hyndman, a geographer at York University who has studied conditions in these camps, refugees were housed in bleak, isolated camps in semi-arid border regions.[22]

Thousands of other Somalis have fled overseas—many to Canada, where they have settled mainly in Toronto. Here, they have formed a rapidly developing Somali community (**Figure 3.2.2**). According to census data, there were more than 17,000 Somalis in Toronto in 1996, but some scholars estimate that the total was between 35,000 and 40,000 in that year. By 1999, a spokesperson for the Somali Immigrant Aid Organization estimated the size of the Somali community

---

[21] Somali immigrants also self-report their settlement experience on a website funded by Canada's Youth Employment Strategy and produced by the Somali Immigrant Aid Organization. See **http://epe.lac-bac .gc.ca/100/205/301/ic/cdc/somalia/intro.html**.

[22] Jennifer Hyndman, *Managing Displacement: Refugees and the Politics of Humanitarianism.* Minneapolis: University of Minnesota Press, 2000. Hyndman reports that the bleak conditions of these camps are, in fact, part of a deliberate U.N. High Commission for Refugees policy of "humane deterrence," an approach that is designed to reduce refugee flows from Somalia by showing potential migrants how unattractive life as a refugee will be (see pp. 23–24).

Figure 3.2.2 Toronto's Somali community

that recent European immigrants have fared much better in Toronto than recent non-white immigrants from every other continent.[26]

Work based on qualitative methods and interview techniques significantly deepens the picture outlined by statistics. For example, a case study based on interviews concerning the settlement experiences of 21 Somali refugee women who came to Toronto between 1990 and 1997 allows us to clearly see how the refugees themselves view the difficulties they have faced.[27] The study shows that possessing refugee status is itself the first problem because refugees are denied the full rights accorded Canadians. For example, refugees must pay twice as much in college or university tuition fees, are eligible for only temporary work permits, are not eligible for bank loans, are not eligible for Canadian travel documents, and are unable to sponsor family members to immigrate to Canada. In view of these restrictions, it is hardly surprising that one of those interviewed remarked:

> Before we came to this country, we used to work and manage our lives like any other human beings. Now, we are not allowed to work, to struggle for the well being of our children, to get access to education, and to get loans. Why did they welcome us to their country with open arms only to make life more miserable for us?

A second concern voiced by the women interviewed is about the education of their children. Many do not speak English. As one women says, "Even if the child has a good educational background, with a strong base in math and other subjects, still he wouldn't be able to follow along in class because of the language. Language is the key factor...." Another mother noted student and teacher biases: "When I send my little girl to school wearing our Islamic dress, teachers and students make negative comments about her dress, they are showing intolerance."

A third difficulty concerns access to affordable housing in Toronto. There is a six- to eight-year waiting list for subsidized housing, and with recent declines in social assistance payments in Ontario, the women interviewed said that they spent as much as 80 percent of their monthly income on housing. A study by Ransford Danso reports that access to affordable housing was listed as a significant obstacle to settlement by 16 percent of the

in the Greater Toronto Area at approximately 75,000. (If this estimate is correct, it is another illustration of the problems of inaccurate census enumeration.)

Geographers Robert Murdie and Carlos Teixeira from York University, describing this community, have made the following observations:

> When they first arrived in Toronto in the late 1980s, Somalis tended to concentrate in the Dixon Road and Islington Avenue area, also known as Little Somalia. There, large households, together with a tendency to concentrate in order to create a sense of security, have led to overcrowding in apartments that has contributed to cultural clashes and harassment by building managers and property owners.[23]

Certainly, the immigration experience of Somali refugees in Toronto has been a very challenging one, and a number of recent studies have confirmed Opoku-Dapaah's early assessment that they are among the most disadvantaged ethnic minorities in Canada.[24] For example, census analysis conducted by Michael Ornstein of York University's Institute for Social Research in 2000 concluded that more than 62 percent of Somali families in Toronto lived below the poverty line in 1996 and that unemployment rates for people of black, Caribbean, and African origins was 19 percent, or twice the average rate for the city as a whole in that year.[25] A 2003 study of multicultural Toronto, called *The World in a City*, only confirms this picture. In Chapter 4, an economic examination by geographers Valerie Preston, Lucio Lo, and Shuguang Wang using income tax information shows

[23] Robert A. Murdie and Carlos Teixeira, "Towards a Comfortable Neighbourhood and Appropriate Housing: Immigrant Experiences in Toronto." In Paul Anisef and Michael Lanphier (eds.), *The World in a City*. Toronto: University of Toronto Press, 2003, p. 157.

[24] E. Opoku-Dapaah, *Somali Refugees in Toronto: A Profile*. Toronto: York Lanes Press, 1995.

[25] Quoted in Myer Siemiatycki, Tim Rees, Roxanna Ng, and Khan Rahi, "Integrating Community Diversity in Toronto: On Whose Terms?" In Paul Anisef and Michael Lanphier (eds.), *The World in a City*. Toronto: University of Toronto Press, 2003, pp. 418–419.

[26] Valerie Preston, Lucio Lo, and Shuguang Wang, "Immigrants' Economic Status in Toronto: Stories of Triumph and Disappointment." In Paul Anisef and Michael Lanphier (eds.), *The World in a City*. Toronto: University of Toronto Press, 2003, pp. 192–262.

[27] Neita Kay Israelite, Arlene Herman, Faduma Ahmed Alim, Hawa Abdullah Mohamed, and Yasmin Khan, *Settlement Experiences of Somali Refugee Women in Toronto*. Paper presented at the Seventh International Congress of Somali Studies, York University, Toronto, 10 July 1999, available online at www.ceris.metropolis.net/oldvl/other/israelite2.html.

115 Somali and Ethiopian refugees he interviewed in Toronto.[28]

Danso's respondents list two other significant obstacles to settlement. The most important problem (mentioned by 22 percent of those interviewed) was in getting employment. Employers' covert racism, dislike of dealing with those on temporary work permits, and failure to recognize foreign credentials are all cited as impediments that stand in the way of Somali refugee employment. "What is so unique about this 'Canadian experience' every employer is always asking for?" asks one respondent in evident frustration. Another, an individual with a doctoral degree who had been in Toronto for three months, remarked that he was "already facing obstacles finding suitable employment. I am doing odd jobs. It is very difficult to overcome the hidden barriers in Canadian society." When interviewed, he was working as an airport baggage handler.

Most troubling of all is the evidence of discrimination encountered by Somali refugees. Overall, 17 percent of Danso's respondents listed racism as a significant obstacle to settlement, but it is likely that this figure underestimates the problem; the effects of racism cross almost every aspect of the experience in Toronto and so compound the effects of the other difficulties listed above. For example, access to affordable housing is made even more difficult by landlord bias against Somalis. One Somali refugee woman reported, "Sometimes you go to rent an apartment that through the telephone you were assured to be vacant. When they see that you are a Somali, you are told that it has been rented."

We have already seen that Somalis feel a bias against them that affects their employment—what Danso calls a subtle or "courteous" racism. A further illustration is provided by his observation that "many Somalis in Toronto still feel strongly that their community is unfairly targeted by the police and the media."[29]

Danso has argued that for any immigrant group, the movement from "there" to "here" inevitably juxtaposes two kinds of "places" and "identities." In view of what we have seen here, it is hardly surprising that the Somali experience has caused these people to develop a very different approach toward the construction of place and identity from that adopted by many other immigrant groups. Somalis who have sought to participate in the wider Canadian society have generally been rebuffed by the social discrimination and economic inequality that confront them, and their community has therefore had to look inward for its own validation and support. This approach, as one scholar has remarked, "allows them to maintain the identities they established in their homelands rather than accept the racialized identities available to them in Canada."[30]

Recent reports show little overall economic progress. According to a 2008 Statistics Canada study, recent immigrants from African countries have the toughest challenges getting into the Canadian workforce when compared with other immigrant groups. On the basis of 2006 data, the report noted an unemployment rate of 20.8 percent among the 70,000 African immigrants aged between 25 and 54 who had arrived in this country between 2001 and 2006—a rate over four times higher than that found for the Canadian-born population, and twice that for immigrants from either Latin America or Asia (the rate was 8.4 percent for immigrants from Europe).[31]

In commenting on these statistics in an interview conducted in February 2008, Ahmed Hussein, president of the Canadian Somali Association, observed that he was disappointed, but not surprised by the report's findings. He observed that many Somalis experienced a "hard landing" in this country because, finding themselves refugees, they were often unprepared (in terms of language ability or job training, for example) for the conditions found in the country that granted them asylum. Furthermore, he noted, as part of a very recently formed community in this country, Somali immigrants to cities such as Toronto lacked a support network where they might find help—with accommodation, employment, and language skills. "It's a recent community that doesn't have the community support and individual support that might be available for other recent immigrants," he said.[32]

[28] Ransford Danso, "From 'There' to 'Here': An Investigation of the Initial Settlement Experiences of Ethiopian and Somali Refugees in Toronto." In Alan Nash (ed.), *Geography and Refugees,* a special issue of *GeoJournal* 56(1), 2002, pp. 3–14.

[29] Ibid., p. 9. On this point, see also Myer Siemiatycki, Tim Rees, Roxanna Ng, and Khan Rahi, "Integrating Community Diversity in Toronto: On Whose Terms?" In Paul Anisef and Michael Lanphier (eds.), *The World in a City.* Toronto: University of Toronto Press, 2003, p. 420.

[30] A.M. Kusow, *Migration and Identity Processes among Somali Immigrants in Canada.* Unpublished PhD thesis. Wayne State University, Detroit, 1998; quoted in Neita Kay Israelite, Arlene Herman, Faduma Ahmed Alim, Hawa Abdullah Mohamed, and Yasmin Khan, *Settlement Experiences of Somali Refugee Women in Toronto.* Paper presented at the Seventh International Congress of Somali Studies, York University, Toronto, 10 July 1999, available online at www.ceris.metropolis.net/oldvl/other/israelite2.html.

[31] Statistics Canada, "Study: The 2006 Canadian Immigrant Labour Market: Analysis by Region or Country of Birth." *The Daily,* 13 February 2008, pp. 5–7, www.statcan.gc.ca/daily-quotidien/080213/dq080213b-eng.htm. The statistics in this report should be studied in conjunction with the fine series of metropolitan maps (showing immigrant arrivals between 2001 and 2006 as a percentage of population in 2006) contained in Robert Murdie, "Diversity and Concentration in Canadian Immigration: Trends in Toronto, Montreal and Vancouver, 1971–2006." University of Toronto, Cities Centre, *Research Bulletin* 42, March 2008, www.NeighbourhoodChange.ca.

[32] Charles Lewis, "African Immigrants Face Tough Challenges in Canada, Says Report." *Montreal Gazette,* 13 February 2008.

Somewhat more optimistically, the Statistics Canada data show that immigrants from Africa who had been in Canada in 2006 for longer than 10 years have a much lower rate of unemployment (7.6 percent) than those more recently arrived. Known as the "period of residence" effect, and a general result of sufficient time to acquire the necessary language and employment skills, this phenomenon holds the promise of a brighter economic future for those Somalis who have just immigrated to Canada.

Perhaps the last word should be reserved for one Grade 12 student who was born in Somalia but now lives in an area of apartment housing on the corner of Dixon Road and Kipling Avenue. Interviewed in September 2007, she compared her former homeland, where the constant threat of being caught in crossfire made it impossible to wander outside, with her current neighbourhood. "Nobody fights here. It's peaceful," she remarked.[33]

[33] Michele Henry, "4 City Blocks." *Toronto Star*, 6 September 2007, L10.

International Forced Migration

The African slave trade is a classic example of international forced migration. This migration stream was integral to European economic expansion from the seventeenth through the nineteenth century. The huge fortunes made in the sugar trade, for example, were earned on the backs of African slaves working the sugar plantations of Brazil, Guyana, and the Caribbean. **Figure 3.13** shows those regions of the world to which slaves from Africa were transported from the seventeenth to the nineteenth century. Other prominent examples of international forced migration include the deportation of Armenians out of Eastern Anatolia to other parts of the Ottoman Empire during World War I and the expulsion of Jews from Germany preceding World War II. At the end of that war in 1945, 12 million people of more than 20 nationalities found themselves scattered across Europe as displaced persons. An additional 14 million ethnic Germans fled or were deported from Eastern Europe to what would become West Germany. During the first Arab-Israeli War of 1948, almost one million Palestinian Arabs fled

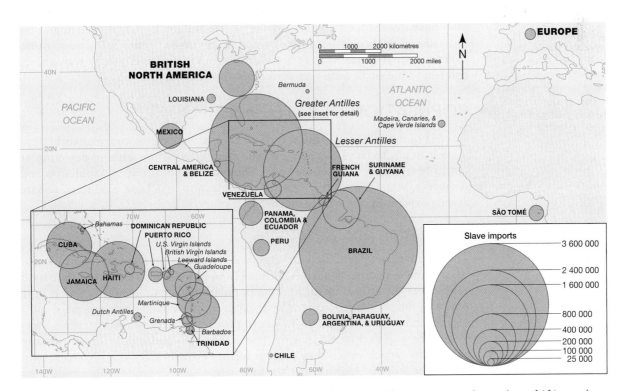

Figure 3.13   African slave trade, seventeenth through nineteenth century   This map portrays the numbers of Africans who were carried off into slavery to Europe and various regions in the New World, mainly Brazil (3,647,000 slaves), the Greater Antilles (2,421,000), and the Lesser Antilles (1,619,000). It should also be noted that a substantial number of slaves died during the transatlantic crossing.   (*Source:* Philip D. Curtin, *The Atlantic Slave Trade*, ©1969. Reprinted by permission of The University of Wisconsin Press.)

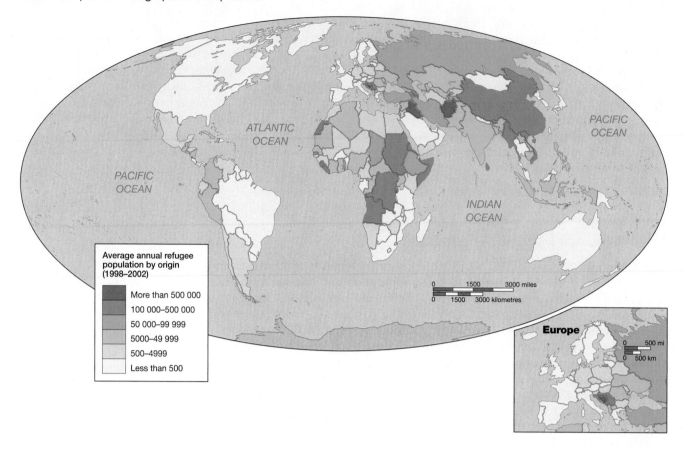

Figure 3.14 Refugee-sending countries, 1998–2002 War is certainly the most compelling factor in forcing refugee migration. Shown are the sending countries, those whose internal situations propelled people to leave. What is perhaps most distressing about this graphic is that refugee populations have increased over the last decade almost exclusively in the periphery. (*Source:* www.unhcr.org/4125cb8c4.html.)

from the territory of the new state of Israel. Their second- and third-generation descendants still live in refugee camps in surrounding countries, where high birth rates have swelled their numbers to almost five million. Clearly, forced migration is a sad reality throughout history—and it continues: **Figure 3.14** shows those countries where residents have been forced from their homelands by war, abuse, and fear in the single four-year period between 1998 and 2002.

POPULATION DEBATES AND POLICIES

One big question occupies the agenda of population experts studying world population trends today: How many people can Earth sustain without depleting or critically straining its resource base? The relationship between population and resources, which lies at the heart of this question, has been a point of debate among experts since the early nineteenth century.

Population and Resources

The debate about population and resources originated in the work of an English cleric named Thomas Robert Malthus (1766–1834), who theorized that food supply was the critical factor limiting population growth. He insisted that "the power of the population" (or, as he also put it, "the passion between the sexes") "is indefinitely greater than the power of the earth to produce subsistence." Inevitably, the population would grow faster than the food supply and eventually exhaust it—which would then prevent further growth. Fifty years later, Darwin saw in the work of Malthus the key to how evolution worked—the struggle for existence. Geographers note that Malthus used data from the work of Alexander von Humboldt (see Chapter 1) to illustrate his case.

We must see the work of Malthus in the historical context within which it was written. Technological innovations in English agriculture and industry were

Migrant Farm Workers in Canada

Migrant labourers, or "guest workers" as they are sometimes called, have played an important part in the economy of many countries. For example, Jonathan Crush, a geographer at Queen's University in Kingston, has written extensively about how South Africa's gold mines have depended on cheap migrant labour from neighbouring countries. Yet the host countries are not the only beneficiaries of this process, as the example of the Philippines shows. Filipino emigrants working in other countries send a substantial amount of money every year back to the Philippines. Indeed, it is estimated that approximately 15 percent of the entire Philippine population are dependent on overseas sources of income.[34] Nevertheless, the reliance of one country on migrant labour recruited from another is a controversial policy as the migrants are often exploited and their home countries drained of labour and talent.

In view of such controversy, it is perhaps surprising to learn that Canada has long had a migrant labour program, albeit a small and relatively unpublicized one. The program, known as the Seasonal Agricultural Workers Program (SAWP), began in 1966 when 264 men were recruited from Jamaica to work temporarily in Canada. Since then, the number of recruits has grown to 20,000 men and women from the Caribbean and Mexico who spend from six weeks to eight months working on one of 1,600 farms across Canada (**Figure 3.3.1**).

The program certainly has a number of benefits. First, the program helps Canadian farmers to remain competitive as it allows them to pay only minimum wage for physically demanding jobs that many Canadians no longer are willing to perform. Second, the localities in Canada where SAWP workers temporarily reside benefit from their presence. One Simcoe, Ontario, farmer involved in the program estimates that the farm output generated by every migrant labourer he employs supports the jobs of three Canadians in related packing and transport activities. He estimates that SAWP migrants spend two-thirds of their income in the area—a "$32 million bounty each year for local shopkeepers, restaurateurs and providers of telephone, banking and other services." A Simcoe discount store manager told researchers from the University of Guelph that the period when SAWP migrants are making purchases before they return home is "literally like Christmas in September."

Third, many of the SAWP workers state that the program benefits them economically. Despite the fact that migrant farm workers usually earn only minimum wage in Canada, the economic disparity between the economies of Canada and Mexico or the Caribbean makes the

Figure 3.3.1 Migrant workers in Ontario

migrant labour program financially worthwhile for them. As an example, consider the remarks of Irena Gonzalez, a migrant farm worker who has come from Mexico to pick tomatoes for four months in Ontario every year since 1989.[35]

In Mexico, we're paid by the day, thirty pesos ($6 to $7 a day). But we have to fill fifteen or twenty pails. The time it takes depends on how fast you move your hands. But in Canada, we're paid by the hour, $7 an hour, and you can work as many hours as you want. If we work eight hours, which is what the contract says, we get $56, which is seven times as much as we get in Mexico.

Not all commentators agree that the program is so beneficial, and some have pointed to several major disadvantages with Canada's guest worker program. First, the dependence on low-wage employment may harm Canadian farmers in the long run by making the industry less efficient and harm Canadian farm workers by depressing the average wages in the agricultural sector.

Second, migrants often do not speak up when they are not treated properly for fear of losing their contract, which is governed by strict terms of employment. Under the SAWP, workers do not have the rights of Canadian citizens and are unable to gain immigrant status in Canada. Assigned a specific employer (who provides accommodation), they can only change jobs if their embassy and both the original and the new employers agree. Although they pay employment insurance in Canada (amounting to $3.4 million per year), workers cannot collect benefits because unemployed SAWP workers are usually repatriated within 24 hours. Workers in the SAWP are not covered by Ontario's health and safety legislation, and they do not have the right to bargain collectively. Professor

---

[34] R.T. Jackson, "The Cheque's in the Mail: The Distribution of Dependence on Overseas Sources of Income in the Philippines." *Singapore Journal of Tropical Geography* 11, 1990, pp. 76–86.

[35] Deborah Barndt, *Tangled Routes: Women, Work and Globalization on the Tomato Trail*. Aurora, ON Garamond Press, 2002, p. 162.

Kerry Preibisch, a University of Guelph sociologist who has examined the program, calls these rules "extra-economic coercions" that make workers dependent on the subjective goodwill of their employers.

Complaints filed at the Simcoe migrant workers' support centre illustrate that such concerns are justified: substandard accommodations, unhealthy conditions, and unfair wage differences between SAWP workers and Canadian workers are frequent complaints; others include a man who almost lost a leg to an infection he was told to ignore; workers forced to escape their lodgings at night and walk an hour to phone home; supervisors berating employees; and so on. Given these concerns, the fact that many continue to return to Canada year after year cannot be seen as a complete vindication of the program: SAWP workers are simply taking the best of a series of poor options available to them, options that diminish year by year as globalization and trade liberalization continue to erode agricultural wages both in this country and abroad.

eliminating traditional forms of employment faster than new ones could be created. This led to a widespread belief among wealthy members of English society that a surplus of unnecessary workers existed in the population. The displaced and impoverished farmworkers became a heavy burden on charity, and the so-called Poor Laws were introduced to control begging and regulate public behaviour. After centuries of authorities trying to "people" lands and increasing the population so as to have more agricultural labour available, a new perspective was forming: one that saw population as a potential problem that needed to be carefully managed.

Population, Resources, and the Environment

The debate about the relationship between population and resources continues to this day, with the term *resources* now being conceived more broadly to include food, water, land, energy, minerals, etc. Neo-Malthusians—people today who share Malthus's perspective—predict a population doomsday: they believe that growing human populations the world over, with their potential to exhaust Earth's resources, pose the most dangerous threat to the environment. Although they point out that the people of core countries consume the vast majority of resources, they and others argue that only strict demographic control everywhere, even if it requires severely coercive tactics, will solve the problem.

A more moderate approach argues that people's behaviours and governmental policies are much more important factors affecting the condition of the environment and the status of natural resources than population size. Proponents of this approach reject casting the population issue as a biological one in which an ever-growing population will inevitably create ecological catastrophe. They also reject framing it as an economic issue in which technological innovation and the sensitivities of the market will regulate population increases before a catastrophe can occur. Rather, they see the issue as a political one—one that governments have tended to avoid dealing with because they lack the will to redistribute wealth or the resources to reduce poverty, a condition strongly correlated with high fertility. Conversely, some analysts have recently argued that ecological problems may exacerbate or even cause political crises. Much of the work of Canadian political scientist Thomas Homer-Dixon has examined the background to crises in, for example, Chiapas (Mexico) and Rwanda in terms of ecological crises of food and human security.

Population Policies and Programs

Contemporary concerns about population—especially whether too many people exist for Earth to sustain—have led to the development of international and national policies and programs. A *population policy* is an official government policy designed to affect any or all of several objectives, including the size, composition, and distribution of population. The implementation of a population policy takes the form of a *population program*. Whereas a policy identifies goals and objectives, a program is an instrument for meeting those goals and objectives.

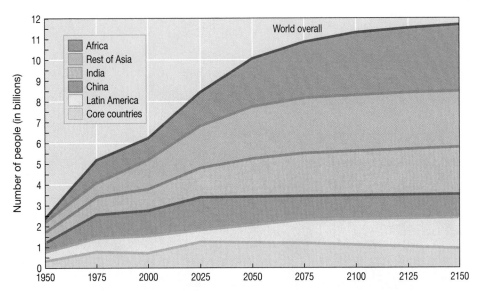

Figure 3.15   World population projection by region   In this projection, population continues to expand in the periphery, though in some regions more than in others. Africa is projected to experience the greatest growth, followed by Asia (not including China or India), where growth is expected to level off by 2150. Less dramatic growth is expected to occur in Latin America, while in the core, population numbers remain constant or drop slightly. Though the total number of people in the world will be dramatically greater by 2150, the forecast indicates a levelling off of world population.   (Printed with permission from the Continuum International Publishing Company. I. Hauchler and P. Kennedy [eds.] © 1994.)

Most of the international population policies of the last three decades have been directed at reducing the number of births worldwide through family-planning programs. The desire to limit fertility rates is a response to concerns about rapidly increasing global population—an increase that is being experienced overwhelmingly in the periphery and semiperiphery. Accompanying this situation of imbalanced population growth between the core and the periphery are gross social and economic inequalities as well as overall environmental degradation and destruction.

Figure 3.15 provides a picture of the recent history and a reasonable projection of the future of world population growth by region. The difference between the core and the periphery is dramatically illustrated. Also striking is the acceleration of growth. In 1999, for example, the world contained 6 billion people, but by 2011, it contained 7 billion people (see also Table 3.1). In comparison, over the course of the entire nineteenth century, fewer than one billion people were added to the population. **Figure 3.16** shows a projection of world population in the year 2020.

The geography of projected population growth is noteworthy. Over the next century, population growth is predicted to occur almost exclusively in Africa, Asia, and Latin America, whereas Europe and North America will experience very low and in some cases zero population growth (as Figure 3.15 shows).

United Nations conferences were held in Bucharest (1974) and Mexico City (1984) to develop population policy at the global level, but the core and the periphery found it difficult to arrive at an agreement. The most recent meeting was held in Cairo in 1994 as the International Conference on Population and Development, the new name reflecting the realization that those two factors must be seen in conjunction. The Cairo conference focused on the fact that birth rates in almost every country on Earth were dropping—in many cases significantly so. Recognizing that a levelling off of the population was possible in the foreseeable future, conference participants from both the core and the periphery were in agreement that efforts to bring down the growth rates must continue so that human numbers will peak sooner rather than later. The policy that emerged from the Cairo conference called for governments not simply to make family-planning programs available to all but also to take deliberate steps to reduce poverty and disease; improve educational opportunities, especially for girls and women; and work toward environmentally sustainable development (**Figure 3.17**).

The goals established at the Cairo meeting have been embraced and extended in the most recent international population conference, which was held at the United Nations in September 2000 as part of the "U.N. Millennium

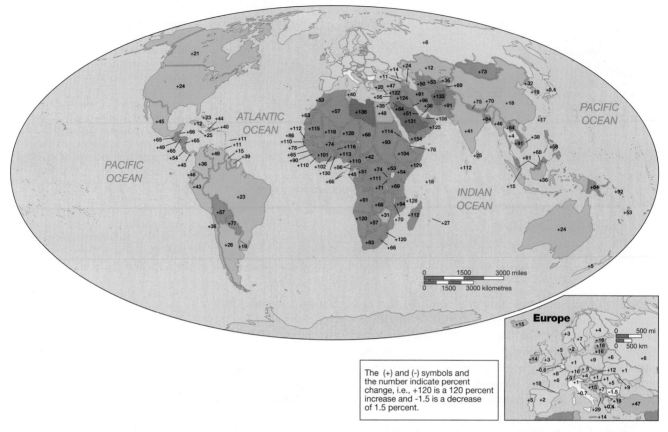

Figure 3.16 World population, 2020 This map provides a sense of how much the populations of various countries are expected to change by the year 2020. Although the populations of nearly all countries are expected to increase, it is clear that some populations will grow far more dramatically than others. Notice the substantial growth expected in Saudi Arabia and Afghanistan in contrast to the United States and Europe, where little if any population growth will occur. Italy, for example, is expected to lose population, whereas the Netherlands will grow by only 5 percent.

Figure 3.17 International Conference on Population and Development, 1994 The conference in Cairo had the important effect of insisting on the link between level of development and population growth. At the conference, much discussion ensued about improving the status of women to help control population. However, core and peripheral countries often disagreed about the most appropriate means to halt the present trend of global population expansion.

Summit Conference." At that summit, the "Millennium Declaration" adopted by 189 nations made a commitment to achieve eight key "Millennium Development Goals" by 2015. These goals are as follows:

1. Eradicate extreme poverty and hunger.
2. Achieve universal primary education.
3. Promote gender equality and empower women.

4. Reduce child poverty.
5. Improve maternal health.
6. Combat HIV/AIDS, malaria, and other diseases.
7. Ensure environmental sustainability.
8. Develop a Global Partnership for Development.[36]

As these goals suggest, the issues of population, economy, human rights, and environment all interrelate, and if action is required on one issue (such as population policy), it must inevitably involve progress on almost all of the other goals if change is to be truly effective, sustainable, and fair. To that end, in 2001 the member nations of the United Nations charged the Secretary-General to report annually on the progress made toward the achievement of the Millennium Development Goals. At a Millennium Development Goals Summit in New York in 2010, the United Nations conceded that progress has been slow and that several goals will not be reached in many countries; nonetheless, the international community reaffirmed their commitment to strive toward achieving these goals by 2015. Regardless of whether the goals will be met or not, one beneficial outcome of the campaign is that debates on overpopulation are finally placed in the larger contexts of poverty, education, economics, ecology, and women's rights.

Demographers and policy-makers take care to remind us that controlling fertility is not exclusively a female issue. However, they also stress that a close relationship exists between women's status and fertility. Women who have access to education and employment tend to have fewer children because they have less of a need for the economic security and social recognition that children are thought to provide. In Botswana, for instance, women with no formal education have, on average, 5.9 children, whereas those with four to six years of school have just 3.1 children. In Senegal, women with no education give birth to an average of 7 children. In contrast, the average number of children born to a woman with 10 years of education drops to 3.6. The numbers are comparable for Asia and South America.

More equality between men and women inside and outside the household is also believed to have a significant impact on reducing fertility. Enabling voluntary constraints that give both men and women a choice, and educating them about the implications of such choices, appears to be an especially successful program for small islands—such as Bali, Barbados, and Mauritius—with historically high population growth rates. In Mauritius, in just 24 years (between 1962 and 1986), the introduction of voluntary constraints lowered the total fertility rate from 5.8 to 1.9. It is hardly any wonder, then, that the 1994 population conference in Cairo placed such a clear and well-received emphasis on (1) improving the rights, opportunities, and economic status of girls and women as the most effective way of slowing down global population growth, and (2) rejecting coercive measures, including government sterilization quotas, that force people to violate their personal moral codes.

When trying to improve women's status relative to men's, it is necessary to take a closer look at a particularly grim issue: why is there an excess of male children in parts of the periphery? Sadly, many cultures value boys more highly than girls and parents may take more or less covert measures to ensure that more boys are born and survive infancy—particularly so when the number of children is limited by authorities, as in China. In 2000, the official Chinese census reported 116.9 boys born for every 100 girls, but in some regions, the ratio is as high as 135 to 100. It is estimated that approximately 100 million more females worldwide would be alive today were it not for a preference for male children, which results in prenatal choices to abort females, biased health care, unequal nutritional provision, and female infanticide.

---

[36] United Nations Development Program, "About the Millennium Development Goals," www.undp.org/mdg/basics.shtml.

When reading about the success of the Chinese One-Child Policy in reducing population growth, we thus need to keep in mind that this reduction is gender-biased—and that the resulting gender imbalances have long-term social and economic consequences: by 2020, as many as 40 million Chinese bachelors will be unable to find wives, have children, and provide a family home for their aging parents who depend on their sons in old age.

In summary, success at slowing population growth in the periphery appears to be very much tied to enhancing the possibility for a good quality of life and empowering people, especially women, to make informed choices. But a better quality of life may require altering—even reducing—the consumption practices of populations in the core to make more resources available to populations in the periphery (see the discussion of the Ecological Footprint in Chapter 4).

Population, Health, and the Environment

medical geography: a subdiscipline of geography that studies the interconnections between population, health, and the environment

The study of the interconnections between population, health, and the environment is the subject of **medical geography**. This broad area of research has traditionally been made up of two quite distinct approaches (the study of the cause and spread of disease and the study of the provision and consumption of health care), to which modern geographical work adds two more (the study of the social construction of health and the study of the effects of environmental change).

The Study of the Cause and Spread of Disease By mapping patterns of disease, geographical analysis has been able to pinpoint possible causes of illness. The most celebrated early example is the work of Dr. John Snow. In the 1850s, he examined the geographical pattern of cholera cases in London, England, and showed that they were clustered around a water pump contaminated by sewage. His findings disproved the *miasmic theory*, which claimed that disease was the result of breathing foul air that had been in contact with putrefied bodies and decaying vegetation. One of the earliest works of medical geography in Canada, *The Medical Topography of Upper Canada,* a work written by John Douglas in 1819, claimed that disease in Ontario was the result of such miasmas, and such a view was prevalent across nineteenth-century Canada (**Figure 3.18**).

epidemiological transition: a theory stating that the prevailing forms of illness changed from infectious to degenerative types as the demographic transition occurred

The connection between disease incidence and geographical patterns continues to be much explored by geographers. The focus is now on the ecology of diseases, their ecological relations with their agents of transmission, known as *vectors* (which have their own environmental constraints), and the environments in which both disease and vector interact with human populations.

These connections have many implications. The importance of these associations from a broader environmental perspective will be considered in Chapter 4. Here, let us briefly note their importance from the perspective of the world-system approach we are using in this book: when trying to explain the differences between the health experiences of the core and the periphery, medical geographers use the epidemiological transition model (**Figure 3.19**).

Figure 3.18 Nineteenth-century attitudes toward disease This magazine illustration shows that miasmic theory thought diseases to be caused by foul or malodorous air (*miasma* is Greek for "pollution," while Italian *malaria* literally means "bad air"). Modern medicine, however, stresses the roles of bacteria and viruses in causing contagious diseases.

Humans probably first experienced many infectious and parasitic diseases following the domestication of animals, such as pigs, sheep, and goats, approximately 10,000 years ago. Such illnesses as influenza and small pox are, in this sense, a by-product of the first agricultural revolution. **Epidemiological transition** is the theory stating that the prevailing forms of illness changed from infectious to degenerative types as the demographic transition occurred. During the first phases of that transition, it is argued that high death rates are mainly caused by very high rates of infectious and parasitic diseases. This contrasts with the situation after the transition when, according to this theory, mortality is mainly the result of degenerative diseases caused by aging, changing lifestyles, and environmental toxicity. It will be part of the periphery's challenge to see if it can pass through the demographic transition without bringing on itself these so-called diseases of modernization.

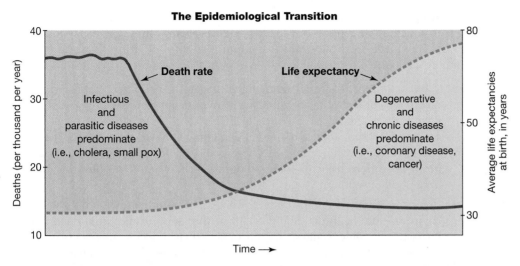

The Epidemiological Transition

Figure 3.19 The epidemiological transition As societies move through the demographic transition, the prevailing form of illnesses changes from infectious and parasitic diseases to the degenerative diseases caused by modernization and urban life: those of aging, changing lifestyle, and toxic substances in the environment. (*Sources:* Diagram based on a written description in Dhruva Nagnur and Michael Nagrodski, "Epidemiologic Transition in the Context of Demographic Change: The Evolution of Canadian Mortality Patterns." In Frank Trovato and Carl F. Grindstaff [eds.], *Perspectives on Canada's Population: An Introduction to Concepts and Issues.* Toronto: Oxford University Press, 1994, pp. 118–135.)

The connection between disease incidence and spatial pattern is also explored by those medical geographers who examine the diffusion of diseases. We have already seen examples in Chapter 1 of cholera diffusion in nineteenth-century North America and the global spread of the HIV-1 virus in the late twentieth century. A contemporary example is the work of Professor Tinline of Queen's University in Kingston, Ontario. Using advanced diffusion theory, combined with GIS techniques, he has been able to develop computer models that predict the spread of rabies outbreaks in Ontario, thereby aiding the provincial government's attempts to control such outbreaks. Other diseases such as West Nile virus and Lyme disease that have been spreading northward into Canada recently are also being investigated by geographers.

The Study of the Provision and Consumption of Health Care The examination of the locations of hospitals, physicians, clinics, and nurses across Canada at a variety of scales of analysis has enabled Canadian medical geographers, such as Alun Joseph and Mark Rosenberg, to show the considerable spatial discrepancies in health care provision that exist across this country. Simply put, urban areas have a better provision of health care than do rural areas, and richer urban areas have a better provision of services than do poorer urban areas. These discrepancies have raised questions about the social justice of such spatial inequalities and prompted analyses of their ultimate causes. They also prompted further research into the provision of health care for certain groups, such as single parents, people with disabilities, and Aboriginal communities, who, because of their disadvantaged position in society, now find themselves further marginalized by where they live. These types of discrepancies also exist at a world scale. For example, the variation in the global distribution of doctors indicates the degree to which inequalities exist between the core and the periphery of the world-system.

The Study of the Social Construction of Health *Health care* and *medical care* are not the same. Nor are they objective or value-free concepts. In fact, ideas of good health and the nature of illnesses are defined by our social norms. Our medical traditions are an outcome of our views about nature and science. For these reasons, the forces of industrialization and consumption that are embedded in both the world-system and demographic transition models have fundamentally altered what we consider to be "good health" and our view of how to achieve it.

Environmental Change   An issue of great current concern is the effect of global environmental change on our health and well-being. In a recent paper on this topic published in the journal *Canadian Geographer,* John Eyles and Susan Elliott highlighted the following three aspects as important:[37]

- *Climate change.* If global warming continues as predicted, a wide range of direct and indirect effects will result. Government estimates suggest that annual heat-related deaths could rise from 240 to 1,140 in Montreal, from 230 to 1,220 in Toronto, and from 80 to 500 in Ottawa. Respiratory-related disorders and increases in waterborne infections could result. It has been suggested that hotter conditions have allowed pathogens, such as the West Nile virus, to gain a foothold in southern Ontario, Manitoba, and Quebec (**Figure 3.20**).

- *Pollution.* Eyles and Elliott stated that air pollution is arguably the major environmental health issue in Canada at this time. Studies in Hamilton, Ontario, for example, suggest that particulate matter in the air results in about 70 cases of premature deaths per year and 300 additional hospital admissions.

- *Psychosocial effects.* We must not overlook the qualitative aspects of environmental change. Our fear of change, the context in which change occurs, and its impacts on our wider community all affect how we are able to deal with environmental changes and the extent to which they will affect our sense of well-being.

Examples from many other parts of Canada can be cited (especially in Arctic Canada where, as Chapter 4 shows, global warming threatens Inuit livelihood). Whatever the example, however, the interconnectedness of the environment means we are *all* affected.

The interrelations between climate change, population, and health are profound, and the growing volume of research being conducted on their interconnections illustrates how important it is to have a basic understanding of the issues involved (see **Human Geography and Climate Change 3.4—Population and Health**).

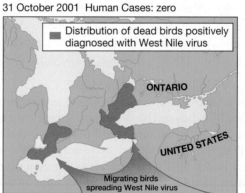

31 October 2001 Human Cases: zero

Figure 3.20   The beginnings of West Nile virus in Canada   West Nile virus (WNV) is carried by mosquitoes and is spread when they bite any of several bird and mammal species. Crows, ravens, blue jays, and magpies are particularly susceptible, as are horses and human beings. In humans, WNV can cause West Nile fever and, in a very few number of cases, develop into fatal inflammations of the brain or spinal cord. WNV was first identified in the West Nile district of Uganda in 1937. Since then, it has slowly spread throughout the Mediterranean and the temperate parts of Europe. The first reported cases in North America occurred in New York City in August 1999. Spread from there by migrating birds, WNV first reached Canada in 2001, when a number of dead birds in Southern Ontario were diagnosed with the disease. The first human cases in this country occurred in Ontario and Quebec in 2002, and six people died that year from the effects of the disease. Most experts suggest that WNV is in Canada to stay because global warming will likely increase the range of infected mosquitoes and birds.   (*Sources:* "Le virus du Nil bientôt terrassé?" *Le Devoir,* 25 April 2005, A2; and Helen Branswell, "Summer's Blight, West Nile, Here to Stay." *Globe and Mail,* 13 May 2005, A11.)

---

[37] J. Eyles and S.J. Elliott, "Global Environmental Change and Human Health." *Canadian Geographer* 45(1), 2001, pp. 99–104.

Human Geography and Climate Change

Population and Health

The consensus within the Fourth Assessment Report of the Intergovernmental Panel on Climate Change (IPCC) concludes that global climate change will likely result in significant climatic shifts.[38] Given the close relationship between climate, environment, and health, climate change is expected to have both direct and indirect effects on the health of Canadians.

Direct health effects of an extreme climatic event can include injuries related to storms and gastrointestinal diseases or cholera brought about by flooding.[39] Direct effects also include increased heat-related stress illnesses and death during extreme heat events.[40] The European heat wave of 2003, which has been attributed to climate change, was directly linked to nearly 15,000 deaths in France alone,[41] with neighbouring European countries experiencing similar increases in mortality at the same time. Most of these deaths were amongst the old (aged 75 and over). In Canada, Riedel's national health impact assessment of climate change points to similar increases in heat-related mortality.[42] Extreme heat events with concurrent poor air quality are also associated with more intense asthma attacks, increased rates of asthma, and cardiovascular disease.[43]

Indirect effects of climate change on human health are likely more complex in their origins and relationships, impacting on health through a multiplicity of avenues including air, water, and food quality and availability.[44] Warmer temperatures are, for example, likely to be associated with increased allergens and air pollution due to more frequent and intense smog episodes which aggravate asthma and other respiratory conditions. Perhaps the most worrisome impact of climate change on health is associated with changing disease distribution and incidence.[45] Warmer climates are expected to allow diseases to move northward and beyond where they are historically located. Mosquitoes or other disease-carrying organisms can also expand their breeding area and the length of time they can survive in a season. Consequently, diseases such as West Nile virus and

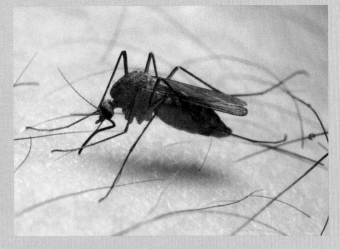

Figure 3.4.1 Mosquitoes as disease carriers Mosquitoes can transmit West Nile virus, a potentially harmful virus, to humans. Climate change will allow the range of mosquitoes and other disease-carrying insects to expand and place humans at risk for a greater length of time.

Eastern and Western Equine Encephalitis (both transmitted by mosquitoes), Lyme disease, and Rocky Mountain Spotted Fever (both transmitted by ticks) will likely be more common in future years, will have a longer season, and be found over an increasingly wide geographical area (Figure 3.4.1). For example, as temperature determines the northern limits for the tick responsible for Lyme disease, it is expected to spread out of its current reservoirs in southwestern Ontario, British Columbia, and Nova Scotia and extend northwards by approximately 200 km by 2020.[46] Tropical diseases including malaria, dengue fever, yellow fever, and encephalitis that are not typically associated with northern environments may also emerge with increased regularity. Given the high likelihood that climate change will result in warmer temperatures and increased precipitation in northern latitudes including Canada,[47] human health and climate change are also linked through water- and food-borne diseases. Water-borne diseases such as Legionnaires disease typically increase during warmer, rainy, and humid weather.

The impacts, burden, and ability to cope with climate change will be inequitably shared across the population. Groups including the poor, Aboriginals, and immigrants will be more vulnerable to climate change, with existing health inequities continued or magnified. The negative health impacts of climate change are expected to be greatest within **vulnerable populations**, including the very young, the old, and those with existing health conditions. Residents of northern Canada, including Canada's

[38] IPPC 4th Assessment Report, 2007 (http://www.ipcc.ch/index.html).

[39] A. Greer, V. Ng, and D. Fisman, "Public Health: Climate Change and Infectious Diseases in North America: The Road Ahead," *Canadian Medical Association Journal* 178(6), 2008, pp. 715–722.

[40] J.M. Balbus and M.L. Wilson, *Human Health and Global Climate Change*. Arlington VA: PEW Center, 2000.

[41] IPPC 4th Assessment Report, 2007, p. 397.

[42] D. Riedel, "Human Health and Well-being," in D. Lemmen and F. Warren (eds.), *Climate Change: Impacts and Adaptation— A Canadian Perspective*. Ottawa, ON: Climate Change Impacts and Adaptation Directorate, Natural Resources Canada, 2004, pp. 151–171.

[43] IPPC 4th Assessment Report, 2007.

[44] Greer, "Public Health: Climate Change and Infectious Diseases in North America."

[45] Balbus and Wilson, *Human Health and Global Climate Change*.

[46] Greer, "Public Health: Climate Change and Infectious Diseases in North America."

[47] IPPC 4th Assessment Report, 2007.

Inuit peoples, are also particularly vulnerable to climate change, as Canada's Arctic regions are expected to warm faster than other regions. A warming Arctic will lead to melting permafrost, loss of sea ice, and melting of glaciers, with impacts on animal and plant habitats. For the Inuit, changing environmental conditions, including loss of snow cover and sea ice, means securing traditional food sources may be more difficult and increased risk associated with travel. Changing climate will also impact animal migrations, access to hunting grounds, and the availability of animal food sources. At the same time, plant species and animals from the south will move northward, further disrupting local ecosystems.[48]

---

[48] Greer, "Public Health: Climate Change and Infectious Diseases in North America."

With climate change, the increased incidence of disease and illness may place heavy burdens on Canada's health infrastructure due to the increased disease prevalence. The impact of extreme climate events and climate-related natural disasters on the health of Canadians can be minimized with appropriate planning for extreme events. Dealing with indirect effects is less easy to implement and requires long-term planning and adaptation.

—K.B.N.

vulnerable populations: populations that include common characteristics making them more susceptible to "fall through the cracks," including the very young, the old, and those with existing health conditions

The Geography of Canadian Health[49]

Population experts regard life expectancy as one of the basic indicators of the overall health of a population, and one that allows reliable comparisons to be made between places and over time. We should therefore feel extremely pleased that the 1998 U.N. Human Development Report ranked Canada as the top country among its 174 members in terms of human development (as measured in terms of life expectancy, educational attainment, and adjusted income). By 2010, however, Canada had slipped to eighth place. The reason is not that conditions in this country worsened (in fact, all measured indicators continue to improve), but that other countries have seen more improvement and that this improvement has been more even across all segments of the population.

This statement about equality points us to the single most significant point to be made about the geography of health in Canada (or elsewhere for that matter): people with higher incomes generally live longer than people with lower incomes. In other words, the geography of health is simply one manifestation of the spatial inequalities generated by Canada's *economic* geography. In 1991, for example, Canadian men in the highest quarter of the income distribution could expect, on average, to live 6.3 years longer and 14.3 more years without disability than those in the lowest quarter (for women, the differences were 3 and 7.6 years, respectively). Experts remark that it is the relative distribution of income in a given society, rather than the total income, that is the most important determinant of health status. If this is so, then the impacts on marginalized and disadvantaged groups can be profound. For example, the life expectancy of the Status Indian population in 1990 was seven years less than that for the overall Canadian population in 1991. Sadly, by 2001, that difference had narrowed by only 0.4 years—one of the reasons why Canada has slipped in the Human Development Index ranking.

The geography of Canadian health can be examined at a number of scales. At the countrywide level of analysis, detailed calculations by Statistics Canada enable us to compare directly the mortality data obtained from health districts across the country. (These data were expressed in terms of age-standardized rates per 100,000 population in 1996. Statistics Canada notes that this procedure allows for a more meaningful comparison of rates because it adjusts for variation

---

[49] Parts of this section are based on *Toward a Healthy Future: Second Report of the Health of Canadians*, prepared by the Federal, Provincial, and Territorial Advisory Committee on Population Health for the Meeting of Ministers of Health, Charlottetown, PEI, September 1999. Health Canada: Ottawa, 1999, pp. ix, 14, and 41. Canada's current status can be checked in the latest United Nations Human Development Report, available at **http://hdr.undp.org**.

TABLE 3.4 The Geography of Health in Canada, 1996

National Health Indicators	Average	Low Regions	High Regions
Total mortality*	668.9	Halton (ON) 585	Nunavut 1082
All cancers*	185.7	Vancouver/ Richmond 154	Nunavut 327
Breast cancer*	28.3	Yukon 16.7	Peace River (BC) 42
All circulatory diseases*	245.8	Northwest (AB) 167	Grenfell (NF) 363
All respiratory diseases*	59.8	Halton (ON) 41.7	Nunavut 209
Average life expectancies (at birth)	78.3	Nunavik (QC) 65.4 Nunavut 69.8	Richmond (BC) 81.2

*Age-standardized rates per 100,000 population
Sources: The Geography of Health in Canada from Health Indicators 1999 from "Health Indicators," October 2002, volume 2002, number 2, Catalogue number 82-221-SIE. (These data can be accessed at **http://secure.cihi.ca/cihiweb/splash.html**. In addition, Statistics Canada publishes periodic reports on special issues, such as the health status of immigrants, the Aboriginal population, and socioeconomic factors. The annual report *How Healthy Are Canadians?* is available at **www.statcan.gc.ca/pub/82-003-s/4060579-eng.htm**.)

in population age structures over time and across geographic areas.) A summary of these data is given in **Table 3.4**. The average total mortality in Canada in 1996 was 669 per 100,000 people. As we have said before, averages can obscure considerable variations: in this case, the Halton health region in Ontario had only half the mortality of the Nunavut region. Overall, in provincial terms, mortality rates in 1996 dropped from east to west, from a high of 753 per 100,000 in Prince Edward Island to a low of 623 per 100,000 in British Columbia, a drop of 21 percent in this indicator of health.

If we consider mortality from the major groups of illnesses, we see, again, considerable variation around the national averages. We also see that the locations of the highs and lows across the country tend to differ by types of illness. The Peace River region of British Columbia has high levels of breast cancer, at 42 per 100,000; the Northwest health region of Alberta has low levels of mortality from circulatory diseases. Clear patterns are not always easy to identify. Indeed, some of the highest rates of breast cancer deaths in Canada occur next door to some of the lowest rates (the North and South Eastman districts of Manitoba, with rates of 18.7 and 37.1 per 100,000, respectively). Nevertheless, Nunavut's high levels of mortality, from a number of causes, and the Halton (ON) and Richmond (BC) areas' low levels of mortality do indicate some of the major outlines of Canada's medical geography.

Because of this, when we turn to regional patterns of life expectancies for 1996 (**Figure 3.21**), it is not surprising to find Nunavut (with an average life expectancy at birth of 69.8 years) and Richmond (81.2 years) at opposite ends of the spectrum. The variations between parts of Saskatchewan (with above average life expectancies) and parts of the St. Lawrence Valley west and east of Montreal (with below average life expectancies) are also worth noting, since they are indicative of some important underlying patterns. We can sharpen our focus on the geography of health by moving to a smaller scale and examining, as a case study, the city of Montreal.

Data for average life expectancies at birth, calculated for Montreal's Centre local de services communautaires (CLSC) regions, for the years 1994 to 1997, indicate that people on the west of the island can expect to live, on average, almost a decade longer than those in some east-end communities (**Figure 3.22**). This variation, from a life expectancy of 81.3 years in the Lac Saint-Louis CLSC region to one of 70.7 years in the Des Faubourgs CLSC region, is one that closely follows patterns of income. In the Lac Saint-Louis area, only 1 percent of all age groups rely on social assistance, whereas in the Des Faubourgs region, as many as 40 percent receive welfare.

Figure 3.21 Life expectancy at birth, by health region, 1996
(*Source:* Statistics Canada, *Health Indicators* 1009 [3], December 2001, Catalogue No. 82-221-XTE, available online at **www.statcan.ca**.)

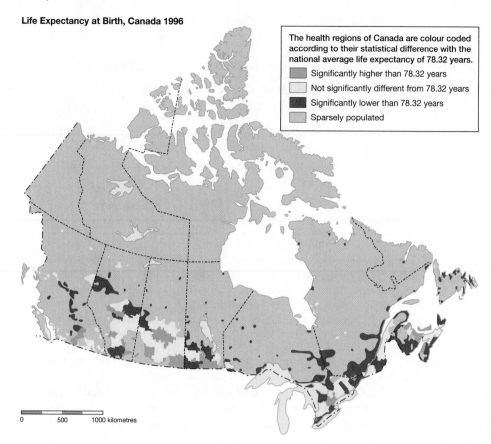

Life Expectancy at Birth, Canada 1996

The health regions of Canada are colour coded according to their statistical difference with the national average life expectancy of 78.32 years.

- Significantly higher than 78.32 years
- Not significantly different from 78.32 years
- Significantly lower than 78.32 years
- Sparsely populated

0   500   1000 kilometres

Figure 3.22 Life expectancies on the island of Montreal This map shows life expectancies at birth, for both sexes combined, using 2001–2005 data for the 29 CLSC health districts of the island of Montreal. Considerable variations across the city can be seen, and the 10-year difference between the city centre and the western suburbs is a long-standing feature. (*Source:* The Centre local de services communautaires (CLSC) data are given on "Les CLSC d'un coup d'oeil," Direction de la santé publique de Montreal-Centre at **www.santepubmtl.qc.ca/Portrait/Les29/carteesperance.html**.) For more recent information, see the Foundation of Greater Montreal's annual publication *Greater Montreal's Vital Signs: 2006* at **www.fgmtl.org/en/VitalSigns/index.htm**.

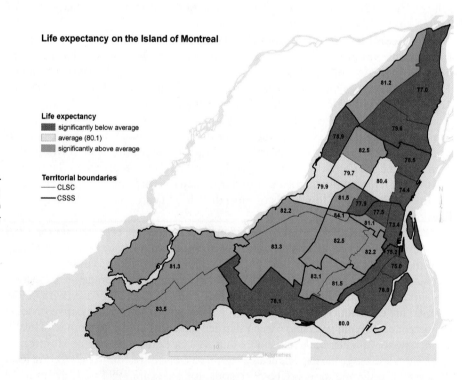

Life expectancy on the Island of Montreal

Life expectancy
- significantly below average
- average (80.1)
- significantly above average

Territorial boundaries
—— CLSC
—— CSSS

In seeking to explain the existence and persistence of these patterns, medical geographers have generally favoured two types of explanation. The first, a behavioural (or lifestyle) hypothesis, argues that these geographical differences (or spatial inequalities) in health arise because certain groups of people more commonly engage in health-threatening activities (such as smoking) and less commonly participate in health-promoting activities (such as sports or eating a healthful diet) than other groups in the population. As a headline in the 30 May 2001 issue of the *Montreal Gazette* covering this topic bluntly explained it, "Poor people tend to smoke more, eat less healthy food."[50]

The second explanation approaches the pattern of health inequalities from a structuralist perspective and challenges the assumptions of the lifestyle hypothesis. From this perspective, the operation of the economy and society as a whole dictates people's quality of life. For example, less wealthy people, exposed to health hazards where they live or work, may find themselves effectively denied access to high-quality health care facilities simply because such resources tend to be located in more wealthy parts of town. As the medical geographer S. Martin Taylor has observed, "the higher mortality rates for men in the north end of Hamilton, for example, raise questions about exposure to hazards in the local workplace, a heavily industrial area. Equally, they may reflect limits in discretionary time and income as well as limited access to resources and facilities which would support engagement in positive health behaviour."[51]

Certainly, Canadian medical geographers have observed that there are marked discrepancies in the provision of medical services and that a more equitable spatial pattern, across city and country alike, is one possible and necessary step toward solving Canada's health care problems. The search for the underlying causes of the patterns shown in Canada's medical geography brings us back full circle to the traditional medical geographer's concerns with patterns of spatial association. A provisional list must surely put the various advantages and disadvantages of urban and rural living in the balance, together with the spatial inequalities inherent in the basic differences that are embedded in Canada's economic geography. Once again, we clearly see the importance of place, this time in our consideration of Canadians' health.

CONCLUSION

The geography of population is directly connected to the complex forces that drive globalization. And, since the fifteenth century, the distribution of the world's population has changed dramatically as the capitalist economy has expanded, bringing new and different peoples into contact with one another and setting into motion additional patterns of national and regional migrations. When capitalism emerged in Europe in the fifteenth century, the world's population was experiencing high birth rates, high death rates, and relatively low levels of migration or mobility. Five hundred years later, birth, death, and migration rates vary—sometimes quite dramatically—from region to region, with core countries experiencing low death and birth rates and peripheral and semiperipheral countries generally experiencing high birth rates and fairly low death rates. Migration rates vary within and outside the core. These variations reflect the level and intensity of political, economic, and cultural connectedness between the core and the periphery.

The example of formerly colonized peoples migrating to their former ruling countries in search of work provides insights into the dynamic nature of the world economy and shows the important role that people play in acting out the dynamics of geographical variety.

In the final analysis, death rates, birth rates, and migration rates are the central variables of population growth and change. These indicators tell us much about transforming regions and places as elements in a larger world-system. Globalization has created many new maps as it has unfolded; the changing geography of population is just one of them.

---

[50] See also "Montrealers Die Younger: Life Span among Lowest in Canada." *Montreal Gazette*, 5 July 2002, A1, A4.

[51] S.M. Taylor, "The Geography of Urban Health." In L. Bourne and D. Ley (eds.), *The Changing Social Geography of Canadian Cities*. Montreal and Kingston: McGill-Queen's University Press, 1993, pp. 309–325. (The quotation is from p. 317.)

MAIN POINTS REVISITED

- Population geographers draw on a wide array of data sources to assess the geography of populations. Chief among these sources is the census, although other sources include vital records and public health statistics.

  Census collection methods vary from country to country and are often conducted in different years, making it difficult to compare different places.

- Population geographers are largely concerned with the same sorts of questions as other population experts study, but they also investigate "the why of where": *why* do particular aspects of population growth and change (and problems) occur *where* they do, and what are the implications of these factors for the future of places?

  A geographical perspective is sensitive to the important influences of place and sees geographical factors as an important part of an explanation for population growth and change.

- Two of the most important factors that make up population dynamics are birth and death. These variables may be examined in simple or complex ways, but in either case, the reasons for the behaviour of these variables are as important as the numbers themselves.

  Birth and death rates are fairly crude measures of population change. Population geographers expand on these rates by looking at such factors as the particular experiences of certain cohorts or ethnic groups and how those factors influence birth and death rates.

- A third crucial force in population change is the movement of populations. The forces that push populations from particular locations, as well as those that pull them to move to new areas, are key to understanding the resulting new settlement patterns. Population migration may not always be a matter of choice.

  Migration is one of the most important factors affecting the distribution of world population today. For some countries whose birth rates are especially low, migration is one way of reversing that trend.

- As a generalization, world demographic patterns are easily described within a world-system framework. They are an important aspect of the very different economic and social "spaces" that this system produces. High birth rates and death rates are a feature of today's periphery; low birth rates and death rates a feature of the core. The discrepancy in economic and political terms between them generates substantial flows of migrants and refugees.

  This suggests that the differences we see in population patterns across the globe are the result of the same set of processes that have created (and are created by) the world-system. It also suggests that continued globalization may accentuate these differences rather than remove them.

- Perhaps the most pressing issue facing scholars, policy-makers, and other interested individuals is the one articulated at the International Conference on Population and Development, held in Cairo in 1994: how many people can the world adequately accommodate with food, water, clean air, and other basic necessities for the enjoyment of happy, healthy, and satisfying lives?

  Many policies have been advanced to address what some observers feel is an overpopulated world. One important factor that is widely seen to be effective in curbing high birth rates is the education of the female population.

- Whether at the world, country, or local scale of analysis, the work of those geographers studying the interactions between population, health, and the environment shows us that the principal explanation for varying spatial patterns of health is variation in income distribution.

  Spatial inequalities are related to differing patterns of disease incidence and affect people's relative access to health care facilities.

Key Terms

adaptability (p. 120)
administrative record linkage (p. 100)
age–sex pyramid (p. 104)
aging (p. 105)
baby boom (p. 102)
census (p. 99)
cohort (p. 104)
crude birth rate (CBR) (p. 108)
crude death rate (CDR) (p. 110)
crude density (arithmetic density) (p. 102)
demographic transition (p. 114)
demography (p. 99)
dependency ratio (p. 104)
doubling time (p. 109)
eco-migration (p. 117)

emigration (p. 116)
environmental refugees (p. 117)
epidemiological transition (p. 134)
family reconstitution (p. 100)
fertility (p. 109)
forced migration (p. 117)
geodemographic analysis (p. 104)
gross migration (p. 116)
guest workers (p. 122)
immigration (p. 116)
infant mortality rate (p. 111)
internal migration (p. 116)
international migration (p. 116)
life expectancy (p. 112)
medical geography (p. 134)
middle cohort (p. 104)

migration (p. 116)
mobility (p. 115)
natural decrease (p. 111)
natural increase (p. 111)
net migration (p. 116)
old-age cohort (p. 104)
participation rate (p. 106)
pull factors (p. 116)
push factors (p. 116)
resiliency (p. 120)
total fertility rate (TFR) (p. 109)
vital records (p. 100)
voluntary migration (p. 117)
vulnerability (p. 120)
vulnerable populations (p. 138)
youth cohort (p. 104)

Additional Reading

Beaujot, R. *Population Change in Canada: The Challenges of Policy Adaptation.* Toronto: McClelland and Stewart, 1991.

Bouvier, L., and C. DeVita. "The Baby Boom—Entering Midlife," *Population Bulletin* 46(3), 1991, 2–33.

Castles, S., and M.J. Miller. *The Age of Migration: International Population Movements in the Modern World.* London: Macmillan, 1993.

Eyles, J., and S.J. Elliott. "Global Environmental Change and Human Health," *Canadian Geographer* 45(1), 2001, 99–104.

Foot, D., and D. Stoffman. *Boom, Bust and Echo 2000: Profiting from the Demographic Shift in the New Millennium.* Toronto: Macfarlane Walter and Ross, 1998.

Greer, A. *The People of New France.* Toronto: University of Toronto Press, 1977.

Harris, C. *The Resettlement of British Columbia: Essays on Colonialism and Geographical Change.* Vancouver: UBC Press, 1997.

Mann, C.C. "How Many Is Too Many?" *Atlantic Monthly*, February 1993, 47–67.

Miron, J. *Housing in Postwar Canada: Demographic Change, Household Formation, and Housing Demand.* Kingston and Montreal: McGill-Queen's University Press, 1988.

Nash, A.E. "Environmental Refugees: Consequences and Policies from a Western Perspective," *Discrete Dynamics in Nature and Society* 3, 1999, 227–238.

Nash, A.E., and K. Noonan-Mooney. "Environmental Refugees," *Encyclopaedia of Environment and Society.* Thousand Oaks, CA: Sage Publications, 2007, 590–591.

Statistics Canada. *Report on the Demographic Situation in Canada, 2005 and 2006.* Ottawa: Statistics Canada, 2008.

Taylor, S.M. "The Geography of Urban Health." In L. Bourne and D. Ley (eds.), *The Changing Social Geography of Canadian Cities.* Montreal and Kingston: McGill-Queen's University Press, 1993, 309–325.

Toward a Healthy Future: Second Report of the Health of Canadians, prepared by the Federal, Provincial and Territorial Advisory Committee on Population Health for the Meeting of Ministers of Health, Charlottetown, PEI, September 1999. Ottawa: Health Canada, 1999.

Trovato, F., and C.F. Grindstaff (eds.). *Perspectives on Canada's Population: An Introduction to Concepts and Issues.* Toronto: Oxford University Press, 1994.

Discussion Questions and Research Activities

1. The distribution of population is a result of many factors, such as employment opportunities, culture, water supply, climate, and other physical environmental characteristics. Look at the distribution of population in your province. Is it evenly distributed, or are the majority of people found in only a few cities? What role do you think these various factors have played in influencing where people live in your province? Can you think of other reasons for this distribution? How has the effect of the various factors changed with technological innovation, for example in communication and transportation? Can you detect influences of globalization and trade liberalization on the distribution of population?

2. Immigration is an important factor contributing to the increase in the population of Canada. Chances are your great-grandparents, grandparents, parents, or even you immigrated to, or migrated within, your country of residence. Construct your family's immigration or migration history by relying both on your family's oral history and generally available information about the migration movement of which your family was a part. What were some of the push and pull factors influencing your family's decision to immigrate to or migrate within your country? What barriers to integration, if any, did they face: language difficulties, racial discrimination, ethnic prejudice, religious segregation, economic exclusion? How did they adapt to life in their new country? Did they use strategies similar to those described in this chapter?

3. Every few years, UNESCO publishes data on global refugee statistics indicating both sending and receiving countries among other variables. Identify one country that has been a large sender of refugees and the matching country that has been the largest receiver of those refugees. The UNESCO data provide information on not only the numbers of refugees, but also their age, gender, and other variables. Discuss some of the demographic implications for both countries if the refugee population were not to be allowed to return to the sending country. What would be the impact on the age–sex structure of the population, its future dynamics, the dependency ratio, or the socioeconomic conditions of the countries involved?

MyGeosciencePlace

Visit **www.mygeoscienceplace.ca** to find chapter review quizzes, videos, maps, and much more.

4

Nature, Society, and Technology

Eight glasses of water

One of the most crucial elements in the relationship between people and their environment is water. We obviously can't survive without drinking it, but there also are large quantities of "hidden" water in just about everything else we consume. Take your breakfast, for instance: it took 140 litres of water to produce your cup of coffee, 250 litres for your glass of milk, and 1,000 litres for the orange juice. That means that by 8 A.M. you have already consumed 14 bathtubs full of water—and you haven't even showered yet! Put on your new T-shirt and you are adding another 25 bathtubs—and the same goes for the hamburger you eat for lunch. The water embedded in our food and consumer products is called virtual water, and Canadians use more than twice the global average. Much of this virtual water is "exported" along with the product: thus the orange juice we consume in Canada puts a strain on the water supply in California, Spain, or wherever the oranges were grown in irrigated groves. Evidently, this makes (virtual) water one of the most heavily traded resources—but does that mean that water should also be treated as a commodity, that is, a tradeable resource with a market price determined by supply and demand? Consider the consequences: without abundant water, we in the core could not live the luxurious lives we currently enjoy; without clean water, however, those in the periphery die. It is therefore important to question what our lives would be like if the price of water would put it out of our reach.

Although this may seem a far-fetched question for those of us who enjoy very low water costs, populations in the periphery have been feeling the effects of escalating water prices for a long time. The 2010 U.N. Human Development Report states that 1.2 billion people do not have adequate access to water and that another 1.6 billion face economic water shortages. Almost two-thirds of the people lacking access to clean water survive on less than $2 a day. In fact, these statistics are two sides of the same coin: poor people in urban areas rarely have access to piped water and therefore must pay horrendous prices to mobile water merchants, whereas their neighbours in the rich parts of town pay low rates for piped municipal water.

One of the biggest challenges of the twenty-first century will be how to ensure access to adequate supplies of quality drinking water for everyone. In fact, experts around the world have begun to talk about a global "water crisis," which is occurring not because there is a physical shortage but because water is rapidly turning from a public good into a privatized commodity with steeply rising prices. Originally, the privatization of water (as opposed to the provision of water through publicly owned utilities) was touted as a way of bringing equitable access and efficiency to all water users; instead, it has led to increased prices and accessibility problems for poor and marginalized peoples not only in the global periphery but in peripheral areas of many core countries as well.

In response to the global water privatization movement and its negative effects on price and accessibility, critics are increasingly arguing that water should be seen as a human right and that corporations are not capable of guaranteeing that right. It is important to be aware that the conflict over who should provide safe water (and at what cost) is occurring in cities and towns throughout the core as well as in the periphery. Besides issues of access and public safety, many of those opposing water privatization argue that conflicts over water are really about fundamental questions of democracy. In particular, if water is no longer a public good, who will make the decisions that affect our future access to it, and who will be excluded? This question is an especially significant one as climate change is expected to have dramatic impacts on water quality and quantity throughout the world.

Water, then, is an apt illustration of the many ways in which humans interact with their environment and how this interaction is mediated by society, mainly through technology, but also through politics, economics, culture, religion, and consumption. All of which, of course, are the very subject of human geography. In this chapter, we explore the ways in which society has used technology to transform and adapt to nature, together with the impact of those technological adaptations on humans and the environment.

MAIN POINTS

- Nature, society, and technology constitute a complex relationship. In this chapter, we will take the view that nature is both a physical realm and a social creation.

- Because we regard nature as a social creation, it is important to understand the many social ideas of nature present in society today and especially the history of those ideas. The most prominent idea of nature in Western culture is the belief that humans should dominate nature, an idea derived from the Judeo-Christian tradition.

- Social relationships with nature have developed over the course of human history, beginning with the early Stone Age. The early history of humankind included people who revered nature as well as those who abused it. Urbanization and industrialization have had extremely degrading impacts on the environment.

- The globalization of the world economy has meant that environmental problems are also global in their scope: deforestation, air pollution, overfishing, and global climate change, for example, affect us all. Many new ways of understanding nature have emerged in the last several decades in response to these serious global crises.

NATURE AS A CONCEPT

As discussed in Chapter 1, a simple model of the nature–society relation is that nature limits or shapes society. This model is known as *environmental determinism*. A second model posits that society also shapes and controls nature, largely through technology and social institutions. This second model, explored in this chapter, emphasizes the complexity of nature–society interactions.

Interest in the relationships between nature, society, and technology has steadily intensified over the last three decades as people everywhere have been experiencing more frequent and severe effects of environmental degradation. Although a turnaround in the state of the environment clearly is a long way off, some very important and significant improvements have been achieved, mainly through the creation of new international institutions to facilitate and monitor environmental improvements. Examples include the curbing of ozone-depleting substances through the Montreal Protocol or the global phaseout of leaded gasoline. Another example is the North American Commission on Environmental Cooperation, a body established under NAFTA in 1994. Based in Montreal, it monitors the ecological effects of liberalized trade in Canada, the United States, and Mexico.

Equally significant is the growing concern for sustainability that expresses itself in a number of practices and objectives that governments, corporations, and public and private organizations are developing. Among these new practices and objectives are: environmental restoration, green urban development, renewable energy sources, sustainable tourism, "greening" the commodity supply chain, sustainable agriculture, "greening" government practices, the emergence and growth of carbon markets, sustainable buildings, and "green marketing" (which unfortunately includes the phenomenon of "greenwashing").

Finally, there is evidence that concern for the environment has spread from the scientific community to the public and from the core to the periphery. For instance, in 1998, the International Environmental Monitor survey was coordinated by Environics International Ltd. (now GlobeScan Inc.) of Toronto. With more than 35,000 interviews in 30 countries, the survey was the largest of its kind ever conducted. Taken together, the countries surveyed represent over two-thirds of the world's population and GDP. Majorities in 27 of 30 countries surveyed, ranging from 91 percent in Greece to 54 percent in India, said environmental laws as currently applied in their country "don't go far enough." Overall concern about the environment was higher than it had been in a similar survey taken in 1992 (**Figure 4.1**). And it continues to rise: A 2001 update of the survey found that "environmental pollution is seen as the single greatest threat to future generations, ahead of economic hardship and war." In fourth place follows another environmental issue: the depletion of natural resources.[1]

The growing concern about the state of the environment reflects a worrisome reality: despite repeated attempts to address environmental problems, they not only persist but are getting worse. In his book *The Enemy of Nature*, Joel Kovel reminds us that "the era of environmental awareness, beginning roughly in 1970, has also been the era of greatest environmental breakdown."[2] Since 1970:

- global consumption of oil, coal, paper, and fish has roughly doubled
- consumption of natural gas has roughly tripled
- the number of cars has tripled, while air traffic has increased sixfold

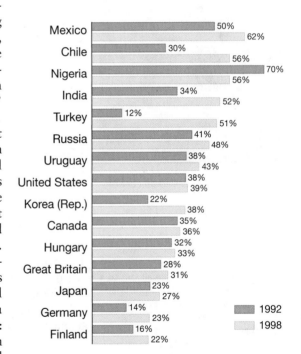

Figure 4.1 Rising levels of environmental concern In the 1998 International Environmental Monitor survey, there was increased environmental concern in 13 of 15 countries that had been surveyed in 1992. When asked to describe how concerned they were about the environment, the percentages shown in the bar graph answered "a great deal." Note that levels of concern appear to be higher in peripheral countries than in core countries: could this mean that populations in rich countries are more insulated from the immediate effects of environmental problems?

---

[1] You can see the results of the survey at www.globescan.com/news_archives/iem01pr.pdf.

[2] J. Kovel, *The Enemy of Nature*, 2nd ed. Black Point, NS: Fernwood Publishing, 2007, pp. 1–3. The quotation is from p. 3.

4.1   Geography in the Information Age

In Beijing alone, more than 700,000 new cars were registered in 2010—almost 2,000 cars every single day! When the city government announced that it would limit new registrations to a total of 240,000 in 2011, the shares of German car makers (who had benefited disproportionately from the soaring car sales) tumbled at the Frankfurt stock exchange.

Figure 4.2   Rachel L. Carson (1907–1964)   Rachel L. Carson was a professional biologist who worked for the U.S. Fish and Wildlife Service. Many people credit her as a key figure in the emergence of what is now known as the *environmental movement*. Her 1962 book, *Silent Spring* (the title alludes to a future in which songbirds are poisoned by pesticides), was instrumental in changing attitudes toward the widespread and carefree use of synthetic pesticides such as DDT. Carson called these substances "biocides" to stress the then emerging realization that their poisonous effects cannot be limited to "pests" but harm other organisms too. In birds, exposure to DDT causes brittle eggshells that break under the weight of the brooding bird, while in humans it is assumed to cause cancer. The United States and Canada banned DDT in 1972 and 1974, respectively, but Mexico did not follow until 2000. Carson did not live to see the bans: she died in 1964—of cancer.

These surges in consumption (and associated resource use and pollution) have several causes. First, some of these increases may be traced back to the doubling of the global population during the same period. Second, changes in consumption and lifestyle patterns in many core countries require increasing amounts of resources per capita. In Canada, for instance, the average house size has doubled since 1970, whereas the number of people per household has dropped from 4 to 2.5. Third, the swelling middle class in countries such as China and India are increasingly purchasing consumer items such as cars and air conditioners that require large amounts of resources to produce and run. In China in particular, car ownership is exploding: to provide roads for the new cars, China built 25,000 kilometres of new highways between 2001 and 2005 alone—that is more than twice the entire length of Autobahn in all of Germany, the country with the fourth-longest highway network in the world!

Do these increases in consumption and resource use at least reflect a similar increase in equality, health, and well-being? Sadly, the answer is "no": according to the United Nations, more people in India have access to a cell phone than to a toilet. And worldwide, since 1970, Third World debt has increased eightfold and the gap between rich and poor nations has doubled, leaving more of the world's poor population to disproportionately suffer the effects of environmental degradation.

In summary, people the world over are not only concerned about the increasing frequency and magnitude of environmental problems they experience, they are also beginning to wonder whether the reason for the situation worsening so rapidly is that humans have a flawed view of the nature–society relationship. This has led to attempts to rethink this relationship (**Figure 4.2**). In the past, technology has usually emerged as the apparent solution to our environmental problems, but now the continued and even intensified application of technology no longer seems to solve them (**Figure 4.3**). As a result, researchers and activists have begun to ask different questions and abandon the assumption that technology is the *only* solution.

Environmental thinkers, including a number of geographers, are suggesting that we should consider nature not as something that sits apart from humans but as inseparable from society. They believe that nature and questions about the environment need to be considered in conjunction with both society and technology because these are the most important influences on how we think about nature and how we identify sources and solutions to environmental problems. Such an approach—uniting nature, society, and technology as interactive components of a complex system—enables us to ask new questions and consider new alternatives to current practices with respect to nature. Before asking new questions about nature, we first define key terms and look at different approaches to the concept of nature. We then examine how changing conceptions of nature have translated into very different uses of it and adaptations to it.

Nature, Society, and Technology Defined

The central concepts of this chapter—nature, society, and technology—have very specific meanings. Although we discuss the changing conceptions and understandings of nature in some detail, we hold to one encompassing

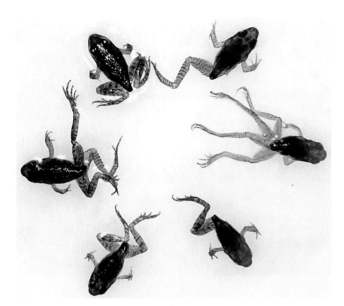

Figure 4.3 Deformities in frogs Although DDT and other substances that are now known to be harmful have been banned, many others continue to be used, even if we are not certain of their possible effects on the ecosystem. A 2005 study by a Pennsylvania State University scientist published in the Proceedings of the National Academy of Sciences found that the combination of pesticide contamination and parasite infection has caused missing legs and extra legs in wood frogs in 43 states in the United States and 5 provinces in Canada. It is believed that exposure to agricultural chemicals may weaken amphibian immune systems, making the frogs more vulnerable to parasitic infection leading to limb deformities. Studies such as this one reveal how incomplete our understanding of the complex structure of our environment still is.

position: **nature** is not only the physical universe that includes human beings; it also is a social creation, which is to say that the many different understandings of nature are the product of different times and different needs. Hence, nature is not only objects; it is a reflection of society in that philosophies, belief systems, and ideologies shape the way people think about nature and the way they use it.

nature: a social creation as well as the physical universe that includes human beings

Society is the sum of the inventions, institutions, and relationships created and reproduced by human beings across particular places and times. Society's relationship with nature is just one of the relationships created and reproduced by society, and it varies from place to place among different social groups. Moreover, the relationship between nature and society is two-way: society shapes people's understandings and uses of nature at the same time that nature shapes society. The amount of shaping by society is dependent to a large extent on the state of technology and the constraints on its use at any given time.

society: the sum of the inventions, institutions, and relationships created and reproduced by human beings across particular places and times

The relationship between society and nature is usually mediated through technology. Knowledge, implements, arts, skills, and the sociocultural context all are components of technology. If we accept that all these components are relevant to technology, then we can provide a definition that has three distinguishable, though equally important, aspects. **Technology** is defined as

technology: physical objects or artifacts, activities or processes, and knowledge or know-how

- physical objects or artifacts (for example, the plow)
- activities or processes (for example, plowing)
- knowledge or know-how (for example, knowing how to make a plow)

This definition recognizes tools, applications, and understandings as critical components of the processes and outcomes of the human production of technology. The manifestations and impacts of technology can be measured in terms of such concepts as level of industrialization and per capita energy consumption. We now look at two recent attempts of quantifying the human impact on the environment in those terms.

The first is the $I = PAT$ formula, an attempt to distinguish the various sources of social impacts on the environment. The formula relates human population pressures on environmental resources to the level of affluence and access to technology in a society. More specifically, the formula states that $I = PAT$, where I (impact on Earth's resources) is equal to P (population) times A (affluence, as measured by per capita income) times T (a technology factor). For example, the differential impact on the environment of different households' energy use would equal the number of people per household times the per capita income of the household times the type of technology used to provide energy for that household (**Figure 4.4**).

Figure 4.4 Affluence differences in various households As the $I = PAT$ formula suggests, a household's level of affluence plays an important role in its impact on the global environment. The first two pictures show families in front of their homes with all of their possessions displayed around them. The extensive range of possessions shows the Icelandic family (a) as far more affluent than the Guatemalan family (b). The Icelandic family possesses two radios, one stereo, two televisions, one VCR, one home computer, two automobiles, and a private airplane. The Guatemalan family possesses one battery-operated radio and no telephone but would like to acquire a television set—if they can get electricity service. However, as the next two pictures show, differences in affluence and impact between two households in the *same* country can be just as stark: Pictures (c) and (d) show two Chinese families in their dining rooms with a week's worth of food arrayed around them. Look closely for the differences. The Dong family from Beijing (c) is upwardly mobile and aspiring to be middle class, and their weekly groceries reflect their higher level of affluence (far more processed food and even a couple of French baguettes). The Cui family of Weitai Village (d), 100 kilometres east of Beijing, consume much larger amounts of local produce and freshly butchered meats than their urban counterparts. Although both families possess refrigerator-freezers, the technology and energy required to produce, distribute, and market the processed foods the Dongs consume in a week indicate a greater impact on the environment than the locally sourced foods eaten by the Cuis.

Each variable in the formula—population, affluence, and technology—should be seen as complex; otherwise, some erroneous conclusions can be drawn. For example, with regard to population numbers, it is generally believed that fewer people on the planet will result in fewer direct pressures on resources. Some argue, however, that increases in world population numbers are quite desirable because a larger population means more minds and more labour can be put toward solving present and future problems. Clearly, there is no simple answer to the question of how many people are too many people.

Affluence also cannot simply be assessed in terms of less is better. Certainly, increasing affluence is a drain on Earth's resources and a burden on Earth's ability to absorb waste. Yet, determining how much affluence is too much is difficult. Furthermore, evidence shows that core countries, with high levels of affluence, are more effective than the poor countries of the periphery at protecting their environments. Unfortunately, core countries often do so by exporting their noxious industrial processes and waste products to peripheral countries. At the same time, by exporting polluting industries and the jobs that go with them, core countries may also be contributing to a rise in the level of affluence of peripheral countries. Given what we know from the historical development in core countries, such a rise may foster a set of social values, attitudes, and behaviours that would ultimately protect the environment. It is difficult to identify the moment when an environmental consciousness goes from being a luxury to being a necessity. The role of affluence in terms of environmental impacts is, like that of population, difficult to assess.

Not surprisingly, the technology variable is no less complicated than population or affluence. Technology affects the environment in three ways:

- through the harvesting of resources
- through the emission of wastes in the manufacture of goods and services
- through the emission of waste in the consumption of goods and services

Technology is complex because it can work two ways: as a solution and as a problem. Such is the case with nuclear energy, widely regarded as a cleaner and more efficient energy source than coal or oil. Producing this energy also creates hazards, however, which scientists are still unable to prevent, as we will discuss later in this chapter.

The second attempt to quantify human impact is the **ecological footprint**. It provides a measure of the biologically productive land area (biocapacity) required to support a given population by providing for its needs and absorbing its wastes. It allows us to visualize the growth and scale of the impact humans have on Earth in terms of sustainability. Because people use resources from all over the globe, the footprint calculation includes all the cropland, fisheries, and other natural resources required to produce the products consumed by a population, wherever on the planet they may be drawn from. According to the *Ecological Footprint Atlas 2010*, Canada's footprint is 7.01 hectares per capita, a figure exceeded only by seven other countries in the world, including the United States (8.0 hectares) and the United Arab Emirates (at the top of the list with 10.68 hectares). At the other extreme we find countries such as Afghanistan and Bangladesh with 0.62 hectares. The global average is 2.7 hectares, but there are only 1.8 hectares of biocapacity available for each person on the planet—which means that the global population currently uses 50 percent more resources than is sustainable. Finally, because the ecological footprint is measured per capita, we also need to take into consideration the size of national populations to appreciate its true dimensions: half the total global footprint can be attributed to only 10 countries, with the United States using 21 percent and China using 24 percent of the global biocapacity.[3]

ecological footprint: a measure of the biologically productive land area needed to support a population by providing for its needs and absorbing its wastes

Now that we understand the scale of the human impact on the planet, we are almost ready to examine the specific human impacts on the natural environment. First, though, we need to look at how differing social attitudes such as religion, science, philosophy, and politics can shape human behaviour that leads to such impacts. This will help us understand that humankind, in its uses and abuses of the environment, is as much influenced by prevailing ideas about nature as by the realities of nature.

Religious Perspectives on Nature

In a 2003 essay entitled "Engaging Religion in the Quest for a Sustainable World," Garry Gardner argues that all religious traditions involve ideas about nature.[4] Defining religion in the most general terms as "an orientation to the

---

[3] The atlas is available at **www.footprintnetwork.org**, a website that also allows you to calculate your personal ecological footprint.
[4] Garry Gardner, "Engaging Religion in the Quest for a Sustainable World." In Linda Starke (ed.), *State of the World 2003*. New York: Norton, 2003, pp. 152–75. The quotations are from pp. 153 and 154.

cosmos and to our role in it," Gardner suggests three major ways religious beliefs can affect our attitudes toward the environment.

First, the fundamental worldview of religions shapes beliefs about the natural world and its importance. The proper relationship between humans and the environment and the real value of environmental protection are therefore among the many concepts that may be rooted in particular theologies.

Second, religious rituals in many societies can affect the ways in which natural resources are used. "Before stripping bark from cedar trees, for instance, the Tlingit Indians of the Pacific Northwest perform a ritual apology to the spirits they believe live there, promising to take only what they need," Gardner notes. As another example, some anthropologists suggest that religious injunctions against certain foods may well have started as attempts to prevent the unhealthful effects of eating animals reared in poor environmental conditions.

Third, ethical systems derived from religious beliefs may influence how environmental resources are used and how they are distributed across society. In this respect, ethical systems whose prime goal is an equitable distribution of resources among people can reduce overconsumption and lead to a more sustainable use of the environment. Dietary practices, such as vegetarianism, also illustrate how ethics can influence our use of animals and plants. On the financial markets, so-called ethical funds allow investors to support environmentally friendly businesses.

These connections between religious belief and attitudes toward the environment show not only the importance of understanding the role of the world's religions in environmental matters but also the need to appreciate that religions reflect many possible perspectives on human relationships to nature. This appreciation is especially valuable in such a country as Canada, with its great variety of religions and enormous diversity of environments.

The **Taoist perspective on nature**, for example, clearly emphasizes valuing nature for its own sake, not for the utilitarian purposes to which it might be put. An ancient Chinese religion, Taoism emphasizes harmony with nature and views the natural world not as an exploitable resource but as a complex life process to be respected and appreciated.

A **Buddhist perspective on nature** teaches that nothing exists in and of itself, and everything is part of a natural, complex, and dynamic totality of mutuality and interdependence. Humans have a special role in the totality in that they alone are capable of reflection and conscious action. It is up to human beings, therefore, to care for all life, human and nonhuman, and to safeguard the integrity of the universe.

An **Islamic perspective on nature** teaches that authority over nature is given to humans by Allah (God) not as an absolute right but as a test of obedience, loyalty, and gratitude to Allah. Abuse of Earth is opposed to the will of Allah; stewardship of it shows respect and fulfills the will of Allah.

The Judeo-Christian tradition has exerted considerable influence on Western ideas about nature. Generally, the **Judeo-Christian perspective on nature** holds that nature was created by God and is subject to God in the same way that a child is subject to parents. "Man" (by which pre-twentieth-century environmental philosophies meant males *exclusively*) was also created by God but made in God's own image, and so man is separate from, and superior to, nature in this regard.

Indigenous religious traditions in North and South America and Africa also conceptualize nature differently, and there was a widespread system of belief on these continents before European contact. An **animistic perspective on nature** is the belief that natural phenomena—both animate and inanimate—possess an indwelling spirit or consciousness. For many indigenous peoples, humans cannot be separated from nature, and the natural cannot be separated from the supernatural (**Figure 4.5**). The Cree, for instance, believe in an unending cycle of reciprocity between humans and animals based on respect. According to

Taoist perspective on nature: the view that nature should be valued for its own sake, not for how it might be exploited

Buddhist perspective on nature: the view that nothing exists in and of itself and everything is part of a natural, complex, and dynamic totality of mutuality and interdependence

Islamic perspective on nature: the view that the heavens and Earth were made for human purposes

Judeo-Christian perspective on nature: the view that nature was created by God and is subject to God in the same way that a child is subject to parents

animistic perspective on nature: the view that natural phenomena—both animate and inanimate—possess an indwelling spirit or consciousness

Figure 4.5 Conflicting environmental perceptions Pictured here is a member of the Algonquin First Nation attempting to prevent a logging truck from passing along a forest road. In conflict here are opposing perceptions of the forest: some members of the band see it as a place of spiritual renewal, whereas lumber companies see it as the source of harvestable commodities.

this worldview, a hunter is successful because the animal chooses to give itself to the hunter who has behaved with respect toward the animal and its spirit. Through this spirit, the animal may then become part of the hunter, "dissolving any discernable boundary between person and the animal and between the natural and spirit worlds," anthropologist Naomi Adelson writes.[5]

One elder from Whapmagoostui (a Cree community at the mouth of the Great Whale River in northern Quebec) provided this account in an interview with Adelson:[6]

> The people would . . . take care of what they had killed very well and handle it with respect so that they did not anger the spirits of the animals. If they handled the killed animals with respect, they would be successful in their hunts and the spirits of the animals would be happy to give food to them. . . . It is said that when someone really angered the animal that he depended on for food, the animal would leave that person for good and starvation resulted.

The Concept of Nature and the Rise of Science and Technology

In a very influential essay written in 1967, Lynn White argued that the prevalent view in Judeo-Christian thinking that humans should dominate nature was one of the main causes of the current ecological crisis because it gave humanity free rein to exploit nature for industrial purposes.[7] Many critics now suggest that this view is too simplistic an interpretation. Their reasons are an important caution to remember when we examine the general connections between people's religious beliefs and their environmental attitudes.

First, a multiplicity of views exists within all religious traditions. The Judeo-Christian tradition, for example, deals not only with domination over nature but

[5] Naomi Adelson, *"Being Alive Well": Health and the Politics of Cree Well-Being*. Toronto: University of Toronto Press, 2000, pp. 67–70. The quotation is from p. 68.
[6] Ibid. The quotation is from p. 71.
[7] Lynn White Jr., "Historical Roots of Our Ecological Crisis." *Science* 155, 1967, pp. 1203–1207.

Figure 4.6 The Tower of the Winds Architecture is one of the ways in which we can learn about belief systems of past historical periods: buildings often display symbolic representations of the deity, humanity, and nature, as well as what was perceived to be their proper relationship to one another. Dating from the first or second century B.C., the Tower of the Winds is the oldest intact building remaining from Greek's Classical Period. Built to support a weather vane and house a water clock, its eight sides show allegorical images of the eight *anemoi* or wind gods revered by the Greeks. The name of the northern wind god, *boreas*, is still used today as in the term "boreal forest," while the scientific instrument used to measure wind speeds is called *anemometer*. Evidently, ideas and terminologies relating to nature, although arising in specific places and at specific times, also persist in many ways.

also teaches environmental stewardship (as the story of Noah and the Ark illustrates). Second, not all people practise religious beliefs with equal intensity. Third, many people cannot always practise their environmental beliefs (religious or otherwise) because of the pressures of everyday life.

Finally, it is possible that Lynn White was wrong about the date when the separation of humans from nature occurred. Noted geographer Clarence Glacken, in his influential study *Traces on the Rhodian Shore*, a book published in the same year as White's essay, demonstrates that the ancient Greeks were the original source of the idea that nature is separate from humans (**Figure 4.6**). Glacken argues that it was from the Greeks that we inherited the belief that a fundamental distinction exists between humans and nature, with nature being defined as anything not fabricated by humans.

Whatever the direct connection between religion and environmental crises, an important indirect connection was created in the core European countries in the sixteenth century, when Christian theology was conscripted to legitimize the goals and methods of the emerging science and technology. Before 1500, Europeans held two complementary views of nature as an organism: one that saw nature as providing for humans in a beneficent way, like a nurturing mother; the other was of a violent and uncontrollable nature that could threaten human lives, like an unpredictable fury. In both views, nature was regarded as female.

Francis Bacon (1561–1626) and Thomas Hobbes (1588–1679) were English philosophers who, as prominent promoters of science and technology, were influential in changing the prevailing view of nature as a (female) organism. Borrowing from Christian ideology, they advanced a view of nature as something subordinate to humans—something to be exploited through the application of new technologies, including pumps, windmills, chains, gears, and ratchets that helped in mining, draining, and cutting the treasures of Earth.

As feminist environmental historian Carolyn Merchant writes:

> The change in controlling imagery was directly related to changes in human attitudes and behavior toward the earth. Whereas the nurturing earth image can be viewed as a cultural constraint restricting the types of socially and morally sanctioned human actions allowable with respect to the earth, the new images of mastery and domination functioned as cultural sanctions for the denudation of nature.[8]

This meant that nature could now be seen as a storehouse of resources, an entity to be exploited rather than respected. For several centuries, this view of nature as a mere instrument of humans remained more or less unchallenged in Western culture, at the same time undergirding processes such as colonialism, the Industrial Revolution, and globalization. It was only with the emergence of environmental philosophies that the pendulum began to swing back toward a more respectful attitude toward nature.

Environmental Philosophies and Political Views of Nature

Our review of environmental philosophies begins with Henry David Thoreau (1817–1862), the American naturalist and activist, who perhaps best illustrates the Western incorporation of North American Aboriginal conceptions of nature combined with other emerging ecological approaches. Thoreau lived and studied the natural world around the town of his birth, Concord, Massachusetts, during the middle decades of the nineteenth century. He is most famous for his book *Walden*, which chronicles the two years he spent living and observing nature in solitude in a house he built on Walden Pond, a few kilometres from Concord. Thoreau represents one of the first alternatives to the "humans-over-nature" approach that characterized his times. He embraced European notions of **romanticism**, a philosophy that emphasized interdependence and relatedness between humans and nature and saw all creatures (and not just humans) as infused with a divine presence.

romanticism: the philosophy that emphasizes interdependence and relatedness between humans and nature

Early in the twentieth century, writers and politicians drew on the ideas of Thoreau and others to advocate the wise use of natural resources and the conservation of natural environments. The view that nature should be conserved for future generations is one that has persisted to the present. **Conservation** holds that natural resources should be used wisely and that society's actions with respect to the natural world should be actions of stewardship, not exploitation. One example of a group with these views is the Sierra Club, a well-established private organization with chapters throughout Canada and the United States. It possesses an extensive legal division that litigates cases of corporate or individual violations of environmental regulations.

conservation: the view that natural resources should be used wisely and that society's effects on the natural world should represent stewardship, not exploitation

A more extreme position, **preservation** is an approach to nature advocating that certain habitats, species, and resources should remain off-limits to human use, regardless of whether the use maintains or depletes the resource in question. The philosophy of such groups as the International Fund for Animal Welfare (IFAW) is closely aligned with the preservationist perspective. Whereas the Sierra Club takes its opponents to the courtroom, the IFAW, a Canadian-based group that has taken up the leadership of the anti-seal hunt protest, relies more on active protest and the publicity that generates. Other Canadian preservationist groups employ extralegal tactics—often called *ecoterrorist tactics*—such as driving spikes into trees to discourage logging. Indeed, the anti-sealing Sea Shepherd Conservation Society, under its leader, Canadian environmentalist Paul Watson, actively promotes the use of "quick strike" actions to halt what they regard as government or corporate abuses of the environment (which may, in fact, be perfectly legal though counter to a preservationist philosophy). In 2008, their ship, the *Farley Mowat,* was seized by Fisheries and Oceans Canada off the coast of Newfoundland on charges of endangering the safety of seal hunters by sailing too close to them.

preservation: an approach to nature advocating that certain habitats, species, and resources should remain off-limits to human use, regardless of whether the use maintains or depletes the resource in question

---

[8] C. Merchant, *The Death of Nature*. San Francisco: Harper and Row, 1979, pp. 2–3.

Figure 4.7 Controversy over Clayoquot Sound, British Columbia Canadian environmental activists have made the preservation of British Columbia's temperate rain forests a global environmental issue. Aided by powerful European environmental lobbyists who persuaded consumers to boycott manufacturers that use Canadian lumber from old-growth forests, these Canadian activists have ensured that Canadian forestry companies pay much greater attention to environmental concerns in their forestry practices.

Founded in Vancouver in 1979, Greenpeace is an environmental organization with global reach, meaning that both its membership and its areas of emphasis are international. Focusing on environmental polluters and combining the strategies of both the Sierra Club and the IFAW, Greenpeace utilizes oppositional tactics as well as formal international legal actions. In its membership (with the world headquarters in Amsterdam and regional offices in most major industrial countries) as well as its objectives (halting environmental pollution worldwide), Greenpeace articulates the belief that places are interdependent and that what happens in one part of the globe affects us all.

Such organizations as the IFAW and Greenpeace are practical illustrations of the new approaches to understanding human interactions with nature that have arisen in environmental philosophy since the publication of *Silent Spring* 50 years ago. These new approaches—environmental ethics, ecofeminism, and deep ecology—take the view that nature is as much a physical universe as it is a product of social thought. All are new and different ways of understanding how society shapes our ideas about nature. Increasingly, their combined efforts are leading to successes, such as the campaigns against the use of fur, factory farms, or the logging of old-growth forests in British Columbia's Clayoquot Sound (**Figure 4.7**).

environmental ethics: a philosophical perspective that prescribes moral principles as guidance for our treatment of nature

■ **Environmental ethics** is a philosophical perspective that prescribes moral principles as guidance for our treatment of nature. What exactly these principles are is a matter of controversy between the different schools of thought in environmental ethics, but all agree that society has a moral obligation to treat nature according to the rules of moral behaviour that exist for our treatment of one another. An aspect of environmental ethics that has caused a great deal of controversy is the perspective that animals, insects, trees, rocks, and other elements of nature have rights in the same way as humans do. If the moral system of our society insists that humans have the right to a safe and happy life, then it is argued that the same rights should also be extended to nonhuman nature. Such a perspective would of course have far-reaching consequences for the way in which humans treat and use nature.

ecofeminism: the view that patriarchal ideology is at the centre of our present environmental malaise

■ **Ecofeminism** holds that patriarchy—a system of social ideas that values men more highly than women—is at the root of our present environmental malaise. As Carolyn Merchant's work (noted previously) has suggested, patriarchy has not only equated women with nature but also established the subordination and exploitation of both. Ecofeminism has been widely embraced in the periphery, where women are primarily responsible for the health and welfare of their families in environments that are being rapidly degraded. The unifying objective in all of ecofeminism is to dismantle the patriarchal biases in Western culture and replace them with a perspective that values both cultural and biological diversity.

■ **Deep ecology** is an approach to nature revolving around two key ideas: self-realization and biospherical egalitarianism. The first idea sees humans as identifying with a larger organic unity or "Self" that transcends their individual being. In this view, the universe is not merely a collection of matter and energy, but just as much a complex and diverse set of relationships. Or, as a deep ecologist might say: you are the universe, and the universe is you. The second idea regards humans as no more valuable or important than any other species: humans and their interests should not be given preferential treatment. In sum, deep ecologists hope that the belief that all things are internally related can enable society to treat the nonhuman world with respect and not simply as a source of raw materials for human use.

deep ecology: an approach to nature revolving around two key ideas: self-realization and biospherical egalitarianism

Although none of these philosophies is a panacea to our environmental problems, each one offers an important critique of our current relationship with nature. More than anything, however, each serves to remind us that environmental crises are complex and that simple, technology-based solutions will no longer suffice to mitigate humanity's ever-growing impact on the environment. With a better understanding of how ideas can shape human behaviour toward the environment, we are now ready to examine the effects humans have wrought on the environment over the course of their history.

THE TRANSFORMATION OF EARTH BY ANCIENT HUMANS

Although the previous discussion might suggest that Earth remained relatively unaffected by human action until well into the early modern period, this section will provide evidence that contemporary humans have inherited an environment that was significantly affected by the practices of even our earliest ancestors.

Paleolithic Impacts

Although humans are thought to have emerged approximately six million years ago, the earliest evidence about people–environment relationships dates from the **Paleolithic period** (literally, the "old" [*paleo*] "stone" [*lithic*] age), so called because this was the period when chipped-stone tools first began to be used. According to archaeologists the Paleolithic period runs from 2.5 million to 10,000 years ago—or roughly the same time frame as the geological period known as the Pleistocene.

Paleolithic period: the period when chipped-stone tools first began to be used

Living on the land in small groups as hunters and gatherers, early Paleolithic people mainly foraged for wild food and killed animals and fish for their survival. Hunting under these conditions could not support a growing population, however. It is estimated that on the African grassland, only two people could survive on the vegetation and wildlife available within about a 4 square kilometre area. To help ensure survival, early Paleolithic people constantly moved over great distances, which ultimately made them a dispersed species.

Tools and cave paintings from the Stone Age give evidence of the importance of hunting to these early peoples. Because they lived in small bands and moved frequently and in wider and wider ranges, it is tempting to conclude that they had very little impact on their environment. It does appear, however, that Paleolithic people did in fact change the landscape through the frequent use of fire.

They used it to attract game, to herd and hunt game, to deflect predators, to provide warmth, and to encourage the growth of vegetation that would attract grazing animals, such as antelope and deer.

For thousands of years following their settlement of North America, Canada's Aboriginal peoples practised various forms of hunting and gathering adapted to available local resources. On the west coast, for example, abundant fishing resources supported the Haida villages on the Queen Charlotte Islands. In the North, the Inuit had developed the sophisticated harpoon technology needed to hunt seals and survive in the Arctic. Across the Prairies, indigenous peoples trapped bison, as evidenced by the site at Head-Smashed-In Buffalo Jump (Alberta), which began to be used 5,700 years ago and has been designated one of this country's UNESCO World Heritage sites (**Figure 4.8**). Across much of what is now Ontario and Quebec, indigenous peoples supported themselves through a combination of fishing, hunting (of moose and deer), and gathering. On the southern and northeastern coasts of Newfoundland, the Beothuks fished and hunted for seals and other sea mammals and birds.

Neolithic Peoples and Domestication

The credit for the development of agriculture goes to the Neolithic peoples, also known as the late Stone Age peoples. Although the transition between them and the Paleolithic peoples occurred about 10,000 years ago, it is not known exactly when Neolithic peoples shifted from hunting and gathering to cultivating certain plants and taming and herding wild animals. Scholars call this period the First Agricultural Revolution. Climatically, we know that for many regions of the globe, this period coincides with the end of the last Ice Age, which means that spring slowly began to occur in places that had not experienced it for thousands upon thousands of years.

It was just at this time that environmental conditions made possible the domestication of plants and animals, which both enabled and required a sedentary lifestyle based in permanent settlements. The first domestication successes of the Neolithic peoples were with the most docile animals (herbivores) and the hardiest plants (those with large seeds and a tolerance to drought).

American cultural geographer Carl Sauer (see Chapter 1) is the individual most associated with the geographical study of domestication (**Figure 4.9**). Sauer suggested that those areas of the world where domestication first occurred "are to be sought in areas of marked diversity of plants or animals, where there were varied and good raw materials to experiment with . . . [which] implies well-diversified terrain and perhaps also variety of climate." On this basis, he suggested that domestication probably occurred first in the lands now known

Figure 4.8 Massive animal kills Paleolithic hunters appear to have used features of the landscape to aid them in hunting large game. Archaeologists believe that the mounds of skeletal remains of large animals found at various sites (such as at Head-Smashed-In Buffalo Jump, Alberta) are evidence of this. It is not clear whether hunters and their kin were even able to consume all the animal flesh made available through such killing methods. It has been speculated that such gross killing methods may have led to the extinction of some species. (*Source:* Arthur Lidov/National Geographic Society Image Collection.)

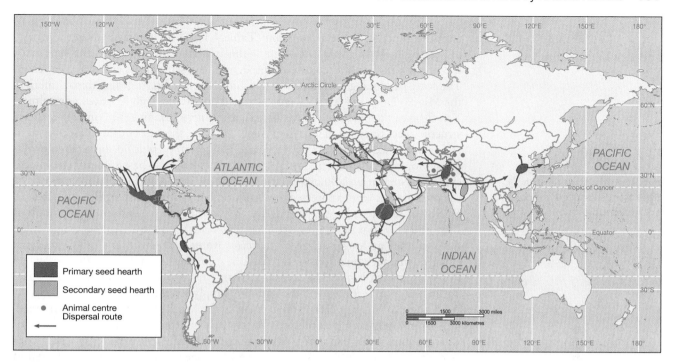

Figure 4.9   Areas of plant and animal domestication   Plant and animal domestication did not predominate in any one continent but occurred in several areas across the globe. The origins of plant and animal domestication, however, are not definitively known, and much of what is represented on this map is speculative. Archaeological evidence to date supports the distribution shown here and developed in the mid-twentieth century by Carl Sauer.   (*Source: J.M. Rubenstein, The Cultural Landscape: An Introduction to Human Geography, 7th ed., Prentice Hall © 2003, p. 319. Adapted from Carl O. Sauer, Agricultural Origins and Dispersals, with permission of the American Geographical Society.*)

as "The Fertile Crescent" approximately 10,000 years ago. In river valleys in what are now parts of Iran and Iraq, the slightly wetter conditions than today (probably caused by the end of the last glaciations) allowed wild grasses to grow and feed small groups of people. Having the time to devote to the selection of better-yielding grasses, the population was eventually able to domesticate what were to become important grain crops (principally wheat). Indeed, Sauer stressed that domestication could not have been the result of people driven by hunger because they would not have had the time to devote to the careful choice and tending of plants over a considerable period of time.

The emergence of agriculture was a process that changed the course of human history and had important environmental impacts—both negative and positive. One negative impact was the simplification of ecosystems as the multiplicity of wild species began to be replaced by fewer cultivable crops. An **ecosystem** is a community of different species interacting with one another and with the larger physical environment that surrounds them. Along with the vast number of wild species lost, the opportunity to understand their role in the wider ecosystem (and potential benefit to humans) has also gone. On the positive side, increased yields of cultivated food crops helped to sustain population growth.

ecosystem: a community of different species interacting with one another and with the larger physical environment that surrounds them

Early Settlements and Their Environmental Impacts

Perhaps the most significant aspect of plant and animal domestication is that it eventually enabled a surplus to be produced. In turn, this permitted the formation of human settlements in which small groups—probably craftspeople and political and religious elites—were able to live off the surplus without being directly involved in its production. Eventually, growing numbers of people, bolstered by increasing surpluses, were able to expand human settlement to places where water was available and the land could be cultivated.

Irrigation is one of the most significant ways that humans have been able to alter the limits of their environment (**Table 4.1**). Throughout much of the world, in fact, agriculture could not occur without irrigation. Following the success of the Fertile Crescent, agriculture diffused, and new settlements emerged as a result. The food-producing mini-systems of China, the Mediterranean, Meso-America, the Middle East, and Africa were sustained largely through irrigated agriculture. Yet, despite the existence of a vast irrigation network and the complex societal structure necessary for maintaining such a system, the cities of the Mesopotamian region collapsed around 4,000 years ago. Although there is no undisputed explanation for why this occurred, many researchers believe—based on archaeological evidence—that it was due to environmental mismanagement. **Deforestation** (the removal of trees from a forested area without adequate replanting) led to increased erosion of soil from logged hillsides, which in turn led to **siltation** (the buildup of sand and clay in a natural or artificial waterway). As the irrigation canals filled with silt, they no longer delivered sufficient water to the fields and the soil became clogged with accumulations of salt leached from the soil. Agriculturalists switched to barley, which is more salt-resistant than wheat, but the ultimate result was a significant drop in yields and thus in food supply for the population.

Other early urban civilizations, such as the Maya society in Central America, are also thought to have collapsed because of environmental mismanagement of water (**Figure 4.10**). Similarly, environmental change is now being seriously considered as a factor in the collapse of the Mycenaean civilization that occurred in Greece about 1200 B.C. The evidence is hardly new and comes from a wide variety of sources. For example, Aristotle (384–322 B.C.) writes that "at the time of the Trojan War . . . the land of Mycenae was good and highly esteemed. Now, however . . . [it] is dried up and therefore lies idle."[9] Similarly, archaeological evidence shows that a large dam was built outside Tiryns in the thirteenth century B.C., probably to divert flood water around the city's citadel (**Figure 4.11**). Archaeologists such as Curtis Runnels have speculated that this flooding was caused in the first

deforestation: the removal of trees from a forested area without adequate replanting

siltation: the buildup of sand and clay in a natural or artificial waterway

TABLE 4.1   World Irrigated Area since 1700

Area (in thousands of square kilometres)	Date (A.D.)
1700	50
1800	80
1900	480
1949	920
1959	1,490
1980	2,000
1981	2,130
1984	2,200
2000	2,780
2007	2,860

Source: W. Meyer, *Human Impact on the Earth.* Cambridge: Cambridge University Press, 1990, p. 59. *Original source:* B.G. Rozanov, V. Targulian, and D.S. Orlow, "Soils." In B.L. Turner II, W.L. Clark, R.W. Kates, J.E. Richards, J.T. Matthews, and W.B. Meyer (eds.), *The Earth Transformed by Human Action.* 1990. Cambridge: Cambridge University Press. Updated from the FAO Statistical Yearbook 2009, **http://www.fao.org/economic/ess/publications-studies/statistical-yearbook/fao-statistical-yearbook-2009/a-resources/en/.**

[9] Eberhard Zangger, "Prehistoric Coastal Environments in Greece: The Vanished Landscapes of Dimini Bay and Lake Lerna." *Journal of Field Archaeology* 18(1), 1991, pp. 1–15. The quotation is from p. 13.

Figure 4.10 The Maya pyramid at Altun Ha, Belize This temple site was excavated by Dr. David Pendergast of the Royal Ontario Museum. The classic Maya civilization collapsed suddenly during the century following A.D. 900. At its height, population densities of up to 400 people per square kilometre were supported by a variety of crops and cultivation practices, most important among them being the cultivation of domesticated maize and a form of wetland agriculture involving the construction of raised fields. Some experts blame the collapse on the environmental mismanagement of water; other scholars point to political upheavals as the cause of this sudden decline. Whatever the cause, the forest quickly took back the land once so intensely cultivated.

place by increased water runoff as the surrounding landscape was transformed into agricultural fields. Other signs of environmental change can be found in the layers of soil formed all around the Mediterranean by the deposition of materials that were eroded by the clearing of land for early agriculture (**Figure 4.12**). Our provisional conclusion from this survey must be that, throughout human history, environmental degradation has been an almost unavoidable result of civilization.

In the following section, we examine the period of European expansion and globalization. Although many other important cultures and civilizations affected the environment in the intervening period, the impacts of their technological developments were much the same as those we have already described. The period of European colonialism, however, had a profoundly different impact from preceding periods in extent, magnitude, and kind. Furthermore, it set the stage for the kinds of environmental problems contemporary society has inherited, perpetuated, and magnified.

Figure 4.11 The Mycenaean dam at Tiryns Dating from about 1300 B.C., this dam near the Mycenaean town of Tiryns in Greece's Peloponnese peninsula provides clear evidence of human interference with the environment. Indeed, some archaeologists speculate that the dam was needed to protect the town from flooding by a stream that had greatly increased in volume as a result of land clearance for agriculture.

Figure 4.12 Ancient soils near Sparta, Greece All around the Mediterranean, evidence of environmental change can be seen in the form of ancient deposits of soils, clearly indicated by their different colours. In the 1980s, scholars such as Dr. Claudio Vita-Finzi suggested that at least two main episodes of such deposition have occurred, each associated with periods of greater-than-average rainfall. Experts now suggest that the older episode was likely naturally induced (perhaps during an interglacial period), while the more recent is likely the result of human-induced soil erosion caused by the spread of agriculture between 10,000 and 8,000 years ago.

EUROPEAN EXPANSION AND GLOBALIZATION

Europe provides a powerful example of how a society with new environmental attitudes was able to transform nature in ways vastly different from any in previous human history. These new attitudes drew from a newly emerging science and its contribution to technological innovation; the consolidation of the population around cultural and religious beliefs; and, most important, the development of a capitalist political and economic system.

Initially, European expansion occurred within its continental boundaries, driven mainly by an increase in population: from 36 million in A.D. 1000 to more than 45 million in 1100, and more than 60 million in 1200 to about 80 million by 1300 (**Figure 4.13**). As the population increased, agricultural settlement was extended to take up all readily available land, and then some. In England, Italy, France, and the Netherlands, for example, marshlands were drained and the sea was pushed back or the water table lowered to create new land for agriculture and settlement. In addition, more animals were reared for food, more minerals and other resources exploited for a variety of needs, and more forested land cleared. When the period of internal expansion ended in the fourteenth century, the forested area in Western and Central Europe had been reduced from 90 percent to 20 percent. The immediate reason for the end of the internal expansion was the bubonic plague, also known as the Black Death, which almost halved Europe's population within the span of a few years around 1350.

It took more than a century to recover from the depopulation but, by the fifteenth century, Europe initiated its second phase of expansion. This time it was an external expansion that changed not only the global political map but launched a 500-year period of environmental change that continues to this day. European external expansion, *colonialism,* was the response to several impulses, ranging from self-interest to altruism. Europeans were fast running out of land, and, as we saw in Chapter 2, explorers were being dispatched by monarchs to conquer new territories and enlarge their empires while collecting taxes from the monarchs' new subjects. Many of these adventurous individuals were searching for fame and fortune or fleeing religious persecution. Behind European external expansion was also the Christian impulse to missionize and bring new souls into the kingdom of God. Other forces behind European colonialism included the need to expand the emerging system of trade by creating new markets, which ultimately meant increased wealth and power for a new class of people—the merchants—as well as for the aristocracy.

Over the centuries, Europe came to control increasing areas of the globe. Two cases illustrate how the introduction of European people, ideologies, technologies, plant species, pathogens, and animals changed not only the environments into which they were introduced but also the societies they encountered.

Disease and Depopulation in the Spanish Colonies

Little disagreement exists among historians that the European colonization of the New World was ultimately responsible for the greatest loss of human life in history, primarily through diseases the colonizers brought with them. New World populations, including Canada's First Peoples, had been isolated for millennia from the Old World and so their immune systems had never encountered some of the most common European diseases.

Geographer W. George Lovell, of Queen's University in Kingston, Ontario, has examined the role disease played in the depopulation of some of Spain's New World colonies from the point of initial contact until the early seventeenth century, using several cases to illustrate his point.[10]

In one example, Lovell describes how Hernán Cortés made contact with the Aztec, a complex civilization in Central Mexico whose achievements in architecture, mathematics, and astronomy easily surpassed those of the Spanish colonizers (**Figure 4.14**). In 1521, Cortés captured their capital city, Tenochtitlán, a sprawling city of 200,000 inhabitants located on an island in a lake. The presence of the Spaniards triggered a devastating outbreak of smallpox among the population. An Aztec text provides a graphic description of the disease:

> While the Spaniards were in Tlaxcala, a great plague broke out here in Tenochtitlán. It began to spread during the thirteenth month [30 September–19 October 1520] and lasted for 70 days, striking everywhere in the city and killing a vast number of our people. Sores erupted on our faces, our breasts, our bellies; we were covered with agonizing sores from head to foot. . . .
>
> A great many died from this plague, and many others died of hunger. They could not get up and search for food, and everyone else was too sick to care for them, so they starved to death in their beds.[11]

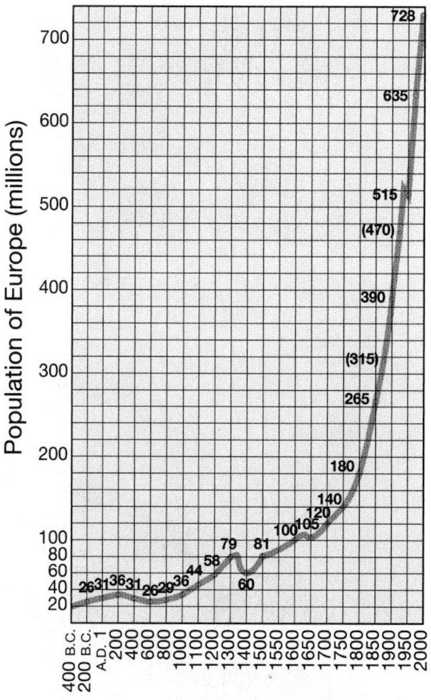

In another example, Lovell describes the Jesuits' missionizing efforts in northern Mexico during a slightly later period. Contact with Spanish conquistadors in advance of the missionaries had already reduced indigenous populations by perhaps 30 percent to 50 percent. Now that the Jesuits gathered dispersed groups of the population into single locations around a mission, conditions for the outbreak of disease were created and mortality climbed to 90 percent. Sadly, missionizing seems to have killed the Aboriginal inhabitants whose souls it was claiming to save. Eventually, the disease was diffused beyond the initial area of contact as traders carried it across long-distance trade routes to the periphery of the Maya empire. The Maya were not defeated by European technological superiority but by the ravages of diseases against which they possessed no natural defences (**Figure 4.15**).

Lovell provides similar descriptions of disease impacts in Mayan Guatemala and the Central Andes of South America that led to devastating depopulation, a phenomenon scholars refer to as **demographic collapse**. The ecological effect of the population decline was the transformation of many regions from productive agriculture to abandoned land. Many of the Andean terraces, for example, were abandoned, and dramatic soil erosion ensued. In contrast, large expanses of cleared land eventually returned to forests in some areas, such as the Yucatán, in present-day Mexico.

Old World Plants and Animals in the New World

Our second illustration concerns the phenomenon known as **ecological imperialism,** or the deliberate introduction of exotic plants and animals into ecosystems as part of the process of colonization. The interaction between the Old and New Worlds resulted in both the intentional and the unintentional introduction of new crops and animals. Europeans brought from their homelands many plants and animals that were exotics (that is, species unknown to American

Figure 4.13 Population growth in Europe This graph shows the growth of the European population from 400 B.C. to A.D. 2000. The increase in human numbers at the beginning of the 1500s was an important push to exploration and colonization beyond the confines of the continent. The dip in the graph from 1300 to 1400 is partially explained by the bubonic plague epidemic known as the Black Death, but food shortages also played a significant role in this population decline. (*Source:* Adapted from C. McEvedy and R. Jones, *Atlas of World Population History.* London: Allen Lane, 1978, fig. 1.2, p. 18.)

demographic collapse: phenomenon of near genocide of indigenous populations

ecological imperialism: introduction of exotic plants and animals into new ecosystems

---

[10] W.G. Lovell, "Heavy Shadows and Black Night: Disease and Depopulation in Colonial Spanish America." *Annals, Association of American Geographers* 82, 1992.

[11] W.G. Lovell, 1992, p. 429, quoting from M. Leòn-Portilla, *The Broken Spears: The Aztec Account of the Conquest of Mexico.* Boston: Beacon Press, 1962, pp. 92–93.

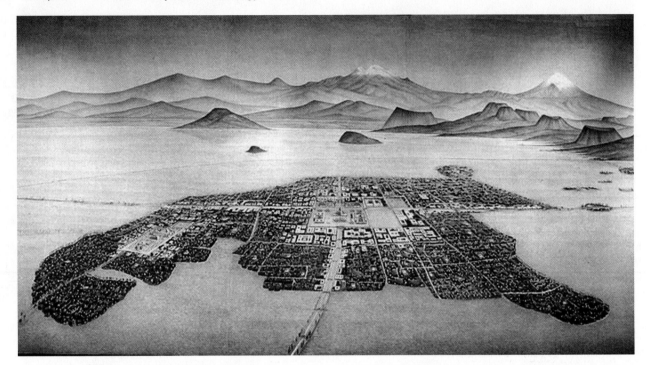

Figure 4.14   "Tenochtitlán," circa 1500   This famous contemporary painting by Miguel Covarrubias of the Aztec capital city of Tenochtitlán illustrates the existence of dense social, cultural, and political activity in the core of the city with agricultural fields on the periphery, particularly to the north (the top of the painting). Agricultural goods were also imported from the area surrounding the capital beyond the shores of the lake. With a population of 200,000, it was roughly twice the size of Seville, then Spain's largest city. When Cortés came upon the capital he noted that ". . . in Spain there is nothing to compare with it."

Figure 4.15   The population of the Cuchumatán Highlands, Guatemala, 1520–1825   This graph shows the demographic collapse of northern Guatemala's Aboriginal population after European contact.   (*Source:* W. George Lovell, *Conquest and Survival in Colonial Guatemala: A Historical Geography of the Cuchumatán Highlands, 1500–1821.* Montreal and Kingston: McGill-Queen's University Press, 1985, p. 146.)

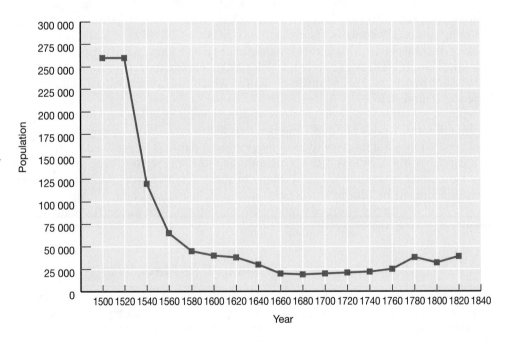

ecosystems) so that they might continue to farm using animals and plants with which they were familiar. For example, the Spanish introduced wheat as well as horses, cattle, and pigs. These introductions altered the environment, particularly as the emphasis on select species led to a reduction in the variety of plants and animals that constituted local ecosystems.

In addition, the European settlers inadvertently introduced exotic species that were more hardy and soon crowded out the less competitive indigenous species. As with the human population, the indigenous populations of plants, birds, and mammals had few defences against European newcomers and were some-times seriously reduced or even made extinct through contact. In New Zealand, for example, newspapers described a "sparrow pest" within 12 years of their introduction. Other examples include pigeons and starlings; mammals, such as rats and pigs; and weeds, such as the dandelion and thistle.

However, contact between the Old and the New Worlds was an exchange— a two-way process—and New World crops and animals were likewise introduced into the Old World. As part of what environmental historian Alfred Crosby has called "the Columbian Exchange," maize, potatoes, tobacco, cocoa, tomatoes, and cotton were all brought back to Europe, crops that had profound benefits for the European population.

The introduction of new animal species provided the New World not only with additional sources of protein but also with additional animal power. Before the Columbian Exchange, the only important sources of animal energy were the llama and the dog. The introduction of the horse, ox, and donkey created a virtual power revolution in the New World. These animals, through their eventual death or slaughter, also provided fibres, hides, and bones to make various tools, utensils, and coverings. Most significant in its environmental impact, however, was the ox.

Land that had escaped cultivation because the indigenous digging sticks and tools were unable to penetrate the heavy soil and matted root surface became available to an ox-drawn plow. As a consequence, the indigenous form of inten-sive agricultural production (small area, many labourers) was replaced by exten-sive production (large area, fewer labourers). This transformation, however, also had negative impacts, such as increased rates of soil destabilization and erosion.

It is important to note here that environmental degradation did not begin with European contact. The popular image of indigenous peoples living in har-mony with nature, having only a minimal impact on their environment, has been shown to be flawed. Polynesian contact with Hawaii, for example, had pro-found effects on the islands' ecosystems. The pigs the Polynesians introduced ate native flora, and their digging around created pools of water in which insects bred, which subsequently decimated native birds. In reality, different groups of indigenous peoples had very different impacts, and it is erroneous to conflate the thousands of groups into one romanticized caricature.

In New England, for example, before European contact, groups existed that hunted for wild game and gathered wild foods. More sedentary types also existed, living in permanent and semi-permanent villages, clearing and plant-ing small areas of land. Hunter-gatherers were mobile, moving with the seasons to obtain fish, migrating birds, deer, wild berries, and plants. Agriculturalists planted corn, squash, beans, and tobacco and used a wide range of other natu-ral resources. The economy was a fairly simple one based on personal use or on barter (trading corn for fish, for example). The idea of a surplus was foreign here: people cultivated or exploited only the amount of land and resources that they needed to survive. Land and resources were shared in common, without such concepts as private property or land ownership. Fire was used to clear land for planting, as well as for hunting. Although vegetation change did occur, it was minimal and reversible.

The Aztecs of Mexico and the Incas of Peru were responsible for dramatic environmental modifications through cultivation techniques that included the irrigation of dry regions and the terracing of steep slopes. As we have seen, irrigation over several centuries will result in the salinization of soils. In the lowland tropics, intensive agricultural practices resulted in widespread defor-estation as people cut and set fire to patches of forest, planted crops, and then moved on when soil fertility declined. A surplus was key to the operations of both societies, because tribute by ordinary people to the political and religious elite was required in the form of food, animals, labour, or precious metals. The construction of the sizeable Inca and Aztec empires required the produc-tion of large amounts of building materials, specifically wood and mortar.

Concentrated populations and the demands of urbanization meant that widespread environmental degradation existed in the Americas before European contact and the Columbian Exchange.

As the pace of development of the world-system quickened, so did the extent of ecological imperialism increase (**Figure 4.16**). In the earliest stages, flows of plants and animals were mainly toward the core. Much of this movement occurred not because of any utilitarian purpose but because of the attraction of Europe's wealthy to the rare and exotic. The Dutch fascination with tulips may serve as an example: a native of Central Asia, the plant had rapidly spread from Turkey to the Netherlands by 1565. Tulip mania afflicted that country to such an extent during the early seventeenth century that one bulb was worth the price of a townhouse in Amsterdam! Another example is the European potentates' passion for menageries. During the Middle Ages, one king of Portugal shipped an Indian elephant to the pope, and there are records of live polar bears being sent from Greenland as part of that colony's tribute. Finally, wealthy people could also afford to recruit plant collectors to bring back new species for the botanical gardens they were beginning to establish at this time.

Movement of Plants

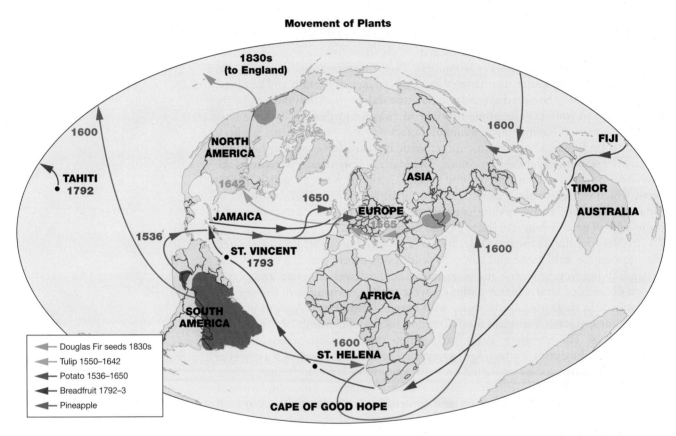

Figure 4.16 Ecological imperialism The movement of plants occurred on an ever-increasing scale as the core of the world-system extended its grasp into the periphery. The consequences of these movements were often unforeseen, because the introduction of flora into new ecosystems often disturbed the subtle balances of nature. Early transfers, such as the diffusion of the tulip from the foothills of Central Asia to Holland, were affected more by Europe's quest for the exotic than any utilitarian objective. However, as the core developed overseas colonies, plants with agricultural or commercial value (such as the potato) were exchanged between core and periphery. As Europe's colonial empires grew, plant transfers increasingly occurred about the periphery itself: by 1600, the pineapple had been spread across Spanish and Portuguese territories and was virtually ubiquitous across the tropics. By the 1790s, Captain Bligh's transfer of the breadfruit from Tahiti to St. Vincent showed plants could be moved halfway round the world in under a year. Indeed, one of the greatest nineteenth-century collectors, David Douglas, sent the plants he had collected in British Columbia between 1825 and 1834 back to England via the Pacific. The Douglas fir, named after him, was but one of more than 200 species he collected for the Royal Horticultural Society, based at Kew Gardens in England. (*Sources*: Map compiled by author from the following: R.A. Howard, "Captain Bligh and the Breadfruit." *Scientific American* 188[3], March 1953, pp. 88–94; W.H. McNeill, "American Food Crops in the Old World." In H.J. Viola and C. Margolis [eds.], *Seeds of Change*. Washington, DC: Smithsonian, 1991, pp. 43–59; Anna Pavord, *The Tulip*. London: Bloomsbury, 1999; K.F. Kiple and K.C. Ornelas [eds.], *The Cambridge World History of Food*, vol. 2. Cambridge: Cambridge Unversity Press, 2000, p. 1834; J. Grimshaw, *The Gardeners Atlas*. Willowdale, ON: Firefly, 1998, p. 11.)

It is only when the core begins to integrate the periphery into an expanding economic system that we begin to see the far more utilitarian exchange of plants and animals occurring between the Old and New Worlds. What this means is that at this stage, the core directs the diffusion. Because of this, as Alfred Crosby has argued, the most successful exchanges were those with countries that most closely replicated the European environment and its traditional livestock-rearing and grain-growing practices. Conversely, European farmers took some time to accept the potato because they were unused to eating tubers.

But the story does not end here. As the core developed colonial empires at a global scale, so were plants and animals moved between colonies and between different parts of the periphery without recourse to the core. One example is the pineapple, carried by both the Portuguese and Spanish across their colonies and spread throughout most of the tropical world by 1600. Another is the breadfruit, which the British moved from Tahiti to St. Vincent to feed their slaves there more efficiently. The ever-increasing grasp and greater sophistication of ecological imperialism had some interesting consequences:

■ Botanical gardens were developed around the world. No longer the playthings of the idle rich or attempts to re-create the Garden of Eden, botanical gardens were now developed so that plants could be collected and acclimatized before the next stage of their transfer. The Dutch East India Company's garden at Cape Town was a vital link in this chain, which included Kew Gardens in England and the botanical gardens on St. Vincent in the Caribbean (the oldest in the Western Hemisphere).

■ The movement of greater numbers of species, in shorter time periods, further and further afield, greatly accelerated the pace of change.

■ The breaking down of the world's major biogeographic barriers (such as Wallace's Line between Borneo and Sulawesi, which marks the divide between Asian and Australian fauna and flora) in such a concerted manner meant that

  – entirely new combinations of plants and animals were being assembled for the first time in environments where natural controls were lacking. The introduction of rabbits to Australia and of starlings to North America led to population explosions of those species.

  – many plants we call "weeds" (such as the dandelion) became almost global in distribution. These accidental introductions were particularly successful in new ecological areas precisely because the establishment of Western types of agriculture in new settings re-created the ecological niches (such as open or cleared ground) that such plants favour.

  – the flora and fauna of different parts of the world became increasingly homogenized. The tropics now look the same everywhere because they are the product of species assembled from across the equatorial world, but originally they looked quite different. Bananas, royal palm trees, and pineapples seem so much a part of the Hawaiian landscape that it is a shock to discover that these are all introduced species. By the same token, Canadian gardens in the summer are made up almost entirely of introduced species, and yet they are now so familiar to us that we can no longer sense how "out of place" they really are.

As we have seen by the transfer of plants and animals and the subsequent interactions with nature, we have begun to make the world look the same wherever we are: we have, in this sense, homogenized space and created familiar places. This type of place making is therefore directly tied to changing attitudes to nature on the one hand and to the expansion of the world-system on the other hand. (The term *place making* is examined in Chapter 6.)

HUMAN ACTION AND RECENT ENVIRONMENTAL CHANGE

No other transition in human history has had the impact on the natural world that industrialization has. When we couple industrialization with its frequent companion, urbanization, we have the two processes that, more than any others, have revolutionized human life and brought about far-reaching ecological changes. For the first time in history, these changes have moved beyond a local or a regional scale to affect the entire globe. In this section, we explore some of the dramatic contemporary environmental impacts that industrial technology and urbanization have produced. In doing so, we focus on three issues of environmental geography: energy use, land-use change, and the exploitation of natural resources (using the state of the world's fisheries as an example).

The Impact of Energy Needs on the Environment

Certainly the most central and significant technological breakthrough of the Industrial Revolution was the discovery and utilization of fossil fuels—coal, oil, and natural gas. Although the very first factories in Europe and North America relied on water power to drive the machinery, it was hydrocarbon fuels that provided a more constant, dependable, concentrated, and also mobile source of power. At present, the world's population relies most heavily on nonrenewable energy resources, which include fossil fuels and nuclear ones, but renewable resources, such as wood and solar, hydroelectric, wind, and geothermal power, are beginning to increase in importance.

According to their publication *Key World Energy Statistics 2010,* the Paris-based International Energy Agency estimates that the largest proportion of the world's current supply of primary energy, 33 percent, comes from oil; 27 percent from coal (and related materials, such as peat); 21 percent from natural gas; 10 percent from wood and waste; 6 percent from nuclear power; 2 percent from hydroelectricity; and less than 1 percent from a mixture of renewable sources that includes wind, solar, and geothermal sources.[12] The production and consumption of these available resources, however, is geographically uneven, as **Figure 4.17** shows. Fifty percent of the world's oil supplies are from the Middle East (which will change as the Alberta oil sands ramp up production), and most of the coal is from the Northern Hemisphere, mainly from the United States, China, and Russia. Nuclear reactors are predominantly a phenomenon of the core: France, the United States, and Japan together generate more than half of all the nuclear-generated electricity in the world.

The consumption side of energy also varies geographically. It has been estimated that current annual world energy consumption is equal to what it took about 1 million years to produce naturally. In one year, global energy consumption is equal to about 1.3 billion tonnes of coal. This is four times what the global population consumed in 1950 and 20 times what it consumed in 1850. And, as the $I = PAT$ formula suggests, the affluent core regions of the world far outstrip the peripheral regions in energy consumption. With nearly four times the population of the core regions, the peripheral regions account for less than one-third of global energy expenditures. Yet, consumption of energy in the peripheral regions is rising rapidly as globalization spreads industries, energy-intensive consumer products such

[12] International Energy Agency, *Key World Energy Statistics 2010.* Paris: International Energy Agency, 2010, p. 6 (available at **www.iea.org**).

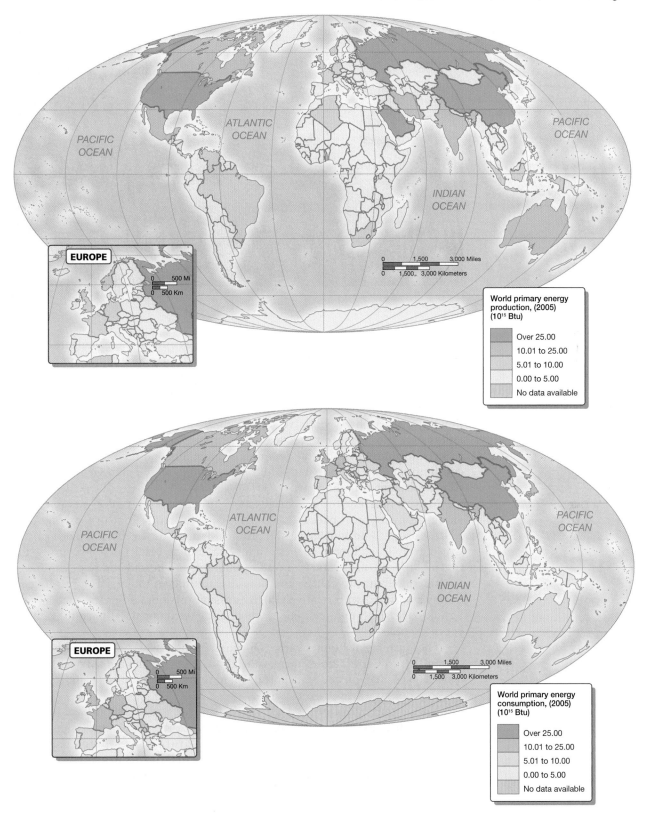

Figure 4.17 World production and consumption of energy, 2005 These paired maps provide a picture of the uneven distribution of the production and consumption of energy resources around the world. The United States is the largest producer and consumer of a range of energy resources. Notice that although the Middle East and North African countries as well as Nigeria are important producers of energy resources, their consumption (as well as that of the rest of the African continent, excluding South Africa) is very low. Japan produces a negligible amount of the total of world energy resources but consumes a relatively high share.   (*Source:* Adapted from *Energy Information Agency, International Energy Annual 2005*, Tables E1 and F1. www.eia.doe.gov/iea/wepbtu.html.)

Figure 4.18 Traffic in Bangkok, Thailand In many cities of Southeast Asia, such as Manila, Jakarta, and Hanoi, people spend several hours each day battling traffic. In Bangkok, it can take three to five hours to travel from one section of the city to another because of traffic congestion. An additional outcome of increasing automobile use in the periphery is rising rates of urban air pollution. In Mexico City, air pollution from motor vehicles is so severe that respiratory ailments are increasing, and residents with respiratory problems are routinely warned to stay indoors on hot summer days.

as automobiles and air conditioners, and energy-intensive agricultural practices into all regions of the world. It has been projected that the peripheral regions will become the dominant consumers of energy within a few decades (**Figure 4.18**).

Rising levels of energy consumption in both the nations of the core and those of the periphery will have serious global implications for climate change unless steps can be taken to reduce the consumption of fossil fuels and practical renewable alternatives can be found. (For a detailed look the impact of energy consumption and the possible solutions available, see **Human Geography and Climate Change 4.1—Energy**).

Most important for our discussion, however, is that every stage of the energy conversion process—from discovery to extraction, processing, and utilization—has an impact on the physical landscape. In the coalfields of the world, from Cape Breton to western Siberia, mining results in a loss of vegetation and topsoil, in erosion and water pollution, and in acid and toxic drainage. It also contributes to cancer and lung disease in coal miners. The burning of coal is associated with relatively high emissions of soot and gases, such as carbon dioxide and sulphur dioxide, which are environmentally harmful in high concentrations.

The burning of home-heating oil, diesel, and gasoline launches harmful chemicals into Earth's atmosphere, causing air pollution and related health problems. The production and transport of oil have resulted in oil spills and substantial pollution to water and ecosystems.

Natural gas is one of the least noxious of the hydrocarbon-based energy resources because it is converted relatively cleanly. Now supplying nearly one-quarter of global commercial energy, natural gas is predicted to be the fastest-growing energy source in the twenty-first century. Significant deposits of natural gas have been discovered in Alberta and off the coast of Nova Scotia. Plans are currently being made to pipe liquefied gas from these sources to the large market for this clean fuel in urban Canada and the eastern United States. Although preferred to oil and coal, natural gas is not produced or consumed without environmental impacts either. The risk of explosions at natural gas conversion facilities is significant, and leakages of gas from distribution systems contribute to the deterioration of Earth's atmosphere.

At the midpoint of the twentieth century, nuclear energy for civilian use was widely promoted as an alternative to fossil fuels. It was seen as the answer to the

Energy

Energy plays a fundamental role in day-to-day human activity, powering our cars, lights, and entertainment. Since the Industrial Revolution, much of the world relies on fossil fuels such as oil, gas, and coal to meet its energy needs. At the same time, fossil fuels are significant sources of greenhouse gas (GHG) emissions, with their combustion releasing carbon dioxide (CO_2) and nitrous oxide (NOX) into the atmosphere, two key greenhouse gases. Their use is responsible for approximately 70 percent of greenhouse gas emissions, and 80 percent of all CO_2 emissions, with coal producing proportionately more CO_2 emissions than either oil or gas.[13]

The economies of the core countries are heavily dependent on the use of fossil fuels, having the highest per capita use. However, the most rapid growth in the use of fossil fuels is occurring in the semiperiphery, driven in part by the economic development of countries such as Mexico, Brazil, India, and China. China's rapid industrialization, for example, is responsible for about one-third of the growth in the world's oil consumption, making it the world's largest source of greenhouse gases, ahead of the United States.[14] The Intergovernmental Panel on Climate Change (IPCC) estimates that global demand for energy will increase by 65 percent between 2004 and 2030, largely driven by the increasing energy needs of the industrializing countries of the periphery and semiperiphery. Given the growing demand for energy, greenhouse gas emissions are expected to increase for the foreseeable future.[15]

Like other industrialized core countries, Canada's economy is closely linked to fossil fuels. It has large coal reserves, and its oil reserves are second only to those of Saudi Arabia, enabling the country to be a net exporter of energy.[16] As a source of oil, much of the interest is now focused on northern Alberta's **oil sands**, a mixture of bitumen (a type of oil), sand, clay, and water. Energy companies are rushing to develop the estimated 174 billion barrels of recoverable oil, driven by rising crude oil prices, increased concern over the global supply of oil, and increased demand (**Figure 4.1.1**).

Canada's fossil fuel production sector represents 13 percent of Canada's overall GHG emissions, with the oil sands development alone accounting for 5 percent, making it the single largest contributor of GHG in Canada.[17] The reason is that the extraction of oil from the oil sands

Figure 4.1.1 Mining Alberta's oil sands Increased energy demand and limited reserves of easily accessible fossil fuels have led to an expansion of production in Northern Alberta's oil sands. (*Source:* © 2005 The Pembina Institute, Photographer: David Dodge. With permission)

[13] Intergovernmental Panel on Climate Change, *IPPC 4th Assessment Report: Climate Change 2007* (www.ipcc.ch/index.htm).

[14] Paul Krugman, "Dealing with the Dragon," *New York Times,* 4 January 2008, A12.

[15] *IPCC 4th Assessment Report: Climate Change 2007.* The projections assume "business as usual," which means no significant changes in the efficiency of energy use.

[16] D. Woynillowicz, C. Severson-Baker, and M. Raynolds, *Oil Sands Fever: The Environmental Implications of Canada's Oil Sands Rush.* Drayton Valley, AB: The Pembina Institute, 2005 (www.pembina.org).

[17] The Pembina Institute (www.pembina.org/oil-sands/os101/climate).

is very resource intensive: the equivalent of one barrel of oil has to be expended to extract three barrels of oil. Even as the level of greenhouse gas emissions per barrel of oil produced has been reduced with improved production techniques, new development has undercut these gains. Thus, even under the best-case scenarios, GHG emissions will increase substantially in the coming years as the oil sands industry looks to significantly increase production.[18] Estimates from Environment Canada project that oil sands operations could account for almost half of the increase in Canada's greenhouse gas emissions from 2006 to 2020.[19]

The growth of Alberta's oil sands raises interesting political and economic questions. Ottawa's desire to take action on GHG emissions through carbon taxes, for instance, risks slowing the economy or alienating western provinces. Similarly, whom are the emissions attributed to? Alberta becomes the largest source of emissions, but Alberta's production of oil and gas feeds consumption elsewhere. At the same time, California and other jurisdictions have moved to promote cleaner (e.g., lower carbon footprint) sources of energy, meaning that they may not buy Alberta oil.[20]

Finding energy supplies to match the expected growth in energy demand without increasing greenhouse gases is both difficult and costly. Conventional fossil fuels are not equally distributed across the globe, and new sources are typically costly to develop given their increasingly remote and often geographically challenging locations, such as the proposed oil drilling in the Arctic. Moreover, many of the new reserves are found offshore and at increasing depths below the ocean. The technical and safety challenges associated with offshore and deep sea drilling were highlighted by the three months it took to cap the Deepwater Horizon oil gusher in the Gulf of Mexico in 2010.

To date, much of the growth in energy demand has been met with coal-fired power plants, which are comparatively inexpensive and easy to build with existing technology while utilizing a widely available and inexpensive resource, despite increased GHG emissions. For instance, every 7 to 10 days, China is opening a new coal-fired power plant large enough to power almost all households in Montreal. At this pace, China's coal consumption is set to double every five years—along with GHG emissions.[21] Fortunately, China is also quickly becoming a leader in the development of various renewable energy sources such as solar and wind power.

Biofuels, or fuels made from plant material including corn, soy, and sugar cane, have been seen as a particularly environmentally friendly alternative to fossil fuels, reducing both greenhouse gas emissions and dependence on foreign oil reserves. The attraction of biofuels was based on the assumption that they were **carbon neutral**: any carbon released during their burning was equivalent to the carbon absorbed when the plants grew. Recent research has, however, argued that almost all biofuels are not as "green" as they may seem.[22] In fact, they may release as much or more greenhouse gases as conventional fuels once the full cost of production is taken into account. These full costs include the destruction of natural ecosystems for planting of biofuel crops such as corn, soy bean, or sugar cane, planting and fertilizing, refining crops into fuel, and their transportation to market. The development of biofuels may also push food prices higher as farmland is used for fuel rather than food production, and they were partially blamed for food riots in several peripheral nations in early 2008. Biofuels may also result in the destruction of natural ecosystems as new and often marginal lands are cleared for food or fuel production, potentially contributing to soil erosion and longer-term land degradation. Given the often over stated benefits of biofuels, it may be better to leave land in its natural state or to reforest,[23] as these more natural states typically absorb more carbon than cropland.

In the face of mounting concerns with the use of biofuels, governments must rethink energy policies. European governments have moved to reduce subsidies for biofuels, supporting only those that are environmentally sustainable and that yield a true **carbon benefit**, or the reduction in carbon dioxide emissions for the same quantity of fuel.[24] The greater the carbon benefit, the fewer GHG emissions. At the same time, however, questions emerge as to what alternative energy sources should be supported. Sugar cane, for instance, is transformed much more efficiently into biofuel than corn or soybean. Agricultural or forest industry wastes may also provide more efficient methods of fuel production, and research in this area continues.

Hydroelectric, solar, wind, and nuclear power are among the other energy options that are available and may help to reduce greenhouse gas emissions, but they too come with concerns. Hydroelectric energy, for example, has been criticized because of its land-use impacts. The Three Gorges Dam in China has resulted in environmental problems including water pollution and landslides and the displacement of 1.13 million people from their villages and livelihoods.[25] Similar concerns and outcomes

[18] Ibid.

[19] Ibid.

[20] Felicity Barringer, "California Will Offer Plan to Cut Harmful Emissions," *New York Times,* 26 June 2008, A8.

[21] Keith Bradsher and David Barboza, "Pollution from Chinese Coal Casts a Global Shadow," *New York Times,* 11 June 2006, A1.

[22] T. Searchinger, R. Heimlich, R.A. Houghton, F. Dong, A. Elobeid, J. Fabiosa, S. Tokgoz, D. Hayes, and T. Yu, "Use of US Croplands for Biofuels Increases Greenhouse Gases through Emissions from Land-Use Changes," *Science*, February 29, 2008, 319, pp. 1238–240.

[23] R. Righelato and D.V. Spracklen, "Carbon Mitigation by Biofuels or by Saving and Restoring Forests?" *Science*, 17 August 2007, 317, p. 902.

[24] Elisabeth Rosenthal, "Europe, Cutting Biofuel Subsidies, Redirects Aid to Stress Greenest Options," *New York Times*, January 22, 2008, A3. See also J.K. Bourne, "Growing Fuel: The Wrong Way, The Right Way," *National Geographic*, October 2007.

[25] Jim Yardley, "Chinese Dam Projects Criticized for their Human Costs," *New York Times*, 19 November 19, 2007, A4.

were experienced in Northern Quebec with the building of the La Grande hydroelectric system during the 1980s and 1990s. Flooding and river diversion resulted in the loss of traditional Cree lands and population displacement, although more recent hydroelectric projects in the area have been more sustainable.[26]

Renewable energy sources such as solar and wind power are currently small but growing energy providers, but they can only provide power when environmental conditions allow either wind capture or solar collection. Although research continues to improve the efficiency of solar power technology, current technology means that the true cost of solar power exceeds its returns. Wind generation has been criticized for its visual impacts on the landscape and concerns that migrating birds and bats may be killed by the rotating blades.

Nuclear energy has also been identified as an alternative energy source that is "green." Several jurisdictions, such as Ontario and the United Kingdom, are actively pursuing expansion of nuclear power plants given the increased need for energy and the desire to minimize greenhouse emissions. But nuclear energy comes with negative public perceptions and fears, both of security and of the technology, due to events such as the 2011

---

[26] J.F. Hornig, *Social and Environmental Impacts of the James Bay Hydroelectric Project.* Montreal: McGill-Queen's University Press, 1999.

Fukushima core meltdowns. The long-term disposal of radioactive waste, which remains toxic and radioactive for centuries, along with the decommissioning of the reactors themselves, poses additional long-term concerns and questions, and Canada has yet to articulate a policy for dealing with nuclear waste.

Although fossil fuels provide the majority of the world's energy supply, government and industry are actively searching for ways to eliminate greenhouse gases through energy conservation and alternative energy sources. The choices, however, are not clear cut, with each energy option having its own implications, and future choices will likely represent a compromise between continued use of conventional energy sources such as oil, gas, and coal, and renewable energy sources such as wind energy or solar power.

—K.B.N.

oil sands: a mixture of bitumen (a type of oil), sand, clay, and water

biofuels: fuels made from plant material including corn, soy, and sugar cane

carbon neutral: any carbon released upon burning is equivalent to the carbon absorbed when the plants grew

carbon benefit: the reduction in carbon dioxide emissions for the same quantity of fuel

---

expanding energy needs of core countries, especially since the supply of uranium worldwide was thought to be more than adequate for centuries of use (**Figure 4.19**). It was not until serious accidents at nuclear power plants began to occur, such as at Chernobyl in Ukraine in 1986 and Fukushima in Japan in 2011, that concerns about reactor safety led to a questioning of the nuclear option. Since these accidents, some core countries have drastically reduced or eliminated their reliance on nuclear energy. Another problem is the disposal of nuclear waste generated in

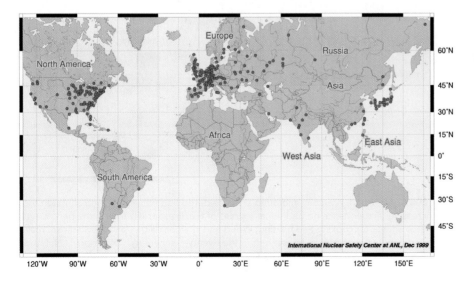

Figure 4.19 World distribution of nuclear reactors, 2005
Most of the dependence on nuclear power is concentrated in core countries. South America and Africa together contain only four nuclear reactors. Whereas some peripheral countries, such as India, are enthusiastic about increasing their nuclear energy production, some core countries (Germany and Switzerland, for example) are phasing out nuclear power. Australia, where there is a very strong antinuclear movement, is one of the few core countries to have rejected nuclear power altogether. (*Source:* "Map of Nuclear Power Reactors: World Map"; available from International Nuclear Safety Center at Argonne National Laboratory (**www.insc.anl.gov/pwrmaps/map/world_map.php**).

173

the reactors: to this day, no permanent storage site for highly radioactive waste exists anywhere on the planet.

Although nuclear power problems are largely confined to the core, the periphery is not without its own energy-related environmental problems. Because a large proportion of populations in the periphery relies on wood for their energy needs, the demand for fuelwood has risen in tandem with population growth. One of the most immediate environmental impacts of wood burning is air pollution. But the most alarming environmental problem related to wood burning is the rapid depletion of forest resources. With the other conventional sources of energy (coal, oil, and gas) being too costly or unavailable to most peripheral households, wood is the only alternative. The demand for fuelwood has been so great in many peripheral regions that forest reserves are being rapidly used up (**Figure 4.20**).

Fuelwood depletion is extreme in the highland areas of Nepal as well as in Andean Bolivia and Peru. The clearing of forests for fuelwood in these regions has led to serious steep-slope soil erosion. In sub-Saharan Africa, where 90 percent of the region's energy needs are met by wood, overcutting of the forests has resulted in denuded areas around rapidly growing cities. And although wood gathering is usually associated with rural life, it is not uncommon for city dwellers to use wood to satisfy their household energy needs as well. It is now estimated that city dwellers in Niamey, the capital of Niger, travel from 50 to 100 kilometres to gather wood. The same goes

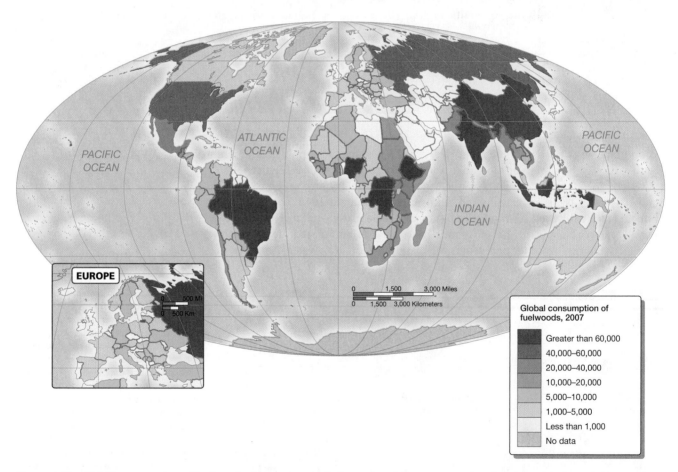

Figure 4.20 Global consumption of fuelwoods, 2007 Firewood, charcoal, and dung are considered traditional fuels, and although their availability is decreasing, dependence on them is increasing. Dependence on traditional sources of fuel is especially high in the periphery. In Africa, for example, they are the most important energy source for cooking and heating. Wood and charcoal, although renewable sources, are replenished very slowly. Acute scarcity will be a certainty for most African households in the twenty-first century. (Data from U.N. Food and Agricultural Organization, *State of the World's Forests 2007*, Annex, Tab. 4, Rome, 2007. **ftp://ftp.fao.org/docrep/fao/009/a0773e/a0773e10.pdf**).

for inhabitants of Ouagadougou in Burkina Faso, where the average haul for wood is also over 50 kilometres.

Hydroelectric power was also once seen as a preferred alternative to the more obviously environmentally polluting fossil fuel sources. It is no exaggeration to state that the wave of dam building that occurred throughout the world over the course of the twentieth century has improved the overall availability, quality, cost, and dependability of energy (**Figure 4.21**). Unfortunately, however, dams built to provide hydroelectric power (as well as water for irrigation, navigation, and drinking) for the burgeoning cities of the core and to encourage economic development in the periphery and semiperiphery have also had profound negative environmental impacts. Among the most significant of these impacts are changes in downstream flow, evaporation, sediment transport and deposition, mineral quality and soil moisture, channelling and bank scouring, and aquatic plants and animals, as well as changes in human health.

The construction of dams also dramatically alters the surrounding landscape, sometimes with serious consequences such as geological tremors caused by the enormous weight of the water behind the dam. Furthermore, as the rising waters of the reservoir drown the vegetation, decomposition processes in the increasingly acidic water produce methyl mercury, a poisonous substance that

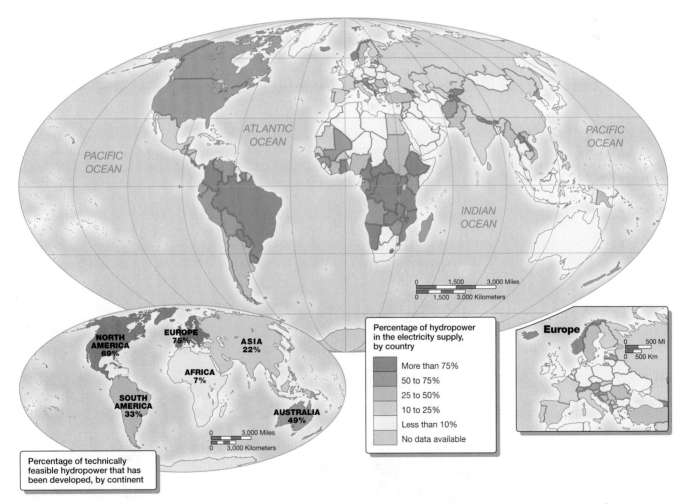

Figure 4.21   Percentage of hydropower in the electricity supply by country, 2002   Although the great dam-building era for core countries is now largely completed, many peripheral countries, in a bid to participate more actively in the world economy, are building dams. A few countries are almost exclusively dependent on the electricity produced from dams. These include Norway, Nepal, Zambia, Ghana, Paraguay, and Costa Rica. Although the electricity produced by dams is environmentally benign in terms of emissions, the construction of large dams can be extremely destructive to the environment and can dislocate large numbers of people. Still, given the increasing need for electricity in rapidly developing peripheral countries, hydropower is becoming a more attractive energy option for many of them because of the uncertain supply of oil in the future. The larger map shows the amount of hydropower that is currently available; the smaller one shows the potential for hydropower development, especially for peripheral regions.

bioaccumulates in the aquatic food chain and ultimately harms humans that eat fish caught in the reservoir or downstream. The impounded waters can also incubate mosquitoes, which carry diseases, such as malaria and West Nile virus. In light of these and various other environmental and social problems, many argue that new dam projects should not be undertaken without a clear strategy for preventing or alleviating them.

To make matters more complex, many large-scale dam projects are located on Aboriginal lands, which means that these problems disproportionally affect indigenous populations, whereas the produced electricity benefits mainly urban populations. An example of the increasing controversy over dam construction is the James Bay Project in Quebec, approximately 1,000 kilometres north of Montreal. Begun in the 1970s, the expansive system of dams now produces as much electricity as Belgium, but it pits the interests of electricity consumers as far away as New York City against the concerns of the 5,000 Cree whose livelihood is altered by the reservoirs (**Figure 4.22**).

One of the reasons hydroelectric power continues to be appealing, however, is that it produces few atmospheric pollutants compared with fossil fuels. Indeed, coal and gas power stations as well as factories, automobiles, and other forms of transportation are largely responsible for the increasingly acidic quality of Earth's atmosphere (see **Human Geography and Climate Change 4.2—Legislating for Climate Change: Kyoto, Cancun, and Onward**). Increasing the level of acids in the atmosphere are sulphur dioxide, nitrogen oxides, and hydrocarbons, among other gases, which are released into the atmosphere from motor vehicle exhaust, industrial processes, and power generation (based on fossil fuels). If these gases reach sufficient concentrations and are not effectively dispersed in the atmosphere, acid rain can result.

Acid rain is the wet deposition of acids on Earth created by the natural cleansing properties of the atmosphere. Acid rain occurs as the water droplets in clouds absorb certain gases, which later fall back to Earth as acid precipitation. Also included under the term *acid rain* are acid mists, acid fogs, and smog. The effects of acid rain are widespread. Throughout much of the Northern Hemisphere, for example, forests are being poisoned and killed and soils are becoming too acidic to support plant life. Lakes are becoming acidic in North America and Scandinavia. As if this were not enough, the Great Lakes that serve much of the population of Ontario have become increasingly polluted with heavy metals and other toxic substances that are normally locked in soils but become

acid rain: the wet deposition of acids on Earth created by the natural cleansing properties of the atmosphere

Figure 4.22 Dams in Quebec Using an extensive system of large dams in the James Bay and Great Whale watersheds, Quebec has become an important producer of hydroelectricity. Once considered an environmentally friendly source of power, dam projects are becoming increasingly controversial as people learn more about their drawbacks. These include the destruction of Aboriginal lands, the disruption of fish stocks, and the problems of silt accumulation. Other critics observe that more efficient energy conservation would remove the need for any further dam construction.

Human Geography and Climate Change

Legislating for Climate Change: Kyoto, Cancun, and Onward

Since the 1992 Earth Summit in Rio de Janeiro, Brazil, the international community has sought to ensure economic development without further threatening the global environment. At the Rio Earth Summit, 167 nations ratified the Framework Convention on Climate Change with the aim of finding ways to reduce the amount of greenhouse gases (GHG). An additional and equally critical aim of the Summit was to ensure that the burden of protecting the environment would be shared equitably across all nations.

In December 1997, these nations began to address the problem of balancing global economic development and environmental protection more substantively by forging the Kyoto Protocol. The Protocol marked the first time that attempts were made to limit the amount of GHG emissions generated by core countries through legislative and binding measures. The aim of the Protocol was to cut the combined emissions of greenhouse gases from core countries by roughly 5 percent from their 1990 levels by 2012. It also specified the amount each core nation would contribute toward meeting that reduction goal. Nations with the highest carbon dioxide (CO_2) emissions—the United States, Canada, Japan, and most European nations—were expected to reduce emissions by a range of 6 to 8 percent.

The Kyoto Protocol was historic in that it was the first and only binding international agreement to reduce GHG. Since Kyoto, world leaders have met on a number of occasions to negotiate the second phase of the Kyoto Protocol (with the first ending in 2012). Climate talks in Copenhagen (2009) marked a deadline for completing these talks and setting GHG reduction targets for the post-2012 period. However, the Copenhagen Accord was largely seen as a failure, agreed upon by only 25 countries (and not including Canada), and it was never ratified by the United Nations. A year later, the U.N. Climate Summit in Cancun, Mexico, also failed to deliver a global climate agreement, although countries did commit to action and international cooperation on adaptation to climate change; agreed on measures to reduce emissions from deforestation and forest degradation in peripheral countries; agreed to accelerate the development and transfer of technology that would reduce GHG to the periphery; and agreed to continued commitment to the Green Climate Fund that will finance adaptation and mitigation efforts in peripheral countries. However, they could not reach agreement on reducing carbon emissions, and no replacement for the Kyoto Protocol was agreed upon, with Canada portrayed as a key roadblock to finding agreement on the issue given its demands that peripheral and semiperipheral countries such as China and India also bear responsibility for GHG reduction.

In Canada, movement toward reduction of GHG has been equally problematic, despite Canadians' concern with climate change (**Figure 4.2.1**) and desire to see strong action on the issue (see **Human Geography and Climate Change Box 12.3—Climate Change and Social Action**), and despite the fact that Canada ranks in the top 10 of GHG emitters.[27] While Canada ratified the Kyoto Protocol in a vote in the House of Commons on December 10, 2002, ongoing disagreements between the different levels of government over the implementation of the Kyoto Protocol, including methods to reduce emissions and disagreements between provinces, meant that the agreement rather was in trouble. Alberta, for instance, was strongly opposed to the implementation of the protocol owing to fears that its oil-rich economy would be seriously harmed if emission reductions were enforced. On the other hand, Quebec, with its abundance of hydroelectric power, strongly supported the agreement, believing it would benefit from being seen as a provider of "clean" energy to the United States. The election of Stephen Harper's Conservative government in January 2006 effectively ended Canada's participation in the agreement.

Instead, the federal government set out to create a "Made in Canada" strategy to deal with climate change.[28] Announced in April 2007 and formalized in March 2008, Canada's *Turning the Corner* framework was supposed to commit the country to reducing greenhouse gas emissions 20 percent by 2020 from 2006 levels.[29] It included mandatory reductions for industry, along with additional new measures to address the oil sands and electricity sectors, two key greenhouse gas emitting sectors. Other policies to reduce emissions, including new vehicle fuel efficiency standards and consumer appliance standards, would also be introduced. To achieve these reductions, the plan provided incentives for industry and individual Canadians to reduce greenhouse emissions. In addition, new oil sand operators starting after 2012 would be required to have carbon capture and storage capabilities, and the construction of inefficient coal-fired electricity generation would not be allowed.

Critics of the policy immediately questioned the new greenhouse targets and the policy's feasibility. It was unclear, for instance, whether the targeted reductions were achievable within 10 years, a timeline not all that different than that laid out in the Kyoto Protocol. Others argued that the targeted reduction levels were too low. On a technical front, it was unclear whether CO_2 capture and storage, whereby carbon emissions are pumped into underground reservoirs rather than released into the atmosphere, is safe

---

[27] Claire Demerse, *Our Fair Share*. Drayton Valley, AB: The Pembina Institute, April 2009.

[28] Steve Soloman, "Deep by Shortsighted?" *Globe and Mail*, April 14, 2006, A14.

[29] See www.ec.gc.ca.

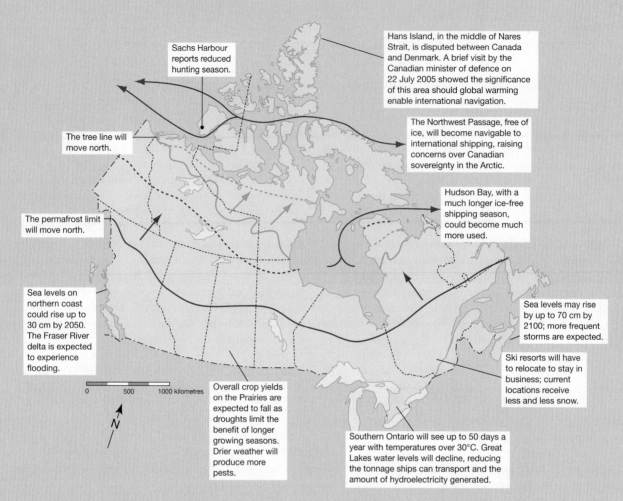

Sachs Harbour reports reduced hunting season.

Hans Island, in the middle of Nares Strait, is disputed between Canada and Denmark. A brief visit by the Canadian minister of defence on 22 July 2005 showed the significance of this area should global warming enable international navigation.

The tree line will move north.

The Northwest Passage, free of ice, will become navigable to international shipping, raising concerns over Canadian sovereignty in the Arctic.

The permafrost limit will move north.

Hudson Bay, with a much longer ice-free shipping season, could become much more used.

Sea levels on northern coast could rise up to 30 cm by 2050. The Fraser River delta is expected to experience flooding.

Sea levels may rise by up to 70 cm by 2100; more frequent storms are expected.

Ski resorts will have to relocate to stay in business; current locations receive less and less snow.

0   500   1000 kilometres

N

Overall crop yields on the Prairies are expected to fall as droughts limit the benefit of longer growing seasons. Drier weather will produce more pests.

Southern Ontario will see up to 50 days a year with temperatures over 30°C. Great Lakes water levels will decline, reducing the tonnage ships can transport and the amount of hydroelectricity generated.

Figure 4.2.1 Impact of climate change in Canada The projected increase in global temperatures associated with the greenhouse effect will have many effects on Canada, some of which are shown on this map. Average temperatures in some regions of the country could rise by as much as 5° to 10°C. Even now, evidence suggests that polar bears have suffered from the reduction of winter sea ice on which they hunt. The Inuvialuit community of Sachs Harbour on Banks Island now reports more than a month's reduction in their average winter hunting season. The projected melting of Canada's Arctic ice and permafrost will also affect the global community because it will contribute to a global rise in sea levels. The spread of West Nile virus across southern Canada may be aided by warmer summers, which allow mosquitoes to thrive and transmit the disease.   (*Sources:* Geoffrey J. Matthews and Robert Morrow Jr., *Canada and the World: An Atlas Resource*, 2nd ed. Scarborough, ON: Prentice Hall, 1995, p. 61; Government of Canada, *Think Climate Change*, Ottawa, 1001 [Catalogue En56-169/2001E]. Further details on regional impacts and a video about Sachs Harbour [*Sila Alangotok: Inuit Observations on Climate Change*] are available at www.climatechange.gc.ca/.)

and viable as a technology in a cost-effective way,[30] and a Canadian demonstration project raised further questions.[31] Ultimately, the federal government never ratified the *Turning the Corner* framework. The NDP-sponsored Climate Change Accountability Act (Bill C-311) was passed by the House of Commons in 2010 but was ultimately killed in the Senate by the Conservatives.[32] The Act would have committed Canada to reduce GHG emissions 25 percent below 1990 levels by 2020 and to an 80 percent reduction

by 2050. To its credit, the federal government did announce vehicle fuel efficiency standards in April 2010, but it has yet to introduce other regulations to deal with GHG emissions and climate change.

The failure to lead at the federal level has been partially offset by movement at the provincial level, with provincial governments charting their own course independent of Ottawa.[33] In 2008, Manitoba became the first provincial government to confirm its commitment to

[30] Elisabeth Rosenthal, "Europe Turns Back to Coal, Raising Climate Fears," *New York Times*, April 23, 2008, A6.

[31] Nathan VanderKlippe, "Gas Not Leaking from Carbon Project: Review," *Globe and Mail*, January 19, 2011, A7.

[32] Gloria Galloway, "Tory Senators Kill Climate Bill Passed by House," *Globe and Mail*, November 17, 2010, A5.

[33] See, for example, *Provincial Power Play: Breaking Away from Federal Inaction on Climate Change*. David Suzuki Foundation, 2008. See also: *Highlights of Provincial Greenhouse Gas Reduction Plans*. Drayton Valley, AB: The Pembina Institute, 2009.

reaching Kyoto targets for greenhouse gas emissions by 2012,[34] and Quebec became the first province to introduce a **carbon tax**, which is a tax on emissions of CO_2 and other greenhouse gases.[35] Similarly, the Western Climate Initiative,[36] which includes states and provinces along the western rim of North America, is meant to combat climate change. Despite these measures, Canada's GHG emissions have continued to increase.

The legacy of Kyoto and later attempts to curb GHG emissions is therefore limited. Although it has initiated new discussions and actions to curb emissions, the United States never signed the treaty, and both Canada and Australia backed away from commitments to greenhouse gas reductions. Globally, responses to climate change remain mired in political arguments over causes, responsibility, and participation, as witnessed by the comparative failures of Copenhagen and Cancun. Kyoto, for instance, placed the burden of reducing global climate change on the core countries most responsible for the buildup of greenhouse gases. At the same time, industrializing countries, including China and India, were expected to play a role, although Kyoto set no binding limits on their emissions and did not establish a mechanism or timetable for these countries to take on such limits voluntarily. As discussions continued, most industrialized countries stated that developing nations, including large industrializing nations such as India and China, must participate in emission reduction and that reductions would be binding. Peripheral and semiperipheral countries continue to reject this condition, however, citing their own need for economic development and their inability to pay for new technology. The Harper government has also clearly stated that any Canadian policies will reflect any climate regulations adopted in the United States, meaning progress will likely be slow. Further international disagreement on GHG reductions is likely.

—K.B.N.

[34] Joe Friesen, "Manitoba's Kyoto Bill Will Be a First in Canada," *Globe and Mail*, April 12, 2008, A5.

[35] Fannie Olivier, "Gore Praises Quebec's Environmental Record," *Globe and Mail*, April 5, 2008, A3.

[36] See their website at www.westernclimateinitiative.org/.

carbon tax: a tax on emissions of CO_2 and other greenhouse gases

soluble under acidic conditions and so find their way into water bodies where they bioaccumulate (**Figure 4.23**).

Before giving up all hope that the use of energy can ever be anything but detrimental to the environment, it is important to realize that alternatives to fossil fuels, hydroelectric power, and nuclear energy do exist. Renewable energy derived from the sun, the wind, Earth's interior (geothermal sources), and the tides has been found to be clean, profitable, and dependable. Japan, the United States, and Germany all have large-scale solar energy production facilities, whereas Iceland, Italy, Japan, the United States, Mexico, New Zealand, and the Philippines all

Figure 4.23 Pollution of Lake Ontario The disposal of industrial waste, municipal drainage, and agricultural runoff into the Great Lakes has contributed to elevated levels of toxic substances (such as dioxins, mercury, and pesticides) in those waters. Although recent environmental legislation has led to a decline in current effluents, it will take many years before the amounts of harmful chemicals already present in the lakes have dissipated to levels that no longer threaten the health of the more than 40 million people that surround and depend on this ecosystem. Despite such measures, however, many problems remain. For example, the continued release of sewage into the lakes often poses a nuisance for communities downstream—as this photograph of a closed recreational beach in Toronto (south of Woodbine) shows, and until more sustainable solutions are discovered, it is likely that such closures will continue to be an annual event. Photo: © Dick Hemingway

derive some of their energy production from geothermal sources. Tidal power barrages are currently operational in France, China, Russia, South Korea, and Annapolis Royal, Nova Scotia, with another major project in South Korea promising to double the global production of tidal power by 2012. The biggest success story in renewable energy, however, is wind energy.

Wind power generation has enjoyed a meteoric rise over the last decade. From its beginnings in Denmark and Germany in the 1980s, the wind power industry has now developed into a globalized business with remarkable growth rates. Between 2005 and 2010, installed wind power generating capacity worldwide tripled. Canada grew its installations fivefold (mainly through wind farm development in Alberta, Ontario, and Quebec), enough to power 1 million Canadian homes. This pales in comparison to China, however, which increased its capacity twentyfold during the same period—it is now the biggest producer of wind energy worldwide. The example of India is equally instructive: it is now the fifth-largest producer of wind energy in the world and its Suzlon Energy—a company founded only in 1995—is now the third-largest manufacturer of wind turbines in the world.

Impacts of Land-Use Change on the Environment

In addition to industrial pollution and steadily increasing demands for energy, the environment is also being dramatically affected by pressures on the land. The clearing of land for fuel, farming, grazing, resource extraction, highway building, energy generation, and war all have significant impacts on land. Land may be classified into five categories: forest, cultivated land, grassland, wetland, and areas of settlement. Geographers understand land-use change as occurring in either of two ways: conversion or modification. *Conversion* is the wholesale transformation of land from one use to another (for example, the conversion of forested land to settlement). *Modification* is an alteration of existing cover (for example, when a grassland is overlaid with railroad tracks or when a forest is thinned but not clear-cut). As human populations have increased and the need for land for settlement and cultivation has also increased, changes to the land have followed.

One of the most dramatic impacts of humans on the environment is loss or alteration of forest cover on the planet caused by the clearing of forests over millennia to make way for cultivation and settlement. Forests are not only cleared to provide land to accommodate increases in human numbers, but they are also exploited for the vast resources they contain. The approximate chronology and estimated extent of the clearing of the world's forests since pre-agricultural times is portrayed in **Table 4.2**. The table shows that the forested area of the world has been reduced by about 8 million square kilometres since pre-agricultural times, an area equivalent to four-fifths of the territory of Canada.

The permanent clearing and destruction of forests, known as *deforestation*, is currently occurring most alarmingly in the world's rain forests. **Figure 4.24** shows the global extent of deforestation. The U.N. Food and Agricultural Organization has estimated that rain forests globally are being destroyed at the rate of one football field (0.5 hectare) per second.

Today, rain forests cover less than 7 percent of the land surface, half of what they covered only a few thousand years ago. Destruction of the rain forests, however, is not just about the loss of trees, a renewable resource that is being eliminated more quickly than it can be regenerated. It is also about the loss of the biological diversity of an ecosystem, which translates into the potential loss of biological compounds that may have great medical value. The destruction of rain forests is also about destabilizing the oxygen and carbon dioxide cycles of the forests, which may have long-term effects on global climate. Much of the destruction of the South American rain forests is the result of peripheral countries' attempts at economic development. **Figure 4.25** (on p. 182) illustrates another aspect of the problem—the clear-cutting of forests in Canada. Demands for more sustainable

TABLE 4.2 Estimated Area Cleared (1,000 km²)

Total Region or Country	Pre-1650	1650–1749	1750–1849	1850–1978	1990–2000	2000–2005	Estimate
North America	6	80	380	641	0	1	1,108
Central America	15	30	40	200	+4*	3	288
Latin America and Caribbean	12	100	170	637	42	45	1,006
Australia, New Zealand, and the South Pacific	4	5	6	362	4	4	385
Former USSR	61	150	260	575	—	—	1,046
Europe	176	54	186	18	+9	+7	481
Asia	732	190	606	1,220	8	10	2,766
Africa	126	24	72	469	44	40	775
Total Estimate	1,132	633	1,720	4,185	85	96	7,855

*"Plus" sign indicates a growth, not loss, of total forest area (× 1,000 km²).

Sources: Adapted from B.L. Turner II, W.C. Clark, R.W. Kates, J.F. Richards, J.T. Mathews, and W.B. Meyer, *The Earth as Transformed by Human Action: Global and Regional Changes in the Biosphere over the Past 300 Years.* Cambridge: Cambridge University Press, 1990, p. 180; U.N. Food and Agricultural Organization, *State of the World's Forests*, 2007, pp. 109–115.

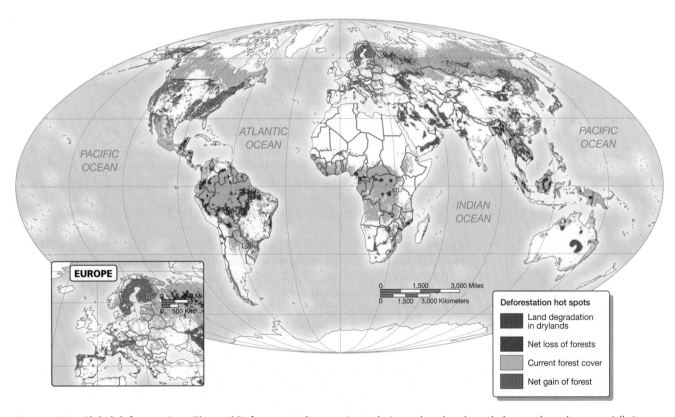

Figure 4.24 Global deforestation The world's forests are disappearing or being reduced or degraded everywhere, but especially in tropical countries. Since agriculture emerged about 10,000 years ago, human activities have diminished the world's forest resources by about 25 percent. Whereas forests once occupied about one-third of Earth's surface, they now take up about one-quarter. Playing an important role in the global ecosystem, they filter air and noise pollution, provide a habitat for wildlife, and slow down water runoff, helping to recharge streams and groundwater. They also influence climate at local, regional, and global levels.   (*Source:* Adapted from E.B. da Silva, GeoScience Blog: The World of Geography, "World Deforestation," Map. http://images.wri.org/sdm-gene-02-deforestation.jpg.)

Figure 4.25 Clear-cutting in British Columbia Views like this one have mobilized groups, such as Greenpeace, against Canadian forestry practices. Although making some concessions and supporting research into more environmentally acceptable methods, the forest industry continues to log large parts of its timber licences in this way.

forestry practices have long dogged this industry, and yet for many parts of Canada's periphery, the clear-cutting of forests for lumber or pulp and paper is still a crucial economic activity. In Canada, at present, 1 million hectares are harvested (90 percent by clear-cutting) and replanted each year.

Great geographical variability exists with respect to human impacts on the world's forests. In most of the core regions, net clearance of the forests has been replaced by regeneration. Yet, for most of the periphery, clearance has accelerated to such an extent that one estimate shows a 50 percent reduction in the amount of forest cover since the early twentieth century.

Cultivation is another important component of global land use, which we deal with extensively in Chapter 8. However, a few points about the environmental impacts of cultivation are pertinent here. During the past 300 years, the land devoted to cultivation has expanded globally by 450 percent. In 1700, the global area of land under cultivation was about the size of Argentina. Today, it is the size of the entire continent of South America. Although the most rapid expansion of cropland since the mid-twentieth century has occurred in the peripheral regions, the amount of cropland in the core regions has either held steady or been reduced. The expansion of cropland in the peripheral regions is partly a response to growing populations and rising levels of consumption worldwide. It is also partly due to the globalization of agriculture (see Chapter 8), which has "outsourced" some of the food production destined for core populations to regions in the periphery. Conversely, the reduction of cropland in some core regions is partly a result of this globalization and partly the result of a more intensive use of cropland—utilizing more fertilizers, pesticides, and farm machinery—and new crop strains.

Grasslands are also used productively the world over for livestock grazing. As **Figure 4.26** shows, most grassland occurs in arid and semi-arid regions that are unsuitable for farming, the result of either lack of water or poor soils. Some grasslands, however, occur in more rainy regions where tropical rain forests have been removed and replaced by grasslands. Approximately 42 million square kilometres of land surface are currently taken up by grasslands.

Human impacts on grasslands are largely of two sorts. The first is the conversion of grasslands to other uses, most frequently settlement. The second impact, triggered partly by an increase in global trade and consumption of beef, is the widespread overgrazing of grasslands. In its most severe form, overgrazing can lead to **desertification**, the degradation of land cover and damage to the soil and water in grasslands and arid and semi-arid lands. One of the most severe cases of

desertification: the degradation of land cover and damage to the soil and water in grasslands and arid and semi-arid lands

Figure 4.26 African grasslands Also known as *savannas*, these grasslands include scattered shrubs and isolated small trees as well as extensive herds of roaming animals, such as gazelles, giraffes, zebras, wildebeests, antelopes, and elephants.

desertification has been occurring in the Sahel region of Africa since the 1970s. The degradation of the grasslands bordering the Sahara Desert, however, has not been a simple case of careless overgrazing by thoughtless herders. Severe drought, land decline, recurrent famine, political instability, and the breakdown of traditional systems for coping with disaster have all combined to create increased pressure on fragile resources, resulting in a loss of grass cover and extreme soil degradation (**Figure 4.27**).

Human impacts on wetland environments have also been numerous. The most widespread, however, has been the draining or filling of wetlands and their conversion to other land uses, primarily settlement and cultivation. One reliable estimate places the total area of the world's wetlands at about 8.5 million square kilometres

Figure 4.27 Desertification in sub-Saharan Africa Desertification is a mounting problem in many parts of the world, but especially in Africa south of the Sahara Desert. Overgrazing on fragile arid and semi-arid rangelands and deforestation without reforestation are thought to be the chief causes of desertification in this part of Africa.

with about 1.5 million square kilometres lost to drainage or filling. In Australia, all of the original 20,000 square kilometres of wetlands have been lost to conversion.

The Exploitation of the World's Fisheries

Fishing has always been an important activity, and current statistics show that it remains so on a global scale. For example, data presented in the Food and Agriculture Organization's *The State of the World's Fisheries and Aquaculture* for 2006 show that the annual total volume of fish caught in all the world's rivers and oceans has risen consistently every year since the 1950s (**Figure 4.28**). Indeed, the volume for 2004, some 95 million tonnes, represented the largest annual amount of fish ever caught, according to the FAO.[37]

According to FAO statistics for 2004, China (16.9 million tonnes) and Peru (9.6 million tonnes) were the top countries, followed by the United States (5.0 million tonnes), and Chile (4.9 million tonnes) (**Figure 4.29**). Canada ranked nineteenth with a total capture of 1.17 million tonnes in 2004.

Beneath these statistics lies a story that the FAO has been very keen to stress: it appears that the world's fisheries have almost reached the limits of their production, and these very high totals are not sustainable over the long term. Simply put, there is a growing body of evidence that global fish stocks are now being depleted faster than they can replace themselves. For example, in its 2002 report, the FAO observes that only 25 percent of the world's marine fish stocks are "moderately exploited" or "underexploited." The state of the remaining 75 percent makes for depressing reading: 47 percent are "fully exploited," 18 percent are "overexploited," and 10 percent are "significantly depleted."

Among the last group are the North Sea herring (whose numbers collapsed in the 1970s), the Atlantic blue fin tuna (which has declined from 250,000 fish in 1975 to 20,000 in recent years), and—of particular concern to Canadian fishers—the North Atlantic cod. Once the most important fish stock in the region, the cod population declined by a factor of 100 between 1990 and 1994. The species is now officially classed as endangered and, as the FAO observes, has failed "to respond to the drastic management measures that have been adopted. . . ." These particular stocks have clearly surpassed their **maximum sustainable yield** (**MSY**), a figure defined as the equilibrium between a fish's biological productivity and the level of the fishing effort. The attempt to net more will harm the ability of the species to maintain its population and before long result in a reduced catch.

maximum sustainable yield (MSY): the equilibrium between a fish population's biological productivity and the level of fishing effort; theoretically, the MSY for a fish stock is the largest number that can be caught while ensuring that enough remain for a productive fishery next year

Figure 4.28 The world's rising catch of fish, 1950–2004 The Food and Agricultural Organization's statistics show a rising global volume of fish caught since the 1950s. Note: This graph shows the total for the world's "capture" fisheries (inland and marine). It does not include figures for aquaculture. (*Source:* Food and Agriculture Organization of the United Nations, "The World's Rising Catch of Fish 1950–2004" from *State of the World's Fisheries and Aquaculture 2006.* Available at www.fao.org.)

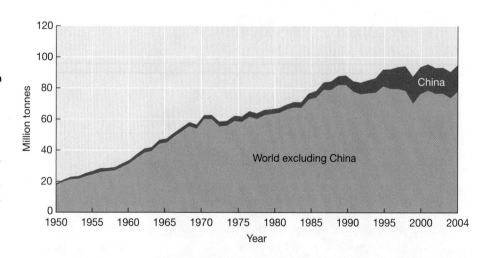

[37] Data from the Food and Agriculture Organization of the United Nations can be found on the website at **www.fao.org**, where a wealth of other statistics and reports on fisheries can be consulted. The statistics used here are from Part 1 of their report, *State of the World's Fisheries and Aquaculture 2010.*

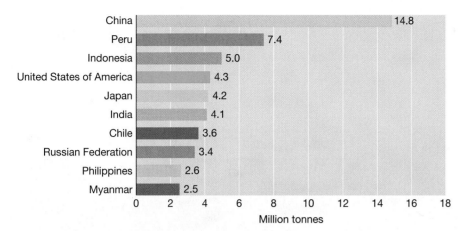

Figure 4.29 Marine and inland capture fisheries: Top 10 producer countries in 2004 In a year in which the total catch was 95.0 million tonnes, the leading country (China) caught 16.9 million tonnes. Canada ranked nineteenth, with a total catch of 1.17 million tonnes. Note: Figures for aquaculture are excluded. (*Source:* Food and Agriculture Organization of the United Nations, "Leading Fishing Nations by Size of Catch in 2004" from *State of the World's Fisheries and Aquaculture 2010.* Available at www.fao.org.)

How could the world's fisheries have reached such a state? Two very thoughtful reports by the internationally respected Worldwatch Institute suggest that the present situation is the almost inevitable outcome of two competing factors: (1) the world's *overcapacity* to fish and (2) the *resource depletion* of marine stock.[38] In a nutshell, too many fishers are chasing a decreasing number of fish. Let us consider each of these factors in turn.

Overcapacity The FAO defines the term **fishing capacity** as "the ability of a fleet to catch fish" and notes that this capacity can be most easily measured by counting the number of boats in a fishing fleet.[39] Between 1970 and 1992 the size of the world's fishing fleet doubled both in terms of tonnage (to 26 million tonnes) and number of vessels (to 3.5 million). Such totals, according to the Worldwatch Institute, mean that the world has twice the fishing capacity it needs to meet present demands—in other words, a large *overcapacity* (or *excess capacity*) exists. This situation, which is both economically and environmentally unsustainable over the long term, is the result of six main factors that have affected the growth of global fishing since the 1950s.

fishing capacity: the ability of a fleet to catch fish, most easily measured by counting the number of boats in a fishing fleet

1. *Open access to fisheries.* Historically, beyond 5 kilometres (3 miles) from the coast (the range a cannon could fire), the world's oceans and their fisheries were open to all. Because no one country or person "owned" the fish stocks in these waters, fishers could catch as much as they wanted and had no incentive to conserve stocks. The "tragedy of the commons," Garret Hardin's term for the complete exhaustion of a common resource through open access, was not a frequent problem because many fisheries developed informal customs that regulated fishing activities and because fishing vessels were too small to affect fishing stocks and technology was in its infancy. However, traditional practices of open access could not hope to regulate fishing capacity once technology began to change.

2. *Technological change.* The development of the "factory trawler" by European shipbuilders in the 1950s revolutionized fishing. Their enormous stern-mounted trawl nets enabled such ships to catch far more than traditional fishing boats did, and their ability to process and freeze their catch on board meant that they could stay at sea for months (**Figure 4.30**). Freed from the

---

[38] Peter Weber, "Protecting Oceanic Fisheries and Jobs." In Linda Starke (ed.), *State of the World 1995.* New York: Worldwatch Institute and Norton, 1995, pp. 21–37; Anne Platt McGinn, "Promoting Sustainable Fisheries." In Linda Starke (ed.), *State of the World 1998.* New York: Worldwatch Institute and Norton, 1998, pp. 59–78.

[39] FAO, "Excess Capacity and Illegal Fishing: Challenges to Sustainable Fisheries—What Is Fishing Capacity?" *FAO Newsroom, Focus on the Issues,* 2004, available online at **www.fao.org/newsroom/en/focus/2004/47127/article_47132en.html**.

Figure 4.30 Trawler This view of Klaksvik harbour in the Faroe Islands in the North Atlantic shows a deep-sea trawler moored beside a fish-processing plant. Like Greenland, the Faroe Islands are a constituent country of the kingdom of Denmark. Between 2004 and 2008, Danish-flagged trawlers were denied access to ports in Newfoundland and Labrador in retaliation for what Canada considered overfishing in international waters off Canada's eastern coast. Denmark has been unwilling to respect the Northwest Atlantic Fisheries Organization (NAFO) fishing quotas in that zone. The ban was reinstated in February of 2010 after disagreements over quotas of northern shrimp could not be resolved.

need to return to port frequently, these huge industrial trawlers are "free to roam the globe in search of profits."[40]

3. *National claims to fishing grounds.* Since 1976, to protect their domestic fleets from the effects of competition from foreign factory trawlers, an increasing number of countries have been extending their fisheries' jurisdictions. The 1982 U.N. Convention on the Law of the Sea (UNCLOS) is an international treaty that was formally ratified in November 1994 to support this move. UNCLOS grants coastal nations the right to use and develop fisheries within a 200-nautical-mile Exclusive Economic Zone (EEZ) (**Figure 4.31**). Ironically, perhaps, this development has, in many cases, harmed rather than protected the world's fisheries:

   ■ The oceans *outside* the EEZ now face increased pressures and virtually uncontrolled fishing. FAO statistics do not distinguish between catches made within EEZs and those outside. However, an analysis of those 116 oceanic species that occur principally in the high seas show that catches of oceanic species nearly tripled, from 3 million tonnes in 1976 to 8.5 million tonnes in 2000. Regional agreements do exist for the high seas, but these are unenforceable, as Canada discovered in August 2004, when Denmark refused to abide by the shrimp quotas allocated by the Northwest Atlantic Fisheries Organization.

   ■ The exclusion of foreign fleets from the EEZ initially obscured the need to conserve stocks *within* the EEZ. Indeed, freed from the depredations of foreign factory trawlers, many domestic fisheries initially appeared far more sustainable than their stocks actually were, and the necessary decision to control domestic fleets through quotas and fleet reductions was therefore sadly delayed by many countries, including Canada.

   ■ Migratory fish do not observe EEZ boundaries and are therefore very hard stocks to manage successfully. For example, the Pacific Coast Salmon Treaty between Canada and the United States attempts to allocate fairly the salmon catch between fishers in British Columbia and Alaska. Agreement is never easy, however; Canadian fishers charge

---

[40] Anne Platt McGinn, "Promoting Sustainable Fisheries." In Linda Starke (ed.), *State of the World 1998*. New York: Worldwatch Institute and Norton, 1998, p. 66.

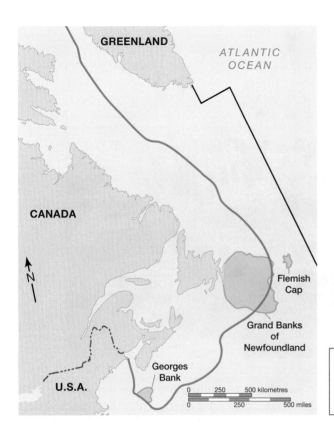

Figure 4.31   Canada's 200-nautical-mile Exclusive Economic Zone (EEZ)   (*Source:* Claude Emery, *The Northern Cod Crisis.* Library of Parliament: Ottawa, 1992, p. 3. It is available online at http://dsp-psd.tpsgc.gc.ca. Fisheries and Oceans Canada. Reproduced with the permission of Her Majesty the Queen in Right of Canada, 2006.)

that Alaskan vessels are catching salmon that are on their way to spawn in British Columbian waters, thereby unduly reducing the size of the resource. The July 1997 blockade of a U.S. ferry in Prince Rupert by 100 British Columbian commercial fishing boats provides a telling example of how difficult such agreements are to maintain (**Figure 4.32**).

■ Those countries unable to fully exploit their EEZ were permitted to grant harvesting rights to other countries. Stocks that might otherwise have been left alone have now become the target of the fleets of the developed nations capable of fishing on a global scale. In 1996, for example,

Figure 4.32   Blockade of U.S. ferry in Prince Rupert, July 1997   Angered by the failure of talks over the allocation of fish stocks between the United States and Canada, BC fishers took matters into their own hands and prevented an American ferry from leaving Prince Rupert.

Figure 4.33 Traditional fishers in Brazil

the European Union paid US$250 million for access agreements with a number of coastal African states, and nearly 1,000 European vessels now fish those waters. This arrangement often heavily affects traditional small-scale fisheries, threatening local livelihoods in many parts of the developing world (**Figure 4.33**).

4. *Economic development policies.* Although many countries were extending their control over their adjacent waters, international development agencies were increasingly lending the developing countries the money to develop their fisheries (**Figure 4.34**). Between 1970 and 1989, the developing nations' share of the world fishing fleet rose from 27 percent to 58 percent, and for the first time, those countries became not only an important part of the fishing world but also a major contributor to its growing overcapacity. Any attempts to reduce the world's fishing capacity will therefore have a disproportionate effect on the poorer countries of the periphery unless such policies are sensitively managed.

Figure 4.34 Fish market, Bequia, St. Vincent Fishing activity has been promoted in many developing countries by Western development policies. This picture shows a fish market built with Canadian support on the Caribbean island of Bequia (part of St. Vincent and the Grenadines).

5. *Growing demand.* In a 2004 report, the FAO noted that the world's fisheries provide 16 percent of the total animal protein consumed by the world's population. Demand has risen steadily since 1950 because (until recently) fish protein represented a cheaper alternative to meat, and many countries (the former Soviet Union, for example) found it cheaper to feed their population by fishing than by farming. Moreover, because most countries now subsidize their fishers (the FAO estimates that the world fleet is subsidized with US$54 billion per year), the true cost of the fishing industry is not always seen in the price of fish. Governments may choose to subsidize fisheries for a variety of reasons: to ensure an affordable supply of protein for their populations, to remain competitive on the export market (over one-third of the global fish production is traded internationally), to prevent unemployment in coastal regions, or to prop up strategically important shipbuilding industries. The growing global population puts further stresses on the fish stocks: if food supplies are to remain at the per capita levels they are now, an increasing share of the global catch will be needed for direct human consumption rather than as animal feed for meat production.

6. *Resource depletion.* As the world's capacity to fish has been increasing, the world's fish stocks have been diminishing. For some species, stocks have become so low that they face extinction. The decline of the world's marine and river fishery stocks is due to a series of both direct and indirect causes, the most important of which are overfishing and the effects of changing environments and pollution on fish populations. Let us briefly consider these factors.

   ■ *Decline.* How can the total amount of fish caught in recent years be the highest on record if fish stocks have been declining? The answer is simple: as the catches of individual species have declined, they have been replaced by other species pursued at greater depths or more remote locations. In other words, increasing global totals mask a dramatic decline of many species and have prevented many people from realizing the true state of the world's fisheries. The declining size of fish that are caught and the collapse of particular fisheries are each indicative of a diminishing natural resource.

   ■ *Environmental threats.* Fish numbers can be affected by a range of environmental effects, principally pollution, habitat destruction, and global warming. Since 60 percent of the world's population now live within 100 kilometres of the sea, marine ecosystems are under increasing threat from the damage that development can cause, including the discharge of human and industrial wastes.

It is surprising, perhaps, to see the statement "climate change will have a greater impact on the health of the world's fisheries than overfishing itself."[41] Yet, there are already examples to demonstrate the likelihood of such a future. Off the coast of Southern California, sea temperatures have risen by 0.8°C in the past 40 years. This change has led to the decline of plankton on which fish feed and the almost total collapse of the anchovy industry. In similar fashion, the recurring *El Niño* phenomenon has very deleterious effects on the Peruvian anchoveta stock.

Aquaculture has been the most rapidly growing sector of the world fishing industry in the past 20 years (**Figure 4.35**). However, its growth potential may be ultimately limited by environmental problems. The possibility of fish diseases spreading from farmed stock to wild stock and the damage caused by aquaculture to coastal habitats (for example by the highly concentrated deposition of

---

[41] Anne Platt McGinn, "Promoting Sustainable Fisheries." In Linda Starke (ed.), *State of the World 1998*. New York: Worldwatch Institute and Norton, 1998, p. 63.

Figure 4.35 Aquaculture is a growing industry in Canadian waters.

feces) are but two of the concerns raised. An additional issue has arisen in 2010 with the introduction of a genetically modified "turbo salmon" that grows twice as fast as its wild counterpart.

Faced with the mounting evidence that the world's fisheries are unsustainable, it is important that we consider what options we have for changing the present situation. Solutions have run the gamut from community-based control of local fisheries (as in the Philippines, for example) to market-based strategies that limit access by privatizing fishing rights (for instance, the individual transferable quota or ITQ). The two most obvious suggestions are that governments should immediately stop subsidizing their fishers and reduce the size of their fishing industries. Yet, few governments in the countries of the core or the periphery have felt able to jeopardize the only means of livelihood in many of their coastal communities. Sadly, many governments have found it cheaper to continue to subsidize fishing in remote regions than to develop economic diversification strategies or to confront the political consequences of closing entire communities (see **Geography Matters 4.3—Changing Places: The Effects of Resource Depletion and Technological Change on the Geography of Atlantic Canada**). However, as many observers have stated, until we place the needs of the fish populations first, we will not be able to return fish stocks to sustainable levels. For too long, the fishing industry has profited by borrowing at the expense of the environment; if sensitive strategies are not developed soon, the time will come when that debt must be repaid.

The combustion of fossil fuels, the destruction of forest and fishery resources, the damming of watercourses, and the massive change in land-use patterns brought about by the pressures of globalization—industrialization being the most extreme phase—contribute to environmental problems that now reach enormous proportions: they have become truly global. Geographers and others use the term **global change** to describe the combination of political, economic, social, historical, and environmental problems with which human beings across Earth must grapple. Very little, if anything, has escaped the embrace of globalization, least of all the environment.

In fact, no other period in human history has transformed the natural world as profoundly as have the past 500 years. Although we reap the benefits of a modern way of life, it is critical to recognize that these benefits have not been without cost—and that these costs have accrued disproportionately to the poor. A growing political consciousness of this lamentable fact has resulted in a movement known as environmental justice.

Activists in the **environmental justice** movement consider the pollution of their neighbourhoods through such elements as nearby factories and hazardous

global change: combination of political, economic, social, historical, and environmental problems at the world scale

environmental justice: movement reflecting a growing political consciousness, largely among the world's poor, that their immediate environs are far more toxic than those in wealthier neighbourhoods

Changing Places: The Effects of Resource Depletion and Technological Change on the Geography of Atlantic Canada

The effects of changing technology and resource exploitation on human settlement patterns and people's sense of place are well illustrated by the evolution of the fisheries of Atlantic Canada (**Figure 4.3.1**). A brief examination of these particular changes will show how space and place are profoundly governed by environmental and economic considerations and how these considerations, in turn, are affected by our approaches to place.

Fishing has been a way of life in Atlantic Canada for centuries, and it began with the Aboriginal fisheries. Archaeological evidence from L'Anse Amour in Labrador and Port au Choix in Newfoundland indicates that a sophisticated technology for catching fish in estuaries using toggling harpoons and nets supported small, seasonal coastal settlements as early as 7500 B.C. (**Figure 4.3.1a**).

This pattern of settlement and resource use was slowly undercut by the entry of Europeans into the fisheries, beginning with the Basque exploitation of whales and cod in the Gulf of the St. Lawrence in the 1500s (**Figure 4.3.1b**). From the seventeenth century onward, Britain and France created a migratory fishery to develop the resources of their new colonies. Under this system, vessels arrived every year to fish and dry their catch on shore for transport back the same year to Europe. Such a system of dependency, articulated by core countries and understandable only in terms of European economic space, resulted in no permanent settlers in Atlantic Canada. The effects of newly introduced European diseases and brutality on the Aboriginal population also removed many traces of the previous settlement pattern.

There is evidence that the migratory fisheries in some areas soon showed clear signs of depletion. For example, one early eighteenth-century observer remarked, "Though there be Harbours and conveniences on shoare for the making of Fish there is not fishing ground or can constantly be fish enough for so many Boates as they have kept."[42] Despite such warnings, Europe's increasing population provided a ready market for dried cod and became the impetus for a greater exploitation of the fisheries off Canada's Atlantic coasts. One way to increase yields was to be among the first on the fishery each year; another was to fish the unexploited stocks of the Grand Banks and Labrador. To that purpose, small permanent settlements were established on the coasts of Newfoundland and Labrador and by 1675, there were about 1,700 overwinterers on the English coast of Newfoundland.

Such settlements, called outports, became the main type of place associated with the exploitation of the fisheries until the 1950s. Small clusters of houses, fish-drying areas, fishing huts, and jetties composed the typical outport (**Figure 4.3.1c**). Built of wood, the impermanence of individual structures (houses were even hauled to new locations) belied the intimate connection such places had with the landscape. With their orientation to the coast and their lack of any other focus, the geography of such settlements indicates their total reliance on the sea for their support. Ironically, perhaps, despite the fact that the very existence of these communities depended on an increasingly globalized market (dried cod was traded in Europe, Africa, the Caribbean, and the United States), the outports were otherwise almost completely isolated. Often located in remote coves that were hard to reach by land, outports suffered from a lack of road access and development of their hinterlands. This only added to the self-reliance of outports and the development of localized customs, traditions, and dialects.

By 1864, the Newfoundland fishery was showing signs of decline. The average catch per fisherman had dropped by 25 percent, and many blamed overfishing by the "swarms of French and American ships . . . seen busily employed dragging forth the treasures of the deep."[43] One important result was that most fishers withdrew from the Labrador fishery, which was left to the Newfoundlanders, and began fishing the banks off Nova Scotia and Newfoundland using new fishing methods. In the 1870s, for example, vessels from Lunenburg sailed to the Grand Banks, where their dories collected the cod from baited trawl lines known as "ganglings." The town quickly flourished on the strengths of this new technology and its newly developed rail links to the emerging markets in New England and central Canada (**Figure 4.3.2**). The fact that the region's outports, not having such links, found themselves increasingly bypassed proved to be an ominous sign of the future.

Twentieth-century changes spelled the end not only of the North Atlantic cod but also of the outports that had so long depended on it. Certainly, nothing could have prepared the Canadian and the Newfoundland and Labrador fishing industry for the shock of the introduction of steam trawlers after 1914, onboard refrigeration units in the 1930s, and the enormous factory-freezer vessels developed from the 1960s. The greater capacity and speed of these new vessels rapidly shifted the

[42] Original spelling, punctuation, and grammar are retained. Quoted in C. Grant Head, *Eighteenth Century Newfoundland: A Geographer's Perspective*. Toronto: McClelland and Stewart, 1979, pp. 5–36.

[43] Raymond B. Blake, *From Fishermen to Fish: The Evolution of Canadian Fishery Policy*. Toronto: Irwin Publishing, 2000, p. 19.

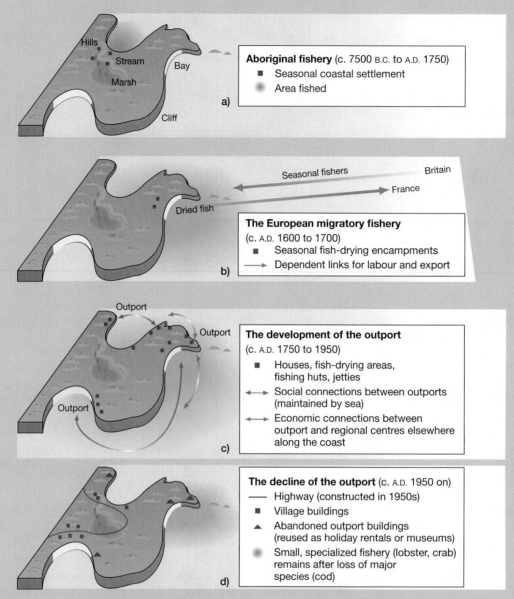

Figure 4.3.1 Changing places: A model of the evolution of the fisheries of Atlantic Canada and its effects on place This idealized sequence of diagrams shows how changes in the exploitation of Atlantic Canada's fisheries have fundamentally altered that region's meaning of "place" over the centuries. The changes are shown in four simplified stages, (a) to (d). In (a), the early Aboriginal fishery, we find an essentially self-contained, seasonal community located at the head of a bay, based on estuary fishing, and drawing its sense of place from the local environment. That situation is fundamentally altered by European contact. The development of a migratory fishery, (b), creates a series of temporary places that are not homes and that have no connection with their location. Rather they are part of a settlement system that is organized (or "articulated") around British and French ports. They have turned their backs on Canada and draw their meaning as places from their dependency on Europe. The transition from this system to one focused on more regionally based trade, (c), sees the replacement of Europe with the trading hubs of Atlantic Canada (such as Halifax or St. John's) and the growth of permanent settlements or outports. Small and often very remote, these outport communities drew their sense of place from their maritime location. Oriented toward the sea, from which came their livelihood, and located often on rugged peninsulas to reach the expanding fisheries, outports were strung out along the coast and had little connection with the inland interior. Indeed, they maintained social and economic ties with other outports more easily by sea than they did by land. In such a milieu, the classic outport sense of place was developed based on very local social practice and knowledge of the environment. However, as (d) shows, this situation begins to change by the 1950s. The isolation of the outports was ended by the construction of inland highways, and their economic purpose was eliminated by, first, the focusing of fish processing in larger and larger centres, and, second, by the cod moratoria of the 1990s. In fact, the outports were abandoned; houses were rebuilt along the new highways, and streets now face inland—the source of their new identity. Meanwhile, nostalgia for the past ensures that the meaning of place is once more transformed—in this case, as abandoned outports become "places of memory."

focus from the traditional salted fish to new markets in fresh and frozen fish. This shift ended local production by individual fishers and required capital-intensive, industrialized processes based on packing and cold storage facilities in a limited number of centres. The fact that most of the European fleets were subsidized by their own governments made it hard for Canadians to compete and especially hard for outport production

Figure 4.3.2   Lunenburg, Nova Scotia

Figure 4.3.3   The outport as a place of memory   Newfoundland as a place of nostalgia is celebrated in countless photographs such as this view.

(which depended on small, labour-intensive production techniques) to reduce costs or become more efficient. Importantly, the shift also hastened the ultimate collapse of the cod fishery by increasing the demands placed on this resource.

As early as the 1950s, following its joining the Confederation, Newfoundland and Labrador endeavoured to move people from outports to larger centres where they could be provided with access to schools, hospitals, and electricity (**Figure 4.3.1d**). The outrage this caused in some circles, however, showed many politicians how important the "attachment to place" could be, and it framed both federal and provincial policy until the cod moratorium of 1992. The outport way of life had by now become the stuff of tradition, a memory hallowed by those who had left to find work elsewhere and celebrated in academic research and literature. In effect, the meaning of place was undergoing another transformation: at the same time that the outport was losing its relevance in economic space, it was beginning to serve as a place of memory with which to resist the processes of modernization sweeping the region (**Figure 4.3.3**).

"It is like coming home to another place and time," writes McGill architect Robert Mellin in his fascinating 2003 study of the small outport of Tilting on Fogo Island, 13 kilometres off the northeastern shore of Newfoundland.[44] Writer E. Annie Proulx used local dialect and customs to convey the uniqueness of such places in her novel *The Shipping News,* while the book's film adaptation, using another approach, relied on use of the distinctive landscapes of the Newfoundland and Labrador coast for the same purpose. A third example, and one which draws directly on geographic concepts, is the work *Places of Presence* by artist Marlene Creates, in which she uses photographs, found objects, and "memory maps" to show how the Newfoundland outport, such as Lewisporte, "is not an abstract physical location, but a *place,* charged with personal significance, shaping the images we have of ourselves."[45]

For the outport to endure as a place with such meaning, fishing had to be defended as a way of life. This meant that despite evidence of a declining fishery (**Figure 4.3.4**) and the clear need to reduce not only the foreign fleets within Canada's 200-nautical-mile limit but also the number of Canadian fishers, reductions to Canada's own exploitation of its fisheries were put off until it was too late. Despite the obvious inefficiencies, the need to preserve jobs in the outports also meant that a greater number of fish plants were supported than were needed, and a rationalization of the industry into fewer major processing centres was delayed. The fact that the social and economic role of the outport had to be protected at the expense of the environment illustrates the dilemma facing policy makers in those years.

With almost no cod to harvest, many of the outports are now redundant. It is estimated that perhaps as many as 1,200 such communities across Atlantic Canada are in this position. Their populations are now faced with hard decisions on whether to leave the outport or to stay and retrain in the hope that new employment opportunities will develop. Some communities will survive through the development of new fisheries for crab and such, but the opportunities will be limited: strictly controlled access to scarce fishing quotas will undoubtedly make such communities far more economically polarized than before. But many others will disappear, their disappearance warning us that unless we learn to protect the needs of the fish populations before we consider our own needs, we can expect further fundamental changes in place.

[44] Robert Mellin, *Tilting: House Launching, Slide Hauling, Potato Trenching, and Other Tales from a Newfoundland Fishing Village.* New York: Princeton Architectural Press, 2003, p. 2.

[45] Marlene Creates, *Places of Presence: Newfoundland Kin and Ancestral Land.* Killick Press: St. John's, NF, 1997, p. 6.

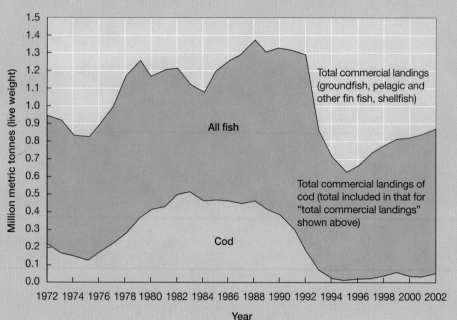

Figure 4.3.4 Canada's declining cod fishery, 1972–2002 This graph shows government data for all commercial landings by live weight (in metric tonnes) in the Atlantic region (Nova Scotia, New Brunswick, Prince Edward Island, and Newfoundland and Labrador) and Quebec. The effects of the decline in cod fishing are clear, as is the growing exploitation of other species (especially shellfish) since the early 1990s. (*Source:* This graph is based on data from Fisheries and Oceans Canada, Statistical Services, 1972–2002, available online at **www.dfo-mpo.gc.ca/communic/ statistics.**)

waste dumps to be the result of a structured and institutionalized inequality that is pervasive in both core and periphery. They see their struggles as distinct from the more middle-class and mainstream concerns of such groups as the Sierra Club and Greenpeace. These activists have come to conceptualize their struggles as rooted in their disadvantaged economic status in the worldwide capitalist system. Thus, these struggles are not about quality-of-life issues, such as whether any forests will be left to hike in, but about issues of sheer economic and physical survival. According to the United Nations University and the International Red Cross, the number of environmental refugees now exceeds the number of refugees fleeing war or persecution, and may be as high as 200 million in 2050[46] (see **Geography Matters 4.4—Disasters**). As a result, the answer to the questions raised by environmental justice activists must be directed toward the redistribution of economic and political resources. Such questions are not easily resolved in a court of law but speak to more complex issues, such as the nature of racism, of sexism, and of capitalism as a class-based economic system.

CONCLUSION

The relationship between society and nature is very much mediated by institutions and practices, from technology to religious beliefs. In this chapter, we have seen how the nature–society relationship has changed over time and how the globalization of the capitalist world economy has had more of a widespread and profound impact on attitudes and practices, but also on the environment, than any cultural or economic system that preceded it. In short, the environment has been globalized along with the economy. We can now speak of a global environment in which not only the people but also the physical environments in which they live and work are linked in increasingly complex ways.

---

[46] See the United Nations University website at **www.ehs.unu.edu/file/get/4170**.

Disasters

On May 2 and 3, 2008, tropical cyclone Nargis hit southern Myanmar (Burma) with almost no warning (**Figure 4.4.1**). As many as 130,000 people were killed. Reports from the United Nations Children's Fund (UNICEF) noted that at least 1.5 million people were affected by the storm and its aftermath. The storm struck towns and farmland along the banks of the Irrawaddy River, and its impacts were probably magnified by this area's dense human settlement and by the clearance of coastal mangrove forests that might have buffered the wind-driven waves. However, in terms of worsening the cyclone's effects, nothing could compare with Myanmar's own government and its decision to reject outside aid. In one telling example, the World Food Programme (potentially the largest emergency relief supplier in these cases) was only able to deliver one-fifth of the 375 tonnes of food a day that it estimated had to be airlifted into the country because its planes were denied access. Simple steps (such as the provision of water purification units) would have enabled more to survive and others to recover more quickly, but they could not be taken. Similarly, longer-term reconstruction measures (including the construction of provisional housing and the re-equipping of farms and fishing boats) were not possible.[47]

Only 10 days later, on May 12, 2008, an extremely powerful earthquake in Sichuan in southwestern China highlighted the differences in response. With as many as

Figure 4.4.1 The aftermath of tropical cyclone Nargis This picture, taken a month after the cyclone hit the southern Irrawaddy delta region of Myanmar on May 2–3, 2008, shows homes damaged in Nyaung Wai village in the township of Kyauktan 49 kilometres south of Yangon.

75,000 to 100,000 people killed, many towns and villages virtually levelled, and many of the area's roads rendered impassable, providing relief proved challenging. Within three days, however, the government had ordered over 100,000 troops into the areas most affected by the disaster and international relief operations were allowed immediate access. Japan, for example, was able to send an earthquake response team, and funds raised by Canadian charities were quickly dispatched to Sichuan.[48]

The impact of a disaster always raises many questions: Why did it happen? What can we do to help? What does the disaster mean? Some of these questions are more immediate than others—certainly, the most urgent would be, how can we best get aid to the victims?[49] More important in the long term are questions that investigate how we can successfully deal with or even prevent such disasters in the future. For instance, what does the disaster reveal about long-term environmental changes, the structure of society, and the distribution of economic wealth, all of which fundamentally influence how a disaster will affect a population and how quickly it can recover.

Geography is uniquely situated to deal with both types of questions—those that deal with immediate problems and those that focus on the more long-term or root problems. For example, knowledge of Earth's processes enables physical geographers (or geomorphologists) to understand the conditions of slope formation, soil cohesion, and amounts of rainfall that will lead to catastrophic mudslides in specific hilly regions, such as in Peru or British Columbia.

But beyond this, an understanding of the economic processes that structure the spaces of the world-system (see Chapter 2) allows geographers to realize that the actual impact of such disasters is related to the ability of the local population to cope: Peruvian villagers have less financial ability to recover from the loss of their houses and fields than do many who have bought ocean-view properties in Vancouver. In this sense, the effects of disasters map the inequalities of the world-system because they point to regions that lack, or are denied, the resources to respond to a crisis.

The reluctance of people to leave areas that are prone to disaster is itself a phenomenon that modern geography is able to examine. The love of place (or *topophilia*) that we will look at more fully in Chapters 5 and 6 is one that binds people so strongly to areas that they love that even knowledge of almost certain disaster will not prompt

[47] United Nations Children's Fund, "UNICEF on the Ground in Myanmar Delivering Life-Saving Supplies." Press release, accessed July 18, 2008, at www.unicef.ca/portal/SmartDefault.aspx.

[48] "Days of Disaster: Two Natural Disasters, Two Very Different Responses," *The Economist*, May 15, 2008.

[49] A useful introduction to the provision of aid is Adrian Ward, Raymond Apthorpe, and John Borton (eds.), *Evaluating International Humanitarian Action: Reflections from Practitioners*. London and New York: Zed Books, 2001.

them to move away or evacuate. Examples of this behaviour include the refusal of long-term residents to leave the slopes of Mount St. Helens immediately before the volcanic eruption and the continuing desire of Winnipeggers to remain in that city despite the obvious threats of Red River floods in the future.[50]

Finally, geographers have begun to understand that because the natural environment and the human realm are so intimately connected, disasters are created by how individual societies use and interact with the natural world. Mudslides, according to this interpretation, are as much a result of human activity (logging, farming, or building on steep slopes) as they are of natural causes. In this sense, disasters are a direct result of the "political ecology" of an area (a term defined in Chapter 9), the result perhaps of how a particular economic system forces the poor to farm on land of no commercial value (such as on steep slopes). In this manner, the economic system itself can become a cause of the deforestation or unsustainable farming that such groups must employ to support themselves. (We will explore ideas of political ecology further in Chapter 5, and we will provide some interesting examples from the work of Canadian scholar Thomas Homer-Dixon concerning his theory of environmental scarcity in Chapter 9.)

We have already seen in this chapter how the idea that humans and nature are separate has been seen by scholars as a major cause of our inability to realize how intimately human activity and the natural environment interconnect. The very word *disaster* perpetuates that mind-set because it implies that a separate natural force has wreaked devastation on a passive and uninvolved population. It interprets the world from a human point of view, where nature is almost seen as an enemy, a threat that somehow can be "fixed" if we can get the engineering right. But this may be the wrong way to think—perhaps the phrase *extreme natural event* might be more useful to our understanding.

Certainly, the latest work by disaster scholars suggests that the impact of such an extreme natural event (be it flood or earthquake) only becomes a disaster to the extent that our economy has placed people in the path of that catastrophe, to the extent that our cultures view nature as a separate entity or threat, and to the extent that our own societies are unable to rebuild themselves. In this sense, then, although many natural events are out of our hands, disasters are socially constructed.

It is therefore imperative that we turn our attention to root causes (such as poverty and social inequality) that create or heighten the *socio-economic vulnerability* of the populations who are most at risk. For this reason, the analysis of such types of social or economic vulnerability has engaged the attention of most leading scholars in the field of disaster research since 1983, when Kenneth Hewitt (professor of geography and environmental studies at Wilfrid Laurier University) first developed the concept. More recent work by geographers has contributed to this type of analysis by defining *spaces of vulnerability*—those areas in which socioeconomic circumstances predispose populations to a crisis.[51] In this approach, disasters are more explainable in terms of the "normal" order of things (that is, the distribution of wealth or power in a society) than in terms of the accidental geophysical features of a place.[52]

With these thoughts as background, let us now consider two other recent disasters as examples of the challenges that such catastrophes place on human society: the 2004 Indonesian tsunami, one of the worst floods in human history, and the 2005 Hurricane Katrina, one of the worst disasters in North American history.

The 2004 Indonesian Tsunami

"On 26 December 2004 an earthquake measuring 9.0 on the Richter Scale struck the far western coast of northern Sumatra, triggering massive tidal waves, or tsunamis, that hit coastal areas in countries all round the Indian Ocean Rim—from Indonesia to Somalia, a total of 226,000 people are presumed to have died in the disaster."[53]

The sheer scale of the disaster caused by the tsunami is hard to grasp. However, reports provided by the International Federation of the Red Cross and Red Crescent Societies (IFRC) in their *World Disasters Report 2005* allow us to begin to see a picture of the tragedy and its aftermath in South Asia (**Figures 4.4.2a** and **4.4.2b**).

In Aceh itself, the Indonesian region closest to the epicentre of the earthquake that triggered the tsunami, the devastation was enormous, the result of both quake damage and flooding because of the tidal wave along the coasts. The IFRC reports that on Aceh, the disaster left 164,000 people dead or missing and more than 400,000 homeless. The scale of the disaster meant that settlements scattered along hundreds of kilometres of coast were cut off, and relief workers found it extremely hard to reach survivors in time.

[50] The cost of Winnipeg's new floodway is estimated at $665 million. Julius Strauss, "Money Flows to Stem the Tide of Winnipeg's Roaring Red," *Globe and Mail*, September 15, 2005, p. A3.

[51] Kenneth Hewitt (ed.), *Interpretations of Calamity*. Winchester, MA: Allen and Unwin, 1983.

[52] An excellent introduction to research on disasters is Anthony Oliver-Smith, "Theorizing Disasters: Nature, Power and Culture." In Susanna M. Hoffman and Anthony Oliver-Smith (eds.), *Catastrophe and Culture: The Anthropology of Disaster.* Santa Fe: School of American Research Press, 2003, pp. 23–47. A more challenging exposition of the ideas in this paragraph is found in the work of the eminent geographer David Harvey, *Justice, Nature and the Geography of Difference.* Cambridge, MA: Blackwell, 1996.

[53] The quotation is taken from an International Federation of the Red Cross and Red Crescent Societies 2005 summary of the interactive map (see www.ifrc.org/what/disasters/response/tsunamis/map.asp). The summary concludes that by mid-2005, the Red Cross and Red Crescent had spent more than US$456 million on tsunami relief efforts and that more than 1 million people had received aid. The December 2005 issue of the *Geographical Journal* contains five very valuable analyses by geographers on the effects of the tsunami.

(a)   (b)

Figure 4.4.2   (a) Before the Indian Ocean tsunami; (b) aftermath of the Indian Ocean tsunami

The report observes that because of the extent of this disaster, "it rapidly became the most reported and well-funded disaster in history," a situation that ironically had its own surprising consequences. For example, the unprecedented levels of aid led to what the IFRC report calls a "struggle for beneficiaries" as each of the 200 aid agencies in the region tried to find people to help and to very limited information-sharing among groups as each "jealously guarded their information to protect their niche." Most agencies flocked to the devastated west coast of Aceh, to the detriment of more than 150,000 people displaced on the east coast, who received far less help.

Interestingly, the IFRC reports that "although international agencies were right in guessing that water, food, and shelter would be survivors' initial needs, they were wrong to assume these needs would not be covered by the Indonesians themselves. Agencies did little to suppress the myth of disaster victims dependent on external aid to survive."[54]

In the wake of the tsunami, Canadians were among the many who responded generously to the crisis. As but one illustration of this, according to a June 23, 2005, report from UNICEF, Canadian individuals, businesses, schools, and other organizations raised a total of C$23 million for UNICEF's tsunami work, a figure that was increased by a further C$15 million from the Canadian International Development Agency, to fulfill the government's pledge to match private donations. In all, it is estimated that the government matched about C$150 million in donations for relief efforts for the tsunami victims.[55]

Canadian efforts did not stop with financial aid. Geography students from the University of Ottawa teamed up with Ottawa-based web-mapping company DM Solutions Group to respond to a request from the Indian government to create a tsunami disaster mapping portal. Constructed within a week, this website aimed to help those involved in tsunami reconstruction and relief work by providing important geographical information, such as road maps, earthquake epicentres, and mortality statistics.[56]

Hurricane Katrina

"It's as if the entire Gulf Coast were obliterated by the worst kind of weapon you can imagine," said U.S. President George W. Bush of the devastation of Hurricane Katrina.[57]

At eight o'clock on the morning of Monday, August 29, 2005, the eye of Hurricane Katrina hit the Mississippi Delta, a few kilometres east of New Orleans on the Louisiana coast, with the force of a category 4 hurricane. Meteorologists believe that with wind speeds of 215 kilometres per hour and a diameter more than 320 kilometres across, this hurricane was, in fact, the most powerful ever to have hit the United States. The consequences for New Orleans and surrounding states were immediate and severe (**Figures 4.4.3a** and **4.4.3b**).

Overall estimates on the economic consequences of the disaster suggest that the total cost of rebuilding the region will be more than US$100 billion, making Hurricane Katrina the most costly disaster in U.S. history and the costliest that insurers have ever faced.[58]

[54] The International Federation of Red Cross and Red Crescent Societies, *World Disasters Report 2005*. Geneva: IFRC, 2005. The quotation is from Chapter 4, "Information Black Hole in Aceh," available online at **www.ifrc.org/publicat/wdr2005/chapter4.asp.**

[55] Jane Taber and Brian Laghi, "Ottawa to Match Quake Aid," *Globe and Mail*, October 12, 2005, p. A1.

[56] The website is **www.dmsolutions.ca/solutions/tsunami.html** and is described more fully in Jan Dutkiewicz, "Map Aid," *Canadian Geographic* 125(2), 2005, p. 30.

[57] Quoted in "Katrina." Special issue, *National Geographic*, September 2005, p. 43. The paragraphs that follow draw on material in this publication, which contains a very valuable collection of maps, photographs, and analyses of the hurricane.

[58] Insurance estimates are from "Assessing the Damage." *The Economist*, 17 September 2005, p. 73.

(a)

(b)

Figure 4.4.3 (a) The gulf coast; (b) the aftermath of Hurricane Katrina

The total may well be higher when the full impact is computed. In the New Orleans area alone, 500,000 workers were evacuated and 150,000 properties were damaged. The local tourist industry (worth US$7 billion per year) was destroyed, and local fishing fleets (responsible for 30 percent of the U.S. seafood market) have been largely eliminated. Shipping was interrupted, ports destroyed, and the Gulf's oil and gas installations so badly hit that experts predicted a 30 percent rise in heating oil prices.

The effects of Hurricane Katrina have been enormous. From Louisiana to Florida, an area of more than 145,000 square kilometres was declared a federal disaster area. Within the first two weeks after the hurricane hit, the U.S. federal government approved a total of US$62.3 billion in disaster relief.

But perhaps the last word on the hurricane should go to Pierce Lewis, emeritus professor of geography at Pennsylvania State University, who writes of the power of place in any future rebuilding: "Whether we rebuild New Orleans or not is an ethical and aesthetic question—one not to be answered glibly by politicians or academic savants. Despite what doomsayers have proclaimed, New Orleans was not destroyed. The community of people called New Orleans has dispersed for a time, and many (if not most) will return to their beloved city."[59]

The Future

In seeking to understand what disasters mean, we can do no better than to continue with the remarks of geographer Pierce Lewis:[60]

> When attention was drawn to the perilousness of New Orleans, those who noted the fact usually shrugged, remarking with enthusiasm on the ability of man to conquer nature. To be sure, people said, the engineers had seemingly "solved" the problem of river flooding. But nobody could divert a hurricane from hitting New Orleans head-on. Scientists at Louisiana State University and elsewhere had warned that New Orleans' luck simply could not hold, but those warnings were taken with the same kind of optimistic insouciance that had long been among Orleanians' most endearing qualities. Technology had solved the problem in the past. Would it not do so in the future?

In fact, New Orleans was a disaster waiting to happen. Technology and a willful ignorance of the environment had enabled settlement to occur in a low-lying area, and much of that settlement was of poorer people who could only afford to live in areas of the city below sea-level. These people did not have the resources to be able to evacuate when the need arose. In this way, when an extreme natural event in the form of Hurricane Katrina hit the Louisiana coast, its effects were translated into those of a disaster by the circumstances of the economy and the society that it hit. In this sense, any rebuilding of the city is problematic because, as described in *The Economist*, "the more cash that is spent rebuilding New Orleans, the more foolhardy Californians will be about where they build in their earthquake-prone state, confident that the government will bail them out if the 'Big One' strikes."[61]

The tsunami that hit Indonesia and South Asia in December 2004 can be similarly interpreted. There, an extreme natural event, an earthquake, set off a chain of natural events that were turned into a disaster by the many ways in which local socioeconomies in the region have been required to respond to the global economy. For example, experts have commented that the removal of mangrove swamps in favour of shrimp farming had the unforeseen side effect of removing natural coastal defences in many parts of the region—defences that would have dampened and perhaps eliminated the tidal wave's effects on some coastal communities. The over-reliance on local fishing and tourism as economic

---

[59] Quoted in "Katrina." Special issue, *National Geographic*, September 2005, p. 101.
[60] Ibid.
[61] "Hurricane Katrina: Whoaaah," *The Economist*, 17 September 2005, p. 14.

activities (both encouraged by international aid agencies) had led to increased populations in the most vulnerable areas of the region: the coastal belts. Finally, through urbanization and rural emigration, there had been a substantial increase in the size of the coastal communities in this region. What this all means is that the coastal areas of South Asia support a large number of people with limited economic means—people who are therefore very vulnerable to flood disasters.

Most commentators argue that the number of such disasters is likely to increase in the future, not only because global warming is likely to increase the strength and frequency of natural hazards (such as category 4 and 5 hurricanes, whose frequency has doubled in the last 35 years)[62] but also because the populations living in coastal regions are growing rapidly. In other words, we are creating the "perfect storm" for future catastrophes unless we can address the root causes of social and economic vulnerability that cause disasters.

In a piece comparing the 2004 tsunami and Hurricane Katrina, Johan Schaar of the International Federation of the Red Cross and Red Crescent Societies wrote:

> Whether you are from Banda Aceh or New Orleans, your assets in physical, material and social terms—that is, wealth, insurance and the ability to rely on others—will determine your ability to recover. Resilience is as much a community as an individual quality, and as we can see in Aceh and Louisiana, it is invariably the most vulnerable among us—the poor, the sick, the elderly and the isolated—who fare the worst when disaster strikes. . . . That is why poverty alleviation and disaster reduction are mutually reinforcing and must go hand in hand if we want to ensure safety and security for all.[63]

[62] See "Frequency and Ferocity of Hurricanes Increasing Dramatically," *Globe and Mail*, September 21, 2005, p. A16. On floods not associated with hurricanes or tsunamis, see S.N. Jonkman, "Global Perspectives on Loss of Human Life Caused by Floods," *Natural Hazards* 34, 2005, pp. 151–75.

[63] Johan Schaar, *Hurricane Katrina-Tsunami Recovery Comparisons*. International Federation of Red Cross and Red Crescent Societies, Opinion piece, September 13, 2005, available online at **www.ifrc.org/ docs/News/opinion05/05091301/index.asp.**

Although we must be careful not to generalize and romanticize, we can say that many ancient humans apparently displayed a reverential attitude toward the natural world, an attitude still evident among indigenous populations in many parts of the world. With the emergence of Judaism and, later, Christianity, humans adopted a more dominant attitude toward nature. The expansion of European trade, followed by colonization and eventually industrialization, broadcast worldwide the belief that humans should take their place at the apex of the natural world. The Judeo-Christian attitude toward nature as it was taken up by the emergence of the capitalist economic system is the most pervasive shaper of nature–society interactions today.

Besides exploring the history of ideas about nature, this chapter has also shown that society and nature are interdependent and that events in one part of the global environmental system affect conditions in the system across space and time. The nuclear accident in Chernobyl taught us this lesson when nuclear fallout from Ukraine was spread throughout the globe within days of the reactor meltdown—yet its effects persist even today, almost 30 years later, in countries that are thousands of kilometres from the accident site. In Ukraine itself, radioactive fallout has been absorbed not only into the bodies of meltdown survivors but also into the bodies of their children born after the disaster.

Finally, this chapter has also shown that past events continue to shape the contemporary state of society and nature, and that nature–society relationships are truly two-way interactions. Again, Chernobyl is an apt example: as of 2011, the abandoned "ghost city" of Pripyat in the irradiated zone around Chernobyl will be marketed as a tourist destination. As contemporary society reframes the destruction of nature by technology as a tourist attraction, we are powerfully reminded that our idea of nature is a social creation and that this might reveal more about our society than we care to admit.

MAIN POINTS REVISITED

■ Nature, society, and technology constitute a complex relationship. In our view, nature is both a physical realm and a social creation.

Recognizing that nature, society, and technology are interactive requires us also to acknowledge that humans are not separate from nature but an integral part of it.

■ Because we regard nature as a social creation, it is important to understand the many social ideas of nature present in society today and especially the history of those ideas. The most prominent idea of nature in Western culture is the belief that nature is an entity to be dominated by humans, an idea derived from the Judeo-Christian tradition.

Just because the Judeo-Christian tradition is a dominant view of nature does not mean it is the only one, nor that it is superior to other views. It does mean, however, that we need to come to terms with how that tradition shapes our views and beliefs about nature if we want to change them.

■ Social relationships with nature have developed over the course of human history, beginning with the early Stone Age. The early history of humankind included people who revered nature as well as those who abused it. Urbanization and industrialization have had extremely degrading impacts on the environment.

Although other societies have had substantial impacts on nature, the extent and degree of the contemporary core society's impact on the environment is unprecedented. Just as peripheral countries aim to achieve the level of prosperity enjoyed in the core, their economic practices also have similar environmental impacts. The result is that although core countries have begun to limit their negative environmental impacts, peripheral countries, in many ways, are just beginning to produce their own significant environmental problems.

■ The globalization of the world economy has meant that environmental problems are also global in their scope: deforestation, air pollution, overfishing, and global change, for example, affect us all. Many new ways of understanding nature have emerged in the last several decades in response to these serious global crises.

Some of the most disturbing problems have to do with extensive land-use changes, such as deforestation, as well as with widespread air pollution from the burning of fossil fuels, which many scientists believe are leading to global climate change. In response to these serious global crises, many new ways of understanding nature have emerged in the last several decades, offering insight into our world as a complexly integrated natural system.

Key Terms

acid rain (p. 176)
animistic perspective on nature
   (p. 152)
biofuels (p. 173)
Buddhist perspective on nature (p. 152)
carbon benefit (p. 173)
carbon neutral (p. 173)
carbon tax (p. 179)
conservation (p. 155)
deep ecology (p. 157)
deforestation (p. 160)
demographic collapse (p. 163)

desertification (p. 182)
ecofeminism (p. 156)
ecological footprint (p. 151)
ecological imperialism (p. 163)
ecosystem (p. 159)
environmental ethics (p. 156)
environmental justice (p. 190)
fishing capacity (p. 185)
global change (p. 190)
Islamic perspective on nature (p. 152)
Judeo-Christian perspective on
   nature (p. 152)

maximum sustainable yield (MSY)
   (p. 184)
nature (p. 149)
oil sands (p. 173)
Paleolithic period (p. 157)
preservation (p. 155)
romanticism (p. 155)
siltation (p. 160)
society (p. 149)
Taoist perspective on nature (p. 152)
technology (p. 149)

Additional Reading

Blake, R.B., *From Fishermen to Fish: the Evolution of Canadian Fishery Policy*. Toronto: Irwin, 2000.

Cartwright, J. "Can Canada Afford Its Forest Industry?" *Policy Options* 17(9), November 1996, 5–18.

Chiotti, Q. "An Assessment of the Regional Impacts and Opportunities from Climate Change in Canada," *Canadian Geographer* 42, 1998, 380–393.

Coates, P. *Nature: Western Attitudes Since Ancient Times*. Berkeley: University of California Press, 1998.

Collingwood, R. *The Idea of Nature*. London: Oxford University Press, 1960.

Commission for Environmental Cooperation. *The North American Mosaic: A State of the Environment Report*. Montreal: Commission for Environmental Cooperation, 2001.

Crosby, A.W. *The Columbian Exchange: Biological and Cultural Consequences of 1492*. Westport, CT: Greenwood Press, 1972.

Crosby, A.W. *Ecological Imperialism: The Biological Expansion of Europe, 900–1900*. Cambridge: Cambridge University Press, 1986.

de Villiers, M. *Water: The Fate of Our Most Precious Resource*. Toronto: Stoddart, 1999.

Diamond, I., and G.F. Orenstein. *Reweaving the World: The Emergence of Ecofeminism*. San Francisco: Sierra Club Books, 1990.

Diamond, J. *Guns, Germs and Steel: A Short History of Everybody for the Last 13,000 Years*. London: Jonathan Cape, 1997.

Draper, D. *Our Environment: A Canadian Perspective*, 2nd ed. Scarborough: Nelson, 2002.

Draper, D., and B. Mitchell, "Environmental Justice Considerations in Canada," *Canadian Geographer* 45(1), 2001, 93–98.

Glacken, C. *Traces on the Rhodian Shore*. Berkeley: University of California Press, 1967.

Gould, P. *Fire in the Rain: The Democratic Consequences of Chernobyl*. Cambridge: Polity Press, 1990.

Homer-Dixon, T. (ed.). *Environment, Scarcity and Violence*. Princeton: Princeton University Press, 1993.

Hughes, J.D. *Pan's Travail: Environmental Problems of the Ancient Greeks and Romans*. Baltimore: The Johns Hopkins University Press, 1994.

Lovell, W.G. "Heavy Shadow and Black Night: Disease and Depopulation in Colonial Spanish America," *Annals of the Association of American Geographers* 82(3), 1992, 426–443.

Kovel, J. *The Enemy of Nature*, 2nd ed. Black Point, NS: Fernwood Publishing, 2007.

Marsh, G.P. *Man and Nature*. New York: Scribner, 1964.

McKenzie, J.I. *Environmental Politics in Canada*. Toronto: Oxford University Press, 2002.

Merchant, C. *The Death of Nature: Women*. San Francisco: Harper & Row, 1979.

Oelschlager, M. *The Idea of Wilderness: From Prehistory to the Age of Ecology*. New Haven: Yale University Press, 1991.

Peters, R.L., and T.E. Lovejoy. *Global Warming and Biological Diversity*. New Haven: Yale University Press, 1992.

Simmons, I.G. *Environmental History: A Concise Introduction*. Oxford: Blackwell, 1993.

Smith, M., and L. Marx. *Does Technology Drive History? The Dilemma of Technological Determinism*. Cambridge, MA: MIT Press, 1995.

Thomas, W.L. (ed.). *Man's Role in Changing the Face of the Earth*. Chicago: University of Chicago Press, 1956.

Turner, B.L. II, et al. *The Earth Transformed by Human Action: Global and Regional Changes in the Biosphere over the Past 300 Years*. New York: Cambridge University Press, 1990.

Vita-Finzi, C. *The Mediterranean Valleys: Geological Changes in Historical Times*. Cambridge: Cambridge University Press, 1969.

Wilson, A. *The Culture of Nature: North American Landscape from Disney to the Exxon Valdez*. Toronto: Between the Lines, 1991.

Worster, D. *Nature's Economy: A History of Ecological Ideas*. Cambridge, UK: Cambridge University Press, 1977.

Discussion Questions and Research Activities

1. Many communities have begun to produce an index of environmental stress, which is a map of the toxic sites of a city or region. One way to plot a rudimentary map is to use the local phone book as a data source. Use the Yellow Pages to identify the addresses of environmentally harmful and potentially harmful activities, such as dry-cleaning businesses, gas stations, automotive repair and car-care businesses, aerospace and electronic manufacturing companies, and agricultural supply stores. Can you think of additional categories of businesses where noxious chemicals may be produced or applied? Compile a map of these activities to begin to get a picture of your locale's geography of environmental stress. Can you discern a spatial pattern, for example a clustering of such businesses in a particular part of your town? Why might they be located there and not elsewhere? How might this relate to concerns for environmental justice?

2. Locate and read a natural history of the place where your college or university is located. What sorts of plants and animals dominated the landscape in the past? Do any of them continue to survive in altered form or unaltered from that period? What are some of the most common introduced exotic species, and what kinds of effects have they had on the native flora and fauna? Why were they introduced? What are some of the most important agricultural crops in your area, and where in the world did they originate?

3. Colleges and universities are large generators of waste, from plain paper waste to biomedical and other sorts of wastes, which can have significant environmental impacts. Identify how your college or university handles this waste stream and how you, as a member of the academic community, contribute to it. Where does the waste go when it leaves the university/ college? Is it separated? Recycled? Locally deposited? Does it go out of the province? If it does, find out why: is there no local facility, or is the waste being treated as a resource? Remember to trace the stream of all the types of waste, not just the paper.

MyGeosciencePlace

Visit **www.mygeoscienceplace.ca** to find chapter review quizzes, videos, maps, and much more.

5

Mapping Cultural Identities

Cosplay fans dressed as their favourite characters, China

"You've toppled the undead armies of the Lich King and brought Arthas to his knees. Now the breaker of worlds, Deathwing, has burst forth from the heart of the Maelstrom and unleashed his rage upon the land and sea. Azeroth has been changed forever, and you must enter the elemental planes in an epic quest to stop the Destroyer from shattering the world itself."[1]

This is the world of the online game World of Warcraft (WOW), an online role-playing video game set in the fantasy Warcraft universe. Globally, 11 million subscribers participate by assuming roles as Warcraft heroes who interrelate in a vast, challenging experience. Thousands of players are able to converge across the globe within the same virtual world where they band together or fight against each other in epic battles, competing for power and glory. This phenomenon of multiple players involved interactively in online play is known as MMORPG, which is an acronym for "Massively Multiplayer Online Role-Playing Game."

It may seem strange to use the example of video games to talk about cultural geography, but the games provide an excellent entry point into the complexity of culture, its globalization, and the new geographies that are being produced around rapidly developing technologies. For example, not only does World of Warcraft have its own virtual geography, but it can also be understood as a culture: "There is a vast community of gamers waiting for you to join their ranks on the World of Warcraft community website. Discuss the game with fellow players, get the latest news, and discover much, much more."[2] In other words, an online community envelops the virtual WOW world. In this community as in the game landscape, people learn and cultivate a unique pattern of interaction that is governed by a shared set of meanings unique to this environment. In other words, they behave according to the norms deemed appropriate for this culture—a culture that only exists online but nonetheless feels real to millions of participants.

This prompts further questions: Who determines what constitutes "proper" behaviour? What effect, if any, does the extended presence of people in the increasingly sophisticated virtual environments have on their real life? At what point does the virtual world we encounter and create in games or online begin to influence and shape our offline culture? And what happens to those who cannot participate online because of a lack of access?

---

[1] From the official website of Blizzard Entertainment (**http://us.blizzard.com/en-us/games/cataclysm/**).

[2] Ibid.

With regard to globalization, the fact that players come from all over the world and join in one online event demonstrates how technology is changing the ways cultural practices come into contact (and possibly influence each other) across great distances. Still, each player experiences the event differently depending on their nationality, age, viewing venue, level of skill, gender, and a whole host of other variables. In fact, this difference is exploited by some players in the core who want to "level-up" (improve their relative standing in the game community) without spending the necessary time and effort: they simply hire professional players in semiperipheral "sweat labs" to serve as their stand-ins. Unequal core–periphery relations thus extend into the virtual world as well.

We begin our investigation of cultural geography by asking how geographers have explored the concept of culture and what insights they have gained from these explorations. We then explore the questions: What counts as culture? How do geographers study it? What are the effects of the increasing dominance of American cultural practices across the world, and in particular in Canada? Because of the size of the task, it will take us two chapters fully to answer these questions.

In this chapter, we will examine how language, religion, and issues of *group* identity (such as nationalism and multiculturalism) shape and are shaped by cultures and, in the process, are responsible for the creation of cultural regions. In Chapter 6, we will investigate the many ways in which *individuals* interpret for themselves the distinct landscapes of these cultural regions.

MAIN POINTS

- Though culture is a central, complex concept in geography, it may be thought of as a way of life involving a particular set of skills, values, and meanings.

- Geographers are particularly concerned about how place and space shape culture and, conversely, how culture shapes place and space. They recognize that culture is dynamic and is contested and altered within larger social, political, and economic contexts.

- Like other fields of contemporary life, culture has been profoundly affected by globalization. However, globalization has not produced a homogenized culture so much as it has produced distinctive impacts and outcomes in different societies and geographical areas as global forces are modified by local cultures.

- Contemporary approaches in cultural geography seek to understand the roles played by politics and the economy in establishing and perpetuating cultures, cultural landscapes, and global patterns of cultural traits and cultural complexes.

- Cultural geography has been broadened to include analysis of gender, class, ethnicity, stage in the life cycle, and so on, in recognizing that important differences can exist within as well as between cultures.

- Cultural ecology, an offshoot of cultural geography, focuses on the relationship between a cultural group and its natural environment.

- Political ecologists also focus on human–environment relationships but stress that relationships at all scales, from the local to the global, are intertwined with larger political and economic forces.

CULTURE AS A GEOGRAPHICAL PROCESS

Geographers, anthropologists, and other scholars who study culture, such as historians, sociologists, and political scientists, agree that culture is a complex concept that intersects with a host of social, political, economic, historical, and geographical factors. But what is culture? Many valid definitions are possible. One simple understanding of culture is that it is a particular way of life, such as a set of skilled activities, values, and meanings surrounding a particular type of economic practice. Or, to take a second example, the way of life established by a religious belief can also form the basis for culture, as in the case of the Amish and Mennonite cultures. Scholars also describe culture in terms of classical standards and aesthetic excellence in, for example, opera, ballet, or literature. Finally, the term *culture* is also used to describe the range of activities that characterize a particular group, such as working-class culture, corporate culture, or teenage culture. Although all these understandings of culture are accurate, for our purposes they are not inclusive enough.

Broadly speaking, **culture** is a shared set of meanings that are lived through the material and symbolic practices of everyday life. The "shared set of meanings" can include values, beliefs, practices, and ideas about religion, language, family, gender, sexuality, and other important identities (**Figure 5.1**). Culture is often subject to re-evaluation and redefinition, and ultimately transformation from both within and outside a particular group. As with many other processes discussed in this book, globalization can increase the speed and frequency with which such transformations are occurring.

Culture is a central concept in geography, although our understanding of its meaning and its impact has changed considerably over the last three decades.

culture: a shared set of meanings that are lived through the material and symbolic practices of everyday life

Figure 5.1   Maori men with traditional tattoos   These indigenous men of New Zealand are dancing a *haka*, a traditional war dance meant to display aggressiveness and fearlessness. The dancers use facial contortions to deride their enemy. Note the tattoos, known as *ta moko*, used as signs of identification, rank, genealogy, tribal history, eligibility to marry, beauty, and ferocity.

What has remained the same, though, is that geographers seek to understand the manifestations and impacts of culture on geography—and of geography on culture. Whereas anthropologists, for example, are concerned with the ways in which culture is created and maintained by human groups, geographers are interested in how place and space shape culture—and how culture shapes place and space. (We will look more closely at the development of the cultural tradition in geography in the following section, in which we discuss the debates surrounding culture within the discipline.)

For much of the twentieth century, geographers, like anthropologists, have focused their attention on the material manifestations of culture (e.g., buildings) as opposed to its less tangible symbolic or spiritual manifestations (e.g., ideas or music). Only in the last 30 or so years have geographers begun to look beyond culture as a "thing" or an effect that can be identified in the landscape and started to pay more attention to culture as an idea, practice, or process.

As with agriculture, politics, and urbanization, globalization has also had complex effects on culture. Such terms as *world music* and *international television* are a reflection of the sense that the world has become a very small place indeed, and people everywhere are sharing aspects of the same culture through the widespread influence of television and other media. Yet, as pointed out in Chapter 2, although powerful homogenizing global forces are certainly at work, the world has not become so uniform that place no longer matters. With respect to culture, just the opposite is true. Place matters more than ever in the negotiation of global forces, as local forces confront globalization and translate it into unique place-specific forms (see **Geography Matters 5.1—The Culture of Hip-Hop**).

Nothing perhaps better illustrates this than music, which has both the formalism to preserve traditional cultural forms and the fluidity to adopt new characteristics. For example, the traditional French lyrics and tunes of the Acadians deported from Nova Scotia were merged in the Cajun music of Louisiana with African and Aboriginal-American rhythms, and played on a variety of instruments—including the French fiddle, the German accordion, and the washboard, a local addition. This distinctive style, with variants such as zydeco, was altered yet again and became part of "world music" when Paul Simon combined it with the rhythmic pulses of South Africa's Ladysmith Black Mambazo in his 1986 *Graceland* album. International attention has not harmed traditional Cajun music, which, if anything, has enjoyed renewed interest in the last 20 years as Cajuns have sought to re-establish their regional identity as a French-speaking culture in North America. Cajun-inspired music has, in turn, found a ready ear in Quebec, as the popularity of Zachary Richard indicates. Another example that shows how traditional forms of culture are continually adapted and recombined to produce new meanings is the practice of tattooing and the role it now plays in certain youth cultures (**Figures 5.1** and **5.2**).

The place-based interactions occurring between culture and political and economic forces are at the heart of cultural geography today. **Cultural geography** focuses on the ways in which space, place, and landscape shape culture at the same time that culture shapes space, place, and landscape. As such, cultural geography demarcates two important and interrelated parts. Culture is the ongoing process of producing a shared set of meanings, whereas geography is the dynamic setting in which groups operate to shape those meanings and, in the process, to form an identity and conduct their lives. Geography in this definition can be as small as the micro-space of the body and as large as the macro-space of the globe—or indeed as pervasive as the virtual space of the Internet.

Figure 5.2 Youth culture The term *culture* is also used to describe a range of practices characterizing a group. Pictured here is a youth culture known as *goth*, who have adopted the traditional indigenous practices of tattooing and body piercing as a cultural marker of their own, together with hairstyle and dress, as well as a distinctive philosophy and music. Yet, culture is more than just the physical distinguishing aspects of a group. It is also a way in which groups derive meaning and attempt to shape the world around them.

cultural geography: study of the ways in which space, place, and landscape shape culture at the same time that culture shapes space, place, and landscape

The Culture of Hip-Hop

Hip-hop is a popular manifestation of contemporary cultural practices among U.S. big-city and especially inner-city youth. From there, it has spread spatially (to other places) and socially (to other segments of the population). Characterized to some extent by graffiti art, and earlier on by break dancing, hip-hop is understood globally through rap music and a distinctive idiomatic vocabulary. Like most nations, hip-hop has its forebears, including boxer Muhammad Ali, Jamaican Rastafarian and reggae musician Bob Marley, and funkster James Brown.

But it also has much older roots in the West African storytelling culture known as *griot*. Hip-hop enlarged upon those origins and now is both appreciated and produced on six continents. It is a cultural practice that has truly globalized, not because its practitioners have migrated far and wide, but because its culture has diffused via telecommunications and the music and film industries. Hip-hop has become a cultural phenomenon that exists beyond geography in the music, the clothes, and the language of its practitioners.

Music is the heart and soul of the hip-hop nation, and the geography of U.S. hip-hop—its hearth area—can be crudely divided into East Coast, West Coast, South Coast, and a region in and around Detroit where white rap-metal groups have become popular. But hip-hop has broken out of its regional boundaries and transcended national boundaries as well, for example spreading from the West Coast region into Vancouver. Today, hip-hop graffiti art can be found in urban areas as distant as Australia and South Africa, and rap music is as popular in the Philippines as it is in Paris.

But hip-hop is also very clearly about the more local space of the neighbourhood, or "the 'hood"—rap's dominant spatial trope. Although rap and dancing are central to hip-hop, the local context in which the story, music, or dance unfold is also critical. As hip-hop cultural theorist Murray Forman argues, "Virtually all of the early descriptions of hip-hop practices identify territory and the public sphere as significant factors, whether in visible artistic expression and appropriation of public space via graffiti or b-boying [break dancing], the sonic impact of a pounding bass line, or the discursive articulation of urban geography in rap lyrics [and films]."[3] Hip-hop, then, is very much about claiming space and place!

Hip-hop is effectively about how space and place shape the identities of rappers in particular but also African Americans more generally, showing how race, space, and place come together to produce the contradiction of "home" as a locus of roots and the foundation of personal history but also as a site of devaluation vis-à-vis

the dominant white society. Most recently, a hybrid form of rap metal has emerged in the Detroit metropolitan area, which contains large numbers of African Americans and working-class whites who lost their jobs in the restructuring of the automobile industry. The rap-metal genre confirms that, although hip-hop culture has its roots in the African American experience, it derives much of its power from issues of poverty and class.

The most controversial (but also most popular and lucrative) of all hip-hop genres is "gangsta rap," pioneered in the late 1980s by artists like Ice T and groups such as N.W.A. Gangsta lyrics are said to glorify promiscuity, violence, misogyny (hatred of women), gang culture, rape, drug dealing, and other acts of criminal behaviour. Gangsta artists respond, however, that they are merely retelling the reality experienced by young inner-city African Americans (**Figure 5.1.1**).

Figure 5.1.1 Rapper 50 Cent Curtis James Jackson, III, is better known by his stage name, 50 Cent. Born in Queens, New York, 50 Cent began drug dealing at the age of 12. He grew up without a father and was raised by his mother, Sabrina Jackson, a cocaine dealer, who gave birth to him at the age of 15. Sabrina raised Jackson until he was 8, when she was murdered. Following his mother's death, he was raised by his grandparents, spending much of his youth selling drugs, experiencing several arrests, being shot nine times, and serving a prison term. His biography starkly reflects the controversial lyrics in his songs as well as those of other gangsta rappers.

---

[3] M. Forman, "Ain't No Love in the Heart of the City: Hip-Hop, Space, and Place." In M. Forman and M.A. Neal (eds.), *That's the Joint! The Hip Hop Studies Reader*. New York: Routledge, 2004, p. 155.

Cultural critic bell hooks turns the condemnation of gangsta rap on its head by pointing out that gangsta rap does not exist in a vacuum but is an extension of white, male-dominated, capitalist society.[4] She argues that it is far easier to attack gangsta rap than the culture that produces and reproduces it (through white, middle-class consumption of the music). Simultaneously, hooks points out that although we are repelled by the misogyny promoted by gangsta rappers, we fail to see it everywhere else—including within mainstream Western culture.

Hip-hop as a youth-oriented cultural product has become widely commercialized in core countries by multinational corporations. Still, in many parts of the world, it is a fully homegrown phenomenon. Interestingly, rather than homogenizing local cultures, the global spread of hip-hop from the United States outward has tended to create hybrid and synthetic forms of music, adjusting to local cultures and struggles. What is most consistent about the rap music produced in the periphery is that it has become a focal point for the underprivileged to unite and challenge the oppressive quality of the status quo. For example, Emmanuel Jal, a former child soldier in Sudan's People's Liberation Army, uses rap as a way of educating the world about the struggles that oppressed people face in Africa: political injustice, government terror, war, as well as the hope of freedom from these tyrannies.

[4] b. hooks, "Sexism and Misogyny: Who Takes the Rap?" *Z Magazine*, February 1994, pp. 26–29, **http://race.eserver.org/misogyny.html**.

An example of the two-way relationship between geography and culture in a non-physical space is the ubiquity of Facebook and other online social media. These virtual networks have revolutionized the way we communicate with each other, as friendship groups and circles obscure the boundaries between online and offline domains. Cultural scholars who study them believe that social media are not turning us into "virtual creatures" that exist only in the ether of the Internet but rather into hybrid creatures with a foot in both the virtual and the real world.

This hybridity enables us to be in more than one place at any one time and to connect to others whom we may never meet in person but with whom we may form significant relationships or merely passing ones. In fact, it may even enable us to be more than one person: you could be a student sitting in class or reading this text and at the same time be a more or less different "online" person that exists only through the laptop or smartphone in front of you. Whatever the degree of overlap between our "real" and "virtual" characters, these virtual interactions change us, perhaps only in small ways, but those ways can and often do add up to something quite substantial.

But beyond the virtual space, Facebook and the Internet are also a perfect example of the two-way relationship between physical space and culture. Consider how our virtual cultural practices can change the arrangement and use of physical space: the more time we spend online shopping or "meeting" with friends, the less busy our stores and streets become, which has immediate consequences for shopping opportunities or our feeling of personal safety. Conversely, the changed space now changes our cultural practices: with fewer brick-and-mortar stores to go to and feeling less safe on the less busy streets, we elect to do even more socializing or shopping online.

We should also mention the increasing privacy concerns arising from our intense use of social media. Their open access means that anyone from stalkers to employers to marketing companies and the police can use the sites to gain access to members' personal information. Not surprisingly, because these networking sites allow users from all over the world to express their opinions and engage with other users, the same cultural fault lines that occur in everyday spaces are also drawn within cyberspace, though the connections can be far more extensive and immediate.

At this point, we can summarize our understanding of culture as follows: culture is a process that is shaped by and shapes politics, the economy, and society. It can be enduring as well as newly created, but it is always influenced by a whole range of interactions as groups maintain, change, or even create traditions

5.1   Geography in the Information Age

This textbook illustrates how quick the pace of change in ICT and the associated behaviours has become: the previous edition still contained a lengthy explanation of Facebook, and put its number of subscribers at 50 million worldwide. By 2011, that number had ballooned to 800 million people—likely including every one of you!

Recent events have demonstrated the very concrete political potential of social networks for mobilizing people and support and thus facilitating change. During the 2008 U.S. presidential campaign, Obama supporters were able to mobilize supporters and fundraise by connecting individuals with similar interests and goals through a "snowball" system. More recently, the "Facebook revolutions" in northern Africa have shown how social networks can be used to organize opposition movements "below the radar" of the authorities.

from the material of their everyday lives. As a result, there is no purpose in categorically differentiating between hip-hop and Hinduism, as both are significant expressions of culture and both are of interest to geographers. (Note, though, how the capitalization of the word *Hinduism* expresses the persistence of traditional evaluations!)

In the remainder of this chapter, we consider how culture and geography interact by examining the geography of religion, the geography of language, and the various ways in which group identity is inscribed on the cultural landscape. Before we do so, however, it is necessary to define some of the categories and terms geographers use when they discuss the interaction of culture and space.

CULTURAL LANDSCAPES, TRAITS, SYSTEMS, AND REGIONS
The Cultural Landscape

Geographers are interested in the interactions between people, culture, space, place, and landscape. One of the "founding fathers" of what we now call cultural geography was Carl Sauer (**Figure 5.3**). He was particularly interested in trying to understand how a culture expresses itself in the **cultural landscape**, a characteristic and tangible outcome of the complex interactions between a human group—with its own practices, preferences, values, and aspirations—and a natural environment. Sauer differentiated the cultural landscape from the natural landscape. He emphasized that the former was a "humanized" version of the latter, such that the activities of humans resulted in an identifiable and understandable alteration of the natural environment (**Figure 5.4**). In making such connections, Sauer was influenced by the work of George Perkins Marsh, whose 1864 book, *Man and Nature*, was one of the first to explore the links between human action and environmental change. **Figure 5.5** illustrates Sauer's notion of the cultural landscape.

For roughly five decades, scholars working in cultural geography largely followed Sauer's important ideas about culture. His approach to the cultural landscape was ecological, and his many published works reflect his interest in trying to understand the myriad ways that humans transformed the surface of Earth. In his own words:

> The cultural landscape is fashioned from a natural landscape by a cultural group. Culture is the agent, the natural area is the medium, the cultural landscape is the result. Under the influence of a given culture, itself changing through time, the landscape undergoes development, passing through phases, and probably reaching

Figure 5.3   Carl Sauer (1889–1975) Carl Sauer spent his career as a geographer at the University of California, Berkeley. He rejected environmental determinism as a way of understanding human geography and emphasized the uniqueness of landscape through the impact of both cultural and physical processes.

cultural landscape: a characteristic and tangible outcome of the complex interactions between a human group and a natural environment

Figure 5.4   Masai village, Kenya   The cultural landscape, as defined by Carl Sauer, reflected the way that cultural and environmental processes came together to create a unique product. Pictured here is a small village where herding is the major occupation. The village is enclosed by thorny brambles and branches harvested from the surrounding area. Within the enclosure, the dwellings are arranged in a unique circular pattern, with the animal pens in the middle of the settlement for easy observation by the residents. This cultural landscape reflects the needs of the herder society that created it by modifying the natural landscape.

Figure 5.5   Sauer's cultural landscape
This illustration is a graphic representation of the ways in which the natural landscape is formed and then transformed into a specific cultural landscape. First, physical factors shape the natural landscape. Then people—through culture—reshape the natural landscape into a cultural landscape that meets their needs. This reshaping creates specific cultural forms (such as population distributions, patterns, and housing) that together make up the characteristics of a cultural landscape that is specific to a particular group of people.   (*Source:* Adapted from C. Sauer, "The Morphology of Landscape." In J. Leighly [ed.], *Land and Life: Selections from the Writings of Carl Ortwin Sauer.* Berkeley, CA: University of California Press, 1964, pp. 315–50.)

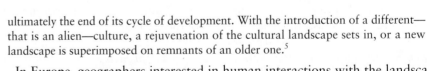

Factors		Forms	
Geological		Weather	
Climatic	**Time** →	Land Surface Soil Drainage Mineral resources Sea and coast	**Natural landscape**
Vegetational		Plants	

Factor	Medium	Forms	
Culture → **Time** →	Natural landscape →	Population Density Mobility Housing Plan Structure Production Communication	**Cultural landscape**

historical geography: the study of the geography of the past

ultimately the end of its cycle of development. With the introduction of a different—that is an alien—culture, a rejuvenation of the cultural landscape sets in, or a new landscape is superimposed on remnants of an older one.[5]

In Europe, geographers interested in human interactions with the landscape produced slightly different approaches. For example, in Great Britain, the approach to understanding the human imprint on the landscape was given the term *historical geography.* Very simply defined, **historical geography** is the study of the geography

---

[5] C. Sauer, "The Morphology of Landscape." In J. Leighly (ed.), *Land and Life: Selections from the Writings of Carl Ortwin Sauer.* Berkeley, CA: University of California Press, 1964, pp. 315–50.

of the past. One of its most famous practitioners was H.C. Darby, who attempted to understand how past geographies changed, or evolved, into more recent geographies (**Figure 5.6**). He most successfully implemented his historical approach to geography by developing a geography of the *Domesday Book*. William the Conqueror ordered the survey that became known as "Domesday" (from the Saxon word *dom,* or "judgement") to be compiled in 1085 so that he could have an inventory of his new possessions in England. The book provides a rich catalogue of the ownership of every tract of land and of the conditions and contents of the lands at that time, and even the number of people that lived there (**Figure 5.7**). For geographers like Darby and those scholars influenced by his approach, such data are invaluable for reconstructing the political, economic, and social forces that shaped past geographies.

In France, Paul Vidal de la Blache developed an approach to cultural geography that centres on the livelihood practices of a group (**Figure 5.8**). Called *genre de vie* (or "ways of living"), these practices are seen to shape physical, social, and psychological bonds. This approach emphasizes the need to study small, homogeneous areas to uncover the close relationships that exist between people and their immediate surroundings. De la Blache constructed complex descriptions of pre-industrial France that demonstrated how the various *genres de vie* emerged from the possibilities and constraints posed by local physical environments. Subsequently, he wrote about the changes in French regions brought on by industrialization, observing that regional homogeneity was no longer the unifying element. Instead, the increased mobility of people and goods had produced new, more complex geographies wherein previously isolated *genres de vie* were being integrated into a competitive, industrial economic framework. Anticipating the widespread impacts of globalization, Vidal de la Blache recognized how people in various places struggled to mediate the big changes that were transforming their lives.

What unifies all of these approaches is that they placed the cultural landscape at the heart of their study of human–environment interactions. They differ, however, in the emphasis they place on different landscape components and the importance of the role they assign to the physical environment.

Figure 5.6   Professor Sir Henry Clifford Darby (1909–1992) H.C. Darby argued that historical geography is an essential foundation for the study of all human geography. His own studies of past geographies were published in a series of *Domesday Geographies of England.*   (*Source:* Preston E. James and Geoffrey J. Martin, *All Possible Worlds: A History of Geographical Ideas,* 2nd ed. New York: John Wiley and Sons, 1981, p. 211.)

genre de vie: a functionally organized way of life that is characteristic of a particular cultural group

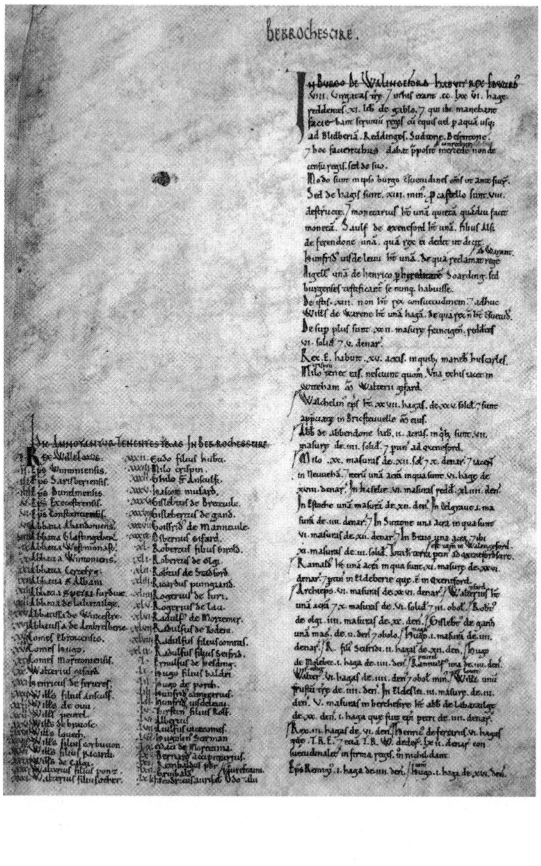

Figure 5.8   Paul Vidal de la Blache (1845–1919)   Vidal de la Blache was a founder of the *Annales de géographie,* an influential academic journal that fostered the idea of human geography as the study of people–environment relationships. His most long-lasting conceptual contribution was *genre de vie,* which is the lifestyle of a particular region reflecting the economic, social, ideological, and psychological identities imprinted on the landscape. (*Source:* Preston E. James and Geoffrey J. Martin, *All Possible Worlds: A History of Geographical Ideas,* 2nd ed. New York: John Wiley and Sons, 1981, p. 211.)

Figure 5.7   Domesday Book   Pictured here is a page from the *Great Domesday Book* that shows the accounts for Berkshire County in England. The listing begins with the lands belonging to the King, followed by the lands of the bishops of Winchester, Salisbury, and Durham, then the lands of the Abbot of Abingdon, and lastly those of the great lay barons. *Domesday Book* reveals an elaborate feudal structure of land-holding from the King down. Under this system, land was supposedly held directly or indirectly by the King, who stood at the top of the feudal ladder. He granted land called *fiefs* to his chief barons, bishops, and abbots. To geographers, such sources reveal important information not only about the form and structure of the landscape but also about the society that created this structure.

Cultural Traits

cultural trait: a single aspect of the complex of routine practices that constitute a particular cultural group

Geographers' interest in culture as a geographical factor ranges from single attributes to complex systems. One simple aspect of culture is the concept of a **cultural trait,** which is a single aspect of the complex of routine practices that constitute a particular cultural group. Examples include distinctive styles of dress, dietary habits, or styles of architecture. Peter Ennals and Deryck Holdsworth have shown how the single cultural trait of architecture can be studied and how it can contribute to the broader identification of cultural regions in this country (**Figure 5.9**). In the areas of Canada first occupied by Europeans, settlers built houses that were very similar in style and building technique to those found in the areas of Europe from which they had come. In Newfoundland and Labrador, versions of English and Irish cottages were erected. In Acadia and Quebec, houses were built that copied the regional patterns found in France at the time.

Obviously, having no time to experiment and heavily conditioned by their own images of what a house should look like, these early settlers simply

a. Vancouver: bungalow style

b. Prairie farmhouse

c. Ontario farmhouse

d. Quebec farmhouse

e. Nova Scotia

f. Newfoundland and Labrador

g. Toronto: "bay and gables" style

h. Montreal: duplex design

0   500   1000 kilometres

Figure 5.9 Vernacular architectural regions in Canada Geographers have shown that architectural style is an important characteristic of the cultural region and that differences in architecture are one way of distinguishing different cultural regions. This map shows the major types of *vernacular* (that is, "everyday") residential architecture found in Canada at the end of the nineteenth century. The pattern reflects the traditional, or "folk," architectural styles of Canada's major European colonizers, adapted to this country's environment and modified over time as more recent ideas about fashionable style diffused across Canada.   (*Sources:* Based on redrawings by Karine Arakelian. House types a and c–f based on Peter Ennals and Deryck W. Holdsworth, "The Look of Domestic Building, 1891." In William Dean et al., *Concise Historical Atlas of Canada.* Toronto: University of Toronto Press, 1998, Plate 30; house types b, g, and h from Peter Ennals and Deryck W. Holdsworth, *Homeplace: The Making of the Canadian Dwelling over Three Centuries.* Toronto: University of Toronto Press, 1998, pp. 195–196, 210.)

replicated the styles they knew. In this way, at least, Canada was "a simplification of Europe overseas," as some Canadian cultural geographers have described it. Certainly, as we shall see in Chapter 6, these settlers were engaged in their own version of "place making" and re-creating in this country a world they knew.

From about 1850, however, another element is added to the mix—that of fashion. By then, many Canadian settlers had become a little more prosperous and could afford to rebuild their houses in the styles affected by new ideals of domestic privacy and by the "polite" architecture of the neo-Georgian houses Canada's elite were building for themselves. In this way, Ennals and Holdsworth argue, earlier *folk* styles were replaced by what they call *vernacular* architecture. This "everyday" or "common" architecture, developed in Canada, maintains a set of distinct regional styles, ranging from the exuberance of the porches of Lunenburg, Nova Scotia, to the "eyebrow" designs of the nineteenth-century Ontario farmhouse with its distinctive dormer window. The latter has become so quintessentially Ontarian that its design elements are echoed in many contemporary subdivisions (**Figure 5.10**).

Increased immigration and growing urbanization in the nineteenth century did little to erode these patterns. In fact, they added their own distinctive contributions, because the need to adapt vernacular styles to the high-density demands of Canada's cities was met in different ways. In Montreal, for example, the duplex and triplex styles were developed, designs almost unique in North America, possibly inspired by the city's Scottish immigrants with their memories of Glaswegian tenement life. In Toronto, the classic farmhouse morphed into the gothic row house. During early twentieth-century expansion in Vancouver, the bungalow, perhaps inspired by immigrants from California, was the leading suburban form of housing.

Meanwhile, out on the Prairies, history was repeating itself with new waves of immigration. By the late nineteenth century, settlers from Central Europe were building farmhouses in the styles of their homelands. From Verigin, Saskatchewan, to Dauphin, Manitoba, the farm architecture of Ukraine, Poland, and Russia was adopted as the design for barns, houses, and churches. Prosperity, when it occurred, was marked this time by the purchase of plans or prefabricated houses from mail-order companies. The vernacular architecture of the Prairies thus arose from a literally off-the-shelf, central Canadian design made in Toronto that could be seen in countless small towns across the west.

A preference for rational planning and the lure of profit from mass production erased regional differences in new construction styles during the second half of the twentieth century. However, postmodernism's rejection of uniformity (see Chapter 6) and the real estate industry's realization that "difference sells" have rekindled interest in Canadian regional patterns of vernacular architecture in recent times (**Figure 5.10**).

Figure 5.10 The present preserves the past These houses in a new Orangeville, Ontario, subdivision echo architectural elements from earlier styles.

Cultural Systems

cultural system: a collection of interacting elements that, taken together, shape a group's collective identity

Whereas a cultural trait is a *single* aspect of the routine practices of a group, the **cultural system** refers to a *collection* of interacting components that, taken together, shape a group's collective identity. A cultural system includes traits, territorial affiliation, and shared history, as well as other more complex elements, such as language. In a cultural system, it is possible for internal variation to exist in particular elements at the same time that broader similarities lend coherence. For example, Christianity unites all Protestant religions, and yet the practices of particular denominations vary. And, although Mexicans, Bolivians, Cubans, and Chileans exhibit variations in pronunciation, pitch, stress, and other aspects of vocal expression, they all speak Spanish. This means they share a key element of a cultural system (which, for these nationalities, also includes Roman Catholicism and a Spanish colonial heritage).

Cultural Regions

cultural region: the area within which a particular cultural system prevails

A **cultural region** is the *area* within which a particular cultural system prevails. In this area (which may be quite small, or extensive, or even discontinuous), certain cultural practices, beliefs, or values are more or less practised by the majority of the inhabitants. Illustrations of cultural regions abound in Canada. For example, parts of New Brunswick, Nova Scotia, and Prince Edward Island compose the Acadian cultural region (**Figure 5.11**). The population of this cultural region is made up mainly of a long-settled community of French-speaking, Roman Catholic people who have a series of distinct cultural traits, as we have already seen, in connection with music, folk architecture, and, as we shall see below, language.

To take another example, the Manitoba lowlands were settled by hundreds of thousands of immigrants from continental Europe in the years before 1914. The settlers' adherence to an agricultural way of life and to their Central European traditions serves to define this area as a cultural region. At a finer scale of analysis, this region is, in fact, made up of a great variety of subregions—each the home of a distinctive culture, which gives a specific flavour to a particular community. For instance, Mennonites came to the area from southern Russia in the 1870s, creating very distinctive agricultural landscapes around Winkler, Altona, and Steinbach. They re-created a European-style nucleated village form and open-field system of collective farming, whereas Anglo-American immigrants favoured dispersed settlement on land that was individually farmed.[6] Although abandoned as a way of life in the 1920s, these settlement forms gave a social cohesion to Mennonite society that has contributed to the retention of their language and culture in this region of varied cultures. In describing this variety, John Warkentin has written, "Distinctive communities such as Icelanders at Gimli, Mennonites in Southern Manitoba, Ukrainians in the Dauphin area, French in St. Boniface and St. Pierre, Métis in southeast Manitoba, and Ontarians in Portage la Prairie are still visible"[7] (**Figure 5.12**).

To these well-known and established examples, we should add those that are currently coalescing around shared cultural values. Around Nelson, in southeast British Columbia, for example, a long countercultural or "alternative" tradition has attracted a considerable number of artists, environmentalists, and community activists in recent years. Their impact on the landscape can be seen in developments as varied as the renovation of old Main Street stores into cooperatively

Figure 5.11   The Acadian region
The Acadian region of Canada preserves its cultural heritage through many visual reminders, as this picture of the Acadian flag at Grand Pré illustrates. The gold star at the top is the Stella Maris (Star of the Sea). The national park at Grand Pré, Nova Scotia, is a memorial to the deportation of the Acadians in 1755.

[6] Yossi Katz and John C. Lehr, *The Last Best West: Essays on the Cultural Geography of the Canadian Prairies.* Jerusalem: Magnes Press, 1999.

[7] John Warkentin, *A Regional Geography of Canada: Life, Land and Space,* 2nd ed. Scarborough: Prentice Hall, 2000, p. 403.

Figure 5.12   Ukrainian Catholic Church, Dauphin, Manitoba

run stores selling local art and the individually designed houses and organic farms that can be found scattered along the nearby Slocan Valley.

As we said in our brief introduction to cultural systems, religion and language are two of the key components of a cultural system for most of the world's people. We will now look at them in more detail, followed by an examination of the role of society.

Geography and Religion

Two key components of a cultural system for most of the world's people are religion and language. **Religion** is a belief system and a set of practices that recognize the existence of a power higher than humans. Although religious affiliation is perhaps on the decline in parts of the world's core regions, it still acts as a powerful shaper of daily life, from eating habits and dress codes to coming-of-age rituals and death ceremonies in both the core and the periphery. And, like language, religious beliefs and practices change as new interpretations are advanced or as new spiritual influences are adopted.

The most important influence on religious change has been conversion from one set of beliefs to another. Especially in the 500 years since the onset of the Columbian Exchange, conversion of all sorts has escalated throughout the globe. In fact, since 1492, traditional religions have become dramatically dislocated from their sites of origin through missionizing and conversion as well as diaspora and emigration. Whereas missionizing and conversion are deliberate efforts to change the religious views of a person or people, diaspora and emigration involve the involuntary and voluntary movement of people who bring their religious beliefs and practices to their new locales.

Diaspora is a spatial dispersion of a previously homogeneous group. The processes of global political and economic changes that led to the massive movement of the world's populations over the last five centuries have also meant the dislodging and spread of the world's many religions from their traditional sites of practice. Religious practices have become so spatially mixed that it is a challenge to present a map of the contemporary global distribution of religion that reveals more than it obscures. This is because the global scale is too gross a level of resolution to portray the wide variation that exists between and within religious practices. **Figure 5.13** identifies the contemporary distribution of what are considered by religious scholars to be the world's major religions because they contain the largest number of practitioners globally. As with other global-scale representations, the map is useful in that it helps present a generalized picture.

religion: belief system and a set of practices that recognize the existence of a power higher than humans

diaspora: a spatial dispersion of a previously homogeneous group

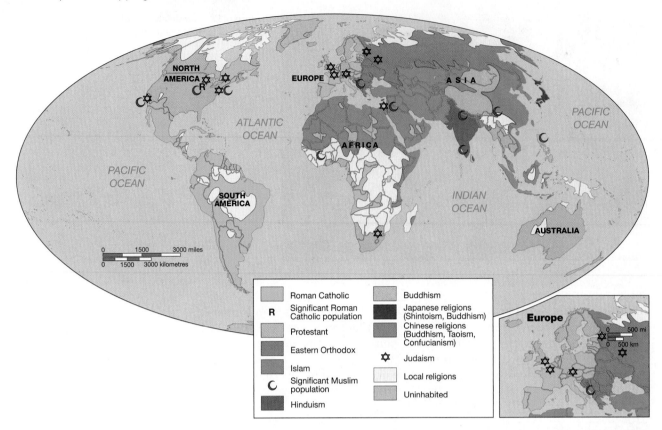

Figure 5.13   World distribution of major religions   The map shows a generalized picture of the world's major religions. Most of the world's peoples are members of one of these religions. Not evident on this map are the local variations in practices, as well as the many other different religions that are practised worldwide. (Although known in the West primarily as philosophies, Taoism and Confucianism both also developed religious traditions and so are included on this map.)

Figure 5.14 identifies the source areas of four of the world's major religions and their diffusion from those sites over time. The map illustrates that the world's major religions originated and diffused from two fairly small areas of the globe. The first, where Hinduism and Buddhism (as well as Sikhism) originated, is an area of the lowlands of the subcontinent of India drained by the Indus (Punjab on the map) and Ganges Rivers. The second area, where Christianity and Islam (as well as Judaism) originated, is in the deserts of the Middle East.

Religious beliefs are organized and codified, often based on the teachings and writings of one or more founders. And it is important to recognize that the world's religions contain all sorts of variation within them. For example, Christians may be Catholics or Protestants, but even within these large groups there exists a great deal of variation. The same is true for all religions.

Hinduism was the first religion to emerge, among the peoples of the Indo-Gangetic Plain, about 4,000 years ago. Buddhism and Sikhism evolved from Hinduism as reform religions, with Buddhism appearing around 500 B.C. and Sikhism developing in the fifteenth century. Buddhism dispersed to other parts of India and was carried by missionaries and traders to China (100 B.C. to A.D. 200), Korea and Japan (A.D. 300–500), Southeast Asia (A.D. 400–600), Tibet (A.D. 700), and Mongolia (A.D. 1500). Not surprisingly, as Buddhism spread, it developed many different regional forms, such that Tibetan Buddhism is distinct from Japanese Buddhism.

Christianity, Islam, and Judaism all developed among the Semitic-speaking people of the deserts of the Middle East. Like the Indo-Gangetic religions, these three religions are also related. Although Judaism is the oldest, it is the least widespread. Judaism originated about 4,000 years ago, Christianity about 2,000 years ago, and Islam about 1,300 years ago. Judaism developed out of the

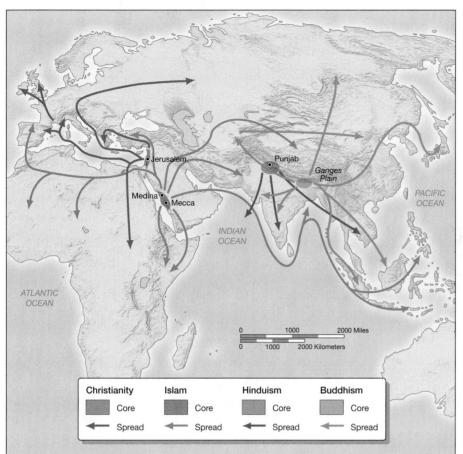

Figure 5.14 Origin areas and diffusion of four major religions
The world's major religions originated in a fairly small region of the world. Judaism and Christianity began in present-day Israel and Jordan. Islam emerged from the western Arabian peninsula (in present-day Saudi Arabia). Buddhism and Hinduism originated on the Indian subcontinent. The source areas of the world's major religions are also the cultural hearth areas of agriculture, urbanization, and other key aspects of human development.

cultures and beliefs of Bronze Age peoples and was the first monotheistic (belief in one God) religion. Christianity developed in Jerusalem among the disciples of Jesus; they proclaimed that he was the Messiah expected by the Jews. As it spread from its hearth area, Christianity's diffusion was helped by missionizing and imperial sponsorship.

Many other religions figure prominently in the cultural lives of people around the world. Among them are Confucianism, Taoism, Shintoism, Mormonism, Zorastrianism, and Jansenism, as well as Voodoo, Rastafarianism, and animism, among many others. The point is that faith, a trusting belief in a transcendent reality or a supreme being, is a profoundly powerful force in guiding people's actions and attitudes and shaping the worlds in which they live. Faith is also a significant element of globalization as disparate belief systems come into contact, in some cases causing tension and even violent conflict as new religions are introduced among populations who are adherents of a different one.

An excellent illustration of the global forces behind the changing geography of religion is the Columbian contact with the New World. Before Columbus and later Europeans reached the continents of North and South America, the people living there practised, for the most part, various forms of animism and related rituals. They viewed themselves holistically, as one part of the wider world of animate and inanimate nature. They used religious rituals and charms to guide and enhance the activities of everyday life as well as the more extreme situations of warfare. Shamanism, in which spiritually gifted individuals are believed to possess the power to control preternatural forces, is one important aspect of the belief system that existed among Native American populations at the time of European contact (**Figure 5.15**).

European contact with the New World was, from the beginning, accompanied by Christian missionizing efforts directed at changing the belief systems of the Aboriginal peoples and converting them to what the missionizers believed to

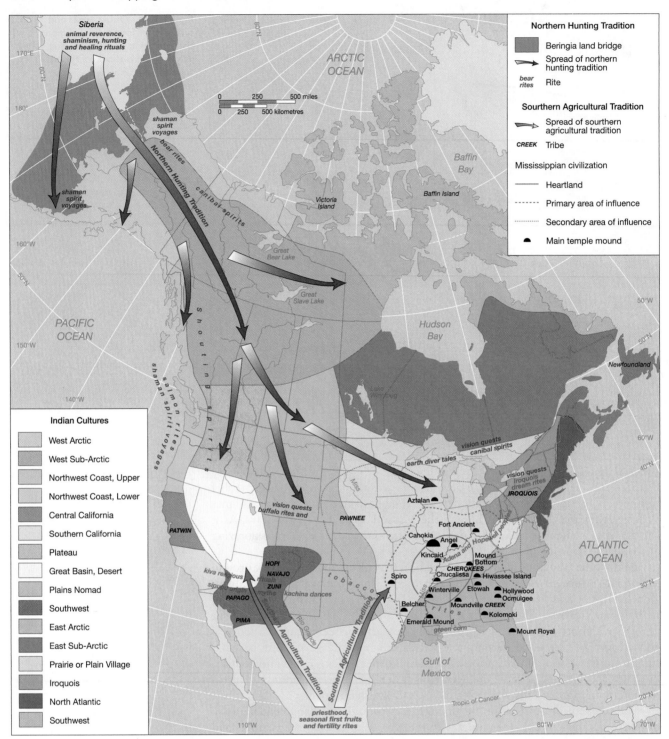

Figure 5.15 Pre-Columbian religions in North America   Before European contact, the indigenous populations in North America had developed a range of religious practices. Religious traditions based on agrarian practices diffused from south to north, while those religious traditions based on hunting diffused from north to south.   (*Source:* B.E. Carroll, *The Routledge Historical Atlas of Religion in America.* New York: Routledge, 2000, pp. 15–16.)

be "the one true religion" (**Figure 5.16**). Religion, especially for the Spanish colonizing agents, was especially important in integrating the indigenous population into the feudal system.

Perhaps what is most interesting about the present state of the geography of religion is how, during the colonial period, religious missionizing and conversion flowed from the core to the periphery. In the current postcolonial period, however, the opposite is becoming true. For example, the fastest-growing religion in

Figure 5.16   Mission at Sainte-Marie-Among-the-Hurons   This historically exact re-creation was built in the 1960s on the actual site of a seventeenth-century Jesuit mission to the Hurons, in what is now Midland, Ontario.

the United States today is Islam, and it is in core countries that Buddhism is making the greatest number of converts. Although Pope John Paul II was the most widely travelled pontiff in Roman Catholic history, the same can be said for the Tibetan Buddhist religious leader, the Dalai Lama, who is also a tireless world traveller for Buddhism. The Papacy's efforts are mostly directed at maintaining Roman Catholic followers and attempting to dissuade their conversion to other religions, such as evangelicalism in the United States and Latin America. We should also note that the bulk of the world's Roman Catholics will be located in Latin America if present population growth trends continue (see Chapter 3).

The Geography of Canada's Religions

The geography of Canada's religions is—as you might expect—a product of this country's history of colonialism and recent immigration (**Figure 5.17**). Following European contact, the original pattern of Aboriginal faiths and belief systems found across Canada was slowly replaced by the dominant Christian faiths of the French and British colonizing powers. For instance, New France (Quebec and Acadia) was peopled by settlers who brought the Roman Catholic faith of France with them. Conversely, substantial parts of Newfoundland and Labrador were settled by Protestant fishing people from England. When Britain gained control of Canada after 1760, immigrants from Britain and the United States brought with them into Ontario the Protestant denominations of Christianity that they practised (**Figure 5.18**).[8]

The legacy of this history can be seen to this day at the national level (**Table 5.1**) as well as on the provincial level: census data from 2001 show that in Newfoundland and Labrador, 60 percent of people over age 15 record their religious affiliation as Protestant. In Quebec, conversely, 83.2 percent of people over age 15 record their religious affiliation as Roman Catholic. In Ontario, we find that 34 percent are affiliated to Roman Catholicism and 35 percent record a Protestant affiliation.[9] However,

---

[8] An excellent introduction is provided in Robert Choquette's study *Canada's Religions*. Ottawa: University of Ottawa Press, 2004. See especially Chapter 18 ("Immigration and Religions," pp. 377–407) and Chapter 19 ("Alternative Religions," pp. 409–430).

[9] When interpreting these data, Statistics Canada cautions that the census asked respondents to report "a specific denomination or group, even if they were not practising members of their group. Consequently, these data indicate only religious affiliation." We cannot, therefore, rely on these data to provide a clear indication about changing levels of faith (religiosity) in the population and must use other information, such as measures of attendance at religious services (provided in Statistics Canada's General Social Survey). The 2001 census data are reported in Statistics Canada, *2001 Census: Analysis Series. Religions in Canada*. Ottawa: Minister of Industry, May 2003, Catalogue No. 96F0030XIE2001015; this report is also available online at **www12.statcan.ca/english/census01/products**.

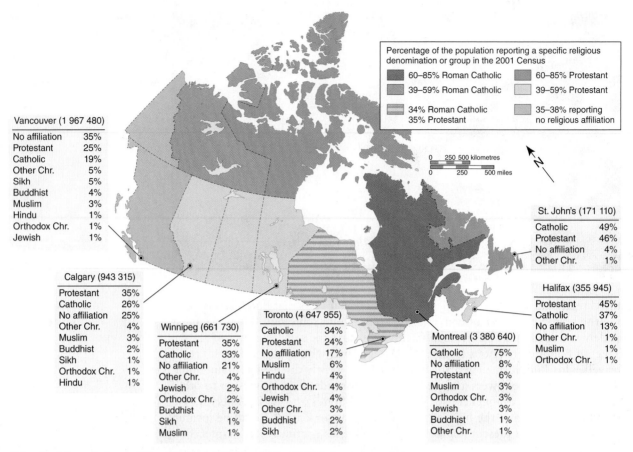

Vancouver (1 967 480)

No affiliation	35%
Protestant	25%
Catholic	19%
Other Chr.	5%
Sikh	5%
Buddhist	4%
Muslim	3%
Hindu	1%
Orthodox Chr.	1%
Jewish	1%

Calgary (943 315)

Protestant	35%
Catholic	26%
No affiliation	25%
Other Chr.	4%
Muslim	3%
Buddhist	2%
Sikh	1%
Orthodox Chr.	1%
Hindu	1%

Winnipeg (661 730)

Protestant	35%
Catholic	33%
No affiliation	21%
Other Chr.	4%
Jewish	2%
Orthodox Chr.	2%
Buddhist	1%
Sikh	1%
Muslim	1%

Toronto (4 647 955)

Catholic	34%
Protestant	24%
No affiliation	17%
Muslim	6%
Hindu	4%
Orthodox Chr.	4%
Jewish	4%
Other Chr.	3%
Buddhist	2%
Sikh	2%

Montreal (3 380 640)

Catholic	75%
No affiliation	8%
Protestant	6%
Muslim	3%
Orthodox Chr.	3%
Jewish	3%
Buddhist	1%
Other Chr.	1%

St. John's (171 110)

Catholic	49%
Protestant	46%
No affiliation	4%
Other Chr.	1%

Halifax (355 945)

Protestant	45%
Catholic	37%
No affiliation	13%
Other Chr.	1%
Muslim	1%
Orthodox Chr.	1%

Notes: City data are for Census Metropolitan Areas (CMAs); population totals are from sources cited.
"Catholic" includes Roman Catholic, Eastern Catholic, Polish National Church, and Old Catholic.
"Other Christian" refers to those respondents to the 2001 Census who reported their affiliation as "Christian" without further elaboration.
"No religious affiliation" includes agnostic, atheist, humanist, "no religion," and other responses to the Census, such as Darwinism.
Religious groups or denominations of less than 1 percent of CMA population are not reported.
Totals may not add to 100 percent because of rounding of data.

Figure 5.17   The distribution of religions in Canada, by province and territory, 2001   This map shows the leading religious denomination or group in each province or territory, according to the affiliations expressed by the population in the 2001 census. In broad terms, the map shows that the Roman Catholic and Protestant denominations of Christianity still dominate in most parts of the country, except for British Columbia and Yukon, where those individuals expressing "no religious affiliation" form the largest single group in the population. This pattern is repeated at the city level, although a greater diversity of religious affiliation occurs in cities that have become major centres for recent immigration. Indeed, city diversity is greater than can be shown here because some religious affiliations, such as Baha'i, Jain, Rastafarian, Scientology, and Aboriginal spirituality, are too small to be included in the city data (city data do not show groups with less than 1 percent of the CMA's population). Note that on the 2001 census, individuals were asked to report their affiliation to a specific religious denomination or group, even if they were not practising members of that group. These data can therefore show only broad patterns of religious affiliation and not, for example, the proportion attending religious services or functions in Canada or the degree of devotion across the country.   (*Sources:* Map compiled from provincial and territorial data in Statistics Canada, *2001 Census: Analysis Series. Religions in Canada.* Ottawa: Minister of Industry, May 2003, Catalogue No. 96F0030XIE2001015, available online at **www12.statcan.ca/english/census01/products;** and from city data, including 2001 CMA population sizes adjusted in 2003, in Statistics Canada, *2001 Census: Topic-Based Tabulations. Religions in Canada,* Table 95F0450XCB2001004, available online at **www12.statcan.ca/english/census01/products/standard/themes.**)

since the inception of the non-discriminatory immigration policy in 1967, this pattern has been increasingly diluted as people from a wide variety of religious backgrounds have immigrated to Canada.

Of the 1.8 million new immigrants who came to Canada during the 1990s, 32 percent reported affiliations to religions other than Christianity (15 percent were Muslim, 7 percent Hindu, 5 percent Sikh, and 5 percent Buddhist). Whereas the share of Protestant and Roman Catholic denominations is declining (from 80 percent of the population in 1991 to 72 percent of the population in 2001), the size of other religious groups in Canada is increasing. Canada's Muslim population, for instance, has seen the largest growth and has doubled from 253,265 in

Figure 5.18 Protestant religion in Canada Established by dissident Quakers in Ontario in the early nineteenth century, the small community of Sharon still retains the original Quaker meeting house constructed in what was believed to be the image of Solomon's Temple.

TABLE 5.1 Canada's Religions by Affiliation Numbers for Major Religious Denominations, 1991 and 2001

Religious Denomination	2001	%	1991	%	% Change 1991–2001
Roman Catholic	12,793,125	43.2	12,203,625	45.2	4.8
Protestant	8,654,845	29.2	9,427,675	34.9	−8.2
Christian Orthodox	479,620	1.6	387,395	1.4	23.8
Christian*	780,450	2.6	353,040	1.3	121.1
Muslim	579,640	2.0	253,265	0.9	128.9
Jewish	329,995	1.1	318,185	1.2	3.7
Buddhist	300,345	1.0	163,415	0.6	83.8
Hindu	297,200	1.0	157,015	0.6	89.3
Sikh	278,415	0.9	147,440	0.5	88.8
No religion	4,796,325	16.2	3,333,245	12.3	43.9

*Total includes persons who report "Christian" as well as those who report "Apostolic," "Born Again," and "Evangelical."

Source: Statistics Canada, *2001 Census: Analysis Series. Religions in Canada.* Ottawa: Minister of Industry, May 2003, Catalogue No. 96F0030XIE2001015, available online at **www12.statcan.ca/census01/products.** Census data for 2006 can be found at **www12.statcan.ca/census-recensement/2006/rt-td/index-eng.cfm.**

1991 to 579,640 in 2001. The Orthodox family of Christian churches (479,620 in 2001) reported an increase of 24 percent in its numbers since 1991 because of the arrival of Serbian Orthodox emigrants from the Balkans.

As might be expected, much of this growth has taken place in the leading destinations for immigration and has focused on Canada's major metropolitan centres. According to 2001 census data, Ontario is now the home to 73 percent of Canada's Hindu population, 61 percent of the Muslim community, and 38 percent of the Sikh population. The majority of Canada's Sikh community is found in British Columbia (**Figure 5.19**).

Canada's religious geography has also been affected by the growing number of people who report that they have no religious affiliation. As Figure 5.17 shows, the majority of the population of both British Columbia and Yukon report that they have "no religious affiliation." Before 1971, less than 1 percent of Canada's total population made such a declaration. However, by 2001, that number had risen to 16 percent (4.8 million people). There are a variety of reasons for this decline. Statistics Canada observes that many immigrants from China and Taiwan do not claim a religious affiliation.

Figure 5.19 Sikh temple, Surrey, British Columbia

Robert Choquette, one of the leading authorities on Canada's religions, notes the increase in "new age" religious movements, which may be seen as outside the categories of more traditional religions. Whatever the causes, it is interesting to note that 40 percent of those declaring "no affiliation" in 2001 were under the age of 24.

A declining number of young people report an affiliation with either Protestant or Roman Catholic Christianity, and increases in other faiths because of immigration have combined to mean that the average ages of Canada's religious communities are also changing. The median age of Canada's population in 2001 was 37 years. However, the median age for Canada's Presbyterians was 46 years, and 41.5 years for Canada's Jewish population (**Figure 5.20**). Conversely, those faiths

Figure 5.20 Synagogue, Montreal

experiencing growth have much lower medians. For example, in 2001 Canada's Muslim population had a median age of 28 years, the Sikh community had a median age of 30, and the Hindus had a median age of 32 years.

The distribution of religions in Canada is only one aspect of the geographical study of religions in Canada. In recent years, a number of scholars have examined the contribution of religions to the creation of social and cultural geography. For example, the buildings used by religious groups to conduct their worship are a very tangible indicator of that group's presence in the community and contribute to the creation of distinct cultural landscapes. Consider, for example, the part played by Roman Catholic churches in rural Quebec or Sikh *gurdwaras* (temples) in suburban Vancouver in creating a sense of place in those areas.

The growing number and diversity of religions have affected this country's geography in another way because they have influenced our ability to appreciate other cultures and their traditions. Robert Choquette writes: "The transformation of Canada from a Christian monochrome to a religious kaleidoscope during the second half of the twentieth century meant that a growing number of diverse world views and theologies appeared."[10] In particular, he notes that the teachings of Christianity, Islam, and Judaism (which have a *linear* or historical view of time) contrast greatly with Eastern religions (which see time in *cyclical* terms). The former, he argues, also place more value on this world, which is seen as redeemable, whereas the latter emphasize the need to escape the limitations of this world. We have already seen (in Chapter 4) how these different perspectives affect our view of the environment. Seen in these terms, Canada has been enriched by the variety of insights gained from its growing number of religions. As Choquette concludes:

> Their presence made Canadians become aware that there are other worldviews competing with their traditional Christian one. When added to the growing secularism of Canadian society during the same period, the result was the transformation of Canada from a Christian bastion to a secular society where all religions became private.[11]

Sacred Spaces

Sacred space includes those areas recognized by individuals or groups as worthy of special attention because they are the sites of special religious experiences or events. Sites are designated as sacred to distinguish them from the rest of the landscape, which is considered ordinary or profane. Sacred space does not occur naturally; rather, it is assigned sanctity through the values and belief systems of particular groups or individuals. Geographer Yi-Fu Tuan insists that what defines the sacredness of a space goes beyond the obvious shrines and temples: sacred spaces rise above the commonplace and interrupt ordinary routine (**Figure 5.21**).

sacred space: an area recognized by individuals or groups as worthy of special attention as a site of special religious experiences or events

One particularly "geographic" aspect of certain religions is the obligation to make a pilgrimage to a sacred place to renew one's faith or to demonstrate devotion. Perhaps the most well-known pilgrimage is the *hajj*, the obligatory once-in-a-lifetime journey of Muslims to Mecca. For one month every year, the city of Mecca in Saudi Arabia swells from its base population of 150,000 to more than 1,000,000 as pilgrims from all over the world journey to fulfill their obligation to pray in the city and receive the grace of Allah. In India, many of the sacred pilgrimage sites for Hindus are concentrated along the banks of the Ganges, India's holiest river.

Pilgrimages to sacred sites are made all over the world, and Christian Europe is no exception. The most visited sacred site in Europe is Lourdes, at the base of

---

[10] Robert Choquette, *Canada's Religions*. Ottawa: University of Ottawa Press, 2004, p. 378.
[11] Ibid., p. 380.

Figure 5.21 Buddhist monastery in Bhutan This monastery, built on a mountainside at over 3,000 metres elevation, is an example of an elaborately constructed and highly maintained sacred site. For Bhutanese Buddhists, such monasteries and temples are holy places that are sites of worship and important Buddhist rituals.

the Pyrenees in southwest France, not far from the Spanish border (**Figure 5.22**). Another sacred site that attracts pilgrims throughout the world is the city of Jerusalem, and the Holy Land more generally. As is the case with most sacred spaces, the codes that are embedded in the landscape of the Holy Land may be read quite differently by different religious and even secular visitors:

> Each group brings to Jerusalem their own entrenched understandings of the sacred; nothing unites them, save their sequential—and sometimes simultaneous—presence at the same holy sites. For the Greek Orthodox pilgrims, indeed, the precise definition of the site itself is largely irrelevant; it is the icons on display which are the principal focus of attention. For the Roman Catholics, the site is important in that it is illustrative of a particular biblical text relating to the life of Jesus, but it is important only in a historical sense, as confirming the truth of past events. Only for the Christian Zionists does the Holy Land itself carry any present and future significance, and here they find a curious kinship with indigenous Jews.[12]

If we want to make geographical sense of the phenomenon of sacred space, it is useful to consider a very simple model (**Figure 5.23**). In this model, we hypothesize a very early time when almost all of Earth's surface was considered sacred, and contrast this with the present day, when very little of its surface is so considered. In between lies a long period of transition, one affected by many changes in religion and spirituality. We should note that many other changes were occurring during this transition period, including changing attitudes to nature (see Chapter 4) and to material wealth (see Chapter 7).

Figure 5.22 Source areas for pilgrims to Lourdes This map shows the points of origin of European, group-organized pilgrims to Lourdes in 1978. These represent only about 30 percent of all pilgrims to Lourdes, most of whom travel to the shrine on their own. Improved transportation (mainly by train) and the availability of organized package trips have contributed to a marked increase in the number of pilgrims visiting. Despite ongoing improvements in transportation, the map clearly shows the effects of friction of distance (see Chapter 1). (*Source:* C.C. Park, *Sacred Worlds*. London: Routledge, 1994, p. 284.)

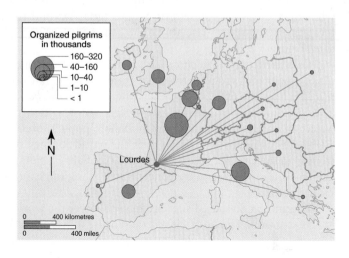

---

[12] J. Eade and M. Sallnow (eds.). *Contesting the Sacred*. London: Routledge, 1991, p. 14.

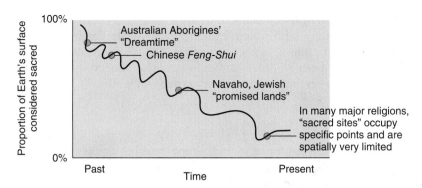

Figure 5.23 A model of sacred space This diagram shows how changes over time may have affected society's changing views of sacred spaces.

Let us illustrate our model with some examples from groups we have discussed elsewhere in this book, looking first at the period the whole Earth was considered sacred. The Australian Aborigine interprets the entire surface of Earth as embodying aspects of the Creation, an event occurring during the Dreamtime. Hills and caves, for example, are where creatures of the Dreamtime have slept or hidden. The Dreamtime can be called to mind by travelling through the landscape on routes known as "Songlines," travels that celebrate the landscape (and creation) in song.

In another manner, Chinese *feng-shui* practitioners recognize the sacredness of the entire Earth's surface as they seek to interpret its energy lines and most propitious landscapes. In China, the early use of the lodestone (a forerunner of the compass) enabled early *feng-shui* geomancers to interpret Earth's magnetic variations as lines of energy across its surface. The topography of that surface can also be interpreted. In a widely quoted paper on this topic, University of Victoria geographer David Lai describes how *feng shui* was used to locate the first Chinese cemetery in Victoria. In general terms, for example, the close resemblance of a range of hills to the forms of a dragon and a tiger is considered by *feng-shui* interpreters to be an advantage for houses or graves located nearby. This is because these two animals symbolize respectively the yang and yin energies present in nature, and their occurrence together at such locations shows that these two energies will be kept in abundance and harmony.[13]

Other groups believe that they have been given their homeland as a sacred trust, to inhabit it as a chosen people. This division of Earth in some way implies that not all space is seen as sacred, at least in the eyes of the group in question. Jewish belief in the "promised land" is one example. Another is the North American Navaho's belief that their appointed territory lies between four sacred mountains. For the Blackfoot, certain locations in the Alberta foothills, where Spirit Beings changed into human form and gave them their sacred ceremonies, are considered special places. As the Blackfoot people explained at a recent exhibition at Calgary's Glenbow Museum that they curated: "These places provide physical evidence that the events really happened and are part of Blackfoot history. Sacred places connect the Blackfoot to our territory, are part of our identity and are the basis of our claim to this territory."[14]

With the development of Islam, Christianity, and Buddhism, ideas of sacred space became more focused into specific locations. Those parts of Earth touched by the deity are more valued than those places that were not. A geography of sacred and profane spaces begins to unfold. Places of pilgrimage and shrines, as mentioned previously, articulate that space and serve to connect us with the sacred. Indeed, it is worth noting that it is necessary *to go* to church, temple, synagogue, or mosque because in some way these are more sacred places than the

---

[13] Chuen-yan David Lai, "A *Feng Shui* Model as a Location Index," *Annals Association of American Geographers* 64, 1974, pp. 516–513.

[14] *Nitsitapiisinni: The Story of the Blackfoot People.* Toronto: Key Porter, 2001, p. 50.

everyday or profane world in which many of us live. Various Western "new age" spiritualities seek to bring us full circle by seeing the whole Earth as sacred once more. It is significant that in doing so, many of the traditions of Canada's Aboriginal peoples have been co-opted. Others—perhaps influenced by today's environmental concerns—see nature in spiritual terms.

Geography and Language

Geographers have also been interested in understanding other aspects of cultural systems, such as language. Language is an important focus for study because it is a central aspect of cultural identity. Without language, cultural accomplishments could not be transmitted from one generation to the next. Moreover, language itself reflects the ways in which different groups understand and interpret the world around them. Finally, the distribution and diffusion of languages tells much about the changing history of human geography, European expansion, and the impact of globalization on culture. Before looking more closely at the geography of language and the impacts of globalization on the changing distribution of languages, however, it is necessary to become familiar with some basic vocabulary.

language: a means of communicating ideas or feelings by means of a conventionalized system of signs, gestures, marks, or articulate vocal sounds

dialects: regional variations from standard language, in terms of accent, vocabulary, and grammar

language family: a collection of individual languages believed to be related in their prehistoric origin

language branch: a collection of languages that possess a definite common origin but have split into individual languages

language group: a collection of several individual languages that are part of a language branch, share a common origin, and have similar grammar and vocabulary

Language is a means of communicating ideas or feelings by way of a conventionalized system of signs, gestures, marks, or articulate vocal sounds. In short, communication is symbolic, based on commonly understood meanings of signs or sounds. Within standard languages (also known as *official languages* because they are maintained by offices of government, educational institutions, and the courts), regional variations, known as **dialects,** exist. Dialects emerge and are distinguishable through differences in pronunciation, grammar, and vocabulary that are place-based in nature.

For the purposes of classification, languages are divided into families, branches, and groups. A **language family** is a collection of individual languages believed to be related in their prehistoric origin. About 50 percent of the world's people speak a language that originated from the Indo-European family. A **language branch** is a collection of languages that possess a definite common origin but have split into individual languages. A **language group** is a collection of several individual languages that are part of a language branch, share a common origin in the recent past, and have relatively similar grammar and vocabulary. For instance, Spanish, French, Portuguese, Italian, Romanian, and Catalan are a language *group*, classified under the Romance *branch* as part of the Indo-European language *family*.

Language is probably one of our greatest cultural creations and, as we shall see, a creation that is inherently geographical in its place-marking and place-making abilities. Through language, we describe our world in our own words and, by our use of that language, provide others with some indication of where we are from. Regional accents can enable those familiar enough with our language to tell exactly where within a region we were brought up. And, within the vocabulary and structure of our languages, we preserve a faint memory of where our distant ancestors originated. Let us briefly consider the most important aspects of each of these three points.

The Memory of Language Language is such a sophisticated cultural creation that it retains a memory of its past within its present form. One of the first people to realize this was Sir William Jones, an employee of the British East India Company. In 1786, he recognized the close similarities between Sanskrit (an extinct East Indian language retained for sacred use) and many European languages, both extinct (such as Latin) and extant (such as English or French). In **Table 5.2** you will see the often astonishing similarities in vocabulary among these languages.

Jones asserted that all of these languages are related to one another (the "Indo-European" language family, **Figure 5.24**) and that they have all descended

TABLE 5.2 Vocabulary Comparisons between Some Indo-European and Non–Indo-European Languages

English	French	Greek	Sanskrit	P-I-E†	Japanese
two	deux	duo	dva	*duwo	ni
three	trois	treis	tryas	*treyes	san
four	quatre	tettares	catvaras	*kwetwores	yon
ten	dix	deka	dasa	*dekmt	jyu
cow [ox]	vache	bous	gauh	*kwou	usi
field	champ	agros	ajras	*agras	hatake
water	eau	hudor	udan	*wedor	mizu
father	père	pater	pita	*pater	chichi
god	dieu	theos	devas	*dyeus	kami
wheel [chariot]	roue [wheel, chariot]	roda	ratha	*roto	sharing

†P-I-E: Proto-Indo-European
*denotes a reconstructed word in P-I-E

The proto-Indo-European language may have originated about 6,000 years ago in a steppe region somewhere between the Black Sea and the Caspian, or in Anatolian Turkey. Its vocabulary (here shown by the use of an asterisk to denote a reconstructed word) has been reconstructed by linguistic experts on the basis of correspondences between daughter languages (the name given to those languages that are descended from a common original) and known rules of linguistic change over time. P-I-E is believed to be the ancestor of extinct languages (such as Latin and Sanskrit) and many languages of the Indo-European family (such as English, French, and Hindi) currently spoken in the world today. The difference between these languages and those from other language families can be seen in the comparison with Japanese.

Sources: J.P. Mallory, *In Search of the Indo-Europeans.* London: Thames and Hudson, 1989; Colin Renfrew, *Archaeology and Language: The Puzzle of Indo-European Origins.* London: Cape, 1987; T.V. Gamkrelidze and V.V. Ivanov, "The Early History of Indo-European Languages," *Scientific American*, March 1990, pp. 110–16; and P. Tieme, "The Indo-European Language," *Scientific American*, October 1958, pp. 63–74.

from a now lost language called "proto-Indo-European." The passage of time and the migration of peoples, who then lost contact with one another, have been sufficient to change proto-Indo-European into the many languages of the Indo-European language family we hear today. (Note that the *present* global distribution of Indo-European languages is much greater than that shown in Figure 5.24, which describes the situation *before* European expansion and globalization carried the languages of the colonizers around the world.)

We do not know exactly where the proto-Indo-European language had its **cultural hearth**, that is, where it first developed; we do know, however, that it spread across almost all of Europe, missing only four areas (see Figure 5.24). Finnish, Estonian, and Hungarian are members of the Uralic language family (a non-Indo-European language believed to have originated in the northern Urals around 6000 B.C.). The Basque language of northeastern Spain and southwest France is an **isolate**, a language that has no known relationship with any other and cannot be assigned to a language family. We can gain an impression of how different Basque is from its vocabulary for the numerals 1 through 10, which are *bat, bi, hiru, lau, bost, sei, zazpi, zortzi, beheratzi,* and *hamar*. Recent genetic research by L.L. and F.C. Cavalli-Sforza also indicates how distinct the Basques are from all other Europeans.[15] One intriguing possibility is that they are

cultural hearth: the geographical origin or source of innovations, ideas, or ideologies (term coined by geographer Carl Sauer)

isolate: a language that has no known relationship with any other and cannot be assigned to a language family

[15] L.L. and F.C. Cavalli-Sforza, *The Great Human Diasporas: The History of Diversity and Evolution.* Reading, MA: Addison-Wesley, 1995.

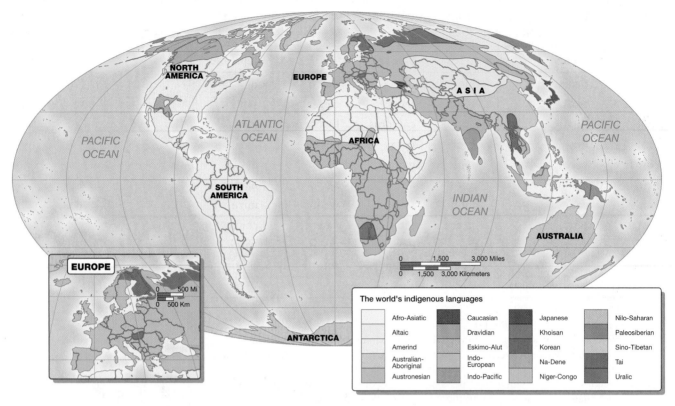

Figure 5.24   World distribution of major languages and major language families   Classifying languages by family and mapping their occurrence across the globe provides insights about human geography. For example, we may discover interesting cultural linkages among seemingly disparate cultures widely separated in space and time. We may also begin to understand something about the nature of population movements across broad expanses of time and space.   (*Sources:* Reprinted with permission from Prentice Hall, E.F. Bergman, *Human Geography: Cultures, Connections, and Landscapes,* © 1995, p. 240. Western Hemisphere adapted from *Language in the Americas* by Joseph H. Greenberg with the permission of the publishers, Stanford University Press, 1987 by the Board of Trustees of the Leland Stanford Junior University. Eastern Hemisphere adapted with permission from David Crystal, *Encyclopedia of Language.* New York: Cambridge University Press, 1987.)

descended from a pre-Neolithic people who were not completely absorbed by a westward-moving, Indo-European–speaking Neolithic people.

The story of Europe's indigenous languages is only one of many that linguists have attempted to unravel. Work on the languages of the Pacific, for example, seems to support the current theories of migration and settlement we examined in Chapter 1. Indeed, it was Captain Cook who first recognized the similarities between Hawaiian and the indigenous languages of the South Pacific islands he knew. Alone among the great navigators of his day, he believed that these apparently "primitive" peoples had the ability to navigate the great distances involved (see Chapter 1) and saw that the connection of language supported his view.

Let us now consider Canada. Historical linguists speculate that the thousands of indigenous languages that probably existed in the Americas on the eve of European contact can be divided into just three groups. These are known as the Amerindian, Na-Dene, and Eskimo-Aleut language families. Languages within each of these families can still be found within what is now Canada (see Figure 5.24). Scholars also believe that there may have been three separate phases of migration from Asia to the Americas (see Chapter 4).

Putting these two ideas together has led to speculation that these three language families might be descended from three "proto-languages" brought over at different times by Asian settlers to the New World. Certainly, the fact that Eskimo-Aleut is both the least differentiated of the language families (its only member is the Inuit language, Inuktitut) and the most recent arrival in Canada (moving across the Canadian Arctic about 4,000 years ago) is evidence for this claim. Amerindian and Na-Dene, however, were introduced into this continent at least 10,000 years ago and rapidly developed into the hundreds of indigenous languages of the Americas. The fact that Canada's West Coast contains a far greater number of Aboriginal languages than either the Prairies or the Eastern Woodlands is probably a result of the much longer time that languages had to develop in British Columbia.

Language and Regional Identity Because language is an intrinsic part of culture, it is not surprising that language has always been seen as an important characteristic of the cultural region. Many groups strongly identify with their language and use it as a means to establish ethnic, regional, and national differences.

Canada is no exception in this regard. Indeed, many see disputes over language as a particularly distressing part of this country's identity. **Figure 5.25**

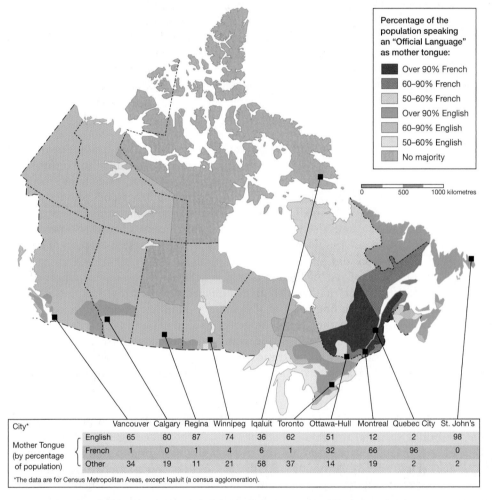

City*		Vancouver	Calgary	Regina	Winnipeg	Iqaluit	Toronto	Ottawa-Hull	Montreal	Quebec City	St. John's
Mother Tongue (by percentage of population)	English	65	80	87	74	36	62	51	12	2	98
	French	1	0	1	4	6	1	32	66	96	0
	Other	34	19	11	21	58	37	14	19	2	2

*The data are for Census Metropolitan Areas, except Iqaluit (a census agglomeration).

Legend for map:

Percentage of the population speaking an "Official Language" as mother tongue:
- Over 90% French
- 60–90% French
- 50–60% French
- Over 90% English
- 60–90% English
- 50–60% English
- No majority

0   500   1000 kilometres

Figure 5.25 The distribution of language across Canada: mother tongue by province and territory
This map shows one way of providing an overview of Canada's language geography. It does this by showing the percentage of people in an area who, in the 1986 census, reported that they used one of the official languages (French or English) as their mother tongue. Using data from small areal units (Statistics Canada's "census divisions"), the map gives a much more detailed picture than is possible from one based on provincial or territorial divisions. The map clearly shows the regions in Canada where these languages predominate (for example, French in southern parts of Quebec and English in Newfoundland). It also allows us to see those areas where neither official language is used as the predominant language by the majority (in Nunavut, northern Saskatchewan, and northeastern Ontario, because of the importance of Aboriginal languages in those regions). In addition, the map shows those regions where the official languages, although in a majority, are less dominant than in other parts of Canada (for example, in northern Alberta and northern Quebec). Such maps, however, cannot show the more detailed patterns that exist within urban communities, places where the many mother tongues of recent immigration make their greatest impact on the pattern of Canada's languages. To do that, data for a selection of cities has been added to show the variation that exists across this country.   (*Sources:* David H. Kaplan, "Population and Politics in a Plural Society: The Changing Geography of Canada's Linguistic Groups," *Annals of the Association of American Geographers* 84[1], 1994, pp. 52–53. The material is used permission of Blackwell Publishing Ltd. City data are from Statistics Canada's "1996 Census: Community Profiles," available at **www12.statcan.gc.ca/census-recensement/index-eng.cfm**.)

mother tongue: the first language learned at home in childhood and still understood by the individual at the time of the census (as defined by Statistics Canada)

official languages: languages (in Canada, English and French) in which the government has a legal obligation to conduct its affairs, and in which the public has the right to receive federal services

anglophone: a person whose mother tongue is English

francophone: a person whose mother tongue is French

allophone: a person whose mother tongue is neither English nor French

shows the provincial and territorial distribution of the leading languages spoken as a **mother tongue,** or first language learned at home in childhood and still understood, across this country. Canada has two **official languages,** English and French, in which the business of the federal government is conducted. Government policies of "multiculturalism" indicate a tolerance of other languages, but the reality of the workplace shows that a proficiency in English or French is an important determinant of an individual's economic success. As a result, although recent immigrants to this country are not required to learn the official languages, many decide to do so.

According to the 2006 census, 18 million Canadians reported English as their mother tongue, an increase of 3 percent since 2001 and of almost a third since 1971. This English-speaking, or **anglophone,** portion of the population made up about 60 percent of the country's population in 1996 (approximately the same proportion of Canadians it represented in 1971). A considerable range existed around this national average. The highest proportion of anglophones was found in Newfoundland and Labrador (where 98.6 percent of the population recorded their mother tongue as English), and the lowest in Quebec (9.2 percent). Provinces with large recent immigrant populations, such as Ontario and British Columbia, recorded anglophone figures of 74.6 percent and 78.9 percent, respectively.

The size of Canada's **francophone,** or French-speaking, population was 6.9 million in 2006. Although this figure has increased in absolute terms since 1971, as a proportion of the total population of Canada, it has fallen from 29 percent in 1951 to 22.1 percent in 2006. (Quebec's low francophone fertility rates and the relatively small number of francophone immigrants to Canada are the main causes of this decline.) According to 1996 census figures, 86 percent of Canada's francophones lived in Quebec (where they represent 82 percent of that province's population).

In Quebec, the use of French is very much seen as an intrinsic part of the "nationalist project" and is also an established part of provincial government policy. All of the leading provincial political parties have been conscious of the minority position of the French language in Canada and North America as a whole. Realizing that this position was further weakened by a decline in the provincial birth rate among francophones and an increase in the number of **allophone** immigrants to the province (those whose mother tongue is neither English nor French) who chose to adopt English, the government has taken steps to encourage the greater use of French in Quebec. Through such legislation as Bill 101, the government has acted to ensure the use of French in government, in public schools, and even on street signs. A provincial agency (Office québécois de la langue française) has the responsibility for monitoring public compliance (**Figure 5.26**). Although initially the target of much opposition, especially from Quebec's large anglophone and allophone communities, which represented 8.8 percent and 9.7 percent of Quebec's population in 1996, this policy has now become accepted as a fact of life in the province, one that no political party can afford to oppose. However, as **Figure 5.27** shows, it takes more than government policy to create a truly integrated, bilingual society.[16]

Outside of Quebec, the francophone population totals 970,000 and is found mainly in the two provinces of Ontario and New Brunswick, where it is declining in relative size. "Language islands," to use geographer Donald Cartwright's phrase, that historically contained significant numbers of francophones just inside

Figure 5.26 Office québécois de la langue française Quebec's watchdog on language monitors compliance with provincial legislation promoting French. Among the most publicized prosecutions in recent years have been cases where store signs did not use French or, if more than one language was used, French did not have the largest font size.

---

[16] A well-received discussion of these issues in English can be found in the recent work of two scholars at Montreal's Institut national de la recherche scientifique. Annick Germain and Damaris Rose, *Montréal: The Quest for a Metropolis.* Chichester: Wiley, 2000, Chapter 7, "Language, Ethnic Groups, and the Shaping of Social Space," especially pp. 230–247.

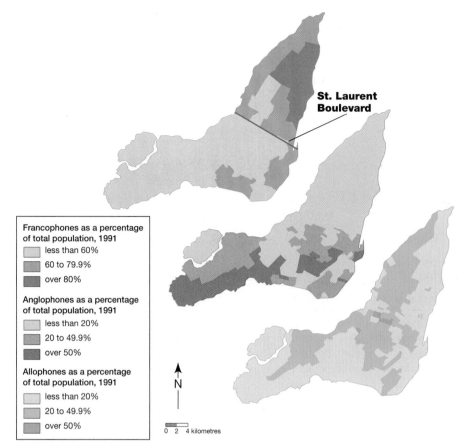

St. Laurent
Boulevard

Francophones as a percentage
of total population, 1991
□ less than 60%
■ 60 to 79.9%
■ over 80%

Anglophones as a percentage
of total population, 1991
□ less than 20%
■ 20 to 49.9%
■ over 50%

Allophones as a percentage
of total population, 1991
□ less than 20%
■ 20 to 49.9%
■ over 50%

N

0 2 4 kilometres

**Figure 5.27   The language divide in
Montreal**   As these maps based on 1991
census data show clearly, the English- and
French-speaking populations of Montreal
(the anglophone and francophone communities) maintain separate existences.
The traditional boundary of St. Laurent
Boulevard can still be seen as demarcating
these two groups. Straddling the "two sol-
itudes," the allophone communities (made
up of people who speak neither English
nor French as their mother tongue) have
developed language geographies of their
own.   (*Sources:* L. Lo and C. Teixeira, "If Quebec Goes . . . The 'Exodus' Impact," *Professional
Geographer* 50, 1998, pp. 481–498. The material is used by permission of Blackwell Publishing Ltd. Further information, including mother
tongue maps for 1996, can be found in Julie
Archambault, Damaris Rose, and Anne-Marie
Séguin, *ATLAS: Immigration and Metropolis*, on
the website of the Montréal Centre for Interuni-
versity Research on Immigration, Integration and
Urban Dynamics at http://im.metropolis.net.)

the Ontario border (from Hawkesbury to Cochrane) and anglophones within
Quebec (such as the Eastern Townships) have steadily eroded over the years to
leave a much starker geographical divide between French-speaking Quebec and
the rest of the country.

Bilingualism in English and French, a necessary feature of the language
islands, is also the hallmark of a federal government policy to show Quebec that
Canada as a whole could also be a home for francophones. The 1996 census
records that 17 percent (4.8 million) of the country's population were bilingual
in English and French, a figure that had increased from 13 percent in 1971.
The highest rates of bilingualism were recorded in Quebec (38 percent of the
population) and New Brunswick (33 percent). Urban centres, such as Montreal
(50 percent), Ottawa-Hull (44 percent), and Sudbury (40 percent), also have
sizeable bilingual populations.

In terms of Canada's allophone population, the 2006 census records that
there were 6.3 million people in this country who spoke neither English nor
French as their mother tongue. This represents 20.1 percent of the total population, a figure that had risen from 13 percent in 1971, fuelled by Canada's
large immigration flows from countries where neither English nor French
is spoken (see Chapter 3). Indeed, as **Table 5.3** shows, there were significant
changes. In Canada, in 1971, the leading allophone languages most often spoken
at home (the **home language**) were German, Italian, and Ukrainian. In 1996,
the top three were Chinese, Italian, and Punjabi. By 2006, 1.03 million people
(or 3.3 percent of the population) reported a Chinese language as their mother
tongue, an increase of almost 162,000 since the 2001 census. Punjabi was the
fourth most frequently reported allophone mother tongue in the country, while
Urdu had posted the fastest increase since 2001, rising from 87,000 speakers in

home language: the language
most often spoken at home by an
individual (as defined by Statistics
Canada)

TABLE 5.3 Canada's Top 10 Home Languages, 1971 and 1996
(Excluding English and French)

1971 Home Language	Number	1996 Home Language	Number
1. Italian	425,230	1. Chinese	630,520
2. German	213,350	2. Italian	258,050
3. Ukrainian	144,755	3. Punjabi	182,895
4. Greek	86,825	4. Spanish	173,040
5. Chinese	77,890	5. Portuguese	142,975
6. Portuguese	74,760	6. Polish	137,330
7. Polish	70,960	7. German	134,615
8. Hungarian	50,670	8. Arabic	118,605
9. Dutch	36,170	9. Tagalog (Filipino)	111,865
10. Yiddish	26,330	10. Vietnamese	102,905
Aboriginal languages	122,205	Aboriginal languages	146,120

Source: Statistics Canada, *1996 Census Results Teacher's Kit* (**www.statcan.gc.ca/ kits-trousses/edu01_0001-eng.htm**). The 1996 results combine single and multiple responses to the question about which language (other than English or French) is spoken most often at home.

2001 to reach 156,000 in 2006. Overall, by 2006, allophones for the first time represented fully 20 percent of Canada's population.[17]

The discrepancy between mother tongue and home language provides demographers and statisticians with a way of recording the degree of **language shift** that has occurred as newcomers slowly take up one of this country's official languages. The 1996 census data, for example, shows us that 40 percent of allophones spoke English or French at home, a figure somewhat smaller than in 1991, perhaps because of the relative youth of the current immigrant cohorts in this country.

Given the recent pattern of immigration, it is not surprising to see that Toronto has the highest proportion of allophones. According to 2006 census data, in that city, 44 percent of the population has a mother tongue other than English or French. A very similar result (41 percent) is noted for Vancouver. Montreal, however, with 22 percent of its population now allophone, has proportionally fewer non-French, non-English residents.

Canada's Aboriginal languages are among the most endangered in the world.[18] As of 1996, only 3 of the 50 Aboriginal languages currently spoken in this country can be considered secure, and at least a dozen are on the brink of extinction. Over the years, the number of native language speakers has been reduced through slaughter and disease, forced assimilation in residential schools, and the economic and political necessity of learning English or French. The death in 1829 of the last known speaker of the Beothuk language of Newfoundland and Labrador was but the first of a series of Aboriginal language extinctions that continues to this day. For example, the British Columbian languages of Haida (with only 240 speakers left in 1996), Tlingit (145), and Kutenai (120) are almost certain to join that list in the very near future.

language shift: an indicator of the number of people who adopt a new language, usually measured by the difference between mother tongue and home language populations

[17] Information from the 2006 census about Canada's language composition and links to more detailed material can be found at **www12.statcan.ca/census-recensement/2006/rt-td/lng-eng.cfm** and in the publication "2006 Census: Immigration, Citizenship, Language, Mobility and Migration," *The Daily,* December 4, 2007 (see **www.statcan.gc.ca/daily-quotidien/071204/dq071204a-eng.htm**).

[18] S.A. Wurm (ed.), *Atlas of the World's Languages in Danger of Disappearing.* Paris: UNESCO Publishing, 1996, p. 23.

TABLE 5.4   Inuit Words for Snow

The language of the Inuit is called *Inuktitut*, and *Inuit* means "the people" in that language.

anuigaviniq:	very hard, compressed, or frozen snow
apijaq:	snow covered by bad weather
apigiannagaut:	the first snowfall of autumn
katakartanaq:	snow with a hard crust that gives way under footsteps
kavisilaq:	snow roughened by rain or frost
kinirtaq:	compact, damp snow
mannguq:	melting snow
masak:	wet, falling snow
matsaaq:	half-melted snow
natiruvaaq:	drifting snow
pukak:	crystalline snow that breaks down and separates like salt
qannialaaq:	light-falling snow
qiasuqaq:	snow that has thawed and refrozen with an ice surface
qiqumaaq:	snow whose surface has frozen after a light spring thaw

Source: Aboriginal Times 6(8), April 2002, p. 44.

The 1996 census records approximately 800,000 Aboriginal people in Canada (a figure that, as Chapter 3 noted, is somewhat incomplete). Of this total, 25 percent reported that they spoke an Aboriginal language as a mother tongue. Of these, the majority spoke Cree (76,475), Ojibway (22,625), or the languages of the Inuktitut language family (26,840). However, when asked about the language most used at home, only 15 percent of the total in 1996 used an Aboriginal language. This statistic gives us an indication of the measure of *language shift* into English or French that is occurring.

As Mary Jane Norris has recently remarked in a study of Canadian Aboriginal languages, the loss of language does not equate with the death of a culture, but it can severely handicap its future.[19] The vocabulary that each language develops is unique, and its loss therefore diminishes a people's ability to describe phenomena in terms most appropriate to it. Perhaps the most famous illustration of this point is the number of words that the Inuit have for *snow* (**Table 5.4**), a range of vocabulary brought about by the importance of snow in their way of life. Given how important language is to a sense of cultural identity, the issue of language extinction has to be a very important one that should concern us—whether it occurs in the global core or in the periphery (**Figure 5.28**).

Dialects   The use of English and French in Canada provides us with a further insight into the place-making abilities of language. This is because the way in which these languages are now spoken in Canada differs sufficiently from the way they are spoken in England and France that native speakers on either side of the Atlantic can tell them apart. In fact, both have developed Canadian versions, or dialects, based on distinct accents, vocabulary, and grammar. Similarly,

---

[19] The paragraphs on Aboriginal languages are based on M.J. Norris, "Canada's Aboriginal Languages," *Canadian Social Trends*, Statistics Canada, Catalogue No. 11-008, January 13, 1998, pp. 8–16; and Statistics Canada, "1996 Census: Aboriginal Data," *The Daily*, 1998 (**www.statcan.ca/Daily/English/980113/d980113.htm**). The distinctions between Aboriginal languages and language families are from these sources, as are the English spellings used here.

Figure 5.28 Extinct and threatened languages in Africa It is not absolutely certain how many languages are currently spoken worldwide: the estimates range between 4,200 and 5,600. Although some languages are being created through the fusion of an indigenous language with a colonial language, such as English or Portuguese, indigenous languages are mostly dying out. Although only Africa is shown in this map, indigenous languages are dying out throughout the Americas and Asia as well.

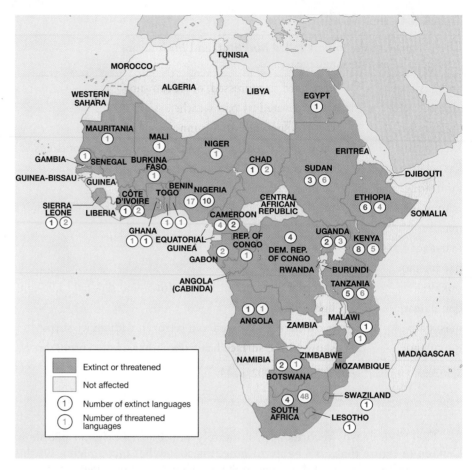

Spanish and Portuguese have developed distinct New World variants. Indeed, we could sum up this phenomenon as "new worlds, old words."

Clearly, these differences must have been caused in some way by the emigration experience. Scholars have identified two general processes, and we can easily see them at work in the Canadian case:

- *When people move, their language escapes the changes in vocabulary, grammar, or pronunciation that occur in the region of origin.* The various experiences of the French language in Canada well illustrate this point. The majority of the original French settlers of Quebec came from north of the Loire River in France, a region where a variety of northern French dialects were spoken. The bulk of those who had earlier settled the Acadian regions of Nova Scotia, Prince Edward Island, and New Brunswick came from western France, between the Loire and the Pyrenees, where southern dialects of French were spoken (**Figure 5.29**). These differences have been preserved in the two regional dialects of French that developed in Canada (for example, Acadian French retains the southern Loire verb *éparer*, meaning "to hang a net out to dry," whereas Quebec French uses the verb *étendre*). A variant of Acadian French is the Cajun dialect of Louisiana, in the southern United States, where many Acadians settled after their deportation from Nova Scotia.

At the same time that these dialects were consolidating in Canada, they were being made obsolete in France itself. Following the French Revolution of 1789, the central government suppressed the various regional dialects and languages of France in the belief that the use of one language (Parisian French) would unite the country and promote egalitarianism. From 1789 onward, therefore, the French spoken in Canada has preserved older forms of French than found in France itself. The Quebec French verb *gager*, meaning "to bet," has long been replaced by the verb *parier* in France. Sinclair Robinson and Donald Smith's very useful dictionary of Quebec and Acadian French

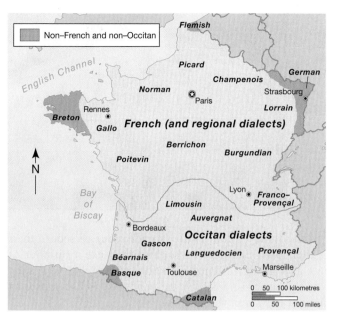

Figure 5.29 The languages of France in 1789 We think of France as having one unified language. On the eve of the French Revolution, however, language diversity in France was not so dissimilar from other European regions that were consolidating into states. Once a central government was created, it eliminated the multiplicity of local languages and dialects because a common language made it easier to collect taxes, enforce laws, and teach new citizens. (*Source*: D. Bell, "Lingua Populi, Lingua Dei," *American Historical Review*, 1995, p. 1406.)

shows how extensive the differences between these long-separated forms of French have now become.[20]

Another look, this time with the forms of French spoken on Caribbean islands that were once French colonies (such as Saint Lucia), reveals equally fascinating glimpses of language change. In these cases, versions of French brought by early eighteenth-century colonists merged with African languages spoken by slaves imported to run plantations and with English (when the island switched hands in the 1760s) to create a creole language that, although it follows its own rules, contains a vocabulary that draws on old forms of French.

- *When people move, their language undergoes considerable changes in vocabulary as people adapt to their new surroundings.* We can illustrate this process by the experience of the English language in Newfoundland and Labrador. Settled from the seventeenth century onward by English-speaking fishing people from southwest England and Ireland, the Newfoundland and Labrador environment was very different from anything these people had experienced before. A great variety of words were needed to describe this particular new world.[21] Many new words were created, for example for types of fish (*caplin*), or the many forms of ice Newfoundlanders and Labradorians encountered (*ballicatter, clumper, quarr, sish, slob*). Evidence from 1578 even suggests that the word *penguin* was first developed in Newfoundland and Labrador to describe the now extinct Great Auk and may derive from the Welsh *pen gwyn* ("white head").

CULTURAL NATIONALISM

The protection of regional languages is part of a larger movement in which geographers and other scholars have become interested. The movement, known as **cultural nationalism,** is an effort to protect regional and national cultures from the homogenizing impacts of globalization. Cultural nationalism is one manifestation of a much wider set of beliefs known as nationalism. The idea of nationalism (defined and more fully explored in Chapter 9) holds that individuals share

cultural nationalism: an effort to protect regional and national cultures from the homogenizing impacts of globalization

---

[20] Sinclair Robinson and Donald Smith, *Practical Handbook of Quebec and Acadian French.* Toronto: Anansi, 1984.

[21] G.M. Story, W.J. Kirwin, and J.D.A. Widdowson, *The Dictionary of Newfoundland English.* Toronto: University of Toronto Press, 1982.

Figure 5.30 The United States in Canada This image of a Kentucky Fried Chicken restaurant in Quebec illustrates the influence of U.S. products on Canadian society and culture. Because Canada is the nearest northern neighbour to the United States, it is not surprising that Canada is probably more heavily influenced by U.S. culture than any other country in the world. It should be pointed out, however, that the flow is not one way.

an identity with others of the same nation. Nations endeavour to secure their identities by promoting their own distinctiveness, and they use a number of ways to achieve this. Some groups may attempt isolationism as a way of sealing themselves off from what they see as undesirable influences. Other groups may attempt to legislate the flow of ideas and values.

Maintaining Cultural Borders: Canada and the United States Not only the periphery is resisting cultural imperialism. Australia, Britain, France, and Canada all have formally attempted to erect barriers to U.S. cultural products. This is especially true for Canada, which continues to struggle to maintain an independent cultural identity beyond the shadow of the United States. To this purpose, Canada has developed an extensive and very public policy of cultural protection against the onslaught of U.S. music, television, magazines, films, and other art and media forms (**Figure 5.30**). Besides regulating how much and what type of U.S. culture can travel north across the border, the Canadian government also sponsors a sort of "affirmative action" grant program for this country's own cultural industries.

Multiculturalism in Canada One way in which Canada has sought to distance itself from U.S. cultural policies has been to develop policies based on the concept of multiculturalism. Such policies enable different cultures to maintain their distinctiveness (as in the Canadian cultural mosaic model), rather than to require them to be assimilated (as in the American melting pot model) into the mainstream French- or English-speaking cultures. This approach has become especially valuable as the number and diversity of immigrants into this country have increased and as the sizes of ethnocultural communities within Canada have grown (see, for one example, Chapter 3 on the experiences of the Somali community in Toronto).

Jean Burnet's concise explanation of multiculturalism in Canada notes that the term *multiculturalism* is used in at least three senses:

1. To refer to a society, such as Canada's, that is characterized by ethnic or cultural heterogeneity

2. To refer to a country's ideal of equality and mutual respect for its minorities

3. To refer to federal government policies proclaimed in 1971 and set out in the Canadian Multiculturalism Act of 1988, which aims "to recognize all Canadians as full and equal participants in Canadian society"[22]

Burnet's reflection on the value of these policies is also worth noting. Multicultural policies since 1971 have not met the needs of all immigrants (especially visible minority groups), since they were tailored much more to the needs of long-established ethnic groups of European background. "Nevertheless," he argues, "the introduction of the term and what has been called 'the multicultural

---

[22] Jean Burnet, "Multiculturalism." *The Canadian Encyclopedia*, online edition: Historica Foundation, **www.thecanadianencyclopedia.com**.

Figure 5.31 Canada's multiculturalism
Traditional institutions, such as the Royal
Canadian Mounted Police, are recognizing that Canada's increasingly multicultural population requires that diversity
be reflected in their hiring policies.

movement' have been important in calling attention to an important type of
diversity within society and engendering recognition of it."[23]

Of course, there have been criticisms of this policy over the years. Critics have
seen multiculturalism as a way of either distracting Canadians from the implications of official bilingualism, diluting the political clout of francophone Canada, or
"bribing" Canada's ethnic communities with cultural blandishments rather than
any real financial aid. Certainly, the experience of groups such as Toronto's Somali
community (see Chapter 3) makes it clear that whatever the effects such policies
have had, they have not yet been able to fully combat the social and economic
discriminations that many such groups face. The adoption of multicultural hiring
goals by many Canadian organizations and institutions serves as another illustration of the challenges that still confront many ethnic communities (**Figure 5.31**).

One important issue that has attracted a lot of attention is the extent to
which policies of multiculturalism produce a framework for the creation of
minority rights. Authors, such as Neil Bissoondath, have written forceful critiques of these policies, arguing that by empowering minorities, the policies have
given them more rights than the majority has. William Kymlicka provides a very
well thought out answer to this question in his book *Multicultural Citizenship:
A Liberal Theory of Minority Rights*. He suggests that in "multination" or
"polyethnic" states, it is necessary to protect ethnocultural minorities from the
political and economic power of the majority.[24] This can be done through the
use of multicultural policies that either promote the self-government of particular groups (he cites the example of Canada's Aboriginal peoples) or advance
the "polyethnic rights" of ethnocultural communities (such as permitting dress
codes or minority languages).

A good example of the first type, according to Kymlicka, is Aboriginal groups
that have been accorded rights of self-government (see Chapter 9). Examples of
the second include policies that have been developed by provincial and territorial school boards to enable young Sikh males to carry small ceremonial daggers,
known as *kirpan*.

Although now abandoned, the 2005 Ontario proposal to recognize *sharia*-
based tribunals in family arbitration cases illustrates very clearly some of

---

[23] Ibid.
[24] William Kymlicka, *Multicultural Citizenship: A Liberal Theory of Minority Rights*. Oxford:
Oxford University Press, 1995, pp. 3–48.

the dilemmas of multicultural policy.[25] In proposing to recognize differences (the right of the Muslim community to follow its own teachings regarding divorce), the province appeared to disavow universal rights (the rights of women). It is hardly surprising, therefore, that scholars have recognized that countries with significant multicultural communities, such as Canada, must grapple with what are essentially the challenges of the postmodern state (see Chapter 9).

CULTURE AND IDENTITY

In addition to exploring cultural forms, such as religion and language, and movements, such as cultural nationalism, geographers have increasingly begun to ask questions about other forms of identity. This interest largely has to do with the fact that certain long-established and some more recently self-conscious cultural groups have begun to use their identities as a way of asserting political, economic, social, and cultural claims.

Ethnicity and the Use of Space

ethnicity: a socially created system of rules about who belongs and who does not belong to a particular group based on actual or perceived commonality

Ethnicity is one way in which geographers are exploring cultural identity. **Ethnicity** is a socially created system of rules about who belongs to a particular group based on actual or perceived commonality, such as language or religion. A geographic focus on ethnicity is an attempt to understand how it shapes and is shaped by space, and how ethnic groups use space with respect to mainstream culture. For cultural geographers, territory is also a basis for ethnic group cohesion (see Chapter 9 for more on territory). For example, cultural groups—ethnically identified or otherwise—may be spatially segregated from the wider society in ghettos or ethnic enclaves (see Chapter 11). Or these groups may use space to declare their subjective interpretations about the world they live in and their place in it. The use of the city streets by many different cultural groups demonstrates this point (**Figure 5.32**).

Nineteenth-century immigrants to U.S. cities used the streets to broadcast their ideas about life in their adopted country. Ethnic parades in the nineteenth century—such as St. Patrick's Day for the Irish and Columbus Day for the Italians—were often very public declarations about the stresses that existed among classes, cultures, and generations.

At the height of late nineteenth-century immigration, the Irish and many other immigrant groups, such as the Italians, Greeks, Poles, and Slavs, were largely shunned and vilified by the host society and were relegated to low-paying jobs and poor housing. Publicly ridiculed in newspapers, these groups took to the streets to re-interpret the city's public spaces, even if only for a day. Released from a strict work routine of 10 to 15 hours a day, participants and spectators could use the parade to promote an alternative reality of pride and festivity, acquiring a degree of power and autonomy that was not possible in their workday lives. Because of their festive and extraordinary nature, nineteenth-century parades temporarily helped to change the world in which they occurred.

The same can be said of cultural parades in the twentieth century. Montreal's St. Jean Baptiste Day parade is a barometer of separatist feelings and is often a highly politically charged event. Irish-American gay and lesbian groups in Boston and New York, with their own interpretations of "Irishness," have been turned away from St. Patrick's Day parades by the more mainstream interpreters of the term. Such a confrontation between ethnicity and sexuality also highlights how difficult it is to separate cultural identity into distinct categories. In different places, for different historical reasons, the complex combinations of cultural identities of race, class, gender, and sexual preference result in unique and sometimes powerful expressions.

Figure 5.32 Parade in Montreal
Many ethnic groups use city parades as an opportunity to promote pride and an alternative picture of what it means to belong to an ethnic group. This photo shows members of Montreal's Temple Hare Krishna in their annual *Ratha Yatra* parade along St. Laurent Boulevard. Known as "the Main," this street was traditionally the first place immigrants lived on when they reached the city, and it still constitutes a major divide between Montreal's anglophone and francophone populations.

---

[25] Karen Howlett, "Islamic-Law Plan Will Respect Rights, Ontario Says," *Globe and Mail*, September 7, 2005, A5.

Race and Place

Prevailing ideas and practices with respect to race have also been used to understand the shaping of places and responses to these forces.[26]

Race is a problematic classification of human beings based on skin colour and other physical characteristics. Biologically speaking, however, no such thing as race exists within the human species. Yet, consider the categories of race and place that correspond to "Chinese" and "Chinatown." Powerful Western ideas about Chinese as a racial category enabled the emergence and perpetuation of Chinatown as a type of landscape found throughout many North American cities (**Figure 5.33**). In this and other cases, the visible characteristics of hair, skin, and bone structure made race into a category of difference that was (and still is) widely accepted and often spatially expressed.

The mainstream approach to an ethnic neighbourhood is to see it as a spatial setting for systems of affiliation more or less chosen by *minority* people with similar skin colour. Recently, cultural geographers have begun to turn this approach around and see ethnic neighbourhoods as spaces that express and affirm the *dominant* society's sense of identity. For example, from the perspective of white society, nineteenth-century Chinatowns were the physical expression of what set the Chinese apart from Caucasians. The distinguishing characteristics revolved around the way the Chinese looked, what they ate, their non-Christian religion, their opium consumption, gambling habits, and other "strange" practices. A recent study by Ban Seng Hoe of the history of the Chinese laundry in Canada shows that discrimination against the Chinese often worked at spatial scales much smaller than that

race: a problematic classification of human beings based on skin colour and other physical characteristics

Chinatown, Vancouver, 1907—The marginalization of the Chinese population of Vancouver, British Columbia, had strong racial and ethnic undercurrents that surfaced in illustrations such as this one, published in 1907. Note how the white settlements are pictured as airy, light, and single-family, whereas the Chinese domiciles are labelled as "warrens" "infested" by thousands of Chinese.

Figure 5.33 Chinatown, Vancouver, 1907 Rather than depicting the real conditions in Vancouver's Chinatown, this illustration actually reflects what the "Vancouver white workingman" thought Chinatown looked like. In other words, it reflects the notions and prejudices of the mainstream Canadian society at the time. (*Source:* K. Anderson, "The Idea of Chinatown: The Power of Place and Institutional Practice in the Making of a Racial Category," Annals of the Association of American Geographers 77(4), 1987, pp. 580–598.)

[26] Adapted from K. Anderson, "The Idea of Chinatown: The Power of Place and Institutional Practice in the Making of a Racial Category," *Annals of the Association of American Geographers* 77(4), 1987, pp. 580–598.

of a Chinatown. He shows that many Chinese immigrants established laundries in a large number of communities across Canada during the early part of the twentieth century; however, this way of making a living almost always caused antagonism from the local residents:

> The City of Calgary, for example, stipulated that no Chinese laundries would be allowed to operate on certain streets. In 1905, the Calgary Central Labour Union condemned Chinese laundries as a menace to public health, and *The Calgary Herald* demanded that the Chinese laundries be cleared in order to avoid an epidemic.[27]

Place—Chinatown—maintained and manifested differences between Caucasian and Chinese societies. Furthermore, place continues to be a mechanism for creating and preserving local systems of racial classification within defined geographical confines. The homelands of South Africa are another illustration of the interaction of race and place, though at a much larger scale.

Gender

gender: a category reflecting the social differences between men and women rather than the anatomical differences that are related to sex

Gender is an identity that has received a great deal of attention by cultural geographers within the last three decades. **Gender** is a category reflecting the social differences between men and women. As with other forms of identity, gender implies a socially created difference in power between groups. In the case of gender, the power difference gives males an advantage over females and is socially and culturally created (or learned) rather than biologically determined. As with other forms of identity, class position can intensify the power differences among and between groups. Furthermore, the implications of these differences are played out differently in different parts of the world.

Among South Asia's poor, for example, women bear the greatest burden and the most suffering. South Asian societies are intensely patriarchal, though the form that patriarchy takes varies by region and class. The common denominator among the poor throughout South Asia is that women not only have the constant responsibilities of motherhood and domestic chores but also have to work long hours in informal-sector occupations (**Figure 5.34**). In many poor communities,

Figure 5.34 Indian women in the informal sector Many women in South Asia are self-employed as small vendors in the daily markets. Others do home-based work such as weaving and dyeing cloth or embroidering or sewing garments. Nearly all workers in the informal sector, whether male or female, lack any sort of social protection such as health or unemployment insurance.

[27] Ban Seng Hoe, *Enduring Hardship: The Chinese Laundry in Canada*. Gatineau: Canadian Museum of Civilization, 2003, p. 55.

90 percent of all production occurs outside of formal employment, and more than half of it is the result of women's efforts. In addition, women's property rights are curtailed, their public behaviour is restricted, and their opportunities for education and participation in the waged labour force are severely limited. Women's subservience to men is deeply ingrained within South Asian cultures, and it is manifested most clearly in the cultural practices attached to family life, such as the custom of providing a dowry to daughters at marriage. The preference for male children is reflected in the widespread (but illegal) practice of selective abortion and female infanticide. Within marriages, many (but by no means all) poor women are routinely neglected and maltreated. More extreme are the cases—usually reported only when they involve middle-class families—of "bride burning," whereby a husband or mother-in-law fakes the accidental death (kitchen fires are favoured) or suicide of a bride whose parents had defaulted in their dowry payments. Several thousand such deaths are reported in India each year, and this is almost certainly only a fraction of the real incidence.

The picture for women in South Asia, as elsewhere, is not entirely negative, however, and one of the most significant developments has been the emergence of women's self-help movements. Perhaps the best-known of these is the Grameen Bank, a grassroots organization formed to provide small loans to the rural poor in Bangladesh. Another is the Self-Employed Women's Association (SEWA) in India, which has made a major contribution to building self-confidence and self-reliance among poor working women by mobilizing and organizing them.

If we turn to examples from the developed world, we can see that geographical studies in Canada have paid special attention to how our city spaces have become gendered and how this has affected our use and appreciation of place. These studies have shown that the suburbs were seen as "female" space; the downtown and industrial areas as "male" space.[28] This simple dichotomy was created in Canada by nineteenth-century and twentieth-century constructions of gender in which residential space was seen as the site of social reproduction and private life, and commercial and industrial space as the site of economic reproduction and public life. Under gender stereotypes prevalent at the time, the former site became identified as female space; the latter site as male space (**Figure 5.35**).

Although such constructions of gender relations are entirely artificial, their existence has a series of real implications. Scholars have, for example, pointed out that the unquestioning assumption by city planners that the suburbs are still entirely a domestic or female space means that city regulations often forbid the creation of small business in suburban zones. These rules are based on old preconceptions that there is no need for economic activity ("male" work) in residential areas ("female" space). These preconceptions could not envisage the need for people to create paid employment where they live (the mixture of private or domestic and public or economic spheres). Home businesses, for example, are precluded because they are "male" use of "female" space—despite the obvious opportunities for home-based work in the Information Age.

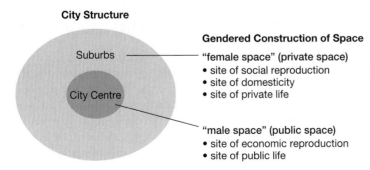

City Structure

Suburbs

City Centre

Gendered Construction of Space

"female space" (private space)
• site of social reproduction
• site of domesticity
• site of private life

"male space" (public space)
• site of economic reproduction
• site of public life

Figure 5.35 The gendered construction of space This simple model shows the ways in which nineteenth-century and twentieth-century constructions of gender in Western societies affected how those societies created and used landscapes, such as the city. Men, as breadwinners, inhabited a very different social world from that of women, and this affected not only their economic roles but also their geographic experiences in our cities.

---

[28] See, for example, Suzanne Mackenzie, "Restructuring the Relations of Work and Life: Women as Environmental Actors, Feminism as Geographic Analysis," *Gender, Place and Culture* 6(4), 1999, pp. 417–430.

5.2   Geography in the Information Age

The recent rise in "telework" or "telecommuting" is occurring under the radar of these zoning regulations as the home offices in which the work is done are not officially places of work.

feminist geography: a field that examines the extent to which women and men experience spaces and places differently and how these differences themselves are part of the social construction of gender as well as that of place

Until recently, the only sub-discipline within geography that concerned itself with the importance of gender in space, place, or environmental concerns was **feminist geography**, a field concerned to examine "the extent to which women and men experience spaces and places differently and to show how these differences themselves are part of the social construction of gender as well as that of place," to quote Linda McDowell's 1999 definition of the field.

Beginning in the early 1980s in Canada, Britain, and the United States, "Women in Geography" study groups became established and took their place among the more long-standing activities of organizations such as the American Association of Geographers and the Canadian Association of Geographers (where the group is known as the Canadian Women and Geography Group, or CWAG).

Initially concerned with studying how the lives of men and women differed geographically, much of the early work conducted by feminist geographers showed how the gender categories "male" and "female" created different spatial experiences for men and women. Thus, for example, Susan Hanson and Geraldine Pratt's studies of commuting patterns in North American cities showed that a clear distinction existed between the travel behaviour of men and women. Women would, as their data showed, take many short trips during the middle of the day across the city, whereas men would take long trips at the beginning and end of the day.

Such studies showed that different geographic opportunities (or "life spaces") existed for men and women, and many geographers have continued in this research vein. Other feminist geographers have more recently gone beyond demonstrating that a clear difference exists to exploring the underlying societal reasons *why* those differences exist and the processes that sustain their continued existence. To take Hanson and Pratt's work again as an example, the commuting pattern they documented had nothing to do, they suggest, with an intrinsic difference between men and women. Rather, it was caused by the economic and social demands on those whom late twentieth-century North American society had assigned the duties of either child care (a female-designated activity) or work in the paid labour force (a male-designated task).

Armed with these insights, a "third wave" of gender-sensitive geographical research is now underway and is beginning to use the insight that gender is equally as socially constructed as space or place to examine the life spaces of other gender categories.

Gender categories based on gay, lesbian, and other identities also create their own geographies. In Canada, for example, research has shown how Montreal's Gay Village has created a district in the city where gay men are able to meet and socialize in bars and clubs with less animosity from the general public than elsewhere. The higher-than-average income that many gay Canadian couples enjoy has enabled many gay people who live in the village to embark on an extensive rejuvenation of the area's housing stock and to support an increasingly expensive range of restaurants. In these ways, the urban landscape of the area has been visibly transformed over the past 30 years or so (**Figure 5.36**). Indeed, the city of Montreal has become so accepting of the village that it actively promotes its presence in its tourist literature.

Figure 5.36 Montreal's "Gay Village" This building, known as the Complexe Bourbon, incorporates a café and a restaurant. It is located on the corner of rue St. Catherine and rue Alexandre de Sève in the heart of Montreal's "Gay Village." The building flies multicoloured flags recalling the rainbow, an emblem of gay culture.

CULTURE AND THE PHYSICAL ENVIRONMENT

Although interest in culture and the built environment has become prominent among geographers over the last several decades, a great deal of attention continues to be paid to culture and the physical environment. As with Sauer's original concept of the cultural landscape, geographers continue to focus their attention on people's relationships to the natural world and how the changing global economy disrupts or shapes those relationships. In this section, we look at two related but distinct ways of understanding the relationship between culture and the natural environment—cultural ecology and political ecology.

Cultural Ecology

Cultural ecology is the study of the relationship between a cultural group and its natural environment. Cultural ecologists study the material practices (food production, shelter provision, levels of biological reproduction) as well as the nonmaterial practices (belief systems, traditions, social institutions) of cultural groups. Their aim is to understand how cultural processes affect adaptation to the environment. Whereas the traditional approach to the cultural landscape focuses on human impacts on the landscape or its form or history, cultural ecologists seek to explain how cultural processes affect adaptation to the environment. **Cultural adaptation** involves the complex strategies human groups use to live successfully as part of a natural system. Cultural ecologists recognize that people are components of complex ecosystems, and that the way they manage and consume resources is shaped by cultural beliefs, practices, values, and traditions as well as by larger institutions and power relationships.

The cultural ecology approach incorporates three key points:

- Cultural groups and the environment are interconnected by systemic interrelationships. Cultural ecologists must examine how people manage resources through a range of strategies to comprehend how the environment shapes culture, and vice versa.

- Cultural behaviour must be examined as a function of the cultural group's relationship to the environment through both material and nonmaterial cultural elements. Such examinations are conducted through intensive fieldwork.

cultural ecology: the study of the relationship between a cultural group and its natural environment

cultural adaptation: the use of complex strategies by human groups to live successfully as part of a natural system

■ Most studies in cultural ecology investigate food production in rural and agricultural settings in the periphery to understand how change affects the relationship between cultural groups and the environment.[29]

These three points illustrate the way in which cultural geographers go about asking questions, collecting data, and deriving conclusions from their research. They also show how cultural ecology is both similar to and different from Sauer's approach to the cultural landscape, described at the beginning of the chapter: both share an emphasis on culture, but in cultural ecology the cultural processes of particular groups, rather than the imprint that culture makes on the landscape, have come to take centre stage. As a result, cultural ecologists look at food production, demographic change and its impacts on ecosystems, and ecological sustainability. Additionally, the scale of analysis is not on cultural areas or cultural regions but on small groups' adaptive strategies to a particular place or setting.

The impact of Spanish agricultural innovations on the culture of the indigenous people of the Central Andes region of South America (an area encompassing the mountainous portions of Peru, Bolivia, and Ecuador) presents an excellent case study in cultural ecology.[30] The transformation of Andean culture began when Pizarro arrived in Peru from Spain in 1531 and set about vanquishing the politically, technologically, and culturally sophisticated Inca empire. The Spaniards brought with them not only domestic plants and animals (mainly by way of Nicaragua and Mexico) but also knowledge about how to fabricate the tools they needed and a strong sense of what was necessary for a "civilized" life.

By 1620, however, the indigenous Andean people had lost 90 percent of their population and had been forced to make significant changes in their subsistence lifestyles (an illustration of demographic collapse as discussed in Chapter 4). The Inca Empire, with its large population base, had once engaged in intensive agriculture practices, including building and maintaining irrigation systems, terracing fields, and furrowing hillsides. With the severe drop in population and consequent loss of labour power, the survivors turned to pastoralism because herding requires less labour than intensive agriculture. Ultimately, it was the introduction of Old World–domesticated animals that had the greatest impact on the Central Andes (**Figure 5.37**), another example of ecological imperialism (see Chapter 4).

Of the range of animals the peasants could have incorporated into their agricultural practices (including cattle, oxen, horses, donkeys, pigs, sheep, goats, rabbits, and turkeys), only a few animals were widely adopted. Sheep were by far the most important introduction and were kept by Andean peasants as early as 1560. In many areas, sheep herding soon replaced the herding of indigenous animals, such as llamas and alpaca. By the seventeenth century, at elevations below 3,500 metres, sheep herding had been fully integrated into peasant economies and practices.

Adoption of sheep herding was facilitated by several factors. Sheep wool was oilier than that produced by native animals, a quality that made wool clothing more water resistant. Sheep also provided a source of meat, tallow, and manure for farm plots and could become an important source of food to a family in times of flood, frost, or drought. Sheep had a higher fertility level and a lower mortality rate than native herd animals and did not require large inputs of labour to manage. Finally, unlike crops, sheep could be marched to market on their own feet—no small advantage in the rugged terrain of the Andes.

Pigs and goats also proved popular because they fit well into available niches of the peasant economy. Rabbits, however, even though they produced more meat, never replaced the native guinea pigs. Guinea pigs retained a high cultural value as they continued to be a featured food at Aboriginal ceremonies celebrating life-cycle

Figure 5.37 Bolivian herders, Lake Titicaca Though sheep are not indigenous to the Andes, they have been widely adopted in this region since the Columbian Exchange. Sheep are well adapted to the high altitudes and provide wool and meat. Shown here are young girls of the Lake Titicaca region of Bolivia returning at day's end from herding.

---

[29] K. Butzer, "Cultural Ecology." In G.L. Gaile and C.J. Wilmot (eds.), *Geography in America*. Columbus, OH: Merrill Publishing Co., 1989, p. 192.

[30] Adapted from D. Gade, "Landscape, System, and Identity in the Post-Conquest Andes," *Annals of the Association of American Geographers* 82(3), 1992, pp. 461–477.

events and curing rites. Likewise, cows, though valued by the Spanish colonists, never became important to indigenous ways of life. Cows did not do well at higher altitudes or on steep terrain, and it was difficult to find appropriate fodder for them during the dry season. They also constituted a high risk, for they were an expensive investment, and loss or theft created economic hardship for the owner.

The pattern of selective adoption among Central Andean peasants also extended to plants. Of the approximately two dozen crops they could have adopted, Andean peasants adopted only about half. Peasants based their planting decisions on usefulness, environmental fit, and competition from other plants. For example, of the various grain crops that were available (rye, barley, oats, and wheat), Andean peasants adopted only wheat and barley. Andean peasants began to cultivate these grains in the highlands as early as the 1540s.

Both wheat and barley found a good ecological "fit" within the Central Andes and could be integrated into the fallow cycles that the peasants had long practised. These crops also had the advantage of supplementing the peasants' array of foods because they complemented—rather than competed with—cultivation of indigenous crops such as maize and potatoes (**Figure 5.38**).

By the 1590s, a "bundle" of Spanish cultural traits had thus been integrated into the Central Andean rural cultural complex, creating a hybrid rural culture. The hybridized culture—and cultural landscape—combined a much simplified version of Spanish material life with important (though altered) Inca practices of crop growing, herding, agricultural technology, and settlement patterns. That this hybrid cultural complex remains identifiable today, even after four centuries and in the face of contemporary globalizing forces, is due to a combination of factors: the peasants' strong adherence to custom, their geographical isolation, and the poverty of their circumstances.

Following the three points outlined earlier, cultural ecologists have been able to understand complex relationships between cultural groups and their environment, showing how choices are shaped by both culture and environmental conditions. Some critics have argued, however, that this conceptual framework of cultural ecology leaves out other intervening influences of the relationship between culture and the environment, namely, the impact of the political and economic institutions and practices.

Political Ecology

During the 1980s, cultural ecologists began moving away from a strict focus on a particular group's interactions with the environment, instead placing that relationship within a wider context. The result is political ecology, the merging of political economy with cultural ecology. **Political ecology** stresses that human–environment relationships can be adequately understood only by reference to the relationship of patterns of resource use to political and economic forces. Just as with the study of agriculture, industrialization, urbanization, and comparable geographical phenomena, this perspective requires an examination of the impact of the state and the market on the ways in which particular groups use their resource base.

Political ecology incorporates the same human–environment components analyzed by cultural ecologists. Yet, because political ecologists frame cultural ecology within the context of political and economic relationships, political ecology is seen to go beyond what cultural ecologists seek to understand.

Two studies of farming on St. Vincent and the Grenadines, an island nation in the Caribbean, illustrate this difference (**Figure 5.39**).[31] You will remember from Chapter 4 that St. Vincent (its Botanic Gardens, specifically) was the place to which Captain Bligh brought the breadfruit specimens that he had transported from the Pacific. The Botanic Gardens remained a centre for agricultural innovation in the

Figure 5.38 Andean potatoes in the marketplace The Andean region boasts hundreds of varieties of potatoes. The potato is one of the New World plants introduced into Europe following the Columbian Exchange. Forced reliance on the potato in nineteenth-century Irish agriculture led to disaster, however. The Great Potato Famine of the 1840s caused widespread mortality and migration. Many died, and many others migrated to the United States, reducing Ireland's population to levels from which it still has not recovered.

political ecology: an approach to cultural geography that studies human–environment relationships through the relationships of patterns of resource use to political and economic forces

---

[31] Adapted from L. Grossman, "Soil Conservation, Political Ecology, and Technological Change on Saint Vincent," *Geographical Review* 87, 1997, p. 353; and L. Grossman, *The Political Ecology of Bananas: Contract Farming, Peasants, and Agrarian Change in the Eastern Caribbean.* Chapel Hill: University of North Carolina Press, 1998.

Figure 5.39   St. Vincent and the Grenadines   St. Vincent and the Grenadines are part of the island chain of the Lesser Antilles in the Caribbean Sea. The total population is about 116,400, occupying about 240 square kilometres.

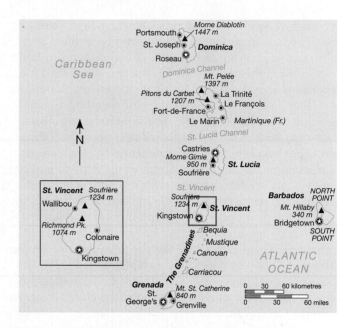

islands into the twentieth century, and St. Vincent's leading export crop of the inter-war years—arrowroot—was first grown experimentally there.

Government reports from the 1940s stressed that soil erosion was the leading agricultural problem on St. Vincent. Official documents often blamed inappropriate farming methods as the cause. However, Grossman's study of this period shows that more astute commentators realized that the political and economic constraints faced by the island's peasantry contributed to soil loss during this period. The best land was owned by large agricultural estates, so many of the islanders were forced to farm on slopes too steep for agriculture. Because average holdings were too small to support them, farmers could not afford to leave any land fallow. And because of the constant fear of eviction, farmers could not risk long-term measures needed to conserve the soil. Every one of these factors forced peasants to employ methods that increased soil erosion.

In recent years, agriculturalists on the main island of St. Vincent have shifted to banana production for export at the same time that local food production has begun to decline (**Figure 5.40**). Without recognizing the impacts of politics and the wider economy, it would be impossible to understand why these two processes are occurring simultaneously. Disincentives and incentives have both played a role. Disincentives to maintain local food production include marketing constraints, crop theft, competition from inexpensive food exports, and inadequate government agricultural extension assistance. Incentives to produce for export include state subsidies for export-oriented agriculture and access to credit for banana producers, as well as a strong British market for Caribbean bananas. As a result, local food production, although faced with the same environmental conditions as banana production, does not enjoy the same political and economic benefits. Because production for export is potentially more lucrative and an economically safer option, and to some extent because of changing dietary preferences, local food production has become a less attractive option for agriculturalists.

As the St. Vincent case illustrates, the political ecology approach provides a framework for understanding how the processes of the world economy affect local cultures and practices. The St. Vincent case also indicates how government policies and economic demand in the global economy shape local decision making. Furthermore, local cultural practices (especially dietary) are being abandoned as people develop a taste and preference for low-cost and convenient imported agricultural commodities (including flour and rice). Unfortunately, however, production for export also opens up the local economy to the fluctuations of the wider global economy. Recent changes in European Union policy on banana imports, for example, are having negative effects on banana

Figure 5.40   St. Vincent: banana production

production in St. Vincent. And those policy changes themselves are a response to American insistence that European states no longer grant banana producers in their Caribbean ex-colonies preferential access to the huge European market. St. Vincent's banana industry is therefore but another pawn in the politics of trade that globalization has caused.

GLOBALIZATION AND CULTURAL CHANGE

The discussion of cultural geography in this chapter raises one central question: how has globalization changed culture? We have seen that it affects different cultural groups differently and that different groups respond in different ways to these changes. With so much change occurring for so long, however, we must still ask ourselves what impact, overall, globalization is having on the multiplicity of cultural groups that inhabit the globe.

Anyone who has ever travelled between major world cities—or, for that matter, anyone who has been attentive to the backdrops of movies, television news stories, and magazine photojournalism—will have noticed the many familiar aspects of contemporary life in settings that, until recently, were thought of as being quite different from one another. Airports, offices, and international hotels have become notoriously alike, and their similarities of architecture and interior design have become reinforced by near-universal dress codes of the people who frequent them. The business suit, especially for males, has become the norm for office workers throughout much of the world. Jeans, T-shirts, and athletic footwear, meanwhile, have become the norm for young people as well as those in lower-wage jobs. The same automobiles can be seen on the streets of cities throughout the world; the same popular music is played on local radio stations; and many of the movies shown in local theatres are the same. Some of the TV programming is also the same—not just the music videos on MTV but also CNN's news, major international sports events, children's programs, drama series, and sitcoms. The same brand names also show up in stores and restaurants: Coca-Cola, Perrier, Carlsberg, Nestlé, Nike, Seiko, Sony, IBM, Nintendo, and Microsoft, to list just a few. Everywhere there is Chinese food, pita bread, pizza, classical music, rock music, and jazz.

It is these commonalities that provide a sense of familiarity among the inhabitants of the "fast world" that we described in Chapter 2. From the point of view of cultural nationalism, the "lowest common denominator" of this familiarity is often seen as the culture of fast food and popular entertainment that emanates from the United States. Popular commentators have observed that cultures around the world are being Americanized, or "McDonaldized," which represents the beginnings of a single global culture that will be based on material consumption, with the English language as its medium (**Figure 5.41**).

There is certainly some evidence to support this point of view, not least in the sheer numbers of people around the world who view *Sesame Street,* drink Coca-Cola, and eat at Subway franchises or similar fast-food chains. Meanwhile, U.S. culture is

Figure 5.41 McDonald's in Poland The U.S. franchise restaurant McDonald's is becoming a fixture on the landscape of formerly communist Eastern European countries, such as Poland. Although menu prices are quite high by local standards, frequenting places like McDonald's is a sign of status and personal prosperity in Poland and other previously communist countries, such as Romania and the Czech Republic.

increasingly embraced by local entrepreneurs around the world. Travel writer Pico Iyer, for example, describes finding dishes called "Yes, Sir, Cheese My Baby" and "Ike and Tuna Turner" in a local cafeteria in Guangzhou, China.[32] It seems clear that U.S. products are consumed as much for their symbolism of a particular way of life as for their intrinsic value. McDonald's burgers, along with Coca-Cola, Hollywood movies, rock music, and NFL and NBA insignia, have become associated with a lifestyle package that features luxury, youth, fitness, beauty, and freedom.

The economic success of the U.S. entertainment industry has helped reinforce the idea of an emerging global culture based on Americanization. In 1996, the entertainment industry was a leading source of foreign income in the United States, with a trade surplus of US$23 billion. Similarly, the United States transmits much more than it receives in sheer volume of cultural products. In 1995, the original versions of more than half of all the books translated in the world (more than 20,000 titles) were written in English. In terms of international flows of everything from mail and phone calls to press-agency reports, television programs, radio shows, and movies, a disproportionately large share originates in the United States.

Neither the widespread consumption of U.S. and U.S.-style products nor the increasing familiarity of people around the world with global media and international brand names, however, adds up to the emergence of a single global culture. Rather, what is happening is that processes of globalization are exposing the inhabitants of both the fast world and the slow world to a common set of products, symbols, myths, memories, events, cult figures, landscapes, and traditions. Although people living in Tokyo, Toronto, Turin, or Timbuktu may be perfectly familiar with these commonalities, they do not necessarily use or respond to them in uniform ways. Equally, it is important to recognize that cultural flows take place in all directions, not just outward from the United States. Think, for example, of European fashions in U.S. stores; of Chinese, Indian, Italian, Mexican, and Thai restaurants in U.S. towns and cities; and of U.S. stores selling craft goods from the periphery.

A Global Culture?

The answer to the question "Is there a global culture?" must therefore be "no." Although an increasing familiarity exists with a common set of products, symbols, and events (many of which share their origins in a U.S. culture of fast food and popular entertainment), these commonalities become configured in different ways in different places rather than constituting a single global culture. The local interacts with the global, often producing hybrid cultures. Sometimes traditional, local cultures become the subject of global consumption; sometimes it is the other way around. This is illustrated very well by the case of two suqs (linear bazaars) in the traditional medieval city of Tunis in North Africa. Both suqs radiate from the great Zaytuna Mosque, which has always been the geographical focal point of the old city. One suq, which was once *the* suq, leads from the mosque to the gateway that connects the medieval core to the French-built new city, where most tourists tend to stay. The second sets off at right angles to another exit from the formerly walled city.

> The first suq now specializes in Tunisian handicrafts, "traditional" goods, etc. It has kept its exotic architecture and multicoloured colonnades. The plaintive sound of the ancient nose flute and the whining of Arabic music provide background for the European tourists in their shorts and T-shirts, who amble in twos and threes, stopping to look and to buy. Few natives, except for sellers, are seen. The second suq, formerly less important, is currently a bustling madhouse. It is packed with partially veiled women and younger Tunisian girls in blouses and skirts, with men in knee-length tunic/toga outfits or in a variety of pants and shirts, with children everywhere. Few foreigners can be seen. The background to the din is blaring rock and roll music, and piled high on the pushcarts that line the way are transistor radios, watches, blue jeans (some prewashed), rayon scarves, Lux face and Omo laundry soaps.[33]

---

[32] P. Iyer, *Video Nights in Kathmandu: Reports from the Not-So-Far East*. London: Black Swan, 1989.

[33] J. Abu-Lughod, "Going Beyond Global Babble." In A.D. King (ed.), *Culture, Globalization, and the World-System*. Basingstoke, England: Macmillan, 1991, p. 132.

CONCLUSION

Culture is a complex and exceedingly important concept within the discipline of geography. A number of approaches exist to understand culture. It may be understood through a range of elements and features from single traits to complex systems. Cultural geography recognizes the complexity of culture and emphasizes the roles of space, place, and landscape and the ecological relationships between cultures and their environments. It distinguishes itself from other disciplinary approaches, providing unique insights that reveal how culture shapes the worlds we live in at the same time that the worlds we inhabit shape culture.

Two of the most universal forms of cultural identity are religion and language. Despite the secularization of many people in core countries, religion is still a powerful form of identity, and it has been used to buffer the impacts of globalization. Globalization has caused dramatic changes in the distribution of the world's religions as well as interaction between religions. Perhaps most remarkable, conversion to religions of the periphery is now underway in the core.

The 500-year history of globalization has resulted in the steady erosion of many regional languages and heavy contact and change in the languages that persist. A substantial number of languages that exist worldwide are threatened, and some governments are taking action to protect official and regional languages against the onslaught of globalization. Not only are religion and language at risk from globalization, but other forms of cultural expression, such as art and film, are as well.

Cultural geographers are also interested in understanding how culture shapes groups' adaptations to the natural environment. The aim of cultural ecology is to understand how the availability of resources and technology, as well as value and belief systems, shape the behaviours of cultural groups as active modifiers of, and adapters to, the natural environment. Recently, geographers have begun to pay attention to the role of politics and the wider economy in understanding the relationship between adaptive strategies and the natural world. This approach is known as *political ecology*.

Different groups in different parts of the world have begun to use cultural identities, such as gender, race, ethnicity, and sexuality, as a way of buffering the impacts of globalization on their lives. It is also the case that when the impacts of globalization are examined at the local level, some groups suffer more harm or reap more benefits than others. The unevenness of the impacts of globalization and the variety of responses to it indicate that it is unlikely that a monolithic global culture will wipe out all forms of difference.

Finally, it is useful to remember the point made at the beginning of this chapter: it will take us two chapters fully to appreciate the ways in which geography and culture interact. In this chapter, we have considered how language, religion, and issues of group identity (such as nationalism and multiculturalism) shape and are shaped by cultures, and in the process are responsible for the creation of cultural regions. In Chapter 6, we will look at the ways in which individuals interpret and navigate the distinct landscapes of these cultural regions.

MAIN POINTS REVISITED

- Though culture is a central, complex concept in geography, it may be thought of as a way of life involving a particular set of skills, values, and meanings.

  Culture includes youth styles of dress as well as operatic arias and slang and ecclesiastical languages.

- Geographers are particularly concerned about how place and space shape culture and, conversely, how culture shapes place and space. They recognize that culture is dynamic and is contested and altered within larger social, political, and economic contexts.

  The places in which cultural practices are produced shape cultural production as much as cultural production shapes the places in which it occurs.

- Like other fields of contemporary life, culture has been profoundly affected by globalization. However, globalization has not produced a homogenized culture so much as it has produced distinctive impacts and outcomes in different societies and geographical areas as global forces come to be modified by local cultures.

Although U.S. culture, especially commercialized culture, is widely exported around the globe, it is important to recognize that foreign cultural practices affect the United States and other parts of the world as well. The French influence on Argentina, for instance, is much more pronounced than is the U.S. influence.

■ **Contemporary approaches in cultural geography seek to understand the roles played by politics and the economy in establishing and perpetuating cultures, cultural landscapes, and global patterns of cultural traits and cultural complexes.**

For example, the state often facilitates the import or export of cultural practices, such as movies or music, so that economic growth can be enhanced.

■ **Cultural geography has been broadened to include analysis of gender, class, ethnicity, stage in the life cycle, and so on, in recognizing that important differences can exist within as well as between cultures.**

What geographers find important about these identities are the ways in which they are constructed in spaces and places, and how those particular geographies shape the identities.

■ **Cultural ecology, an offshoot of cultural geography, focuses on the relationship between a cultural group and its natural environment.**

It recognizes that culture is significantly shaped by the physical environment in which it occurs at the same time that certain cultures shape the ways its participants interact with the environment.

■ **Political ecologists also focus on human–environment relationships but stress that relationships at all scales, from the local to the global, are intertwined with larger political and economic forces.**

Political ecologists consider the influence of the state in shaping cultural practices since the state plays an increasingly important role in our everyday lives.

Key Terms

allophone (p. 230)
anglophone (p. 230)
cultural adaptation (p. 243)
cultural ecology (p. 243)
cultural geography (p. 206)
cultural hearth (p. 227)
cultural landscape (p. 209)
cultural nationalism (p. 235)
cultural region (p. 214)
cultural system (p. 214)
cultural trait (p. 212)

culture (p. 205)
dialects (p. 226)
diaspora (p. 215)
ethnicity (p. 238)
feminist geography (p. 242)
francophone (p. 230)
gender (p. 240)
genre de vie (p. 211)
historical geography (p. 210)
home language (p. 231)
isolate (p. 227)

language (p. 226)
language branch (p. 226)
language family (p. 226)
language group (p. 226)
language shift (p. 232)
mother tongue (p. 230)
official languages (p. 230)
political ecology (p. 245)
race (p. 239)
religion (p. 215)
sacred space (p. 223)

Additional Reading

Anderson, K. *Vancouver's Chinatown: Racial Discourse in Canada, 1875–1980.* Montreal: McGill-Queens University Press, 1991.

Bebbington, A. "Movements, Modernizations, and Markets: Indigenous Organizations and Agrarian Struggles in Ecuador." In R.P. and M. Watts (eds.), *Liberation Ecologies: Environment, Development, Social Movements.* London: Routledge, 1996.

Cartwright, D.G. "The Divided Continent: Political, Population, Ethnic and Racial Division." In F.W. Boal and S.A. Royle (eds.), *North America: A Geographical Mosaic.* London: Arnold, 1999, 103–122.

Crawford, M. "The World in a Shopping Mall." In M. Sorkin (ed.), *Variations on a Theme Park: The New American City and the End of Public Space.* New York: The Noonday Press, 1992, 3–30.

Cronon, W. *Changes in the Land: Indians, Colonists, and the Ecology of New England.* New York: Hill and Wang, 1983.

Ennals, P., and D.W. Holdsworth. *Homeplace: The Making of the Canadian Dwelling over Three Centuries.* Toronto: University of Toronto Press, 1998.

Ennals, P., and D.W. Holdsworth. "The Look of Domestic Building, 1891." In R.L. Gentilcore (ed.), *Historical Atlas of Canada,* vol. 2. Toronto: University of Toronto Press, 1993, plate 6.

Hiro, D. *Holy Wars: The Rise of Islamic Fundamentalism.* New York: Routledge, 1989.

Ingram, J. *Talk, Talk, Talk.* Toronto: Viking Penguin, 1992.

Ingram, J. *The Talk Show.* (A set of four 60-minute audio cassettes, based on a radio series of that name.) Toronto: CBC Radio, 1993.

Jackson, P. *Maps of Meaning: An Introduction to Cultural Geography.* London: Unwin Hyman, 1989.

Kalman, H. *A Concise History of Canadian Architecture.* Don Mills: Oxford University Press, 2000.

Katz, C., and J. Monk. *Full Circles: Geographies of Women over the Life Course.* London: Routledge, 1993.

Katz, Y., and J. Lehr. *The Last Best West: Essays on the Historical Geography of the Canadian Prairies.* Jerusalem: Magnes Press, 1999.

Lachapelle, R., and J. Henripin. *The Demolinguistic Situation in Canada: Past Trends and Future Prospects.* Montreal: Institute for Research on Public Policy, 1982.

Leyshon, A., D. Matless, and G. Revill (eds.). *The Place of Music.* New York: Guilford Press, 1998.

Moore, D. "Contesting Terrain in Zimbabwe's Eastern Highlands: Political Ecology, Ethnography, and Peasant Resource Struggles," *Economic Geography* 69(4), 1993, 380–401.

Rocheleau, D.E., B.P. Thomas-Slayter, and E. Wangari. *Feminist Political Ecology: Global Issues and Local Experiences.* London and New York: Routledge, 1996.

Roy, O. *The Failure of Political Islam.* Cambridge, MA: Harvard University Press, 1994.

Saunders, R. "Kickin' Some Knowledge: Rap and the Construction of Identity in the African-American Ghetto," *Arizona Anthropologist* 10, 1993, 21–40.

Underwood, D. *Oscar Niemeyer and the Architecture of Brazil.* New York: Rizzoli International, 1994.

Ward, P. *A History of Domestic Space: Privacy and the Canadian Home.* Vancouver: UBC Press.

Warkentin, J. "Chapter 6: Interpreting Canadian Landscapes." In *A Regional Geography of Canada: Life, Land and Space.* Scarborough: Prentice Hall, 2000, 144–172.

Women & Geography Study Group. *Geography and Gender: An Introduction to Feminist Geography.* London: Hutchinson, 1984.

Wood, J.D. *Making Ontario: Agricultural Colonization and Landscape Re-creation before the Railway.* Montreal and Kingston: McGill-Queen's University Press, 2000.

Zimmerer, K. "Human Geography and the 'New Ecology': The Prospect and Promise of Integration," *Annals of the Association of American Geography* 84(1), 1994, 108–125.

Discussion Questions and Research Activities

1. Using *Billboard Magazine* (the news magazine of the record industry), construct a historical geography of the top 20 singles over the last half century to determine the way in which different regions of the world have risen and fallen in terms of their significance. You should also determine an appropriate interval for sampling—every three to five years is an acceptable one. You may use the hometown of the recording artist or the headquarters of the recording studio as your geographical variable. Once you have organized your data, you should be able to answer the following questions: How has the geography you have documented changed? What might be the reasons for these changes? What do these changes mean for the regions of the world that have increased or decreased in terms of their musical prominence?

2. Ethnic identity is often expressed spatially through the existence of neighbourhoods or business areas dominated by members of a particular group. One way to explore the spatial expression of ethnicity in a place is to look at newspapers over time. In this exercise, you will look at ethnic change in a particular neighbourhood over time. You can do this by using your library's holdings of local or regional newspapers. Examine change over at least a four-decade period. To do this, you must identify an area of the city in which you live or some other city for which your library has an extensive newspaper collection. You should trace the history of an area you know is now occupied by a specific ethnic group. How long has the group occupied that area? What aspects of the group's occupation of that area have changed over time (for example, school, places of worship, sports activities, age of the households)? If different groups have occupied the area, what might be the reasons for the changes?

3. College and university campuses generate their own cultural practices and ideas that shape behaviours and attitudes in ways that may not be obvious at first glance. For this exercise, you will observe a particular practice that occurs routinely at your college or university, such as important rituals of college/university life, sports events, and even class discussions. Who are the participants in this practice? What are their levels of importance? Are there gender, age, or status differences in the implementation of this ritual or practice? What are the time and space aspects of the practice? Who controls its production? What are the intended outcomes of the practice? How does the practice or ritual contribute to the maintenance or disruption of order in the larger culture?

4. Find a description of a coming-of-age ceremony for any part of the world. Summarize that description and then compare it to one you have either experienced directly or have observed in Canada. What are the differences and similarities between your experience and the one you read about? What might be some of the reasons for these?

MyGeosciencePlace

Visit **www.mygeoscienceplace.ca** to find chapter review quizzes, videos, maps, and much more.

6

Interpreting Places and Landscapes

Thames Town Development, Shanghai, China

Wish to live in Australia—without leaving Beijing? Beijing residents can now buy a home in Sydney Coast, a subdivision that offers its residents a "seven-day Australian-style villa life." "Designed by Australian experts, the project presents a kind of simple and fresh lifestyle," says a brochure for the new development. "Taking a walk along the streets in Sydney Coast, you will get a true sense of Australia."

Beijingers who would prefer to live in California can move into the Yosemite subdivision—or wait for the completion of Napa Valley, a new development under construction about 50 kilometres outside Beijing. Napa Valley attempts to capture a Californian Mediterranean lifestyle of laid-back, al fresco leisure. "Rustic stone is widely used, with rich stucco colors, along with wood shutters and wrought-iron accents, to create an intimate scale and village-like feel," according to Napa Valley's architects and planners.

For those craving to re-create life in seventeenth-century France, there is Chateau Regalia, located on Beijing's northern outskirts. In both form and decoration, Chateau Regalia's homes are an eccentric amalgam of French Baroque and neoclassical architecture. And yes, there's Canada, too: Vancouver Forest is a new subdivision of homes that mimics a typical neighbourhood in British Columbia. It was built by Canadian architects, using Canadian materials to create a mini Canada.

The craze has also caught on in Shanghai, where there are many more tract homes built in foreign styles. Thames Town, just outside Shanghai, is one of seven satellite towns built by the municipal government to house 500,000 people (the other six are themed with architectural styles adopted from Italy, Spain, Canada, Sweden, Holland, and Germany). Thames Town includes a gothic church, village green, and mock-Tudor pub selling real ale. Built from scratch in little over three years, the suburb encapsulates five centuries of British architecture with half-timbered Tudor-style residences at the centre, shops in Victorian redbrick warehouses on the waterfront, and gabled Edwardian houses bordered by privet hedges, manicured lawns, and leafy roads.[1]

The success of these themed neighbourhoods points to a number of interesting questions. To begin with, why do wealthy Chinese consumers prefer these fake Western urban landscapes to the local architectural styles? Why do these neighbourhoods possess such prestige and allure? Underneath

---

[1] Based on D. Elsea, "China's Chichi Suburbs: American-style Sprawl All the Rage in Beijing," *San Francisco Chronicle*, April 24, 2005.

these questions of style and authenticity are some more fundamental issues: why do urban landscapes across the world look so different in the first place, and at the same time so similar? What historical legacies are expressed in them, and what globalizing forces are working to homogenize them?

Geographers suggest that an important reason why human landscapes are so distinctive is that they have been shaped by different cultures. Cultures may respond differently to the challenges of the physical realm, and different cultural attitudes toward living arrangements or land ownership can have very different impacts on the "look of the land." In short, that "look of the land" is what geographers have called the *cultural landscape*. In this chapter, we explore the relationships between people, landscapes, and places to assess how individuals and groups experience their environments, create places, and find meanings in the cultural landscapes they create. We also discuss the forces that seem to be eroding the differences between places, making them look increasingly similar and even "placeless."

MAIN POINTS

- Landscape serves as a kind of archive of society. It is a reflection of our culture and our experiences. Like a book, landscape is a text that is written by individuals and groups and read by them as well.

- The language in which a landscape is written is a kind of code. The code or codes are signs that direct our attention toward certain features and away from others.

- The written code of landscape is also known as *semiotics*. Codes signify important information about landscapes, such as whether they are accessible or off-limits or are oriented toward work or play.

- In addition to understanding how the environment shapes (and is shaped by) people, geographers seek to identify how it is perceived and understood by people.

- Different cultural identities and status categories influence the ways in which people experience and understand their environments, as well as how they are shaped by—and are able to shape—them.

- The emergence of the most recent phase of globalization has occurred in parallel with a transition from modernism to postmodernism.

- Modernism as a historical period embraced scientific rationality and optimism about progress.

- Postmodernism, the name for the contemporary period, revolves around an orientation toward consumption and emphasizes the importance of multiple perspectives.

BEHAVIOUR, KNOWLEDGE, AND HUMAN ENVIRONMENTS

In addition to attempting to understand how the environment shapes and is shaped by people, geographers also seek to identify how it is perceived and understood by people and how people ascribe meaning to landscape and places. Arguing that there is an interdependence between people and places, geographers explore how individuals and groups acquire knowledge of their environments and how this knowledge shapes their attitudes and behaviours. Much of what we as humans know about the environment we live in is learned through direct and indirect experience. At the same time, our environmental knowledge is also acquired through a filter of personal and group characteristics, such as gender, stage of the life cycle, religious beliefs, ethnicity, and where we live. In this chapter, we take the key geographical concepts of landscape, space, and place and explore the ways in which people understand them, create them, and operate within them.

What Is Landscape?

Generally speaking, *landscape* is a term that can mean different things to different people. For some, the term brings to mind the design of formal gardens and parks, as in landscape architecture. For others, landscape signifies a bucolic countryside or even the organization of plantings around residences and public buildings. For still others, landscape calls to mind the artistic rendering of scenery, as in a landscape painting. Geographers think of landscape as a comprehensive product of human action such that every landscape is a complex repository of society. What that means is that each landscape is a collection of evidence about our character and experience, our struggles and triumphs as humans: for better or worse, landscape reflects our humanity.

Landscapes reflect the lives of ordinary people as well as the more powerful, and they reflect their dreams and ideas as well as their material lives. To understand better how exactly landscapes do this, we can distinguish different categories of landscape types based on the elements contained within them.

Ordinary landscapes (or **vernacular landscapes,** as they are sometimes called) are the everyday landscapes that people create in the course of their lives together. From parking lots and trailer parks to tree-shaded suburbs and the patchwork fields of prairie farms, these are landscapes that are lived in and changed continuously. In turn, they influence and change the perceptions, values, and behaviours of the people who live and work in them. Just because these landscapes are "ordinary," however, does not mean that they are simplistic or do not carry complex messages. Take the example provided by the landscapes of contemporary American (and, to a somewhat lesser degree, Canadian) suburbia. They are conservative utopias of bigness and ostentation, characterized by master-planned developments, simulated settings, and conspicuous consumption (**Figure 6.1**). They are landscapes of seemingly casual displays of wealth, dominated by a presumed correlation between the size of the house/lot/car and the social standing of the owner.

The point is that ordinary landscapes, as geographers such as Don Mitchell have established, are instruments of social and cultural power that make political–economic structures appear as if they were simply given and inevitable. As powerful complexes of signs, the landscapes of contemporary American suburbia have naturalized an ideology of competitive consumption, moral minimalism, and disengagement from notions of social justice and civil society—the peculiar mix of political conservatism and social libertarianism that is the hallmark of much of contemporary suburban America. Popular HBO television shows such as *The Sopranos, Weeds,* and *Big Love,* and the landscapes they produce for viewers, confirm this representation of American suburbia, but they also complicate it by showing suburbia as filled with a diversity of people with a range of moral commitments who are engaged in a variety of legal and criminal activities. All three shows are mentioned here because they help to undermine a monolithic

ordinary landscapes (vernacular landscapes): the everyday landscapes that people create in the course of their lives

Figure 6.1 Conspicuous consumption in suburbia The dominant theme in upscale residential developments in North America is size and ostentation.

image of suburbia and to complicate homogenized images of the most ordinary landscape we encounter in our daily lives.

Symbolic landscapes represent the particular values or aspirations that the builders and financiers of those public landscapes want to impart to a larger public. Parliament Hill in Ottawa, for example, with its neo-gothic style of architecture, is intentionally designed to invoke the British tradition of parliamentary democracy (**Figure 6.2**). In Washington, DC, the neo-classical architecture of the federal government buildings is intended to suggest the democratic and republican traditions of Classical Greece and Rome (**Figure 6.3**).

Geographers also speak about "landscapes of power," such as gated communities; "landscapes of despair," such as homeless encampments; and **derelict landscapes**. The latter are landscapes that have experienced abandonment, misuse, disinvestment, or vandalism. We may think of such places as part of the "Landscapes of Fear" that Yi-Fu Tuan has described in his 1979 study, places that our culture has taught us to be afraid of.

symbolic landscapes: representations of particular values or aspirations that the builders and financiers of those landscapes want to impart to a larger public

derelict landscapes: landscapes that have experienced abandonment, misuse, disinvestment, or vandalism

Landscape as a Human System

Geographers now recognize that many layers of meaning are embodied in each and every landscape, meanings that can be expressed and understood differently at different times. Put another way, many cultural landscapes exist in any single place. Consider the example of a family visiting a park: the children's perceptions of their world (in this case, the playground) are different from those of their parents, and girls may see their world differently from boys, even in the same family.

Figure 6.2 Parliament buildings, Ottawa With their neo-gothic style, these buildings were designed to evoke a sense of the British traditions of government. In this way, they represent an example of the use of symbolic space.

Figure 6.3   Lincoln Memorial   The Lincoln Memorial, like the other public buildings, monuments, and statuary around the Mall in Washington, DC, is intended to convey a sense of sobriety, authority, and the power of democratic principles first developed in ancient Greece.

The realization that there may be as many different landscapes in a place as there are individuals beholding it has led geographers to appreciate the role of individual subjectivity in the study of landscape, also known as the **humanistic approach.** The humanistic approach in geography places the individual—especially individual values, meaning systems, intentions, and conscious acts—at the centre of analysis.

The humanistic approach's focus on the perceptions of individuals is an important counterweight to the tendency to talk about a social group or society as if they thought, felt, and acted all the same. In other words, the humanistic approach avoids the stereotyping of people on the basis of certain characteristics. Nevertheless, some critics argue that humanistic research has limited utility because the results only apply to the individual and thus are hard to generalize to the level of the group or population. The tension between these viewpoints reminds us that there is not one single correct or right approach and that we need to be open to a variety of perspectives when studying any phenomenon in human geography.

How would we do this in the case of studying landscape? We could combine the humanistic focus on individual motivations and actions with an approach that considers the role of larger forces, such as culture, gender, and the government, and the ways in which these forces enhance or constrain individuals' lives. Much recent cultural geographical work, therefore, conceptualizes the relationship of people and the environment as *interactive*, not one-way, and emphasizes the role that landscapes play in shaping and reinforcing human practices. This most recent conceptualization of landscape is more dynamic and complex than the one Carl Sauer advanced, and it encourages geographers to look outside their own discipline—to anthropology, psychology, sociology, and even history—to fully understand its complexity.

humanistic approach: places the individual—especially individual values, meaning systems, intentions, and conscious acts—at the centre of analysis

Landscape as Text

Such a dynamic and complex approach to understanding landscape is based on the conceptualization of **landscape as text,** by which we mean that, like a book, landscape can be read and written by groups and individuals. This approach departs from traditional attempts to categorize landscapes based on the different elements they contain. The landscape-as-text view holds that landscapes do not simply exist "out of nowhere." Rather, there are "writers" who produce landscapes and give them meaning, and there are "readers" who consume the messages embedded in landscapes. The messages embedded in landscapes can be read as signs about values, beliefs, and practices, though not every reader will take the same message from a particular landscape (just as people may differ in their interpretation of a passage from a book).

These ideas can be understood by considering how individuals experience or value landscapes. A child sees a park very differently from the way an adult does—the pile of sand in the corner is a playground for the former and a hazard for the latter. Landscapes mean different things to different people. In short, landscapes both produce and communicate meaning, and one of our tasks as geographers is to interpret those meanings. Later in this chapter, in the section

landscape as text: the idea that landscapes can be read and written by groups and individuals

"Coded Spaces," we provide an extended example of the "writing" and "reading" of two landscapes: the shopping mall and the capital city of Brazil, Brasília. First, however, we must establish how places and spaces are given meaning by individuals and by different social and cultural groups.

THE AESTHETICS OF LANDSCAPE

We continually strive to alter, or to improve, landscapes and places we have control over. We improve them according to some received standard of taste, or **aesthetic**, which is itself both culturally and historically determined. Standards of taste are influenced by many things—most importantly, by our changing attitudes to nature (see Chapter 4), our desire to appear *au courant* with the latest styles, and the diffusion of such fashions. As individuals, we have most control over the design of our houses and our gardens. Because we have already looked at vernacular architecture (see Chapter 5), let us now look at the garden, a topic that will enable us to consider not only the everyday garden of the average Canadian but also the grand "landscape gardens" of the core's wealthy, whose gardens have so often set the standards of fashions, which the periphery has subsequently followed.

aesthetic: culturally determined standard of beauty and good taste

The Evolution of Garden Design

Many cultural geographers have studied the evolution of the European landscape garden. Their work emphasizes the importance of controlling enough resources to improve a landscape on a large scale, and how the resulting landscape was radically altered over time according to the prevailing garden aesthetic. Such landscapes reflect the elite's ability to control space as they wished and, in doing so, to use the landscape itself to send a visible message of their wealth and power (see "Coded Spaces" later in this chapter). Changes in our attitudes to the landscape also suggest how our attitudes to nature in general are culturally constructed.

We will take a brief look at how the European landscape garden has evolved because those changes have most influenced Canadian garden aesthetics and still have powerful control over the way we perceive and appreciate nature. However, we must not overlook the fact that there are several other great gardening traditions in the world (including the Islamic, Japanese, and Chinese traditions). Nor must we fail to appreciate that their influence has begun to spread in Canada as increased immigration to this country has brought with it different cultural attitudes concerning nature (**Figure 6.4**).

Figure 6.4 Chinese garden, Vancouver

Research shows us that the European landscape garden has gone through four basic phases (**Figure 6.5**). Using very approximate dates, they are as follows:

- *The "Italian garden": nature domesticated (the dominant European style from about 1550–1650).* In its small scale and very controlled planting in rectangular beds around the owner's villa, this type reflected a desire to

(a) The "Italian garden": nature domesticated, 1550–1650

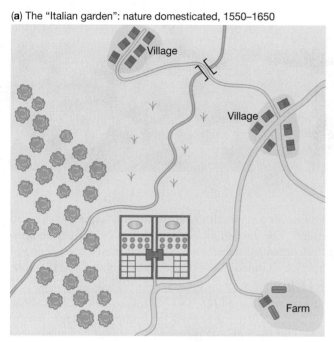

(b) The "French garden": nature subdued, 1650–1720

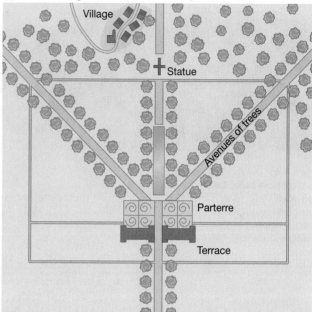

(c) The "English garden": nature triumphant, 1720–1850

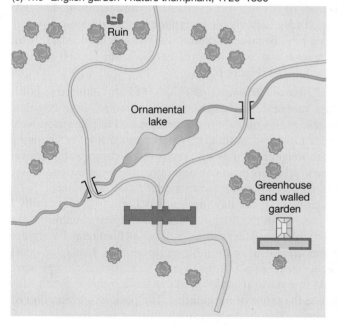

(d) The "city park": municipal nature, 1850–present

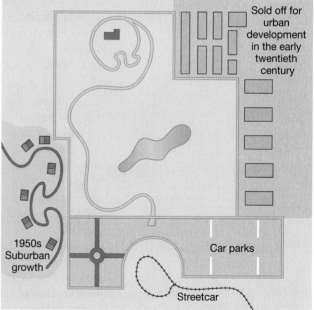

Figure 6.5　The evolution of the landscape garden　This sequence of illustrations shows how the design of the landscape garden has changed over 500 years in response to changing aesthetics. Drawn to the same scale, these illustrations show the general elements of redesign that occurred to one idealized garden over the period. A considerable number of gardens in Western Europe underwent many of these transformations, but not all of them experienced all of the changes shown here. Beginning from small, walled gardens (a), landowners expanded and redesigned their properties during the late seventeenth century. Long, straight avenues of trees symbolized their power—a power that removed villages that stood in the way of design (b). Between 1720 and 1850, more romantic views of nature led to garden re-landscaping based on curvilinear paths and lakes, irregular plantings of trees, and vast sweeps of park-like grass (c). Ruins (fake or genuine) were a popular garden feature of the time. By the beginning of the twentieth century, many owners of large properties could no longer afford the upkeep of their estates. Many estates were sold to municipalities, which redeveloped them for housing and city parks, linked by streetcar (and then by car) to the city centre (d).

Figure 6.6   The Italian landscape garden: Isola Bella, Lake Maggiore, Italy   Begun in 1632 by Count Borromeo, the gardens of his baroque palace are considered a classic seventeenth-century Italian garden design.

domesticate nature. Fountains and small linear ponds (or "canals") showed water was also controlled. The garden's clear separation from outside indicated the fear that an uncontrolled nature, or wilderness, still existed beyond the walls. Typical examples included many of the mansions of the Italian nobility of the day (**Figure 6.6**).

■ *The "French garden": nature subdued (1650–1720).* Gardens such as those at Versailles, developed by Le Nôtre for Louis XIV, had one message: nature had been "subdued." Beyond the intricate geometric plantings and topiary of the garden around the house, the surrounding landscape was turned into a series of straight avenues of trees that radiated out from the house. The wilderness became a park and a very visible metaphor of the Sun King's power across France and its empire. Because imitation was the best (and safest) form of flattery, this design style was soon adopted by the lesser French nobility and spread throughout Europe (**Figure 6.7**).

■ *The "English garden": nature triumphant (1720–1850).* Geometric landscapes, especially on a vast scale, did not suit the "romantic" aesthetic that was developing in Britain at this time. Industrialization and urbanization were contributing to a sense of loss and nostalgia for nature. In this set of changing attitudes, nature was no longer feared as wild but loved because, as the antithesis of the industrial world, it was primitive and pure, uncorrupted and closer to God. To show this, garden design turned to a celebration of nature.

The leading practitioner of the new design was Lancelot "Capability" Brown, so named because of his expression that he saw "great capability" for improvement in a particular landscape. The gardens at Blenheim Palace are among his most famous creations. In his designs, no straight lines of avenues or roads were allowed, irregular plantings of trees in scattered clumps were preferred, and at least one natural-looking lake was *de rigueur*. Small hills were created to enhance the sense of irregularity. The park was even allowed to run right up to the house's front door to suggest that it was surrounded by nature (**Figure 6.8**).

The obvious contradiction that an entirely created landscape could not be "natural" did not seem to detract from the experience of these gardens. In fact, the main landscape aesthetic of the period, the **picturesque**, inspired by eighteenth-century landscape painters in the Romantic tradition, was characterized by the celebration of the natural world found in the work of eminent landscape artists, such as Lorrain, Turner, and Constable in England and Thomas Cole and the Hudson Valley School in the United States.

picturesque: a landscape design inspired by eighteenth-century landscape painters in the Romantic tradition

Figure 6.7 The French landscape garden: Versailles Designed for Louis XIV by his gardener, André Le Nôtre, this garden clearly shows how long, straight avenues and perspectives were imposed on the landscape. The intention was not only to produce an aesthetic in which nature was subdued but also to show in a very visible way the power of the French king.

- *The "city park": municipal nature (1850–present).* The slow decline in the economic fortunes of the core's elite made it too expensive for them to support large houses and gardens. However, nature was to find another champion, this time from those urban reformers who thought its soothing aesthetic effects should be made available to a wider range of people. From the 1850s onward, public interest in the use of city parks as "breathing spaces" led many municipalities to develop public gardens. Design and size varied greatly, with the more formal layouts of earlier generations at least as popular as the more informal. Often, these gardens were connected by streetcar routes to the city centre and became the focus of a fairground of attractions, such as can be found at Copenhagen's famous Tivoli Gardens (**Figure 6.9**).

Figure 6.8 The English landscape garden Petworth Park in the south of England was landscaped by Capability Brown and painted by Turner.

Figure 6.9 Tivoli Gardens, Copenhagen This city centre park combines a garden and amusement park.

Canadian Garden Design

Each of the last three of these European landscapes has had an influence on Canadian garden design. The "French school," as might be expected, found early expression in Nova Scotia (**Figure 6.10**). For example, in her recent history of Canadian gardening, Carol Martin describes how "the leading citizens of Louisbourg . . . had neither the means nor the ability to recreate the magnificent gardens of France but their gardens showed the influence of contemporary French design" in their symmetry and contrasting colour of plantings in the design.[2]

The "English style" was used in the private gardens of some nineteenth-century industrialists, but its main influence in Canada was felt in the growing number of public parks and gardens developed across the country that incorporated its aesthetic. Promoted by such groups as the City Beautiful and Garden City movements (see Chapter 11), a number of these parks were designed by leading landscape architects. For example, in 1877, the architect of New York's Central Park, Frederick Law Olmsted, was hired to design Mount Royal Park in Montreal (**Figure 6.11**). As Martin observes, "drawing heavily on the English landscape tradition, he saw parks as natural landscapes—but natural landscapes improved by design."[3] The main improvements Olmsted made to Mount Royal were to weave curvilinear paths around the hillside to its summit, creating many opportunities for breathtaking views on the way up. Olmsted's influence continued in Canada through the work of his students, Henry Englehart (who designed Mount Pleasant Cemetery in Toronto in 1874) and Frederick Todd (who designed Winnipeg's Assiniboine Park in 1908 and Wascana Park around the Saskatchewan legislative building in 1905).

Of course, there were no ambitious goals or resources for all municipal parks. The majority of parks served the basic purpose of public recreation without the demands of major landscaping projects. By the 1850s, there were city parks in Kingston, Toronto, Hamilton, and Niagara-on-the-Lake, and in 1870 the Halifax Public Gardens were founded. By establishing gardens at strategic points, the Canadian Pacific Railroad spread the new idea of beautifying public spaces across the country by the beginning of the twentieth century.

But however modest the garden, the message that these gardens represented "nature improved" was never far from the surface. In a very perceptive essay

[2] Carol Martin, *A History of Canadian Gardening*. Toronto: McArthur and Company, 2000, pp. 40–42.
[3] Ibid., p. 79.

Figure 6.10   Louisbourg, Nova Scotia   Gardens within the fortress are inspired by the French landscape garden tradition.

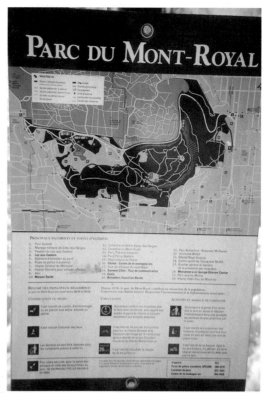

Figure 6.11   Mount Royal Park, Montreal   Landscaped by Frederick Law Olmsted, this park's design is inspired by the English landscape garden tradition.

about the Galt Gardens Park in Lethbridge, a 4-hectare park established in 1885, David Garneau writes that "prairie gardens, especially floral gardens, are acts of will imposed on the wilderness." The park, he notes, has not preserved the prairies but supports non-indigenous grasses, trees, and flowers—all of which have to be artificially irrigated if they are to grow. Galt Gardens are, he concludes, "an imitation of—or compensation for the lack of—proper, European and Eastern Canadian type, nature/landscape."[4]

It is perhaps surprising to read that this nineteenth-century aesthetic still has a powerful hold over us today, and even more surprising that it should so influence us in Canada, of all countries, where there is wilderness to spare. Yet, our own private gardens, the length and breadth of this country, are a visible testimony that we value landscapes that are "acts of will imposed upon the wilderness." The supreme example, and the most visible part of our garden, is the front lawn (**Figure 6.12**). Socially considered as neither completely public nor completely private space, it must be kept free of all weeds, mowed to within a few millimetres above ground all summer, and watered every few days during its growing season. This manicured front lawn also owes its origins to the English landscape garden and, despite (or maybe because of?) its inappropriateness to our climate, has become a hallmark of the successful garden in Canada.

Many people have argued that the sign of a "Canadian aesthetic" is the ability to appreciate true wilderness or landscapes untouched by people. But it is important to realize that this view is itself a learned ability: the ability to appreciate untouched wilderness is an aesthetic every bit as culturally constructed as the European views we have considered. This brings us to the question of how an aesthetic is actually constructed in practice.

Figure 6.12   The suburban lawn   This tract of grass is a mainstay of suburban Canada. Canadians spend millions of dollars on fertilizers and pesticides to keep their lawns looking perfect, producing a landscape that is anything but natural.

---

[4] David Garneau, "Nature Redux: Multiple Natures." In *Nature Redux*. Lethbridge: Southern Alberta Art Gallery, 1996, pp. 52–53.

The Construction of an Aesthetic

In his wonderful book *How the Canyon Became Grand*, Stephen Pyne tells us that the sixteenth-century Spanish explorers who made the first European discovery of the Grand Canyon spent only a few sentences describing it in their report to the Spanish king. Pyne suggests that this is because they did not know what to make of it. They had no cultural frame of reference in which to place it, and so words, literally, failed them. Annie Dillard tells us that in the eighteenth century, "when educated European tourists visited the Alps, they deliberately blindfolded their eyes to shield themselves from the evidence of the earth's horrible irregularity."[5] Yi-Fu Tuan, in his study *Landscapes of Fear*, adds that Europeans feared mountains because they were the realm of ghosts and robbers. On a more prosaic level, Tuan suggests that mountains were not valued because they were of little use for farming. Yet today, canyons and mountain ranges are among the landscapes that inspire the most awe and admiration. Why and how did this change or "reconstruction" occur?

The answer lies partly in the Romantic rejection of industrialization we have already discussed and partly in the opening up of the North American frontier. Let us look at each briefly. A number of eighteenth-century writers and artists argued that the ill effects of industrialization on the human body, mind, and soul could only be counterbalanced by exposing people to nature in its original state. The knowledge that something existed outside human control served to show that industry had its limits, and the fear of nature's elemental power caused people to forget humanity in a contemplation of the infinite. Landscapes that had the power to induce this sense of the **sublime**, or awe, were the ones to be most valued. As a result, *elemental nature*, the nature of windswept coasts, storms, rugged mountains, deserts, glaciers, and snow, became reinterpreted by the late eighteenth century: rather than God-forsaken wilderness, they now represented God's best handiwork. Perhaps that was the reason why Franklin's ill-fated search for Canada's Northwest Passage was so celebrated—the expedition through the Arctic vastness was as sublime as anything Coleridge's *Ancient Mariner* could manage. In Europe itself, mountains became sought-after destinations from the 1830s on, and it was from Switzerland that the Canadian Pacific Railroad recruited the first mountain guides to take their Banff Hotel visitors into the Rockies (**Figure 6.13**).

The sublime was an aesthetic particularly suited to the Canadian landscape, and it came to dominate in painting, photography, and fiction. It is the sublime landscape that we are taught to value, and it is that which our national parks,

sublime: a landscape so impressive that it inspires awe or wonder

Figure 6.13 The Canadian Rockies from the highway south of Rogers Pass Awe-inspiring views of vast and monumental mountain landscapes, such as this, are considered sublime.

---

[5] Annie Dillard, *Pilgrim at Tinker Creek*. New York: Harper Perennial, 1998, p. 141 [originally published 1974].

from the Rockies to Gros Morne in Newfoundland, seek to preserve. The vast Canadian landscape and the challenges its cold and often rugged environment presents combine to produce the unique mix of beauty and fear that this aesthetic requires. Literary theorists from Margaret Atwood to Northrop Frye have written about the position that myths of the North have held in the Canadian imagination. From the 1920s, artists, such as Emily Carr and the Group of Seven, repudiated picturesque depictions of landscape to establish a national art "created in the spirit of northern lands" as Lawren Harris, one of the group's founders, said.

It has been said that Canadians have *endured* rather than *conquered* nature in their settlement of this country. South of the border, however, the opposite would be a better generalization of public opinion in the late nineteenth century: to American society, nature was to be conquered. Scholars suggest this different attitude resulted in a different evolution of the sublime. By the time settlement reached the Rockies, Americans were feeling uneasy that wilderness had vanished. In his celebrated "frontier thesis," Frederick Jackson Turner claimed in 1892 that American society had been animated by the "frontier" experience. On the frontier, Turner argued, Americans learned values of hard work and self-reliance. However, the disappearance of the vast tracts of "uninhabited" lands in the west spelled the inevitable end of the frontier.

In a recent thought-provoking essay, environmental historian William Cronon argues that Americans replaced the loss of a real wilderness with an imaginary one in which elemental nature ruled. The energizer of America became preserved in the sublime aesthetic. Landscape painters of this period produced stirring scenes of mountain scenery, the types of views photographer Ansel Adams later was to make iconic in his pictures of the Yosemite Valley. It is significant that the first American national parks were created in this period and that they preserve not the ordinary landscapes, but the spectacular. Yosemite, the Yellowstone Gorge, the Grand Canyon—these are the views Americans are told to value.

These examples show that the perception and appreciation (or rejection) of landscape is culturally constructed: we learn what to find aesthetically pleasing, awe-inspiring, or fearsome by taking our cues from others around us, or from literature, art, or any other cultural representation of our surroundings. As we will see in a later section, this construction can also be intentionally manipulated.

PLACE MAKING/PLACE MARKETING

Some social scientists believe that humans, like many other species, have an innate sense of territoriality. The concept of **territoriality** refers to the persistent attachment of individuals or peoples to a specific location or territory. This concept is important to geographers because it can be related to fundamental place-making forces. The specific study of people's sense of territoriality is part of the field of **ethology**, the scientific study of the formation and evolution of human customs and beliefs. The term is also used to refer to the study of the behaviour of animals in their natural environments. According to ethologists, humans carry genetic traits produced by our species' need for territory. Territory provides a source of physical safety and security, a source of stimulation (through border disputes), and a physical expression of identity. These needs add up to a strong territorial urge, which can be seen in the claims made by gangs to neighbourhood turf, for instance (**Figure 6.14**). Ethologists argue that the territorial urge can also be observed in cases where people become frustrated because of overcrowding. They become stressed and, in some circumstances, begin to exhibit aggressive or deviant behaviour. Crowding has been linked by ethologists and environmental psychologists to everything from vandalism and assault to promiscuity, listlessness, and clinical depression.

Although such claims are difficult to substantiate (as is the whole notion that humans have an inborn sense of territoriality), the idea of territoriality as a product of *culturally* established meanings is supported by a large body of scientific evidence. Some of this evidence comes from the field of **proxemics**, the study of the social and cultural meanings that people give to personal space. These

territoriality: the persistent attachment of individuals or peoples to a specific location or territory

ethology: the scientific study of the formation and evolution of human customs and beliefs

proxemics: the study of the social and cultural meanings that people give to personal space

Figure 6.14 Graffiti as territorial markers Graffiti are used by neighbourhood gangs to establish and proclaim their identity. Some graffiti also function as simple territorial markers that help to stake out turf in high-density environments where there exist few other clues about claims to territory.

meanings make for unwritten territorial rules (rather than a biological urge) that can be seen in the microgeography of people's behaviour. It has been established, for example, that people develop unwritten protocols about how to claim space. One common protocol is simply regular use (think of students always choosing the same seat in a classroom). Another is through the use of spatial markers such as a newspaper or a towel to reserve a space in a reading room or on a beach.

There are also bubbles, or areas, of personal space that we try not to invade (or allow to be invaded by others). Varying in size and shape according to location and circumstance, these bubbles tend to be smaller in public places and in busier and more crowded situations; they tend to be larger among strangers and in situations involving members of different social classes; and they tend to vary from one social class or cultural group to another.

At larger spatial scales, territoriality is mostly a product of forces that stem from political relations and cultural systems. This dimension of territoriality underpins a great deal of human geography. All social organizations and the individuals who belong to them are bound at some scale or another by formal or informal territorial limits. Many of them—nations, corporations, unions, clubs—actually claim a specific area of geographical space under their influence or control. In this context, territoriality can be defined as any attempt to assert control over a specific geographical area to achieve a degree of control over other people, resources, or relationships. Territoriality is also defined as any attempt to fulfill socially produced needs for identity, defence, and stimulation. Territoriality covers many different phenomena, from the property rights of individuals and private corporations to the neighbourhood covenants of homeowners' associations; the market areas of commercial businesses; the heartlands of ethnic or cultural groups; the jurisdictions

6.1 Geography in the Information Age

The ubiquitous use of cell phones is destabilizing some of our carefully ordered bubbles because a larger personal space is required to keep phone conversations private. Similarly, when we text in the presence of another person, we unilaterally introduce a third, "virtual" person to the shared personal space. Just like in the 1990s when we needed to learn about spatial privacy when entering PINs or passwords at ATMs or computers, we now have to develop new spatial protocols for "properly" using cell phones. These examples show how important the spatial dimension is to social interaction, even in the age of instant telecommunications across great distances. In fact, far from eliminating the importance of space, place, and distance, the new technologies actually present us with an entirely new set of challenges to the way we order space.

of local, provincial, and national governments; and the reach of transnational corporations and supranational organizations.

Territoriality thus provides a means of fulfilling three social and cultural needs:

- the regulation of social interaction
- the regulation of access to people and resources
- the provision of a focus and symbol of group membership and identity

Territoriality fulfills these needs because, among other things, it facilitates classification, communication, and enforcement. We can classify people and/or resources in terms of their location in space much more easily than we can classify them in relation to personal or social criteria. All that is necessary to communicate territory is a simple marker or sign that constitutes a boundary. This, in turn, makes territory an efficient device for determining whether people are subject to the enforcement of a particular set of rules and conditions: if they are inside the boundaries, they are; if they are outside, they are not.

Territoriality also gives tangible form to power and control but does so in a way that directs attention away from the personal relationships between the controlled and the controllers. In other words, rules and laws become associated with particular spaces and territories rather than with particular individuals or groups whose interests those rules serve. Finally, territoriality allows people to create and maintain a framework through which to experience the world and give it meaning. Bounded territories, for example, make it easier to differentiate "us" from "them."

Sense of Place

The bonds established between people and places through territoriality allow people to derive a pool of shared meanings from their lived experience of everyday routines. People become familiar with one another's vocabulary, speech patterns, gestures, humour, and so on. Often, this carries over into people's attitudes and feelings about themselves and their locality. When this happens, the result is a self-conscious sense of place. The concept of a **sense of place** refers to the feelings evoked among people as a result of the experiences, memories, and symbolism that they associate with a given place. It can also refer to the character of a place as seen by outsiders—its unique or distinctive physical characteristics or its inhabitants.

For *insiders,* this sense of place develops through shared dress codes, speech patterns, public comportment, and so on. It also develops through familiarity with the history and symbolism of particular elements of the physical environment, for example, the birthplace of someone notable, the location of a particularly well-known event, or the expression of community identity through community art. Sometimes, the sense of place is deliberately fostered by the construction of symbolic structures, such as monuments and statues. Often, it is the outcome of people's familiarity with one another and their surroundings. Because of this consequent sense of place, insiders feel at home and "in place."

For *outsiders,* such details add up to a sense of place only if these places are distinctive enough to evoke a significant common meaning for those with no direct experience of them. Consequently, visits to Niagara Falls, Toronto's CN Tower, Quebec City, or the Canadian Rockies can bring meaning to people who have no direct connection with them because these Canadian places have become familiar to them through television, films, and the promotional activities of the tourist industry. Manhattan, in New York City, is another setting that carries a strong sense of place to outsiders: many people feel a sense of familiarity with the skyline, busy streets, and distinctive commercial districts that together symbolize the heart of the American business world (**Figure 6.15**).

Think for a moment of your own "sense of place"—think about places that you are attached to and why they are special to you. Going to school, visiting places as a child, your first kiss, a major argument—all of these memories are indelibly associated in our minds with the places where they occurred. In this way, places become engrained with our memories and provide a way to concretize memory. It is because

sense of place: feelings evoked among people as a result of the experiences and memories that they associate with a place and the symbolism they attach to it

Figure 6.15 Manhattan's financial district This pre–September 11 image of the financial district, which was often portrayed in films and advertising, conveyed a sense of the confidence and authority of American corporate capitalism, as well as the role of the city as the world's financial centre. Since the destruction of the twin towers of the World Trade Center, this image now brings with it a series of other feelings, including patriotism and outrage.

we each have such unique and powerful associations with place that even the least imposing landscapes or locations are valued by someone. It is not the outward appearance, or objective value, that creates a sense of place, but our own personal engagement with such places. We can illustrate this easily enough from our own experience. How many of us have dutifully gone with a friend to see some place that was important to that friend and come away wondering what the fuss was about? As the proverb says, "Beauty (or, in this case, place) is in the eye of the beholder."

This insight is important because it reminds us that loss of place can also be traumatic. Consider, for example, the damming of the Columbia River in British Columbia, which led to the flooding of 14 communities in the late 1960s. The creation of the Hugh Keenleyside Dam, west of Castlegar, raised the level of the Arrow Lakes and forced the removal of more than 2,000 people living in the flooded part of the Columbia Valley (**Figure 6.16**). In total, 615 households and 269 small farmsteads and ranches were affected. At the hearings held to launch the project, many of those to be evicted complained about the loss of livelihood and the inadequate compensation proposed. Significantly, many spoke passionately also about the loss of their community, their home, and their place. One individual observed:

> It is not the financial loss that hurts. What hurts is that you are losing the land on which you had worked, where you know every bit of it, where you get accustomed to it, you know how to farm it. It is full of remembrances, of your failures and successes. It becomes a part of you.[6]

Imagine how much more traumatic the loss of place must be for the thousands of Cree displaced by the James Bay dam project who have few local alternatives to their traditional lifestyle!

Experience and Meaning

The interactions between people and places raise some fundamental questions about the meanings that people attach to their experiences: How do people process information from external settings? What kind of information do they use? How do new experiences affect the way they understand their worlds? What meanings do particular environments have for individuals? How do these meanings influence behaviour? Although there are no complete answers to these questions, it is clear that people not only filter information from their environments through

Figure 6.16 Keenleyside Dam, Castlegar, B.C. Part of an extensive flood control scheme begun in the 1960s to regulate the flow of the Columbia River, this dam flooded large parts of the Arrow Lakes Valley in the southeast interior of British Columbia.

---

[6] Quoted in J. Douglas Porteous and Sandra E. Smith, *Domicide: The Global Destruction of Home.* Montreal and Kingston: McGill-Queen's University Press, 2001, p. 171.

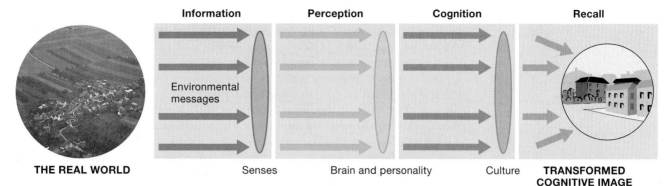

| Information | Perception | Cognition | Recall |

THE REAL WORLD   Senses   Brain and personality   Culture   **TRANSFORMED COGNITIVE IMAGE**

Environmental messages

neurophysiological processes but also draw on personality and culture to produce cognitive images of their environment, pictures or representations of the world that can be called to mind through the imagination (**Figure 6.17**). Cognitive images are what people see in the mind's eye when they think of a particular place or setting.

Two of the most important attributes of cognitive images are that they both simplify and distort real-world environments. Research on the ways in which people simplify the world through such means has suggested, for example, that many people tend to organize their cognitive images of particular parts of their world in terms of several simple elements (**Figure 6.18**):

Paths: the channels along which they and others move (for example, streets, walkways, transit lines, canals)

Edges: barriers that separate one area from another (for example, shorelines, walls, railroad tracks)

Districts: areas with an identifiable character (physical and/or cultural) that people mentally "enter" and "leave" (for example, a business district, an ethnic neighbourhood)

Nodes: strategic points and foci for travel (for example, street corners, traffic intersections, city squares)

Landmarks: physical reference points (for example, distinctive landforms, buildings, monuments)

Figure 6.17 The formation of cognitive images People form cognitive images as a product of information about the real world experienced directly and indirectly and filtered through their senses, their brain, their personality, and the attitudes and values they have acquired from their cultural background.   (*Source:* R.G. Golledge and R.J. Stimpson, *Analytical Behaviour Geography.* Beckenham: Croom Helm, 1987, fig. 3.2, p. 3.)

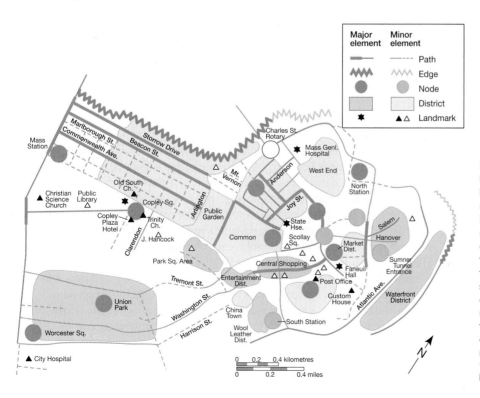

Figure 6.18 Cognitive image of Boston This map was compiled by Kevin Lynch, one of the pioneer researchers into cognitive images, from interviews with a sample of Boston residents. Lynch found that the residents of Boston used similar elements to structure their cognitive images of the city. He produced ingenious maps, such as this one, to demonstrate the collective "mental map" of the city, using symbols of different boldness to indicate the proportion of respondents who had mentioned each element. (*Source:* K. Lynch, *The Image of the City.* Cambridge, MA: M.I.T. Press, 1960, p. 146.)

For many people, individual landscape features may function as more than one kind of cognitive element. A highway, for example, may be perceived as both an edge and a path in a person's cognitive image of a city. Similarly, a train station may be seen as both a landmark and a node.

Distortions in people's cognitive images are partly the result of incomplete information. Once we go beyond our immediate living area, there are few spaces that any of us know in complete detail. Yet, our worlds—especially for those of us in the fast world who are directly tied to global networks of communication and knowledge—are increasingly large in geographical scope. As a result, these worlds must be conceived, or cognized, without many direct stimuli. We have to rely on fragmentary and often biased information from other people and from books, magazines, television, and the Internet. Distortions in cognitive images are also partly the result of our own biases. What we remember about places, what we like or dislike, what we think is significant, and what we impute to various aspects of our environments all are a function of our own personalities, our experiences, and the cultural influences to which we have been exposed.

Images and Behaviour

Cognitive images are compiled, in part, through behavioural patterns. Environments are "learned" through experience. Meanwhile, cognitive images, once generated, influence behaviour. In the process of these two-way relationships, cognitive images are constantly changing. Each of us also generates, and draws on, different kinds of cognitive images in different circumstances.

Such elements as districts, nodes, and landmarks are important in the kinds of cognitive images that people use to orient themselves and to navigate within a place or region. The more of these elements an environment contains—and the more distinctive they are—the more legible that environment is to people and the easier it is to get oriented and navigate. In addition, the more first-hand information people have about their environment and the more they are able to draw on secondary sources of information, the more detailed and comprehensive their images will be. By contrast, the narrower and more localized people's images are, the less they will tend to venture beyond their home area: their behaviour becomes circumscribed by their cognitive imagery in a kind of self-fulfilling prophecy.

People's images of places are also important in shaping particular aspects of their behaviour. Research on shopping behaviour in cities, for example, has shown that customers do not necessarily go to the nearest store or the one with the lowest prices: they also are influenced by the configuration of traffic, parking, and pedestrian circulation. Even more important, shopping behaviour, like many other aspects of behaviour, is influenced by people's values and feelings. One of the strongest influences on shopping patterns relates to the imagery evoked by retail environments. As we will see in a later section, the significance of this has clearly not been lost on the developers of shopping malls, who spend large sums of money to establish the right atmosphere and image for their projects.

Shopping behaviour is one narrow example of the influence of place imagery on behaviour that we can all relate to, but other examples can be drawn from virtually every aspect of human geography, and at every spatial scale. One such example is the way that people respond to environmental hazards, such as floods, droughts, earthquakes, storms, and landslides, and come to terms with the associated risks and uncertainties. Some people tend to change the unpredictable into the knowable by imposing order where none really exists (resorting to folk wisdom about weather, for example), while others deny all predictability and take a fatalistic view. As a result, some people tend to underestimate the risk involved in living in an area prone to natural hazards, whereas others tend to overestimate the risk.

Finally, one aspect of cognitive imagery is of special importance in modifying people's behaviour, namely, the sentimental and symbolic attributes ascribed to places. Through their daily lives and through the cumulative effects of cultural influences and significant personal events, people build up affective bonds with places. They do this simultaneously at different geographical scales: from the home, to the neighbourhood and locality, to the national country.

The tendency for people to do this has been called *topophilia*. **Topophilia** literally means "love of place" and is a term often associated with the work of Yi-Fu Tuan, the geographer who pioneered work on this idea. Geographers use it to describe the complex of emotions and meanings associated with particular places that, for one reason or another, have become significant to individuals. The result is that most people have a home area, hometown, or home region for which they have a special attachment or sense of identity and belonging.

Over the past 20 years, however, people and "their" places have been confronted with change on an unprecedented scale and at an extraordinary rate. As we saw in Chapter 2, globalization has generated a world within which commonalities among places are intensifying. The more that places change, the more they seem to look alike, the less they are able to retain a distinctive sense of place, and the less they are able to sustain public social life. Trying to both stem and profit from this homogenization, developers have created theme parks, shopping malls, and festival marketplaces; renovated historic districts; and designed neotraditional villages and neighbourhoods that are supposed to bring back that feeling of uniqueness. But the more developers have competed to provide distinctive settings and the larger and more spectacular their projects have become, the more convergent the results. The inevitable outcome is that the "authenticity" of places is undermined. City spaces, in particular, become inauthentic and "placeless." As a result, the experience of spectacular and distinctive places, physical settings, and landscapes has become an important element of consumer culture that is marketed to us with increasing intensity—like the Beijing residential developments described in the opening paragraphs of this chapter.

topophilia: the emotions and meanings associated with particular places that have become significant to individuals

Place Marketing

Economic and cultural globalization has meant that places and regions throughout the world are increasingly seeking to influence the ways in which they are perceived by tourists, businesses, media firms, and consumers. As a result, places are increasingly being reinterpreted, re-imagined, designed, packaged, and marketed (see **Geography Matters 6.1—Place Marketing: Niagara Falls, Ontario**). Through place marketing, sense of place has become a valuable commodity, and culture has become an important economic activity in itself. Furthermore, culture has become a significant factor in the ability of places to attract and retain other kinds of economic activity. Seeking to be competitive within the globalizing economy, many places have sponsored extensive makeovers of themselves, including the creation of pedestrian plazas, cosmopolitan cultural facilities, festivals, and sports and media events. Meanwhile, the question of who does the re-imagining and cultural packaging, and on whose terms, can become an important issue for local politics.

6.2   Geography in the Information Age

A "branded" Internet presence now is an absolute must for places trying to promote themselves in the global marketplace for tourism and commerce. At the same time, the Internet is also an unprecedented "truth tool," as it enables individuals to post their own assessments and recommendations of which places to visit and which to avoid. With information practically limitless, free of charge, and immediately available, the challenge is no longer how to obtain information but how to determine whether it is reliable and trustworthy. In addition, because there is an increasing amount of outdated information that has simply been "abandoned" on web pages that are no longer actively maintained, more timely information is increasingly drowned out.

Place Marketing: Niagara Falls, Ontario

A fascinating example of place marketing is Niagara Falls, Ontario, because as a place it has been marketed in a number of very different ways over the years.[7] Tourism at Niagara began as early as the 1820s, and as a suitably sublime landscape, the Falls were the main attraction (**Figure 6.1.1**). As one scholar has observed, Niagara was the most-often painted subject in early North American art. There quickly developed, however, additional attractions, such as museums of curiosities and billiard rooms. The boat *Maid of the Mist* (named after a fake legend of Aboriginal sacrifice) began its trips to the base of the Falls as early as the 1840s. In 1859, the great Blondin crossed over them on a tightrope. Many people have gone over them in a barrel. Famous for being famous, Niagara was on every visiting celebrity's itinerary. In short, Niagara was spectacle as well as spectacular.

By the 1930s, the Falls' reputation as a tourist destination, its proximity to large centres of population, and its image as an icon of sublime beauty all combined to turn Niagara into a major destination for honeymooners. Its scenic attractions had even been further enhanced by the addition of a landscaped park, designed by Frederick Law Olmsted, around the top of the Falls.

After the hiatus of the Second World War, Niagara's tourist business developed into a multi-million-dollar business, with up to 13 million visitors a year in the 1950s. The 1953 film *Niagara* about a honeymoon (in which, according to the press releases of the time, both the Falls and Marilyn Monroe starred) confirmed the Falls' connection with honeymooners in the public's mind. Niagara's position as the honeymoon capital of North America was seemingly secure.

But by the end of the 1960s, the boom was over. In 1967, the year of Montreal's Expo 67, Niagara motel owners experienced a 50 percent drop in business, a drop from which they never recovered. A 1968 survey revealed that only 3 percent of visitors were honeymooners. Niagara's old image had largely disappeared from popular culture, to be replaced by one it tried not to promote. According to Karen Dubinsky, to many observers at the time, Niagara Falls was in danger of becoming tawdry and cheap, a capital of kitsch that everyone denied visiting.

Yet, by the end of the twentieth century, Niagara reinvented itself yet again. Its renaissance, this time, was owed to the opening of Casino Niagara in Niagara Falls, which in 1997, its first year of operation, attracted 10 million visitors. However, the prospect that gambling will result in a substantial and long-term revival of tourism in the region seems unlikely on the basis of some preliminary research that suggests gamblers spend little money outside the immediate area of the casino. Nevertheless, a second, even larger casino complex opened in 2004, confirming Karen Dubinsky's conclusion that "it certainly looks as though the next version of Niagara Falls will owe more to Las Vegas than to Disneyland."[8]

Figure 6.1.1 Niagara Falls For 200 years, Niagara has been a tourist attraction. However, the nature of the attraction has changed several times. As a place, Niagara has marketed itself in different ways—from honeymoon destination to casino venue.

---

[7] The paragraphs on Niagara are based on Karen Dubinsky, *The Second Greatest Disappointment: Honeymooning and Tourism at Niagara Falls*. Toronto: Between the Lines, 1999.

[8] Ibid., p. 245.

Central to place marketing is the deliberate manipulation of material and visual culture in an effort to enhance the appeal of places to key groups. These groups include the upper-level management of large corporations, the higher-skilled and better-educated personnel sought by expanding high-technology industries, wealthy tourists, and the organizers of business and professional conferences and other income-generating events. In part, this manipulation of culture depends on promoting traditions, lifestyles, and arts that are locally rooted; in part, it depends on being able to tap into globalizing culture through new cultural amenities and specially organized events and exhibitions with global draw. Some of the most widely adopted strategies for the manipulation and exploitation of culture include funding for facilities for the arts, investment in public spaces, the re-creation and refurbishment of distinctive settings, such as waterfronts and historic districts, the expansion and improvement of museums (especially with blockbuster exhibitions of spectacular cultural products that attract large crowds and can be marketed with commercial tie-ins), and the designation of historic landmarks.

Examples of the re-creation and refurbishment of distinctive settings, such as waterfronts, can be found in many cities. Examples include the development of Vancouver's Expo site, Toronto's Queen's Quay, and the redevelopment of Halifax's waterfront (which includes tourist attractions, such as the Historic Properties, the Maritime Museum of the Atlantic, and Pier 21, the museum of immigration) (**Figure 6.19**). Examples of the re-creation and refurbishment of historic districts are even more widespread—so widespread, in fact, that they have become a mainstay of the heritage industry. This industry, based on the commercial exploitation of the histories of peoples and places, is now worldwide, as evidenced by the involvement of the United Nations Educational, Scientific, and Cultural Organization (UNESCO) in identifying places for inclusion on world heritage lists. Quebec City, one of Canada's leading heritage attractions (**Figure 6.20**) has joined such places as Jerusalem and Old Havana as a site recognized as culturally and historically significant by UNESCO.

In countries with a high density of historic districts and settings, place marketing relies heavily on the heritage industry. For instance, in the United Kingdom, there are 373,000 buildings of historical interest, almost 20,000 monuments, 1,500 parks and gardens, and 17 world heritage sites. Every year, more than 200 million tourists visit designated heritage sites in the United Kingdom, spending about $50 billion on entry fees, retail sales, travel, and accommodations.

Figure 6.19 Halifax Waterfront

Figure 6.20 Quebec City
One of Canada's leading heritage attractions, Quebec City is on UNESCO's list of world heritage sites.

It is difficult to calculate the so-called "economic multiplier" effects of heritage tourism. There is no doubt that some of the benefits of heritage tourism "trickle down" through a region's economy, but not all spending will. Hotel stays, for example, may benefit the corporation that owns the hotel rather than the locality. Moreover, hotel workers themselves are (on average) less well paid than many workers outside the tourism industry, which means that they have less money to spend locally than a workforce that depends on, for example, automotive manufacturing or IT development. It is for such reasons that tourism is not always an easy or viable alternative when factories close and their rusting shells are recycled as industrial heritage sites.

One important aspect of the influence of the heritage industry on spaces, places, and landscapes is the tendency for historic districts and settings to be re-created, imitated, simulated, and even reinvented according to commercial considerations rather than principles of preservation or conservation. As a result, contemporary landscapes contain increasing numbers of inauthentic settings: places that are as much the product of contemporary material and visual culture as they are of any cultural heritage (**Figure 6.21**).

Figure 6.21 Las Vegas The boundaries between the heritage industry and the leisure and entertainment industries have become increasingly blurred, with the result that a great deal of investment has been channelled toward the creation of inauthentic "historic" settings whose characteristics owe as much to movies and popular stereotypes as to historic realities. Shown here is the Venetian Hotel in Las Vegas.

Figure 6.22 Kimberley, B.C. This community in the interior of British Columbia has adopted a (Disneyfied) Austrian style of architecture to celebrate its mountain location.

In Canada, a number of towns have "borrowed" another cultural heritage to heighten tourist appeal. The Okanagan valley community of Osoyoos in British Columbia has adopted Spanish-American architecture to advertise its unusually warm microclimate. Kimberley, also in British Columbia, has emphasized its mountain location by developing an "Austrian"-style town square, or *Platz* (**Figure 6.22**).

The intriguing example of Shelburne, Nova Scotia, suggests that we now even value the replica over the real! Settled in 1783, the town still has a considerable number of genuine vernacular buildings of that period. Partly on the strength of this, in 1994, Shelburne was chosen to be the location for the film *The Scarlet Letter*, set in seventeenth-century New England. To fully re-create the appearance of such a place, the filmmakers built a number of additional structures in the style of the period. These buildings were so "authentic" that when shooting was over, the town petitioned the movie company to leave them standing. These replica buildings are now advertised on the town's website as an "authentic" tourist attraction: "Why not tour part of the remaining set and experience an authentic historic market square? You can pick up a self-guided tour brochure at the tourist bureau or, for a small fee, participate in a guided tour replete with a myriad of fascinating details."[9]

Less specific than place marketing, but just as evocative, is the ability to market an entire region using some of the many components of the cultural region (see Chapter 5) as selling points. The ability of music, for example, to conjure up an image of a country or region in our minds is well known. In recent years, Cape Breton—settled by Highland Scots in the late eighteenth and early nineteenth centuries—has been so successful in promoting the Cape Breton fiddle and old-style piping that it has become internationally recognized as an important homeland for Celtic music. Celtic music and its associated cultural and tourist activities have become a major resource and leading employer on the island, according to a University College of Cape Breton report.

Finally, we must also mention the redevelopment of industrial heritage areas into postindustrial business and "lifestyle" areas. The most prominent example is the London Docklands, whose remaking in the 1980s was a deliberate attempt by then prime minister Margaret Thatcher not simply to market this part of London to global investors and tourists but to create a symbol of the United

---

[9] "Historic Shelburne: Where Canada's History Comes Alive!" (**www.historicshelburne.com**).

Figure 6.23 London Docklands
(a) Before the advent of deep draft container vessels, ocean-going ships were able to steam up the Thames to the port facilities right in the heart of London. In the London dockyards, more than 30,000 labourers loaded and unloaded the ships, making the Docklands the commercial heart of the British Empire. In the late 1960s, specialized ports using new container technologies made the Docklands obsolete. In 1981, the London Docklands Development Corp. was created by the central government and given extensive powers to redevelop the derelict dock areas. (b) Prior to the gigantic Chinese urban redevelopment projects of recent years (for example, for the 2008 Beijing Olympics), the Docklands were the largest urban redevelopment scheme in the world, with millions of square feet of office and retail space and substantial amounts of new housing. The photo shows the office complex of Canary Wharf, a development largely begun by the Canadian Reichmann family.

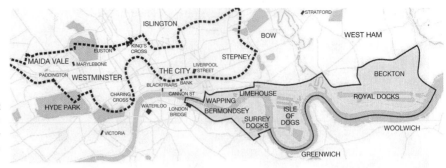

Kingdom as a rejuvenated, postindustrial economy (**Figure 6.23**). Purpose-built high-rise office complexes created an alternative to the crowded financial district of the "City" in central London, while many of the old warehouses were converted into high-priced condominium lofts for commute-free living.

CODED SPACES

As we discussed in an earlier section of this chapter, landscapes are embedded with meaning, which can be interpreted differently by different people and groups. To interpret or read our environment, however, we need to understand the language in which it is written. We must learn how to recognize the signs and symbols that go into the making of landscape. The practice of writing and reading signs is known as **semiotics**.

semiotics: the practice of writing and reading signs

Semiotics in the Landscape

Semiotics assumes that innumerable signs are embedded or displayed in landscape, space, and place, sending messages about identity, values, beliefs, and practices. The signs that are constructed may have different meanings for those who produce them and those who read, or interpret, them. Some signs are so subtle as to be recognizable only when pointed out by a knowledgeable observer; others may be more readily available and more ubiquitous in their spatial range. For example, semiotics enables us to recognize that university students, simply by the way they dress, send messages to one another and the wider world about who they are and what they value. For some of us, certain types, such as jocks, preps, emos, gamers, hipsters, or tree-huggers, are readily identifiable by their clothes, hairstyle, or footwear; by the bags they carry; or even by the food they eat. Semiotics, however, is not only about the concrete signs that people convey with their bodies or their behaviours. Messages are also deployed through the landscape and embedded in places and spaces. In this section, we will consider two examples of coded spaces to show the importance of this concept: the shopping mall and the city plan.

The Shopping Mall as Coded Space   Consider the very familiar landscape of the shopping mall. Although there is certainly a science to the size, scale, and marketing of a mall based on demographic research as well as environmental and architectural analysis, more exists to a mall than these concrete features. The placement and mix of stores and their interior design, the arrangement of products within stores, the amenities offered to shoppers, and the ambient music all combine to send signals to the consumer about style, taste, and self-image (**Figure 6.24**). Called by some "palaces of consumption," malls are complex semiotic sites, directing important signals not only about what to buy but also about who should shop there and who should not.

   To fully appreciate the role shopping malls play in the Canadian economy, consider the following statistics: there are almost 5,000 shopping centres in Canada, which together account for almost half of all non-automotive retail sales. They employ more than 1.2 million people, representing almost 10 percent of Canada's non-agricultural work force. Ninety-two percent of Canadians visit a mall at least once a month, with the average being 2.25 visits per month.[10] Evidently, shopping is an integral part of Canadian life. Yet, as much as we seem to enjoy shopping, there persists for a great many of us an explicit disdain for shopping and the commercialism and materialism that accompany it. Thus,

Figure 6.24   Place Canada Trust mall in downtown Montreal   Developers of shopping malls know that consumer behaviour is heavily conditioned by the spatial organization and physical appearance of retail settings. As a result, they find it worthwhile to spend large sums creating what they consider to be the appropriate atmosphere for their projects.

---

[10] International Council of Shopping Centres (**icsc.org**).

shopping is a complicated activity that is full of ambivalence. It is not surprising, therefore, that developers have promoted shopping as a kind of tourism. The mall is a "pseudoplace" meant to encourage one sort of activity—shopping—by projecting the illusion that something else besides shopping (and spending money) is actually going on. Because of their important and complex function, malls are places with rich semiotic systems expressed through style, themes, and fantasy. Malls are designed to convey different messages to particular subsets of the population, such as the very wealthy or teenagers. Most malls therefore possess a kind of sociocultural geology, where the lowest level of the mall is a landscape with lower-middle-class semiotics, whereas the more elaborate and pricey upper levels are a landscape more consistent with affluence.

However complex the messages that malls send, one message is consistent across class, gender, age, ethnicity, and other cultural boundaries: consumption is a predominant aspect of globalization. Indeed, malls are the early twenty-first century's spaces of consumption, where just about every aspect of our lives has become a commodity. Consumption—or shopping—defines who we are more than ever before, and what we consume sends signals about who we want to be. Advertising and the mass media tell us what to consume, equating ownership of products with happiness, a good sex life, social standing, and success in general. Within the space of the mall, these signals are collected and re-sent. The architecture and design of the mall are an important part of the semiotic system shaping our choices and moulding our preferences. As architectural historian Margaret Crawford writes:

> All the familiar tricks of mall design—limited entrances, escalators placed only at the end of corridors, fountains and benches carefully positioned to entice shoppers into stores—control the flow of consumers through the numbingly repetitive corridors of shops. The orderly rows of goods along endless aisles continuously stimulates the desire to buy. At the same time, other architectural tricks seem to contradict commercial consideration. Dramatic atriums create huge floating spaces for contemplation, multiple levels provide infinite vistas from a variety of vantage points, and reflective surfaces bring near and far together. In the absence of sounds from the outside, these artful visual effects are complemented by the "white noise" of MUZAK and fountains echoing across enormous open courts.[11]

Some of the "tricks" that "seem to contradict commercial consideration" are those of place making. They are needed because we are reluctant to consider malls as real "places" (in Yi-Fu Tuan's sense of "places" as "space filled with meaning"). Rather, we tend to see malls as bland, or mundane, spaces of "placelessness" (to use Toronto geographer Edward Relph's useful term). They are commercial spaces of franchises and chains that could be anywhere. For malls to succeed commercially, we must be persuaded that these drab collections of concrete are not the "machines for consumption" they really are. Only then are we comfortable enough to think about what we might buy there.

Jon Goss has written that to conceal the contradiction in our society between conspicuous consumption and contempt for consumerism, a mall needs us to disconnect from the reality of shopping. We do not want to know about the true circumstances in which the objects we buy were made or distributed, for to do so will diminish the object's value in our eyes, and our own value as discriminating purchasers in the eyes of other people. Malls must therefore mystify the true connection between the ideals and reality of consumption—a "trick" that many successful malls perform by creating a "sense of place."[12] Consequently, malls provide an excellent opportunity to see "place making" at work.

---

[11] M. Crawford, "The World in a Shopping Mall." In M. Sorkin (ed.), *Variations on a Theme Park*. New York: Noonday Press, 1992, p. 14.

[12] Jon Goss, "The Magic of the Mall: An Analysis of Form, Function, and Meaning in the Contemporary Retail Built Environment," *Annals of the Association of American Geographers* 83, 1993, pp. 18–47. The quotations that follow are on pp. 19, 27, 22, 33, and 31.

What, according to geographers, should we be looking for next time we go to the mall? Goss argues that malls create a sense of place by creating allusions to the following:

- *The traditional "main street" of small-town North America.* This entails not only design references (such as the use of cobblestones, awnings, lamp posts, and street signs) but also the creation of a feeling of public space in the mall (such as a bandstand, park benches, or a speakers' corner).

- *Carnivals or open-air markets.* Malls achieve this illusion of more friendly exchange through the use of market handcarts, sidewalk sales, street artists and travelling performers, "quayside" scenes, and even carousels. The sense of fun this conveys is part of the fantasy of consuming, and is seen to its logical excess in the West Edmonton Mall and in Las Vegas.

- *Nature.* To increase people's comfort levels and to disguise the mall's links to consumption, references to nature are made through the use of plants, artificial lighting, mirrors, and fountains (see Figure 6.24 on p. 277).

In a detailed study of the West Edmonton Mall, Jeff Hopkins shows us how to read some of the semiotics embedded in the retail landscape.[13] The stores create in us a sense of place through the following:

- *Their simple allusion to place names.* So, one part of the West Edmonton Mall is called "Bourbon Street." The name alone makes the link with any associations we may have of the real city of New Orleans.

- *Their general allusion to a distant time period*—such as the 1920s—or general type of place—such as "the Wild West"—through statues, other decorative details, or music.

- *The replication of a specific place*—the West Edmonton Mall's "Fantasyland" makes direct reference to Disneyland. Again, this is achieved through architecture and design, colour, lighting, statues, and so on.

By 2011, this mega-mall just outside Edmonton, Alberta, consisted of more than 800 stores, 100 restaurants, two hotels, and numerous recreational facilities (including a wave pool, dolphin lagoon, and ice rink), and the world's largest parking lot. Every year, more than 30 million visitors find their way to the mall.[14] Obviously, much more than shopping is going on in this mall. Fortunately or unfortunately, the majority of Canadian malls do not rise to the excesses of the West Edmonton Mall and do not aspire to be tourist destinations. Nevertheless, for many of us, even the most lacklustre mall is still a place to hang out.

Depending on our perspective, however, we can each interpret the landscape quite differently, and the mall is no exception in this regard. Not surprisingly, the homeless will be less concerned with how a mall creates a sense of place than with how it can provide warmth and shelter. It would be a mistake, however, to interpret the park benches and open spaces of the mall as an indication of public space in which one can remain. Malls are private space, and security personnel will soon appear to move those people who misinterpret the signals.

In fact, ambiguities about public and private space are deliberately fostered by malls to make us feel at home when we make our purchases. These ambiguities have been strengthened by the recent development in Canada of covered, combined retail and pedestrian spaces, such as the skywalks of Halifax and Calgary and the "underground cities" of Montreal and Toronto (**Figure 6.25**).

---

[13] Jeffrey S.P. Hopkins, "West Edmonton Mall: Landscape of Myths and Elsewhereness," *Canadian Geographer* 34, 1990, pp. 2–17.

[14] The West Edmonton Mall has a very useful website, at which maps, photos, and information about the mall can be found (**www.wem.ca**).

Figure 6.25 Toronto's underground city
Underground tunnels and shops are becoming frequent features of such Canadian cities as Toronto, as this diagram shows. They are not only creating new retail opportunities but new forms of urban spaces as well. (*Source:* City of Toronto Economic Development—Small Business & Local Partnerships Office.)

Officially called the "PATH: Downtown Walkway," Toronto's underground city in 2011 comprised 28 kilometres of tunnels beneath the city core, lined with over 1,200 stores and services and frequented by over 100,000 pedestrians a day. Five thousand people now work in this underground city, which started with a single tunnel as early as 1900. Montreal's underground city is even more extensive, with more than 30 kilometres of tunnels comprising over 1,700 shops and services. Both, linked to underground transit systems via a number of stations, have considerable hinterlands, drawing on distant residential districts or nearby office towers. Designed to enable pedestrians to avoid the demands of the Canadian winter and summer, both networks are creating a new environment in which some people never get outdoors. Outside, meanwhile, streets become lifeless—a challenge for retailers and planners alike.

These forms of retailing present growing difficulties over the use of public and private space. For example, although the tunnels of the Toronto underground city seem to be a continuous public space, they actually are a mosaic of 35 private spaces that are individually owned and controlled. The retailers' desire to attract customers by creating the illusion of a public space is an invitation contradicted by the store owners' rights of exclusion. The tunnels are private property and, as such, are covered by the rights of private property owners against trespass (legislation which, in Ontario, for example, enables owners to evict "undesirables," such as skateboarders or street people). On the other hand, recent legal decisions have shown that public right can be extended to such private spaces. This is because, in Canadian law, a public space need not be public property, and even in underground cities, individuals have constitutionally guaranteed freedoms of expression and peaceful assembly. In such clearly contested terrain, it is not surprising that the signals the landscape gives are ambiguous and depend heavily on our intentions and who we are.

Malls, condominium developments, neighbourhoods, university campuses, and any number of other possible geographical sites possess codes of meaning. By linking these sites with the forces behind globalization, it is possible to interpret them and understand the implicit messages they contain. And it is certainly not necessary to restrict our focus to sites in the core.

The City Plan as Coded Space Consider Brasilia, the capital city of Brazil. As early as independence from Portugal in 1822, Brazilian politicians began suggesting that a new capital be established on the central plateau in the undeveloped interior of the country, but the seat of government was not officially transferred to the new capital of Brasilia until 1960. A symbol of the taming of the wild interior of the country and the conquest of nature through human ingenuity, Brasilia is also a many-layered system of signs conveying multiple and frequently contradictory messages. Interestingly, Brasilia, intended to symbolize a new age in Brazilian history, was also literally an attempt to construct one. That is why its plan and its architecture are so self-consciously rich with messages meant to transform Brazilian society through a new and radical form of architecture. To launch both the idea and the reality of a "city in the wilderness," the Brazilian government sponsored an international design contest hoping to encourage the development of a new vision for the new capital (and by extension a new society). The winner of the contest was engineer Lucio Costa. His original plan was a simple sketch of three essential elements: a cross created by the intersection of two highway axes, an equilateral triangle superimposed on this cross that defined the geographical area of the city, and two terraced embankments and a platform. By using a cross to designate the location and orientation of Brasilia, Costa was suggesting a holy origin for Brasilia, the new city in the wilderness.

In a semiotic reading of Costa's plan for the city, the sign of the Christian cross suggests that Brasilia was to be built on a sacred site, an important endorsement for the founding of a new capital. Second, the sign of the cross also makes an important semiotic connection to two ideal types found in ancient civilizations, as anthropologist John Holston writes:

> The first is considered one of the earliest pictorial representations of the idea of city: the Egyptian hieroglyph of the cross within the circle, itself an iconic sign standing for "city." . . . The second is the diagram of the templum of ancient Roman augury, a circle quartered by the crossing of two axes. It represents a space in the sky or on earth marked out . . . for the purpose of taking auspices. Hence it signifies a consecrated place, such as a sanctuary, asylum, shrine, or temple.[15]

Many other observers of the plan have said that it resembles an airplane (**Figure 6.26**). The plan shows that the residential districts were to be located along the wings and administrative government offices on the part corresponding with the fuselage. The commercial district was to be constructed at the intersection of the wings and the fuselage, with a cathedral and museum along the monumental axis. Like the sign of the cross, the significance of an airplane

Figure 6.26 Aerial view of Brasilia This aerial view of Brasilia clearly shows the symmetrical plan of the city, resembling an airplane.

---

[15] J. Holston, *The Modernist City: An Anthropological Critique of Brasilia.* Chicago: University of Chicago Press, 1989, p. 71.

Figure 6.27 Palacio de Alvorada, Brasilia The official residence of the president of Brazil combines the homogenized international style of modernist "glass-box" architecture with culturally distinctive artistic elements, such as the sweeping colonnades pictured here.

is obvious. Politicians and planners envisioned Brasilia as both the engine and the symbol of the rapid modernization of the country. The image of an airplane in flight was an exciting, soaring, uplifting, and speedy means of achieving modernization.

All of Brasilia's major public buildings were designed by the internationally famous Brazilian architect Oscar Niemeyer. The residential axes were designed with clusters of apartment buildings, each cluster surrounding a set of recreational facilities, school buildings, and shopping areas. The University of Brasilia was also part of the early vision of the city, as was the creation of a lake and the official home of the president of the country, the Palacio de Alvorada, or the Palace of Dawn (**Figure 6.27**).

The architecture of Brasilia, like that of other capitals, contains both subtle and more explicit messages about the society that conceived them. The exclusively modernist architectural style of Brasilia (as opposed to the neo-classical style of Washington, DC, for example) was intended to convey the modernist utopian ideal of technological progress and an egalitarian society: Niemeyer's architectural designs were conceived to *transform* colonial Brazilian society by projecting modernism and innovation through bold new urban images. This egalitarianism was never achieved, though, and the city itself embodies the tension between ideal and reality: the migrant workers who came to construct the city and live out their own dreams there have been relegated to ever-growing *favelas* (or squatter settlements) surrounding the city. Thus, although the original plan and architecture were intended to send a message about the aspirations of the new Brazil, the contemporary structure of the city contradicts those dreams with the harsh realities of poverty and inequality. The lesson to be learned is that not all the signs in a given place are consistent, even when planners and designers have complete control over their projects: social and political realities can disrupt the plan and insert very different messages, and readers do not always interpret signs in ways the creators intended (**Figure 6.28**).

The examples of the shopping mall and the city of Brasilia illustrate how we can read or decode landscapes by interpreting the signs and symbols they project within specific settings. In the next section, we look at the broader context of the intellectual, economic, and political dimensions of society that influence the ways in which people think about themselves and about the places they inhabit.

Figure 6.28 The landscape of Brasilia Just like other purpose-designed new capital cities (e.g., Astana in Kazakhstan, Yamoussoukro in Ivory Coast, or Abuja in Nigeria) Brasilia is designed to make a statement about the country it represents: dynamic, modern, grand. Aesthetic beauty (in the modernist style), a sense of permanence, and the expression of power are among the primary messages of these designed landscapes. Note, however, how these messages can be undermined by everyday users superimposing their own patterns of use. In this photograph, the many lighter-coloured footpaths reveal the presence of poorer, non-motorized citizens carving their own informal transportation routes into the official, car-dominated landscape.

POSTMODERN SPACES

Since the 1980s, many commentators on cultural change have noted a broad shift in cultural sensibilities that seems to have permeated every sphere of creative activity, including art, architecture, advertising, philosophy, clothing design, interior design, music, cinema, literature, television, and urban design. This shift, broadly characterized as a shift from modernism to postmodernism, has involved both avant-garde and popular culture. It seems to have originated in parts of the world's core countries and is currently spreading throughout the rest of the world. The shift to postmodern cultural sensibilities is of particular importance to cultural geography because of the ways in which changed attitudes and values have begun to influence place making and the creation of landscapes.

Modernism and Postmodernism

Throughout the world, the philosophy of modernism has been one of the major influences on the interdependencies between culture, society, space, place, and landscape for the last century. **Modernism** is a forward-looking view of the world that emphasizes reason, scientific rationality, creativity, novelty, and progress. Its origins can be traced to the European Renaissance and the emergence of the world-system of competitive capitalism in the sixteenth century, when scientific discovery and commerce began to displace sociocultural views of the world that were backward-looking—views that emphasized mysticism, romanticism, and fatalism. These origins were consolidated into a philosophical movement during the eighteenth century, when the so-called Enlightenment established the widespread belief in universal human progress and the sovereignty of scientific reasoning.

At the beginning of the twentieth century, this philosophy developed into a more widespread intellectual movement. Around the turn of the twentieth century, there occurred a series of sweeping technological and scientific changes that not only triggered a new round of spatial reorganization (see Chapter 2) but also transformed the underpinnings of social and cultural life. These changes included the telegraph, the telephone, the x-ray, cinema, radio, the bicycle, the internal combustion engine, the airplane, the skyscraper, relativity theory, and psychoanalysis. Universal human progress suddenly seemed to be a much more realistic prospect.

Nevertheless, the pace of economic, social, cultural, and geographical changes was unnerving, and the outcomes uncertain. The intellectual response, developed among a cultural avant-garde of painters, architects, novelists, and photographers, was a resolve to promote modernism through radical changes in culture. These ideas were first set out in the "Futurist Manifesto," published in 1909 by the Italian poet Filippo Marinetti. Gradually, the combination of new technologies and radical design contributed to the proliferation of landscapes of modernism. In a general sense almost all of the place making and landscapes of the early and mid-twentieth century are the products of modernism, with the most striking being modernist urban landscapes (**Figure 6.29**).

Throughout most of the twentieth century, a confident and forward-looking modernist philosophy remained virtually unquestioned, with the result that places and regions everywhere were heavily shaped by people acting out their notions of rational behaviour and progress. Rural regions, for example, bore the imprint of agricultural modernization. The hedgerows of traditional European field patterns were torn up to make way for landscapes of large, featureless fields in which heavy machinery could operate more efficiently (**Figure 6.30**). Peripheral areas within the core, and (more generally) within developing countries, sought

modernism: a forward-looking view of the world that emphasizes reason, scientific rationality, creativity, novelty, and progress

Paris, France: Les Halles

Toronto's downtown landscape

Figure 6.29 Urban landscapes of modernism These photographs of the subterranean Les Halles shopping mall in Paris and the Toronto skyline reflect the pervasive influence of modernist architecture on the central areas of large cities throughout the world's core regions.

postmodernism: a view of the world that emphasizes an openness to a range of perspectives in social inquiry, artistic expression, and political empowerment

to remake traditional landscapes through economic modernization. Economic development and social progress were achieved through a modern infrastructure of highways, airports, dams, harbours, and industrial parks.

Postmodernism is a view of the world that emphasizes openness to a range of perspectives in social inquiry, artistic expression, and political empowerment. Postmodernism is often described in terms of cultural impulses that are playful, superficial, populist, pluralistic, and spectacular. Many commentators see it as the result of a reconfiguration of sociocultural values that has accompanied the reconfiguration of the political economy of the core countries of the world. In this context, postmodernism has been described as the "cultural clothing" of the postindustrial economy.

Postmodernism abandons modernism's emphasis on economic and scientific progress, arguing that modernism's failure to deliver such progress is indicative of its flaws. Because of this, postmodernism also rejects the value of grand universal theories. Instead, postmodernism favours the unique and values difference—both aspects that appeal to geographers and students of "place making." To others, the appeal of postmodernism is its emphasis on living for the moment. Above all, postmodernism is consumption-oriented. This has made for sociocultural environments in which the emphasis is not so much on ownership and consumption as such but rather on the possession of particular combinations of things and on the style of consumption. Postmodern society has been interpreted as a "society of the spectacle," in which the symbolic properties of places and material possessions have assumed unprecedented importance.

The stylistic emphases of postmodernism include eclecticism, decoration, parody, and a heavy use of historical and vernacular motifs—all rendered with

Figure 6.30 Rural landscape of modernism This photograph of rural East Anglia, Great Britain, shows a landscape that is the product of agricultural modernization. Urban land uses—commuter homes and the cooling towers of a power station, in this case—have encroached into the countryside. In addition, many of the traditional hedgerows in much of East Anglia have been torn out, and small land holdings have been consolidated to create a "prairie" landscape of large fields in which modern agricultural equipment can operate efficiently.

Figure 6.31 Landscape of postmodernity This photograph shows the Piazza d'Italia in New Orleans, one of the first public projects in the United States to consciously celebrate an eclectic, over-the-top decorative approach to design. The architecture of this square borrows heavily from various Classical and Italianate styles and recombines them.

a self-conscious stylishness. In architecture, for example, the modernist aphorism "Less is more" is itself parodied: "Less is a bore." Since the mid-1970s, postmodernism has been manifest in many aspects of life, from architecture, art, literature, film, and music to urban design and planning. It is now reflected in the landscapes of some places and regions, especially in more affluent settings. Some of the most striking of these postmodern landscapes are found in the redeveloped waterfronts, revitalized downtown shopping districts, and neo-traditional suburbs of major cities (**Figure 6.31**).

Globalization and Postmodernism

As we saw in Chapter 2, economic globalization has brought about a generalization of forms of industrial production, market behaviour, trade, and consumption. This economic interdependence is also tied into several other dimensions of globalization, many of which have reinforced and extended the commonalities among places. Three of these dimensions are especially important. First, mass communications media have created global culture markets in print, film, music, television, and particularly the Internet. Indeed, the Internet has created an entirely new *kind* of space—cyberspace—with its own "landscape" (or technoscape) and its own embryonic cultures (see **Geography Matters 6.2—The Cultural Geography of Cyberspace**). The instantaneous character of contemporary communications has also made possible the creation of a shared, global consciousness from the staging of such global events as royal weddings, the Olympic Games, and the World Cup. Second, mass communications media have diffused certain values and attitudes toward a wide spectrum of sociocultural issues, including citizenship, human rights, child rearing, social welfare, and self-expression. Third, international legal conventions have increased the degree of standardization and level of harmonization not only of trade and labour practices but also of criminal justice, civil rights, and environmental regulations.

These commonalities have been accompanied by an increased importance of material consumption within many cultures. This is where globalization and postmodernism meet, with each reinforcing the other. People's enjoyment of material goods now depends not only on their physical consumption or use. It is also linked to the role of material culture as a social marker. A person's home, car, clothes, reading, viewing, eating, and drinking preferences; choice of vacations; and even model of cell phone are all increasingly interpreted as indicators of that person's social distinctiveness and sense of style. This means

The Cultural Geography of Cyberspace

The rapid growth of the Internet is of great cultural significance, for it has created the basis for a massive shift in patterns of social interaction, a seedbed for new forms of human consciousness, and a new medium for cultural change. Culture is fundamentally based on communication, and in cyberspace we have an entirely new form of communication: written, visual, and aural, but also multi-directional, networked, open to all, and uncensored.

At face value, the Internet represents the leading edge of the globalization of culture. In broad terms, the culture propagated by the Internet is very much core-oriented. With most Internet communication conducted in English, the Internet portends a global culture based on English as the universal world language—although this is quickly changing with the dramatic increase in the number of Chinese Internet users. For the time being, however, the Internet still very much reflects its origins in affluent Western educational establishments and corporations. It also carries a heavy emphasis on core-area cultural values, such as novelty, spectacle, fashion, material consumption, and leisure.

It is unlikely, however, that the Internet will simply be a new medium through which core-area values and culture are spread. As an agent of cultural change, the Internet is a unique space with its own landscape of web pages and wayfinding methods; its own vocabulary, syntax, and style; its own economy; and its own netiquette for regulating virtual social interactions. These changes, however, are uneven in their impact because of the digital divide. It is also very possible that these new technologies will actively undermine businesses in the periphery, which have, until now, been protected by their very remoteness. Moreover, the Internet allows some new twists on old core–periphery relationships—relationships in which the periphery and its inhabitants are systematically disadvantaged or exploited. Consider, for example, the example of a website on prostitution in Havana, Cuba. This website, operating from a host server in Finland, was perfectly clear about its function as a tourist guide to the re-emerging sex market in Havana. Written in English by Italian correspondents, the site provided detailed information on locations, specializations, and prices, together with tips on how to handle the local police. Although undoubtedly something of a boost for Havana's sex industry, the overall result was to intensify the economic exploitation and cultural domination of the periphery by the core.

In some places and regions, there is resistance to the cultural globalization associated with cyberspace. The Quebec government, already sensitive about the influence of English-language popular culture, has actively sought ways of allowing Francophones to use the Internet without submitting to English, the dominant language of websites. The French government has even gone so far as subsidizing an all-French alternative to the Internet—Minitel, an online videotext terminal that plugs into French telecommunication networks.

In much of Asia, the Internet's basic function as an information-exchange medium clashes with local cultures in which information is a closely guarded commodity. Whereas many Canadian and U.S. websites feature lengthy government reports and scientific studies, as well as lively debates about government policy, comparable Asian sites typically offer little beyond public relations materials from government agencies and corporations. In puritanical Singapore, political leaders, worried that the Internet will undermine morality, have taken to reading private email as part of an all-out effort to beat back the menace of online pornography. Fearful that the Internet will foment political rebellion, Chinese officials have limited the access to it to ensure that the Chinese portion of the Internet can easily be severed from the world in the event of political unrest.

The Chinese government's desire to control access to the Internet was clearly shown during the 2008 Olympic Games held in Beijing. Despite the commitments China had made to the International Olympic Committee (IOC) that it would allow unfettered access to the Internet to the foreign media who had come to Beijing to cover the games, many journalists reported that they had been unable to access websites, including those that discussed Taiwan, Tibet, or the protests in Tiananmen Square; reporters also noted access was denied to the websites of Amnesty International, the British Broadcasting Corporation's Chinese language news, and some Hong Kong–based newspapers.[16] Similarly, during the North African "Facebook revolutions" of 2011, the Chinese authorities prevented the spread of information about the popular uprisings for fear that its own citizens might feel encouraged to start their own "Jasmine Revolution."

---

[16] See, for example, Andrew Jacobs, "China to Limit Web Access During Olympic Games," *New York Times*, July 31, 2008; Edward Cody, "IOC Allows China to Limit Reporters' Access to Internet," *Washington Post*, July 31, 2008.

that there must be a continuous search for new sources of style, and distinctiveness must occur. The wider the range of foods, products, and ideas from around the world—and from past worlds—the greater the possibilities for establishing such style and distinctiveness. It also means that new products must be produced that can deliver this novelty, which in turn means that the product cycle

6.3 Geography in the Information Age

Perhaps most important, the Internet empowers individuals (rather than social groups or institutions), allowing millions of people to say whatever they want to one another, free (for the first time in history) from government control. As such, the Internet can be a potentially important vehicle for the spread of participatory democracy. But authoritarian regimes are fully aware of this potential, too, and so they launch their own propaganda through paid mouthpieces—or they simply cut access to the Internet to prevent the spread of unwanted information. The struggle between these uses of the Internet was powerfully illustrated by the wave of "Facebook revolutions" across the Arab world in 2011.

During 2009 alone, the number of Chinese Internet users jumped by one-third to 389 million. In absolute numbers, that increase was equivalent to the entire population of Germany. Only one year later, by early 2011, 457 million Chinese were online—450 million of them via broadband! Already, two-thirds of Chinese netizens connect to the Internet via smartphones, which means they have leapfrogged the expensive infrastructure requirements of cable connections and are set for even more explosive growth: the penetration rate still is only 34 percent, compared with 75 percent and more in industrialized core nations.

becomes shorter all the time: no sooner have we bought the latest product than it already is "so last year."

Given that material consumption is so central to the repertoire of symbols, beliefs, and practices of postmodern cultures, the "culture industries"—advertising, publishing, communications media, and popular entertainment—have become important shapers of spaces, places, and landscapes. Because the symbolic meanings of material culture must be shared, advertising has become a key component of contemporary culture and place making. In addition to stimulating consumer demand, advertising has always had a role in teaching people how to dress, how to furnish a home, and how to signify status through groupings of possessions.

In fact, in a postmodern world this "teaching" function may well be the dominant one. In the 1970s and 1980s, the emphasis in advertising strategies shifted away from presenting products as newer, better, more efficient, and more economical (in keeping with modernist sensibilities) to identifying them as the means to self-awareness, self-actualization, and group stylishness (in keeping with postmodern sensibilities). Increasingly, products are advertised in terms of their association with a particular lifestyle rather than in terms of their intrinsic utility. Campaigns rely on stereotypes of particular places or kinds of places (especially exotic, spectacular, or "cool" places) in creating the appropriate context or setting for their product. Images of places therefore join with images of global food, architecture, pop culture, and consumer goods in the global media marketplace. Advertisements thus both instruct and influence consumers not only about products but also about spaces, places, and landscapes.

One result of these trends is that contemporary cultures increasingly rely not only on material consumption but also on *visual* and *experiential* consumption—the purchase of images and the experience of spectacular and distinctive places, physical settings, and landscapes (think of the West Edmonton Mall). Visual consumption can take the form of magazines, television, movies, sites on the World Wide Web, tourism, window shopping, people watching, or visits to galleries and museums. The images, signs, and experiences that are consumed may be originals, copies, or simulations (See **Geography Matters 6.3—Restaurants as Places and Objects of Consumption**).

Restaurants as Places and Objects of Consumption

One interesting aspect of the increasing trend toward the consumption of experiences is the emergence of restaurants as significant cultural sites. The cultural historian Rebecca Spang has shown how restaurants developed in late eighteenth-century Paris, as eating shifted from the domestic sphere to the public realm, and became increasingly commodified as society industrialized. Today, restaurants often are powerful cultural and geographical symbols in their own right. For example, the dining experience in a particular restaurant can be an important symbolic good as the social standing of celebrity customers can transfer to other patrons. Consequently, restaurants and the act of public dining themselves can be both theatre and performance. Finally, restaurant design also contributes to a city's visual style as architects and interior designers, restaurant consultants, and restaurant-industry magazines adapt global trends to local styles to create local "hot spots" (Figure 6.3.1).

Increasingly, restaurants also represent a synthesis of the global and the local by bringing together a global and a local labour force (immigrant owners, chefs, and waiters, as well as locals) and clientele (tourists and business travellers, as well as locals). Evidently, restaurants, and food in general, are powerful place-makers. Spang notes how the use of menus and of specific names for dishes allows restaurateurs to "pin down" space and time. In her words, menus become an "atlas."

The connection between food, identity, and place is obviously intense, a fact that is particularly well reflected by the increasing number of "ethnic" restaurants. Originally developed to serve traditional home cooking from its country of origin to local immigrant groups, the ethnic restaurant served as a clear cultural geographical marker of that group's spatial presence in an area.

In recent years, "ethnic" cuisines have become so much sought after by the wider public that ethnic restaurants have greatly increased in number (Figure 6.3.2). The ethnic restaurant phenomenon has been such a success because it has taken the ability of food to convey place and used it as a marketing device. It has, in other words, *commodified* cuisine and place (Figure 6.3.3). To aid this endeavour, appropriate architectural motifs, styles of writing, music, and folk costume are often used by the restaurant to indicate the place or country it represents (Figure 6.3.4).

Ethnic restaurants have also been so successful because they counter the homogenization of the chain restaurant experience with an emphasis on "exotic" or unique cuisines from different or unusual places in the world. In other words, postmodernism's celebration of place is counterbalancing globalization's erosion of difference.

Figure 6.3.1 Consumption in style The postmodern emphasis on novelty and the consumption of experience and style has meant that restaurants have moved far beyond simply providing food: they have become sites of conspicuous consumption where "being seen" is a big part of the reason for going out to dine.

(a)

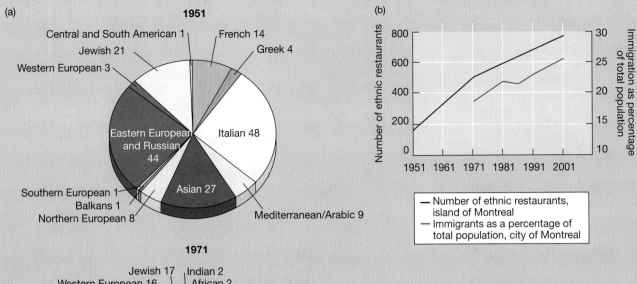

1951

Central and South American 1
Jewish 21
Western European 3
French 14
Greek 4
Eastern European and Russian 44
Italian 48
Southern European 1
Balkans 1
Northern European 8
Asian 27
Mediterranean/Arabic 9

(b)

— Number of ethnic restaurants, island of Montreal
— Immigrants as a percentage of total population, city of Montreal

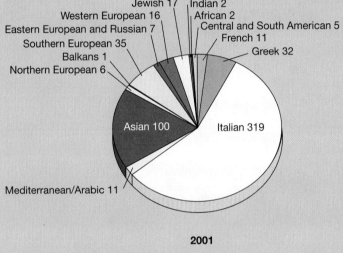

1971

Jewish 17
Indian 2
Western European 16
African 2
Eastern European and Russian 7
Central and South American 5
Southern European 35
French 11
Balkans 1
Greek 32
Northern European 6
Asian 100
Italian 319
Mediterranean/Arabic 11

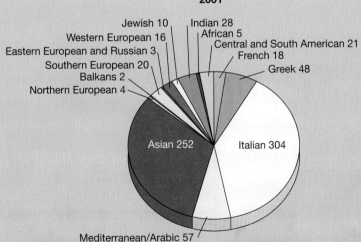

2001

Jewish 10
Indian 28
Western European 16
African 5
Eastern European and Russian 3
Central and South American 21
Southern European 20
French 18
Balkans 2
Greek 48
Northern European 4
Asian 252
Italian 304
Mediterranean/Arabic 57

Figure 6.3.2   Increase in number of ethnic restaurants in Montreal, 1951–2001   These pie charts show the increasing number and diversity of ethnic restaurants on the island of Montreal from 1951 to 2001. What has caused these changes? Some experts believe that increases in immigration over those years are a major factor (see graph (b) above). Other experts suggest that an increasing trend toward diversity (itself an outcome of postmodernism) is a major explanation.   (*Source:* Alan Nash, "From Spaghetti to Sushi: An Investigation of the Growth of Ethnic Restaurants in Montreal, 1951–2001," *Food, Culture and Society* 12[1], 2009. The author is grateful to Geneviève Aboud, Megan Lewis, and Jake Fogels for their help in this research.)

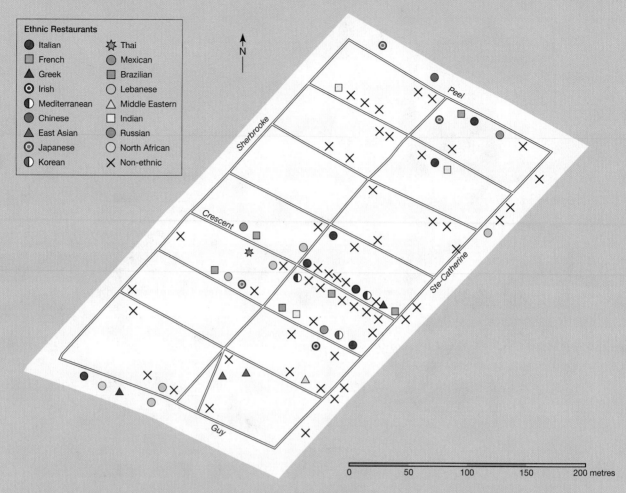

Figure 6.3.3 **Ethnic restaurants** This map of a few blocks of downtown Montreal shows the enormous popularity and variety of ethnic restaurants in Canada's large urban and metropolitan centres. (*Source:* Marie-Michelle Belanger, Concordia University, B.A. Honours Essay, Department of Geography, April 2002.)

Figure 6.3.4 **Ethnic restaurants** This view of ethnic restaurants on Toronto's Queen Street West shows how architectural motifs and sign writing are used to convey a sense of other places.

6.4 Geography in the Information Age

The increasing globalization of food production has caused regional food producers to legally protect the names of foods that are synonymous with their region of origin. For example, the vintners of the Champagne region in France went to court to ensure that only their product may be called Champagne. Similarly, only prosciutto (cured ham) from the Italian region of Parma may carry the protected Parma name. The EU has established "Protected Designations of Origin" or PDOs, which are particularly widespread among cheeses: Gorgonzola, Roquefort, and Feta, for example, must be produced in the regions with the same names. In this way, the value of places, as it is embodied in food, is protected. This idea has carried through into advertising campaigns for Canadian cheeses. For example, we are told that by eating Oka cheese, we can "taste the beauty of the land."

6.5 Geography in the Information Age

Beware: *Ethnic food* is a spongy term that often says little more than "not from here" or "exotic." It is thus instructive to look at Canada's regional specialties with an open mind and wonder whether some of these may not be considered "exotic" too by people in other places: Newfoundland's cods' tongues, Nova Scotia lobster, Quebec's poutine, Ontarian maple syrup, Niagara ice wines, Winnipeg's cinnamon buns, Saskatoon berry pie, Alberta beef, British Columbia's smoked salmon, and Northern bannock—such a list conveys "difference" just as much as it does regional identities!

The significance of the increased importance of visual consumption for place making and the evolution of landscapes is that such settings as theme parks, shopping malls, festival marketplaces, renovated historic districts, museums, and galleries have all become prominent as centres of cultural practices and activities. The number of such settings has proliferated, making a discernible impact on metropolitan landscapes. The design of such settings, however, has had an even greater impact on metropolitan landscapes. Places of material and visual consumption have been in the vanguard of postmodern ideas and values, incorporating eclecticism, decoration, a heavy use of historical and vernacular motifs, and spectacular features in an attempt to create stylish settings that are appropriate to contemporary lifestyles.

Although the idea of the emergence of a single global culture is too simplistic, we must acknowledge that the postmodern emphasis on material, visual, and experiential consumption means that many aspects of contemporary culture transcend local and national boundaries. Furthermore, many of the residents of the fast world are world travellers—either directly or via TV or Internet—so that they are knowledgeable about many aspects of other cultures. This contributes to **cosmopolitanism**, an intellectual and aesthetic openness toward divergent experiences, images, and products from different cultures.

Cosmopolitanism is an important geographic phenomenon because it fosters a curiosity about all places, peoples, and cultures, together with at least a

cosmopolitanism: an intellectual and aesthetic openness toward divergent experiences, images, and products from different cultures rudimentary ability to map, or situate, such places and cultures geographically, historically, and anthropologically. It also suggests an ability to reflect on different places and societies. Furthermore, cosmopolitanism allows people to locate their own society and its culture in terms of a wide-ranging historical and geographical framework. For travellers and tourists, cosmopolitanism encourages both the willingness and the ability to take the risk of exploring off the beaten track of tourist locales. It also develops in people the skills needed to interpret other cultures and to understand their visual symbolism. Ultimately, this appreciation of other cultures may also contribute to an acceptance of difference as we learn to see beyond our own culture's norms and accept other people's ways of life as equally "normal."

CONCLUSION

Geographers study the interdependence between people and places and are especially interested in how individuals and groups acquire knowledge of their environments, and how this knowledge shapes their attitudes and behaviours. People ascribe meanings to landscapes and places in many ways, and they also derive meanings from the places and landscapes they experience. Different groups of people experience landscape, place, and space differently. For instance, the experience that rural Sudanese children have of their landscape and the way in which they acquire knowledge of their surroundings differ from how middle-class children in a Canadian suburb learn about and function in their landscape. Furthermore, both landscapes elicit a distinctive sense of place that is different for those who live there and those who visit or see the place as outsiders.

As indicated in previous chapters, the concepts of landscape and place are central to geographical inquiry. They are the result of intentional and unintentional human action, and every landscape is a complex reflection of the operations of the larger society. Geographers have developed categories of landscape to help distinguish among the different types that exist. Ordinary landscapes, such as neighbourhoods and drive-in movie theatres, are ones that people create in the course of their everyday lives. By contrast, symbolic landscapes represent the particular values and aspirations that the developers and financiers of those landscapes want to impart to a larger public. An American example is Mount Rushmore in the Black Hills of South Dakota, designed and executed by sculptor Gutzon Borglum. Chiselling the heads of George Washington, Thomas Jefferson, Theodore Roosevelt, and Abraham Lincoln into the granite face of the mountain, Borglum intended to construct an enduring landscape of nationalism in the wilderness. That he did so on part of the Lakota Sioux's sacred mountains is an irony no longer lost on us. (The current effort to complete an enormous sculpture of the famous Sioux chief Crazy Horse in the southern Black Hills demonstrates a recognition of the First Nations' much earlier presence in that landscape.)

More recently, geographers have come to regard landscape as a text, something that can be written and read, rewritten, and reinterpreted. The concept of landscape as text suggests that more than one author of a landscape can exist, and different readers may derive different meanings from what is written there. The idea that landscape can be written and read is further supported by the understanding that the language in which the landscape is written is a code. To understand the significance of the code it is necessary to understand semiotics, or the language in which the code is written. The code may be meant to convey many things, including a language of power or of playfulness, a language that elevates one group above another, or a language that encourages imagination or religious devotion and spiritual awe.

The global transition from modernism to postmodernism has altered cultural landscapes, places, and spaces differently as individuals and groups have struggled to negotiate the local impacts of this widespread shift in cultural sensibilities. The shared meanings that insiders derive from their place or landscape have been disrupted by the intrusion of new sights, sounds, and smells as values, ideas, and practices from one part of the globe have been exported to another. The Internet and the emergence of cyberspace have resulted in the emergence of new spaces of interaction that have neither distinct historical memory attached to them nor well-established sense of place. Because of this, cyberspace carries with it some unique possibilities for cultural exchange. It remains to be seen, however, whether access to this new space will be truly open—or whether the Internet will become another landscape of power and exclusion.

MAIN POINTS REVISITED

- **Landscape serves as a kind of archive of society. It is a reflection of our culture and our experiences. Like a book, landscape is a text that is written by individuals and groups and read by them as well.**

  It is therefore possible to have one landscape convey different meanings for different groups. Landscapes can be constructed to reflect the everyday worlds of social groups as well as to represent power and the values of a particular society.

- **The language in which a landscape is written is a kind of code. The code or codes are signs that direct our attention toward certain features and away from others.**

  To interpret our environment, we must learn how to read the codes that are written into the landscape.

- **The written code of landscape is also known as** *semiotics.* **Codes signify important information about landscapes, such as whether they are accessible or off-limits or are oriented toward work or play.**

  Landscapes as different from each other as shopping malls and national capitals can be understood in terms of their semiotics.

- **In addition to understanding how the environment shapes (and is shaped by) people, geographers seek to identify how it is perceived and understood by people.**

  People not only filter information from their environments through neurophysiological processes but also draw on personality and culture to produce cognitive images of their environment—pictures or representations of the world that can be called to mind through the imagination.

- **Different cultural identities and status categories influence the ways in which people experience and understand their environments, as well as how they are shaped by—and are able to shape—them.**

  Among the most important of these are the cultural identities of class, gender, age, and ethnicity. Often, these identities come together in a group, and their influence in combination becomes central to our understanding of how group identity shapes space and is shaped by it.

- **The emergence of the most recent phase of globalization has occurred in parallel with a transition from modernism to postmodernism.**

  This transition involves a shift in cultural sensibilities that affects every sphere of creative activity, from art and architecture to television and urban design. It seems to have originated in parts of the world's core countries and is currently spreading throughout the rest of the world.

- **Modernism as a historical period embraced scientific rationality and optimism about progress.**

  Modernism has been one of the major influences on culture, society, space, place, and landscape for the last century.

- **Postmodernism, the name for the contemporary period, revolves around an orientation toward consumption and emphasizes the importance of multiple perspectives.**

  In contrast to modernism's emphasis on economic and scientific progress, postmodern cultural sensibilities focus on living for the moment, emphasizing the *style* of consumption.

Key Terms

aesthetic (p. 258)
cosmopolitanism (p. 291)
derelict landscapes (p. 256)
ethology (p. 265)
humanistic approach (p. 257)
landscape as text (p. 257)

modernism (p. 283)
ordinary landscapes (vernacular landscapes) (p. 255)
picturesque (p. 260)
postmodernism (p. 284)
proxemics (p. 265)

semiotics (p. 276)
sense of place (p. 267)
sublime (p. 264)
symbolic landscapes (p. 256)
territoriality (p. 265)
topophilia (p. 271)

Additional Reading

Aziz, L. "The Great Canadian Feast: A Celebration of Family Traditions from Canadian Kitchens." In *Canadian Geographic*. Toronto: Key Porter Books, 2002.

Burnett, R. *The Global Jukebox: The International Music Industry*. New York: Routledge, 1996.

Carney, G.O. (ed.). *Fast Food, Stock Cars, and Rock 'n' Roll: Place and Space in American Pop Culture*. Lanham, MD: Rowman & Littlefield, 1995.

Cronon, W. "Telling Tales on Canvas: Landscapes of Frontier Change." In J.D. Prown et al. (eds.), *Discovered Lands, Invented Pasts: Transforming Visions of the American West*. New Haven: Yale University Press, 1992, 37–87.

Davidson, J. *Phobic Geographies: The Phenomenology and Spatiality of Identity*. Aldershot, UK: Ashgate, 2003.

Dodge, M., and R. Kitchin. *Atlas of Cyberspace*. London: Pearson, 2001.

Dunlay, K. "The Celtic Revival in Cape Breton." In E. Koskoff (ed.), *The Garland Encyclopedia of World Music, Volume 3: The United States and Canada*. New York: Garland, 2001, 1127–1131.

Gaylor, H. (ed.). *Niagara's Changing Landscapes*. Ottawa: Carleton University Press, 1994.

Gayton, D. *The Wheatgrass Mechanism: Science and Imagination in the Western Canadian Landscape*. Saskatoon: Fifth House Publishers, 1990.

Gold, J.R., and S.V. Ward (eds.). *Place Promotion: The Use of Publicity and Marketing to Sell Towns and Regions*. New York: Wiley and Sons, 1994.

Golledge, R.G., and R.J. Stimpson. *Spatial Behavior: A Geographic Perspective*. New York: Guilford Press, 1996.

Graham, B., G.J. Ashworth, and J.E. Tunbridge. *A Geography of Heritage: Power, Culture and Economy*. New York: Oxford University Press, 2000.

Harmon, K. (ed.). *The Pacific Northwest Landscape: A Painted History*. Seattle: Sasquatch Books, 2001.

Hopkins, J. "Excavating Toronto's Underground Streets: In Search of Equitable Rights, Rules, and Revenues." In J. Caulfield and L. Peake (eds.), *City Lives and City Forms: Critical Research and Canadian Urbanism*. Toronto: University of Toronto Press, 1996, 63–81.

Jackson, E., and D. Johnson (eds.). "Feature Issue: The West Edmonton Mall and Mega-malls," *Canadian Geographer* 35(3), 1991.

James, W.C. *Locations of the Sacred: Essays on Religion, Literature and Canadian Culture*. Waterloo, ON: Wilfrid Laurier University Press, 1998.

Kearns, G., and C. Philo (eds.). *Selling Places*. Oxford: Pergamon Press, 1993.

Morley, D., and K. Robins. *Spaces of Identity*. London: Routledge, 1995.

Osborne, B. "Images of People, Place and Nation in Canadian Art." In D. Cosgrove and S. Daniels (eds.), *The Iconography of the Past*. Cambridge: Cambridge University Press, 1988.

Price, J. *Flight Maps: Adventures with Nature in Modern America*. New York: Basic Books, 1999, 167–206.

Pyne, S. *How the Canyon Became Grand*. New York: Penguin, 1998.

Schama, S. *Landscape and Memory*. New York: Vintage Books, 1995.

Shields, R. *Places on the Margin: Alternative Geographies of Modernity*. London and New York: Routledge, 1991.

Shurmer-Smith, P., and K. Hannam. *Worlds of Desire, Realms of Power*. London: Edward Arnold, 1994.

Simpson-Housley, P., and G. Norcliffe (eds.). *A Few Acres of Snow: Literary and Artistic Images of Canada*. Toronto: Dundurn Press, 1992.

Spang, R. *The Invention of the Restaurant: Paris and Modern Gastronomic Culture*. Cambridge, MA: Harvard University Press, 2000.

Tuan, Y.F. *Landscapes of Fear*. Minneapolis: University of Minnesota Press, 1979.

Urry, J. *Consuming Places*. London: Routledge, 1995.

Williams, A. (ed.). *Therapeutic Landscapes: The Dynamic between Place and Wellness*. Lanham, MD: University Press of America, 1999.

Zelinsky, W. "The Roving Palate: North America's Ethnic Restaurant Cuisines," *Geoforum* 16, 1985, 51–72.

Zukin, S. *The Cultures of Cities*. Cambridge, MA: Blackwell, 1995.

Discussion Questions and Research Activities

1. Write a short essay (500 words, or two double-spaced, typed pages) that describes, from your personal perspective, the sense of place that you associate with your hometown or province. Write about the places, buildings, sights, and sounds that are especially meaningful to you. Why they are meaningful to you? Why might they be "meaningless" to other people?

2. Draw up a list of the top 10 places in Canada in which you would like to live and work; then draw up a list of the bottom 10 places in which you would least like to live. How do these lists compare with the lists of your friends and members of your family? Why might your preferences be different from theirs?

3. On a clean sheet of paper and without reference to maps or other materials, sketch a detailed map of the town or city in which you live. When you have finished your sketch, analyze it. Does your sketch contain nodes? Landmarks? Edges? Districts? Paths? How does your sketch compare with the reality shown in a published city map?

4. Your campus provides an institutional landscape that has been "written" to convey certain important relationships. "Read" your campus landscape, and discuss the most powerful sites versus the least powerful ones as well as the groups or academic disciplines that occupy them. Map what you think are the most powerful and important places and sites and the least powerful and important ones. Why do different places and sites fit into each category? Are there significant differences in architecture, location (central or on the edges of campus), or accessibility? How might your reading of the campus landscape differ from readings created by other members of the campus community (as well as outsiders)?

MyGeosciencePlace

Visit **www.mygeoscienceplace.ca** to find chapter review quizzes, videos, maps, and much more.

7

The Geography of Economic Development

The Teck smelter in Trail, British Columbia

Its tall smokestack is visible for kilometres. The size of the zinc–lead smelter at Trail, one of the largest in the world, exemplifies the importance of economic activity in our use of the landscape, the ways in which that activity has traditionally trumped our concerns for the environment, and the ways in which the development of place, space, and region are affected by the economy.

An economic geographer, visiting the town of Trail, inevitably asks some important geographical questions: Why is the smelter here? What does it produce? Who owns it? Where are its markets? What are its effects on the local environment and the local economy? Economic geographers also examine where its raw materials, power, and labour come from; where the markets for its products are located; and how these locations in turn may have influenced the decision to build the smelter here. Economic geographers examine how the smelter is connected to the various networks of transportation and communication. They are interested in the history of the smelter and the fact that production has been occurring here for more than a century, making the smelter an integral part of the local economy. At the same time, because the smelter is only 15 kilometres from the United States, cross-border pollution issues make the smelter the subject of international considerations. Other key concerns are how new technologies challenge the roles of location and distance and how its operation fits into the scenarios of global climate change and international environmental obligations.[1]

A visiting economic geographer, seeing that the size of the smelter is out of proportion to the small town of Trail (where about 7,000 people live), would also examine the smelter's global-regional-local connections. The smelter is clearly part of a much larger economic picture, as it evidently does not produce just for this town. Its size hints at an economic system in which long-distance trade is a key component and at a culture that permits the local economic exploitation of the environment at such a scale to meet far-flung demand.

Our visitor to Trail—certainly if he or she has spent some time in the town and bought a coffee or gas—might also wonder why such a large industrial plant has not become the foundation for more extensive and diversified industrial development. Indeed, the visitor might wonder why the downtown boasts more thrift stores than high-end retail establishments. How and why is the local population affected by global processes, and are these effects distributed equally?

The study of economic geography looks for answers to all of these questions by approaching economic development as an inherently uneven geographic phenomenon. In this chapter, we try to understand why and how this uneven economic development is interconnected with the shaping of places and regions worldwide.

---

[1] Information about the Trail smelter is available from the website of Teck Resources at **www.teck.com**.

- The geography of economic development is the cumulative outcome of decisions guided by fundamental principles of land use, commercial and industrial location, and economic interdependence.

- Geographically, the single most important feature of economic development is that it is highly uneven.

- Successive technology systems have rewritten the geography of economic development as they have shifted the balance of advantages between regions.

- Geographical divisions of labour have evolved with the growth of the world-system of trade and politics and with the changing locational logic of successive technology systems.

- Regional cores of economic development are created cumulatively, following some initial advantage, through the operation of several basic principles of spatial organization.

- Spirals of economic development can be arrested in various ways, including the onset of disinvestment and deindustrialization, which follow major shifts in technology systems and in international geopolitics.

- The globalization of the economy has meant that patterns and processes of local and regional economic development are much more open to external influences than before.

- Tourism has increasingly come to represent a major industry at a world scale and offers the potential for local economic development in forms as various as ecotourism and visits to Aboriginal cultural sites.

WHAT ECONOMIC DEVELOPMENT MEANS

Economic development is often discussed in terms of levels and rates of change in prosperity, as reflected in bottom-line statistical measures of productivity, incomes, purchasing power, and consumption. Increased prosperity is only one aspect of economic development, however. For human geographers and other social scientists, the term *economic development* refers to processes of change involving the nature and composition of the economy of a particular region, as well as to increases in the overall prosperity of a region. These processes can therefore involve three types of changes:

- changes in the structure of the region's economy (for example, a shift from agriculture to manufacturing)

- changes in forms of economic organization within the region (for example, a shift from socialism to free-market capitalism)

- changes in the availability and use of technology within the region

Economic development is also expected to bring with it some broader changes in the economic well-being of a region. The most important of these changes is the capacity of the region to improve the basic conditions of life (through better housing, health care, social welfare systems, and the provision of public services) and the physical framework, or infrastructure, on which the economy rests.

Economic Development and the Environment

In addition, we must not overlook the interactions between the economy and the environment, which we know are intimately linked. For example, heightened levels of pollution may diminish the region's overall prosperity, whereas an increase in ecotourism might turn forests previously considered wilderness into a valued economic resource. It is therefore important that the integrity and sustainability of a region's environment are not harmed and that environmental considerations are made integral to decisions about economic development. As we saw in Chapter 4, philosophies of nature affect how we exploit Earth and its species for industrial purposes. We can contrast the "traditional" approach to economic growth (one that ignores the environment) with a "new" approach that endeavours to achieve economic growth through sustainable development, in the following manner:

The Traditional Economy	*The New Economy*
– consumes renewable and nonrenewable resources	– recycles, replaces, and reduces its use of renewable and nonrenewable resources
– treats the environment as a "free good"	– prices the use of the environment (through environmental audits)
– uses the environment to absorb pollution	– costs the price of pollution (through emission credits)
– considers any environmental action as a cost	– considers environmental action part of the price of doing business and, increasingly, as a business opportunity
– regards "place" as simply a location	– regards "place" as a locus of interconnections at the global, regional, and local scales
– regards "space" only in economic terms	– regards "space" as the arena in which those interconnections operate

One of the great challenges—and opportunities—of your generation will be to restructure our current growth-oriented, resource-devouring economy into one that is sustainable and based on qualitative growth.

The Unevenness of Economic Development

Geographically, the single most important feature of economic development is that it is *uneven*. At the global scale, this unevenness takes the form of core–periphery contrasts within the evolving world-system, a competitive economic system that is heavily influenced by cultural and political factors (see Chapter 2).

Global Core–Periphery Patterns   At the global scale, levels of economic development are usually measured by economic indicators, such as gross domestic product, gross national product, and gross national income. **Gross domestic product (GDP)** is an estimate of the total value of all materials, foodstuffs, goods, and services that are produced by a country in a particular year. To standardize for countries' varying sizes, the statistic is normally divided by total population to produce a *per capita* GDP, which is a good measure for comparing relative levels of economic development. **Gross national product (GNP)** also includes the value of income from abroad (e.g., profits from overseas investments). **Gross national income (GNI)** is measured as GDP minus the taxes and wages a country pays to outside interests, but includes those taxes and wages earned outside its borders by its own businesses or individuals.

In making international comparisons, however, all of these measures can be problematic because they are based on each nation's currency. As a result, it is now common to make comparisons expressed in "international dollars" based on *purchasing power parity* (PPP). In effect, PPP measures how much of a common "market basket" of goods and services each currency can purchase locally.

gross domestic product (GDP): an estimate of the total value of all materials, foodstuffs, goods, and services produced by a country in a particular year

gross national product (GNP): similar to GDP, but also includes the value of income from abroad

gross national income (GNI): similar to GDP, but also includes the value of income from abroad and excludes the taxes and wages a country pays to outside interests

As **Figure 7.1** shows, most of the countries with the highest levels of economic development are found in northern latitudes (very roughly, north of 30°N), which has given rise to another popular shorthand for the world's economic geography: the division between the "North" (the core) and the "South" (the periphery). Viewed in more detail, the global pattern of per capita GNI (measured in the "international dollars" of PPP) is a direct reflection of the core–semiperiphery–periphery structure of the world-system. In 2006, according to the latest estimates available, in almost all the core countries of North America, northwestern Europe, and Japan, annual per capita GNI (in PPP) exceeded $30,000 (Canada: $36,650).

In the periphery, annual per capita GNI (in PPP) typically ranges between $1,000 and $7,000. The gap between the highest per capita GNIs ($71,240 in Luxembourg and $68,440 in Norway), and the lowest ($130 in Liberia and $100 in Burundi) is staggering. Sadly, the gap between the world's rich and poor is also growing wider rather than narrower (**Figure 7.2**). In 1970, the average GNI per capita of the 10 richest countries in the world was 50 times higher than the average GNI per capita of the 10 poorest countries. By 1990, it was a hundred times higher; by 2005, two hundred times; and by 2007, two hundred and fifty times higher.

Geography of Inequality   Geographic inequality in income is reflected—and reinforced—by many aspects of human well-being. Patterns of infant mortality, a reliable indicator of social well-being, show the same steep core–periphery

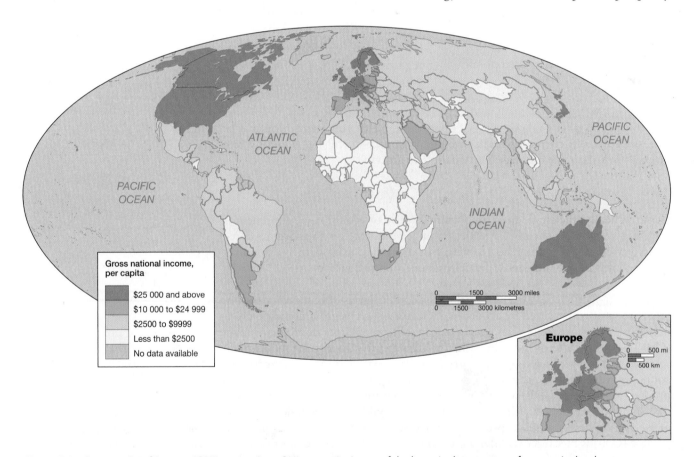

Figure 7.1   Gross national income (GNI) per capita   GNI per capita is one of the best single measures of economic development. This map, based on 2003 data, shows the tremendous gulf in affluence between the core countries of the world economy—like Canada, Norway, and Switzerland, with annual per capita GNI (in PPP "international dollars") of more than $25,000—and peripheral countries like Angola, Haiti, and Mali, where annual per capita GNI was less than $2,500. In semiperipheral countries like South Korea, Brazil, and Mexico, per capita GNI ranged between $5,000 and $10,000.   (*Source:* after map projection, Buckminster Fuller Institute and Dymaxion Map Design, Santa Barbara, CA. The word *Dymaxion* and the Fuller Projection Dymaxion™ Map design are trademarks of the Buckminster Fuller Institute, Santa Barbara, CA, © 1938, 1967 & 1992. All rights reserved.)

7.1 Geography in the Information Age

Patterns of food consumption, one of the most basic of all human needs, reflect another key dimension of inequality in human well-being. Every day, one person in eight goes hungry. In south Asia the rate is one in four, in sub-Saharan Africa even one in three. In terms of sheer numbers, however, there are more chronically hungry people in Asia and the Pacific. The fact that many of them are living in countries that are net exporters (by value) of foods is a telling indictment of the uneven economic structure of the world-system: people and countries that are forced to produce and sell food without being able to properly feed themselves are clearly not equal participants in the global economy.

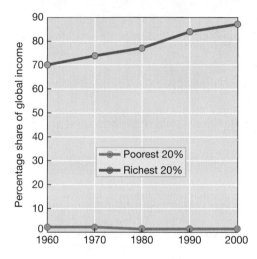

Figure 7.2 Long-term trends in per capita GNI This graph shows the steady divergence in international economic prosperity between the richest and poorest of the world's population. In 1960, the richest 20 percent of the world's population accounted for 70.2 percent of global income, whereas the poorest 20 percent accounted for 2.3 percent: a ratio of 30 to 1. By 1980, the ratio had increased to 45 to 1; by 1990, it was 64 to 1; and by 2000, it was 72 to 1.

gradient (refer back to Figure 3.8 on p. 112). In the industrialized core countries, life expectancy is high and continues to increase. In 2007, life expectancy at birth in Canada, Switzerland, or Australia was 81 years. In contrast, life expectancy in the poorest countries is dramatically shorter. In Africa, life expectancy in many countries has been falling in the last three decades, mainly due to AIDS, war, and poverty. In Mozambique, life expectancy in 2010 was 39 years. In most African countries, only two-thirds of the population can expect to survive beyond age 40.

The United Nations Development Programme (UNDP) has devised an overall index of human development based on measures of life expectancy, educational attainment, and personal income. The index is calculated so that a country with the best scores among all countries in the world on all three indicators would have a perfect index score of 1.0, whereas a country that ranked worst in the world on all three indicators would have an index score of 0.0. **Figure 7.3** shows the international map of human development in 2005. The latest statistics released by the UNDP in 2010 report that Norway, Australia, and New Zealand had the highest overall levels of human development (with scores of 0.938, 0.937, and 0.907, respectively; Canada was ranked eighth with 0.888). The lowest levels were recorded by Niger (0.261), DR of the Congo (0.239), and Zimbabwe (0.140).[2] The same fundamental pattern is repeated across the entire array of indicators of human development: adult literacy, poverty, malnutrition, access to physicians, public expenditure on higher education, telephone lines, Internet users, and so on. Inequality on this scale poses the most pressing, as well as the most intractable, questions of spatial justice.

---

[2] UNDP data can be accessed online at **www.undp.org**.

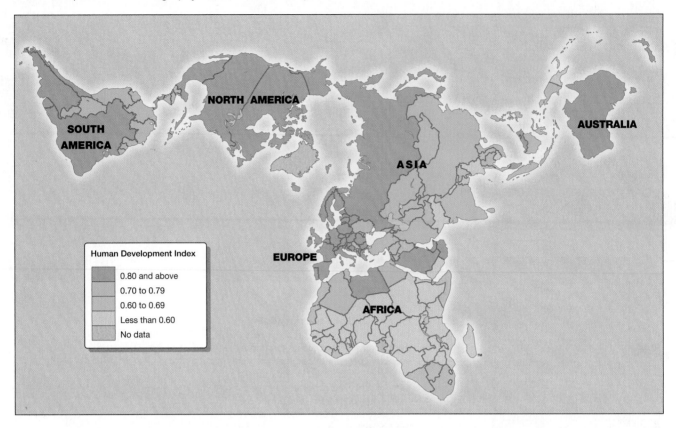

Figure 7.3 An index of human development, 2005 This index, calculated by the UNDP, is based on measures of life expectancy, educational attainment, and personal income. A country with the best scores among all countries in the world on all three measures would have a perfect index score of 1.0, whereas a country that ranked worst in the world on all three indicators would have an index score of zero. Most of the affluent core countries have index scores of 0.9 or more; the worst scores—those less than 0.4—are concentrated in Africa. (*Source:* after map projection, Buckminster Fuller Institute and Dymaxion Map Design, Santa Barbara, CA. The word *Dymaxion* and the Fuller Projection Dymaxion™ Map design are trademarks of the Buckminster Fuller Institute, Santa Barbara, CA, © 1938, 1967 & 1992. All rights reserved.)

These questions of spatial justice are underscored by simple comparisons between the needs of the periphery and the spending patterns in core countries. The UNDP has calculated that the annual cost of providing a basic education for all children in peripheral countries would be in the region of US$6 billion, which is less than the annual sales of cosmetics in the United States. Providing water and sanitation for everyone in peripheral countries is estimated at US$9 billion per year, which is less than Europeans' annual expenditure on ice cream. Providing basic health and nutrition for everyone in the peripheral countries would cost an estimated US$13 billion per year, which is less than the annual expenditure on pet foods in Europe and the United States. Reducing the military expenditures of core countries (in the region of US$1 trillion per year) by less than 10 percent would pay for the costs of basic education; water and sanitation; basic health and nutrition; and reproductive health programs for all people in peripheral countries.

Geography tells us that inequalities exist at levels below that of the global scale. In other words, the sorts of fundamental disparities that we have just seen operating between core and peripheral countries are also operating at regional and local levels. Why is this?

The answer is twofold. First, as we saw in Chapter 2, the operation of the world-system through the interaction of the core and periphery (at global, regional, or local levels) ensures that peripheral regions are kept in a dependent position. A series of processes (economic, political, military, and environmental) work together to benefit core regions at the expense of peripheral areas and, in so doing, create disparities among those regions.

Second, "space" is, in many important ways, a human construction. In Chapter 1, we saw how the development of a railhead in a previously ignored patch of prairie would begin to "create space." Farmers who found themselves close to the railhead paid much less than other farmers to transport their grain to that shipment point. This simple example (in which people pay for transport and land is privately owned) shows that the effects of distance "create" an economic space—one in which farmers nearest the railhead will make higher profits than those on the periphery. In more general terms, geography tells us that it is through such *spatial processes* that *spatial disparities* are created.

Development and Gender Inequality   Core–periphery patterns are also reflected in indicators that measure economic development by *gender inequality*. In 2010, the UNDP established a new gender-sensitive development index that adjusts the overall human development index for such factors as maternal mortality, prevalence of contraception, female participation in the labour force, and percentage of parliamentary seats held by women. Using 2008 data, the top countries were the Netherlands, Denmark, Sweden, and Switzerland. The lowest were Niger, DR of the Congo, and Yemen. Although this clearly reflects the by now familiar core–periphery pattern, there is by no means a direct correlation between economic prosperity and gender empowerment: creating equal opportunities for women does not necessarily require high levels of economic development.

Women are, in fact, playing a central and increasingly large role in processes of development and change in the global economy as globalization appears to increase their level of participation in the formal labour force. But increasing participation does not always mean less discrimination: on average, women earn 40 to 50 percent less than men for the same work. They also tend to work longer hours than men—12 to 13 hours a week more (counting both paid and unpaid work) in Africa and Asia. In many peripheral countries, women constitute the majority of workers in the manufacturing sector created by the new international division of labour. As well, it is increasingly women who keep households afloat in a world economy that has resulted in localized recession and intensified poverty (**Figure 7.4**).

Children are even more vulnerable than women to the effects of uneven development, whether it is malnutrition, lack of sanitation, health care, or lack of safety and security. In many peripheral countries, child labour is also an integral part of the

Figure 7.4   Women in development   The changing global economy has placed unprecedented demands on women. (a) Large firms producing for export tend to employ women in assembly-line jobs because they can be hired for lower wages than men. In fact, many factories will only hire women and justify that practice by claiming that women work more nimbly and deftly on account of their smaller hands. (b) In times of rapid economic change and adjustment, women are typically called upon to help sustain household incomes, in addition to their traditional household responsibilities. When employed, women are often more vulnerable than men, as they are disproportionately concentrated in occupations with little or no training or job security and few opportunities for advancement. This photo shows women peeling and grading cashew nuts by hand at a large processing factory in Mtwara, Tanzania, which employs 2,400 women. The workers are paid by the weight of the nuts they process and this works out to approximately US$1.80 per day.

Figure 7.5 Child labour A 13-year-old girl makes fireworks at a factory at Sivakasi, India. One in twelve of the world's children (180 million young people aged 5 to 17) are involved in the worst forms of child labour—hazardous work, slavery, forced labour, the military, commercial sexual exploitation, and illicit activities. Of these children, 97 percent are in peripheral and semiperipheral countries.

Figure 7.6 Persistent poverty The poorest country in the Western Hemisphere, Haiti has hundreds of thousands of very young children who have been handed over to "host" families by desperately poor parents lured by the promise of a better life. Instead, the children receive no education and are forced to do hard, menial jobs; oftentimes they are forbidden to join the host family for meals and sleep on concrete or dirt floors with little clothing. Host families often throw them out on the street when they reach 15 years of age (by law the age to receive a wage) and replace them with younger children.

very process of development: according to International Labour Organization (ILO) estimates, more than 250 million children between the ages of 5 and 14 are sent out to work, many of them in dangerous conditions (**Figure 7.5**). The ILO also estimates that around 1 million children work in small-scale mining and quarrying around the world. Although most of these children live in peripheral countries, hundreds of thousands of underage workers are exploited in sweatshops, farm fields, and other workplaces in core countries, including up to 1.5 million children in the United States, as estimated by the United Nations Children's Fund (UNICEF). Globally, an estimated 114 million children of primary school age are not enrolled in school, depriving one in five children of an education. They become exposed to exploitation and abuse and miss out on developing the knowledge and employable skills that could lift them and their own children out of the poverty cycle (**Figure 7.6**).

Regional Patterns Inequality in economic development often has a regional dimension. Initial conditions are a crucial determinant of regional economic performance. Scarce resources, a history of neglect, lack of investment, and concentrations of low-skilled people all combine to explain the lagging performance of certain areas. In some regions, for example, initial disadvantages are so extreme as to constrain the opportunities of individuals born there. A child born in the Mexican state of Chiapas, for example, has much bleaker prospects than a child born in

Mexico City. The child from Chiapas is twice as likely to die before age five, less than half as likely to complete primary school, and 10 times as likely to live in a house without access to running water. On reaching working age, he or she will earn 20 to 35 percent less than a comparable worker living in Mexico City.

Accordingly, the UNDP noted in its 2005 report that "in many countries regional disparities are a major source of inequality." In addition, as the UNDP observes, "living in a rural area is, in many countries, a marker for disadvantage." Poverty rates are usually higher, and the provision of public services (such as health care, schools, and citizen support agencies) is far lower. In Ghana, for example, the incidence of poverty is 2 percent in Accra, the capital, but 70 percent in the rural hinterlands, where only one in five residents have access to piped water (compared to four out of five urban residents).[3]

Although globalization can help even out regional disparities, it can also lead to increasing regional inequality. In China, for example, disparities have widened dramatically between the export-oriented regions of the coast and the interior (see **Geography Matters 7.1—China's Economic Development**). The transition economies of the countries of the former Soviet Union and its Eastern European satellites have registered some of the largest increases in regional inequality, and some core countries—especially Sweden, the United Kingdom, and the United States—have also registered significant increases in regional inequality since the 1980s. In Canada, the rising demand for resources (much of it from China) has caused a boom in Alberta, Saskatchewan, and Newfoundland, whereas difficulties in the manufacturing sector have dampened Ontario's economy.

Figure 7.7 shows the provincial and territorial distribution of annual average individual income levels in Canada in 2001. The continuing importance of staple production is shown in the above-national-average income figures for the Yukon and Northwest Territories, British Columbia, and Alberta, where

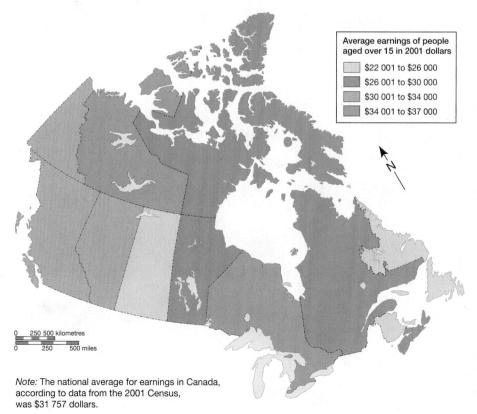

Average earnings of people aged over 15 in 2001 dollars

- $22 001 to $26 000
- $26 001 to $30 000
- $30 001 to $34 000
- $34 001 to $37 000

0   250 500 kilometres
0   250   500 miles

Note: The national average for earnings in Canada, according to data from the 2001 Census, was $31 757 dollars.

Figure 7.7   Provincial and territorial differences in average earnings: Canada in 2001   (*Source: Average Earnings of the Population* [*2001 Census*]. Adapted from the Statistics Canada website: **http://www40** .statcan.gc.ca/l01/cst01/labor50a-eng.htm.)

---

[3] United Nations Development Programme, *Report 2005*. New York: UNDP, 2006; the quotations are from pp. 2, 59, and 60.

China's Economic Development

Under the leadership of Deng Xiaoping (1978–1997), China dismantled its Communist-style central planning in favour of private entrepreneurship and market mechanisms and began integrating itself into the world economy. Since 1992, China has opened the door to foreign investment and normalized trading relationships with the United States and the European Union. In 2001, China was admitted to the World Trade Organization, allowing China to trade more freely than ever before with the rest of the world.

As a result of the opening, China has completely reorganized and revitalized its economy: year after year, China's manufacturing sector has been growing by 10 percent and more—which means it doubles in size every five to seven years! In 2010, China surpassed Germany as the world's third-largest economy after the United States and Japan.

China's increased participation in world trade has created an entirely new situation within the world economy. The Chinese economy's size makes it a major producer, and its labour costs have stayed flat for many years because there seemed to be an endless supply of people willing to work for 60 cents an hour (only recently has the inflationary pressure forced the government to order a rise in wages). This means that Chinese manufacturers, operating with low wages, have imposed a deflationary trend on world prices for manufacturers, forcing everyone to be more competitive and thus further intensifying the process of globalization. Meanwhile, the rapid expansion of consumer demand in China has begun to drive up commodity and energy prices in the world market.

Nowhere have China's "open-door" policies had more impact than in south China, where the Chinese government has deliberately built upon the prosperity of Hong Kong, the former British colony that was returned to China in 1997, and the established trade and manufacturing of Macão, a Portuguese colony that was returned to China in 1999. Geographically speaking, the coastline of south China also provides many protected bays suitable for harbours, and a series of ports has developed, providing an interface with the world economy.

Today, the cities and special economic zones of south China's "Gold Coast" provide a thriving export-processing platform that has driven double-digit annual economic growth for much of the past two decades. The city of Shenzhen (**Figure 7.1.1**) has grown from a population of a few thousand in 1970 to 8.5 million in 2007, with an additional 2 million in the surrounding municipalities. Such growth both reflects and generates the rise of a substantial middle class with significant spending power (**Figure 7.1.2**); it has also created significant inflation, especially in real estate prices (**Figure 7.1.3**).

Much of China's manufacturing growth has been based on a strategy of import substitution. In spite of China's membership in the World Trade Organization

(which has strict rules about intellectual property), a significant share of China's industry is based on counterfeiting and reverse engineering (making products that are copied and then sold under different or altered brand names). Copying everything from DVDs, movies, designer clothes and footwear, drugs, motorcycles, and automobiles to high-speed magnetic levitation trains saves Chinese industry enormous sums in research and development and licensing fees, while saving the country even greater sums in imports.

Foreign investors, meanwhile, are keen to develop a share of China's rapidly expanding and increasingly affluent market: by 2015, China is expected to surpass Japan as the second-largest market for consumer goods. The automobile market is particularly attractive to Western manufacturers as China already is the largest auto market and producer in the world: from 2009 to 2010 alone, production jumped from just under 14 million to over 18 million cars!

Much of the foreign investment in China comes from elsewhere within East Asia. Japan, Taiwan, and South Korea, having developed manufacturing industries that undercut those of the Western core countries, now face competition and deindustrialization themselves. In response, they move their production to cheaper Chinese

Figure 7.1.1   Shenzhen   The skyline of the city of Shenzhen, a city that only 40 years ago was a small town not even the size of Trail, BC, the community we considered at the beginning of the chapter.

Figure 7.1.2 New affluence A saleswoman waits for customers at an outlet of the French fashion brand Hermès in Shanghai. China's economic boom has led to a rapid increase in the size of the country's middle class, up nearly 25 percent in the past two years from 65 to 80 million people.

Figure 7.1.3 Real estate boom In the rapidly growing regions of coastal China, house price inflation has risen as high as 9.5 percent a month. Shown here is a small fishing village near Sanya Harbour in Hainan province, where new luxury buildings are displacing the older homes and their inhabitants.

factories: more than 10,000 Taiwanese firms have established operations in China, investing an estimated US$150 billion. Pusan, the centre of the South Korean footwear industry that in 1990 exported US$4.3 billion worth of shoes, is full of deserted factories. South Korean footwear exports are down to less than US$700 million, whereas China's footwear exports have increased from US$2.1 billion in 1990 to US$24 billion in 2007.

Similarly, Japanese electronics giants have expanded operations in China even as they have shed tens of thousands of workers at home. Toshiba's factory in Dalian illustrates the logic. Toshiba is one of about 40 Japanese companies that have built large-scale production facilities in a special export-processing zone established around Dalian in the early 1990s with generous financial support from the Japanese government and major Japanese firms. By shifting production of digital televisions here from its plant in Saitama, Japan, in 2001, Toshiba cut labour costs per worker by 90 percent.

Although China's economic growth is certainly dizzying, we must keep in mind that it is very uneven. True, some regions have gone through an extraordinary transformation, but others are lagging far behind. In Guangdong province, near Hong Kong, for example, industrial growth, real estate development, and investment in highway construction have increased by an average of 15 to 25 percent per year throughout the past decade while incomes and consumer spending have skyrocketed. Once known mainly for its abundant and high-quality long-grain rice, Guangdong now imports rice from Thailand. Along Guangdong's Pearl River Delta, it is difficult to photograph one of the classic rice paddies without capturing a construction site as well.

Meanwhile, other regions are not sharing in the upsurge. The remote northwestern province of Gansu, for example, is one of the poorest regions in China with an income per capita 40 percent below the national average. Because of its interior location far away from port facilities, few factories are located here. With poor soils highly susceptible to erosion, low and erratic rainfall, and few off-farm employment opportunities, a high proportion of its inhabitants live in poverty.

Other regions are struggling to make the transition: in the southwestern province of Sichuan, there remain more than 20,000 state-owned enterprises, most of which are not able to keep pace with China's economic transformation. Exports from the region's textile factories have declined. The region's economy had become increasingly depressed even before the severe disruption of the 2008 earthquake that killed at least 80,000 and made 4.8 million homeless. Although the official unemployment rate is just 3 percent, the actual rate is closer to 20 percent.

resource extraction (based on gold and diamonds, lumber, and oil) has become the mainstay of the regional economy. Although somewhat lower, average individual income levels in Ontario are also above the national average, illustrating the continuing importance of core and periphery relationships in the Canadian economy.

Resources and Technology

The example of Canada's regional differences illustrates how resource endowment can influence patterns of economic development. Key resources include cultivable land, energy sources, and valuable minerals. These key resources and—just as importantly—the *combinations* of energy and minerals crucial to economic development are distributed unevenly. A lack of natural resources can, of course, be remedied through international trade (Japan's success is a prime example of this). For most countries, however, the resource base remains an important determinant of development.

Cultivable Land   The distribution of cultivable land represents an important basis for economic development. Much more than half of Earth's land surface is unsuitable for any productive form of arable farming: poor soils, short growing seasons, arid climates, mountainous terrain, forests, and conservation limit the extent of agricultural land across much of the globe. As a result, the distribution of the world's cultivable land is highly uneven, being concentrated in Europe, west-central Russia, eastern North America, the Australian littoral, Latin America, India, eastern China, and parts of sub-Saharan Africa. In detail, of course, some of these regions may be marginal for arable farming because of marshy soils or other adverse conditions, whereas irrigation often extends the local frontier of productive agriculture. We also have to bear in mind that not all cultivable land is of the same quality.

Energy   One particularly important resource in terms of the world's economic geography is energy. The major sources of commercial energy—oil, natural gas, and coal—are all very unevenly distributed across the globe. Most of the world's core economies are reasonably well off in terms of energy production, the major exceptions being Japan and parts of Europe (refer back to Figure 4.17 on p. 169). Most peripheral countries, on the other hand, are energy poor. The major exceptions are Algeria, Ecuador, Gabon, Indonesia, Libya, Nigeria, Venezuela, and the Gulf states—all major oil producers. Because of this unevenness, energy has become an important component of world trade: oil is now the most important single commodity in world trade, making up more than 20 percent of the total by value in 2008.

For many peripheral countries the cost of importing energy represents a heavy burden, sometimes using up a quarter or more of their export revenues. Few peripheral countries can afford to consume energy on the scale of the developed economies, so patterns of commercial energy consumption tend to mirror the fundamental core–periphery cleavage of the world economy (see Figure 4.17). In 2005, energy consumption per capita in Canada was 20 times that of India, 35 times that of Mozambique, and over 230 times that of Niger.

But this look at commercial energy does not tell the whole story yet: 1.5 billion people in peripheral countries depend on collecting fuelwood as their principal source of energy (refer back to Figure 4.20 on p. 174). The collection of wood fuel causes considerable deforestation, and the problem is most serious in densely populated locations, arid and semiarid regions, and cooler mountainous areas, where the regeneration of shrubs, woodlands, and forests is particularly slow. Nearly 100 million people in 22 countries (16 of them in Africa) cannot meet their minimum energy needs even by overcutting remaining forests.

Valuable Minerals   A high proportion of the world's key raw materials is concentrated in Canada, Russia, the United States, South Africa, and Australia. This is largely a result of geology, but it is also partly a function of these countries' political and economic stability, which has enabled a much more intensive exploration of resources. On the other hand, political instability in much of postcolonial Africa, Asia, and Latin America has seriously hindered the exploration and exploitation of resources. We should bear in mind, therefore, that this distribution reflects only the currently *known* resource base.

7.2 Geography in the Information Age

In his study of French Guiana called *Space in the Tropics*, Peter Redfield shows how technology can also change the value of *territory* as a resource. In the nineteenth century, the country was regarded as such an unattractive, disease-ridden wilderness by Europeans that they located a prison colony there. By the late twentieth century, however, that "wilderness" had become reinterpreted as a "pristine jungle," valued for its ecotourism potential. In addition, the country's position close to the Equator made it the perfect launch site for the European Space Agency.[4]

___

[4] Peter Redfield, *Space in the Tropics: From Convicts to Rockets in French Guiana*. Berkeley: University of California Press, 2000. For further discussion of the themes raised in this book, see the review by Alan Nash in *GeoJournal* (56) 2003, pp. 241–242.

We should also recognize, as Chapter 4 has shown, that our attitudes toward science and technology (and hence our view of resources) are a product of our own particular culture. Modern Canadian society, for example, is built on a clear distinction between the human and the natural world and is founded on a series of economic principles that stress the importance of private ownership, profit maximization, and competition. Such societies will have a very different approach to the sustainable development of global resources than, for example, the Inuit narwhale hunters, whose culture frames a very different economic geography—one that is founded on common property, a non-exploitive use of renewable resources, and a respect for nature.

We should also bear in mind that the significance of particular resources is often tied to particular technologies and the state of the environment. As these change, the geography of economic development is "rewritten." One important example of this was the switch in industrial energy sources from coal to oil, gas, and electricity in the twentieth century. When this happened, coalfield areas in Atlantic Canada found their prospects for economic development dashed, whereas oil field areas in Alberta suddenly had potential. More recently, technological improvements and a decline in more easily exploited resources have led to the development of that province's oil sands deposits, despite the huge refining costs and environmental impacts.

Regions and countries that are heavily dependent on one particular resource are particularly vulnerable to the consequences of technological change. They are also vulnerable to fluctuations in the price set for their product on the world market. These vulnerabilities are particularly important for a number of Canadian mining industries and Canadian farmers. You will recall from Chapter 2 that the staples thesis lists such vulnerability as one of the challenges of Canadian economic development. Globally, these vulnerabilities are particularly important for countries whose economies are especially dependent on nonfuel minerals, such as the Democratic Republic of the Congo (copper), Mauritania (iron ore), Namibia (diamonds), Niger (uranium), Sierra Leone (diamonds), Togo (phosphates), and Zambia (copper).

Technology Systems   As you will recall from Chapter 2, technological innovations in energy, transportation, and manufacturing processes—called *technology systems*—have been important catalysts for changes in the pattern of economic development. They have allowed a succession of expansions of economic activity in time and space. As a result, many existing industrial regions have grown bigger and more productive. Industrial development has also spread to new regions, whose growth has become interdependent with the fortunes of others through a complex web of production and trade. As each new technology system creates new requirements for natural resources as well as labour forces and markets,

7.3   Geography in the Information Age

We can combine the ideas of "creating" space and technology systems by looking at the spatial changes enabled by cell phone technology. In many parts of northern and rural Canada, remote communities or individual homeowners for the longest time were disadvantaged when it came to accessing telecommunication systems because it was either physically impossible or prohibitively expensive to run cables to their locations. This not only reduced the attractiveness of those locations as residences but also limited what kind of businesses could locate there. Now, more advanced satellite systems make it possible for remote locations to connect to the "fast world" just as easily and quickly (and almost as cheaply) as a suburban business park in Calgary—which opens up new opportunities for businesses and jobs. Similarly, many peripheral countries are currently "leapfrogging" over the "wired" stage of telecommunications, thus skipping the expensive infrastructure requirements.

it tends to favour different regions and different kinds of places, thus rewriting the geography of economic development and shifting the balance of advantages among countries, regions, and places.

Early technology systems diffused outwards in a "pulse" of innovation that took changes outwards from the core to the periphery. In the process, technology systems became part of broader economic forces that tied the global core and periphery together. However, by the time a technology eventually diffused to more remote locations, a newer technology had already supplanted it in the countries of the core. For instance, canals were still being built in Canada in the 1830s, at a time when they were being replaced by railroads in Britain. This "lag" illustrates one of the mechanisms that made it difficult for peripheral countries to simply "catch up" with core countries.

THE ECONOMIC STRUCTURE OF COUNTRIES AND REGIONS

The relative share of primary, secondary, tertiary, and quaternary economic activities determines the *economic structure* of a country or region. **Primary activities** are those concerned directly with natural resources of any kind; they include agriculture, mining, fishing, and forestry. **Secondary activities** are those that process, transform, fabricate, or assemble the raw materials derived from primary activities, or that reassemble, refinish, or package manufactured goods. Secondary activities include steelmaking, food processing, furniture making, textile manufacturing, automobile assembly, and garment manufacturing. **Tertiary activities** are those involving the sale and exchange of goods and services; they include warehousing; retail stores; personal services, such as hairdressing; commercial services, such as accounting and advertising; and entertainment. **Quaternary activities** are those dealing with the handling and processing of knowledge and information. Examples include data processing, information retrieval, education, and research and development (R&D).

Geographical Divisions of Labour

Variations in economic structure—according to primary, secondary, tertiary, or quaternary activities—reflect *geographical divisions of labour*. Geographical divisions of labour are national, regional, and locally based economic specializations that have evolved with the growth of the world-system of trade and politics

primary activities: economic activities that are concerned directly with natural resources of any kind

secondary activities: economic activities that process, transform, fabricate, or assemble the raw materials derived from primary activities, or that reassemble, refinish, or package manufactured goods

tertiary activities: economic activities involving the sale and exchange of goods and services

quaternary activities: economic activities that deal with the handling and processing of knowledge and information

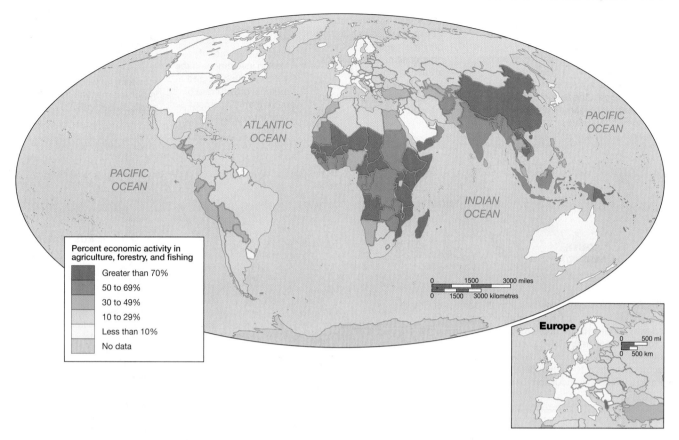

Figure 7.8   The geography of primary economic activities   Primary economic activities are those that are concerned directly with natural resources of any kind. They include agriculture, mining, forestry, and fishing. The vast majority of the world's population, concentrated in China, India, Southeast Asia, and Africa, is engaged in primary economic activities. This map shows the percentage of the labour force in each country that was engaged in primary employment in 2002. In some countries, including China, primary activities account for more than 70 percent of the workforce. In contrast, primary activities always account for less than 10 percent of the labour force in the world's core countries, and often for less than 5 percent.

(see Chapter 2), the exploitation of environmental resources, and the locational needs of successive technology systems. They represent one of the most important dimensions of economic development. For instance, countries whose economies are dominated by primary-sector activities tend to have a relatively low per capita GDP. The exceptions to the rule are oil-rich countries, such as Saudi Arabia, Qatar, and Venezuela. Where the geographical division of labour has produced national economies with a large secondary sector, per capita GDP is much higher (as, for example, in Argentina and Korea). The highest levels of per capita GDP, however, are associated with economies that are *postindustrial*: economies where the tertiary and quaternary sectors have grown to dominate the workforce, with smaller but highly productive secondary sectors.

As **Figure 7.8** shows, the economic structure of much of the world is dominated by the primary sector (that is, primary activities such as agriculture, mining, fishing, and forestry). In much of Africa and Asia, between 50 percent and 75 percent of the labour force is engaged in primary-sector activities. In contrast, the primary sector of the world's core regions is typically small, occupying only 5 to 10 percent of the labour force.

The secondary sector is concentrated in the core countries and in semiperipheral countries, where the world's specialized manufacturing regions are located (**Figure 7.9**). In 2005, core countries accounted for almost three-quarters of world manufacturing value added (MVA). This share has been slowly decreasing, however, as globalization processes have changed the international division of labour. The core countries had an average annual growth rate for MVA of

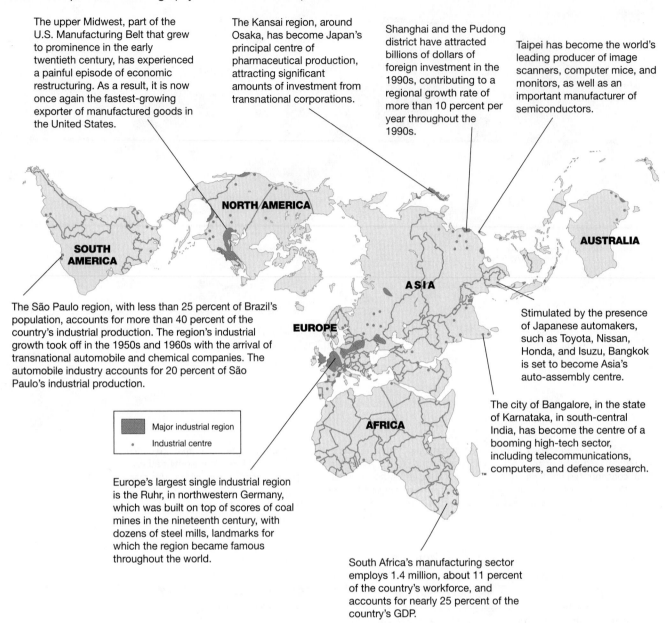

The upper Midwest, part of the U.S. Manufacturing Belt that grew to prominence in the early twentieth century, has experienced a painful episode of economic restructuring. As a result, it is now once again the fastest-growing exporter of manufactured goods in the United States.

The Kansai region, around Osaka, has become Japan's principal centre of pharmaceutical production, attracting significant amounts of investment from transnational corporations.

Shanghai and the Pudong district have attracted billions of dollars of foreign investment in the 1990s, contributing to a regional growth rate of more than 10 percent per year throughout the 1990s.

Taipei has become the world's leading producer of image scanners, computer mice, and monitors, as well as an important manufacturer of semiconductors.

The São Paulo region, with less than 25 percent of Brazil's population, accounts for more than 40 percent of the country's industrial production. The region's industrial growth took off in the 1950s and 1960s with the arrival of transnational automobile and chemical companies. The automobile industry accounts for 20 percent of São Paulo's industrial production.

Stimulated by the presence of Japanese automakers, such as Toyota, Nissan, Honda, and Isuzu, Bangkok is set to become Asia's auto-assembly centre.

The city of Bangalore, in the state of Karnataka, in south-central India, has become the centre of a booming high-tech sector, including telecommunications, computers, and defence research.

Major industrial region

Industrial centre

Europe's largest single industrial region is the Ruhr, in northwestern Germany, which was built on top of scores of coal mines in the nineteenth century, with dozens of steel mills, landmarks for which the region became famous throughout the world.

South Africa's manufacturing sector employs 1.4 million, about 11 percent of the country's workforce, and accounts for nearly 25 percent of the country's GDP.

Figure 7.9 The geography of secondary economic activities Secondary economic activities are those that process, transform, fabricate, or assemble raw materials, or that reassemble, refinish, or package manufactured goods. As this map shows, the world's largest and most productive manufacturing regions are located in the core regions of Europe, North America, and Japan. Important concentrations of manufacturing industry are located in semiperipheral countries, such as South Korea, Mexico, and Brazil, but the increasing globalization of manufacturing means that patterns are subject to rapid change. (*Source:* Map projection, Buckminster Fuller Institute and Dymaxion Map Design, Santa Barbara, CA. The word *Dymaxion* and the Fuller Projection Dymaxion™ Map design are trademarks of the Buckminster Fuller Institute, Santa Barbara, California, © 1938, 1967, & 1992. All rights reserved.)

around 2 percent from 1990 to 2004, whereas the growth rate in the rest of the world was closer to 7 percent. By 2005, 7 of the 20 biggest manufacturing countries were semiperipheral: China, South Korea, Mexico, Brazil, India, Argentina, and Thailand. By contrast, the share of world MVA for all of Africa has changed little over the last two decades, remaining at about 1 percent.

The growth of manufacturing in Pacific Asia is particularly interesting, as it has generated agglomerations of economic activity at a scale that sometimes crosses national boundaries, as with the Southern China–Hong Kong–Taiwan triangle and the Singapore–Batam–Johor triangle (**Figure 7.10**). The 1,500-kilometre urban belt in northeast Asia that runs from Beijing to Tokyo via Pyongyang and Seoul connects some 80 cities of over 200,000 inhabitants each, encompassing nearly 100 million urban dwellers altogether. In terms of individual countries, China has experienced a dramatic increase in manufacturing production, achieving annual average growth rates during the 1970s, 1980s, and 1990s of about 8 percent, 11 percent, and 14 percent, respectively (see Geography Matters 7.1—China's Economic Development on p. 306). Other Pacific Rim countries, such as Malaysia and Thailand, have also experienced rapid growth in manufacturing production. These shifts are part of a globalization of economic activity that largely has been the result of strategies of large transnational corporations.

The tertiary and quaternary sectors are significant only in the most affluent countries of the core. In Canada, for example, the tertiary and quaternary sectors in 2004 accounted for a total of 74 percent of the labour force, whereas the primary and secondary sectors accounted for 5 and 21 percent, respectively. In every core country, the tertiary sector has grown significantly in the past several decades as consumption and marketing have become the hallmarks of postindustrial economies.

More recently, globalization has meant that knowledge-based activities have become a critical aspect of economic development, resulting in the rapid growth of quaternary industries in core countries (**Figure 7.11**). For the world's core economies, knowledge has become just as important as physical and human resources in determining levels of economic well-being. More than half of the GDP of major core countries is now based on the production and distribution of knowledge. By contrast, for the world's peripheral economies, lack of knowledge—along with a limited capacity to absorb and communicate knowledge—has become an increasingly important barrier to economic development. As a result, economic productivity tends to fall relative to the performance of places and regions in core economies, where new knowledge is constantly generated and rapidly and effectively disseminated.

Stages of Development?

This overall relationship between economic structure and levels of prosperity makes it tempting to interpret economic development in terms of distinctive *stages*. Each region or country, in other words, might be thought of as progressing from the early stages of development, with a heavy reliance on primary activities (and relatively low levels of prosperity), through a phase of industrialization, and on to a "mature" stage of postindustrial development (with a diversified economic structure and relatively high levels of prosperity). This, in fact, is a commonly held view of economic development first proposed by the prominent economist W.W. Rostow (**Figure 7.12**). Rostow's model, like those of most economists, rests on certain simplifying assumptions about the world. As we have seen, however, the real world is highly differentiated, not just in its natural resources but also in its demographics, culture, and politics. The assumptions in Rostow's model fit the experience of some parts of the world, but not all.

Furthermore, Rostow's model perpetuates the myth of "developmentalism," the idea that every country and region will eventually make economic progress toward "high mass consumption" provided that they compete to the best of their ability within the world economy. (It is not coincidental that this idea fits

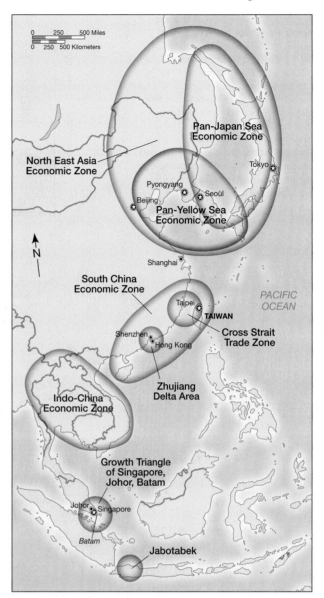

Figure 7.10   Emerging growth zones in Pacific Asia   The globalization of manufacturing industries has spurred the growth of a series of extended metropolitan regions.   (*Source:* Adapted from P. Dicken, *Global Shift*, 4th ed. New York: Guilford, 2003, Figure 3.28, p. 78.)

Figure 7.11 A model of the economic transition In very general terms, most "advanced economies" have moved through the same pattern of change in the employment structure of their workforce. Initially, primary sector activities dominate, but over time, these are replaced by secondary and then tertiary employment as the economy matures. In many core countries, the present competition for increased productivity, coupled with technological innovation, is now leading to the growth of the quaternary sector.

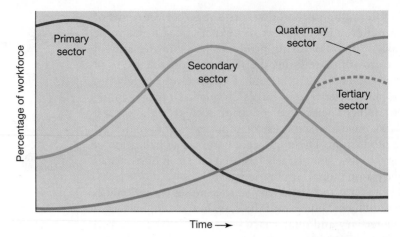

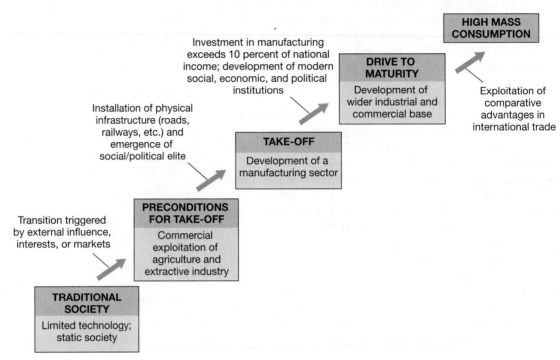

Figure 7.12 Stages of economic development This diagram illustrates a model of economic development based on the idea of successive stages. Each stage is seen as leading to the next, though different regions or countries may take longer than others to make the transition from one stage to the next. According to this view, first put forward by economist W.W. Rostow, places and regions can be seen as following parallel courses within a world that is steadily modernizing. Late starters will eventually make progress, but at speeds determined by their resource endowments, their productivity, and the wisdom of their people's policies and decisions.

well with the globalization mantras of competition and free markets.) The main weakness of developmentalism is that it is simply not reasonable to compare the prospects of late starters to the experience of those places, regions, and countries that were among the early starters. For these early starters the horizons were clear: free of effective competition, free of obstacles, and free of precedents. For the late starters the situation is entirely different. Today's less developed regions must compete in a crowded field while facing numerous barriers that are a direct consequence of the success of some of the early starters.

Indeed, many writers and theorists of international development claim that the prosperity of the core countries in the world economy has been based on *under*development and squalor in peripheral countries. Peripheral countries, it is argued, could not "follow" the previous historical experience of developed countries in stages-of-development fashion because their underdevelopment (that is, exploitation) was a structural requirement for development in the core. The development of Europe and North America, in other words, required the systematic underdevelopment of peripheral countries. By means of unequal trade, exploitation of labour, and profit extraction, the underdeveloped countries became increasingly rather than decreasingly impoverished.

The writings of André Gunder Frank exemplify this critique. Frank rejected the idea that underdevelopment is an original condition, equivalent to "traditionalism" or "backwardness." To the contrary, he argues, it is a condition *created* by integration into the worldwide capitalist system of exchange. The world economy, Frank argues, has been unequally structured since Europeans first ventured out into the world in the sixteenth century. Although the form of the dominance of core over periphery has changed from colonialism and imperialism to neocolonialism, an overall transfer of wealth from periphery to core has continued to fuel growth in some places at the expense of others.

Frank's approach is an example of what can be called "dependency theory." This has been a very influential approach in explaining global patterns of development and underdevelopment. It states, essentially, that development and underdevelopment are reverse sides of the same process: *development somewhere requires underdevelopment somewhere else.* Immanuel Wallerstein's world-system theory (see Chapter 2) takes this kind of dependency into account. According to this perspective, the entire world economy is seen as an evolving market system with an economic hierarchy of states. Sadly, the dependency of peripheral countries is often worsened, rather than alleviated, by the "normal" workings of international trade, debt, and aid in this market system.

International Trade, Debt, and Aid

The geographical division of labour on a world scale means that the geography of international trade is very complex. One significant reflection of the increased economic integration of the world-system is that global trade has grown much more rapidly over the past few decades than global production. Between 1985 and 2005, the average annual growth rate of the value of world exports was twice that of the growth of world production and several times greater than that of world population growth. In other words, more and more of what we consume is transported around the world.

Patterns of International Trade   Patterns of world trade are shifting in response to several factors. In general, trade within and between core regions is growing at the expense of trade between core countries and peripheral countries—with the major exception of trade in oil. Innovations in transport, communications, and manufacturing technology have diminished the friction of distance in trade. Shifts in global politics have also affected the geography of trade, most importantly through the breakup of the former Soviet Union, the increasing integration of Europe, and the rise of China. But perhaps the most important shift in global politics in relation to world trade has been the shift toward open markets and free trade through neoliberal policies propagated by core countries.

The globalization of economic activity has created new flows of materials, components, information, and finished products. As a global system of manufacturing has emerged, significant quantities of manufactured goods are now imported *and* exported across much of the world through complex commodity chains; no longer do developed economies export manufactures and peripheral countries import them (see **Geography Matters 7.2—Commodity Chains**). African countries are an important exception, with many of them barely participating in world trade in manufactures.

The most striking aspect of contemporary patterns of trade is the persistence of the dependence of peripheral countries on trade with core countries that are geographically or geopolitically close. Thus, for example, the United States is the central focus for the exports and the origin of the bulk of the imports of most Central

Commodity Chains

A commodity chain is a network of labour and production processes whose end result is a finished commodity. Global commodity chains link the progression of a commodity from design through procurement of raw materials and production to import or export to the point of sale, distribution for sale, marketing, and advertising. They are often entirely internal to the global operations of transnational corporations.

Advances in telecommunications, management techniques, transportation, informatics, finance, and other services to industry have made possible the segmentation of corporate production lines, as well as services, across

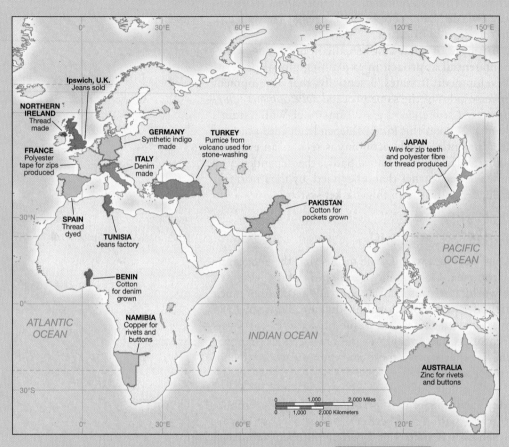

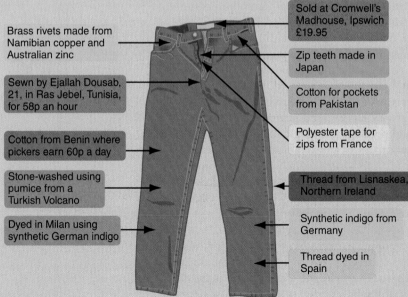

Figure 7.2.1 The making of a pair of Lee Cooper jeans (*Source:* Adapted from A. Hughes and S. Reimer [eds.], *Geographies of Commodity Chains.* New York: Routledge, 2004.)

multiple settings. Manufacturing companies can design a product in one country, have it produced by contractors in various countries continents apart, sell the product with its brand name by telephone or Internet almost anywhere in the world, and have other contractors deliver it. Advances in technology and management have also permitted the reproduction and standardization of services and products on a global basis. Certain patented services, such as fast-food restaurants, rely on computer-regulated technology to deliver a standard service and product over time and geographic space.

Almost every mass-marketed manufactured product involves a complex commodity chain. Take, for example, the manufacture of Lee Cooper jeans (**Figure 7.2.1**). Designed in the United States; advertised globally; and retailed in stores across Europe, the United States, and the metropolises of semiperipheral and peripheral countries, their manufacture draws on labour and products from around the world.

Global commodity chains have three broad types. The first is producer-driven, in which large, often transnational, corporations coordinate production networks. A good example of this is the U.S. pharmaceutical industry. Research and development of drugs are conducted in the United States, but the materials and components are produced, assembled, and marketed in a vertically integrated global commodity chain that involves semiperipheral sites.

A second type of commodity chain is consumer-driven, where large retailers and brand-name merchandisers organize decentralized production networks in a variety of exporting countries, often in the periphery. A good example is the case of Lee Cooper jeans described here. Another good example is the discount chain-store company Walmart, which contracts directly with producers in China for the bulk of its merchandise (which, in the United States, is often sold to the accompaniment of advertising that invokes community-oriented and even patriotic themes).

The third type, the marketing-driven commodity chain, represents a hybrid of the first two types. It involves the production of inexpensive consumer goods—such as colas, beers, breakfast cereals, candies, cigarettes, and infant formula—that are global commodities and carry global brands yet are often manufactured in the periphery and semiperiphery for consumption in those regions. These commodities take their globalized status not only from their recipes and production techniques but, even more important, from their globally contrived cultural identities.

Different forms of commodity chains provide varying opportunities for firms and national economies to enter into and improve their position within the global division of labour. They are an important dimension of the complex transnationalization of economic space. They are also an important dimension of the complex currents of cultural globalization. In addition to facilitating the standardization of products and services (for those who can afford them) around the world, commodity chains also reflect the inequalities that are inscribed into the global economy. If core-country consumers thought for a moment about the origins of many of the products they consume, they might recognize what is happening "down the line," where poverty wages and grim working and living conditions are a precondition for the beginning of many commodity chains. In contrast, those who work on the farms and plantations and in the workshops and factories at the beginning of commodity chains are acutely aware—thanks to contemporary media—of the dramatically more affluent lifestyles of those who will eventually be able to consume the fruits of their labour.

American countries, whereas France is the focus for commodity flows to and from French ex-colonies such as Algeria, Cambodia, Benin, and the Ivory Coast. These flows, however, represent only part of the action for the core economies, whose trading patterns are dominated by flows to and from other core countries.

Patterns of International Debt   In many peripheral countries, debt service—the annual interest on international debts—is a significant handicap to economic development, swallowing up 20 percent or more of all export earnings (**Figure 7.13**). By 2005, the total debt owed by low- and middle-income countries to high-income core countries was just over $2.7 trillion. Core countries are doing extremely well from this aspect of international finance: in 2005, they took in about $514 billion in debt servicing, while giving out less than $60 billion in new loans.

At the root of the international debt problem is the structured inequality of the world economy. The role inherited by most peripheral countries within the international division of labour has been one of producing primary goods and commodities for export to the core countries. An obvious counterstrategy is to attempt to establish a more diversified manufacturing base—a strategy known as import substitution (see Chapter 2). It is a difficult strategy to pursue, however, because it requires vast amounts of start-up capital, which debt-ridden peripheral countries find hard to raise.

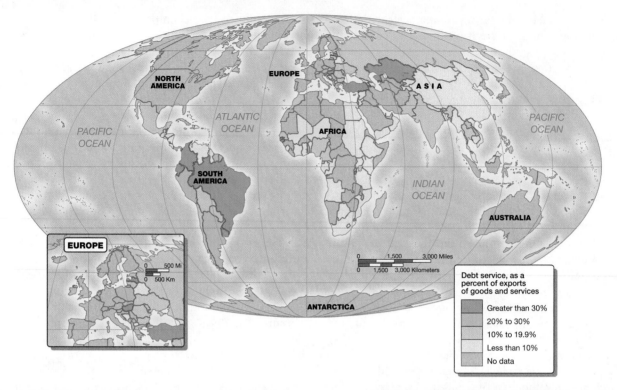

Figure 7.13   The debt crisis   In some countries, the annual interest on international debts (their "debt service") accounts for more than 20 percent of the annual value of their exports of goods and services. Many countries first got into debt trouble in the mid-1970s, when Western banks, faced with recession at home, offered low-interest loans to the governments of peripheral countries rather than being stuck with idle capital. When the world economy heated up again, interest rates rose and many countries found themselves unable to repay the loan or even the interest. The World Bank and the International Monetary Fund (IMF), in tandem with Western governments, worked to prevent a global financial crisis by organizing and guaranteeing programs that eased poor countries' debt burdens. Western banks were encouraged to swap debt for equity stakes in nationalized industries, while debtor governments were persuaded to impose austere economic policies. These policies have helped ease the debt crisis, but often at the price of severe hardship for ordinary people. In dark humour, among radical development theorists, IMF came to stand for "imposing misery and famine."

Patterns of International Aid   Large-scale movements of international development aid began shortly after World War II with the Marshall Plan, financed by the United States to bolster war-torn European countries whose economic weakness, it was believed, made them susceptible to communism. During the 1950s and 1960s, as more peripheral countries gained independence, aid became a useful weapon in cold war offensives to establish and preserve political influence throughout the world. By the late 1960s, the list of donor countries had expanded beyond the superpowers to include smaller countries such as Denmark and Sweden, whose motivation in aid giving must be seen as more philanthropic than political. In addition, there was a greater geographic dispersal of aid, thanks largely to the activities of multilateral financial agencies such as the IMF and the World Bank. Meanwhile, private aid organizations, such as OXFAM, have focused their efforts on emergency aid, on campaigning for debt-relief programs, and on fair trade practices.

The end of the cold war resulted in diminished levels of international aid. Thus, whereas official development assistance from OECD (the Organisation for Economic Co-operation and Development, an association of 34 industrialized countries) countries amounted to nearly 0.5 percent of their total GNI in 1965, it had fallen to 0.25 percent by 2007. Perhaps even more disturbing is the World Bank's assertion that a large proportion of developed countries' pledged aid is "phantom" aid because it ends up going to international consultants and donor countries' own firms. Altogether, around 60 percent of all international aid becomes phantom in this way; in the case of aid from France and the United States, the figure is closer to 90 percent.

Nevertheless, for some countries the impact of aid is clearly significant. Liberia, for example, received aid amounting to 54 percent of its GDP in 2007; and 16 other countries—including Afghanistan, Burundi, Congo, Mozambique, Rwanda, and Sierra Leone—received aid equivalent to more than 20 percent of their GDP. These figures, however, say as much about these countries' extremely small GDP as anything else. They are also exceptions. In general, the poorest countries are by no means the biggest recipients of aid; the amount of aid received per capita is generally very low, and a large share of it is deployed as emergency food aid. In 2002, low-income countries like Burundi, Chad, and Uganda received an average of around US$17 per capita in overseas development assistance. At these levels, aid cannot seriously be regarded as a catalyst for development or as an instrument for redressing core–periphery inequalities.

EVERYTHING IN ITS PLACE: PRINCIPLES OF LOCATION

As geographers have sought to understand and explain local patterns of economic development, they have uncovered some fundamental principles that shape and influence decisions involving the location of economic activities. To the extent that regularity and predictability exist in economic geography, they stem from the logic of these principles.

Principles of Commercial and Industrial Location

Locational decisions in commercial and industrial life are subject to a number of key factors:

- Accessibility to *material inputs*, such as raw materials and energy.
- Availability of *labour* with particular skills.
- *Processing* costs, such as the cost of land and buildings, machinery, wages, and taxes.
- The pull of the *market* for the product or service, which depends on the importance of being near customers.
- The influence of cultural and institutional factors that channel certain activities away from some locations and toward others. The most important of these are *government policies* of one kind or another. It is quite common, for example, for local governments to offer tax breaks to companies to attract investments that will result in the creation of new jobs in the area.

7.4 Geography in the Information Age

The dramatic rise of online shopping is literally changing the landscape of retailing as it alters the importance of location for retailers. For retailers that are able to establish on online outlet, locational constraints are lessened and they can tap into larger markets further afield. At the same time, retailers that depend exclusively on physical stores will find it increasingly harder to compete with the cost advantages of online businesses that need not pay rent for Main Street stores or wages for floor staff. As the resulting store closures are most likely to affect marginally attractive locations, Canadian downtowns that are already struggling will find it even harder to stem the decline of their Main Streets.[5]

[5] For information on online shopping by Canadians, see *The Daily* of Statistics Canada (September 27, 2010): www.statcan.gc.ca/daily-quotidien/100927/dq100927a-eng.htm.

■ The influence of *behavioural considerations* that stem from the objectives and constraints affecting individual decision makers.

The importance and influence of these factors varies according to the type of activity involved. In retailing activities, for example, proximity to specific consumer markets is almost always of paramount importance. For small retailers, behavioural factors are likely to involve the personal values and priorities of business owners—the owner's attachment to a particular neighbourhood, for example, or the owner's desire to locate his or her business at an upscale or central address.

In contrast to the market orientation of retail businesses, manufacturing companies often locate their activities according to the attributes of their inputs (that is, raw materials or components) and outputs (products). Steel production, for example, uses large quantities of iron ore, limestone, coking coal, and water. These basic raw materials lose both bulk and weight as they are transformed into steel. When such weight-losing raw materials are involved in production, it seems most economical to locate the manufacturing plant near the source of those materials. Why transport unnecessary weight?

It was this very insight that in 1909 prompted Alfred Weber to develop a general theory of industrial location. Weber's approach was based on the view that industries attempted to minimize their total transport costs, and that their optimal location would be at the point where this was achieved. This location was somewhere inside a polygon formed by the locations

Figure 7.14   The Sheffield manufacturing region   The growth of Sheffield was largely a result of the locational "pull" of the weight-losing inputs needed for iron and steel manufacturing: limestone, coal, iron ore, and water were all available nearby. A multitude of firms sprang up to use the locally produced high-quality iron and steel in the manufacture of everything from anchors, cutlery, files, and nails to needles, pins, and wire. The photograph shows one of the many ironworks that produced cutlery in Sheffield in the nineteenth century.

of the raw materials and markets. If we assume that transport costs are directly proportional to distance, we can use simple geometry to find the point of lowest total transport costs: the most logical place to locate our factory.

Weber developed some simple rules that indicated where industries would locate. Industries that are based on raw materials, such as coal or iron ore, that lose bulk or weight as they undergo industrial processing, tend to locate near the source of the raw materials. The industrial region around Sheffield, England (**Figure 7.14**), for example, was established on exactly this locational logic. On the other hand, where the manufacturing process adds significant bulk or weight to a product (as, for example, in beer brewing), proximity to markets is more likely the overriding factor.

Many different inputs to different industries exist, however, each with different attributes (such as weight, bulk, form, perishability, and fragility) and different degrees of availability across geographical space. Some inputs (such as bauxite, sulphur, and zinc) are relatively uncommon and very localized; others (water, for example) are much more generally available.

Critics have argued that Weber's model can never capture all of the aspects that go into industrial locational decision making—such as the complexity of

7.5   Geography in the Information Age

Certainly, ours is a very different world to that of Alfred Weber's, and he would be stunned to find that water—a resource he considered so generally available that it could not affect industrial location on its own—is now actively traded around the world in the form of mineral waters such as Perrier from France, San Pellegrino from Italy, and Fiji Water from the South Pacific (where water shortages are chronic).

inputs mentioned above, but also labour costs, government subsidies, or the cachet of a particular location—and should therefore be abandoned as misleading.

Another criticism of Weber's model is that it is largely *ahistorical*—by which we mean that the influences of the past are ignored. To test the validity of this criticism, we return to the example of Sheffield. Although it is true that the presence of iron and steel mills in that city can be explained by the use of Weber's analysis of transport costs, this approach omits the influence of centuries of industrial development. The area around Sheffield had a heritage of innovation in metal work and metallurgical skill that is at least as valuable as the raw materials themselves. In fact, Chaucer's *Canterbury Tales* (written c. 1380) already made reference to cutlery produced there, probably in one of the many small forges dotted along the riverbanks of the area.

In other words, a full explanation for the location of industry is often far more nuanced than we might first imagine, and although the dictates of today's spatial economy obviously have to be considered, we must also pay due regard to the part played by the past in shaping present decision making, as well as the role of interdependencies.

Economic Interdependence: Agglomeration Effects

We can begin by recognizing that in the real world, the various factors of commercial and industrial location all operate within complex webs of *functional interdependence*. These webs include the relationships among different kinds of industries, different kinds of stores, and different kinds of offices. The webs are based on linkages and relationships that tend to follow certain principles. Among the most important principles to human geography are the principles of agglomeration, which influence the locational patterns of economic activities.

Agglomeration is the clustering together of functionally related activities—for example, the cluster of high-tech firms in Silicon Valley (the area between Santa Clara and San Jose, California). In Canada, similar clusters have developed around Ottawa and in the Technology Triangle of Kitchener-Waterloo-Cambridge. **Agglomeration effects** are the cost advantages that accrue to individual firms because of their location within such a cluster. These advantages are sometimes known as *external economies*. **External economies** are cost savings resulting from advantages that are derived from circumstances beyond a firm's own organization and methods of production. For example, it pays to have a wire-making factory located close to a steel mill, not just to save on transporting the steel for the wire but also to save on the cost of reheating the steel and to take advantage of the mill's experienced labour force.

Such situations lead to complex linkages among local economic activities. In relation to any given industry or firm, *backward linkages* are those that develop with suppliers. In our example, the wire-making factory has a backward linkage with the steel mill. The steel mill, in turn, will have backward linkages with its own suppliers—firms that supply raw materials, machinery, specialized maintenance services, and so on. For the steel mill, the wire-making factory is one of a number of *forward linkages* with firms using its output. Others might include can-making firms, tube-making firms, and cutlery firms. In addition, these firms will likely have their own forward linkages. The wire-making factory, for example, will supply local assemblers, finishers, packagers, and distributors. Together, backward and forward linkages often create a threshold of activity large enough to attract ancillary activities. **Ancillary activities** include maintenance, repair, security, and haulage services that serve a variety of industries. **Figure 7.15** summarizes the kinds of linkages that typically develop around a steel production plant.

Where external economies and local economic linkages are limited to firms involved in one particular industry, they are known as **localization economies.** These economies are cost savings that accrue to particular industries as a result of clustering together at a specific location. Examples include sharing a pool of

agglomeration effects: cost advantages that accrue to individual firms because of their location among functionally related activities

external economies: cost savings that result from circumstances beyond a firm's own organization and methods of production

ancillary activities: such activities as maintenance, repair, security, and haulage services that serve a variety of industries

localization economies: cost savings that accrue to particular industries as a result of clustering together at a specific location

Figure 7.15 Backward and forward linkages This diagram illustrates just a few of the complex webs of economic linkages that exist around a steel production plant. In reality, the number of linkages is much greater. (*Source:* M.J. Healey, *Location and Change: Perspectives on Economic Geography.* Oxford: Oxford University Press, 1990. By Permission of Oxford University Press.)

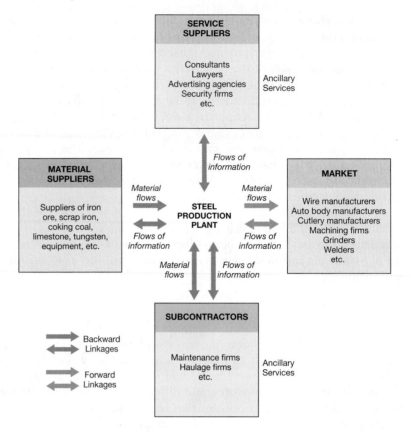

Figure 7.16 The haute couture garment district in Paris Specialized fashion districts like this one on the Boulevard Saint-Honoré in Paris, just north of the Louvre, provide good examples of external economies. Within such a narrow community of interest, close rivalries breed innovation and easy contact among producers helps minimize uncertainty.

infrastructure (fixed social capital): the underlying framework of services and amenities needed to facilitate productive activity

urbanization economies: external economies that accrue to producers because of the package of infrastructure, ancillary activities, labour, and markets typically associated with urban settings

labour with special skills or experience; supporting specialized technical schools; joining together to create a marketing organization or a research institute; and drawing on specialized subcontractors, maintenance firms, suppliers, distribution agents, and lawyers. Where such advantages lead to a reputation for high-quality production, clustering will be intensified because more producers will want to cash in on the reputation. Among the many examples are the Canadian auto industry (in southern Ontario) and Quebec's aeronautic industry (Montreal).

External economies can be derived in three main ways. The first is through external *economies of scale.* By clustering together, firms can collectively support ancillary activities—such as specialized repair firms—that help make all firms more efficient. The second source of external economies is through the atmosphere and easy contact among producers, which can help minimize uncertainty. Thus, for example, small firms in industries in which demand is unpredictable (because it is subject to fashion, for example, or to rapidly changing technologies) tend to cluster to be able to share information as quickly as possible. Examples include women's clothing in Paris (**Figure 7.16**).

The third source of external economies is the **infrastructure** of society, such as roads, highways, railroads, schools, hospitals, shopping centres, and recreational and cultural amenities. The more extensive and sophisticated the infrastructure, the more advantages accrue to the producers: more efficient transportation, more specialized education, more attractive environments for key workers, and so on.

Because larger cities are particularly suited for providing firms with these three opportunities, external economies are often referred to as **urbanization economies,** those accruing to producers because of the package of infrastructure, ancillary activities, labour, and markets that is typically associated with urban settings.

PATHWAYS TO DEVELOPMENT

Patterns of economic development are the product of principles of location and economic interdependence, but—as we already saw in the case of Sheffield—they are also historical in origin and cumulative in nature. Even though the fundamental principles of spatial organization hold steady over time, societal and technological conditions change. As a result, economic geographies that were shaped by certain principles of spatial organization during one particular period are inevitably modified, later on, as the same principles work their way through new technologies and new actors. Thus, we find different pathways of economic development according to various circumstances of timing and location.

Recognizing this, geographers are interested not only in uncovering the fundamental principles of spatial organization but also in relating them to **geographical path dependence**, the historical relationship between present-day activities in a place and the past experiences of that place. A dynamic relationship exists between past and present geographies. In other words, when spatial structures emerge through the logic of fundamental principles of spatial organization, they do so in ways guided and influenced by pre-existing patterns and relationships. One example is provided by the city of Ottawa. Initially a small and remote lumber town, Ottawa developed into a large administrative employment centre once it was designated as the capital of Canada. Its growing population provided both a market and a labour pool for a host of service and small manufacturing industries that were then able to develop in the area. Most recently, the Ottawa area has added high-tech industries to its activities, industries that developed on the basis of federal government grants and the presence of two universities.

These observations lead to an important principle of economic development, the principle of initial advantage. **Initial advantage** highlights the importance of an early start in economic development. It represents a special case of external economies. Other things being equal, new phases of economic development will take hold first in settings that can already offer external economies: existing labour markets, existing consumer markets, existing frameworks of fixed social capital, and so on. This initial advantage will be consolidated by localization economies and so form the basis for continuing economic growth. This sustained growth, in turn, provides the preconditions for initial advantage in subsequent phases of economic development.

For places and regions with a substantial initial advantage, therefore, the trajectory of geographical path dependence tends to be one of persistent growth—reinforcing the core–periphery patterns of economic development found in every part of the world and at every spatial scale. That said, geographers recognize there is no single pathway to development. The consequences of initial advantage for both core and peripheral regions can be—and often are—modified. Old core–periphery relationships can be blurred, and new ones can be initiated.

How Regional Economic Cores Are Created

Regional cores of economic development are created cumulatively, following some initial advantage, through the operation of several of the basic principles of economic geography that we have described. These principles centre on external economies, or agglomeration effects, that are associated with various kinds of economic linkages and interdependencies. The trigger for these agglomeration effects can be any kind of economic development—the establishment of a trading port, or the growth of a local industry or any large-scale enterprise. The external economies and economic linkages generated by such developments represent the initial advantage that tends to stimulate a self-propelling process of local economic development.

Given the location of a new economic activity in an area, a number of interrelated effects come into play. *Backward linkages* develop as new firms arrive to provide the growing industry with components, supplies, specialized services, or facilities. *Forward linkages* develop as new firms arrive to take the finished products of the growing industry and use them as inputs to their own processing, assembly, finishing, packaging, or distribution operations. Together with the initial growth, the growth in these linked industries helps to create a threshold of activity large enough to attract *ancillary industries* and activities (maintenance and repair, recycling, security, and business services, for example).

geographical path dependence: the historical relationship between the present activities associated with a place and the past experiences of that place

initial advantage: the critical importance of an early start in economic development; a special case of external economies

Figure 7.17 Processes of regional economic growth Once a significant cluster of new industry becomes established in an area, it tends to create a self-propelling process of economic growth. As this illustration shows, the initial advantages of industrial growth are reinforced through geographical principles of agglomeration and localization. The overall process is sometimes known as *cumulative causation.*

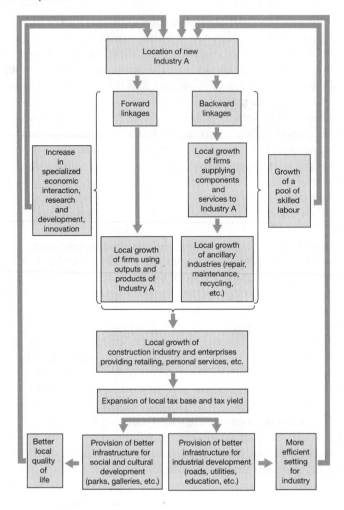

The existence of these interrelated activities establishes a pool of specialized labour with the kinds of skills and experience that make the area attractive to still more firms. Meanwhile, the linkages among all these firms help to promote interaction between professional and technical personnel and allow for the area to support R&D facilities, research institutes, and so on, thus increasing the likelihood of local inventions and innovations that might further stimulate local economic development.

Another part of the spiral of local economic growth is a result of the increase in population represented by the families of employees. Their presence creates a demand for housing, utilities, physical infrastructure, retailing, personal services, and so on—all of which generate additional jobs. This expansion, in turn, helps create populations large enough to attract an even wider variety and more sophisticated kinds of services and amenities. Last, but by no means least, the overall growth in local employment creates a larger local tax base. The local government can then provide improved public utilities, roads, schools, health services, recreational amenities, and so on, all of which serve to intensify agglomeration economies and so enhance the competitiveness of the area in being able to attract further rounds of investment.

Swedish economist Gunnar Myrdal was the 1974 Nobel Prize winner who first recognized that any significant initial local advantage tends to be reinforced through geographical principles of agglomeration and localization. He called the process **cumulative causation** (**Figure 7.17**), meaning the spiral buildup of advantages that occurs in specific geographical settings as a result of the development of external economies, agglomeration effects, and localization economies. Myrdal also pointed out that this spiral of local growth would tend to attract people—enterprising young people, usually—and investment funds from other

cumulative causation: a spiral buildup of advantages that occurs in specific geographical settings as a result of the development of external economies, agglomeration effects, and localization economies

areas. According to the basic principles of spatial interaction, these flows are strongest from nearby regions with the lowest wages, fewest job opportunities, or least attractive investment opportunities. In terms of Canadian regional economic development, these processes are embodied in the theories of metropolitanism (see Chapter 10) and the staples thesis (see Chapter 2).

In some regions or places, this outflow of people and resources is sufficient to trigger a cumulative negative spiral of economic disadvantage. With less capital, less innovative energy, and depleted pools of labour, industrial growth in peripheral regions tends to be significantly slower and less innovative than in regions with an initial advantage and an established process of cumulative causation. This, in turn, tends to limit the size of the local tax base so that local governments find it hard to furnish a competitive infrastructure of roads, schools, and recreational amenities. Myrdal called these disadvantages **backwash effects,** the negative impacts on a region of the economic growth of some other region. These negative impacts take the form, for example, of out-migration, outflows of investment capital, and the shrinkage of local tax bases. Backwash effects are important because they help explain why regional economic development is so uneven and why core–periphery contrasts in economic development are so common. The processes familiar to Canadian economic geographers as "heartland–hinterland" phenomena (see Chapter 2) are specific types of these general core–periphery processes.

backwash effects: the negative impacts on a region of the economic growth of some other region

How Core–Periphery Patterns Are Modified

Although very important, cumulative causation and backwash effects are not the only processes affecting the geography of economic development. If they were, the world's economic geography would be even more starkly polarized than it is now and new economic regions could never develop.

Myrdal himself recognized that peripheral regions do sometimes emerge as new growth regions and partially explained them in what he called *spread* (or trickle-down) *effects*. **Spread effects** are the positive impacts on a region of the economic growth of some other region, usually a core region. This growth creates levels of demand for food, consumer products, and other manufactured goods that are so high that local producers cannot satisfy them. This demand gives investors in peripheral regions (or countries) the opportunity to establish a local capacity to meet the demand. Entrepreneurs who attempt this are also able to exploit the advantages of cheaper land and labour in peripheral regions. If strong enough, these spread effects can enable peripheral regions to develop their own spiral of cumulative causation, thus changing the interregional geography of economic patterns and flows. The economic growth of South Korea, for example, is partly attributable to the spread effects of Japanese economic prosperity. More recently, the Chinese economy benefited from the spread effects of the North American consumer society.

spread effects: the positive impacts on a region of the economic growth of some other region

Another way in which peripheral regions or countries can develop their own spiral of cumulative causation is through a process of *import substitution* (see Chapter 2). In this process, goods and services previously imported from core regions are replaced by locally made goods and locally provided services. Some things are hard to copy because of the limitations of climate or natural resources (Canada being a good example). However, many products and services *can* be copied by local entrepreneurs, thus capturing local capital, increasing local employment opportunities, intensifying the use of local resources, and generating profits for further local investment.

The classic example is in Japan, where import substitution, especially for textiles and heavy engineering, played an important part in the transition from a peripheral economy to a major industrial power in the late nineteenth century. Import substitution also figured prominently in the Japanese "economic miracle" after World War II, this time featuring electronics, optics, and automobile manufacturing. Today countries like Brazil, Peru, and Ghana are seeking to follow the same sort of strategy, subsidizing domestic industries and protecting them from outside competitors through tariffs and taxes. Another example is the Canadian film industry (see Chapter 2).

Core–periphery patterns and relationships can also be modified by changes in the dynamics of core regions—internal changes that can slow or modify the spiral of cumulative causation. The main factor is the development of **agglomeration diseconomies,** the negative economic effects of urbanization and the local concentration of industry. Effects include the higher prices that must be paid by firms competing for land and labour; the costs of delays resulting from traffic congestion and crowded port and railroad facilities; the increasing unit costs of solid waste disposal; and the burden of higher taxes that eventually have to be levied by local governments to support services and amenities previously considered unnecessary—traffic police, city planning, and transit systems, for example.

agglomeration diseconomies: the negative economic effects of urbanization and the local concentration of industry

Deindustrialization and Creative Destruction The most fundamental cause of change in the relationship between initial advantage and cumulative causation is found in the longer-term shifts in technology systems and in the competition among states within the world-system. The innovations associated with successive technology systems generate new industries that are not yet tied down by enormous investments in factories or allied to existing industrial agglomerations. Combined with innovations in transport and communications, this creates *windows of locational opportunity* that can result in new industrial districts, with small towns or cities growing into dominant metropolitan areas through new rounds of cumulative causation. (See **Geography Matters 7.3—A Tale of Two Canadian Towns.**)

Equally important as a factor in how core–periphery patterns are modified are the consequent shifts in the profitability of old, established industries in core regions compared with the profitability of new industries in fast-growing, new industrial districts. As soon as the differential is large enough, some disinvestment will take place within core regions, which, in turn, leads to deindustrialization in formerly prosperous industrial core regions.

deindustrialization: a relative decline in industrial employment in core regions

Deindustrialization involves a relative decline (and in extreme cases an absolute decline) in industrial employment in core regions as firms scale back their activities in response to lower levels of profitability (**Figure 7.18**). This is what happened in the 1960s and 1970s when the Manufacturing Belt in the northeastern United States turned into the "Rustbelt" (**Figure 7.19**). It also occurred in many of the traditional industrial regions of Europe: in France, Belgium, the Netherlands, Norway, Sweden, and the United Kingdom, manufacturing employment decreased by between one-third and one-half from 1960 to 1990. In Canada, restructuring in the 1980s and 1990s affected the industrial region between Windsor and Quebec City, and many isolated resource centres in Canada from Powell River (British Columbia) to Corner Brook (Newfoundland). Similarly, fishing centres on the Atlantic coast suffered an economic collapse as fish stocks dwindled. Wherever restructuring occurs, the plant closures that result from it have serious impacts on their communities and threaten the continued existence of "place," as the slow decline of Newfoundland's outports since the 1950s has all too painfully illustrated (see Chapter 4).

Meanwhile, the capital made available through disinvestment in these core regions becomes available for investment in new ventures based on innovative products and technologies. Old industries—and sometimes entire old industrial regions—are dismantled (or at least neglected) to help fund the creation of new centres of profitability and employment. This process is often referred to as **creative destruction,** something that is inherent to the dynamics of capitalism. Creative destruction is a powerful image, helping us to understand the entrepreneur's need to withdraw investments from activities (and regions) yielding low rates of profit to reinvest in new activities (and, often, in new places).

creative destruction: the withdrawal of investments from activities (and regions) that yield low rates of profit to reinvest in new activities (and new places)

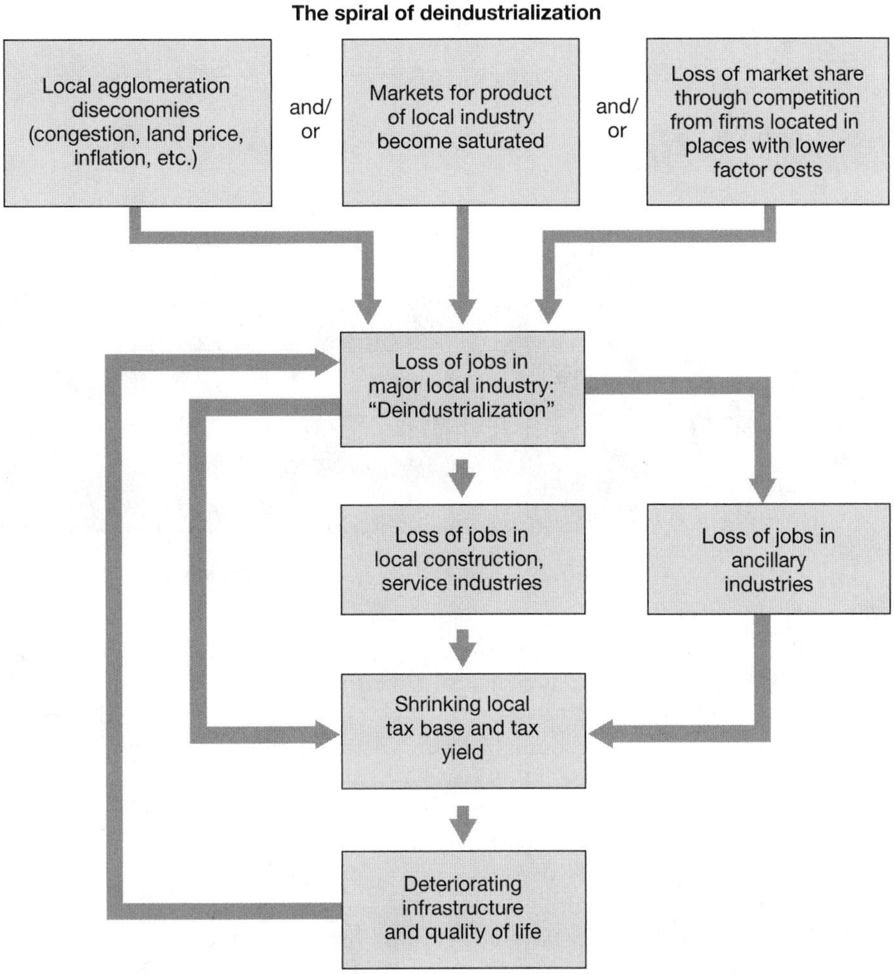

The spiral of deindustrialization

| Local agglomeration diseconomies (congestion, land price, inflation, etc.) | and/ or | Markets for product of local industry become saturated | and/ or | Loss of market share through competition from firms located in places with lower factor costs |

Loss of jobs in major local industry: "Deindustrialization"

| Loss of jobs in local construction, service industries | Loss of jobs in ancillary industries |

Shrinking local tax base and tax yield

Deteriorating infrastructure and quality of life

Figure 7.18   Regional economic decline   When the locational advantages of manufacturing regions are undermined for one reason or another, profitability declines and manufacturing employment falls. This can lead to a downward spiral of economic decline, as experienced by many of the traditional manufacturing regions of Europe during the 1960s, 1970s, and 1980s.   (*Source:* Reprinted with permission of Prentice Hall, from P.L. Knox, *Urbanization,* © 1994, p. 55.)

Figure 7.19   Deindustrialization This derelict steel mill in New Jersey is testament to the downward economic spiral in what was once one of the world's most important heavy manufacturing regions. Unfortunately, many such sites have to be remediated before being redeveloped because their soils and water tables have been contaminated by decades of industrial use.

Antiquated industrial processes have often led to years of toxic accumulations in factory sites, and part of the challenge of creative destruction is generating ways to remediate such properties so that redevelopment of this valuable real estate proceeds. The term **brownfield site** has been used to describe abandoned, idle, or underused industrial and commercial land on which redevelopment is hindered by the effects of contamination (see Figure 7.19).

brownfield site: abandoned, idle, or underused industrial and commercial land on which redevelopment is hindered by the effects of contamination

A Tale of Two Canadian Towns

The 2001 Canadian census reveals in stark form the differences between places that are in areas of economic growth and those that are in areas of decline. We look here at the example of two communities—the towns of Fort McMurray (Alberta), 440 kilometres north of Edmonton, and Trepassey (Newfoundland), 145 kilometres south of St. John's.

Alberta, although not part of the traditional Canadian heartland, is prospering economically and growing demographically. The census shows Alberta grew by 10.3 percent from 1996 to 2001 (to 2.9 million people). The province of Newfoundland and Labrador experienced a 7 percent loss in population over the same period (it now totals 513,000 people). Never part of the Canadian heartland either, this province has supported its population through resource exploitation—in this case, the Atlantic fisheries. The collapse of that resource has meant a downward spiral of disinvestment and deindustrialization for many communities in Newfoundland that were often unable to develop diversified economies. As Newfoundland and Labrador struggles to diversify its economy, the message for Alberta is to do the same.

Figure 7.3.1   Fort McMurray and the oil sands

■ *Fort McMurray.* "It's all fast-paced up here, you're always going, going."

Settled by Europeans in the 1760s as a fur trading centre, in 1963 Fort McMurray had only 1,360 people. During the 1980s and 1990s, growth in demand, the rise in oil prices, and the development of technology to separate oil from sand made the exploitation of the Athabasca Oil Sands worthwhile and Fort McMurray grew into the regional centre for the industry (**Figure 7.3.1**). In the 10 years between 1996 and 2006, the population grew by 83 percent to 64,441, resulting in a severe lack of housing. Many new migrants to Fort McMurray have spent the summer in campgrounds before finding accommodation. Average house prices, until the fall of the price of oil in late 2008, were commonly reported to

be over $600,000. According to a CBC broadcast, the provincial government of Alberta planned to remedy the shortage of affordable housing by releasing enough Crown land in the area to build houses for 40,000 people.

The demand by the oil industry for skilled labour is so great that it has been very hard for the town's service sector to keep employees or pay them competitive wages. One measure of this is that although the province's minimum wage was raised to $8.40 an hour in April 2008, few jobs in Fort McMurray start at less than $15 an hour, a situation that puts pressure on small businesses such as restaurants to meet their payroll without passing on cost increases to their customers.

Growing mainly from in-migration, the town is a young community, with an average age of only 29.4 years, and schools, libraries, sports facilities, and shopping malls are springing up almost overnight. A significant number of those migrants to Fort McMurray are from Newfoundland and Labrador.

■ *Trepassey.* "At nighttime, you can look out of the window for an hour, and you won't see a car go by."

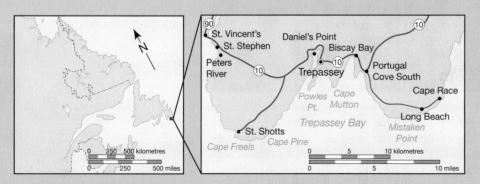

Figure 7.3.2   Trepassey, Newfoundland

Figure 7.3.3 Trepassey, Newfoundland

Established in the seventeenth century on the basis of fishing (**Figures 7.3.2** and **7.3.3**), Trepassey maintained a viable economy until early 1991 when its fish-processing plant closed down. The cod moratoria of 1993 and 1994 (closing the Northern and Gulf cod fisheries) were another devastating blow. The sale of the plant's equipment to Tanzania in 1995 marked a realization that a way of life had ended. It was at this point that almost half the workforce of the town left to work in a meat-packing plant in Alberta or in construction jobs in Ontario and British Columbia.

The census tells the story this way: in 1981, there were 1,473 people in Trepassey. By 1991, the year the plant closed, there were 1,375. In 1996, there were 1,084, and in 2006 only 763. The consequences of this loss of population and economic decline are many. Unemployment rates, which stood at 17 percent when the plant was open, increased to 43 percent by 2001. Average income in 1996 was only $15,885 according to the census. Sea-view houses, which might be worth at least $100,000 in more prosperous communities, stand empty here. There are not enough young people in the area to form a recreational hockey league, and the elementary school closed at the end of 2002 for lack of pupils. Ironically, school dropout rates have fallen from 50 percent, when the plant was open and a fishery existed, to almost 0.

Against this backdrop, regional economic development planners strive valiantly. Reports note the possibilities for tourism, aquaculture, agriculture, information technology, marine-related industries, services and crafts, and manufacturing. That not all of this is wishful thinking is shown by the recent development of 30 jobs in the area (in window manufacturing, marine lighting equipment, and a small iceberg water bottling plant for the President's Choice label). It will, however, be a long time before there will be traffic jams again on Trepassey's streets as there were when 500 people used to set off to work for the fish plant.

Sources: Jill Mahoney and Kevin Cox, "Where the Jobs Are: For Many, 'Go West' Still the Best Advice," *Globe and Mail*, 13 March 2002, pp. A6–A7; Charles Mandel, "Vodka on the Rocks: Newfoundland's Iceberg Harvesting Industry," *Canadian Business*, 24 June 2002, pp. 30–34; *Report for the Trepassey Task Force on Community Economic Development*, December 1999; Jane Robinson, "Women and Fish Plant Closure: The Case of Trepassey, Newfoundland." In C. McGrath, B. Neis, and M. Porter (eds.), *Their Lives and Times; Women in Newfoundland and Labrador: A Collage*. St. John's: Killick Press, 1995, pp. 163–174; The Regional Municipality of Wood Buffalo (Fort McMurray) Community Economic Profile; Syncrude Canada Ltd. (**www.syncrudecom**); (For Statistics Canada data on Trepassey [and many other communities in Canada], go to **www.statcan.gc.ca**, then click on "Community Profiles" and type "Trepassey [town]" in the search box.); Ron Chambers, "Seasonal Slowdown for House Prices in Fort McMurray," *Edmonton Journal*, 15 November 2007; CBC News, "Alberta Launches Plan to House 40,000 in Fort McMurray," 24 June 2008 (**www.cbc.ca/canada/edmonton/story/2008/06/24/edm-fort-land.html?ref=r55**); "Alta. Youths Picky about Jobs Report," *Edmonton Sun*, 14 June 2007. A fascinating documentary film, originally shown on CBC TV on 13 March 2008, entitled "Tar Sands: The Selling of Alberta" is well worth watching for its glimpse of life in Fort McMurray and for its interviews with some of the over 10,000 people it notes have now moved there from Newfoundland to find work, albeit on a temporary basis in some cases (**www.cbc.ca/doczone/tarsands/**).

According to a 1997 report by the National Round Table on the Environment and the Economy, Canada has some 30,000 brownfield sites, ranging from railway yards, junkyards, and garbage dumps to abandoned factories and refineries. Among the many problems that face developers is the question of who should pay to clean up the land. Is it the responsibility of the original industrialist, the current developer, or one of the levels of government? Confusion over jurisdiction has led to sites remaining untouched for years. In some cases, concerns about the high cost of decontamination and environmental investigation have meant that it is more economical for owners to continue to pay taxes on derelict land rather than to attempt to clean up and sell the property.

How to remediate brownfield sites is a challenge for Canadian geographers and planners. Because so many of the sites are in urban locations and already have a basic infrastructure (roads, water, sewage), their redevelopment is an attractive option: the land could be built up with "infill" and high-density housing to reduce sprawl, new office space or retail opportunities could be built, and parks and greenspaces could be created.

As if the problems posed by the redevelopment of brownfield sites are not enough to cope with, many Canadian cities are faced with much wider challenges. This is because the forces that are responsible for the creation of brownfield sites are part of a much wider set of processes of industrial and economic *restructuring* that lead to the *deindustrialization* of old core regions as capital investment moves from developed to less developed regions—usually in search of cheaper labour or locations in which to set up production, but also increasingly in search of places in which environmental standards for manufacturing are lower.

The case of Montreal can serve as a vignette of the effects of deindustrialization and economic restructuring. According to the 2006 census, employment in the metropolitan area of the city grew to 1.83 million jobs, an 8.6 percent increase over 2001. However, this increase masks a decline in the city's textile industries—which lost 10,200 jobs over the five-year period, an average decline of 8.2 percent a year in that sector. Textile manufacturers in Montreal have traditionally relied on immigrant labour to keep their costs down, but even such tactics have failed to allow the industry to compete with manufacturers in developing countries with far cheaper wage rates.

The story is not all gloom, however, because just as these jobs are disappearing, other sectors are growing. Gains of 3,400 have occurred in the amusement and recreation sector, for example, many of them in high-tech computer gaming industries such as Ubisoft—often setting up shop in the very same buildings vacated by closing textile businesses. Growth has also occurred among independent artists, writers, and performers (an additional 1,500 since 2001), and in the performing arts sector (1,500 over the period from 2001 to 2006).

The net result of these processes is that the spatial economy and settlement pattern of a country like Canada are always changing to reflect alterations in economic systems. The survival of towns and regions depends on the extent of their importance to those systems.

Government Intervention   In addition to the processes of deindustrialization and creative destruction, core–periphery patterns can also be modified by government intervention. National governments realize that, without regional planning and policy, the resources of peripheral regions can remain underutilized, whereas core regions can become vulnerable to agglomeration diseconomies. For political reasons, too, national governments are often willing to help particular regions adjust to changing economic circumstances. At the same time, most local governments take responsibility for stimulating economic development within their jurisdiction, if only in order to increase the local tax base.

The nature and extent of government intervention has varied over time and by country. In some countries, special government agencies have been established to promote regional economic development and reduce core–periphery contrasts by investing in infrastructure and providing subsidies for private investment. Other strategies include tax breaks that reduce the cost of labour in peripheral regions or attempts to deal with agglomeration diseconomies in core regions through increased taxes and restrictions on land use.

7.6 Geography in the Information Age

An example of an attempt to deal with agglomeration diseconomies is the Congestion Charge in London, England. To enter the centre of London, cars are charged a daily fee of approximately $20. The intent is to deter cars and ease traffic congestion that causes time delays and costs, which makes city locations less attractive to businesses and their clients.

One of the most widespread governmental approaches to core–periphery patterns involves the exploitation of the principle of cumulative causation through the creation of growth poles. **Growth poles** are places of economic activity deliberately organized around one or more high-growth industries. Economists have noted, however, that not all industries are equal in the extent to which they stimulate economic growth and cumulative causation. The ones that generate the most pronounced effects are known as *propulsive industries*. Examples of propulsive industries include shipbuilding in the 1920s, automobile manufacturing in the 1950s and 1960s, and biotechnology and digital technologies today. The basic idea is for governments to promote regional economic growth by fostering propulsive industries in favourable locations. These locations are intended to become growth poles—places that, given an artificial start, develop a self-sustaining spiral of economic prosperity. In practice, governments often fail to invest in the right industries, and they nearly always fail to invest heavily enough to kick-start the process of cumulative causation.

The British Columbia town of Kitimat provides a Canadian example (**Figure 7.20**). Developed in the 1950s around an aluminium smelter that used hydropower created by the diversion of the Kemano River, the townsite was laid out to accommodate substantial population growth next to that smelter. However, the government's projections that this would become one of the province's largest

growth poles: economic activities that are deliberately organized around one or more high-growth industries

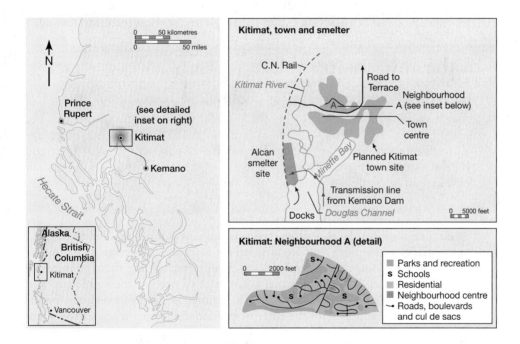

Figure 7.20 Kitimat, British Columbia Originally established in the 1950s as a growth centre based on aluminium smelting, the town of Kitimat, British Columbia, has not seen any significant expansion since. In fact, Kitimat lost 12.6 percent of its population between 2001 and 2006—the census district with the largest population decline in Canada. The photo shows the town centre. (*Source for diagrams:* Based on Ira M. Robinson, *New Industrial Towns on Canada's Frontier.* University of Chicago Research Paper No. 73, 1962. Source for picture: S. Mackenzie.)

centres never materialized—perhaps because of its remoteness or perhaps because such large projects are rarely truly propulsive for the local community (see the example of Trail). In 2007, attempts by the town to require Alcan to pay more for its locally generated hydro illustrate the community's contention that the full benefits of the project are not kept in the region where they are earned.

GLOBALIZATION AND LOCAL ECONOMIC DEVELOPMENT

As we saw in Chapter 2, the globalization of the world economy involves a new international division of labour in association with the internationalization of finance; the deployment of a new technology system (using information technology and robotics, GIS, biotechnology, and other new technologies); and the homogenization of consumer markets.

The dynamics of economic globalization rest on the flows of capital, knowledge, goods, and services between countries. In 2006 (the last year before the financial crisis) companies around the world invested more than US$1.3 trillion in business ventures beyond their own shores. This level of **foreign direct investment** or overseas investments made by private companies was 20 times that of the mid-1970s. Approximately 40 percent of foreign direct investment is targeted at peripheral and semiperipheral countries; the rest is going to core countries. These investments are reflected in increased levels of world trade in goods and services. Between 1975 and 2006, world exports of goods and services increased tenfold.

foreign direct investment: overseas business investments made by private companies

7.7 Geography in the Information Age

The dramatic rate at which economic globalization processes are speeding up is powerfully illustrated by comparing the 2006 figures in this paragraph with the 1998 figures used in the last edition of this book: in 1998, US$400 billion was invested; the foreign direct investment was seven times that of the mid-1970s; and world exports had tripled between 1975 and 1998. In the eight years between 1998 and 2006, all figures tripled!

At a very general level, foreign direct investment can be expected to be good for the places and regions that are targeted for investment. Foreign direct investment increases competition among local producers, forcing them to improve their performance. At the same time, knowledge of new business practices and production technology spreads through the regional economy as regional manufacturers become suppliers to the enterprises funded through foreign investment and as personnel move from one firm to another. The overall effect is for higher levels of productivity all around (**Figure 7.21**).

Figure 7.21 Foreign direct investment and regional economic performance Economic globalization has increased levels of foreign direct investment in many semiperipheral and peripheral regions. Other things being equal, this investment tends to lead to improvements in local economic performance because of the increased competition and new forms of organization introduced by the investors. (*Source:* R. Florida, "Regional Creative Destruction: Production Organization, Globalization, and the Economic Transformation of the Midwest," *Economic Geography*, 1996, fig. 1, p. 317.)

Now that the world economy is much more globalized, the ability to acquire, absorb, and communicate knowledge is more important than ever before in determining the fortunes of places and regions. Patterns of local and regional economic development are much more open to external influences and much more interdependent with economic development processes elsewhere. Shrinking space, shrinking time, and disappearing borders are linking people's lives more intensely and more immediately than ever before. This new framework for economic geography has already left its mark on the world's economic landscapes and has also meant that the lives of people in different parts of the world have become increasingly intertwined.

Not everyone has benefited, however, and the new international division of labour has come under attack by some in industrial countries, where rising unemployment and wage inequality are making people feel less secure about the future. Some workers in core countries are fearful of losing their jobs because of cheap imports from lower-cost producers. Others worry about companies relocating abroad in search of low wages, lax labour laws, and weak or poorly enforced environmental standards.

Most of the world's population now lives in countries that are either integrated into world markets for goods and finance or rapidly becoming so. As recently as the late 1970s, only a few peripheral countries had opened their borders to flows of trade and investment capital. About one-third of the world's labour force lived in countries, such as the Soviet Union and China, with centrally planned economies, and at least another third lived in countries insulated from international markets by prohibitive trade barriers and currency controls. Today, with nearly half the world's labour force among them, three giant population blocs—China, the republics of the former Soviet Union, and India—have entered the global market. Many other countries, from Mexico to Thailand, have already become involved in deep linkages. According to World Bank estimates, less than 10 percent of the world's labour force remained isolated from the global economy in the year 2004. (The World Bank, properly called the International Bank for Reconstruction and Development, is a U.N. affiliate established in 1948 to finance productive projects that further the economic development of member nations.)

The Global Assembly Line

In this and the following sections, we examine some specific impacts of three of the principal components of the global economy: the global assembly line, resulting from the operations of transnational manufacturing corporations; the global office, resulting from the internationalization of banking, finance, and business services; and the pleasure periphery, resulting from the proliferation of international tourism.

Transnationals and Globalization   The globalization of the world economy represents the most recent stage in a long process of internationalization. At the heart of this process has been the emergence of private companies that participate not only in international trade but also in production, manufacturing, and sales operations in several countries. For example, Nestlé, the world's largest packaged-food manufacturer, is the largest company in Switzerland but derives less than 2 percent of its revenue from its home country. Many of these transnational corporations have grown so large through a series of mergers and acquisitions that their activities now span a diverse range of economic activities. *Transnational corporations* (as defined in Chapter 2) are companies with investments and activities that span international boundaries and with subsidiary companies, factories, offices, or facilities in several countries. Today, more than half of all world trade is in the form of intrafirm trade; that is, between different branches and companies of the same transnational conglomerate.

Transnational corporations first began to appear in the nineteenth century, but until the mid-twentieth century there were only a few, most of them U.S.- or

European-based transnationals that were concerned with obtaining raw materials, such as oil or minerals, for their domestic manufacturing operations. The majority of Canada's current transnational corporations grew up as domestic mining companies that developed operations in other countries to increase market share of world trade in their particular commodity. Examples include Teck Resources, owner of the Trail lead–zinc smelter and various mines in Canada, the United States, and Peru; and Barrick Gold, one of the world's largest gold producers. Canadian transnationals that do not have roots in resource extraction include Magna International (an auto parts manufacturer) and Bombardier (manufacturer of subway cars and planes).

Beginning in the 1970s, a sharp increase occurred in the growth of transnational conglomerates not only in the United States but also in Canada, in Europe, in Japan, and even in semiperipheral countries. By 2006, there were about 78,000 transnational corporations in the world. Of these, the top 300 controlled approximately one-quarter of the world's productive assets. Many of the largest transnational corporations are now more powerful, in economic terms, than most sovereign nations. General Motors' economy is larger than Portugal's; Toyota's is larger than Ireland's; and Walmart's annual sales exceed Norway's gross domestic product.

The reason for such growth in the number and scale of transnational conglomerate corporations has been that international economic conditions have changed. A recession, triggered by a massive increase in the price of crude oil in 1973, forced companies everywhere to re-examine their strategies. At around the same time, technological developments in transport and communications provided larger companies with the flexibility and global reach to exploit the steep differentials in labour costs that exist between core and peripheral countries. Meanwhile, these same developments in transport and communications made for increased international competition, which forced firms to search more intensely for more efficient and profitable global production and marketing strategies. Concurrently, a homogenization of consumer tastes (also facilitated by new developments in communications technologies) made it possible for companies to cater to global markets.

It was the consequent burst of transnational corporate activity that has formed the basis of the recent globalization of the world economy. In effect, the playing field for large-scale businesses of all kinds had been marked out anew. Companies have had to reorganize their operations in a variety of ways, restructuring their activities and redeploying their resources *across different countries, regions, and places*. Local patterns of economic development have been recast time and time again as these processes of restructuring, reorganization, and redeployment have been played out (See **Geography Matters 7.4—The Changing Geography of the Clothing Industry**).

Transnationals and Global Assembly Lines   To manufacturers, the advantages of a global assembly line are several. First, a standardized global product for a global market allows them to maximize economies of scale. Second, a global assembly line allows production and assembly to take greater advantage of the full range of geographical variations in costs. Basic wages in manufacturing industries, for example, are between 25 and 75 times higher in core countries than in some peripheral countries. With a global assembly line, labour-intensive work can be done where labour is cheap, raw materials can be processed near their source of supply, and final assembly can be done close to major markets. Third, a global assembly line means that a company is no longer dependent on a single source of supply for a specific component, thus reducing its vulnerability to labour disputes and other disturbances. Fourth, global sourcing allows transnational conglomerates better access to local markets. For example, Boeing has pursued a strategy of buying a significant number of aircraft components in China and has therefore succeeded in opening the Chinese market to its products. Similarly, Volkswagen

The Changing Geography of the Clothing Industry

The clothing industry provides a good example of the way in which local economic geographies are affected by an industry's response to globalization. In the nineteenth century, the clothing industry developed in the metropolitan areas of core countries, with many small firms using cheap, migrant, or immigrant labour. In the first half of the twentieth century, the industry, like many others, began to modernize. Larger firms emerged, their success based on the exploitation of mass-production techniques for mass markets and on the exploitation of principles of spatial organization within national markets. In the United States, for example, the clothing industry went through a major locational shift as a great deal of production moved out of the workshops of New York to big, new factories in smaller towns in the South, where labour was not only much cheaper but less unionized.

The global textile and apparel industry has undergone several shifts in production since the 1950s. The first was from North America and Western Europe to Japan in the 1950s and early 1960s. The second was from Japan to Hong Kong, Taiwan, and the Republic of Korea, which dominated global textile and clothing exports in the 1970s and early 1980s. In the late 1980s, production moved principally to mainland China, but also to Indonesia, Malaysia, the Philippines, Sri Lanka, and Thailand. In the 1990s, new suppliers included India and Mexico, but the largest newcomer in the 1990s was Turkey, whose total of US$3.4 billion in clothing exports placed it fifth in world rankings. By 2005, important new clothing-producing countries (with a billion U.S. dollars or more of exports) included Bangladesh, the Czech Republic, Hungary, Mauritius, Morocco, Poland, Romania, and Vietnam.

Much of this shifting globalization of production was "buyer-driven" by retailers like Walmart and Sears and fashion-oriented apparel companies like Liz Claiborne and H&M. Their cost-reduction strategies led them to retain design and marketing functions but to contract out the actual production of their apparel to firms in low-wage countries. In effect, they became "manufacturers without factories." In an attempt to protect domestic manufacturers, the United States, Canada, and 13 countries in Europe entered into a trade pact called the Multifibre Arrangement (MFA) in 1974 that restricted the amount of imports from any one country. Designed to protect MFA signatories from competition from Japan, Hong Kong, Taiwan, and the Republic of Korea, the import quotas ended up working as a kind of affirmative action program for other countries that had large workforces and low wage rates—hence the spread of production around the world.

The result was that by 1980 more than half of all apparel purchased in the United States was imported (compared to less than 7 percent in 1960). Leisure wear—jeans, shorts, T-shirts, polo shirts, and so on—was an important component of the homogenization of consumer tastes around the world at that time, and it could be produced most profitably by the cheap labour of young women in the peripheral metropolitan areas of the world (**Figure 7.4.1**). Although the retail margin on domestically made clothing sold in Europe and the United States is 70 percent or so, the retail margin on clothing made in workshops in countries like Indonesia and Thailand is 100 to 250 percent.

This globalization of production has resulted in a complex set of commodity chains. Many of the largest clothing companies, such as Liz Claiborne, have most of their products manufactured through arrangements with many different independent suppliers, with no one supplier producing more than a fraction of the company's total output. These manufacturers are scattered throughout the world, making the clothing industry one of the most globalized of all manufacturing activities (**Figure 7.4.2**). In some countries, clothing manufacture is now the primary driver of the economy. Fifty percent of Sri Lanka's export earnings, for example, are derived from clothing, whereas for Bangladesh, El Salvador, and Mauritius the figure is 63 percent, and for Cambodia it is 76 percent. As we have seen, the actual geography of commodity chains in the clothing industry is rather volatile, with frequent shifts in production and assembly sites as companies and their suppliers continuously seek out new locations with lower costs.

Although cheap leisure wear can be produced most effectively through arrangements with multiple

Figure 7.4.1   Cambodian garment workers in a factory in Phnom Penh, Cambodia   The hourly compensation (including benefits) of apparel workers in the United States is around US$10 per hour for a 37-hour week, whereas their counterparts in China work 50 to 60 hours per week and are paid around $1 an hour. Meanwhile, in Bangladesh workers may earn as little as 50 cents per hour.

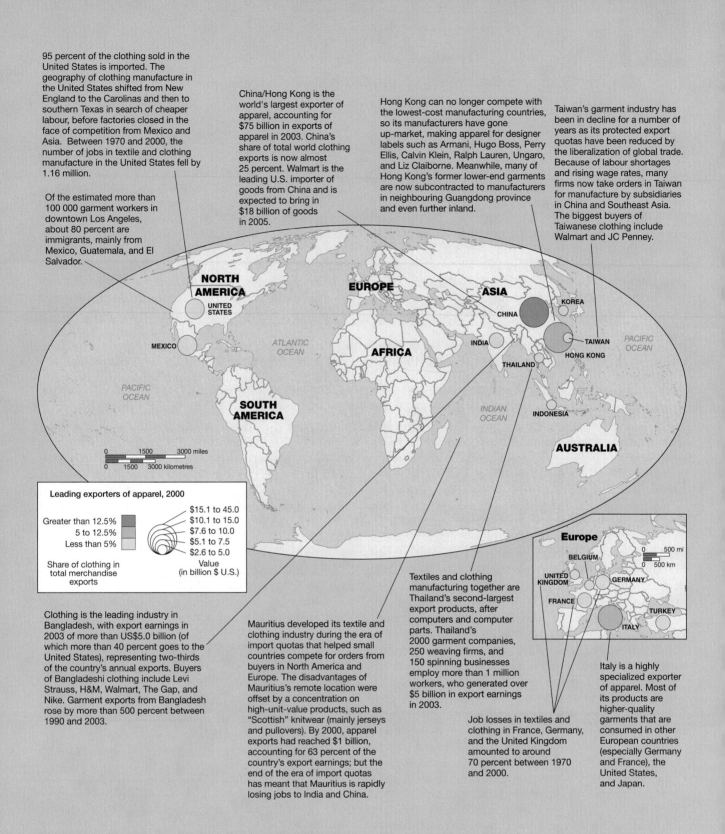

95 percent of the clothing sold in the United States is imported. The geography of clothing manufacture in the United States shifted from New England to the Carolinas and then to southern Texas in search of cheaper labour, before factories closed in the face of competition from Mexico and Asia. Between 1970 and 2000, the number of jobs in textile and clothing manufacture in the United States fell by 1.16 million.

Of the estimated more than 100 000 garment workers in downtown Los Angeles, about 80 percent are immigrants, mainly from Mexico, Guatemala, and El Salvador.

China/Hong Kong is the world's largest exporter of apparel, accounting for $75 billion in exports of apparel in 2003. China's share of total world clothing exports is now almost 25 percent. Walmart is the leading U.S. importer of goods from China and is expected to bring in $18 billion of goods in 2005.

Hong Kong can no longer compete with the lowest-cost manufacturing countries, so its manufacturers have gone up-market, making apparel for designer labels such as Armani, Hugo Boss, Perry Ellis, Calvin Klein, Ralph Lauren, Ungaro, and Liz Claiborne. Meanwhile, many of Hong Kong's former lower-end garments are now subcontracted to manufacturers in neighbouring Guangdong province and even further inland.

Taiwan's garment industry has been in decline for a number of years as its protected export quotas have been reduced by the liberalization of global trade. Because of labour shortages and rising wage rates, many firms now take orders in Taiwan for manufacture by subsidiaries in China and Southeast Asia. The biggest buyers of Taiwanese clothing include Walmart and JC Penney.

Leading exporters of apparel, 2000

Greater than 12.5%
5 to 12.5%
Less than 5%

Share of clothing in total merchandise exports

$15.1 to 45.0
$10.1 to 15.0
$7.6 to 10.0
$5.1 to 7.5
$2.6 to 5.0

Value (in billion $ U.S.)

Clothing is the leading industry in Bangladesh, with export earnings in 2003 of more than US$5.0 billion (of which more than 40 percent goes to the United States), representing two-thirds of the country's annual exports. Buyers of Bangladeshi clothing include Levi Strauss, H&M, Walmart, The Gap, and Nike. Garment exports from Bangladesh rose by more than 500 percent between 1990 and 2003.

Mauritius developed its textile and clothing industry during the era of import quotas that helped small countries compete for orders from buyers in North America and Europe. The disadvantages of Mauritius's remote location were offset by a concentration on high-unit-value products, such as "Scottish" knitwear (mainly jerseys and pullovers). By 2000, apparel exports had reached $1 billion, accounting for 63 percent of the country's export earnings; but the end of the era of import quotas has meant that Mauritius is rapidly losing jobs to India and China.

Textiles and clothing manufacturing together are Thailand's second-largest export products, after computers and computer parts. Thailand's 2000 garment companies, 250 weaving firms, and 150 spinning businesses employ more than 1 million workers, who generated over $5 billion in export earnings in 2003.

Job losses in textiles and clothing in France, Germany, and the United Kingdom amounted to around 70 percent between 1970 and 2000.

Italy is a highly specialized exporter of apparel. Most of its products are higher-quality garments that are consumed in other European countries (especially Germany and France), the United States, and Japan.

Figure 7.4.2 The changing distribution of clothing manufacturing Most of the world's clothing exports come from just a few countries. However, the geography of clothing manufacturing changes rapidly in response to the changing patterns of costs and opportunities within the world economy.

suppliers in peripheral low-wage regions, higher-end apparel for the global marketplace requires a different geography of production. These products—women's fashion, outerwear, and lingerie; infants' wear; and men's suits—are based on frequent style changes and high-quality finish. This requires short production runs and greater contact between producers and buyers. The most profitable settings for these products are in the core countries' metropolitan areas—London, Paris, Stuttgart, Milan, New York, and Los Angeles—where,

has become the dominant foreign car maker in the Chinese market partly because it was one of the first to establish production facilities there.

We can use the example of automobile companies to examine global assembly systems in more detail (**Figure 7.22**). The global production networks of these companies allow them to capitalize on all four advantages listed previously. In addition, they also employ modular manufacturing for their world cars based on a common platform that gives them the flexibility to adapt the interior, trim, body, and ride characteristics to conditions in different countries. Honda, for example, has developed three distinct versions of the Accord—the bigger, family-oriented Accord for North American drivers, the smaller, sportier Accord aimed at young Japanese professionals, and the shorter and narrower Accord, offering the stiff and sporty ride preferred by European drivers.

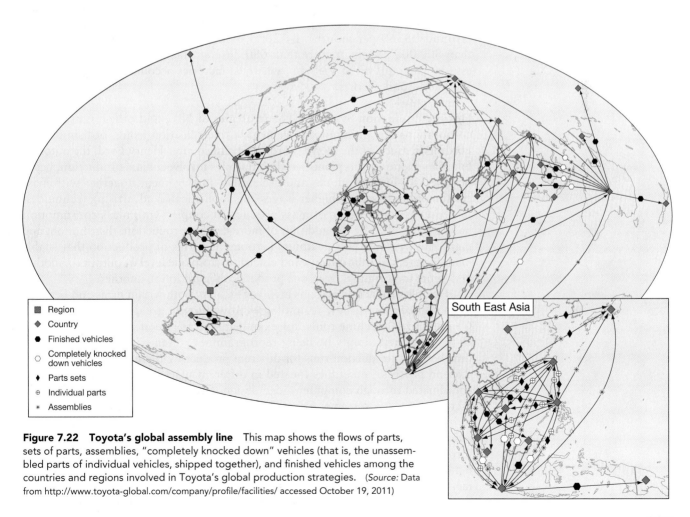

Figure 7.22 Toyota's global assembly line This map shows the flows of parts, sets of parts, assemblies, "completely knocked down" vehicles (that is, the unassembled parts of individual vehicles, shipped together), and finished vehicles among the countries and regions involved in Toyota's global production strategies. (*Source:* Data from http://www.toyota-global.com/company/profile/facilities/ accessed October 19, 2011)

337

7.8 Geography in the Information Age

More than three-quarters of the 60 million motor vehicles that rolled off the production lines in 2010 were made by just 10 transnationals. In order of size, they were Toyota, General Motors, Volkswagen, Ford, Hyundai Kia, PSA Peugeot Citroën, Honda, Nissan, Fiat, and Suzuki. A completely different picture emerges, however, if we ask *where* those cars were produced: China produced nearly as many as the United States, Japan, and Germany taken together! The fact that no Chinese car maker appears among the top 10 indicates the degree to which these transnationals control the international car market.

The global assembly line is constantly being reorganized as transnational corporations seek to take advantage of geographical differences between regions and countries, and as workers and consumers in specific places and regions react to the consequences of globalization. Nike, the athletic footwear and clothing marketer, provides a good illustration. Nike once had its own manufacturing facilities in both the United States and the United Kingdom. Today, however, all its production is subcontracted to suppliers in south and east Asia. The geography of this subcontracting has evolved over time in response to the changing pattern of labour costs in Asia. The first production of Nike shoes took place in Japan. The company then switched most of its subcontracting to South Korea and Taiwan. As labour costs rose there, Nike's subcontracting was spread across more and more peripheral countries—China, Indonesia, Thailand, Malaysia, and Vietnam—in search of low labour costs (around US$60 per month). By 2006, Nike subcontractors employed more than 800,000 people in more than 680 different factories. Nike was the largest foreign employer in Vietnam, where its factories accounted for 5 percent of Vietnam's total exports.

Flexible Production Systems The strategies of Nike and other transnational corporations are an important element in the transition from Fordism to neo-Fordism in much of the world. Fordism is named after Henry Ford, the automobile manufacturer who pioneered the principles involved: mass production, based on assembly-line techniques and "scientific" management, together with mass consumption, based on higher wages and sophisticated advertising techniques. In **neo**-Fordism the logic of mass production coupled with mass consumption has been modified by the addition of more flexible production, distribution, and marketing systems. This flexibility is rooted in forms of production that enable manufacturers to shift quickly and efficiently from one level of output to another and, more importantly, from one product configuration to another.

Flexible production systems involve flexibility both within firms and between them. *Within* firms, new technologies now allow a great deal of flexibility. Computerized machine tools, for example, are capable of producing a variety of new products simply by being reprogrammed, often with very little downtime between production runs for different products. Different stages of the production process (sometimes located in different places) can be integrated and coordinated through computer-aided design (CAD) and computer-aided manufacturing (CAM) systems. Computer-based information systems can be used to monitor retail sales and track wholesale orders, thus allowing producers to reduce the costs of raw materials stockpiles, parts inventories, and warehousing through sophisticated small-batch, just-in-time production and distribution systems. Just-in-time production employs vertical disintegration within large, formerly functionally integrated firms, such as automobile manufacturers, in which daily and even hourly deliveries of parts and other supplies from smaller (often non-unionized) subcontractors and suppliers now arrive "just in time" to maintain "last-minute" and "zero" inventories. The combination of computer-based information systems, CAD/CAM systems, and computerized machine tools has also given firms the flexibility to exploit specialized niches of consumer demand so that economies of scale in production can be applied to upscale but geographically scattered markets.

The Benetton clothing company provides an excellent case-study example of the exploitation of flexible production systems within a single firm. In 1965, Benetton began with a single factory near Venice. In 1968, it acquired a single retail store in the Alpine town of Belluno, marking the beginning of a remarkable sequence of corporate expansion. Benetton is now a global organization with over 6,000 retail outlets in more than 120 countries and with its own investment bank and financial services organizations. It achieved this growth by exploiting computers, new communications and transportation systems, flexible outsourcing strategies, and new production-process technologies (such as robotics and CAD/CAM systems) to the fullest possible extent.

Only about 400 of Benetton's 9,000 employees are located in the company's home base of Treviso, Italy (**Figure 7.23**). From Treviso, Benetton managers coordinate the activities of more than 250 outside suppliers in order to stock its worldwide network of retail outlet franchises. In Treviso, the firm's designers create new shirts and sweaters on CAD terminals, but their designs are produced only for orders in hand, allowing for the coordination of production with the purchase of raw materials. In factories, rollers linked to a central computer spread and cut layers of cloth in small batches according to the numbers and colors ordered by Benetton stores around the world. Sweaters, gloves, and scarves, knitted in volume in white yarn, are dyed in small batches by machines similarly programmed to respond to sales orders. Completed garments are warehoused briefly (by robots) and shipped out directly (via private package delivery firms) to individual stores to arrive on their shelves within 10 days of manufacture.

Sensitivity to demand is the foundation of Benetton's success. Niche marketing and product differentiation are central to this sensitivity, which requires a high degree of flexibility in exploiting new product lines. Key stores patronized by trendsetting consumers (such as the store on the Rue Faubourg St. Honoré in Paris and the megastore on Omotesando Street in Tokyo) are monitored closely, and many Benetton stores' cash registers operate as point-of-sale terminals so that immediate marketing data are available to company headquarters daily. Another notable feature of the company's operations is the way that different market niches are exploited with the same basic products. In Italy, Benetton products are sold through several different

Figure 7.23   Headquarters of the Benetton Group, Villa Minelli, Treviso, Italy

retail chains, each with an image and decor calculated to bring in a different sort of customer.

Between firms, the flexibility inherent in neo-Fordism is achieved through the externalization or outsourcing of certain functions. One way of doing this has been to hire outside consultants, specialists, and subcontractors instead of paying wages and benefits to permanent employees. Another route to externalization involves joint ventures (such as Volkswagen in China); the licensing or contracting of technology; and strategic alliances involving design partnerships, collaborative R&D projects, and the like.

7.9 Geography in the Information Age

Strategic alliances between transnational corporations are an important contributor to the intensification of economic globalization. For example, the Nestlé food company has a number of strategic alliances, including a joint venture with General Mills called Cereal Partners Worldwide (CPW); an alliance with the Walt Disney Company in Europe, the United States, and Latin America; and a joint-venture partnership with the Coca-Cola Company in which the Swiss company cooperates with Coca-Cola in exchanging technologies and in marketing. Nestlé, for example, uses Coca-Cola's distribution network for products such as Nescafé instant coffee.

Maquiladoras **and Export-Processing Zones** The type of international sub-contracting carried out by Nike is encouraged by the governments of many peripheral and semiperipheral countries, who see participation in global assembly lines as a way to help along their own industrialization. They offer incentives, such as tax "holidays" (not having to pay taxes for a specified period), to transnational corporations. In the 1960s, Mexico enacted legislation permitting foreign companies to establish "sister factories"—*maquiladoras*—within 20 kilometres of the border with the United States for the duty-free assembly of products destined for re-export (**Figure 7.24**). By 2001, more than 3,700 such manufacturing and assembly plants had been established, employing more than a million Mexican workers, most of them women, and accounting for more than half of Mexico's exports. Since then, however, brisk competition from China has reduced the number of *maquiladoras* by about 500.

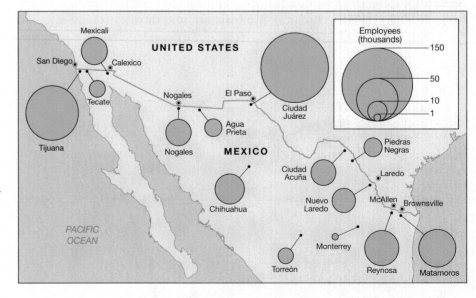

Figure 7.24 Principal *maquiladora* centres on the United States–Mexico border Cheap labour and tax breaks for firms manufacturing and assembling goods for re-export have made many Mexican border towns attractive to U.S. companies. Around a million workers are employed in these maquiladora plants, producing electronic products, textiles, furniture, leather goods, toys, and automotive parts. (*Source:* After P. Dicken, *Global Shift,* 4th ed. New York: Guilford, 2003.)

7.10 Geography in the Information Age

The decline in the number of *maquiladoras* is another example of the constant reorganization of the global assembly line according to the shifting logic of globalization: lower wage rates and better incentives in China have proved more attractive to U.S. manufacturers than the proximity of Mexican assembly plants to their markets. And another change is imminent: the tax breaks that favoured the establishment of the *maquiladoras* are due to expire under the terms of the North American Free Trade Agreement (NAFTA).

One way in which China has been able to attract manufacturing away from Mexican *maquiladoras* is by establishing **export-processing zones (EPZs)**—small areas within which especially favourable investment and trading conditions are created by governments to attract export-oriented industries. These conditions include minimum levels of bureaucracy surrounding importing and exporting, the absence of foreign exchange controls, the availability of factory space and warehousing at subsidized rents, low tax rates, and exemption from tariffs and export duties. In 1985, the International Labour Organization (ILO) estimated a total of 173 EPZs around the world, which together employed 1.8 million workers. In 1998, there were about 850 EPZs with about 27 million employees, 90 percent of whom were women. China alone had 124 EPZs, which together employed 18 million workers. The latest ILO estimate of 2008 puts the number of EPZs at 3,500. The ILO criticizes EPZs because very few of them have any meaningful links with the domestic economies around them, and most trap large numbers of (mostly female) workers in low-wage, low-skill jobs.

export-processing zones (EPZs): small areas within which especially favourable investment and trading conditions are created by governments to attract export-oriented industries

Big-Box Retailing, Chains, and Global Sourcing At the other end of the commodity chain from the farms, mines, *maquiladoras,* and factories of the world are the retail outlets and restaurants where the products are sold and consumed. Traditionally, retailing and food services in core countries have been dominated by small, specialized, independent stores and local cafes, restaurants, pubs, and bars. But the logic of economic rationalization and economies of scale has displaced the traditional pattern of downtown department stores, Main Street shops, corner stores, and local bars with big-box superstores and national and international chains of retail outlets and restaurants. With their cost advantages arising from their big, centralized logistical operations they have not only put small independent stores out of business but are driving the homogenization of consumption, eating, farming, the landscape, the environment, and people's daily lives. The retail sector of most towns and cities is now characterized by external control, the decisions about hiring, labour policies, wages, stock, and menus being made in corporate headquarters far away.

Fast-food restaurants have become icons of this trend. McDonald's alone has more than 30,000 restaurants in more than half of the world's countries. It is the largest purchaser of beef, pork, and potatoes and the largest owner of retail property in the world. In Canada, almost 20 percent of meals are eaten outside of the home, most of them at fast-food restaurants. In the United States, that number is as high as 40 percent, with one in four adults visiting a fast-food restaurant every day. Not surprisingly, the majority of the population is overweight, and the frequency of health problems associated with obesity—such as early-onset diabetes and high cholesterol—is rising rapidly. The cost of these problems to personal well-being and to health care systems is already daunting. Meanwhile, fast food's low-paying service sector has become an increasingly significant component of the economy.

Equally significant in terms of local economies, local development patterns, and global supply chains has been the success of big-box retail outlets such as Best Buy, Staples, Home Depot, and Walmart. To many observers, Walmart has come to symbolize the worst characteristics of globalization, including corporate greed, low wages, the decline of small-town mom-and-pop stores, and the proliferation of sweatshops in less developed countries (see **Geography Matters 7.5— Walmart's Economic Landscape**).

Supermarket chains have also become particularly influential. Their centralized supply chains have not only killed off small local businesses but also impacted local farmers. Supermarket chains rely on big suppliers in agribusiness—national and transnational firms that are often highly subsidized and whose global reach depends heavily on monoculture and intensive husbandry that, in turn, require the frequent use of antibiotics in animals and pesticides, fertilizer, and genetic engineering for crops. As a result, small farmers and fishermen have been squeezed from the market, and with them many traditional local foods have disappeared or are in danger of disappearing. Meanwhile, supermarket shelves are lined with highly processed foods, out-of-season fruit and vegetables, and produce that has travelled a long way and, often, been stored for a while. When the average North American or European family sits down to eat, most of the ingredients have typically travelled at least 2,000 kilometres from farm, processing, packing, distribution, to consumption.

The Global Office

The globalization of production and the growth of transnational corporations have brought about another important change in patterns of local economic development. Banking, finance, and business services are no longer locally oriented ancillary activities but important global industries in their own right that are able to influence local patterns and processes of economic development throughout the world, just like the major transnational conglomerates involved in the global assembly line.

The new importance of banking, finance, and business services was initially a result of the globalization of manufacturing, an increase in the volume of world trade, and the emergence of transnational corporate empires. It was helped along by advances in telecommunications and data processing. Satellite communications systems and fibre-optic networks made it possible for firms to operate key financial and business services 24 hours a day around the globe, handling an enormous volume of transactions. Linked to these communications systems, computers permit the recording and coordination of the data. The world's fourth-largest stock market, the National Associated Automated Dealers Quotation System (NASDAQ) in New York City, has no trading floor at all: telephone and fibre-optic lines connect its half-million traders worldwide.

The global banking and financial network now handles trillions of dollars every day—no more than 10 percent of which has anything to do with the traditional world economy of trade in goods and services. International movements of money, bonds, securities, and other financial instruments have now become an end in themselves because they are a potential source of high profits from speculation and manipulation.

Electronic Offices, Decentralization, and Outsourcing   It is clear that an important shift has occurred in the economic structure of the world's core economies, with the rapid growth of banking, financial, and business services contributing to the expansion of the quaternary sector. What is particularly important from a *geographical* perspective is that this growth has been localized—that is, concentrated in relatively small and distinctive settings within major metropolitan centres. This phenomenon is surprising to some observers, who had expected that new communications technologies would allow for the dispersion of "electronic

Walmart's Economic Landscape

Walmart (Wal-Mart until 2008) is the largest company in the world in terms of revenue, with sales of more than US$250 billion in 2010. It is also the most highly rationalized, centralized retail chain in the world, designed to run like an assembly line. To some, Walmart represents an opportunity to consume high-quality products at low cost from a global market economy. To others, Walmart has displaced McDonald's as the company most closely associated with U.S. political-economic and cultural power, the negative cultural consequences of globalization, and the negative consequences of corporate power.

Walmart was founded on a distinctive—and unusual—geographic marketing strategy, based on a network of stores in small, isolated towns in the American South. From the firm's headquarters in Bentonville, Arkansas, Walmart's founder, Sam Walton, built a retail empire that reflects the values embedded in the small-town rural South: conservatism, idealized views of family and community, and the principles of hard work, frugality, and competitiveness. The company has moved out of the small-town South and into metropolitan markets and international ventures but is still characterized by store locations on the outskirts (**Figure 7.5.1**)—partly because of land costs and tax benefits and partly because of the NIMBYism (NIMBY stands for "Not In My Backyard") associated with established neighbourhoods (**Figure 7.5.2**).

From the start, the emphasis was on a business model that rests on high-volume turnover through low prices. This required a rapid expansion of stores in order to strengthen the firm's position with suppliers, and this, in turn, meant that Walmart quickly developed expertise in logistics—the movement and storage of goods and the management of the entire supply chain, from purchase of raw materials through sale of the final product and back again for the replenishment of goods as they are sold. Walmart put together its own distribution facilities, fleet of trucks, and satellite communications network in order to maximize the supplier discounts required for this business model. Another key feature of Walmart's economic landscape is cost control: pressure is continuously exerted on local governments, employees, and suppliers to get the best deal possible. Walmart's labour policies are virulently anti-union; the stores are deliberately understaffed; there is no grievance policy for employees; vendor agreements are tough; suppliers do not give up ownership of the goods until they are sold to the customer; and suppliers are required to drop prices by as much as 5 percent annually. Suppliers conform to this pressure because they depend on Walmart as their largest (or sole) customer.

The company's rapid expansion and tremendous profitability "allowed it a market power unequalled by any of its large corporate competitors, a power that is reshaping the nature of America's and the world's retail industry."[6] Walmart's low prices have reduced consumer inflation and brought many products within the reach of consumers previously unable to afford them. But there has been a great deal of concern over the impact of Walmart stores on smaller stores and towns because of the many examples of Walmart's predatory pricing having put independent local stores out of business. The result is external control of the local economy. With fewer locally owned businesses, money spent on goods no longer stays within the community but rather is funnelled back to corporate headquarters. At the same time, Walmart wages tend to be significantly lower—in the

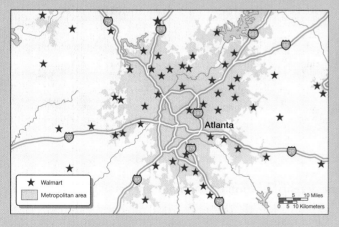

Figure 7.5.1 Walmart stores in the Atlanta metropolitan region Note how they are overwhelmingly located on the outskirts. Since American low-income households are typically concentrated in the inner cities, they are not being served by Walmart's discount stores. (*Source:* Adapted from Figure 2.6 in S.D. Brunn (ed.), *Wal-Mart World.* New York: Routledge, 2006, p. 23.)

Figure 7.5.2 Not In My Backyard Local resistance to a proposed new Walmart store in Blacksburg, Virginia.

[6] E. Rosen, "Wal-Mart: The New Retail Colossus." In S. Brunn (ed.), *Wal-Mart World.* New York: Routledge, 2006, p. 92.

region of 30 percent lower—than in independent, locally owned businesses, so that wages in local labour markets tend to be depressed.

Also, although large retailers such as Walmart carry an extensive array of goods, they often stock only a limited variety of any specific product, thereby leaving the consumer with less choice overall. For example, whereas independent local newsagents typically carry a broad range of magazine titles, big-box chain stores typically concentrate on only the titles with the biggest turnover, in order to maximize profit. The same is true for the sale of CDs and DVDs. So, not only do corporate chains reduce the range of shops available in small towns, they also reduce the choice of goods readily available. This is compounded, in Walmart's case, by the company's censorship, "protecting" consumers from products that the management deems offensive. This includes refusing to sell CDs with parental warning stickers and obscuring the covers of popular magazines like *Redbook, Marie Claire, Cosmopolitan,* and *Rolling Stone.* Because of the enormous size of the Walmart network, some magazines willingly send advance copies to corporate headquarters in Bentonville for approval before publication and will even alter cover artwork to avoid losing sales. "Thus, far from being simply a store, Wal-Mart is also a moral universe external to the community."[7] Walmart advertising campaigns have always emphasized happy staff, customers from cozy families, and support for local communities. Patriotism was a strong theme in the 1990s, the firm's Buy-American campaign coinciding with Walmart becoming China's sixth-largest trading partner. There are, however, no references to fair trade, fair employment, ethical trading, or environmental consciousness.

The most recent development in Walmart's economic landscape has been internationalization. The company entered markets in Mexico, Puerto Rico, and Canada in the early 1990s, later expanding into Hong Kong, Indonesia, Brazil, Argentina, China, Germany, and South Korea. There were mixed results. More recently, the approach has been to acquire "Walmart ready" chains of stores and then convert their operations to the Walmart model, as with the company's takeover of Asda (the United Kingdom's second-largest supermarket chain) in 1999.

Walmart's greatest global impact, though, is through its supply chains. Overall, 50 to 60 percent of the goods Walmart imports into the United States each year by ship come from China, and the home office of Walmart Global Procurement is in Shenzhen, China. The company has a network of over two dozen field offices in other countries and oversees the sourcing of products from more than 5,000 factories in 65 countries, including Bangladesh, Brazil, Guatemala, India, Indonesia, Malaysia, the Philippines, Sri Lanka, and Thailand. The reason, of course, is labour costs. But the "natural" cheapness of labour in these countries is not enough for Walmart; the company systematically imposes pressure on suppliers to reduce costs still further. This, unsurprisingly, has led to abuse and violations of labour laws.

An example that received widespread public attention came to light in 1999 as a result of a report by the National Labor Committee, which revealed that workers in the Liang Shi Handbag Factory in Dongguan City, Guangdong, China, earned as little as 12 cents an hour for 60- to 70-hour weeks producing Kathie Lee Gifford handbags.[8] This was not an isolated example. Recent evidence from *China Labor Watch,* for example, found that four apparel factories in China that supplied Adidas and Walmart were paying their workers just 48 cents an hour—which was not enough to sustain themselves unless they did overtime. A 2007 report by the National Labor Committee, *A Wal-Mart Christmas,*[9] featured Guangzhou Huanya Gift Ltd. Company of Guangdong Province, China, where the 8,000 workers must put in 10- to 12- to 15-hour shifts seven days a week during the long, eight-month busy season manufacturing Christmas ornaments for Walmart. At least half the workers, some 4,000 people, were working 95 hours, including 55 hours of (mandatory) overtime. The legal minimum wage in Guangzhou is 55 cents an hour, but workers were paid by a piece rate, with some workers earning just 26 cents an hour.

---

[7] B. Warf and T. Chapman, "Cathedrals of Consumption: A Political Phenomenology of Wal-Mart." In S. Brunn (ed.), *Wal-Mart World.* New York: Routledge, 2006, p. 165.

[8] China Labor Watch, 2007, "Textile Sweatshops: Adidas, Bali Intimates, Hanesbrands Inc., Piege Co. (Felina Lingerie), Quiksilver, Regina Miracle Speedo, Walcoal America Inc., and Wal-Mart Made In China," **www.chinalaborwatch.org/200711204textile.htm.**

[9] National Labor Committee, 2007, "A Wal-Mart Christmas. Brought to You by a Sweatshop in China," **www.nlcnet.org/article.php?id=498.**

offices" and, with it, the decentralization of an important catalyst for local economic development. A good deal of geographic decentralization of offices has occurred, in fact, but it has mainly involved "back-office" functions that have been relocated from metropolitan and business-district locations to small-town and suburban locations.

Back-office functions are record-keeping and analytical functions that do not require frequent personal contact with clients or business associates. The accountants and financial technicians of main street banks, for example, are back-office

7.11   Geography in the Information Age

The U.S. Postal Service uses optical character recognition software (OCR) to read addresses on mail, which is then bar-coded and automatically sorted to its appropriate substation. Addresses that the OCR cannot read are digitally photographed and transmitted to a computer screen in a back-office facility in a cheap rural location. There a worker deciphers the address and manually types it into a terminal for transmission back to the sorting facility.

workers. Developments in computing technologies, database access, electronic data interchanges, and telephone call routing technologies are enabling a larger share of back-office work to be relocated to specialized office space in cheaper settings, freeing space in the high-rent locations occupied by the bank's front office.

Internationally, this trend has taken the form of offshore back offices. By decentralizing back-office functions to offshore locations, companies save even more in labour costs. For example, Australian mortgage applications can be processed in Bangalore, India, at a fraction of the cost by using cheaper labour and paperless processes.

The logical next step from decentralized back-office functions is outsourcing. The outsourcing of services is one of the most dynamic sectors of the world economy. Outsourced services range from simple business-process activities (for example, data entry, word processing, transcription) to more sophisticated, high-value-added activities (for example, architectural drawing, product support, financial analysis, software programming, and human resource services). India has become one of the most successful exporters of outsourced service activities, ranging from call centres and business-process activities to advanced IT (information technology) services (**Figure 7.25**). More than 150 of the *Fortune 500* companies, for example, now outsource software development to India. In the Philippines, special electronic "enterprise zones" have been set up with competitive international telephone rates for companies specializing in telemarketing and electronic commerce. Mexico, South Africa, and Malaysia have also become important locations for call centres and business-process activities.

Clusters of Specialized Offices   Decentralization is outweighed, however, by the tendency for a disproportionate share of the new jobs created in banking, finance, and business services to cluster in highly specialized financial districts within major metropolitan areas. The reasons for this localization are found in another special case of the geographical agglomeration effects that we discussed earlier in this chapter.

Metropolitan areas such as New York City, London, Paris, Tokyo, Zurich, and Frankfurt have acquired the kind of infrastructure—specialized office space, financial exchanges, teleports (office parks equipped with satellite Earth stations and linked to local fibre-optic lines), and communications networks—that is essential

Figure 7.25   Globalized office work   Employees in a call centre in Bangalore, India.

for delivering services to clients with a national or international scope of activity. These metropolitan areas have also established a comparative advantage both in the mix of specialized firms and expert professionals on hand and in the high-order cultural amenities available (both to high-paid workers and to their out-of-town business visitors).

Above all, these metro areas have established themselves as centres of authority, with a critical mass of people in the know about market conditions, trends, and innovations—people who can gain one another's trust through frequent face-to-face contact, not just in business settings but also in the informal settings of restaurants and bars. They have become world cities—places that, in the globalized world economy, are able not only to generate powerful spirals of local economic development but also to act as pivotal points in the reorganization of global space: control centres for the flows of information, cultural products, and finance that collectively sustain the economic and cultural globalization of the world (see Chapter 10 for more details).

A good example of the clustering of business services in major world cities is provided by advertising services in Europe. In the early 1980s, these services were distributed among major European cities, with Paris, London, Amsterdam, and Stockholm accounting for the headquarters of most firms, but with smaller concentrations in Brussels, Düsseldorf, Frankfurt, and Zürich. By 1990, the headquarters of most advertising agencies in Europe had moved to London, which, along with New York and Tokyo, has become one of the three dominant world cities in the contemporary world-system.

Offshore Financial Centres   The combination of metropolitan concentration and back-office decentralization fulfills most of the locational needs of the global financial network. Some needs—secrecy and shelter from taxation and regulation, in particular—call for a different locational strategy. The result has been the emergence of a series of **offshore financial centres**: islands and microstates such as the Bahamas, Bahrain, the Cayman Islands, the Cook Islands, Luxembourg, Liechtenstein, and Vanuatu that have become specialized nodes in the geography of worldwide financial flows.

The chief attraction of offshore financial centres is simply that they are less regulated than financial centres elsewhere. They provide low-tax or no-tax settings for savings, havens for undeclared income and for hot money. They also provide discreet markets in which to deal currencies, bonds, loans, and other financial instruments without coming to the attention of regulating authorities or competitors. Overall, about 60 percent of the world's money now resides offshore.

The Cayman Islands provide the classic example of an offshore financial centre. This small island state in the Caribbean has transformed itself from a poor, underdeveloped colony to a relatively affluent and modern setting for upscale tourism and offshore finance. With a population of just over 40,000, it has more than 30,000 registered companies. Yet fewer than 75 of the 580 or so registered banks in the Cayman Islands maintain a physical presence on the islands, and only half a dozen offer the kind of local services that allow local residents to maintain chequing accounts or tourists to cash traveller's cheque. Most exist as post office boxes, as nameplates in anonymous office buildings, as fax numbers, or as entries in a computer system. In 2004, over a trillion dollars passed through the Caymans, making it the most successful of all offshore financial centres.

offshore financial centres: islands or microstates that have become specialized nodes in the geography of worldwide financial flows

Tourism and Economic Development

Many parts of the world, including parts of the world's core regions, do not have much of a primary base (that is, in agriculture, fishing, or mineral extraction), are not currently an important part of the global assembly line,

7.12 Geography in the Information Age

Tourism can also be understood as part of a new phase of economic organization. After going through the agrarian, industrial, and service economies, we now enter an "experience economy" based on staging experiences. Apart from tourism, this experience economy comprises sports entertainment, arena rock concerts, fancy megamalls with themed entertainment, and visits to museums and galleries. In addition, new businesses are emerging that are based on selling novel and artificial kinds of experiences. In 11 U.S. locations, American Girl Place offers a combination of attractions specifically targeted at young girls and their dolls: a doll hair salon, a doll bistro with "formal dining atmosphere," a doll hospital, doll care classes, and of course a doll shopping mall with personal shopping services. Their website advertises "Café. Theater. Shops. *Memories.*" (**www.americangirl.com/stores/brand_agplace.php.**)

and are not closely tied into the global financial network. For these areas, tourism can offer the otherwise unlikely prospect of economic development. Geographers (with their interests in the movements of peoples, world regions, and the meaning of "place") have become important contributors to the interdisciplinary study of tourism and leisure and their contribution to economic development.

The globalization of the world economy has been paralleled by a globalization of the tourist industry. Tourism has, in fact, become enormously important: it already is the world's largest nonagricultural employer, with 1 in every 12 workers worldwide involved in transporting, feeding, housing, guiding, or amusing tourists. Between 1970 and 2011, the number of international tourist trips grew sevenfold to almost 1 billion per year, most of which were made by tourists from the more affluent core countries of the world. Spending by U.S., German, U.K., and Japanese tourists accounted for almost 40 percent of total international tourist dollars in 2003, while France, Italy, Canada, and the Netherlands accounted for another 12 percent.

What is most striking, though, is not so much the growth in the number of international tourists as the increased range of international tourism. Thanks largely to cheaper long-distance flights, a significant proportion of tourism is now transcontinental and transoceanic. Although Europe (58 percent) and the Americas (18 percent) continue to be the main tourist destinations, visits to countries in Africa, Asia, and the Pacific have grown to account for almost one-quarter of the industry. This has made tourism a central component of economic development in peripheral and semiperipheral countries with abundant wildlife (Kenya, South Africa), scenery (Nepal, Vietnam), beaches (the Seychelles Islands), shopping (Singapore, Dubai, and Hong Kong), culture (China, India, Japan, and Indonesia), or sex (Thailand).

Although tourism can provide a basis for economic development, it is often a mixed blessing. It certainly creates jobs, but they are often seasonal and pay very little. Dependence on tourism also makes for a high degree of economic vulnerability as tourism, like other high-end aspects of consumption, depends very much on matters of style and fashion. Some places once sought out by tourists because of their remoteness and their "natural," undeveloped qualities, such as Nepal and New Zealand, are now too "obvious" as destinations, whereas Bhutan, Bolivia, Estonia, Patagonia, and Vietnam have been "discovered" and are coping with their first significant growth in tourism. China, meanwhile, is rapidly growing into one of the most popular destinations.

7.13 Geography in the Information Age

In a wider sense, tourism is also a part of the processes of "place making" we discussed in Chapters 5 and 6: tourism demand does not simply exist, it is actively created (as the case of Niagara Falls illustrated). Tourism, like any other human activity, is essentially a social and cultural construct, and the "tourist gaze" (a term coined by sociologist John Urry) can be turned on sites and sights as various as natural phenomena (such as Ayers Rock in Australia or the Grand Canyon), folk housing museums (Upper Canada Village), or the homes of long-dead rock stars (Elvis' Graceland in Memphis). Objectively, what we see is less important than how we see it, and how we use our own biases and frames of reference in that interpretation. In this view, travel does not broaden the mind, it reconfirms what we already know!

Moreover, although tourism is a multi-billion-dollar industry, the financial returns for tourist areas are often not as high as might be expected. The greater part of the price of a package vacation, for example, stays with the organizing company and the airline. Typically, only 40 percent is retained by the tourist region itself. If the package involves a foreign-owned hotel, this number may fall to less than 25 percent.

We can use the cruise ship industry (an industry in which Canada is an important participant) to further illustrate the advantages and disadvantages of package tourism. When three or four of these luxury behemoths each disgorge 2,000 passengers into places such as Skagway or Antigua, in effect doubling the population of the community (**Figure 7.26**), the amount of tourist dollars spent on food, trinkets, and shore excursions can be substantial. In 2005, for example, the cruise ship industry's impact on the British Columbian economy was estimated as $1.2 billion annually, of which $660 million was due to the direct spending of the cruise lines, passengers and crews.[10] Sadly, however, further research has shown that the story is not that simple.

Figure 7.26   Cruise ships anchored in Skagway, Alaska

[10] Ross A. Klein, *Playing Off the Ports: BC and the Cruise Tourism Industry*. Vancouver: Canadian Centre for Policy Alternatives, August 2005. For more information on the Canadian Pacific Cruise Industry, see: Sue Dobson, Alison Gill, and Sam Baird, *A Primer on the Canadian Pacific Cruise Ship Industry*. May 2002 (**www.sfu.ca/cstudies/science/resources/coastalstudies/Cruise_Ship.pdf**).

It is not always apparent, but many of the harbour-side stores and businesses frequented by cruise ship passengers are either owned by the cruise line itself or its local affiliates. In addition, ports are often also obliged to pay the cruise line if they wish the ship to make a stop in their community. Factors such as these mean that much of the revenues apparently earned at port destinations do not, in fact, benefit those communities themselves but flow elsewhere through a process known as "leakage." Other economic drawbacks are that the benefits rarely penetrate far beyond the quayside into the wider community, and that more traditional livelihoods (such as fishing) can be disrupted.

Beyond the economic difficulties, critics have also pointed to the environmental effects of cruise ships dumping raw sewage, garbage, and engine oil, and potentially damaging fragile marine ecosystems such as coral reefs and mangrove swamps. In the final analysis, it may well be that the economic benefits of the cruise ship industry are not worth the environmental price, but many communities depend on the short-term gain to the economy for their economic development strategies.

One strategy to counter the economic, environmental, and social problems of package tourism is "alternative" tourism—tourism that emphasizes self-determination, authenticity, social harmony, preservation of the existing environment, small-scale development, and greater use of local techniques, materials, and architectural styles. Alternative tourism includes ecotourism (birdwatching in Costa Rica, helping endangered sea turtles in Bali, "working" in elephant camps in Thailand, whale watching in Canada [**Figure 7.27**]), cultural tourism (visiting Machu Picchu, the lost city of the Incas), adventure tourism ("exploring" the Amazon), industrial tourism (touring the Potteries district of northern England by canal boat), and Aboriginal tourism (experiencing indigenous cultures).

Ecotourism is probably the most successful form of alternative tourism so far, but it is important to realize that this activity implies more than simply the concept of "sustainable tourism." In addition to that concept, according to the United Nations Environment Programme (UNEP)'s definition, ecotourism: (1) contributes to the conservation of an area's natural and cultural heritage; (2) includes local indigenous communities in its planning; (3) interprets the natural and cultural heritage of the destination to the visitor; and (4) is aimed at small-sized groups (to minimize their impact).[11]

Costa Rica, for example, has protected 30 percent of its territory in biosphere and wildlife preserves so it can use its astonishing biodiversity for ecotourism purposes (Costa Rica has more bird species than all of North America and

ecotourism: an activity which, in addition to following the goals of "sustainable tourism," also (1) contributes to the conservation of an area's natural and cultural heritage; (2) includes local indigenous communities in its planning; (3) interprets the natural and cultural heritage of the destination to the visitor; and (4) is aimed at small-sized groups

Figure 7.27   Whale watching   Following the moratorium on cod fishing and the decline of the Atlantic cod fishery, many fishers turned to alternative sources of employment. Taking tourists to see whales seems a happy fit of environmental tourism and alternative job creation. However, the more whale watchers there are, the greater the threat to the whales (because of engine noise and the boats getting too close), and so this new industry can never make up the shortfall in employment.

[11] United Nations Environment Programme, "Tourism: About Ecotourism," **www.unep.fr/scp/ tourism/sustain**.

more varieties of butterflies than all of Africa). The payoff for Costa Rica is the escalating number of tourists: since 1995, the number of visitors has increased by 10 percent each year, reaching 2 million in 2010. Tourism is now the country's largest source of foreign exchange.

Ecuador is another country that has fostered ecotourism. Two-thirds of all organized travel to Ecuador is handled by members of the Ecuadorean Ecotourism Association, an organization sponsored by the private sector as well as the government in an effort to ensure sustainable development through environmental awareness.

Canada provides a good example of what has become known as *Aboriginal (or indigenous) tourism*.[12] Defined by Butler and Hinch as "tourism activity in which indigenous people are directly involved either through control and/or having their culture serve as the essence of the attraction," Aboriginal tourism has been described by Industry Canada in a 2006 report as "one of Canada's unique strengths," whose development is a "top priority."

According to government estimates, Aboriginal tourism in 2005 generated $474 million in revenue and employed 16,000 people across the country. By using their own culture as an attraction, indigenous peoples foster their own local economic development: tourism can help sustain indigenous lifestyles and regional cultures, arts, and crafts; and it can provide incentives for wildlife preservation, environmental protection, and the conservation of historic buildings and sites. However, tourism can also adulterate and debase indigenous cultures and bring unsightly development, pollution, and environmental degradation. Moreover, in many native communities in Canada, the tourist season coincides with the peak of hunting activities and it therefore does not provide employment when it is most needed during the year. Finally, most research has noted that Aboriginal tourism (like many other forms of tourism) tends to be controlled by non-Aboriginal owners who do not reinvest their profits in the local communities where they are generated.

Aboriginal tourism can also involve exploitative relations that debase traditional lifestyles and regional cultural heritages as they become packaged for outsider consumption. In the process, the indigenous behaviours and artifacts that are made available to an international market of outsiders can lose much of their original meaning. Traditional ceremonies that formerly had cultural significance for the performers are now enacted only to be watched and photographed. Artifacts like masks and weapons are manufactured not for their original use but as curios, souvenirs, and ornaments. In the process, indigenous cultures are edited, beautified, and altered to suit outsiders' tastes and expectations.

CONCLUSION

The growth of alternative tourism in Costa Rica, like the growth of the Cayman Islands as an offshore financial centre and the decline of Nova Scotia's Cape Breton as a manufacturing region, shows that economic development is not simply a sequential process of modernization and increasing affluence. Various pathways to development exist, each involving different ways of achieving increased economic productivity and higher incomes, together with an increased capacity to improve the basic conditions of life. Economic development means not just using the latest technology to generate

---

[12] The material in this section is based, with thanks, upon the work of Andrea Sabelli, "Aboriginal Tourism as an Economic Development Strategy." Honours Essay, Department of Geography, Planning and Environment, Concordia University, Montreal, 2008. In addition, see *Building a National Tourism Strategy*. Ottawa: Industry Canada, 2006; C. Notzke, "Indigenous Tourism Development in S. Alberta, Canada: Tentative Engagement," *Journal of Sustainable Tourism* 12(1), 2004, pp. 29–54; R. Butler and T. Hinch, *Tourism and Indigenous Peoples*. London: ITP, 1996; A. Johnston, *Is the Sacred for Sale? Tourism and Indigenous Peoples*. London: Earthscan, 2005; K. Iankova, "Le tourisme et le développement économique des communautés autochtones du Québec," *Recherches Amérindiennes au Québec* 34(1), 2006, pp. 69–78; J. Altman and J. Finlayson, "Aborigines, Tourism and Sustainable Development," *Journal of Tourism Studies* 4(1), 1993, pp. 39–50.

higher incomes but also improving the quality of life through better housing, health care, and social welfare systems and enhancing the physical framework, or infrastructure, on which the economy rests—all without degrading the environment.

Local, regional, and international patterns and processes of economic development are of particular importance to geographers. Levels of economic development and local processes of economic change affect many aspects of local well-being and so contribute to many aspects of human geography. Economic development is an important place-making process that underpins much of the diversity among regions and nations. At the same time, it is a reflection and a product of variations from place to place in natural resources, demographic characteristics, political systems, and social customs.

Economic development is always an uneven geographical phenomenon. Regional patterns of economic development are tied to the geographical distribution of resources and to the legacy of the past specializations of places and regions within national economies. Nevertheless, such patterns are not fixed or static. Changing economic conditions can lead to the modification or reversal of core–periphery patterns, such as the stagnation of once-booming northern England and the spectacular growth of Guangdong province in southeast China. Over the long term, core–periphery patterns have most often been modified as a result of the changing locational needs and opportunities of successive technology systems. Today, economic globalization has exposed more places and regions than ever to the ups and downs of episodes of creative destruction—episodes played out ever faster, thanks to the way in which new technologies, such as the Internet, have shrunk time and space.

At the global scale, the unevenness of economic development takes the form of core–periphery contrasts within the world-system framework. Most striking about these contrasts today are the dynamism and pace of change involved in economic development. The global assembly line, the global office, and global tourism are all making places much more interdependent and faster changing. Parts of Brazil, China, India, Mexico, and South Korea, for example, have developed quickly from rural backwaters into significant industrial regions. The Cayman Islands have been transformed from an insignificant Caribbean colony to an upscale tourist resort and a major offshore financial centre. Countries, such as Ecuador and Costa Rica, with few comparative advantages suddenly find themselves able to earn significant amounts of foreign exchange through the development of ecotourism. This dynamism has, however, brought with it an expanding gap between rich and poor at every spatial scale—international, regional, and local.

MAIN POINTS REVISITED

- **The geography of economic development is the cumulative outcome of decisions guided by fundamental principles of land use, commercial and industrial location, and economic interdependence.**

  As location decisions are played out in the real world, distinctive geographical linkages and spatial structures emerge.

- **Geographically, the single most important feature of economic development is that it is highly uneven.**

  At the global scale, this unevenness takes the form of core-periphery contrasts. These contrasts raise important issues of spatial justice that are closely bound up with gender inequality and social justice. Similar core–periphery contrasts—and equally important issues of spatial justice—exist at the regional scale.

- **Successive technology systems have rewritten the geography of economic development as they have shifted the balance of advantages between regions.**

Technological innovations in power and energy, transportation, and manufacturing processes have been important catalysts for changes in the pattern of economic development, allowing a succession of expansions of economic activity in time and space. Although many existing industrial regions have grown bigger and more productive, each major cluster of technological innovations tends to create new requirements in terms of natural resources as well as labour forces and markets. As a result, each major cluster of technological innovations has tended to favour different regions and different kinds of places.

- **Geographical divisions of labour have evolved with the growth of the world-system of trade and politics and with the changing locational logic of successive technology systems.**

Geographical divisions of labour are national, regional, and locally based economic specializations in primary, secondary, tertiary, or quaternary activities. The relationship between changing regional economic specialization and changing levels of prosperity has prompted the interpretation of economic development in distinctive stages. In reality, however, various pathways exist to development, as well as various processes and outcomes of development.

■ **Regional cores of economic development are created cumulatively, following some initial advantage, through the operation of several basic principles of spatial organization.**

Any significant initial local economic advantage—existing labour markets, consumer markets, frameworks of fixed social capital, and so on—tends to be reinforced through a process of cumulative causation, a spiral buildup of advantages that occurs in specific geographical settings as a result of the development of external economies, agglomeration effects, and localization economies.

■ **Spirals of economic development can be arrested in various ways, including the onset of disinvestment and deindustrialization, which follow major shifts in technology systems and in international geopolitics.**

The capital made available from disinvestment in core regions becomes available for investment in new ventures based on innovative products and technologies. Old industries—and sometimes entire old industrial regions—have to be "dismantled" (or at least neglected) to help fund the creation of new centres of profitability and employment. This process is often referred to as *creative destruction*.

■ **The globalization of the economy has meant that patterns and processes of local and regional economic development are much more open to external influences than before.**

The globalization of the world economy involves a new international division of labour in association with the internationalization of finance, the deployment of a new technology system, and the homogenization of consumer markets. This new framework for economic geography has meant that the lives of people in different parts of the world have become increasingly intertwined.

■ **Tourism has increasingly come to represent a major industry at a world scale, and offers the potential for local economic development in forms as various as ecotourism and visits to Aboriginal cultural sites.**

Tourism has many economic benefits (in terms of local employment and the creation of new opportunities), but its long-term negatives (in terms of its impact on the environment, and the fact that much of the economic gains do not stay in the community) often outweigh the short-term advantages.

Key Terms

agglomeration diseconomies (p. 326)
agglomeration effects (p. 321)
ancillary activities (p. 321)
backwash effects (p. 325)
brownfield site (p. 327)
creative destruction (p. 326)
cumulative causation (p. 324)
deindustrialization (p. 326)
ecotourism (p. 349)
export-processing zones (EPZs) (p. 341)

external economies (p. 321)
foreign direct investment (p. 332)
geographical path dependence (p. 323)
gross domestic product (GDP) (p. 299)
gross national income (GNI) (p. 299)
gross national product (GNP) (p. 299)
growth poles (p. 331)
infrastructure (fixed social capital) (p. 322)

initial advantage (p. 323)
localization economies (p. 321)
offshore financial centres (p. 346)
primary activities (p. 310)
quaternary activities (p. 310)
secondary activities (p. 310)
spread effects (p. 325)
tertiary activities (p. 310)
urbanization economies (p. 322)

Additional Reading

Barnet, R.J., and J. Cavanagh. *Global Dreams*. New York: Simon & Schuster, 1994.

Blake, R.B. *From Fishermen to Fish: The Evolution of Canadian Fishery Policy*. Toronto: Irwin, 2000.

Britton, J.H. (ed.). *Canada and the Global Economy: The Geography of Structural and Technological Change*. Montreal: McGill-Queen's University Press, 1996.

Castells, M. *The Information Age*, vol. 3. Oxford: Blackwell, 1996–1998.

Castells, M., and P. Hall. *Technopoles of the World: The Making of 21st Century Industrial Complexes*. New York: Routledge, 1994.

Cho, G. *Trade, Aid, and Global Interdependence*. London: Routledge, 1995.

Chodos, R., R. Murphy, and E. Hamovitch. *Canada and the Global Economy*. Toronto: Lorimer, 1993.

Dicken, P. *Global Shift*, 3rd ed. New York: Harper & Row, 1997.

Fennel, D.A. *Ecotourism: An Introduction*. London: Routledge, 1999.

Gibb, R., and W. Michalak. *Continental Trading Blocs: The Growth of Regionalism in the World Economy*. New York: Wiley, 1994.

Hayter, R., and P.D. Wilde (eds.). *Industrial Transformation and Challenge in Australia and Canada*. Ottawa: Carleton University Press, 1990.

Howells, J., and M. Wood. *The Globalisation of Production and Technology*. London: Pinter, 1993.

Hugill, P. *Global Communications Since 1844: Geopolitics and Technology*. Baltimore: Johns Hopkins University Press, 1999.

Knox, P.L., and J. Agnew. *The Geography of the World Economy*, 3rd ed. London: Edward Arnold, 1998.

Norcliffe, G. "Canada in a Global Economy," *Canadian Geographer* 45(1), 2001, 14–30.

Potter, R.B., J.A. Binns, J.A. Elliott, and D. Smith. *Geographies of Development.* London: Longman, 1999.

Smith, N. *Uneven Development: Nature, Capital, and the Production of Space,* 2nd ed. Oxford: Blackwell, 1991.

Taylor, P.J. "The Error of Developmentalism in Human Geography." In D. Gregory and R. Walford (eds.), *Horizons in Human Geography.* Totowa, NJ: Barnes and Noble, 1989, 309–319.

Wallace, I. *A Geography of the Canadian Economy.* Toronto: Oxford University Press, 2002.

World Bank. *World Development Report 1995: Workers in an Integrating World.* New York: Oxford University Press, 1995.

Discussion Questions and Research Activities

1. Although India's per capita income is well below that of Canada (Figure 7.1), India has more people who earn the equivalent of $70,000 a year than Canada does. How can you explain this, and what might be some of the consequences of this from the point of view of economic geography?

2. Figure 7.4 suggests that creating economic opportunities for women does not necessarily require high levels of economic development. Which peripheral countries have a high gender empowerment index score, and which core countries have a relatively low gender empowerment index score? Can you think of explanations for these cases?

3. Write a short essay (500 words, or two double-spaced, typed pages) on any specialized manufacturing region or office district with which you are familiar. Describe the different kinds of firms that are found there, and suggest the kinds of linkages among them that might be considered to be examples of agglomeration effects.

4. Look at the countries advertised as tourist destinations in your daily newspaper. Go to your library and find copies of that newspaper for 1992 and 2002. What was the pattern of tourist destination ads in those years? What explains the differences you see?

MyGeosciencePlace

Visit **www.mygeoscienceplace.ca** to find chapter review quizzes, videos, maps, and much more.

8

Agriculture and Food Production

Searching for food in a Haitian garbage dump. A boy cries after the garbage he had scavenged was stolen from him.

The soaring cost of food, and the increasing numbers of people unable to feed themselves adequately because of it, have been persistently on the news since early 2006. However, a back story about the ramping up of global food prices has been less prominent. This story, which is about finance, investment, stock markets, and profit, is as crucial to understanding the geography of agriculture and the roots of the current food crisis as the farm worker, the crop, and farmland. Market forces—largely in the form of commodities speculation—have been identified by economists and market analysts as significantly implicated in the growing price of food. And yet commodities speculation has received far less media attention than other factors—drought, biofuels popularity, rising new demand, the price of oil, the sinking U.S. dollar—in explaining why many of the world's poorest people are experiencing reduced food and nutrition security.

The modern stock market is the site where the globe's future food prices are determined. Bids by investors on "commodities futures"—for example, the likely price a crop will command at the time of harvest—help to shape the price of any commodity when it is finally offered for sale. Market speculation occurs around food when investors buy, hold, and sell agricultural commodities in order to profit from fluctuations in their prices as opposed to buying them for use or income. Food experts and stock market observers see the recent increase in commodities market speculation as a response to the collapse of the subprime mortgage market in the United States. No longer able to channel investment into the once very profitable real estate sector, investors have turned to commodities—an article or raw material, such as grains or metals, which is interchangeable with another product of the same type and which investors buy or sell, usually through futures contracts.

The International Food Policy Research Institute, in a 2008 publication, points out that investors typically turn to commodities speculation for two reasons. The first is the fact that, historically, commodity investments tend to increase in value when other classes of assets decline. In the second case, many investors believe that the commodity markets are in the midst of a "super cycle," which means that commodity prices will continue to increase for years to come. Commodities, especially food, are seen as relatively safe investments: whereas many commodities can be forgone in a time of crisis, it would be difficult to stop buying food. Because of pressure from the World Bank and the International Monetary Fund, national governments have deregulated trade in agriculture over the last several years, and it is now much easier for the private sector to invest in a global food market.

But how does speculative investment drive up price? Just as with the real estate bubble of the last 15 years, commodity price inflation feeds on itself. The more prices rise and big profits are made, the more others jump on the bandwagon and invest, hoping for big returns. And as the U.S. dollar and other currencies have been sinking, commodities, including gold, oil, and grains, are seen as "hedges"—investments made to reduce risk—against these falling values. In short, as a response to the increasing economic malaise (that is emanating from the United States and its unprecedented budget deficit in particular, but also moving across the global landscape), investors are looking for new ways to improve their chances of turning a profit when interest rates are below the rate of inflation. In the 1990s, investors did this by moving into Internet stocks until that bubble burst in 2001. Then they moved into the property market until that option soured in the mid-2000s, when they shifted to commodities in search of higher returns.

The September 2008 collapse of global financial markets had stock analysts continuing to carefully assess the impact on investment trends to see whether agricultural markets will remain viable. Still, the most crucial question right now about the effects of speculation on commodities markets is whether an agricultural price bubble may yet be underway. If it is, the consequences of it bursting could be severe for farmers and consumers—and not just poor ones—around the world.

As these paragraphs have shown, there is more to agriculture and food production than is obvious at first glance: food production is an integral and highly interdependent part of the world economy and indeed the world-system. In this chapter, we examine the history and geography of agriculture from the global to the household level. We begin by looking at traditional agricultural practices and proceed through the three major revolutions of agricultural change. Much of the chapter is devoted to exploring the ways geographers have investigated the dramatic transformations in agriculture over the last half century as it has become increasingly industrialized through technological, political, social, and economic forces and the effects the globalization of production has had on producing, marketing, delivering, and consuming food.

Most introductory textbooks give considerable attention to tracing the origins of agriculture and the distribution of different agricultural practices across the globe. Although agricultural origins are important, the impacts of twentieth-century political and economic changes in agriculture are so transformative that in this textbook we focus on the state of global agriculture at the beginning of the new millennium instead.

MAIN POINTS

- Agriculture has been transformed into a globally integrated system; the changes producing this result have occurred at many scales and have originated from many sources.

- Agriculture has proceeded through three revolutionary phases, from the domestication of plants and animals, through the agricultural revolution of the mid-eighteenth century, to the latest developments in biotechnology and industrial innovation.

- The increasing ability to manipulate nature has changed how humans view their environment and think about place.

- The introduction of new technologies, political concerns about food security and self-sufficiency, and changing opportunities for investment and employment are among the many forces that have dramatically shaped agriculture as we know it today.

- The industrialized agricultural system of today's world has developed from—and has largely displaced—older agricultural practices, including shifting cultivation, subsistence agriculture, and pastoralism.

- Canadian agriculture, since European settlement began, has always been affected by international markets—first by those of the colonizing powers and later by world markets.

- The contemporary agro-commodity system is organized around a chain of agribusiness components that begins at the farm and ends at the retail outlet. Different economic sectors, as well as different corporate forms, have been involved in the globalization process.

- Transformations in agriculture have had dramatic impacts on the environment, including soil erosion, desertification, deforestation, and soil and water pollution, as well as the elimination of plant and animal species.

TRADITIONAL AGRICULTURAL GEOGRAPHY

The study of agriculture has a long tradition in geography. Because of geographers' interest in the relationships between people and land, it is hardly surprising that agriculture has been of primary concern. Research on agriculture is strongly influenced by geography's commitment to viewing the physical and human systems as interactively linked. Such an approach combines an understanding of spatial differentiation, the importance of place, and the fact that such practices as agriculture affect and are affected by processes occurring at different scales. It also provides geographers with a powerful perspective for understanding the dynamics of contemporary agriculture.

The last four decades have been characterized by major changes occurring in agriculture worldwide. One of the most dramatic changes has been the decline in the number of people employed in farming in both the core and the periphery. Meanwhile, farming practices have been significantly intensified through the use of chemical, mechanical, and biotechnological innovations and applications (**Figure 8.1**). Agriculture has become increasingly integrated into wider regional, national, and global economic systems at the same time that it has become more directly linked to other economic sectors, such as manufacturing and finance (**Figure 8.2**). These changes have been profound and have had many repercussions, ranging from the structure of global finance to the social relations of individual households.

In addition to understanding agricultural systems, geographers are also interested in investigating the lifestyle and culture of different agricultural communities. They and other social scientists often use the adjective **agrarian** to describe the way of life that is deeply embedded in the demands of agricultural production. *Agrarian* not only defines the culture of distinctive agricultural communities

agrarian: referring to the culture of agricultural communities and the type of tenure system that determines access to land and the kind of cultivation practices employed there

Figure 8.1 Pesticide spraying in Nicaragua Pictured here is a plantation in Nicaragua where this group of workers is getting ready to apply pesticides to the crops. Note that they are not wearing any protective gear. Many of the pesticides in use in peripheral countries have been banned in core countries because of human health concerns.

agriculture: a science, an art, and a business directed at the cultivation of crops and the raising of livestock for sustenance and profit

commercial agriculture: farming primarily for sale, not for direct consumption

but also refers to the type of tenure (or landholding) system that determines who has access to land and what kind of cultivation practices will be employed there.

Agriculture is a science, an art, and a business directed at the cultivation of crops and the raising of livestock for sustenance and profit. During the twentieth century, the dominant agricultural system in the core countries has become **commercial agriculture**, a system in which farmers produce crops and animals primarily for sale rather than for direct consumption by themselves and their

Figure 8.2 Agricultural floor of the Chicago Board of Trade Farming has always been tied up with trading. Pictured here is the main site for the global trading of agricultural commodities. Although trade remains an important aspect of agricultural production, it is finance that has had the most significant impact on farming over the last decade.

families. The unique and ingenious methods by which humans have learned to transform the land through agriculture are an important reflection of the two-way relationship between people and their environments: just as geography shapes our choices and behaviours, we are able to shape the physical landscape.

Although there is no definitive answer as to where agriculture originated, we do know that before humans discovered the advantages of agriculture, they procured their food through hunting (including fishing) and gathering. **Hunting and gathering** characterizes activities whereby people feed themselves through killing wild animals and fish and gathering fruits, roots, nuts, and other edible plants. Hunting and gathering are considered subsistence activities in that people who practise them procure only what they need to consume.

As we saw in Chapter 4, subsistence agriculture replaced hunting and gathering activities in many parts of the globe when people came to understand that the domestication of plants and animals enabled them to remain settled in one place rather than having to roam in search of edible wild foods. **Subsistence agriculture** is a system in which agriculturalists consume all they produce. It still is widely practised in the periphery, where it usually takes one of three dominant forms: shifting cultivation, intensive subsistence agriculture, and pastoralism. Worldwide, however, the practice of subsistence agriculture is diminishing as increasing numbers of peasant farmers convert from a subsistence and barter economy to a cash economy: they become incorporated into a globalized economy with a substantial commercial agricultural sector (**Figure 8.3**).

Shifting cultivation, a form of agriculture usually found in tropical forests, is a system in which farmers aim to maintain soil fertility by rotating the fields on which cultivation occurs. Shifting cultivation contrasts with another method of maintaining soil fertility, *crop rotation*, in which the fields under cultivation remain the same but the crops planted are changed to balance the types of nutrients withdrawn from and delivered to the soil.

hunting and gathering: activities whereby people feed themselves through killing wild animals and fish and gathering fruits, roots, nuts, and other edible plants

subsistence agriculture: farming for direct consumption by the producers, not for sale

shifting cultivation: a system in which farmers aim to maintain soil fertility by rotating the fields within which cultivation occurs

Figure 8.3 Global distribution of agriculture, 2005 The global distribution of agricultural practices is illustrated in this map. Notice the dramatic differences between core and periphery with respect to commercial versus subsistence agriculture. The periphery, though it does contain commercial agriculture, is largely dominated by forms of subsistence, while the core countries contain virtually none. The origins of cultivated plants can also be seen here as they are spread across both the Old World and the New. (*Source:* After H. Veregin [ed.], *Goode's World Atlas*, 21st ed. Rand McNally, 2005, pp. 38–39.)

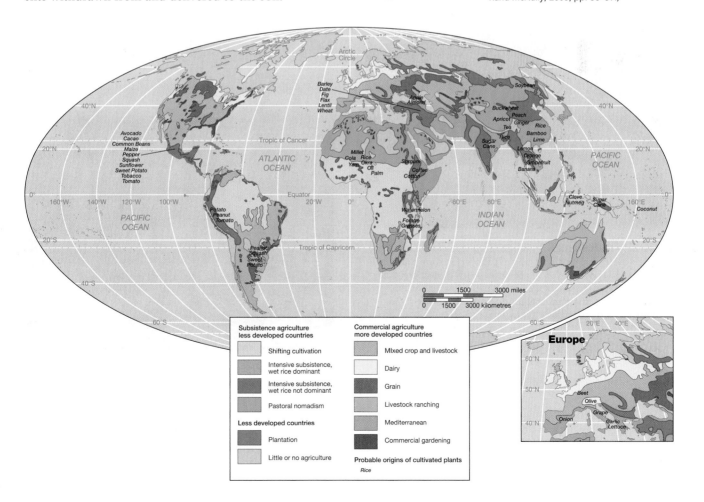

Shifting cultivation is globally distributed in the tropics—especially in the rain forests of Central and West Africa; the Amazon in South America; and much of Southeast Asia. Because tropical soils are poor in nutrients, cultivation can exhaust their fertility in as little as three years. Once the soil nears exhaustion, a new site is identified and the process of clearing and planting, described in the next paragraph, begins again. It may take over two decades for a once-cleared and cultivated site to become tillable again, after decomposition returns sufficient organic material to the soil (**Figure 8.4**).

The typical method for preparing land for shifting agriculture is through slash-and-burn, in which existing plants are cropped close to the ground, left to dry for a period, and then ignited. The burning process adds valuable nutrients to the soil, such as potash, which is about the only readily available fertilizer for this form of agricultural practice. Once the land is cleared and ready for cultivation, it is known as **swidden**. The practice of mixing different seeds and seedlings in the same swidden is known as *intertillage*. Not only are different plants cultivated, but their planting is usually staggered so that harvesting can continue throughout the year. Such staggered planting and harvesting reduces the risk of disasters from crop failure and increases the nutritional balance of the diet.

Shifting cultivation requires no expensive inputs because no manufactured fertilizers, pesticides, herbicides, or heavy equipment are necessary. While it generally is workable when undertaken by small populations on limited portions of land, slash-and-burn becomes ecologically destructive when large numbers of farmers are involved, especially in forests where vulnerable and endangered species occur, as in rain forests (**Figure 8.5**). For example, the use of slash-and-burn techniques to plant marijuana, coca, and opium poppies since the late 1990s has devastated Colombia's portion of the Amazon rain forest.

The second dominant form of subsistence activity is **intensive subsistence agriculture**, a practice involving the effective and efficient use of a small parcel of land to

swidden: land that is cleared using the slash-and-burn process and is ready for cultivation

intensive subsistence agriculture: a practice that involves the effective and efficient use—usually through a considerable expenditure of human labour and application of fertilizer—of a small parcel of land to maximize crop yield

Figure 8.4 Shifting cultivation Shifting cultivation is usually practised in tropical forests. It is a system of agriculture that maintains soil fertility by rotating the fields on which cultivation occurs. This photograph shows a plot under cultivation as well as the burned stumps of the trees that used to occupy the site. Corn and bean shoots are scattered throughout the plot.

Figure 8.5 Slash-and-burn, Xishuangbanna, China Slash-and-burn is a process of preparing low-fertility soils for planting. In the mid-twentieth century, the Xishuangbanna region of China pictured here was a remote tropical rain forest, China's only one. Since then, the government and people of Xishuangbanna have begun to convert the area to rubber tree and sugar cane plantations. Although the transformation has lifted much of the region out of abject poverty, soil erosion is occurring rapidly. Some estimates predict that Xishuangbanna will be a dust bowl in 30 years.

maximize crop yield; a considerable expenditure of human labour and application of fertilizer is also usually involved. Unlike shifting cultivation, intensive subsistence cultivation is often able to support large rural populations. Whereas shifting cultivation is more characteristic of low agricultural densities (see Chapter 3), intensive subsistence usually occurs in Asia, and particularly in those regions where agricultural densities are especially high: India, China, and Southeast Asia.

Whereas shifting cultivation involves the application of a relatively limited amount of labour and other resources, intensive subsistence agriculture requires fairly constant human labour to achieve high productivity from a small amount of land. With population pressures fierce and the amount of arable land limited, intensive subsistence agriculture also reflects the inventive ways in which humans confront environmental constraints and reshape the landscape in the process. In fact, the landscape of intensive subsistence agriculture is often a distinctive one including raised fields and hillside farming through terracing (**Figure 8.6**).

Although not obviously a form of agricultural production, pastoralism is a third, dominant form of subsistence activity associated with a traditional way of life. **Pastoralism** involves the breeding and herding of animals to satisfy the human needs for food, shelter, and clothing. It is usually practised in the cold and dry climates of deserts, savannas (grasslands), and steppes (lightly wooded, grassy plains) where subsistence agriculture is impracticable (**Figure 8.7**). Pastoralism can be either *sedentary* (pastoralists live in settlements and herd animals in nearby pastures) or *nomadic* (they wander with their herds over long distances, never settling in any one place for very long). Although forms of commercial pastoralism (the regularized herding of animals for profitable meat production) exist, for example, among Basque Americans in the basin and range regions of Utah and Nevada and the gauchos of the Argentinean grasslands, we are concerned here with pastoralism as a subsistence activity.

pastoralism: subsistence activity that involves the breeding and herding of animals to satisfy the human needs of food, shelter, and clothing

Figure 8.6 Intensive subsistence agriculture Where usable agricultural land is at a premium, agriculturalists have developed ingenious methods for taking advantage of every square metre of usable terrain. Landscapes like this one (a terraced rice field in Bali, Indonesia) can be extremely productive when carefully tended and can feed relatively large rural populations.

Figure 8.7 Pastoralism In this image, sheep forage near the summer settlement of yurts—circular tents of felt or skins on a collapsible framework—at the base of Tsaast Uul mountain in Mongolia, where pastoralism is the main livelihood. Note the dryness of the landscape. Pastoralism usually occurs where agriculture is not feasible.

Pastoralism is largely confined to parts of North Africa and the savannas of central and southern Africa, the Middle East, and Central Asia. Pastoralists generally graze cattle, sheep, goats, and camels, although reindeer are herded in parts of Eurasia. The type of animal herded is related to the culture of the pastoralists as well as the animals' adaptability to the regional topography and foraging conditions. Many pastoralists practise **transhumance**, the movement of herds according to seasonal rhythms: warmer, lowland areas in the winter and cooler, highland areas in the summer.

transhumance: the movement of herds according to seasonal rhythms: warmer, lowland areas in the winter and cooler, highland areas in the summer

The distinguishing characteristic of pastoralists is that they depend on animals, not crops, for their livelihood. Although the animals are occasionally slaughtered and used directly for food, shelter, and clothing, often they are bartered with sedentary farmers for grain and other commodities. Not surprisingly, pastoralism as a subsistence activity is on the decline as more and more pastoralists become integrated into a global economy that requires more efficient and regularized forms of production.

Like the two other traditional forms of agriculture previously mentioned, pastoralism is not simply a subsistence activity but part of a social system as well. Pastoralists consist of groups of families who are governed by a leader or chieftain. Groups are divided into units that follow different routes with the herds. The routes are well known, with members of the group intimately conversant with the landscape, watering places, and grazing opportunities. This continuous movement, and the different attachment to "place" that it implies, challenges more sedentary societies. As a result, nomadic groups are often persecuted and made to settle down. They have also been forced off the land by competition from other land uses and the state's need to track citizens for taxation and military reasons.

AGRICULTURAL REVOLUTION AND INDUSTRIALIZATION

For a long time, human geography textbooks treated the differences in agricultural practices worldwide as systems to be described and catalogued, as we have just done. In the last three decades, however, new conceptual approaches to the agricultural sector have transformed the ways we view it. Agriculture has become less a human activity to be described through classification and more a complex component of the global economic system to be analyzed.

Increasingly, geographers and others have come to see world agricultural practices as having proceeded through revolutionary phases, just as manufacturing did. As in manufacturing, practices have not been transformed everywhere at the same time. Consequently, some parts of the world are still largely unaffected by certain aspects of agricultural change. By seeing agriculture in this new light, it is possible to recognize that the changes that have occurred in agricultural practices have transformed geography and society as the global community has moved from predominantly subsistence to predominantly capital-intensive, market-oriented practices.

To understand the new agricultural geography, it is necessary to review the history of world agriculture. This history has proceeded in alternating cycles: long periods of very gradual change punctuated by short, explosive periods of radical change. Geographers and others have divided the history of world agriculture into three distinct revolutionary periods.

As we saw in Chapter 4, the *first agricultural revolution* is commonly recognized as founded on the development of seed agriculture and the use of the plow and draft animals (**Figure 8.8**). This probably occurred about 10,000 to 15,000 years ago, depending on the area. Especially important were floodplains along the Tigris, Euphrates, and Nile Rivers, where complex civilizations were built on the fruits of the first agricultural revolution (**Figure 8.9**). Over time, the knowledge and skill underlying seed agriculture and the domestication of plants using other means, such as taking cuttings, diffused outward from these original areas, having a revolutionary impact throughout the world.

It is safe to place the apex of the *second agricultural revolution* historically and geographically alongside the Industrial Revolution in England and Western Europe. Although many important changes in agriculture preceded the Industrial Revolution, none had more of an impact on everyday life than the rise of an industrialized manufacturing sector, the effects of which spread rapidly to agriculture because of the demand for food from a growing urban and industrial population.

On the eve of the Industrial Revolution—in the middle of the eighteenth century—in Western Europe and England, subsistence peasant agriculture was predominant, though partial integration into a market economy was underway. Many peasants were utilizing a crop-rotation system that, in addition to the adoption of fallow crops such as clover (which return nitrogen to the soil) and the application of natural fertilizers, improved soil productivity and led to increased crop and livestock yields. Yields were also greatly increased by the

Figure 8.8 Plowing with yoked oxen and camels In many parts of the world, agriculturalists rely on draft animals to prepare land for cultivation. Using animals to assist in agricultural production was an important element in the first agricultural revolution. By expanding the amount of energy applied to production, draft animals enabled humans to increase food supplies. Many contemporary farmers view draft animals as their most valuable possessions. Pictured here are camels and oxen pulling Sikh farmers' plows in Punjab State, India.

Figure 8.9 Present-day agriculture along the Nile Agriculture along the Nile River dates far back into prehistory. The Nile floodplain was one of the important hearths of domestication, providing the foundation for the growth of complex civilizations in Egypt. The Nile floodplain remains a remarkably productive area even today.

adoption of New World crops, such as the potato, and the addition of new fodder crops, such as the turnip, which enabled much larger herds of sheep and cattle to be raised to feed the growing demands of Europe's increasing population.

At the same time, the feudal landholding system was breaking down and yielding to a new agrarian system, based not on service to a lord but on an emerging system of private-property relations. Finally, communal farming practices and common lands were being replaced by enclosed, individually owned land or land worked independently by tenants or renters.

Such a situation was logical in response to the demands for food production (and the associated opportunities for profit) that emerged from the dramatic social and economic changes accompanying the Industrial Revolution. Perhaps most important of all these changes was the development—through the creation of an urban industrial workforce—of a commercial market for food. Many innovations of the Industrial Revolution, such as improvements in transportation technology, had substantial impacts on agriculture. Innovations applied directly to agricultural practices, such as the new types of horse-drawn farm machinery, improved control over—as well as the quantity of—yields.

The growing demands for food production from an increasingly industrialized and urban population also changed the geographical pattern of agricultural land use around cities: whether a certain crop could be profitably planted in a given location depended on whether that crop could be transported to the urban market cheaply or quickly enough. In one way, this is of course a commonplace observation—the farther away production occurs, the more it costs to transport a product to market—but much agricultural production also put a premium on freshness, and therefore the closer to the market the better. Hence, productive agricultural land close to cities was often devoted to high-value, perishable products such as milk or fruit or leafy vegetables, and producers were prepared to pay high land rents to locate in such areas.

The first scholar to spot these spatial patterns of agricultural land was Johann Heinrich von Thünen, a German landowner. He first published his findings in 1826, but his work languished until it was rediscovered by geographers in the 1960s as part of the interest in *locational analysis* (or *spatial analysis*) that had then gripped the discipline. Like Weber's model of industrial location (discussed in Chapter 7), and the Burgess model of urban land use (introduced in Chapter 11), von Thünen's model argues that an activity (in this case, agricultural land use) is patterned according to distance from a market.

However, as we might expect with such a simple model, substantial criticisms are made: it omits physical factors (such as soil types) and government policies (which subsidize land use or transport). It also assumes that land values are always determined by a rigid economics of space (the kind driven by a market economy). All of this means that the model can only be a general descriptive tool for showing how Europe's agricultural landscapes were reconfigured by the spatial forces of the Industrial Revolution (**Figure 8.10**).

By igniting the second agricultural revolution, the Industrial Revolution changed rural life as profoundly as the sedentary requirements of seed agriculture had transformed hunting and gathering societies. As geographer Ian Bowler writes, this revolution moved rapidly from Europe to other parts of the world:

> From its origins in Western Europe, the new commercialized system of farming was diffused by European colonization during the nineteenth and twentieth centuries to other parts of the world. A dominant agrarian model of commercial capitalist farming was established, based on a structure of numerous, relatively small family farms. From this period can be traced both the dependence of agriculture on manufacturing industry for many farm inputs, and the increasing productivity of farm labour, which released large numbers of workers from the land to swell the ranks of factory workers and city dwellers. Moreover, the production of food surplus to domestic demand enabled establishment of international patterns of agricultural trade.[1]

As **Geography Matters 8.1—Canadian Agriculture** illustrates, this quotation nicely summarizes the development of farming in this country under colonialism.

The *third agricultural revolution* is a fairly recent development that, unlike the previous two, emanates mostly from the New World rather than the Old. Scholars identify the third agricultural revolution as beginning in the late nineteenth century and gaining momentum throughout the twentieth century. Each of its three important developmental phases originated in North America. Indeed, the globalization trends framing all our discussions in this textbook are the very same ones that have shaped the third agricultural revolution. The

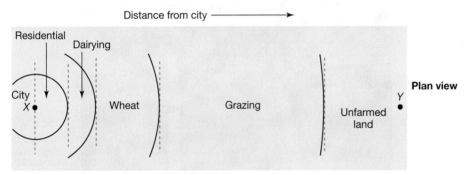

(a) Land-use rings

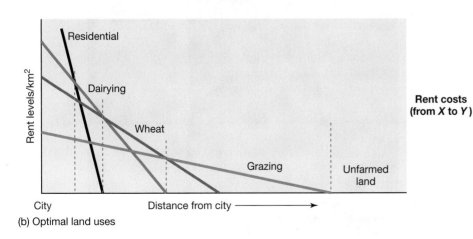

(b) Optimal land uses

Figure 8.10 Von Thünen's model of agricultural location Von Thünen observed that a concentric pattern of agricultural land uses develops around a city (see (a), where only a segment of the full circle is shown for simplicity's sake). The patterns are caused because certain types of agricultural activity can pay more rent per hectare to locate near a city's market than other types (see (b)). (*Source:* Peter Haggett, *Geography: A Global Synthesis.* Harlow, UK: Pearson, 2001, p. 463.)

---

[1] I. Bowler (ed.), *The Geography of Agriculture in Developed Market Economies.* Harlow, UK: Longman Scientific and Technical, 1992, pp. 10–11.

difference between the second and third agricultural revolutions is mostly a matter of degree; so, by the late twentieth century, technological innovations had virtually industrialized agricultural practices.

The three phases of the third agricultural revolution are mechanization, chemical farming with synthetic fertilizers, and globally widespread food manufacturing. **Mechanization** is the replacement of human farm labour with machines. Tractors, combines, reapers, pickers, and other forms of motorized machines have, since the 1880s and 1890s, progressively replaced human and animal labour inputs to the agricultural production process in Canada and the United States. In Europe, mechanization did not become widespread until after World War II. **Chemical farming** is the application of synthetic fertilizers, herbicides, fungicides, and pesticides to enhance yields. Becoming widespread in the 1950s in North America, chemical farming diffused to Europe in the 1960s and to peripheral regions of the world in the 1970s.

Food manufacturing also had its origins in late nineteenth-century North America. **Food manufacturing** involves adding economic value to agricultural products through a range of treatments—processing, canning, refining, packing, packaging, refrigeration, and so on—occurring off the farm and before the products reach the market. The first two phases of the third revolution affected inputs to the agricultural production process, whereas the final phase affects agricultural outputs. Although the first two are related to the modernization of farming as an economic practice, the third involves a complication of the relationship of farms to firms in the manufacturing sector, which had increasingly expanded into the area of food early in the 1960s (**Figure 8.11**). The third also complicates our relationship with our environment because the increased ability to preserve food distances us from the natural rhythms of the farming year. Considered together,

mechanization: the replacement of human farm labour with machines

chemical farming: the application of synthetic fertilizers to the soil and herbicides, fungicides, and pesticides to crops to enhance yields

food manufacturing: adding value to agricultural products through a range of treatments—such as processing, canning, refining, packing, and packaging—that occur off the farm and before they reach the market

Figure 8.11 Food manufacturing
Pictured here are carrots being processed into baby carrots through an assembly-line operation. Food processing is one of the ways in which economic value is added to agricultural products before they reach the market.

Canadian Agriculture

Agriculture in Canada

The Canadian environment places clear limits on agriculture. Large tracts of mountainous terrain and glacial erosion have severely reduced the potential area available for cultivation. Harsh and long winters prohibit most forms of agriculture across northern Canada and restrict the types of farming activity that can be pursued elsewhere in the country.

It is therefore not surprising that most of Canada's productive agricultural land lies within 200 kilometres of the American border or that the total occupied farmland in Canada, according to 2001 Statistics Canada data, represents only 7 percent of the country's total land area. The greatest part of that occupied land, or *ecumene*, lies in the Prairie provinces (Saskatchewan: 39 percent, Alberta: 31 percent, Manitoba: 11 percent), with only 8 percent in Ontario, 5 percent in Quebec, 4 percent in British Columbia, and mere fractions of a percent in the Atlantic provinces—percentages that, as we will see below, also have a significance in terms of the regional policies for Canadian farming (**Figure 8.1.1**).

The 2006 Census of Agriculture counted a total of 229,373 farms—a decline of 7.1 percent since 2001. According to this census, the largest number of farms is found in Ontario (57,211), followed by Alberta (49,431), Saskatchewan (44,329), Quebec (30,675), and Manitoba (19,054). However, in terms of average farm size, the largest farms are found in the Prairies—between 400 and 500 hectares—with farms elsewhere averaging around 100 hectares. Overall, the average farm size in Canada was 295 hectares in 2006.[2]

Without denying the importance of the physical environment or ignoring the potential effects of future climate change under conditions of global warming, it is possible

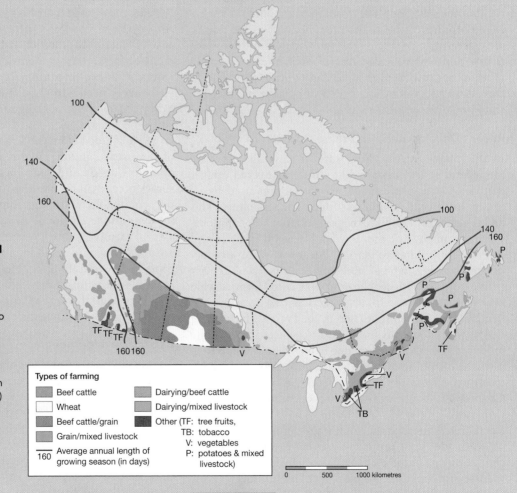

Figure 8.1.1 The agricultural regions of Canada This map shows the limited total area of land farmed in Canada, its concentration along the U.S. border, and its division into two major agricultural systems (the Prairies, and Ontario–Quebec). Specialty crops (such as grape vines in British Columbia's Okanagan region and apples in Nova Scotia's Annapolis Valley) can also be seen.

(*Source:* Geoffrey J. Matthews and Robert Morrow, *Canada and the World: An Atlas Resource*, 2nd ed. Scarborough: Prentice Hall, 1995, pp. 33–34.)

Types of farming

- Beef cattle
- Wheat
- Beef cattle/grain
- Grain/mixed livestock
- Dairying/beef cattle
- Dairying/mixed livestock
- Other (TF: tree fruits, TB: tobacco, V: vegetables, P: potatoes & mixed livestock)

160 Average annual length of growing season (in days)

0   500   1000 kilometres

---

[2] See the *2006 Census of Agriculture* on the website of Statistics Canada (**www.statcan.gc.ca/ca-ra2006/index-eng.htm**). Government policy documents and backgrounders can be found on the website of Agriculture and Agri-Food Canada, the federal government ministry responsible for agriculture, at **www.agr.gc.ca**.

to argue that political decisions, themselves influenced by concerns of globalized trade, currently play a more important role in determining the location and distribution of much of today's farming in Canada. We can look at the changes in Prairie agriculture to illustrate this claim.

Historical Development of Prairie Agriculture

During the nineteenth century, the Canadian Prairies were purposely developed by Canadian politicians as an area of farming settlement. Once drought-resistant forms of wheat had been developed and railroads built, an export-oriented wheat monoculture developed. Quickly realizing how this dependence made them prone to the vagaries of international markets, Prairie farmers agitated for government-subsidized rail shipment rates for their wheat (the Crowsnest Pass Agreement, or "Crow Rate," of 1897) and for a collective grain marketing agency to increase their bargaining power in the global grain market (the Canadian Wheat Board, established in 1935). These political developments had the effect of sustaining wheat cultivation across the Prairies despite the difficult economics of that location (that is, the fact that the Prairies are a long way from markets) and the physical environment (the drought-prone Prairies are not an ideal area for cereal crops, a fact made worse by monocultivation and periodic grasshopper infestations). In other words, without subsidies and political intervention the disadvantages of location and climate might have shut down Prairie wheat farming long ago.

Recent Developments in Prairie Agriculture

In 1995, however, the Crow Rate was abolished because the federal government had to reduce its overall budget deficit and because Canada was being pressured by its trading partners to eliminate subsidies in agriculture. This had the effect of doubling the cost to farmers for shipping Western grain by rail: they now had to pay the true cost of getting their product to market. For many, wheat production became even more of an economically marginal activity than before. To reduce their transport costs, farmers were keen to sell their grain locally, which spurred an increase in hog and beef cattle production in the Prairies. In effect, it was now economically more advantageous to feed locally produced grain to animals and to export those animals than it was to export grain itself (an apt illustration of Weber's locational theory about "weight-losing" industries—see Chapter 7). As a consequence, the production of hogs (Manitoba) and beef (Alberta) have now become fundamental forces restructuring Prairie agriculture.

Consider beef production as an example of these changes. A reshaping of the Canadian beef-processing industry into an "agribusiness" has been underway for some time. Traditionally, cattle raised on ranches of Alberta and British Columbia's interior were shipped live to feedlots in southern Alberta or southwest Ontario for fattening and then were butchered in meat-packing plants in Toronto, Hamilton, and Kitchener-Waterloo. However,

from the 1980s onward, the dominance of large supermarket chains and the sale of ready-to-use foods encouraged the construction of automated nonunionized meat processing plants in the cattle-rearing areas of the West—a locational change that received an additional boost with the abolition of the Crow Rate. By 2001, the total number of cattle in Alberta had increased to 6.6 million (from 5.9 million in 1996), and many of the additional cattle were destined for export to the burgeoning American market (see the discussion of fast food below). However, after the discovery of mad cow disease (bovine spongiform encephalopathy, BSE) in 2003 and 2005 in cows in Alberta, the United States closed its market to Canadian beef, and Alberta cattle farmers were hit hard (**Figure 8.1.2**).[3]

Agriculture in Canadian Life

The centrality of agriculture in Canadian life was once clear to all. It was not only a mainstay of the nineteenth-century economy but also contributed to the ways in which Canadians shaped, or "constructed," their view of the country and of *space* and *place* within it. Again, the Prairies can serve to illustrate.

Harold Troper, in his book *Only Farmers Need Apply,* shows how Sir Clifford Sifton (who became federal minister of the interior in 1896) favoured the recruitment of farmers from Central and Eastern Europe and from the United States for the settlement of the Prairies. He believed people from the industrial and urban areas of Europe had less useful skills and so excluded them (ostensibly the reason Jews and Black Americans were also largely excluded from the Prairies). The perceived needs of rural space, in other words, dictated who could immigrate to Canada and, once these immigrants had created rural "places" in the Prairies, it was believed they would perpetuate Old World agricultural values in a Canadian setting. Sifton was not alone, of course, in believing that a rural farming culture was more honest or moral than an urban or industrial society. Such views have deep roots in Western thinking. He was, unlike many, able to put such ideas into practice and, in so doing, created a farming economy on the Prairies. In geographical terms, he was able to influence the creation of space.

Recent Developments

Today, the memory of these rural places continues to exist in the many examples of vernacular farm buildings and fences that dot the Prairies (see Chapter 5), in the now derelict grain elevators, and in particular in the people, folk tales, and literature of the region (for example, Wallace Stegner's *Wolf Willow,* set in East End, Saskatchewan, and W.O. Mitchell's *Who Has Seen the Wind?*). Yet, statistics show that this agricultural world has been under attack for the last 50 or 60 years and that it now is part of the past.

---

[3] Statistics Canada, "Study: Potential Impact of Mad Cow Disease on Farm Family Income," *The Daily*, 18 June 2004, www.statcan.gc.ca/daily-quotidien/040618/dq040618c-eng.htm.

Figure 8.1.2 Canadian beef industry in crisis Empty feedlots in Alberta in the wake of the mad cow crisis.

Since 1941, the total number of farms in Canada has fallen by two-thirds to 229,373 in 2006. Over the same period, employment in agriculture has fallen from 21 percent of the Canadian population to under 3 percent. Even more telling is the observation that farmers now compose only 10 percent of the total rural population itself—the remainder comprising village dwellers, retirees, and cottagers.

The decline of local grain elevators—to many Canadians an icon of the landscape and agrarian life on the Prairies—is symbolic of the disappearance of rural places. In 1933, there were 5,578 grain elevators across the Prairies. This number fell to 3,117 by 1981, and in 2002 stood at only 588. The reason for the precipitous decline in the last few decades is the restructuring of rail branch lines across the Prairies, which has eliminated the need for many small grain elevators. The new rail system has created a new economic space that has become refocused on a limited number of very large inland grain terminals, many with storage capacities 10 times that of the grain elevators of the 1930s (**Figure 8.1.3**).

What are the causes for these fundamental changes? We can identify a number of major factors:

- *Globalization.* Perhaps the main cause for this decline in the agricultural way of life has been the growing globalization of world trade and the accompanying competition and price pressure.

- *Subsidies.* The increasing liberalization of international trade under such treaties as the General Agreement on Tariffs and Trade (GATT—the precursor of the World Trade Organization, or WTO) and the North American Free Trade Agreement (NAFTA) requires the elimination of domestic subsidies on a range of products and manufactures as part of a way of promoting fairer competition and more open access to the markets of other countries. For Canadian farmers, the loss of subsidies has exacerbated the decline in overall farm income.

(a)

(b)

Figure 8.1.3 The disappearing grain elevator Grain elevators, such as the one shown in (a) at Lang, Saskatchewan, are fast being replaced by fewer and much larger inland grain terminals, such as the one illustrated in (b) at Shaunavon, Saskatchewan.

- *The "cash squeeze."* On the other side of the ledger, farm inputs (such as fertilizers, pesticides, seed, farm machinery, land, labour, and financing) have all increased in cost: from 1974 to 1994, total farm operating costs in Canada rose by 40 percent, while the levels of gross revenue remained approximately the same. Circumstances have now altered somewhat (as noted

369

below), but the challenges of balancing cost and revenue remain.

As a consequence, most Canadian farmers need income from non-farm activities to make ends meet, in effect subsidizing the farm operation's deficit. Many of these non-farm activities are performed by farm women, and their income has enabled many families to continue farming. Historically, women's unpaid labour on the farm itself has always been important, but in recent years, their role has expanded. Farm women are now as likely to operate heavy farm machinery as they are to feed chickens and keep the farm accounts. As Jocelyn Hainsworth, a farm woman who lives in Redvers, Saskatchewan, has written:

> The role of a farm wife as we begin the 21st century has evolved to where she is a chief, and cheap—make that indispensable—source of labour during the busy seasons. I don't ever remember Mom driving the grain truck or even fuelling up the tractor, yet these are considered specifically my jobs on the farm. And it doesn't stop there; I have cultivated and harrowed with both two- and four-wheel drive tractors, and I've run the swather and the grain auger. I haven't used the airseeder to plant a crop and I'm a lot more relaxed hauling the grain back to the bins than I am at the helm of a combine, but there are lots of women who do these jobs too, and excel at them.[4]

In many instances, therefore, changes in farming have resulted in a profound reconfiguration of gender roles in the public and private spheres—in effect, making the Prairies a crucible of social change. Certainly, without the unpaid labour of both farm women and men, many small Prairie farms would be unable to survive economically.

■ *Farm polarization.* Polarization has occurred as those farms that are able to compete pull away from the rest of the pack. These are farms that have been able to increase in size, to specialize, or to increase their capital investments to take advantage of the economies of scale of production. Meanwhile, smaller producers are dropping out of the industry: according to 1996 data, only 3 percent of farms accounted for over 36 percent of gross farm receipts earned that year.

An analysis of farm incomes also allows us to see how Canadian agriculture is currently refocusing its activities in terms of types of agricultural production. Thus, 1991 data show that the four major farm types of beef, dairy, wheat, and other small grains comprised 64 percent of all farms in Canada and accounted for 61 percent of all farm receipts. Such developments are responsible for the increasing division of the country into what economic geographer Iain Wallace has called "two very different

sets of production environments." The first encompasses the three Prairie provinces, where emphasis is placed on grain, oilseeds, and beef production. With these crops, farmers compete in international export markets and are therefore very vulnerable to market fluctuations.

The second production environment comprises the remaining provinces with dairy and poultry production (mainly in Ontario and Quebec), and intensive specialty crops (such as the Niagara and Okanagan Valley soft-fruit and wine industries, and Prince Edward Island's potato crop). Here the producers are not competing internationally or they operate under protective government regulation (for instance, dairy and poultry production in Ontario and Quebec are governed by *supply management systems* whereby demand and supply are kept in balance via regulated markets and the use of production quotas). In contrast to the hinterland location of the Prairie production environment, this second production environment is in the urbanized heartland—a fact that Iain Wallace suggests gives a clear regional dimension to Canadian agricultural policy.[5]

The Future

After decades of declining fortunes, the prospects for many Canadian farmers now look extremely promising—in particular for Prairie grain producers.[6] The reasons for this turnaround are the same that we have discussed in the opening paragraphs of this chapter and of Chapter 1: the soaring demand for food worldwide, which creates more profitable conditions for producers. Forces that for so long have depressed world agricultural prices have now been replaced with a constellation of factors working in the opposite direction, and Canada's farmers clearly stand to benefit.

Four factors are usually identified for the current increase in agricultural prices in Canada:

1. *The increasing demand for grains from India and China.* As living standards rise in Southeast Asia, consumers there are turning to new and more expensive proteins (thereby also permanently changing their diets with higher calorie and more convenience foods—see the discussion of fast food below). As but one example from early 2008, the price of yellow peas (a pulse in much demand in India) rose from $400 a tonne to $600 in just two months. With an estimated 50 million people a year joining the middle classes in China and India, the demand for imported agricultural foodstuffs seems set to increase—and will affect more than simply grain producers. As Donald Coxe, global portfolio strategist for the Bank

[4] Jocelyn Hainsworth, "My Mother's Farm and Mine" (CBC 2002), available on the website **www.cbc.ca/news/work/wherewework/253.html**.

[5] Iain Wallace, *A Geography of the Canadian Economy.* Don Mills, ON: Oxford University Press, 2002. Chapter 3: "Agriculture, Agri-food, and the Rural Economy," pp. 123–139.

[6] These paragraphs are based on Joe Friesen, "Eastern Promises: Asia Is Fuelling a Prairie Agriculture Boom," *Globe and Mail,* 16 February 2008, pp. B1, B4–5.

of Montreal, has noted, "They're adding meat and dairy to their diet and we aren't producing enough feed grains, enough vegetable proteins to supply their needs. Milk is the new oil. Milk demand worldwide is rising faster than oil demand."[7]

2. *The increasing demand from ethanol producers.* Ethanol production now takes up 20 percent of the American corn harvest, and the increasing diversion of cereals into biofuel production in the United States and Canada has created such a competitive market for corn that farmers (who had previously abandoned this crop as not profitable) are eagerly planting additional acreages. Indeed, the price of Saskatchewan farmland, which had been increasing in value by only 1 percent a year over the past 15 years, has jumped by 15 percent in some parts of the province as farmland begins to seem a profitable investment once more.

3. *The increasing effects of climate change.* Recent periods of drought have led to reduced production in parts of the Prairies and contribute to increased prices because not enough surplus from previous years is available to meet the demand prompted by either Asia's demands or biofuels needs.

4. *The rising costs of petroleum.* The increasing cost of gasoline across Canada is being passed straight on to consumers in the form of higher agricultural prices (to pay for the increased costs of transportation and trucking to markets).

However, unlike the first three factors, the increasing cost of gasoline is one that will also work to farmers' disadvantage because it also greatly increases their costs of production and continues problems of "cash squeeze" discussed previously. Similarly, the fact that the price of fertilizers has risen 150 percent during the current period of increasing crop prices will undoubtedly eat into farmers' profits.

In fact, factors like these have led many farmers to treat the present boom with considerable caution. As Keith Gardner, who farms a 525-hectare operation near Virden, Manitoba, remarked about the newfound hope for prosperous times:

> I've been farming since 1977 and we've heard that before. We were told there'd be a shortage of grain to feed the world but it's never really happened. It'd be nice to believe that, but they've been wrong before, haven't they?[8]

Although Canadian agriculture has had a difficult past, it is clear that there are a number of options for the future. However, it is equally clear that these options are only possible if a great deal of effort is expended by the Canadian public. Whether that effort is given or not will provide a measure of how much Canadians really value Canadian agriculture and what value they place

on domestic food security. The range of possible options includes the following:

- *Increasing the cost of food.* At present, Canadians spend less than 10 percent of their after-tax income on food purchased in grocery stores—that is less than we spend on communications such as cable TV, Internet, and cell phones. Inexpensive foods are good for the consumer, but they do not help the farmer.

- *Encouraging farmers to develop forms of food processing.* So far, farmers capture only a fraction of the value added to their product before it is sold in stores. If farmers could sell more "value-added" products themselves (e.g., process their apples into apple pies and sell them in a farm store), they could increase their revenues.

- *Promoting organic or niche forms of farming.* With increasing concern about the environmental damage caused by modern farming, the development of organic farming might represent an alternative in some areas. Data from the 2001 Census of Agriculture show that the organic sector is more popular than ever, but because it still only represents 1 percent (2,230) of all farms, this is a sector that could be developed much further.[9] Other crops, such as ginseng in the British Columbian interior (**Figure 8.1.4**), have proved lucrative—as is the illegal growing of marijuana in that province, which some sources estimate to represent B.C.'s leading crop by value!

- *Promoting alternative uses for agricultural land.* In areas in close proximity to cities, farmers have the option

Figure 8.1.4   A field of ginseng near Lillooet, British Columbia   One of the new developments in farming is to grow organic or niche-market crops. In this case, the demand for herbal products in Canada and abroad has supported the expansion of ginseng cultivation, a high-value crop particularly suited to the dry conditions of British Columbia's southern interior. The crop is grown under a protective black net.

[7] Ibid., p. B4.
[8] Ibid.

[9] A lively debate on this topic followed the initial release of the 2001 Census of Agriculture statistics. See, for example, the remarks of Olds College (Alberta) agrologist Robert Wilson, "Farming Has a Rainbow," *Globe and Mail*, 21 May 2002, p. A17; and Jill Mahoney, "Farmers Take Stock of New Markets," *Globe and Mail*, 16 May 2002, pp. A1, A7.

of devoting parts of their land to uses that may be in demand by urban dwellers. In parts of Britain, for example, once-derelict barns have been converted to expensive second homes or even into office space. Elsewhere, riding stables, "pick your own" fruit and vegetable farms, or maple-sugar lots offer farmers alternative sources of income.

- *Supporting city-oriented farmers' markets and delivery.* A trend that has become increasingly popular in places such as Toronto and Montreal is for groups of people to contract with individual farmers to purchase produce from them for an entire season (see the discussion of *Community-Supported Agriculture* later in this chapter). The benefits are that producers have a sure market and establish connections with people who are committed to supporting local farming. For their part, consumers know exactly where their food has come from and under what conditions it has been grown (often, the preference being for organically and/or humanely produced foods).

- *Promoting the production of "exotic" meats.* The discovery of Canada's first case of mad cow disease in Alberta in May 2003, and the subsequent cost to the Canadian beef industry, has prompted many consumers and producers alike to turn to the certified organic production of cattle or of exotic animals (such as emus or bison) that are believed to be unaffected by the disease.[10]

- *Promoting the importance of farmers as "land resource managers"* (to use Iain Wallace's phrase). If Canadians value the rural life as much as their purchase and use of cottages seem to suggest, then it might be possible to maintain those places through an integrated strategy that benefits recreational users and farmers at the same time. This approach is already practised in the Black Forest region of Germany, where farmers receive subsidies to maintain the typical mosaic landscape of forests and meadows sought by tourists.

Among the most pressing problems in rural Canada (from a policy-maker's perspective) are the decline of the socioeconomic infrastructure in these areas and the emigration of the young—both factors that erode an area's ability to sustain itself. The Social Sciences and Humanities Research Council (SSHRC) has funded 15 university researchers to examine how Canada can rebuild capacity in rural areas (**Figure 8.1.5**). Using 32 research sites,

Figure 8.1.5 Farming near Redvers, Saskatchewan A frequent sight on the Prairies, especially in parts of Saskatchewan, is that of actively farmed land and abandoned buildings: as one farm gives up, its land is bought or leased by a surviving one. It is a very visible outcome of the processes of farm size increase and consolidation, on the one hand, and the movement and reconcentration of the province's once much more dispersed farming population, on the other hand.

the project (known as the New Rural Economy or NRE) explores how we can develop enhanced political institutions, improve service delivery, better manage natural resources, and increase communications in rural centres.[11] It will be interesting to see what answers are produced, but according to Dr. Bill Reimer, the project's director, already three basic lessons are clear:[12]

- Rural Canada is poorly positioned for the new economy, which "requires the ability to extract value from human knowledge, most often acquired through 'global' relationships."

- The social capital and cohesion found in rural Canada can support economic cohesion. The traditional communal values of rural life are not, at first sight, very appropriate resources in a market-based or bureaucratic-based economy. However, in the right context, these values can still be a valuable resource.

- A rural–urban alliance is needed. Despite their differences, it is clear that rural and urban Canada share so many interests (around, for example, the environment, residential space, recreation, and heritage preservation) that to abandon rural Canada to its own devices makes little sense in terms of the greater good.

---

[10] See also the informative essay on Canada's mad cow disease crisis by Ian MacLachlan, "Betting the Farm: Food Safety and the Beef Commodity Chain." In A. Heintzman and E. Solomon (eds.), *Feeding the Future: From Fat to Famine: How to Solve the World's Food Crises.* Toronto: House of Anansi Press, 2004, pp. 37–69.

[11] The website for the New Rural Economy (NRE2) project is at **http://nre.concordia.ca/nre2.htm**.

[12] Bill Reimer, "The New Rural Economy Project: What Have We Learned?" Paper prepared for the Rural Sociological Society, Montreal, July 2003, available online at **http://nre.concordia.ca/nre2.htm**.

8.1   Geography in the Information Age

In a series of books and journal articles based on investigations into problems in rural India and Zimbabwe, geographer Sudhir Wanmali has suggested that one way to maintain important services (such as libraries, banks, and health care) in small rural settings is to make those services mobile so they can move to different towns on different days. This strategy uses flexibility in time to resolve problems with space—a very geographical solution indeed.[13]

these three developmental phases of the third agricultural revolution constitute the industrialization of agriculture.

The Industrialization of Agriculture

The industrialization of agriculture has largely been propelled by advances in science and technology, especially by mechanical as well as chemical and biological innovations. As with industrialization more generally, the industrialization of agriculture has unfolded as the capitalist economic system has become more advanced and widespread. We regard **agricultural industrialization** as the process whereby the farm has moved from being the centrepiece of agricultural production to becoming a mere part of an integrated multilevel (or vertically organized) industrial process that includes production, storage, processing, distribution, marketing, and retailing. Agriculture now is intricately linked to industry and the service sector, forming a complex agro-commodity production system.

> **agricultural industrialization:** the process whereby the farm has moved from being the centrepiece of agricultural production to becoming one part of an integrated string of vertically organized industrial processes including production, storage, processing, distribution, marketing, and retailing

Geographers have helped demonstrate the changes leading to the transformation of an agricultural product into an industrial food product. This transformation has been accomplished not only through the indirect and/or direct altering of agricultural outputs, such as tomatoes or wheat, but also through changes in rural economic activities. Agricultural industrialization involves three important developments:

- changes in rural labour activities as machines replace or improve human labour
- the introduction of innovative inputs—fertilizers, hybrid seeds, agrochemicals, and biotechnologies—to supplement, alter, or replace biological outputs
- the development of industrial substitutes for agricultural products (for example, artificial sweeteners instead of sugar, thickeners instead of cornstarch or flour)

Recall, however, that the industrialization of agriculture has not occurred simultaneously throughout the globe. Changes in the global economic system affect different places in different ways as different countries and social groups respond to and shape these changes. For example, the use of fertilizers and high-yielding seeds occurred much earlier in core-region agriculture than in the periphery, where many places still farm without them. Beginning in the late 1960s, core countries exported a technological package of fertilizers and high-yielding seeds to regions of the periphery in an attempt to boost agricultural production. Known as the **Green Revolution,** this package also included new machines and social institutions, as described in **Geography Matters 8.2—A Look at the Green Revolution**.

> **Green Revolution:** the export of a technological package of fertilizers and high-yielding seeds, from the core to the periphery, to increase global agricultural productivity

However, economic crises, a reduction in government programs, and reduced trade barriers have slowed the progress of the Green Revolution

---

[13] Sudhir Wanmali, *Periodic Markets and Rural Development in India*. Delhi: BR Publishing Corporation, 1981.

A Look at the Green Revolution

The Green Revolution was an attempt by agricultural scientists to find ways to feed the world's burgeoning population. The effort began in 1943, when the Rockefeller Foundation funded a group of U.S. agricultural scientists to set up a research project in Mexico aimed at increasing that country's wheat production. Only 7 years later scientists distributed the first Green Revolution wheat seeds. The project was eventually expanded to include research on maize and rice as well. Norman Borlaug, one of the founders of the Green Revolution, went on to win the Nobel Peace Prize in 1970 for an important component of the project: promoting world peace through the elimination of hunger.

The initial focus of the Green Revolution was on the development of seed varieties that would produce higher yields than those traditionally used in the target areas. However, agricultural scientists soon discovered that, in order for the new plants to thrive, farmers had to deliver nitrogen-based fertilizers in water—which led to the need to build major water and irrigation development projects. Then the scientists discovered that the increased nitrogen and water caused the plants to develop tall stalks that fell over easily, thus reducing the amount of seed that could be harvested. The scientists went back to the drawing board and came up with dwarf varieties of grains that would support the heavy heads of seeds without falling over. Then another problem arose: the short plants were growing close to the ground in very moist conditions, which encouraged the growth of diseases and pests. The scientists responded by developing a range of pesticides.

Thus, the Green Revolution constitutes a package of inputs: new "miracle seeds," water, fertilizers, and pesticides. Farmers had to use all of the inputs—and use them properly—to achieve the yields the scientists produced in their experimental plots. Green Revolution crops, if properly watered, fertilized, and treated for pests, can generate yields two to five times larger than those of traditional crops. In some countries, yields are now high enough to engage in export trade, thus generating important sources of foreign exchange. Furthermore, the creation of varieties that produce faster-maturing crops has allowed some farmers to plant two or more crops per year on the same land, thus increasing their individual production—and wealth—considerably.

Thanks to Green Revolution innovations, rice production in Asia grew 66 percent between 1965 and 1985, and India became largely self-sufficient in rice and wheat by the 1980s. Worldwide, Green Revolution seeds and agricultural techniques accounted for almost 90 percent of the increase in world grain output in the 1960s and about 70 percent in the 1970s. In the late 1980s and 1990s, at least 80 percent of the additional production of grains could be attributed to the use of Green Revolution techniques (**Figure 8.2.1**).

The Green Revolution has not been an unqualified success, however, everywhere in the world. One important reason is that wheat, rice, and maize are unsuitable as crops in many areas, and research on more suitable crops, such as sorghum and millet, has lagged far behind. In Africa, poor soils and lack of water make progress even more difficult to achieve. In recent years scientists have endeavoured to develop seeds with greater pest and disease resistance and more drought tolerance. The International Crops Research Institute for the Semi-Arid Tropics focuses on researching staples of the Sahel region, such as sorghum, millet, pigeon pea, and groundnut. Research on new varieties emphasizes testing under very adverse conditions (such as no plowing or fertilizing) and whether they will provide stable yields over good and bad years. A focus also exists on developing plants that will increase production of fodder and fuel residues, as well as of food, and that give optimal yields when intertilled—a very common practice in Africa. Finally, in the Sahel, scientists are working on crops that mature more quickly to compensate for the serious drop in the length of the rainy season recently experienced in the region.

Several concerns have been raised about the overall benefits of the Green Revolution. The first is that it has decreased the production of biomass fuels—wood, crop residues, and dung—traditionally used in many peripheral areas of the world. For example, in India, as tractors have replaced draft animals, less dung is produced and thus less is available as fuel. Instead, a greater reliance is being placed upon oil to fuel both tractors and other energy needs; this means that if farmers are to be successful, they increasingly must depend upon the most costly of energy resources. The second concern is that the Green Revolution has contributed to a worldwide loss of genetic diversity by replacing a wide range of local crops and varieties with a narrow range of high-yielding varieties of a few crops. The resulting monocultures (planting single varieties over large areas) have made agriculture more vulnerable to disease and pests. Moreover, whereas traditional varieties often have a built-in resistance to the pests and diseases characteristic of an area, the genetically engineered varieties often lack such resistance and need pesticides, which have contributed to ecosystem pollution and worker poisonings (see Figure 8.1). Lastly, the more intensive use of irrigation has created salt buildup in soils (salinization) and water scarcity.

Green Revolution technology has also been blamed for several social problems: it has decreased the need for human labour, creating significant unemployment; it has tended to exclude women, who play important roles

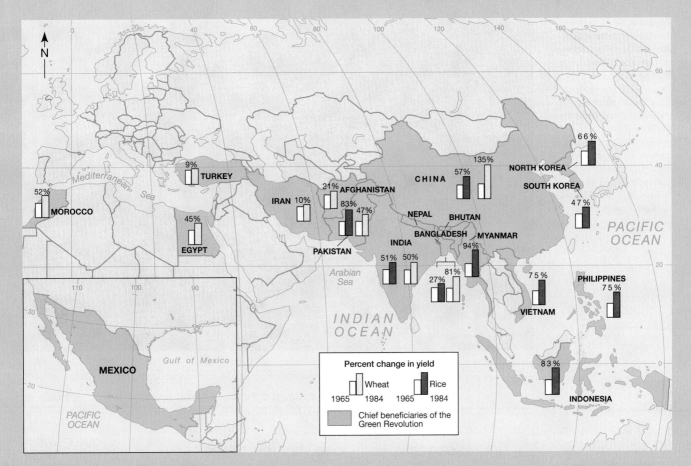

Figure 8.2.1 Effects of the Green Revolution, 1990 This map illustrates the increases in yields brought about by the Green Revolution in Asia and Mexico. Burgeoning populations in these regions mean that increased yields are critical. (*Source:* F. Shelley and A. Clarke, *Human and Cultural Geography*. Dubuque, IA: William C. Brown, 1994, fig. 7.8, p. 196.)

in food production; and it has magnified social inequities by allowing more wealth and power to accrue to a small number of agriculturalists while causing greater poverty and landlessness among poorer segments of the population.

Although the Green Revolution has come under much justified attack over the years, it has focused attention on finding innovative new ways to feed the world's peoples. In the process, the world system has been expanded into hitherto very remote regions, and important knowledge has been gained about how to conduct science and how to understand the role that agriculture plays at all geographical scales of resolution, from the global to the local. In the final analysis, although hunger and famine persist, they would be much worse if the Green Revolution had never occurred.

in many countries. For example, fertilizer use in countries such as Brazil and Mexico has declined with high prices, fewer subsidies, and increased competition from imported corn and wheat, especially from the United States. Many governments have shifted from giving top priority to self-sufficiency in food staples to encouraging crops that are apparently more competitive in international trade, such as fruit, vegetables, and flowers (**Figure 8.12**).

These nontraditional agricultural exports (NTAEs) have become increasingly important in areas of Mexico, Central America, Colombia, and Chile, replacing grain production and traditional exports, such as coffee and cotton. These new crops obtain high prices but also require heavy applications of pesticides and water to meet export-quality standards, and fast refrigerated transport to market. They are vulnerable to climatic variation and to the vagaries of the international

Figure 8.12 Commercial flower production, Argentina Pictured here is a field of allium, flowers that produce a blue, lilac, or purple-coloured bloom, on a flower plantation near Mendoza, Argentina. In the background are vineyards. Once grown only in home gardens, alliums are becoming commercialized all over the world, from Argentina to New Zealand.

market, including changing tastes for foods and health scares about pesticide or biological contamination (again, see Figure 8.1 on p. 358).

Biotechnology and Agriculture

Some observers argue that we are currently in the midst of a Biorevolution, a dramatic shift in agriculture brought about by the genetic engineering of plants and animals. As we saw earlier, ever since the beginnings of plant and animal domestication thousands of years ago, the manipulation and management of biological organisms have been of central importance to the development of agriculture. The central feature of the Biorevolution is **biotechnology**, any technique that uses living organisms (or parts of organisms) to improve, make, or modify plants and animals or to develop microorganisms for specific uses. Recombinant DNA techniques, tissue culture, cell fusion, enzyme and fermentation technology, and embryo transfer are some of the most-talked-about aspects of the use of biotechnology in agriculture (**Figure 8.13**).

A common argument for applying biotechnology to agriculture is the belief that it helps reduce agricultural production costs, as well as acts as a kind of resource-management technique (where certain natural resources are replaced by manufactured ones). Biotechnology has been hailed as a way to address growing concern for the rising costs of cash-crop production; surpluses and spoilage;

biotechnology: any technique that uses living organisms (or parts of organisms) to improve, make, or modify plants and animals or to develop microorganisms for specific uses

---

8.2 Geography in the Information Age

Scientists are also trying to bioengineer plants so that they produce pharmaceuticals, such as therapeutic proteins, medical and veterinary drugs, or vaccines, which would be administered by consuming the modified grain or fruit. It is estimated that there are over 400 "pharma crops" currently at the experimental stage, with many of them secretly field tested in open-air settings. The major disadvantage to farmers is that—once again—only a small part of the crop value will accrue to them.

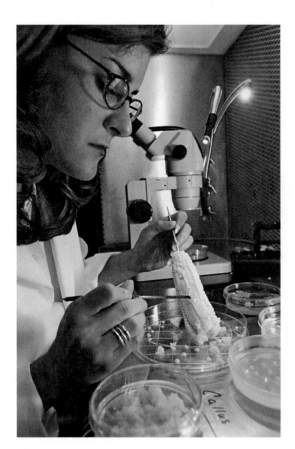

Figure 8.13 Biotechnology Biotechnology laboratories are typically high-technology greenhouses where plants are raised under carefully monitored conditions, from the implanting of special seeds to the applications of fertilizers and water and light. Biotechnology offers both benefits and costs. The benefits include increased yields and more pest-resistant strains, but too often the costs of such technology are too high for the world's neediest populations. In this photograph a Monsanto Corporation worker is extracting corn embryo for the development of a genetically modified crop.

environmental degradation from chemical fertilizers and overuse; soil depletion; and related challenges now facing profitable agricultural production.

Indeed, biotechnology has provided impressive responses to these and other challenges, for example by creating "super plants" that are disease resistant or that produce their own fertilizers and pesticides and can be grown on nutrient-lacking soils. The potential to develop salt-resistant crops may offer a solution to the increasing salinity of the world's soils—a major threat to agriculture in the near future in many countries. Its proponents also believe that biotechnology can enable agricultural production to keep up with food demand from a growing global population.

Just as with the Green Revolution, however, biotechnology may have deleterious effects on peripheral countries (and on poor labourers and small farmers in core countries). For example, biotechnology has enabled the development of plants that can be grown outside of their natural or currently most suitable environment. Yet cash crops are critical to the economic survival of many peripheral nations—such as bananas in Central America and the Caribbean, sugar in Cuba, and coffee in Colombia and Ethiopia (**Figure 8.14**). These and other export crops are threatened by the development of alternative sites of production. Transformations in agriculture have ripple effects throughout the world-system. As an illustration, **Table 8.1** compares the impacts of the Biorevolution and the Green Revolution on various aspects of global agricultural production.

In addition, the availability of technology to these peripheral nations is limited because most advances in biotechnology are the property of private companies. For example, patents protect both the process and the end products of biotechnological techniques. Utilizing biotechnological techniques requires paying fees for permission to use them, and the owners of small farms in both the core and the periphery are unlikely to be able to purchase or use the patented processes. Private ownership of biotechnological processes has resulted in control over food production being removed from the farmer and put into the hands of biotechnology firms, as Monsanto's activities in Canada illustrate (see the discussion of Saskatchewan farmer Percy Schmeiser and his court challenge against Monsanto in Chapter 12).

Figure 8.14 Coffee plantation in Ethiopia For many peripheral countries, the production of cash crops is a way to boost exports and bring in needed income for the national economy. In Ethiopia, coffee has for decades been a cash crop grown for export. Luxury exports, such as coffee, generate some of the capital needed to import staple foods, such as wheat.

TABLE 8.1 Biorevolution Compared with Green Revolution

Characteristics	Green Revolution	Biorevolution
Crops affected	Wheat, rice, maize	Potentially all crops, including vegetables, fruits, agro-export crops, and specialty crops
Other sectors affected	None	Pesticides, animal products, pharmaceuticals, processed food products, energy, mining, and warfare
Territories affected	Some developing countries	All areas, all nations, all locations, including marginal lands
Development of technology and dissemination	Largely public or quasi-public sector, international agricultural research centres (IARCs), R&D millions of dollars	Largely private sector, especially corporations, R&D billions of dollars
Proprietary considerations	Plant breeders' rights and patents generally not relevant	Genes, cells, plants, and animals patentable as well as the techniques used to produce them
Capital costs of research	Relatively low	Relatively high for some techniques, relatively low for others
Access to information	Restricted because of privatization and proprietary considerations	Relatively easy because of public policy of IARCs
Research skills required	Conventional plant breeding and parallel agricultural sciences	Molecular and cell biology expertise as well as conventional plant-breeding skills
Crop vulnerability	High-yielding varieties relatively uniform; high vulnerability	Tissue culture crop propagation produces exact genetic copies; even more vulnerability
Side effects	Increased monoculture and use of farm chemicals, marginalization of small farmer, ecological degradation; increased foreign debt due to decrease in biomass fuels and the increasing reliance on costly, usually imported, petroleum	Crop substitution replacing Third World exports; herbicide tolerance; increasing use of chemicals; engineered organisms might affect the environment; further marginalization of small-farm worker

Sources: Adapted from M. Kenney and F. Buttel, "Biotechnology: Prospects and Dilemmas for Third-World Development," *Development and Change* 16, 1995, p. 70; and H. Hobbelink, *Biotechnology and the Future of World Agriculture: The Fourth Resource.* London: Zed Books, 1991.

Under such circumstances, it becomes possible that the control over world food security could shift from publicly accountable governments to privately held biotechnology firms. Finally, with the refinement and specialization of plant and animal species, women who are currently employed in ancillary activities could face the loss of their jobs. For example, if a grower chooses to plant a bio-engineered type of wheat that does not require winnowing (the removal of the chaff, a normally labour-intensive process), then those labourers who once were involved in that activity are no longer needed.

The Biorevolution in agriculture is so recent that we are just beginning to understand both its negative and positive impacts. At this point, it seems quite clear that these impacts will be distributed unevenly across countries, regions, and locales, and certainly across class, ethnicity, and gender lines. It is still too soon to tell what the overall costs and benefits will be. On the one hand, it seems clear that the advantages include the ability to increase production (especially by permitting growth in different environments) and to reduce the level of pesticide use. On the other hand, the commodification of genes and seed stocks raises the concern that farmers will lose control of their own fields to corporate biotechnology interests.

GLOBAL RESTRUCTURING OF AGRICULTURAL SYSTEMS

When geographers talk about the globalization of agriculture, they are referring to the incorporation of agriculture into the world economic system of capitalism. A useful way to think about the term **globalized agriculture** is to recognize that as both an economic sector and a geographically distributed activity, modern agriculture is increasingly dependent on an economy and set of regulatory practices that are global in scope and organization.

globalized agriculture: a system of food production increasingly dependent on an economy and a set of regulatory practices that are global in scope and organization

Forces of Globalization

Three related processes play a role in the globalization of agriculture:

- The forces—technological, economic, political, and so on—that shape agricultural systems are global in their scope.
- The institutions—trade and finance especially—that most dramatically alter agriculture are organized globally.
- The current form of agriculture reflects integrated, globally organized agro-production systems.

The globalization of agriculture has dramatically changed relationships between and within different agricultural production systems. The result is either eventual elimination of some forms of agriculture (for instance, the decline of shifting cultivation) or the erosion or alteration of systems as they are integrated into the global economy (for example, as described earlier, the erosion in Canada of a national agricultural system based on family farms).

In addition to regulating and assisting agriculture in their own country, governments—especially those of core countries—also directly and indirectly influence the agricultural sectors of other countries, especially those of peripheral countries. Food aid and agricultural development aid are widespread and popularly accepted ways in which core states intervene in the agricultural sector of peripheral states. Such intervention is one way in which peripheral states are incorporated into the global economy.

The Organization of the Agro-Food System

Although the changes that have occurred in agriculture worldwide are complex, we can identify and examine some important indicators of change. Geographers and other scholars interested in contemporary agriculture have noted three prominent and nested forces that signal a dramatic departure from previous forms of agricultural practice: agribusiness, food chains, and integration of agriculture with the manufacturing, service, finance, and trade sectors. **Geography Matters 8.3— The New Geography of Food and Agriculture in New Zealand** illustrates the deployment of these forces in one country.

The concept of agribusiness has received a good deal of attention in the last two decades, and in the popular mind it has come to be associated with large corporations, such as ConAgra, DelMonte, or Cargill. Although transnational corporations (TNCs) are certainly involved in agribusiness, the concept is meant to convey more than a corporate form: **agribusiness** is a system rather than a kind of corporate entity. Indeed, it is a set of economic and political relationships that organizes food production from the development of seeds to the retailing and consumption of the agricultural product. Defining agribusiness as a system, however, is not meant to suggest that corporations are not critically important to the food production process. On the contrary, in the core economies, the transnational corporation is the dominant player operating at numerous strategically important stages of the food production process. TNCs have become dominant for a number of reasons, but mostly because of their ability to negotiate the complexities of production and distribution in many different geographical locations. That capability requires special knowledge of national, regional, and local regulations and pricing factors.

A food chain (a special type of commodity chain) is a way to understand the organizational structure of agribusiness as a complex political and economic system of inputs, processing and manufacturing, and outputs. The **food chain** is composed of five central and connected sectors (inputs, production, processing, distribution, and consumption). External forces such as the state, international trade, the physical environment, or credit and finance, impact those sectors, for example when state farm policies shape inputs, product prices, the structure of the farm, and even the physical environment (remember the example of the Crow Rate subsidy).

The food chain concept illustrates the complex connections among producers and between producers and consumers and regions and places. For example, there are important linkages that connect cattle production in the Prairies, beef-packing plants in High River, Alberta, and the availability of processed hamburger patties in Halifax. Because of such complex food chains, it is now common to find that traditional agricultural practices in peripheral regions have been displaced by expensive, capital-intensive practices.

That agriculture is not an independent or unique economic activity is not a particularly new realization. Beginning with the second agricultural revolution, agriculture began to slowly, but inexorably, be transformed by industrial practices. What is different about the current state of the food system is the way in which farming has become just one stage of a complex and multidimensional economic process. This process is as much about distribution and marketing— key elements of the service sector—as it is about the growing and processing of agricultural products in the primary sector.

Food Regimes and Alternative Food Movements

A **food regime** is the specific set of links that exist between food production and consumption, as well as capital investment and accumulation opportunities. Whereas a food chain describes the complex ways in which specific food items are produced, manufactured, and marketed, the concept of the food regime also describes how a particular type of food becomes dominant during a specific historical period.

Like the agricultural revolutions already described, food regimes are the result of specific political and economic forces operating in a given historical period. For example, the wheat and livestock food regime that characterized global agriculture until the 1960s was the result of the processes of colonization and the industrialization

agribusiness: a set of economic and political relationships that organizes agro-food production from the development of seeds to the retailing and consumption of the agricultural product

food chain: five central and connected sectors (inputs, production, product processing, distribution, and consumption) with four contextual elements acting as external mediating forces (the state, international trade, the physical environment, and credit and finance)

food regime: the specific set of links that exist between food production and consumption, as well as capital investment and accumulation opportunities

The New Geography of Food and Agriculture in New Zealand

The restructuring of international trade, the activities of transnational corporations, and rapid shifts in government policies are affecting agriculture and the rural landscape across the world. For example, agriculture has been transformed through horizontal integration (when farms are consolidated into one large landholding, resulting in the disappearance of small, family-run farms) and through vertical integration (when a company owns the fertilizer and seed companies as well as the food-processing plant and supermarkets).

Geographers such as Richard Le Heron and Guy Robinson have written extensively about how New Zealand agriculture has changed in response to the restructuring of the global food system. They document how New Zealand's agricultural system evolved during the nineteenth century by producing wool and lamb for a guaranteed market in the core economy of the United Kingdom. After World War II, a second regime developed that included dairy cows on small farms and processing of products such as butter for export using refrigerated shipping. By the mid-twentieth century, the New Zealand government was heavily involved in the agricultural system through "marketing boards" that mediated farmers' relationships with international markets through quality controls, price supports, and marketing.

In the 1970s, the shock of the oil crisis (increasing the cost of agricultural inputs) and the loss of the imperial-preference market (when Britain joined the European Community) resulted in further state support for producers. Even though price supports, incentives, and subsidies for inputs such as fertilizers provided more than a third of farm revenues, they could not fully buffer farmers against the increasing cost of inputs and loss of markets for the staples of wool, meat, and dairy. Consequently, some farmers began to diversify into non-traditional exports, such as venison, produced on deer farms, and fruit such as kiwi and Asian pears, responding to a new global food regime of specialty foods and the export of fruit and vegetables (**Figure 8.3.1**).

A dramatic change in domestic agricultural policies in 1984 abruptly removed most price supports, trade protections, and farm subsidies and required farms to pay for extension services, water, and quality inspections. Farm income fell by up to half, debt increased, 10 percent of farms were sold, herds were significantly reduced, and 10,000 farmers protested in front of Parliament. New Zealand agriculture was thrown into a global free market and the full impact of what has been called the "international farm crisis." At the same time, most other developed countries, including the United States, Canada, and the EU, maintained considerable state regulation and support for their agricultural systems, making it even harder for New Zealand farmers to compete globally. Many coped by adjusting herd sizes and changing crop mixes; some

went out of business and their properties were horizontally integrated into larger farms. Transnational agribusiness firms purchased New Zealand agricultural processing enterprises with the goal of supplying growing Asian markets. But New Zealand was also one of the first countries to rethink food production by adopting certification for organic agricultural products and developing a thriving domestic market for sustainably grown foods.

Many geographers are re-examining agriculture in the context of global restructuring and changing government policies and contributing important insights into how the new international geography of food and agriculture is changing the economy and environments of countries such as New Zealand. The geographic perspective allows us to link international trade, regulation, and corporations to the decisions of national and local governments and to the impacts on and responses of agricultural regions, communities, and farm families.

Figure 8.3.1 Kiwi production   These kiwi orchards on the North Island of New Zealand are surrounded by lines of trees that protect the delicate fruit from strong winds. The result is a unique landscape that is completely restructured to meet the needs of the crop.

of agriculture of the late nineteenth century. Employing new industrial technologies (barbed wire, refrigerated freight ships, etc.—see Chapter 2), European core countries turned their colonies into important sources of cheap wheat and meat.

In the last few decades, a new food regime based on a "postmodern diet" of fresh fish, fruit, and vegetables has emerged. Integrated networks of refrigerated food chains deliver these foodstuffs from all over the world to the core regions of Western Europe, North America, and Japan. Echoing the former food networks that characterized nineteenth-century imperialism, peripheral production systems supply core consumers with fish and fresh, often exotic and off-season, produce. Indeed, consumers in core regions expect the full range of fruits and vegetables to be available year round in their produce sections, and unusual and exotic produce has become increasingly popular: just think how many sushi bars have opened in your city lately and how intricate and widespread the food networks are that these restaurants must draw on for their ingredients: fresh fish and crustaceans of various kinds, seaweed, fish roe, Asian vegetables and seasonings, rice, shiitake mushrooms, ginger, wasabi paste, imported Japanese beer and sake, etc.

Alongside the emergence of the food regime based on fresh fish, fruits, and vegetables, it is important to note several other alternative food production and consumption practices taking hold in core regions over the last 25 years and accelerating especially over the last ten: organic farming, local food, and the Slow Food movement. Finally, we also have to address the phenomenon of fast food and its spatial consequences for agriculture worldwide.

Organic farming describes any farming or animal husbandry that occurs without commercial fertilizers, synthetic pesticides, or growth hormones. Organic food production has become a growing force alongside the dominant conventional farming (an approach that uses pesticides and fertilizers, or intensive, hormone-based practices in breeding and raising animals). It is driven by a variety of concerns ranging from opposition to agribusiness and food safety to health concerns and an evolving commitment to food as a gastronomic experience.

Local food (often also organically grown) is food that is produced within a 100-mile (160 kilometre) radius, the so-called food shed. Individuals that want to eat local food ("locavores") can join groups that collect subscriptions and then pay a farmer *up front* to grow food locally for them for a season or a specified time frame. The farmer is then able to purchase seeds, hire workers, cultivate produce and livestock, and deliver the harvest—all without relying on interest-bearing loans. This pre-paid scheme is called Community Supported Agriculture, or CSA. The CSA members, in return for their investment in the farm, receive weekly shares of produce (and sometimes meats, eggs and cheese, flowers, and milk) that reflect the season and the constraints and possibilities of local growing conditions. CSA farms are usually small, independent, and labour-intensive, and the CSA movement is seen as helping to restore the family farm to the national landscapes.

Evidently, the CSA movement has very geographical limitations: the Canadian climate limits the availability of seasonal produce, and products such as chocolate or coffee cannot be procured locally at any time of the year. Moreover, economies of scale mean that certain levels of producer specialization and geographies of regional specialization are more efficient than small-scale local operations. In other words: we could not feed the entire population with this kind of agriculture. Finally, to insist on a dependence on local production runs counter to this country's support for multiculturalism as it would require immigrants to forgo imported foodstuffs necessary in many ethnically inspired cuisines.

One particularly popular way of juxtaposing conventional and alternative agriculture is the concept of "food miles"—a measure of the distance travelled by food items from the farm to the consumer. The term highlights how much we depend on non-local foods—one important indicator of the sustainability of our food production systems.

As an example, consider the 2001 investigation of a team from the Leopold Center for Sustainable Agriculture into food items shipped into Iowa from the Chicago Grain

Terminal building.[14] They discovered that food items had travelled *on average* 2,429 kilometres to get to their Iowa destinations in 1998. This figure represents a 22 percent increase over the situation in 1981, a reflection of the increasing globalization of agriculture that had occurred in that period. Moreover, it was 33 times greater than the "food miles" travelled by food items available through a local CSA.

In similar fashion, 2008 research by Melanie Langlois[15] to establish the food miles required to produce a shepherd's pie in Montreal shows that the average mileage required to assemble all of the ingredients is 4,240 kilometres, a figure mainly due to the Alberta-sourced meat, because the rest of the ingredients were locally derived. Transporting all of these ingredients by truck produced carbon dioxide emissions of 109 grams for each four-serving shepherd's pie.

8.3   Geography in the Information Age

The numbers become even more staggering if we also include all of the packaging materials used in the production of a food item. For example, in her 1995 study "The Well-Travelled Yoghurt Pot," Stefanie Böge of the Wuppertal Institute in Germany showed that the average 150-gram container of yoghurt sold in that country had travelled over 8,000 kilometres if we consider not only the milk but also the plastic for the container and the aluminum for the lid.[16]

For many people, food miles provide an important indicator of the sustainability of their food, and the fact that British supermarkets are beginning to include them on their food labels is a first step to showing not only where that food has come from but also how consumer choice can be a powerful voice in shaping agriculture and agribusiness.

Europe has contributed its own focus to alternative food production and consumption through the *Slow Food* movement: an attempt to preserve the cultural cuisine and the associated food and farming of an ecoregion. Its website declares the following philosophy:

> Slow Food was founded in 1989 to counter the rise of fast food and fast life, the disappearance of local food traditions and people's dwindling interest in the food they eat, where it comes from, how it tastes, and how our food choices affect the rest of the world.
>
> Today, we have over 100,000 members joined in 1,300 convivia—our local chapters—worldwide, as well as a network of 2,000 food communities who practice small-scale and sustainable production of quality foods.[17]

Although the alternative practices of organic farming, local food, and Slow Food signal a shift in food production and consumption, they in no way challenge the dominance of more conventionally produced, distributed, marketed, and consumed food. Moreover, as a number of critics of the movements have pointed out, these alternative practices are largely organized and promoted by white, middle-class members of core regions and exclude poor people simply through cost and associated accessibility. In core countries, the result is that more than any other economic class, poor people turn to cheap, easily accessible food, also known as fast food.

[14] Rich Pirog, Timothy Van Pelt, Kamyar Enshayan, and Ellen Cook, *Food, Fuel, and Freeways: An Iowa Perspective on How Far Food Travels, Food Usage, and Greenhouse Gas Emissions.* Ames, IA: Leopold Center for Sustainable Agriculture, 2001.

[15] Melanie Langlois, unpublished BA Honours Essay, Department of Geography, Planning and Environment, Concordia University, Montreal, 2008.

[16] Stefanie Böge, "The Well-Travelled Yoghurt Pot," *World Transport Policy & Practice* 1(1), 1995, pp. 7–11.

[17] Slow Food, **www.slowfood.com/welcome_eng.lasso**.

Fast food was born in the United States as a product of the post–World War II economic boom and the social, political, and cultural transformations that occurred in its wake. The concept of fast food—standardized edibles that can be prepared and served very quickly, sold in a restaurant, and served to customers in packaged form—was pioneered by brothers Richard and Maurice McDonald in 1948 when they applied industrial organizational principles to food preparation. Looking to shed the labour and material costs of standard restaurant food preparation, they hired unskilled workers to perform a single task in an assembly-line operation—cooking the burger, placing it on the bun, or packaging it for take-out, and so on. Today, fast food is so ubiquitous throughout the world that it is taken for granted—as are the critiques. In fact, so many books and films about fast food and its dietary and labour-related shortcomings have been released in the last decade that we can concentrate here on the interesting perspective it provides on the processes of globalization and development, and on its environmental impacts.

The increased consumption of fast food and many prepared, processed foods—energy-dense, nutrient-poor foods with high levels of sugar and saturated fats—as well as reduced physical activity have raised adult obesity rates threefold or more since 1980 across North America, the United Kingdom, Eastern Europe, the Middle East, the Pacific Islands, Australasia, and China. As this list shows, the obesity epidemic—as it has come to be called—is not restricted to industrialized societies. In fact, the increase is often faster in rapidly developing peripheral countries than in the core. In offering an explanation for the problem, the World Health Organization writes:

> The rising epidemic reflects the profound changes in society and in behavioral patterns of communities over recent decades. While genes are important in determining a person's susceptibility to weight gain, energy balance is determined by calorie intake and physical activity. Thus societal changes and worldwide nutrition transition are driving the obesity epidemic. Economic growth, modernization, urbanization, and globalization of food markets are just some of the forces thought to underlie the epidemic.
>
> As incomes rise and populations become more urban, diets high in complex carbohydrates give way to more varied diets with a higher proportion of fats, saturated fats and sugars. At the same time, large shifts towards less physically demanding work have been observed worldwide. Moves towards less physical activity are also found in the increasing use of automated transport, technology in the home, and more passive leisure pursuits.[18]

Besides the impact on human health worldwide, the rapacious growth of fast-food production and distribution processes is having dramatic effects on Earth's resources, especially forests and farmland. The Beyond Beef Campaign, an international coalition of environment, food safety, and health activist organizations, lists the following facts about beef production and its environmental impacts:

- Beef raised for fast-food hamburgers is one of the largest components of the fast-food sector.

- One quarter-pound of hamburger beef imported from Latin America requires the clearing of 6 square metres of rain forest and the destruction of 75 kilograms of living matter, including 20 to 30 different plant species, 100 insect species, and dozens of bird, mammal, and reptile species.

- Cattle degrade the land by stripping vegetation and compacting the earth. Each kilogram of feedlot steak costs about 15 kilograms of eroded topsoil.

- Nearly half of the total amount of water used annually in the United States goes to grow feed and provide drinking water for cattle and other livestock. Producing a pound of grain-fed steak requires almost 5,000 litres of water.

---

[18] World Health Organization, **www.who.int/dietphysicalactivity/ publications/facts/obesity/en/**.

- Cattle produce nearly 1 billion tons of organic waste each year. The average feedlot steer produces more than 20 kilograms of manure every 24 hours.

- Much of the carbon dioxide released into the atmosphere is directly attributable to beef production: burning forests to make way for cattle pasture and burning massive tracts of agricultural waste from cattle feed crops.

- U.S. cattle production has caused a significant loss of biodiversity on both public and private lands. More plant species in the United States have been eliminated or threatened by livestock grazing than by any other cause.[19]

As these examples of alternative food movements and the fast-food phenomenon show, the impacts of food production and consumption on people and places (not to mention animals!) are complex and far-reaching. As we said at the beginning of this chapter, the study of food is almost by definition a very geographical endeavour. **Figure 8.15** summarizes some of the interconnections between geographical concepts and the subject of food studies.

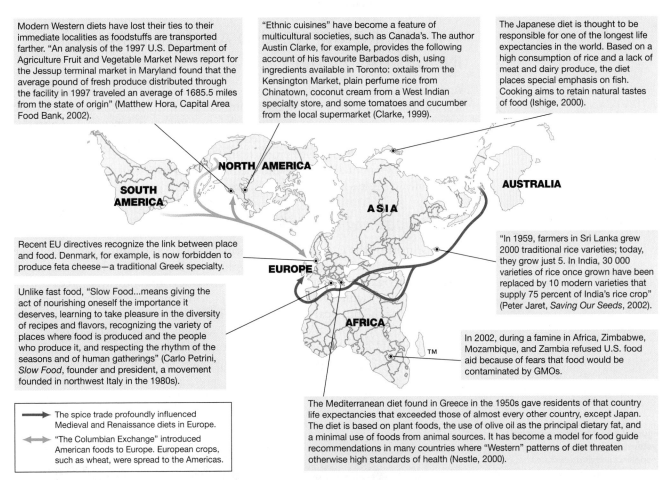

Modern Western diets have lost their ties to their immediate localities as foodstuffs are transported farther. "An analysis of the 1997 U.S. Department of Agriculture Fruit and Vegetable Market News report for the Jessup terminal market in Maryland found that the average pound of fresh produce distributed through the facility in 1997 traveled an average of 1685.5 miles from the state of origin" (Matthew Hora, Capital Area Food Bank, 2002).

"Ethnic cuisines" have become a feature of multicultural societies, such as Canada's. The author Austin Clarke, for example, provides the following account of his favourite Barbados dish, using ingredients available in Toronto: oxtails from the Kensington Market, plain perfume rice from Chinatown, coconut cream from a West Indian specialty store, and some tomatoes and cucumber from the local supermarket (Clarke, 1999).

The Japanese diet is thought to be responsible for one of the longest life expectancies in the world. Based on a high consumption of rice and a lack of meat and dairy produce, the diet places special emphasis on fish. Cooking aims to retain natural tastes of food (Ishige, 2000).

Recent EU directives recognize the link between place and food. Denmark, for example, is now forbidden to produce feta cheese—a traditional Greek specialty.

Unlike fast food, "Slow Food...means giving the act of nourishing oneself the importance it deserves, learning to take pleasure in the diversity of recipes and flavors, recognizing the variety of places where food is produced and the people who produce it, and respecting the rhythm of the seasons and of human gatherings" (Carlo Petrini, Slow Food, founder and president, a movement founded in northwest Italy in the 1980s).

"In 1959, farmers in Sri Lanka grew 2000 traditional rice varieties; today, they grow just 5. In India, 30 000 varieties of rice once grown have been replaced by 10 modern varieties that supply 75 percent of India's rice crop" (Peter Jaret, Saving Our Seeds, 2002).

In 2002, during a famine in Africa, Zimbabwe, Mozambique, and Zambia refused U.S. food aid because of fears that food would be contaminated by GMOs.

The spice trade profoundly influenced Medieval and Renaissance diets in Europe.

"The Columbian Exchange" introduced American foods to Europe. European crops, such as wheat, were spread to the Americas.

The Mediterranean diet found in Greece in the 1950s gave residents of that country life expectancies that exceeded those of almost every other country, except Japan. The diet is based on plant foods, the use of olive oil as the principal dietary fat, and a minimal use of foods from animal sources. It has become a model for food guide recommendations in many countries where "Western" patterns of diet threaten otherwise high standards of health (Nestle, 2000).

Figure 8.15 A world of food This diagram is an attempt to show graphically some of the many geographic issues that the study of food raises. Ethnic and regional cuisines embody ideas of place; the movement of spices and other food illustrates diffusion; standards of diet around the globe illustrate regional patterns of inequality; and, lastly, new approaches to bio-engineering reflect some profound changes in our attitudes toward nature. (*Sources for quotations:* Matthew Hora and Jody Tick, *From Farm to Table: Making the Connection in the Mid-Atlantic Food System.* Washington, DC: Capital Area Food Bank, 2001; Austin Clarke, *Pig Tails 'n Breadfruit: The Rituals of Slave Food, A Culinary Memoir.* Toronto: Random House, 1999; Naomichi Ishige, "Japan." In K.F. Kiple and K.C. Ornelas [eds.], *The Cambridge World History of Food*, vol. 2. Cambridge: Cambridge University Press, 2000, pp. 1175–1183; Peter Jaret, *Saving Our Seeds.* 2002, quoted in Fran McManus and Wendy Rickard [eds.], *Cooking Fresh from the Mid-Atlantic.* Hopewell, NJ: Eating Fresh Publications, 2002; Marion Nestle, *The Mediterranean Diets and Disease Prevention.* In K.F. Kiple and K.C. Ornelas [eds.], *The Cambridge World History of Food*, vol. 2. Cambridge: Cambridge University Press, 2000, pp. 1193–1203; and Carlo Petrini [William McCuaig, Translator], *Slow Food: The Case for Taste.* New York: Columbia University Press, 2003.)

---

[19] Beyond Beef, www.mcspotlight.org/media/reports/beyond.html#9.

Social and Technological Change in Global Agricultural Restructuring

In preceding sections of this chapter, we have shown how the globalization of agriculture has been accomplished through the same kinds of political and economic restructuring that characterized the globalization of industry. Technological change has been of particular importance to agriculture over the last half of the twentieth century as mechanical, chemical, and biological revolutions have altered even the most fundamental of agricultural practices. And, just as restructuring in industry has occurred with innumerable rounds of adjustment and resistance, so has it occurred in agriculture as well.

Besides generating economic competition, the newly restructured agro-commodity production system also fosters conflict and competition within sociocultural systems. For instance, in both core and peripheral locations, men and women, landowners and peasants, different indigenous groups, corporations, and family farmers struggle to establish or maintain control over production and over ways of life.

THE ENVIRONMENT AND AGRICULTURAL INDUSTRIALIZATION

Agriculture always involves the interaction of biophysical and human systems. In fact, it is this relationship that makes agriculture distinct from other forms of economic activity that do not depend so directly on the environment to function. It is also this interactive relationship that requires attention regarding how best to manage the environment to enable the continued production of food. Because the relationship between the human system of agriculture and the biophysical system of the environment is highly interactive, it is important to look at the various ways that each shapes the other.

The Impact of the Environment on Agriculture

Management of the environment by farmers has been steadily increasing over the course of the three agricultural revolutions. In fact, the widespread use of fertilizers, irrigation systems, pesticides, herbicides, and industrial greenhouses suggests that agriculture has become an economic practice that can ignore the limitations of the physical environment (**Figure 8.16**). Yet, it is exactly because agriculture is an economic activity that management of the environment in which it occurs becomes critical. As geographer Martin Parry writes:

> Soil, terrain, water, weather and pests can be modified and many of the activities through the farming year, such as tillage and spraying, are directed toward this. But

Figure 8.16 Modern irrigation system This photo shows a self-propelling irrigation system that can be electronically programmed to deliver different amounts of water at different times of the day or days of the week. Irrigation is just one way that humans have been able to alter the environment to serve their agricultural needs. In many parts of the core, water prices are heavily subsidized for agricultural users in order to ensure food supplies. For many parts of the periphery, however, access to water is limited to the amount of rain that falls and can be stored behind small dams and in impoundments. (*Source:* Agricultural Research Service, USDA.)

these activities must be cost-effective; the benefits of growing a particular crop, or increasing its yield by fertilizing, must exceed the costs of doing so. Often such practices are simply not economic, with the result that factors such as soil quality, terrain and climate continue to affect agriculture by limiting the range of crops and animals that can profitably be farmed. In this way the physical environment still effectively limits the range of agricultural activities open to the farmer at each location.[20]

Though the impact of the environment on agricultural practices that have become heavily industrialized may not at first seem obvious, the reverse is more readily observable. In fact, there are many contemporary and historical examples of the ways that agriculture destroys, depletes, or degrades the environmental resources on which its existence and profitability depend.

The Impact of Agriculture on the Environment

One of the earliest treatises on the impact of chemical pesticides on the environment is Rachel Carson's *Silent Spring*, which identified the detrimental impact of synthetic chemical pesticides—especially DDT—on the health of human and animal populations. Although the publication of the book and the environmental awareness that it generated led to a ban on the use of many pesticides in most industrialized nations, chemical companies continued to produce and market many of these pesticides in peripheral countries. Although some of these pesticides were effective in combating malaria and other insect-borne diseases, many were applied to crops that were later sold in the markets of developed countries. Thus, a kind of "circle of poison" was set in motion, encompassing the entire global agricultural system (**Figure 8.17**).

Some of the most pressing issues facing agricultural producers today are soil degradation and denudation, which are occurring at rates more than a thousand times the natural erosion rates. Although we might tend to dismiss soil erosion as a historical problem of the 1930s Dust Bowl, in reality, the effects of agriculture on worldwide soil resources are dramatic. Unfortunately, most forms of agriculture tend to increase natural erosion, and the losses are more severe in peripheral countries. The loss of topsoil worldwide is a critical problem because it is a fixed resource that cannot be readily replaced. It takes, on average, between 100 and 500 years to generate 10 millimetres of topsoil, and it is estimated that nearly 50,000 million tonnes of topsoil are lost each year to erosion.

Soil erosion because of mismanagement in the semi-arid regions of the world has led to desertification, in which topsoil and vegetation losses have been extensive and largely permanent. As explained in Chapter 4, *desertification* is the spread of desert-like conditions in arid or semi-arid lands resulting from climatic change or human influences. Desertification not only means the loss of topsoil but can also involve the deterioration of grazing lands and the decimation of forests (**Figure 8.18**). In addition to causing

Figure 8.17 Impact of pesticides Pesticides have been shown to have highly damaging impacts on the ecosystem. In addition to fostering pests that are more resistant to chemical suppression, pesticides can kill and cause genetic damage in larger animals, especially birds. One disorder linked to pesticide use is that the shells of bird eggs, such as the one shown here, are not thick enough to remain intact and protect the embryo through the various stages of maturation. The thin shells crack open prematurely, exposing the embryo before it is viable. In the 1960s, many of the most noxious chemicals, such as DDT, were banned in North America. Many peripheral countries, however, continue to allow the sale of such chemicals.

Figure 8.18 Desertification, Gansu, China Severe and largely permanent loss of vegetation and topsoil may result from human activities, such as overgrazing or excessive deforestation. The ravaged landscapes of desertification are a compelling reminder that humans must weigh the implications of their agricultural practices—not always an easy thing to do when ill-informed government policies and grinding hunger and poverty are daily facts of life. The photograph shows a woman walking along the leading edge of the Kumtag desert as it threatens to engulf her onion farm. The sand is advancing at the rate of up to 4 metres a year.

---

[20] M. Parry, "Agriculture as a Resource System." In I. Bowler (ed.), *The Geography of Agriculture in Developed Market Economies*. Harlow, UK: Longman Scientific and Technical, 1992, p. 208.

Agriculture

Climate is closely associated with agriculture: it defines the length of the growing season, average temperatures, and the amount and timing of precipitation. Not surprisingly, climate change becomes an important factor in the long-run variability of agricultural production in developing and developed countries, and is expected to have profound impacts on agricultural production and crop yields through four key dimensions (**Figure 8.4.1**). First, warming will likely reduce food production due to increased heat stress. Even slight increases in temperature will likely reduce crop yields, particularly in tropical latitudes. Moderate temperature increases (1°C–2°C) in mid- to high-latitude regions, such as Canada and Europe, may initially increase crop yields, but further increases in temperature are likely to reduce crop yields.[21]

Second, changing weather and precipitation patterns will alter agricultural patterns. Higher latitudes and the tropics are expected to see increased precipitation, whereas mid-latitudes and semi-arid areas will see less. This means that the impact will predominantly affect agriculturally marginal and semi-arid regions dependent upon rain for agricultural production.[22] Concurrently, the greater frequency of extreme events such as droughts, cyclones, hailstorms, and floods will

Figure 8.4.1   Climate change and food: an integrated framework   The expected impacts of climate change are varied and widespread. It is widely expected that climate change will impact human and natural systems through such things as food and water resources, which in turn will affect economic development and personal livelihoods.   (*Source:* With permission, IPCC.)

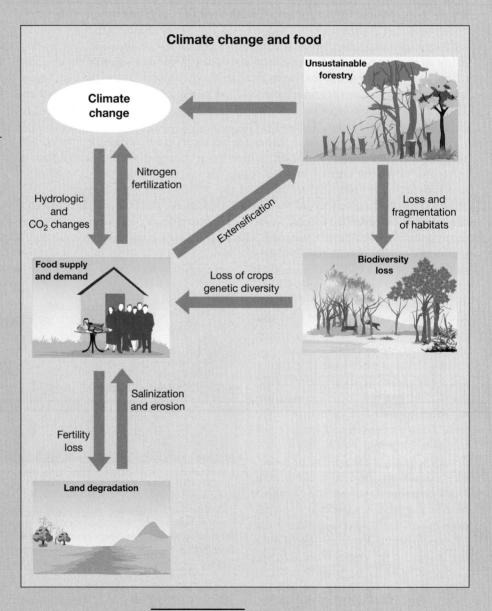

21 IPCC 4th Assessment Report, 2007 (**www.ipcc.ch/index.htm**).
22 Ibid.

388

negatively affect agriculture and potentially devastate crops through higher risks of floods, landslides, and erosion. Such events cannot be anticipated and prepared for, and may be of even greater risk than climate change itself.[23]

Third, changes in weather patterns and warmer average temperatures are likely to modify pests and diseases relative to crops and livestock, impacting economic activities and livelihoods. Rising temperatures will likely expand the range of many agricultural pests and increase their ability to survive the winter and attack spring crops. Recent warming trends in Canada and the United States have resulted in earlier spring activity of insects and the proliferation of some species, such as the mountain pine beetle, which has decimated British Columbia's forest industry and threatens much of Canada's boreal forest. Rising ocean temperatures may reduce the diversity of species and disrupt fish breeding and feeding patterns, as habitats and ranges are reduced. Increased climate extremes may also promote plant disease and pest outbreaks from the tropics to mid-latitudes.[24]

Finally, increasing temperatures will increase evapotranspiration and lower soil moisture levels. For farmers, this means increased reliance on irrigation for crops. If this is compounded by reduced water availability from rainfall, some cultivated areas will become unsuitable for cropping and some grasslands may become increasingly arid, leading to increased risk of food shortages.

Climatic changes are likely to affect agricultural production worldwide. They will not, however, be felt equally across the globe, with variable patterns observed in both the developed and developing world. In Canada, only 2 percent of the labour force is engaged in agricultural production, and agriculture represents less than 4 percent of the country's economy,[25] meaning it can endure a climatic setback more easily than a country like Malawi, where 90 percent of the population lives in rural areas and 40 percent of the economy is driven by rain-fed agriculture.

For the developed and largely temperate world (including North America and Europe), climate change is expected to have neutral or mildly positive impacts. Canada and Northern Europe, for instance, may see increased agricultural production as warming, longer growing seasons, and increased CO_2 concentration (which acts as a "fertilizer" for crops) enable crop production to shift northward, but only in those areas where soil and water conditions allow. In addition, the costs of over-wintering livestock will fall, crop yields will improve, and forests may grow faster. Some negative impacts will also be experienced, with the arid southerly portions of the Canadian prairies (an area commonly referred to as Palliser's Triangle that includes much of southern Alberta and Saskatchewan[26]) and the U.S. plains likely to see decreased agricultural output. Already, drought and annual soil moisture deficits are recurrent problems in this region. More significant increases in temperature (over +2°C) are likely to result in decreased crop yields. The summer 2003 European heat wave, with temperatures approximately 6°C above the long-term mean and reduced precipitation levels, resulted in losses of up to 30 percent for some fruit and grain crops.[27]

The developing world is far more likely to experience the expected negative impacts of climate change. Although higher global temperatures will bring higher rainfall, this will be unevenly distributed, with some areas such as south Asia, northern Latin America, and Africa projected to receive less rainfall than before. The potential loss of farmland due to decreased precipitation and *desertification*, discussed in Chapter 4, will reduce food production. Compounding the problem is the generally lower intensity of agriculture and reduced availability of capital in these regions already, and limited funds to import increasingly expensive staple foods.

The greatest concern centres on Africa and parts of Asia, where even small increases in temperature and small decreases in precipitation will reduce agricultural yields. In Africa, climate change could depress grain production by 2 to 3 percent by 2030, enough to increase the numbers at risk of hunger by 10 million.[28] In India, a country that could be hard hit by climate change, the United Nations Food and Agriculture Organization (FAO) estimates that the country could lose 18 percent of its total grain production. In both cases, this may result in increased dependency on food imports and greater food insecurity. Poor and small-scale subsistence farmers will be especially vulnerable to income or food supply disruptions by crop failure or by extreme events such as drought and floods, given their limited capacity to adapt to changing climate.

Although climate change is not expected to reduce overall global food availability, it will impact crop production, the distribution of food crops, and food security and availability. In Australia, a long-running drought that has been partially attributed to climate change entered its seventh year in 2008, crippling the country's rice production,

[23] Ibid.

[24] Ibid.

[25] Statistics Canada. Statistics based on 2006 Canadian Census (www.statcan.gc.ca).

[26] D.S. Lemmen and F.J. Warren, *Climate Change Impact and Adaptation: A Canadian Perspective*. Ottawa: Climate Change Impacts and Adaptation Directorate, Natural Resources Canada, 2004.

[27] IPCC 4th Assessment Report, 2007 (www.ipcc.ch/index.htm).

[28] Ibid.

forcing farmers off the land, and contributing (along with other factors) to food riots in Haiti, Indonesia, Ivory Coast, Thailand, and other countries that depend on rice as a staple food.[29] Climate change alone is estimated to increase the number of malnourished between 40 and 170 million globally, with the majority located in sub-Saharan Africa.[30] In the face of declining crop yields, many developing countries will become increasingly dependent on food imports. Correspondingly, there will be increased pressure to cultivate marginal land or use unsustainable cultivation practices, which may lead to increased land degradation and reduced biodiversity. Ultimately, changes in crop yields and world food supply patterns raise questions regarding food security. These changes may be more pronounced if other resources such as cropland or water supplies are degraded or depleted. Adaptation of agricultural practices to compensate for climate change will be important.

—K.B.N.

[29] Keith Bradsher, "A Drought in Australia, a Global Shortage of Rice," *New York Times*, 17 April 2008, p. A4.
[30] Ibid.

soil degradation and denudation problems, agriculture affects water quality and quantity through the overwithdrawal of groundwater and the pollution of the same water through agricultural runoff contaminated with herbicides, pesticides, and fertilizers.

The nature–society relationship discussed in Chapter 4 is very much at the heart of agricultural practices. Yet, as agriculture has industrialized, the impacts of agriculture on the environment have multiplied and, in some parts of the globe, have reached the crisis stage. In some regions the agricultural system leads to overproduction of foodstuffs, but in other regions the quantity and quality of water and soil severely limit the ability of a region's people to feed themselves.

Limitations such as these are likely to become even more severe in the future if climate changes as experts predict, although it is possible that not all of the consequences for agriculture will be negative. In some parts of Canada, for example, crop production will probably increase as average temperatures rise; however, because it is also likely that the levels of plant diseases and pests will also increase, the overall effects on agricultural production are difficult to predict (see **Human Geography and Climate Change 8.4—Agriculture**).

8.4   Geography in the Information Age

In the 1980s, core environmental organizations, such as the World Wildlife Fund, offered peripheral countries a "debt-for-nature swap." In these swaps, the organization retired some part of the foreign debt of a peripheral country in exchange for the promise to implement a conservation program to save ecologically sensitive lands from abuse. This usually meant turning the land into a national park or extending the boundaries of an existing park. It turned out, however, that the swaps were not able to address the fundamental causes of environmental degradation in peripheral regions—including extreme poverty, government subsidies for forest clearing, and insecure land tenure. In the final analysis, people who do not have a secure food basis are simply forced to disregard the environment.

CONCLUSION

Agriculture has become a highly complex, globally integrated system. Although traditional forms of agricultural practices, such as subsistence farming, continue to exist, they have been overshadowed by the global industrialization of agriculture. This industrialization has included not only mechanization and chemical and biological modifications but also the linking of the agricultural sector to the manufacturing, service, and finance sectors of the economy. In addition, countries have become important players in the regulation and support of agriculture at all levels, from the local to the global.

The dramatic changes that have occurred in agriculture have affected different places and different social groups. Households in both the core and the periphery have strained to adjust to these changes, often disrupting existing patterns of authority and access to resources. Just as people have been affected by the transformations in global agriculture, so, too, have the land, air, and water.

The geography of agriculture today is a far cry from the way it was organized 100 or even 50 years ago. As the globalization of the economy has accelerated, so, too, has the globalization of agriculture. The future of the global food system is being shaped at this very moment in food science laboratories, in corporate boardrooms, on the street in organized protests, and in homely settlements throughout the world. The biggest issues food policy experts, national governments, consumers, and agriculturalists face revolve around the availability and quality of food in a world where access to safe, healthy, and nutritious foodstuffs is unevenly distributed. For the periphery, the most pressing concern is adequate food supplies to feed growing populations. For the core, there are concerns about food quality in a system that is increasingly industrialized and biologically engineered. Sometimes the solutions to one problem for one population become a new problem for another population.

MAIN POINTS REVISITED

- **Agriculture has been transformed into a globally integrated system; the changes producing this result have occurred at many scales and have originated from many sources.**

  In addition to the restructuring of entire national farming systems, farming households have been transformed as well in core, peripheral, and semiperipheral regions.

- **Agriculture has proceeded through three revolutionary phases, from the domestication of plants and animals, through the agricultural revolution of the mid-eighteenth century, to the latest developments in biotechnology and industrial innovation.**

  These three revolutionary phases have not occurred simultaneously throughout the globe but have been adopted and adapted to differing degrees based on levels of development, culture, and physical geography.

- **The increasing ability to manipulate nature has changed how humans view their environment and think about place.**

  With the development of agriculture, humans began their first sustained efforts to manipulate their environment as a resource. As agriculture developed, the sedentary life that farming required gave new meaning to the values people attached to place.

- **The introduction of new technologies, political concerns about food security and self-sufficiency, and changing opportunities for investment and employment are among the many forces that have dramatically shaped agriculture as we know it today.**

  Two of the most important forces behind these transformations in agriculture have been multinational and transnational corporations and states. The World Trade Organization is another important influence.

- **The industrialized agricultural system of today's world has developed from—and has largely displaced—older agricultural practices, including shifting cultivation, subsistence agriculture, and pastoralism.**

  Although these systems no longer dominate agricultural practices on a global scale, they are still practised in many areas of the world, in some cases alongside more mechanized forms.

- **Canadian agriculture, since European settlement began, has always been affected by international markets—first by those of the colonizing powers and later by world markets.**

  The globalization of trade and the rise of agribusiness is leading to the replacement in Canada of a national farming system based on the family farm, with a system of two production environments based on international exports in the Prairies and supply management elsewhere.

- **The contemporary agro-commodity system is organized around a chain of agribusiness components that begins at the farm and ends at the retail outlet. Various economic sectors, as well as various corporate forms, are involved in the globalization process.**

  No longer the centrepiece in this chain of agricultural organization, the farm is but one of several important components that includes seed and fertilizer manufacturers, food processors, food distributors, and consumers.

■ Transformations in agriculture have had dramatic impacts on the environment, including soil erosion, desertification, deforestation, and soil and water pollution, as well as the elimination of some plant and animal species.

Although most of the core countries have instituted legislation to address some of the problems associated with environmental degradation, these problems exist throughout the global agricultural system to greater and lesser degrees. In peripheral countries, where governments are often too poor to monitor and enforce such legislation, they are being encouraged by international agencies and environmental organizations to limit their degrading practices through relief of part of their national debt.

Key Terms

agrarian (p. 357)
agribusiness (p. 380)
agricultural industrialization (p. 373)
agriculture (p. 358)
biotechnology (p. 376)
chemical farming (p. 366)
commercial agriculture (p. 358)
food chain (p. 380)

food manufacturing (p. 366)
food regime (p. 380)
globalized agriculture (p. 379)
Green Revolution (p. 373)
hunting and gathering (p. 359)
intensive subsistence agriculture (p. 360)
mechanization (p. 366)

pastoralism (p. 361)
shifting cultivation (p. 359)
subsistence agriculture (p. 359)
swidden (p. 360)
transhumance (p. 362)

Additional Reading

Barndt, D. *Tangled Routes: Women, Work and Globalization on the Tomato Trail.* Aurora, ON: Garamond Press, 2002.

Bonanno, A., L. Busch, W.H. Friedland, L. Gouveia, and E. Minzone (eds.). *From Columbus to ConAgra: The Globalization of Agriculture and Food.* Lawrence, KS: University of Kansas Press, 1994.

Boserup, E. *The Conditions of Agricultural Growth: The Economics of Agrarian Change under Population Pressure.* Chicago: Aldine, 1965.

Brody, H. *The Other Side of Eden: Hunters, Farmers and the Shaping of the World.* Vancouver and Toronto: Douglas and McIntyre, 2000.

Found, W.C. "Agriculture in a World of Subsidies." In J.N.H. Britton (ed.), *Canada and the Global Economy: The Geography of Structural and Technological Change.* Montreal and Kingston: McGill-Queen's University Press, 1996, 155–168.

Friesen, G. *The West: Regional Ambitions, National Debates, Global Age.* Toronto: Penguin Canada, 1999.

Goodman, D., and M. Redclift. *The International Farm Crisis.* London: Macmillan, 1989.

Goodman, D., and M. Watts. *Globalising Food: Agrarian Questions and Global Restructuring.* London: Routledge Press, 1997.

Grigg, D.B. *The Agricultural Systems of the World: An Evolutionary Approach.* Cambridge and New York: Cambridge University Press, 1974.

Halweil, B. "Farming in the Public Interest." In C. Flavin, H. French, and G. Gardner (eds.), *State of the World 2002.* New York: W.W. Norton and Company, 2002, 50–74.

Harrison, P. *The Greening of Africa.* London: Paladin Grafton Books, 1987.

Hecht, S., and A. Cockburn. *The Fate of the Forest: Developers, Destroyers and Defenders of the Amazon.* London: Verso, 1989.

Heidenreich, C., and J.V. Wright. "Native Population and Subsistence: Seventeenth Century." In W. Dean, C. Heidenreich, T. McIlwraith, and J. Warkentin (eds.), *Concise Historical Atlas of Canada.* Toronto: University of Toronto Press, 1998, Plate 3.

Heintzman, A., and E. Solomon (eds.). *Feeding the Future: From Fat to Famine: How to Solve the World's Food Crises.* Toronto: House of Anansi Press, 2004.

Hewitt de Alcantara, C. "The Green Revolution as History: The Mexican Experience," *Development and Change* 4(5), 1973, 25–44.

Hobbelink, H. *Biotechnology and the Future of World Agriculture.* London: Zed Books Limited, 1991.

Kloppenburg, J.R., Jr. *First the Seed: The Political Economy of Plant Biotechnology 1492–2000.* Cambridge, England: Cambridge University Press, 1988.

Le Heron, R. *Globalized Agriculture: Political Choice.* Oxford: Pergamon Press, 1993.

McRae, T., C.A.S. Smith, and L.J. Gregorich (eds.). *Environmental Sustainability of Canadian Agriculture: Report of the Agri Environmental Indicator Project. A Summary.* Ottawa: Agriculture and Agri-Food Canada, 2000. (Electronic version available at www.agr.ca/policy/environment/.)

Momsen, J.H. *Women and Development in the Third World.* London and New York: Routledge, 1991.

Pearson, C., and J. Masby. *The Cultivated Landscape: An Exploration of Art and Agriculture.* Montreal and Kingston: McGill-Queen's University Press, 2008.

Persley, G. *Beyond Mendel's Garden: Biotechnology in the Service of World Agriculture.* Wallingford, CT: CAB International, 1990.

Poppendieck, J. *Sweet Charity? Emergency Food and the End of Entitlement.* New York: Viking Press, 1998.

Silversides, B.V. *Prairie Sentinel: The Story of the Canadian Grain Elevator.* Calgary: Fifth House, 1997.

Snow, D.R. "The First Americans and the Differentiation of Hunter-Gatherer Cultures." In B.G. Trigger and W.E. Washburn (eds.), *The Cambridge History of the Native Peoples of the Americas. Volume 1: North America, Part 1.* Cambridge: Cambridge University Press, 1996, 125–199.

Spooner, B. (ed.). *Population Growth: Anthropological Implications.* Cambridge, MA: MIT Press, 1972.

Troper, H. *Only Farmers Need Apply: Official Canadian Government Encouragement of Immigration from the United States, 1896–1911.* Toronto: Griffin House, 1972.

Troughton, M. *Canadian Agriculture.* Budapest: Hungarian Academy of Sciences, 1982.

Vogeler, I. *The Myth of the Family Farm: Agribusiness Dominance of U.S. Agriculture.* Boulder, CO: Westview Press, 1981.

Waithe, D., M. Zafiriou, and D. Niekamp. *Income Inequality in Canada Farm versus Non-Farm Families, 1985–1995.* Ottawa: Agriculture and Agri-Food Canada, 2000.

Wallace, I. *A Geography of the Canadian Economy.* Don Mills, ON: Oxford University Press, 2002.

Discussion Questions and Research Activities

1. Your neighbourhood grocery store is a perfect location to begin to identify the "global" in the globalization of agriculture. Go to the produce section there, document the source of at least 10 fruits and vegetables you find, and illustrate those sources on a world map. Why do you think stores are required to list the provenance of the produce along with the price?

2. The Food and Agriculture Organization (FAO) publishes a range of yearbooks containing statistical data on many aspects of global food production since the mid-1950s. Using the State of Food and Agricultural Production yearbooks, compare the changes that have occurred in agricultural production between the core and the periphery since the mid-twentieth century. You can use just two yearbooks for this exercise, or you may want to use several to get a better sense of when and where the most significant changes have occurred. Once you have identified where the changes have been most significant, try to explain why these changes may have occurred.

3. Your breakfast is the result of the activities of a whole chain of producers, processors, distributors, and retailers whose interactions provide insights into both the globalization of food production and the industrialization of agriculture. Consider the various foods you consume in a typical breakfast, and describe where and by whom they were produced (grown and processed), how they were transported (by whom) from the processing site, and where and by whom they were retailed. Summarize how the various components of your breakfast illustrate the two concepts of globalization and the industrialization of agriculture.

4. The vast majority of Canadians are, as we have seen, not involved with farming activities. How has this separation from agriculture affected how we think about farming, rural life, and nature? Are we realistic or nostalgic?

MyGeosciencePlace

Visit **www.mygeoscienceplace.ca** to find chapter review quizzes, videos, maps, and much more.

9

The Politics of Territory and Space

Beginning after World War II in Europe, the "twinning" of towns and cities provided one way to promote peace and understanding among once-warring countries of that continent. In this example, the small town of Menaggio in northern Italy is twinned with places of equivalent population size in France, Germany, and Brazil, illustrating how twinning is now becoming a worldwide phenomenon.

Even though globalization has made the world a more interconnected whole, it is important to remember that globalization does not necessarily supersede national interests. Canada, for example, although it has benefited economically from its role as part of the global core and its membership in continental pacts such as the North American Free Trade Agreement (NAFTA), nevertheless has expressed its misgivings over the loss of national sovereignty that such arrangements bring with them. Recent events, post 9/11, have also highlighted these contradictions. On the one hand, Canada may benefit from being part of the U.S. global "security umbrella," but, on the other hand, its citizens are thereby subject to a much wider surveillance than before (for example, the new practice of granting American agencies access to Canadian airline passenger lists).

At another scale, at the level of Canadian interests, the possible separation of Quebec has fuelled the growth of federal and provincial political parties dedicated to bringing about the independence of that province and referenda that (in one case) came close to achieving a majority vote for separation from Canada. The desire for independence has not diminished as the world economy has become more integrated. In fact, in some ways, the more obvious presence of that outside world in the day-to-day lives of Quebec's residents could be said to make them more alert to pressures of globalization and therefore more eager to break up the map of Canada to protect their political identity.

As this chapter demonstrates, globalization continues to create new maps; at the same time, established boundaries persist. Exploration, imperialism, colonization, decolonization, and the cold war between East and West are powerful forces that have created national boundaries as well as redrawn them. Much of the political strife that currently grips the globe involves local or regional responses to the impacts of globalization of the economy, aided by the practices of the state. The complex relationships between politics and geography—both human and physical—are two-way relationships. In addition, political geography is not just about global or international relationships. It is also about many other geographic scales and political divisions, from the globe to the neighbourhood, from large, far-reaching processes to the familiar sites of our everyday lives.

MAIN POINTS

- A subfield of the discipline of geography, political geography examines complex relationships between politics and geography (both human and physical).
- Political geographers recognize that the relationship between politics and geography is two-way: political geography can be seen both as the geography of politics and as the politics of geography.

- The relationship between politics and geography is often driven by particular theories and practices of the world's states. Understanding nation-state imperialism, colonialism, and geopolitical theory is key to comprehending how, within the context of the world-system, geography has influenced politics and how politics has influenced geography.

- Political geography deals with phenomena occurring at all scales from the global to the household. Important East–West and North–South divisions dominate international politics, whereas regionalism and similar divisions dominate intra-state politics.

- Political geography recognizes the importance of the environment. Global change and population growth both make it likely that increased competition for future resources will also involve political conflict.

THE DEVELOPMENT OF POLITICAL GEOGRAPHY

Political geography is a long-established subfield in the wider discipline of geography. Aristotle is often taken to be the first political geographer because his model of the state is based on such factors as climate, terrain, and the relationship between population and territory. Other important political geographers—from Strabo to Montesquieu—have promoted theories of the state that incorporated elements of the landscape and the physical environment, as well as the population characteristics of regions. From about the fourteenth through the nineteenth century, scholars interested in political geography theorized that states consolidated and fragmented in response to complex relationships between factors such as population size and composition, agricultural productivity, land area, and the role of the city.

As these factors indicate, political geography at the end of the nineteenth century was influenced by two important traditions within the wider discipline of geography, the people–land tradition and environmental determinism, although different theorists placed more or less emphasis on each of these traditions in their own political geographical formulations. Undoubtedly, the widespread influence of Charles Darwin on intellectual and social life during this period is part of the reason why these factors were identified as central. Darwin's theory of competition inspired political geographers to conceptualize the state as a kind of biological organism that grew and contracted in response to external factors and forces. It was also during the late nineteenth century that foreign policy as a focus of state activity began to be theorized. This new emphasis is called *geopolitics*.

The Geopolitical Model of the State

geopolitics: the state's power to control space or territory and shape the foreign policy of individual states and international political relations

Geopolitics is the state's power to control space or territory and shape the foreign policy of individual states and international political relations. In Germany, geopolitical theory was influenced by Friedrich Ratzel (1844–1904), a geographer trained in biology and chemistry. Ratzel employed biological metaphors, which he adopted from the work of Charles Darwin, to describe the growth and development of the state and formulate his seven laws of state growth:

1. The territory of the state grows with the expansion of the population having the same culture.

2. Territorial growth follows other aspects of development.

3. A state grows by absorbing smaller units.

4. The frontier is the peripheral organ of the state that reflects the strength and growth of the state; hence it is not permanent.

5. States in the course of their growth seek to absorb politically valuable territory.

6. The impetus for growth comes to a primitive state from a more highly developed civilization.

7. The trend toward territorial growth is contagious and increases in the process of transmission.[1]

Ratzel's model portrays the state as behaving like a biological organism: its growth and change are seen as "natural" and inevitable. This organic view of the state has been abandoned since Ratzel advanced his model more than a hundred years ago, but the twin features of power and territory still lie at the heart of political geography—and geopolitics still is one of the cornerstones of twenty-first-century political geography and state foreign policy more generally. In fact, the changes that have occurred in Europe and the former Soviet Union suggest that Ratzel's most important insights about geopolitics are still valid.

Figure 9.1 illustrates Ratzel's conceptualization of the interaction of power and territory through the changing map of Europe from the end of World War I to the present. The fluidity of the maps reflects the instability between power and territory, especially some states' failure to achieve permanence. The most recent map of Europe is a reflection of the precariousness of nation-state boundaries in the post–cold war period. In fact, the 2008 map of Europe has more in common with the 1924 map than with the 1989 map. Estonia, Latvia, and Lithuania have reappeared after decades of forced integration into the Soviet Union. Czechoslovakia has split into the Czech Republic and Slovakia. The former Soviet Union is now the Commonwealth of Independent States, with Russia the largest and most powerful. Yugoslavia has dissolved into several states, but not without much civil strife and loss of life. In fact, the difference between Europe in 1989 and Europe now is far more dramatic than the difference between any other two maps from the previous 50 years.

9.1 Geography in the Information Age

The former Yugoslavia illustrates that these changes are still unfolding: between the last edition of this book and the current one, the number of successor states to the former Yugoslavia increased from five to seven!

Boundaries

Boundaries are important phenomena because they allow territoriality to be defined and enforced and because they allow conflict and competition to be managed and channelled. The creation of boundaries is, therefore, an important element in place making. It follows from the concept of territoriality that boundaries are normally inclusionary (**Figure 9.2**). That is, they are constructed in order to regulate and control specific sets of people and resources *within* those boundaries. Encompassed within a clearly defined territory, all sorts of activity can be controlled and regulated—everything, in fact, from birth to taxes to death. The delimited area over which a state exercises control and that is recognized by other states is called **territory**. Such an area may include both land and water.

territory: the delimited area over which a state exercises control and that is recognized by other states

---

[1] Adapted from Martin I. Glassner and Harm de Blij, *Systematic Political Geography*, 3rd ed. New York: J. Wiley & Sons, 1980, p. 164.

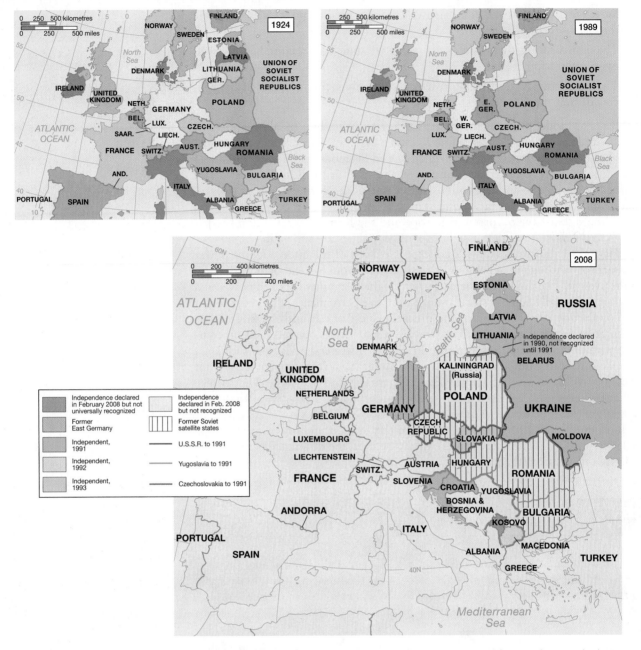

Figure 9.1 The changing map of Europe: 1924, 1989, and 2008 The boundaries of the European states have undergone dramatic changes since World War I. The changing map of Europe illustrates the instability of international politics and the resultant dynamism in the geography of the nation-state system. (*Source:* **http://europa.eu/abc/maps/index_en.htm**. Reprinted with permission from Prentice Hall, from J.M. Rubenstein, *The Cultural Landscape: An Introduction to Human Geography,* 5th ed., © 1996, p. 338.)

Boundaries can also be exclusionary, however, in that they control the flow of people and resources *across* those boundaries. National boundaries, for example, can be used to control the flow of immigrants or the flow of imported goods into the territory (**Figure 9.3**). Municipal boundaries and land-use zoning boundaries can be used to regulate access to upscale residential neighbourhoods, field boundaries can be used to regulate access to pasture, and so on (**Figure 9.4**).

Boundaries can be established in many different ways and with differing degrees of permeability. At one extreme are informal, implied boundaries that are set by markers and symbols but never delineated on maps or set down in legal documents. A good example is the range of a pastoral tribe, or the turf of a city gang marked by graffiti (**Figure 9.5**). At the other extreme are formal boundaries

Figure 9.2 Boundary between Canada and the United States Most boundaries are established to regulate and control specific sets of people and resources within a given territory. Such boundaries need to be clearly identified but do not necessarily need to be fortified. This photograph shows part of the Canada–United States border, a good example of an inclusionary boundary. To an extent, heightened border controls since the events of September 11, 2001, have made the Canada–United States border more like an exclusionary border.

Figure 9.3 Boundary between the United States and Mexico Some boundaries are designed to be exclusionary. The United States–Mexico border is heavily patrolled and lined with barbed-wire chain-link fences along the highly urbanized parts, and aerial surveillance is extensive. In an effort to stem the flow of illegal immigration and narcotics from Mexico, the U.S. government increased the Border Patrol from 5,176 officers in 1996 to 10,000 in 2000 and to more than 20,000 in 2010. This photo shows the United States–Mexico border along the Tijuana River estuary, with Southern California on the left and Mexico on the right.

Figure 9.4 A stone wall in Derbyshire, England Some boundaries, such as this stone wall in Derbyshire, England, contribute significantly to the character of places and regions. In a modern world of featureless agricultural landscapes, traditional field boundaries like these have become potent symbols of regional identity, visible links with past landscapes and past ways of life.

Figure 9.5 Graffiti on walls A frequent sight in most cities, graffiti often serves as a territorial marker.

established in international law, delimited on maps, demarcated on the ground, fortified, and aggressively defended—not only against the movement of people but also of goods, money, and even ideas. An extreme example is the boundary between North and South Korea (**Figure 9.6**). In between the two extremes are formal boundaries that have varying degrees of permeability. The boundaries

Figure 9.6 Border between North and South Korea Some boundaries are virtually impermeable. The border between North and South Korea is highly fortified and heavily patrolled. It was established at the conclusion of the Korean War (1950–1953) between two states that still contest each other's territory. Although occasional talks between the two countries have been held in recent years to declare that war officially over, recent exchanges of heated words and even artillery fire serve as a reminder that this boundary is still very much a disputed one.

Figure 9.7 Berlin Wall The boundary between East and West Germany was virtually impermeable for more than 40 years. This photograph shows the scene on November 12, 1989, when Berliners tore the wall down in celebration of the reunification of Germany.

between the states of the European Union, for example, have become quite permeable as people and goods from member states can now move freely between them.

Impermeability does not necessarily mean immutability, however. The boundary between East and West Germany, part of the "Iron Curtain" for more than 40 years, was as aggressively defended as the present boundary between North and South Korea, and yet it was removed in 1989 when Germany was reunified (**Figure 9.7**). Similarly, the boundaries of the former Soviet Union have been entirely redrawn since 1989, allowing states such as Lithuania, Latvia, and Estonia to reconstitute (see Figure 9.1 on p. 398).

9.2 Geography in the Information Age

Increasingly, boundaries can also be established and secured (as well as attacked!) virtually, through the application of technology. Some states have begun to institute a wide range of practices to secure their borders by electronically screening and assessing those who can cross them. By way of passports that contain RFID (radio frequency identification) chips, as well as retinal scanning, face recognition, and related biometrics (electronic technologies for recognizing an individual based on one or more physical or behavioural traits), state agencies collect and analyze more and more detailed personal information about travellers than ever before. On the basis of that information, risk profiles can be compiled and decisions about permitting border crossings can be largely automated.

Figure 9.8 Straight boundaries A nineteenth-century survey team determined the position of the Canada–U.S. border in southern Manitoba.

Boundary Formation   Generally speaking, formal boundaries tend first to follow natural barriers, such as rivers, mountain ranges, and oceans. Good examples of countries with important mountain-range boundaries include France with Spain (the Pyrenees), and Italy with France, Switzerland, and Austria (the Alps), where the border more or less follows the mountain ridges. Examples of countries with boundaries formed by rivers include China and North Korea (the Yalu Tumen), Laos and Thailand (the Mekong), and Zambia and Zimbabwe (the Zambezi). Similarly, major lakes divide Canada and the United States (along the Great Lakes), France and Switzerland (Lake Geneva), and Kenya and Uganda (Lake Victoria).

9.3   Geography in the Information Age

Sometimes the use of geographical features such as mountain ridges to draw international boundaries can lead to extreme shapes: the territory of Chile, for example, is constrained by the Andes to a very long and thin strip along the Pacific coast, extending over 4,000 kilometres north-south, but on average less than 200 kilometres east-west. This poses numerous challenges in terms of governance, infrastructure, transportation, and communication.

Where no natural features occur, formal boundaries tend to be fixed along the easiest and most practical cartographic device—a straight line. Examples include the western part of the boundary between Canada and the United States (**Figure 9.8**). Straight-line boundaries are also characteristic of formal boundaries that are established through colonization, which is the outcome of a particular form of territoriality. The reason, once again, is practicality. Straight lines were easy to survey and even easier to delimit on maps of territory that had not yet been fully charted, claimed, and settled by Europeans. Straight-line boundaries were established, for example, in many parts of Africa during European colonization in the nineteenth century (see Chapter 2 and Figure 9.16 on p. 410).

Another example is the pattern of townships employed by early surveyors in the mapping and division of land in Canada. According to the *Historical Atlas of Canada,* the first township survey was for Cataraqui Township, just west of Kingston (Ontario), which was completed on October 27, 1783. The system was used across large parts of Ontario and Quebec, where townships were laid out in a chessboard pattern: a typical township being 16 square kilometres and subdivided into *lots* and *concessions*. In western Canada, where settlement occurred later, the township was a square unit of land, 10 kilometres a side, divided into 36 *sections*—each of which was then divided into four *quarter-sections* of 160 acres each (64 hectares). With this rectilinear (that is, linear and rectangular) pattern of land ownership, it also made sense for the boundaries of larger administrative areas—counties and provinces—to be equally rectilinear.

In detail, however, formal boundaries often detour from straight lines and natural barriers to accommodate special needs and claims. Colombia's border, for instance, was established to contain the source of the river Orinoco; Democratic Republic of Congo's border was established to provide a corridor of access to the Atlantic Ocean; and Sudan's border detours to include a settlement, Wadi Halfa.

After primary divisions have been established, internal boundaries tend to evolve as smaller, secondary territories are demarcated. In general, the higher the population density, the smaller these secondary units tend to be. Their configuration tends to follow the same generalizations as for larger units, following physical features, accommodating special needs, and following straight lines where there are no appropriate natural features or where colonization has made straight lines expedient (**Figure 9.9**).

Territories delimited by formal boundaries—nation-states, states, counties, municipalities, special districts, and so on—are known as *de jure* spaces or regions. *De jure* simply means "legally recognized." Historically, the world has evolved from a loose patchwork of territories (with few formally defined or delimited boundaries) to nested hierarchies (**Figure 9.10**) and overlapping systems of de jure territories.

These de jure territories are often used as the basic units of analysis in human geography, largely because they are both convenient and significant units of analysis. They are often, in fact, the only areal units for which reliable data are available. They are also important units of analysis in their own right because of their importance as units of governance or administration. Much regional analysis and nearly all attempts at regionalization, therefore, are based on a framework of de jure spaces.

(a)

(b)

Figure 9.9 Rectilinear boundaries Many of the boundaries between properties and administrative units found across Canada do not follow natural features but are rectilinear. The consequence of surveying techniques used during colonization, these boundaries impose an ordered look on the landscape. The illustrations show boundaries in (a) Alexandria, Ontario, and (b) the Dirt Hills near Kayville, Saskatchewan.

Figure 9.10   Nested hierarchy of de jure territories   De jure territories are constructed at various spatial scales, depending on their origin and function. Administrative and governmental territories are often "nested," with one set of territories fitting within the larger framework of another, as in this example of states, districts, and municipalities in India.

GEOPOLITICS AND THE WORLD ORDER

Arguably, there is no other concept to which political geographers devote more attention than the state. The state is also one of the most powerful institutions—if not the most powerful institution—involved in the process of globalization as it effectively regulates, supports, and legitimates the globalization of the economy.

States and Nations

As described in Chapter 2, the state is an independent political unit with recognized boundaries, even if some of these boundaries may be in dispute. In contrast to a state, a **nation** is a group of people often sharing common elements of culture, such as religion or language, or a history or political identity. Members of a nation recognize a common identity, but they need not reside within a common geographical area. For example, the Jewish nation refers to members of the Jewish culture and faith throughout the world regardless of their place of origin or residence. The term **nation-state** refers to an ideal form consisting of a homogeneous group of people governed by their own state. Thus, in a true nation-state, all people residing in the state belong to the same nation. **Sovereignty** is the exercise of state power over people and territory, recognized by other states and codified by international law.

The idea of the nation-state as a sovereign body controlling space is actually quite a recent idea. Before it arose in eighteenth-century Europe, individual

nation: a group of people often sharing common elements of culture, such as religion or language, or a history or political identity

nation-state: an ideal form consisting of a homogeneous group of people governed by their own state

sovereignty: the exercise of state power over people and territory, recognized by other states and codified by international law

9.4 Geography in the Information Age

Not all territory is defined by boundaries: *frontier regions* are zones of underdeveloped territoriality, areas that are distinctive for their marginality rather than for their belonging. In the nineteenth century, vast frontier regions still existed—major geographic realms that had not yet been conquered, explored, and settled (such as Australia, the American West, the Canadian North, and sub-Saharan Africa). All of these are now largely settled, with boundaries set at a range of jurisdictional levels from individual land ownership to local and national governmental borders. Only Antarctica, virtually unsettled, exists today as a frontier region in this strict sense of the term. Some geographers now see outer space and cyberspace as frontier regions.

rulers forged kingdoms out of groups of followers by offering gifts of land or treasure in return for their military service. The key point here is that an individual's loyalty was to a *person* (the king) not to a physical entity or *space* (the state). From the point of view of political geography, this had two important consequences:

- *A kingdom need not be a unitary whole*, but could be made up of a number of discontinuous parts. The best illustration is the Holy Roman Empire, a powerful political entity ruled by the Holy Roman Emperor during the Middle Ages. At its height, the Empire included large parts of present-day Germany, central Europe, and northern Italy. However, there were many enclaves totally surrounded by the Empire that were not part of the Emperor's domain, and there were parts of the Empire that were outliers from the main part of the Empire.

- *Sovereignty was vested in the ruler's person*. In many medieval countries, the ruler continually travelled around. Wherever he or she was situated, there was the seat of government for the time being. Because, as we have noted, all power flowed from the ruler, or sovereign (the root of the concept of *sovereignty*, of course), the principle developed that power was inherited through royal family lines. Power then became embedded in a few aristocratic families, not in space and certainly not in the people over whom they ruled.

9.5 Geography in the Information Age

As we saw in Chapter 7, the state still is the primary unit of organization for the global economy; in fact, world trade is defined as flows of goods and services between countries, as the words *import* and *export* indicate: they imply the crossing of international boundaries. Recently, however, an increasing amount of world trade is conducted among branches of the same transnational corporations spanning several states, which has all kinds of implications. For example, if an American car maker receives profits from its Canadian operations, where should this profit be taxed? Or, conversely, should the car maker be able to use a financial loss in Canada to offset high profits in the United States and thus lower its taxes payable in the United States?

This arrangement of power persisted until the **Enlightenment**, a major shift in philosophical outlook that occurred in Europe in the eighteenth century. Two events in particular sparked major changes. The American Declaration of Independence (1776) and the French Revolution (1789) both took power from the ruler and transferred it to *the people*. Once power was decoupled from the ruler and vested in the people, a link was soon forged between the area that those people inhabited and the space in which they exercised their sovereign power. In this way, the two concepts of space (state) and people (nation) began to fuse, and the *nation-state* became the most important model for state formation.

In the nineteenth century, because space (the state) was now the only way of defining those people who had sovereignty (the nation), the legitimacy of the nation-state depended on achieving as close a correlation as possible between the two concepts of nation and state. In other words: the spatial extent of the state's territory and the nation's area of settlement had to overlap as much as possible. We can use a simple generalization (or model) to help us understand the two main ways by which the nation-state could achieve that goal (**Figure 9.11**). The first was to ensure, through various means, that all of the people included within the existing boundaries of the state were of the same nation, and to exclude or remove those who were defined as non-members of that particular nation. The second method was to adjust the state's spatial boundaries to encompass all members of the nation, even if they lived outside the present boundaries—obviously a process that often led to the breakup and reconfiguration of states.

To use the more technical terms that political geographers have developed, the rulers of the nineteenth-century nation-states promoted a unified nation using **centripetal forces** to hold the state together. Centripetal forces are those that strengthen and unify the state. The alternative was to witness **centrifugal forces** break the state apart. Centrifugal forces are those that divide or tend to pull apart the state. Centripetal and centrifugal forces employ the same cultural, economic, and political means, but to opposite ends. For instance, newspapers can be used either to cultivate national unity (centripetal effect) or support separatist movements (centrifugal effect).

Let us now look more closely at two of the main strategies that the nineteenth-century nation-state used to establish its political dominance—nationalism and territorial manipulation.

Nationalism   Despite the fact that concepts of *nation, people, folk, race,* and *ethnic group* are all socially constructed, it was crucial for the proponents of the nation-state to believe that their particular *nation* of people developed as a group in a particular place from which they derived an identity and whose identity they now shaped. **Nationalism** is the feeling of belonging to a nation, as well as the belief that a nation has a natural right to determine its own affairs.

To take historic examples, people who lived in eighteenth- and nineteenth-century England (in actuality, a tremendous mixture of peoples of Celtic, Germanic, Scandinavian, and French origin) came to see themselves as the "English race." They believed they had a unique set of traditions, customs, history, language, and—at least according to some—certain distinctive natural abilities. The French of this period saw themselves as the "French race," defined in similar terms, and both the

Enlightenment: an eighteenth-century European movement that sought to replace ideas of authority or explanation drawn from God with those that individual humans could establish through their own reason

centripetal forces: forces that integrate the state

centrifugal forces: forces that can lead to the disintegration of the state

nationalism: the feeling of belonging to a nation as well as the belief that a nation has a natural right to determine its own affairs

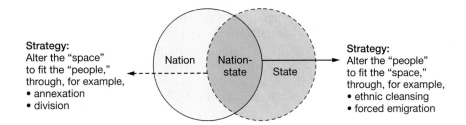

Strategy:
Alter the "space" to fit the "people," through, for example,
• annexation
• division

Strategy:
Alter the "people" to fit the "space," through, for example,
• ethnic cleansing
• forced emigration

Figure 9.11 The nation-state This illustration shows how the nation-state is the product of two different geographical processes. The first attempts to mould the people to the state; the second manipulates the boundaries of the state to fit the space occupied by the people.

French and the English agreed they were from different races. Importantly, both also agreed that the indigenous peoples in their colonies were from different races, and nineteenth-century environmental determinism only served to exaggerate such racist views. The colonized peoples were assigned an inferior status, which denied them the ability and the right to govern their own affairs.

Unfortunately, such practices were by no means confined to the early development of the nation-state. In Germany, the Nazi obsession with purging the country of "non-Aryan" peoples led to the killing of millions of Jews and large numbers of other groups (including Roma, Poles, Ukrainians, and homosexuals) as Germany expanded its borders in the 1930s and 1940s. Horrifically, such practices returned to Europe in the 1990s when Serbia, under nationalist leader Slobodan Milosevic, carried out a concerted policy of "ethnic cleansing" against Muslims in Bosnia and ethnic Albanians in Kosovo. In Africa, the genocide from 1994 to 1995 in Rwanda was an outcome of nineteenth-century colonialism, which originally sowed the seeds of animosity between the Tutsi and the Hutu. In each of these cases, the myth of unique nationhood was perpetuated to justify such atrocities.

It is fascinating—and sometimes deeply disturbing—to see that the means by which many of these myths of nationality were achieved are fundamentally geographical, for they built on many of the place-making activities we have examined in this book. Indeed, since place making is such a powerful aspect of nationalism, we should, on reflection, not be surprised by its importance.

Regional patterns of vernacular house types, folk customs, songs, languages, cuisine, and accents are all pressed into service by nationalists to stamp a land with a particular identity and to use that identity as an indicator of a unique nationality. Even more obvious attempts at claiming a land involve deliberately draping the country with national emblems, such as the country's flag, or building elaborate monuments to enshrine ideas of nationhood. Often such monuments are built right over those established by the nation formerly in control of the territory. For example, Mount Rushmore, a mountain sacred to the Sioux, has been carved into an icon of the nation that has literally "taken" its place.

Of course, we should not be surprised to find this in the United States with its "melting-pot" approach to forging a country from very disparate immigrant communities, an approach that seeks to assimilate people by eliminating cultural differences. By contrast, the Canadian policies of multiculturalism and official bilingualism seek to protect cultural differences between immigrant groups, even to the point of making the recognition of difference itself a hallmark of being Canadian.

British historians Eric Hobsbawm and Terence Ranger have shown, in their study of the creation of nineteenth-century nationalism, that it hardly matters that many of the "unique" traditions used to advance the cause of nationalism are, in fact, myths—as long as we can all agree that these symbols do work to pull people together as a nation. As political scientist Benedict Anderson has argued, a nation is an **imagined community**: we cannot meet everyone in our country, nor will we ever see all of its space; nevertheless, we have no difficulty conceiving of it as a nation because we can imagine it as a group of people mutually bound by shared symbols. Interestingly, as Edward Said (a scholar known for his writings on cultural studies) has shown, we are equally able to use these powers of imagination to construct stereotypes of other nations and to believe firmly in the validity of these invented stereotypes, even if the facts show them to be false.

imagined community: a group of people who believe that they share a common bond and thus are part of the same nation

Fortunately, Canada has been spared the full force of attempts to forge a nation-state within its borders. Yet, we cannot ignore the efforts that were made in the past, some of which leave behind a bitter taste indeed. For example, the banning of Aboriginal languages and the removal of Aboriginal children to residential schools across the Prairies were part of a deliberate attempt to assimilate Canada's indigenous peoples into the Canadian state that lasted well into the

Figure 9.12   Residential schools Residential schools were established by the federal government to assimilate the Aboriginal population through Western education. Management and control of Blue Quills First Nations College, a former residential school pictured here, were assumed by the Aboriginal people in the region in 1971.

second half of the twentieth century (**Figure 9.12**). Similarly, in 1934 and again in 1953, the Canadian government used Aboriginal people to claim sovereignty in the High Arctic when it resettled Inuit communities to the "empty" far north, where they faced ecological conditions for which they were not prepared. The deportation of the Acadians from Nova Scotia in the eighteenth century and the internment of Japanese Canadians in British Columbia's interior in the 1940s were both carried out because of questions over loyalty to the Canadian state (**Figure 9.13**). Our immigration policy, until 1967, was based on overt government racism. Only since the abandonment of that policy, and the official commitment to a policy of multiculturalism in the years that followed, can we truly see Canada as a country that has relinquished the concept of the nation-state as a model for its development.

Nor should we think that the use of the place-making tools of nationalism has been neglected in this country. The so-called Sponsorship Scandal, which led to the establishment of the Gomery Inquiry in 2004, has highlighted the federal

Figure 9.13   Japanese internment camp, New Denver, British Columbia Established during World War II, the internment camp at New Denver was the destination for hundreds of Japanese Canadians who were deported from Vancouver (see Figure 1.6.3). The Nikkei Internment Memorial Centre now stands on the site.

Figure 9.14 The St. Jean Baptiste parade, Montreal

government's program to promote national unity in Quebec through advertising and the use of the federal flag. And if we look to the other side of this divide, as part of the ongoing project of Quebec separation, we see the attempt to create the idea of a Québécois people as a "nation" that has inhabited the land of Quebec since the beginning of the seventeenth century. This endeavour to forge a nation-state uses all of the place-making and cultural devices at its disposal—Québécois folk music, architecture, and heritage have all been vigorously promoted, as has the use of the Quebec flag, the *fleur-de-lys* (**Figure 9.14**). But of all the means by which the nationalist project is advanced in Quebec, none has been more success-ful (or disliked by its detractors) than the insistence that French is the official lan-guage of the province. French is the language of the schools, of government, and of road and store signs. English-language store signs are the targets of graffiti artists and the Office québécois de la langue française (see Chapter 5). Increasingly, in fact, the attempt to create a nation has overtly shifted from an exclusionary focus on those descended from the original French settlers of the province to a more broadly based "cultural nationalism" that embraces anyone sympathetic to its aims.

Territorial Manipulation   The second approach to forging a nation-state has been to adjust the physical boundaries of the state to encompass all the people thought to comprise the nation. Historical examples include the violent expansion of Germany in the years prior to World War II, as it tried to incorporate all of the lands occupied by German-speaking peoples in central Europe into a greater Germany. This involved annexing Austria and claiming German-speaking parts of Czechoslovakia, Poland, Belgium, and France—and ultimately led to war. An-other example is found in the history of Europe's colonization of Africa. Because the nation-state was the model of political geography prevalent at the time when the global core of the world-system was exerting its dominance over the periphery in Africa, the colonizing powers imposed a framework of nation-states on that continent. The problem was that because the imperialists had little understand-ing of the societies they had subdued and—as we have seen—ideas of "nation" are imaginary, the framework was entirely an artificial one. Once decoloniza-tion occurred, the logic of the system fell apart. In fact, the imposed boundaries themselves have become the focus of a large number of conflicts in Africa. Largely being fought in the Democratic Republic of the Congo, the current wars in cen-tral Africa that involve the armies of nine states are a direct consequence of the way in which boundaries were imposed on that region over a century ago.

  The manipulation of boundaries to produce nation-states sometimes has resulted in the breakup of larger entities to form smaller units, the division being made on "ethnic" grounds. For example, the breakup of the large Ottoman and

Austrian "multicultural" empires following World War I led to the creation of much of the political geography of today's Middle East and southeastern Europe, with the creation of such countries as Hungary, Romania, Turkey, Syria, Iraq, and Lebanon. The failure of the victorious powers to accommodate the Kurds, the Jews, and the Palestinians with their own states at that time has led directly to many geopolitical conflicts that continue to vex the international community to this day. The process of decolonization also brought about division on occasion, the best example being the creation of Pakistan as a separate Islamic state when the Indian subcontinent achieved independence from Britain in 1947.

Imperialism, Colonialism, and the North–South Divide

Geopolitics may involve extension of power by one group over another. Two ways in which this is achieved are the interrelated processes of colonialism and imperialism. As we discussed in Chapter 1, imperialism is the extension of state authority over the political and economic life of other territories. Imperialism does not necessarily imply formal governmental control over the dominated area; it can also involve processes by which some countries pressure the independent governments of other countries to behave in certain ways. This pressure may take many forms, such as military threat, economic sanctions, ecological imperialism, or cultural domination (see Chapters 2 and 5).

As Chapter 2 described, over the last 500 years, imperialism has resulted in the political, economic, cultural, and even environmental domination of strong core states over the weaker states of the periphery. Geographers have historically played very central roles in the imperialist efforts of European states. In fact, organizations like the Royal Geographical Societies in England and Scotland were explicitly formed to aid in the expansionary efforts of their home countries. The process of imperialism begins with exploration (**Figure 9.15**), often prompted by a state's perception that a critical natural resource is lacking within its own boundaries. Most, if not all, of the early geographical expeditions undertaken by Europeans were intended to evaluate the possibilities for resource extraction, colonization, and the expansion of empire. Geographers

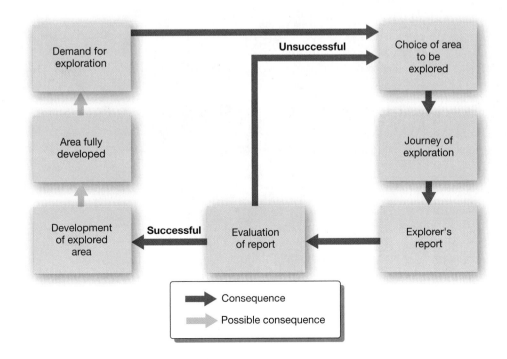

Figure 9.15 Principal steps in the process of exploration This diagram illustrates the main elements in the process of exploration, beginning with a need in the home country that prompts a desire to look outward to satisfy that need. Geographers have figured prominently in the process of exploration by identifying areas to explore as well as actually travelling to those places and cataloguing resources and people. Nineteenth-century geography textbooks are vivid records of these explorations and the often racist ways in which geographers conceptualized the worlds they encountered. Exploration is one step in the process of imperialism; colonization is another. (*Source:* Adapted from J.D. Overton, "A Theory of Exploration," *Journal of Historical Geography* 7, 1981, p. 57.)

were also involved in the development of foreign territories via colonization, the exploitation of indigenous people and resources, or both.

Generally speaking, in the first phases of imperialism, the core exploits the periphery for raw materials. Later, as the periphery becomes developed, colonization may occur, and cash economies are introduced where none have previously existed. The periphery may also become a market for the manufactured goods of the core. Eventually, though not always, the periphery—because of the availability of cheap labour, land, and other inputs to production—can become a new arena for large-scale capital investment. In some cases, it is possible for peripheral countries to rise to semiperipheral status (Mexico, Brazil) or even become part of the core (Canada, the United States, New Zealand, and Australia).

Colonialism differs from imperialism in that it involves formal establishment and maintenance of rule by a sovereign power over a foreign population through the establishment of settlements. The colony does not have any independent standing within the world-system, but it is considered an adjunct of the colonizing power. From the fifteenth to the early twentieth century, colonization constituted an important component of core expansion. The primary colonizing states were Portugal, Spain, the Netherlands, France, and Britain, and they often competed violently with each other for control of territory. Other important states more recently involved in both colonization and imperialist wars include the United States (in the Philippines, Hawaii, and Cuba) and Japan (in Korea and Taiwan).

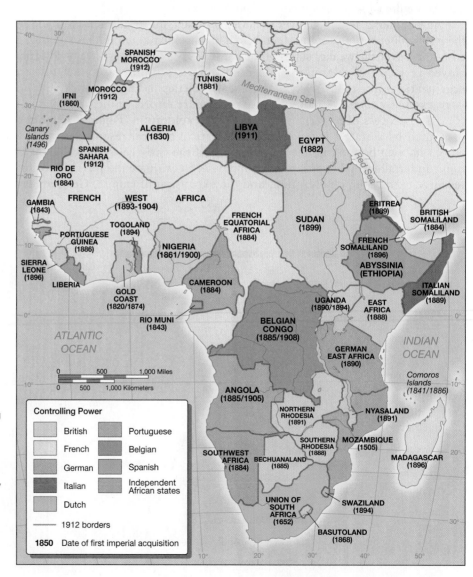

Figure 9.16 European imperialism in Africa, 1496–1912 The partitioning of the African continent by the colonial powers created a crazy quilt that cross-cut pre-existing affiliations and alliances among the African peoples. The Dutch, Belgian, British, French, German, Italian, Portuguese, and Spanish states all laid claim to various parts of Africa and in some cases went to war to protect those claims. (*Source:* Adapted from *Harper Atlas of World History.* New York: HarperCollins, 1992, p. 139.)

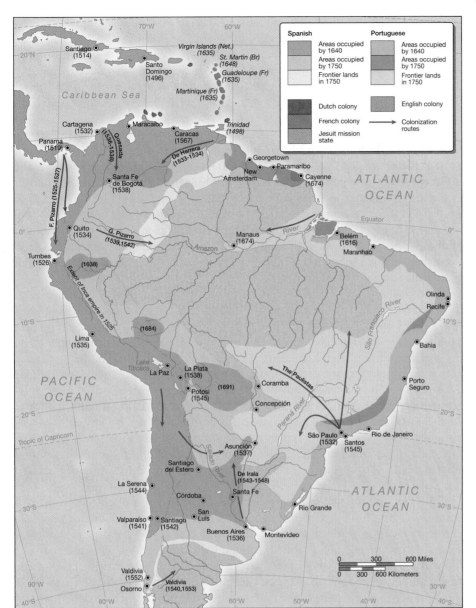

Figure 9.17 Colonization in South America and the Caribbean, 1496–1667 The Spanish and Portuguese dominated the colonization and settlement of South America, with the Dutch, French, and English maintaining only a minor and largely tentative presence. (*Source:* Adapted from *Rand McNally Atlas of World History.* Skokie, IL: Rand McNally, 1992, p. 85.)

Figures **9.16** and **9.17** illustrate the colonies created by European powers in Africa and South America, respectively. Note how almost all of Africa was turned into a patchwork of European colonies: lying within easy reach of Europe, Africa was colonized with the goal of acquiring additional territories and gaining new subjects. Sometimes, the impetus for claiming territory simply was to deny that territory to any competing powers, culminating in the "Scramble for Africa" in the late nineteenth century (see Chapter 2). By contrast, colonization in South America was more focused on securing rich commodity and mineral returns.

To better understand the colonization process and its lasting legacies we can look at three examples: the extension of British rule to India and French rule to Algeria, and the effects of Belgian colonial policies on Rwanda and Central Africa in general. The substantial British presence in India began with the establishment of the East India Trading Company in the mid-eighteenth century. The British government gave the company the power to establish forts and settlements as well as to maintain an army. The company soon established itself in Bombay (now Mumbai), Madras (now Chennai), and Calcutta (now Kolkata). What began as a small trading and manufacturing operation

Figure 9.18 British colonialism in India The British presence in India affected culture, politics, economy, and the layout of cities, as well as numerous other aspects of everyday life. This painting illustrates the way in which Indian and British cultural practices intermingled, changing both in the process (note that the British child is being held by the Indian nanny). Importantly, Indian society absorbed and remoulded many British political and cultural practices so that contemporary Indian government, for example, is a hybrid of British and Indian ideals and practices. In turn, British society continues to be shaped by its colonial history in India, most obviously through the large numbers of Indians who have migrated to Britain, affecting all aspects of society and culture.

burgeoned into a major military, administrative, and economic presence by the British government over time, which did not end until Indian independence in 1947 (**Figure 9.18**). During that 200-year period, the Indian population was brutalized, many were killed, and their society was transformed by British influence. That influence permeated nearly every institution and practice of daily life—from language and judicial procedure to railroad construction and cultural identity.

The reasons why Britain was able to be so callous in its colonial practices are complex. Theorist Edward Said has proposed the concept of Orientalism to explain them, at least in part. For Said, Orientalism is a view that positions the West as culturally superior to the East (the Orient). Said developed the concept to describe the way the West has both historically and contemporarily treated Arabs. This same argument can be applied to the British in India or other Western powers with respect to their colonies: the colonized is seen as inferior and in need of disciplining in the eyes of the supposedly superior and enlightened colonizer. According to this logic, the colonizer even has a moral obligation to colonize and civilize the supposedly inferior.

The postcolonial history of the Indian subcontinent has included partition and repartition as well as the eruption of regional and ethnic conflicts. In 1947, Pakistan split off from India and became a separate Muslim state. In 1971, Bangladesh, previously part of Pakistan, declared its independence. Regional conflicts include radical movements for independence in the states of Kashmir and Punjab. Ethnic conflicts include decades of physical violence between Muslims and Hindus over religious beliefs and the privileging of Hindus over Muslims in the national culture and economy of India. It would be misleading, however, to attribute all of India's current strife to colonialism. Caste also plays a significant role in political conflict. The caste system, which distinguishes social classes based on heredity, preceded British colonization and persists to this day.

The French presence in Algeria is a story of 132 years of colonialism, with accompanying physical violence as well as cultural, social, political, and economic dislocation. French settlers appropriated many of the best agricultural lands and completely transformed Algiers, the capital, into a Westernized city. They also imposed a veneer of Western religious and secular practice over the native and deeply rooted Islamic culture. In the aftermath of the 1954 to 1962 war of independence, there occurred a major exodus of French settlers, many of whose families had lived in Algeria for several generations. With few Westerners in positions of power, important aspects of Islamic society and culture were restored. More recently, Western-oriented politicians, bureaucrats, and citizens have been threatened and killed by radical Islamists who seek to return Algeria to a state governed by strict religious tenets (see Chapter 5 on cultural nationalism).

In both India and Algeria, achieving independence has been a painful and bloody process for both colonizer and colonized. On the Indian subcontinent, an estimated 1 million Hindus and Muslims died in civil war when the British pulled out. For the Algerian war of independence, estimates range from 350,000 to 1.5 million killed—the fact that firm numbers are impossible to ascertain gives an impression of how chaotic the decolonization process was. Our final example of Rwanda shows how the ill effects of colonialism continue to cost lives to this day.

Before the arrival of the Belgians in Rwanda after World War I, a complementary relationship had existed between the Tutsi, who were cattle herders, and the Hutu, who were agriculturists. The Belgians changed this balance by allowing the Tutsi privileged access to education and the bureaucracy, thus establishing a stratified society with the Tutsi on top. In effect, colonialism superimposed a hierarchy on an existing political and social structure that had operated more or less peacefully for centuries. In 1959, the Hutu rebelled, and the Belgians abandoned their Tutsi favourites to side with the Hutu. In 1962, the Belgians ceded independence to Rwanda, leaving behind a volatile political situation that has erupted periodically ever since, most tragically in the 1994 civil war. After a year of violence in which over half a million Tutsi were killed, the Hutu were driven across the border to the Democratic Republic of the Congo (DRC, formerly Zaire) and a new Tutsi-led Rwandan government was formed.

9.6 Geography in the Information Age

U.N. peacekeeping forces caught in the middle of the conflict were unable to prevent the genocide that unfolded. The Canadian general in charge of U.N. forces in Rwanda, General Romeo Dallaire, has described the terrible events in his book *Shake Hands with the Devil*. Dallaire, a seasoned soldier, was so distraught by what he witnessed in Rwanda that years later he tried to take his own life. He has become active in researching issues such as human rights, conflict resolution, humanitarian assistance, and the use of child soldiers. A senator since 2005, he is also an outspoken advocate for soldiers suffering from post-traumatic stress disorder (PTSD) and other mental health effects of war.

The Hutu refugees gathered in camps across the Rwandan border in the DRC. Although run by the United Nations, these camps soon became controlled by armed extremists who used them as bases from which to attack Rwanda. When Rwanda's new Tutsi-led military took matters into its own hands and, with Ugandan support, invaded the DRC to break up the camps, over a million refugees were released (**Figure 9.19**). Many of the extremists

Figure 9.19 Refugees returning to Rwanda Fleeing civil unrest in their own country, Rwandans from the Hutu tribe increasingly sought refuge in the Democratic Republic of the Congo (DRC, formerly Zaire) when the Tutsi-led government assumed power in 1994. Two and a half years later, more than half a million Rwandan refugees in the DRC occupied some of the largest refugee camps in the world. In late 1996, they began streaming back into Rwanda when the Tutsi-led government urged them to come help rebuild the country. Faced with two difficult alternatives—dire conditions in the camps or possible violence in Rwanda—many refugees chose to go home. Tens of thousands of Rwandans moving on foot jammed the road between eastern DRC and Rwanda for over three days.

have since fanned out across Central Africa. The most militant of them are instigating conflict and perpetrating atrocities in Uganda, Congo, and Burundi. Currently, the political situation in Central Africa is one of extreme instability as the Rwandan refugee situation has worsened an already volatile situation in the DRC. All told, since 1994, more than 5 million Africans have lost their lives in the so-called Congo Wars—the bloodiest conflict since World War II.

Clearly, Rwanda's colonial legacy has caused and continues to cause unimaginable human suffering. What has been done to overcome this situation and how successful have these efforts been? To help Tutsis and Hutus work together to rebuild their society and economy, the United Nations established a truth commission, known as the *Gacaca Court System* based on Rwandan traditional justice. Although its work had some important moral impacts, it has not been particularly successful in addressing the structural causes of violence and poverty. Hundreds of thousands of children have become orphans as their parents either died in the atrocities or their mothers were infected with HIV/AIDS through rape and have since died. The country spends more on debt repayments to international banks than it does on education and health. Seventy percent of all households in Rwanda live below the national poverty line. Half the adult population can neither read nor write, and one in three children does not attend school. In fact, the economic situation in Rwanda is worse than it was before the 1994 ethnic cleansing, which does not bode well for the country's long-term political stability. Rwanda indeed presents a sobering example of how colonial policies can continue to thwart peripheral countries and even lead to war decades after decolonization.

The colonization of Africa, South America, parts of the Pacific, Asia, and smaller territories scattered throughout the Southern Hemisphere resulted in a political geographical division of the world into North and South. This **North–South divide** is the differentiation made between the colonizing states of the Northern Hemisphere and the formerly colonized states of the Southern Hemisphere. In the North—roughly the Northern Hemisphere—were the imperialist states of Europe, the United States, Russia, and Japan. In the South—roughly the Southern Hemisphere—were the colonized. Though the equator has been used as a dividing line, it is clear that some so-called southern territories, such as Australia and New Zealand, actually are part of the North in an economic sense. In fact, as you will recall from Chapter 1, we are using a relative measure of space when we divide the world up in this way.

The crucial point is that a relationship of dependence was set up of countries in the South, or periphery, on those in the North, or the core, that began with colonization and persists even today. Very few peripheral countries of the South have become prosperous and economically competitive since achieving political autonomy. Political independence is markedly different from economic independence, and the South remains very much oriented to the economic demands of the North.

North–South divide: the differentiation made between the colonizing states of the Northern Hemisphere and the formerly colonized states of the Southern Hemisphere

9.7 Geography in the Information Age

An example of the one-way orientation from South to North is the transformation of agricultural practices in Mexico as an increasing share of Mexican corn production has become directed not toward subsistence for the local peasant populations but toward luxury consumption in North American markets, particularly for biofuel production. The consequences, as we have mentioned several times already, have been hunger and food riots.

Twentieth-Century Decolonization

Just like colonization did, the process of decolonization has shaped the course of modern world history and geopolitics—and continues to do so. **Decolonization** relates to the re-acquisition of control by colonized peoples over their own territory. The American Revolution (1776–1783) saw the United States break away from Britain and laid the foundation for the United States to become a regional and then a global power. From the early 1800s, the Spanish and Portuguese colonies in Latin America used European styles of government and warfare if necessary to pressure their imperial rulers to grant independence (Brazil, for example, gained independence from Portugal in 1822). Between 1918 and 1960, in a dramatic wave of decolonization, more than 50 countries (with a population of over 800 million at the time) gained independence from European empires (**Figure 9.20**).

For many African and Asian countries, lacking even internal self-government by 1914, the process of decolonization lay less with armed revolts (although these occurred) and more with the development of new local professional elites

decolonization: the re-acquisition of control by colonized peoples over their own territory

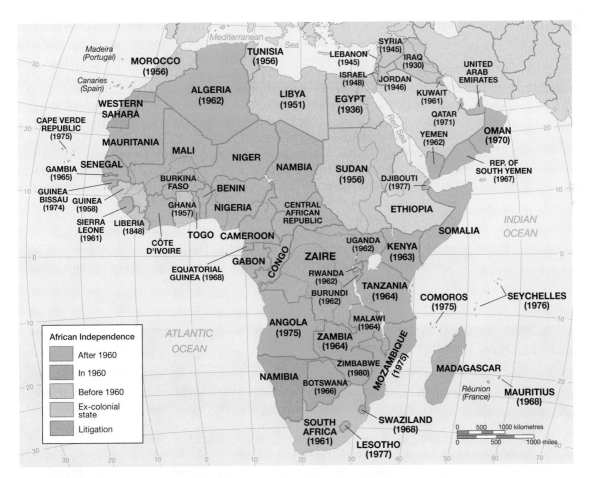

Figure 9.20 Decolonization of Africa, before and after 1960   Britain, France, and Belgium—the dominant European presences in African colonization—were also the first to divest themselves of their colonies. Britain began the process in 1957, when Ghana was granted its independence. France granted independence to its African colonies soon after Britain made the first move. Belgium's and Britain's withdrawal from the remainder of their colonial holdings did not go at all smoothly, with civil wars breaking out. Portugal did not relinquish its possession of Guinea Bissau, Mozambique, and Angola until 1974.   (*Source: The Harper Atlas of World History*, rev. ed., Librairie Hachette, p. 285. Copyright © 1992 by HarperCollins Publishers, Inc. Reprinted by permission of HarperCollins Publishers, Inc.)

and in the establishment of political and military organizations. Such organizations not only served to create a nation that could subsequently claim independence but also acted as a coherent focus for state-wide resistance (which ranged from peaceful civil disobedience, as in the case of Gandhi's campaign for India's independence, to sustained civil war, as in the case of Algeria).

In our discussion so far, decolonization has been seen as only a political step—the formal act of separation. But it is possible to argue that "full" decolonization must involve far more than simply a transfer of sovereignty and political power from one elite to another. We have already seen in Chapter 2 how the core maintains its hegemony over the periphery in the world-system by a variety of means, for example by leaving behind an established European language of government and education system. Certainly, the colonized and the colonizers are tied together in a series of dependent relationships that do not simply end with formal decolonization. Indeed, in more than one case, formal or legal decolonization has merely served as a cloak for business interests in core countries to continue their domination over former colonies using informal means.

Contract farming is one of the mechanisms through which core countries exert influence over peripheral, formerly colonized, countries. Whether the commodity is tea, processed vegetables, fresh flowers, or rice, a contract sets the standards that are involved in producing the commodity for the core market. For example, Japanese firms issue contracts that set the production conditions for the broiler (chicken) industry in Thailand; the United Fruit Company, a U.S. firm, issues contracts for Honduran banana production. Thus, a core country can invoke a new form of colonialism in places it never formally colonized. As explained in Chapter 2, this *neocolonialism* is the domination of peripheral states by core states not by direct political intervention (as in colonialism) but by economic and cultural influence and control.

Other mechanisms that subject the periphery to relations that are little different from those they experienced as colonial subjects include the foreign aid, trade, and investment arrangements originating from core countries. For example, core countries' provision of foreign aid monies, development expertise, and educational opportunities to selected individuals in Kenya has created a class of native civil servants that is in many ways more strongly connected to core processes and networks than those operating within Kenya. This relatively small group of men and women, often foreign educated, now comprises the first capitalist middle class in Kenyan history.

9.8 Geography in the Information Age

For many years, the European Union granted preferential access to its markets to banana producers from former European colonies. When this arrangement came under scrutiny by the WTO (because the United States argued it hindered free competition), European businesses struck individual deals with producers. For example, in 2007, the British supermarket chain Sainsbury's signed a contract with the government of Saint Lucia to buy this Caribbean island's entire banana crop at a "fair trade" price, on condition that the island move toward organic cultivation over the next few years. The deal ensures the British retailer a guaranteed supply of produce that meets its specifications while providing the islanders with a secure demand for their crop. At a time when fair trade and organic practices are becoming fashionable among consumers in core nations (see Chapter 8), the deal also ensures that Sainsbury's maintains an ethical edge over its competitors in the fierce British food retailing market.

| **9.9** | Geography in the Information Age |

Other, somewhat disturbing examples of recent imperialist impulses include attempts to claim and control the surface of the moon, interplanetary space, the virtual realm of the Internet, and the deep ocean floors.

The United States in particular has also used international development projects to promote private enterprise wherever possible. In countries such as Nicaragua and Nepal, American-funded development projects have sought in recent years to replace traditional methods of landholding in favour of the creation of individual title (a process that has often involved the detailed mapping of the countryside). The ensuing creation of a market in land (and the creation of a source of equity for those holding land) are some of the hallmarks of such neoliberal development policies, and may well offer economic development, but at the price of becoming part of an American-led value system. The re-casting of many American values as "universal" or "global ideals" is clearly to the United States' advantage, but it has led to a series of anti-globalization movements across the world, as people seek to turn back what they see as American neo-imperialism.

Finally, we should acknowledge that exploration and colonization continue to occur in Antarctica. This iced landmass is therefore a somewhat exceptional example of ongoing imperialism, where strong states exert power in an area of land where no people and, therefore, no indigenous state power have existed. At present, 15 countries lay claim to territory and/or have established research stations in Antarctica (**Figure 9.21**).

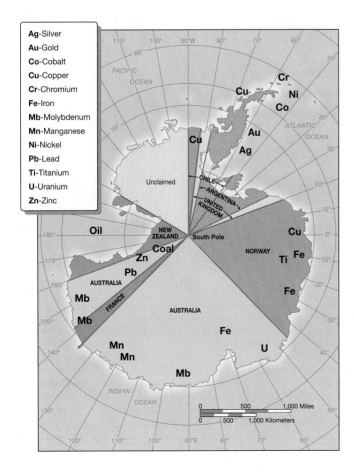

Figure 9.21   Territorial divisions of Antarctica   Even the uninhabitable terrain of Antarctica has become a site for competition among states. The radial lines delineating the various claims bear no relationship to the physical geography of Antarctica; rather, they are cartographic devices designed to formalize and legitimate colonial designs on the region. The overlay provides an indication of the mineral wealth of the continent and the drive behind much of the territorial claims.   (*Source:* Reprinted with permission from Prentice Hall, from J.M. Rubenstein, *The Cultural Landscape: An Introduction to Human Geography*, 5th ed., © 1996, p. 294; and **www.coolantarctica.com/Antarctica_fact_file/science/threats_mining_oil.htm**.)

Heartland Theory Because imperialism and colonialism continue to shape the world political map, it is helpful to understand one of the geographical theories that drove them. By the end of the nineteenth century, numerous formal empires were well established, and imperialist ideologies were dominant. To justify the strategic value of colonialism and explain the dynamic processes and possibilities behind the new world map created by imperialism, the geographer Halford Mackinder (1861–1947) developed a theory. Mackinder was the first professor of geography at Oxford University and director of the London School of Economics. He later went on to serve as a member of Parliament from 1910 to 1922 and as chairman of the Imperial Shipping Committee from 1920 to 1945. With his background in geography, economics, and government, it is not surprising that his theory highlighted the importance of geography to world political and economic stability and conflict.

Mackinder believed that Eurasia was the most likely base from which a successful campaign for control of the world could be launched. He considered its continental heartland to be the "geographical pivot," the location central to establishing global control. Mackinder premised his model on the conviction that the age of maritime exploration was drawing to a close. He theorized that land transportation technology, especially railways, would reinstate land-based power rather than sea prowess as essential to political dominance. Eurasia, which had been politically powerful in earlier centuries, would rise again because it held many resources, was not vulnerable to attack by sea power, and was strategically buffered by an inner and outer crescent of landmasses (**Figure 9.22**).

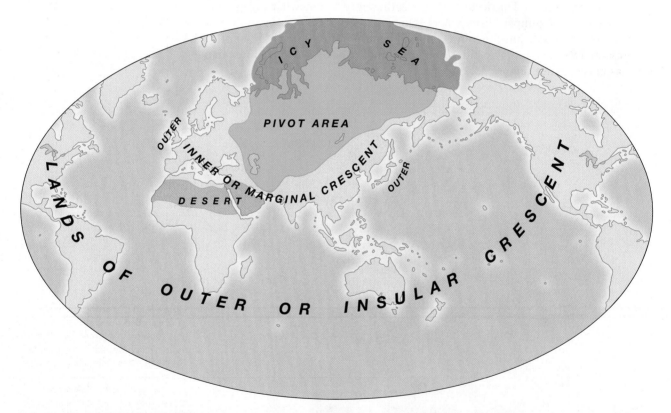

Figure 9.22 Mackinder's heartland theory A quintessential geographical conceptualization of world politics, Mackinder's heartland theory has formed the basis for important geopolitical strategies throughout the decades since its inception. Whereas the pivot area of Eurasia is wholly continental, the outer crescent is mostly oceanic and the inner crescent part continental and part oceanic. It is interesting to compare the Mercator map projection, which Mackinder used to promote his geostrategic theory, with the Dymaxion projection used in this text. This is a classic example of how maps can be used for ideological purposes. The Mercator projection decreases the importance of the northern and southern oceans, which are vast and significant natural barriers. The spatial distortions inherent in the Mercator projection overemphasize the importance of Asia, and the splitting of North and South America (so that they appear on both sides of the map) further exaggerates the centrality of Asia. The Dymaxion projection, as a northern polar representation, de-emphasizes the centrality of any one landmass but exaggerates distances between continents (see Chapter 1). Mackinder's worldview map provides a good example of how cartographic representations can be employed to support ideological arguments. (*Source:* M.I. Glassner and H. de Blij, *Systematic Political Geography*, 3rd ed. New York: J. Wiley & Sons, 1980, p. 291.)

When Mackinder presented his geostrategic theory in 1904, Russia controlled a large portion of the Eurasian landmass beyond the reach of British sea power, and Germany was beginning to challenge Britain for dominance. In an address to the British Royal Geographical Society, Mackinder suggested that the "empire of the world" would be in sight if one power, or combination of powers, came to control the heartland. In particular, he believed that Germany allied with Russia was an alliance to be feared. Mackinder's theory was a product of the age of imperialism, formulated at a time when antagonism was increasing among the core European states, with World War I just around the corner.

As it turned out, Mackinder had ignored the importance of new technologies in his geopolitical assessment, especially the importance of aircraft, which completely altered the vulnerability of places to attack by distant aggressors. Nevertheless, by pointing to the important general observation that "space is power" (or more precisely, that "location confers a strategic advantage dependent on the available technology"), Mackinder's approach paved the way for later geopolitical theories such as the "domino theory" and modern efforts to achieve a "balance of power" between geopolitical power blocs.

The East–West Divide and Domino Theory

In addition to a North–South divide based on imperialism and colonization, the world order of states can also be seen to divide along an East–West split. The **East–West divide** refers to the gulf between communist and noncommunist countries that developed after 1945 and played a significant role in global politics for the next 50 years.

> **East–West divide:** communist and noncommunist countries, respectively

Propelled by the enormous economic and military expansion of the war effort, the United States had assumed the dominant position among countries of the core at the end of World War II. When tensions between East and West escalated into the cold war shortly after 1945, it became the goal of U.S. foreign policy to contain Soviet influence, and Western geopolitics for the next few decades followed an approach that came to be known as the **domino theory**. The domino theory held that if one country in a region chose or was forced to accept a communist political and economic system, then neighbouring countries would fall to communism as well, just as one falling domino in a line of dominoes causes all the others to topple. The antidote to preventing the domino-like spread of communism was economic, political, and military measures that blocked Soviet expansion, including outright military intervention.

> **domino theory:** the belief that if one country in a region chose or was forced to accept a communist political and economic system, then neighbouring countries would fall to communism as well

Adherence to the domino theory began in 1947, when the post-war United States feared communism would spread from Greece to Turkey to Europe. It culminated in the more recent events of U.S. wars in Korea, Vietnam, Nicaragua, El Salvador, and the Persian Gulf. Yet, preventing the domino effect was not just based on military intervention. Cooperation was also emphasized, such as in the 1949 establishment of NATO (North Atlantic Treaty Organization), in which the United States, Canada, and most of the countries of Western Europe allied themselves against Soviet aggression in Europe. Following the end of World War II, core countries set up a range of foreign aid, trade, and banking organizations, such as the World Bank and the IMF. All were intended to open up foreign markets and bring peripheral countries into the global capitalist economic system. The strategy not only improved productivity in core countries but was also seen as a way of strengthening the position of the West in its cold war confrontation with the East.

The collapse of the Soviet Union in 1989 and the consequent end of the cold war effectively left the United States as the only superpower. This reconfiguration has also led to a reframing of world geopolitics, as old views were made redundant. Some theorists, such as Canada's Gwyn Dyer, have speculated that a "war on terror" will provide the West with a new rationale for its approach to other states. If so, the strategic value of countries will be altered to take account of this "new reality" as, for example, the heightened value the United States now gives its relations with Pakistan, Bulgaria, and Turkey. "Extraterritorial spaces," such as Guantanamo Bay (a U.S. base in Cuba), take on new value as places where such a war on terror can escape the sanctions of universal human rights that otherwise limit its reach. An alternative vision, however, places its hopes on a new role for the world's international bodies as a counterbalance to American hegemony.

The New World Order and the Increase in Terrorism With the fall of the Berlin Wall in 1989 and the opening up of former socialist and communist countries, such as China and Russia, to Western-style capitalist economic development, the cold war is widely regarded as over. In March 1991, U.S. President George Bush made a speech referring to a "new world order" following the collapse of the Soviet Union. The notion of the new world order assumes that with the triumph of capitalism over communism, the United States has become the world's only superpower and therefore its policing force. With the political, economic, and cultural dominance of the United States comes the worldwide promotion of liberal democracy and of a global economy predicated on transnational corporate growth through organizations like the World Bank and the World Trade Organization.

However, the sudden shift toward liberal, Western-style democracies and the capitalist consumption practices necessary to the success of the new global economy have created instability in some parts of the world. This instability is especially problematic where the cold war struggle between the United States and the Soviet Union was once waged through proxy wars, in countries that, according to the domino theory, needed to be propped up against the threat of communist takeover. The recent history of Afghanistan provides a telling illustration of this instability and its geopolitical implications (see **Geography Matters 9.1— Afghanistan: From the Cold War to the New World Order**).

The emergence of a new world order has also meant that radical forms of warfare and political practices have replaced more conventional ones. The attacks of September 11, 2001, and the subsequent War on Terror waged by the United States and other governments make clear that terrorism is becoming an increasingly important and lasting factor in global geopolitics.

Terrorism is a complicated concept whose definition very much depends upon social and historical context. A very simple definition is that terrorism is the threat or use of force to bring about political change. It is most commonly understood as actions by individuals or groups of individuals against civilian populations to undermine state practices or institutional organizations. But the state can also be an agent of terrorism, as the original use of the term makes clear. Because terrorism involves violent acts directed against society—whether by antigovernment actors, governments themselves, angry mobs or militants, or even psychotic individuals—it will always mean different things to different people.

9.10 Geography in the Information Age

Recently, the term *ecoterrorism* has been used by the FBI in the United States to prosecute radical environmentalists who have caused injuries or damage to property (for example by setting fire to Hummer dealerships, releasing laboratory animals from research institutions, or spiking trees with nails). Critics have argued that this is a deliberate attempt to vilify and discredit environmental activists.

Afghanistan: From the Cold War to the New World Order

Afghanistan, known in ancient times as Gandhar, was once famous for its wealth, art, and culture (**Figure 9.1.1**). Its trading centres were important links on ancient trading routes between Central Asia and south Asia, and their wealth soon attracted invaders. Alexander the Great swept into Afghanistan—then part of the Persian Empire—in 329 B.C. But invading the mountain passes of Afghanistan is easier than maintaining control of them (**Figure 9.1.2**). The problem, put simply, is physical geography. The country is dominated by the rugged Hindu Kush Mountains, which sweep from the East to the West, petering out near the northwestern city of Herat, where they sink into the desert. Tens of thousands of square kilometres of the Hindu Kush form an intricate and seemingly endless maze of valleys and ravines. Jagged scree-strewn mountains and rugged valleys and caves provide ideal territory in which to fight a guerrilla war against invaders or occupying forces. The problems of topography are compounded by the weather. By late October swirling snow descends on the mountains, sealing off many of the passes, valleys, and high plateaus and making the movement of troops almost impossible until late spring.

Nevertheless, Afghanistan's geopolitical significance has attracted one invader after another. In A.D. 642, Arabs invaded the region and introduced Islam. Arabs in turn gave way to Persians, Turkic Ghaznavids, Mongols, and Mughals. In 1747, Ahmad Shah Durrani

Figure 9.1.2   The Khyber Pass   Over the centuries, the Khyber Pass has been a gateway to Afghanistan's pivotal geopolitical position between Central Asia and south Asia. Persians, Greeks, Mongols, Afghans, and the British have all taken this route, and the surrounding mountains and gulches became the graveyard for many of them.

Figure 9.1.1   Afghanistan   As this map illustrates, Afghanistan is a land-locked, mountainous country sharing borders with six other countries. When war occurred here in the twentieth century, many of the people fled to these neighbouring countries for safety.

consolidated the many chieftainships, petty principalities, and fragmented provinces of the region into the Afghan empire, the predecessor of the modern Afghan state.

Late in the eighteenth century, Afghanistan's geopolitical significance increased still more. For the eastward-expanding Russian empire, Afghanistan represented the last barrier to a thrust toward the rich plains of India. For the British, who were establishing a hold on India, Afghanistan represented a bastion against Russian expansion. Both the Russians and the British desperately wanted to control Afghanistan, and so began the "Great Game"—the struggle between the two imperial powers for control of Afghanistan. The British were able to block the Russians in the Great Game but were not able to establish territorial control. After three wars with the stubborn Afghans, the British finally granted Afghanistan independence in 1921.

A brief period of Afghan independence followed, during which Mohammad Zahir Shah, who reigned from 1933 to 1973, established a relatively liberal constitution. Although Zahir's experiment in democracy produced few lasting reforms, it permitted the growth of extremist political movements, including the communist People's Democratic Party of Afghanistan (PDPA), which had close ideological ties to the Soviet Union, Afghanistan's northern neighbour.

In 1973, a military coup abolished the monarchy and declared Afghanistan a republic, but the badly needed economic and social reforms met with little success. In 1978, a bloody coup led by the PDPA imposed a Marxist-style reform program that ran counter to deeply rooted Islamic traditions. As a result, opposition to the Marxist government emerged almost immediately.

The Soviet Union moved quickly to take advantage of the 1978 coup, signing a new bilateral treaty of friendship and cooperation with Afghanistan that included a military assistance program. Before long, as the opposition insurgency intensified, the PDPA regime's survival was wholly dependent upon Soviet military equipment and advisors. In December 1979, the Soviet Union sent a large airborne force and thousands of ground troops to Kabul under the pretext of a field exercise. More than 120,000 Soviet troops were eventually sent to Afghanistan, but they were unable to establish authority outside Kabul. An overwhelming majority of Afghans opposed the communist regime, and Islamic freedom fighters (*mujahideen*) made it almost impossible for the regime to maintain control outside major urban centres.

Poorly armed at first, the *mujahideen* began receiving substantial assistance in the form of weapons and training from the United States, Pakistan, and Saudi Arabia in 1984. The *mujahideen* exploited Afghanistan's terrain expertly, firing from surrounding ridges to disable the first and last vehicles in the Soviet columns and then slowly picking off the soldiers trapped in the middle. After suffering 15,000 dead and 50,000 wounded, the Soviet Union withdrew its troops in 1989.

As the victorious *mujahideen* entered Kabul to assume control over the city and the central government, a new round of fighting began between the various militia groups that had coexisted uneasily during the Soviet occupation. With the demise of their common enemy, the militias' ethnic, clan, religious, and personality differences resurfaced, and civil war ensued. Large-scale fighting in Kabul and in the northern provinces caused thousands of civilian deaths and created new waves of displaced persons and refugees, hundreds of thousands of whom trekked across the mountains to Pakistan for sanctuary. Eventually, the hard-line Islamist faction of the *mujahideen*, the Taliban (**Figure 9.1.3**), gained control of Kabul and most of Afghanistan. The Taliban regime not only imposed harsh religious laws and mysogynist

Figure 9.1.3 Taliban militiamen The militia that dubbed itself the Taliban (which translates as "students of Islam") emerged in 1994 from the rural southern hinterlands of Afghanistan under the guidance of a reclusive former village preacher, Mullah Mohammed Omar. Fed by recruits from conservative religious schools across the border in Pakistan (most of whom were destitute refugees from the 1979 to 1989 war against the Soviet invasion), the Taliban won military and political support from Pakistan. It rose to power by promising peace and order to a country ravaged by corruption and civil war and the prospect of re-establishing the traditional dominance of the majority ethnic group, the Pashtun.

social practices on the Afghan population but also harboured an entirely new geopolitical force with worldwide implications: Osama bin Laden and his al-Qaeda terrorist network, which was responsible for numerous attacks on the West, including the September 11, 2001, attacks.

The United States, with support from Canada, the United Kingdom, and Australia, invaded Afghanistan in October 2001 as part of its "War on Terror" campaign—a campaign that continues to this day. In fact, the security situation is escalating and casualties are steadily on the rise: more Canadians have died in Afghanistan than in any other mission since the Korean War.

The stability of the country for the Afghan civilian population continues to deteriorate as there is rampant inflation and Taliban violence is spreading. The U.N. Security Mission declared in 2008 that Afghanistan is in danger of becoming a "failed state" unless more resources are invested in shoring up the fledgling democracy.

Geography Matters

State Terrorism in Chechnya

In Chechnya, a region of the northern Caucasus mountain range (**Figure 9.2.1**), clan, not territory, is the traditional form of political organization. Ever since imperial Russia began expanding into the region in the late 1700s, the Sunni Muslim Chechens put up strong resistance, periodically waging holy wars against Christian Russia. When the Russian revolution occurred in 1917, the Chechens did not view the Bolsheviks as an improvement, not least because the newly created Soviet Union formally adopted scientific atheism as its state religion. Following a brief, failed attempt by the people of the North Caucasus and Transcaucasus (including the countries of Armenia, Azerbaijan, and Georgia) to resist Soviet domination, the Soviets decided to divide and conquer by creating administrative regions that cut across clans and ethnic groups. The anti-Soviet Chechens were put in the same region as the Ingush peoples to the south.

The Chechens remained defiant but paid a terrible price for doing so. In the late 1930s, tens of thousands were liquidated by Stalin's purges aimed at suspected anti-Soviet elements. In 1944, after invading German troops were forced to retreat from the North Caucasus, Stalin accused the Chechens of collaborating with the Nazis and ordered the entire Chechen population—then numbering about 700,000—exiled to Kazakhstan and Siberia. Brutal treatment during this mass deportation led to the deaths of more than 200,000 Chechens.

In 1957, Nikita Khrushchev embarked on a program of de-Stalinization that included the rehabilitation of Chechens. But when the Chechens returned, they found newcomers had taken over many of their homes and possessions. Over the next 30 years many of these newcomers withdrew, while the Chechen population consolidated and grew to almost 1 million. When Mikhail Gorbachev initiated his policy of glasnost in 1985, Chechens finally saw a chance for self-determination, and with the breakup of the Soviet Union in 1989, they wasted no time unilaterally declaring their complete independence.

Ingushetia decided to separate from Chechnya in 1992 and signed the Treaty of Federation with Russia. The Russian Federation chose at first to ignore Chechnya's declaration of independence but could not tolerate the possibility of losing the region, particularly since the area around Grozny is one of the Russian Federation's major oil-refining centres and has significant natural-gas reserves. In December 1994, Russian troops invaded Chechnya. The ensuing conflict brought terrible suffering to the Chechen population and resulted in mass migrations away from the fighting. Chechen resistance stiffened, with increased popular support because of the invasion. Russian forces were eventually worn down, and in 1996 the Russian Federation settled for peace, leaving Chechnya with *de facto* independence.

For three years there were protracted negotiations over the nature of the peace settlement. In the summer of 1999, however, after Chechen rebels took the fight to the neighbouring republic of Dagestan and to the Russian heartland with a series of terrorist bombings of apartment blocks, the Russian military effort was renewed. After bitter and intense fighting, during which the Russian army suffered over 400 deaths and nearly 1,500 wounded while hundreds of thousands of Chechens were made homeless and several thousand were dead or missing, Russian troops took the capital, Grozny, in February 2000 (**Figure 9.2.2**). By that time, Grozny was virtually uninhabitable. Since early 2000, Russian Federation troops have maintained control of Grozny, though they continue to be harassed by Chechen

Figure 9.2.1   The Northern Caucasus   This reference map shows the principal features, political boundaries, and major cities of the northern Caucasus.

Figure 9.2.2   Grozny refugees   In December 1999, Chechens were advised by Russian troops to evacuate Grozny, the capital of Chechnya, before it was destroyed.

rebel guerrillas. Although the war has ceased, murders and kidnappings—initiated by both Chechens and the Russian intelligence service—are still commonplace, and organized crime flourishes through the Chechen and Russian mafias throughout the country.

Chechnya provides an instructive example of state terrorism. It also provides an illustration of the complexity of terrorism as a concept by showing that it can be practised by individuals as well as institutions, by rogue forces as well as legitimate ones.

The term *terrorism* was first used during the French Revolution (1789–1795) to describe the new revolutionary government's repression of its own people during the "Reign of Terror." Fifty years later, the term was used to describe revolutionaries who violently opposed existing governments. By the late nineteenth century, it was often applied to militant labour and nationalist political organizations. By the mid-twentieth century, the term was used to describe many left-wing groups, as well as subnationalist (minority groups within the nation-state) or radical ethnic groups. In the 1980s, the violent activity of hate movements in the United States was defined as terrorist, whereas terrorism internationally was seen as a brand of ethnic or subnational warfare sponsored by rogue regimes.

Ethnic and subnational terrorism affects many countries today, including Russia, Uzbekistan, India, China, Colombia, the Philippines, Israel, Sri Lanka, and Palestine. Another ethnic or subnational violent struggle involves the Russian region of Chechnya, where the population has demanded independence. For the Muslim Chechens, Russia is acting as a terrorist state by employing military force to keep them from gaining independence. Chechens believe they have little in common politically, historically, or culturally with Russia. Meanwhile, the Russian state has identified the defiant Chechens as extremists and terrorists (see **Geography Matters 9.2—State Terrorism in Chechnya**).

Although subnational resistance organizations using terrorist tactics continue to operate throughout the world, the most widely recognized terrorism of the new century has religious roots. The September 11 attacks have helped to bring the realities of religious terrorism sharply into public focus. The connection between religion and terrorism is nothing new, as terrorism has been perpetrated by religious fanatics for more than 2,000 years. Indeed, words like *zealot*, *assassin*, and *thug* all stem from fundamentalist religious movements of previous eras.

INTERNATIONAL AND SUPRANATIONAL ORGANIZATIONS

Just as states are key players in political geography, so, too, have international and supranational organizations become important participants in the world-system in the last century. These organizations have become increasingly important in dealing with situations in which international boundaries stand in the way of specific goals. These goals include, among other things, the free flow of goods and information and more cooperative management of shared resources, such as water.

An **international organization** is one that includes two or more states seeking political or economic cooperation with each other. Perhaps the best-known example of an international organization operating today is the United Nations (**Figure 9.23**). Other examples of international organizations include the Organisation for Economic Co-operation and Development (OECD), the Organization of Petroleum Exporting Countries (OPEC), the Association of South-East Asian Nations (ASEAN), and the now-disbanded Council for Mutual

international organization: a group that includes two or more states seeking political or economic cooperation with each other

424

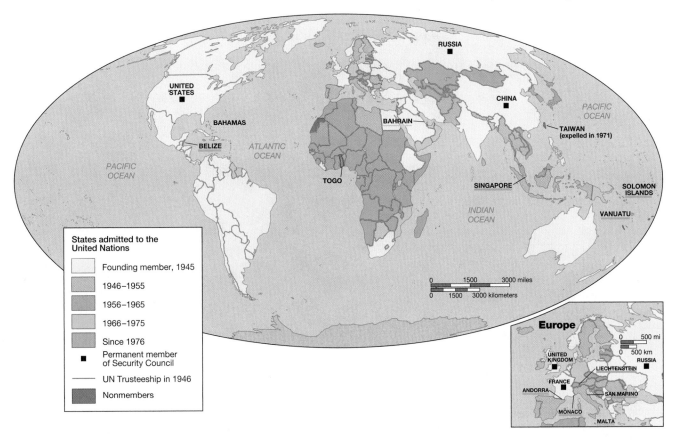

Figure 9.23   U.N. member countries   Following World War II and the demise of the League of Nations, renewed effort was made to establish an international organization aimed at instituting a system of international peace and security. The U.N. Charter was approved in 1945, raising hopes for a more long-lived organization than the ineffective League of Nations. After South Sudan became the 193rd member in 2011, the United Nations now encompasses essentially all recognized states in the world (notable exceptions include Kosovo, Taiwan, the Holy See/Vatican City, and Palestine). At the same time that the United Nations was set up, the United States lobbied for the creation of the IMF and the World Bank. The U.S. government believed that World War II resulted from the collapse of world trade and financial dislocation caused by the Great Depression. The task of the IMF and the World Bank is to prevent economic collapse by providing loans to stabilize currencies and enhance economic growth and trade.

Economic Assistance (COMECON). Though these organizations were formed to accomplish very different ends, they all aim to achieve cooperation while maintaining full sovereignty of the individual states. The countries involved in these organizations are shown in **Figure 9.24**.

The post-war period has seen the rise and growth not only of large international organizations but also of new regional arrangements. These arrangements vary from the highly specific, such as the joint Swiss–French management of Basel–Mulhouse airport, to the more general, such as NAFTA, which joins Canada, the United States, and Mexico into a single trade region. Regional organizations and arrangements now exist to address a wide array of issues, including the management of international watersheds and river basins (such as the International Joint Commission, through which Canada and the United States control the Great Lakes). They also oversee the maintenance of health and sanitation standards, coordinated regional planning, and tourism management. Such regional arrangements seek to overcome the barriers to the rational solution of shared problems posed by international boundaries. They also provide larger arenas for the pursuit of political, economic, social, and cultural objectives.

Unlike international organizations, **supranational organizations** reduce the centrality of individual states. Through organizing and regulating designated operations of the individual member states, these organizations diminish, to

supranational organizations: collections of individual states with a common goal that may be economic and/or political in nature; such organizations diminish, to some extent, individual state sovereignty in favour of the group interests of the membership

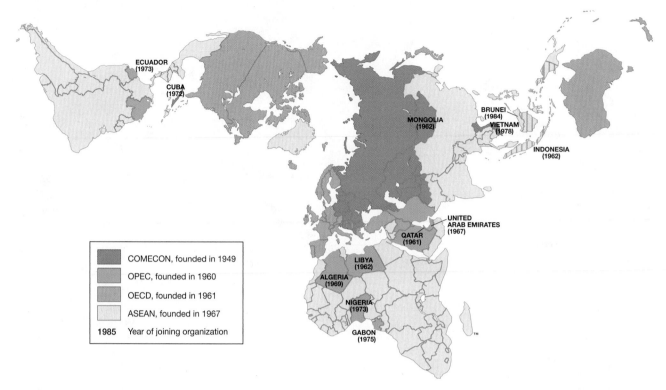

Figure 9.24   International economic groups   OPEC (Organization of Petroleum Exporting Countries) states joined together to foster cooperation in the setting of world oil prices in 1960. ASEAN (Association of South-East Asian Nations), founded in 1967, exists to further economic development in Southeast Asia. The OECD (Organisation for Economic Co-operation and Development), founded by the United States, Canada, and 18 European states in 1961, aims to increase world trade through the provision of financial security. Groupings such as these suggest that the independent state has lost effectiveness in promoting its own and other states' economic progress and stability. Founded in 1949, COMECON (the Council for Mutual Economic Assistance) was the grouping organized to promote trade among former communist and socialist states. It is now defunct.   (*Source:* Map projection, Buckminster Fuller Institute and Dymaxion Map Design, Santa Barbara, CA. The word *Dymaxion* and the Fuller Projection Dymaxion™ Map design are trademarks of the Buckminster Fuller Institute, Santa Barbara, California, ©1938, 1967, & 1992. All rights reserved.)

some extent, individual state sovereignty in favour of the collective interests of the large membership. The European Union (EU) is perhaps the best example of a supranational organization.

At the end of World War II, European leaders realized that Europe's fragmented state system was insufficient to meet the demands and levels of competition building within the world political and economic systems. They endeavoured to create an integrated entity that at the same time would preserve important features of state sovereignty and identity. They also intended to create a more efficient intra-European marketing system and a more competitive entity in global transactions. **Figure 9.25** shows the progression of integration of European countries into the European Union—a direct descendant of the European Economic Community—since 1957.

The EU holds elections, has its own Parliament and court system, and decides whether and when to allow new members to join. Generally speaking, the EU aims to create a common geographical space within Europe in which goods, services, people, and information move freely. Since 2001, a common European currency—the *euro*—is in circulation, and since 2009, the EU also has the equivalent of a foreign minister. However, other indicators of nationalism within the individual member countries continue to be strong. For example, just as the European system of states is on the threshold of dissolving into the larger EU organizational form, national and regional movements (see Chapter 5 and the example of the Basques below) have become potent forces operating against full integration.

Figure 9.25   Map of membership in the European Union   The goal of the European Union is to increase integration and cooperation among the member states. The EU was established on November 1, 1993, when the Maastricht Treaty was ratified by the 12 members of the European Community (Belgium, Denmark, France, Germany, the United Kingdom, Greece, Ireland, Italy, Luxembourg, the Netherlands, Portugal, and Spain. The predecessor to both organizations, the European Economic Community, was originally created in 1957). The Maastricht Treaty established European citizenship for citizens of each member state, enhanced customs and immigration agreements, and allowed for the establishment of a common currency, the euro (further information on the European Union can be obtained from its website, **http://europa.eu/index_ en.htm**). The EU is governed through both supranational European institutions (the European Commission and the European Parliament, both administered by the EU) and the governments of the member states, which send representatives to the Council of Ministers (the main law-making body of the EU). Membership in the EU is much sought after, and numerous European countries have applied and are on the waiting list for admission. The largest expansion in its history occurred in 2004, when the EU admitted 10 new members: Cyprus, the Czech Republic, Estonia, Hungary, Latvia, Lithuania, Malta, Poland, Slovakia, and Slovenia.

Globalization and Transnational Governance: The End of the State?

As we have already noted, globalization has been as much about restructuring the global economy as it has been about reshaping geopolitics. In fact, some globalization scholars believe that the impact of globalization on politics has been so profound that it is leading to the erosion of the powers of the modern state, if not its ultimate disappearance. These scholars, known as hyperglobalists (see Chapter 1), believe that because the modern state is organized around a bounded territory and because globalization is creating a new economic space that is transnational, the state is increasingly incapable of responding to the needs of the new transnational economy. Whether or not we share this view, we must recognize that the state is clearly undergoing dramatic changes that are restructuring its role in local, regional, and global contexts. Moreover, these changes are very much part of recent history.

In the twentieth century, from the end of World War II until 1989, when the Berlin Wall was dismantled, world politics were organized around two superpowers. The capitalist West rallied around the United States, and the communist East around the Soviet Union. But with the fall of the Berlin Wall signalling the "end of communism" as a world force, the bipolar world order came to an end, and a new world order, which is organized around global capitalism, has emerged and increasingly solidified around a new set of political powers and institutions that have recast the role of the state.

We have referred throughout the text, and especially in Chapters 2 and 7, to the importance for the contemporary global economy of such regional and supranational organizations as the EU, NAFTA, ASEAN, OPEC, and the WTO. We have also noted that these organizations are unique in modern history, as they aim to treat the world and different regional clusters as seamless trading areas unhindered by the rules that ordinarily regulate national economies. The increasing importance of these trade-facilitating organizations is the most telling indicator that the world, besides being transformed into one global economic space, is also experiencing global geopolitical transformations. But rather than disappearing altogether, the powers and roles of the modern state are changing as it is forced to interact with these sorts of organizations, as well as with a whole range of other political institutions, associations, and networks (**Figure 9.26**).

The point is not that the state is disappearing, but rather that it must now contend with a whole new set of processes and other important political actors on the international stage as well as within its own territory. For instance, geographer Andrew Leyshon has shown how in the 1980s a transnational financial network was established that is far beyond the control of any one state, even a very powerful state like the United States, to regulate effectively (as the events of the European and American debt crises in 2011 have illustrated). In fact, what the increasing importance of transnational flows and connections—from flows of capital to flows of migrants—indicates is that the state is less a container of political or economic power and more a site of flows and connections.

The increasing importance of flows and connections means that contemporary globalization has made possible a steadily shrinking world. In addition to allowing people and goods to travel farther faster and to receive and send information more quickly, time–space convergence—or the smaller world that globalization has created—means that politics and political action have also become global. In short, politics can at any time move beyond the confines of the state into the global political arena, where rapid communications enable complex supporting networks to be developed and deployed, thereby facilitating interaction and decision making. One indication of the increasingly global nature of politics outside of formal political institutions is the increase in environmental organizations whose purview and membership are global, as discussed in Chapter 4.

Figure 9.26   Growth of states and intergovernmental organizations and nongovernmental organizations in the twentieth century   The number of states has grown steadily over the twentieth century, but intergovernmental organizations (IGOs) and international nongovernmental organizations (INGOs) have experienced dramatic growth, particularly since the 1960s. Although states remain the main forms of national government, they have turned over many of their governing responsibilities to international governing organizations and nongovernmental organizations.

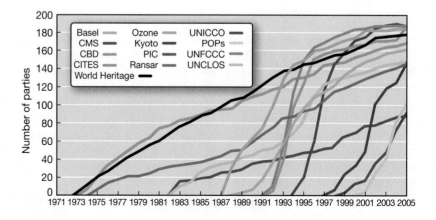

What has been most interesting about the increasing institutionalization of global politics is that it has been less concerned with the traditional preoccupations of relations between states and military security issues; instead, it has been more concerned with issues of economic, ecological, and social security. The massive increases in flows of trade, foreign direct investment, financial commodities, information, tourism, migration, crime, drugs, cultural products, and ideas have been accompanied by the emergence and growth of global and regional institutions whose role is to manage and regulate these flows. The impact of these twin forces on the modern state has been to draw it increasingly into this complex of global, regional, and multilateral systems of governance. And as the state has been drawn into these new activities, it has shed or de-emphasized some of its previous responsibilities, such as maintenance of social welfare.

The involvement of the state in these new global activities, the growth of supranational and regional institutions and organizations, the critical significance of transnational corporations to global capital, and the proliferation of transnational social movements and professional organizations are captured by the term *international regime*. The term reflects the fact that the arena of contemporary politics is now international, so much so that even city governments and local interest groups—from twin-city organizations to car clubs—are making connections and conducting their activities both beyond and within the boundaries of their own states. An example of this is the human rights movement that has gained ascendancy over the last few decades. Human rights, including the rights to justice, freedom, and equality, are considered by most societies to belong automatically to all people.

Until World War II, safeguarding human rights was the provenance of states whose rules and regulations legislated the proper treatment of its citizens, from prisoners to schoolchildren. Since then, nearly all states have come to accept the importance of a comprehensive political and legal framework that focuses on human rights and that allows an international organization to intervene in the operations of a sovereign state if it is in violation of the Universal Declaration of Human Rights adopted by the United Nations in 1948.

In 1998, the United Nations realized another step in the protection of human rights by adopting a treaty to establish a permanent International Criminal Court (ICC), a permanent mechanism to bring to justice the perpetrators of such crimes as genocide, ethnic cleansing, sexual slavery, and maiming. Only seven U.N. members voted against the treaty to establish the ICC: China, Iraq, Israel, Libya, Qatar, the United States, and Yemen.

In the next section, we move from the international level to national, regional, and local levels. Our aim here is to show that political geography occurs at all levels of political organization and that each scale enables significant insights about the politics of geography and the geography of politics.

9.11 Geography in the Information Age

The emergence of human rights as a globally relevant issue is another case study in the importance of new communication technologies for the development of contemporary society. These technologies have enabled groups, organizations, and individuals to discuss issues that concern all people everywhere not only at international conferences and events, but all the time through social networks, email, listservs, and other computer-mediated channels. The phenomenon of different people and groups across the world networking toward a common cause is known as *global civil society*. Global civil society is composed of the broad range of institutions that operate between the private market and the state, most of which are now "at home" on the Internet.

THE TWO-WAY STREET OF POLITICS AND GEOGRAPHY

Political geography can be seen from two perspectives. The first perspective sees political geography as being about the *politics of geography*. This perspective emphasizes that *geography*—or the areal distribution/differentiation of people and objects in space—has a very real and measurable impact on politics. Regionalism, discussed later in this section, provides examples of how geography shapes politics. The politics-of-geography orientation is also a reminder that politics occurs at all levels of the human experience, from the international order down to the scale of the neighbourhood, household, and body.

The second perspective sees political geography as being about the *geography of politics*. In contrast to the first orientation, this approach analyzes how *politics*—the tactics or operations of the state—shapes geography. Mackinder's heartland theory and the domino theory attempt to explain how the geography of politics works at the international level. In the heartland theory, the state expands into new territory in order to relieve population pressures. In the domino theory, as communism seeks new members, it expands geographically to incorporate new territories. Examination of a series of maps of Palestine/Israel since 1923 reveals how the changing geography of this area is a response to changing international, national, regional, and local politics (see **Geography Matters 9.3—The Palestinian–Israeli Conflict**).

The Politics of Geography

Territory is often regarded as a space to which a particular group attaches its identity. Related to this concept of territory is the notion of **self-determination**, which refers to the right of a group with a distinctive politico-territorial identity to determine its own destiny, at least in part, through the control of its own territory.

Regionalism   As we have already seen, it is sometimes the case that different groups with different identities—religious or ethnic—coexist within the same state boundaries. At times, a mismatch between legal and political boundaries and the distribution of populations with distinct identities leads to movements to claim or re-claim particular territories. These movements, whether conflictual or peaceful in their claim to territory, are known as *regional movements*. **Regionalism** is a feeling of collective identity based on a population's politico-territorial identification within a state or across state boundaries.

Regionalism often involves ethnic groups whose aims include autonomy from an interventionist state and the development of their own political power. For example, the Basque people are one of the oldest European peoples, with a distinctive culture and unique language (see Chapter 5). The Basque provinces of northern Spain and southern France have sought autonomy from those states for most of the twentieth century (**Figure 9.27**). Since the 1950s, agitation for political independence has included—especially for the Basques in Spain—terrorist acts. Not even the Spanish move to parliamentary democracy and the granting of autonomy to the Basque provinces could squelch the Basque thirst for self-determination. On the French side, the Basque separatist movement is neither as violent nor as active as the movement in Spain.

We need only look at the long list of territorially based conflicts that have emerged in the post–cold war world to realize the extent to which territorially based *ethnicity* remains a potent force in the politics of geography. For example, the Kurds continue to fight for their own state separate from Turkey and Iraq. Consider also the former Yugoslavia, whose geography has fractured along the lines of ethnicity (**Figure 9.28**). Regionalism also underlies efforts to sever Scotland from the United Kingdom. And, as we have noted earlier, a significant

self-determination: the right of a group with a distinctive politico-territorial identity to determine its own destiny, at least in part, through the control of its own territory

regionalism: a feeling of collective identity based on a population's politico-territorial identification within a state or across state boundaries

Figure 9.27 Basque independence poster This independence poster is plastered over the door of a shop in Donostia (San Sebastian) in one of the Basque provinces of Spain. The poster is a sign of the passionate opposition the Basques have adopted toward the central government in Madrid. Acts of terrorism continue to occur throughout Spain as the Basques maintain their desire for independence. What is most interesting about the sign is that it is written in neither Castilian Spanish (the national language) nor Euskadi (the Basque language), but in English. It appears as if this and declarations like it are directed at international tourists in an attempt to gain the attention of the *global civil society* we discussed earlier.

Figure 9.28 Map of the former Yugoslavia Today, the former Yugoslavia consists of seven nations: Slovenia, Croatia, Bosnia and Herzegovina, Serbia, Montenegro, the former Yugoslav Republic of Macedonia, and the newly separated state of Kosovo. For the most part, the boundaries of the Yugoslav states were laid out only in the twentieth century, across segments of the Austro-Hungarian and Ottoman empires that had acquired a complex mixture of ethnic groups. The history of these boundaries has also been the history of ethnic conflict revolving around claims to territory as well as intolerance for religious differences. As this map shows, with the exception of Slovenia, the new states are home to a mix of nationalities. (*Source:* Redrawn with permission from Prentice Hall, from J.M. Rubenstein, *The Cultural Landscape: An Introduction to Human Geography*, 6th ed., © 1999, p. 260.)

proportion of Quebec's French-speaking population, already accorded substantial autonomy, persists in advocating complete independence from Canada. The politics of geography also finds expression outside Quebec, where regional discontent with Ottawa has led to the creation of political parties, such as the Wildrose Alliance in Alberta or, in the 1990s, New Brunswick's CORE party.

In England and Wales, a *rural versus urban* conflict has been ongoing over the practice of foxhunting. The Hunting Act of 2004 made it illegal to hunt a mammal using a dog, pitting a group called the Countryside Alliance, which sees foxhunting as a seasonal ritual of rural life, against animal rights activists, mostly headquartered in large British cities, and the London-based Parliament.

Throughout the periphery, *rural-to-urban migration* (grossly inflating the populations of cities, such as in Lima, Peru; Nairobi, Kenya; and Jakarta, Indonesia) has generated enormous social and political pressures and poses overwhelming challenges. Policy-makers must ask themselves difficult questions: How much of the country's scarce resources should be devoted to slowing (or reversing) rural out-migration through development projects? What level of resources should be devoted to accommodating the throngs of new urban dwellers, most of whom have worse living conditions in the city than they did in the countryside?

There is also the phenomenon of *competition among cities*, as well as among states, to attract corporate investment (as discussed in Chapter 7). Often corporations play the jurisdictions against each other in attempts to obtain the most attractive conditions for investment. At other times, cities and states compete to induce the government to locate government facilities within their jurisdictions.

The Geography of Politics

An obvious way to show how politics shapes geography is to show how systems of political representation are geographically anchored.

The Palestinian–Israeli Conflict

The Palestinian–Israeli conflict continues to be complex and highly volatile despite persistent regional and international efforts to bring peace to the region. The renewed violence that erupted in the fall of 2000 (and has persisted), just as the peace process seemed to be most promising, underscores the complexity of the problem and the difficulty of resolution. As alluded to earlier, the problem is rooted at least partly in the failure of the victors of World War I, and Britain in particular, to provide the Palestinians with a state of their own when they redrew the boundaries of the region.

The state of Israel is a mid-twentieth-century construction that has its roots in the emergence of **zionism**, a late-nineteenth-century European movement. Zionism's chief objective was the establishment of a legally recognized home in Palestine for the Jewish people. Thousands of European Jews, inspired by the early zionist movement, began migrating to Palestine around 1900. When the Ottoman Empire was defeated in 1917, the British gained control over Palestine and the neighbouring Transjordan area. In the so-called Balfour Declaration, they signalled to the Jewish Diaspora that they would "view with favour the establishment in Palestine of a national home for the Jewish people." This was a problematic promise, however, because the Palestinian people already occupied the area and viewed the arrival of increasing numbers of Jews as an incursion into the sacred lands of Islam. In response to increasing Arab–Jewish tensions in the area, the British decided to limit Jewish immigration to Palestine in the late 1930s through the end of World War II—just as Jewish refugees from Europe were desperately looking for a safe haven.

In 1947, with conflict continuing between the two groups, Britain announced that it had despaired of ever resolving the problems and would withdraw from Palestine in 1948, turning it over to the United Nations. The United Nations, under heavy pressure from the United States, responded by voting to partition Palestine into Arab and Jewish states and designated Jerusalem as an international city, preventing either group from having exclusive control. The Jewish state was to have 56 percent of the mandate of Palestine; an Arab state was to have 43 percent; and Jerusalem, a city sacred to Jews, Muslims, and Christians, was to be administered by the United Nations. The proposed U.N. plan was accepted by the Jews and angrily rejected by the Arabs, who argued that a mandated territory could not legally be taken from an indigenous population.

When Britain withdrew in 1948, war broke out. In an attempt to aid the militarily weaker Palestinians, combined forces from Egypt, Jordan, and Lebanon, as well as smaller units from Syria, Iraq, and Saudi Arabia, confronted the Israelis. Their goal was not only to prevent the Jewish forces from gaining control over additional Palestinian territory but also to wipe out the newly formed Jewish state altogether. This war, which became known as the first Arab–Israeli war, resulted in the defeat of the Arab forces in 1949, and later armistice agreements enabled Israel to expand beyond the U.N. plan by gaining the western sector of Jerusalem, including the Old City. In 1950, Israel declared Jerusalem its national capital, though very few countries have recognized this.

Israel maintained the new borders gained during the first Arab–Israeli war for another 18 years until the Six-Day War in 1967, which resulted in further gains for Israel, including the Sinai Peninsula along the Suez Canal and the Golan Heights in the southwestern corner of Syria. The eastern sector of Jerusalem, previously held by Jordan, was also annexed during the Six-Day War. As **Figure 9.3.1** shows, relatively little territorial change occurred until the 1970s and 1980s, when Israel moved toward reconciliation with Egypt through a series of withdrawals that eventually returned all of Sinai to Egyptian control by 1988.

The territorial expansion of Israel has meant that hundreds of thousands of Palestinians have been driven from their homelands, and the landscape of Palestine has been dramatically transformed. Today, Palestinians live as refugees either in other Arab countries in the region, abroad, or under Israeli occupation in the West Bank (also known as the "Occupied Territory") and the Gaza Strip. The Arabs of the Middle East and North Africa and many other international observers are convinced that Israel has no intention of allowing the diasporic Palestinian population to return to their homelands. By the late 1980s, Palestinians in the West Bank and Gaza Strip had become so angered by Israeli territorial policies and particularly the spreading Israeli settlements that they rose up in rebellion, known as the *intifada* ("uprising"). In addition to the intifada, other Palestinian groups have coalesced in opposition to the Israeli occupation. The Palestinian Liberation Organization (PLO) was formed in 1964 as an organization devoted to returning Palestine to the Palestinians. Since its official recognition, the PLO has become the Palestinian Authority and is seen as the legitimate representative of the Palestinian people. Another, less conciliatory group representing the Palestinian cause is Hamas (Islamic Resistance Movement), whose activities are largely centred in the Gaza Strip.

Since the mid-1990s, hopes for peace in the region have risen and fallen repeatedly. In October 2000, after weeks of very difficult but promising U.S.-sponsored peace negotiations between Yasir Arafat, then chairman of the Palestinian Authority, and Ehud Barak, then Israeli prime minister, violence broke out again in the

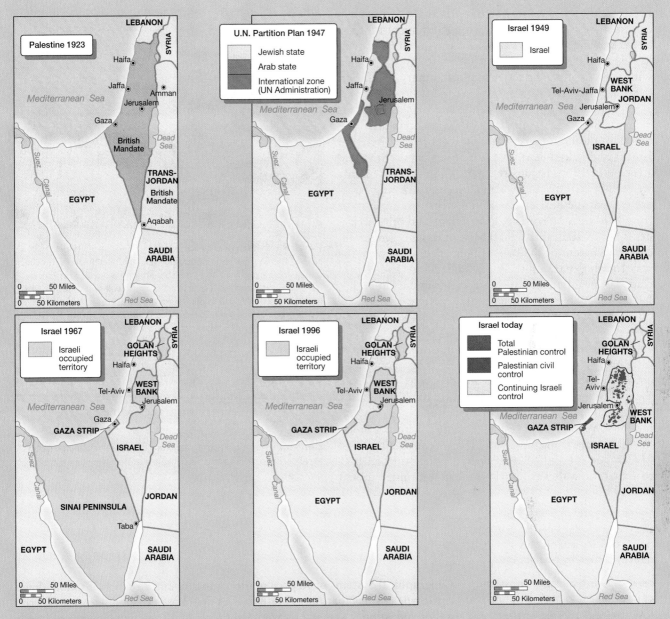

Figure 9.3.1   The changing geography of Israel/Palestine, 1923–2005   Since the creation of Israel out of much of what had been Palestine in 1947, the geography of the region has undergone significant modifications. A series of wars between Israelis and Arabs and a number of political decisions regarding how to cope with both resident Palestinians and large volumes of Jewish people immigrating to Israel from around the world have produced the changing geographies we see here. (*Source:* Reprinted with permission from Prentice Hall, from J.M. Rubenstein, *The Cultural Landscape: An Introduction to Human Geography*, 5th ed., © 1996, p. 233.)

West Bank. This new violence left little hope in Israel, the Occupied Territories, or elsewhere that the Palestinian–Israeli conflict would be resolved anytime in the near future. Renewed hope emerged, however, following the death of Yasir Arafat in November 2004. Arafat was a controversial figure throughout his lengthy political career; his supporters viewed him as a heroic freedom fighter who symbolized the national aspirations of the Palestinian people, but his opponents often described him as a terrorist who promoted violence. His death

made room for a new leader to step forward, one who might negotiate a peace where Arafat could not.

On January 9, 2005, Mahmoud Abbas was elected president of the Palestinian Authority by voters in the West Bank and Gaza, in the first Palestinian election held since 1996. Although the most militant Islamist organizations, Hamas and the Islamic Jihad, boycotted the elections, it is estimated that about 66 percent of eligible voters went to the polls (compared to 61 percent in the 2011 Canadian federal election). Israel has been withdrawing Israeli settlers (many of whom are extremely resistant to leaving) from Palestinian territory, but infighting between Fatah and Hamas in Gaza, following the 2005 election, has spilled into the West Bank, with mass arrests, abductions, and summary executions deepening the discord.

As Israel has begun to cede territory to Palestine (for example, by withdrawing from the Gaza Strip in 2005), it is continuing to construct a physical barrier between Israelis and Palestinians. The Gaza Strip barrier was constructed in 1994. It consists of 52 kilometres of mainly wire fence with posts, sensors, and buffer zones. Israel argues that the barrier is essential to protect its citizens from Palestinian terrorism. Palestinians and other opponents of the barrier contend that its purpose is geographical containment of the Palestinians in order to pave the way for an expansion of Israeli sovereignty and to preclude any negotiated border agreements in the future. But Israel argues that the fence is purely a security obstacle, not a part of a future border.

In 2002, the West Bank wall was begun and, when completed, will seal off that portion of the Palestinian territories from Israel (**Figure 9.3.2**). The barrier cuts across Palestinian settlements and separates them from their livelihood; it also stifles the West Bank's economy because the Palestinians are being cut off from jobs and markets in Israel. As a result, unemployment continues to climb at the same time that GDP per capita plummets. In October 2003, the U.N. General Assembly voted 144 to 4 that the wall was "in contradiction to international

Figure 9.3.2 Israeli security barrier The security barrier, called "the wall" or the "apartheid wall" by Palestinians and other opponents, is a physical barrier consisting of a network of fences, trenches, and, as in this section, a concrete wall eight metres high. Israel's stated purpose in constructing it is to create a zone of security between itself and the West Bank. Palestinians charge that it cuts through lived space, separating villagers from their orchards and labourers from their places of work, for example.

law" and therefore illegal. The World Bank deemed the West Bank "a shattered economic space," where more than half the population lives below the poverty line.

zionism: a late-nineteenth-century European movement to establish a legally recognized home in Palestine for the Jewish people

democratic rule: a system in which public policies and officials are directly chosen by popular vote

territorial organization: a system of government formally structured by area, not by social groups

unitary state: a form of government in which power is concentrated in the central government

confederation: a grouping of independent jurisdictions, such as provinces, into a larger unit that is given separate powers

Geographical Systems of Representation   In a country such as Canada, **democratic rule** ensures that our representatives are chosen by popular vote. **Territorial organization**, a system of government formally structured by area and not by wealth or social group, ensures that we vote where we live. In this way, geography and politics—space and power—are intimately connected.

Canada has inherited this system from Britain and shares this approach to voting and elections with many other countries. But unlike Britain, a **unitary state** (a form of government in which power is concentrated in the central government), Canada is a **confederation** (a grouping of independent jurisdictions, such as provinces, into a larger unit that is given separate powers), a

9.12 Geography in the Information Age

To learn about the geography of the wall and the small scale of the area under dispute, you can take a helicopter ride with a BBC correspondent at **http://www.bbc.co.uk/news/world-middle-east-11139865**.

federal state in which powers are divided between the federal government and the provinces and territories. (Municipal government is under provincial jurisdiction, and the territories are ultimately a federal responsibility.)

As a consequence, Canada is made up of a nested hierarchy of jurisdictions (municipal, provincial and territorial, and federal), each represented by its own spatial unit of representation (*boroughs* or *wards* at a city level, *ridings* at the provincial or territorial and federal level) and its own elected representatives (such as councillors, members of the legislative or national assembly [MLAs or MNAs], and, at the federal level, members of Parliament [MPs]).

At Confederation in 1867, the British North America Act established that the four provinces (Ontario, Quebec, New Brunswick, and Nova Scotia) that composed Canada at the time should have a Parliament comprising two houses. The upper house, the Senate, was to consist of non-elected members appointed to represent their regions. The lower house, the House of Commons, was to be elected by the people. For the purposes of electing the members of the House of Commons (the MPs), the general principle of representation by population was adopted, and the provinces were to be divided into ridings (or seats) for that purpose.

From the very start, the historical compromises at the root of Canadian confederation meant that this general principle has been subject to the need to recognize Canada's diversity, Quebec's status, and the position of the smaller provinces and territories as Canada grew in population size and geographical extent (**Figure 9.29**). The current formula used to determine the **reapportionment** (or allocation) of seats is set out in the Representation Act of 1985 (**Figure 9.30**). Other systems of representation exist throughout the world. For example, many

federal state: a form of government in which powers are divided between the federal government and smaller units of government (such as provinces) within the country

reapportionment: the process of allocating electoral seats to geographical areas

Figure 9.29   Canada's political geography: provinces and territories   (*Source:* Geoffrey J. Matthews and Robert Morrow, *Canada and the World: An Atlas Resource*, 2nd ed. Scarborough, ON: Prentice Hall, 1995, pp. 5–6. See also the National Atlas of Canada's website at **http://atlas.gc.ca/site** where a sequence of maps on the territorial evolution of Canada can be found.)

Figure 9.30 The geography of a federal election This map shows the distribution of federal *ridings* (election districts) in the general election of June 28, 2004, by province and territory. Canada's vast territorial expanse and very uneven population distribution pose difficulties for the creation of ridings that are equal in terms of population. Low population densities in rural and northern areas make it very difficult for ridings to reach national averages for population before they become physically too large for one person (the MP) to represent adequately. For example, the entire territory of Nunavut comprises only one federal riding. It is more than 3 million square kilometres but has a population of only 26,475. The much higher population densities of urban and southern regions mean that there are more ridings in these areas and, all other things being equal, that their interests predominate in the House of Commons. Of the examples shown on the map, the small inner Montreal district of Outremont is the smallest, with an area of only 12 square kilometres, but with a population of 98,722. The challenges of balancing competing spatial interests lie at the heart of electoral geography. (*Source:* Number of electoral districts and district boundaries are taken from the Elections Canada website at **www.elections.ca**.)

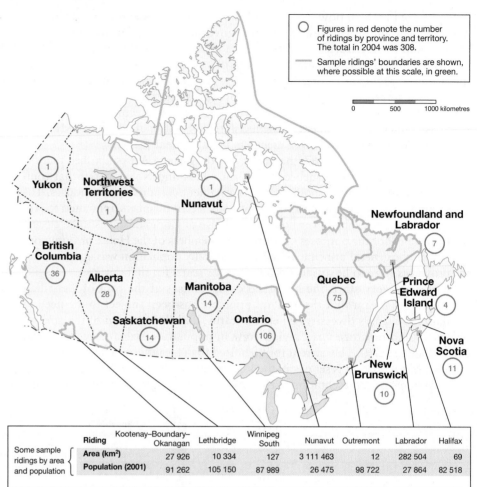

	Riding	Kootenay–Boundary–Okanagan	Lethbridge	Winnipeg South	Nunavut	Outremont	Labrador	Halifax
Some sample ridings by area and population	Area (km²)	27 926	10 334	127	3 111 463	12	282 504	69
	Population (2001)	91 262	105 150	87 989	26 475	98 722	27 864	82 518

electoral systems are based on representing special constituencies in the legislative branch of government. In Pakistan, for example, there are four seats for Christians; four seats for Hindus and people belonging to the scheduled castes; and one seat each for the Sikh, Buddhist, and Parsi communities. The point is that systems of representation are very much tied to the history of a country, with some very sensitive to the way that history and geography (who lives where) come together. These systems are both a product of and an important influence on the political culture of a country.

Politics and the Environment

Canadian political scientist Thomas Homer-Dixon has explored the complex links between the environment, environmental change, and political conflict in a series of studies on environmental scarcity and the causes of civil violence.[2] **Environmental scarcity** is a scarcity of renewable natural resources that, if not addressed by technological, social, or economic means, may cause social disruption or violent conflict. Examining the cases of Chiapas (Mexico), Pakistan, Rwanda, South Africa, Bangladesh/India, Senegal/Mauritania, El Salvador/Honduras, Haiti, Peru, and the Philippines, Homer-Dixon shows how environmental scarcity can be a cause of civil strife and violent conflict. We will look at another of his examples, water

environmental scarcity: a scarcity of renewable natural resources that, if not addressed by technological, social, or economic means, may cause social disruption or violent conflict

---

[2] Thomas Homer-Dixon, *Environment, Scarcity, and Violence.* Princeton: Princeton University Press, 1999.

shortage in the Gaza Strip, to learn how the interactions of population growth (Chapter 3); resource depletion (Chapter 4); religious, ethnic, and linguistic identities (Chapter 5); and political geography can lead to potentially critical situations that will create either conflict or new forms of cooperation between rival groups or states.[3]

With an area of only 365 square kilometres and a population of 1.6 million (up from 1.1 million in 2000), the Gaza Strip region faces a crisis. Simply put, more water is being consumed from Gaza's wells (100 million to 140 million cubic metres per year) than their annual rate of recharge allows on a long-term basis (65 million cubic metres per year). This unsustainable situation is the result of population pressure, intensive agriculture, and—most importantly—a highly inequitable distribution of resources.

Despite its small area, the Gaza Strip has had to accommodate large numbers of Palestinian refugees, often in such places as the Jabalya camp. It is estimated that more than 70 percent of the people living there are descended from refugees who fled the 1948 Arab–Israeli war. With Gaza's population growing at a rate between 5.2 and 6.9 percent per year (one of the highest rates in the world), water consumption will only continue to increase.

Gaza's economy relies on agriculture, but its focus on intensive citrus fruit cultivation makes for a second unsustainable factor. Currently, citrus tree groves occupy 55 percent of the total irrigated land in Gaza, and they use about half the region's agricultural water supply. However, these crops are unlikely to be cultivated for much longer. The continual pumping of water to meet the demands of irrigation has caused Mediterranean sea water to infiltrate into the region's underlying aquifer. The citrus trees cannot tolerate the increased levels of salinity.

The third factor, inequity, arises from the Gaza Strip's political circumstances. In 1967, Israel declared all water resources in the Gaza Strip and West Bank to be state owned and under military control. Palestinian water consumption was limited by orders that prohibited the drilling of new wells without a permit. On the other hand, Israeli settlers in the Gaza Strip faced far fewer restrictions and received subsidies to exploit their water supplies. On average, according to one estimate, Israeli settlers consume 10 times more water than does the Palestinian population. "The net effect of Israel's policies in Gaza," write Kelly and Homer-Dixon, "is to buffer Israelis from the effects of declining levels of water quality and quantity, while Palestinians bear the brunt of water scarcity." They conclude that the effects of this structural scarcity "generate serious friction between these communities."[4]

Unfortunately, the water problems in the Gaza Strip are only a small part of those facing the whole Middle East, the region "of the most concentrated water scarcity in the world," according to Sandra Postel, where 9 out of 14 countries face serious water shortages.[5] Canadian author Marq de Villiers, in his recent award-winning book *Water: The Fate of Our Most Precious Resource*, says that "the Middle East has always been the place where water wars are most probable. Indeed, Israel did have a shooting war with Syria over water, and it is now widely accepted that the 1967 Arab–Israeli war had its roots in water politics as much as it did in national territorialism."[6]

With only one major river in the region, the River Jordan, and only three major groundwater supplies, it is not hard to see why water supplies have become a factor in the geopolitics of the area. For example, Israel now diverts

---

[3] Kimberley Kelly and Thomas Homer-Dixon, "The Case of Gaza." In Thomas Homer-Dixon and Jessica Blitt (eds.), *Ecoviolence: Links among Environment, Population, and Security*. Lanham, MD: Rowman and Littlefield, 1998, pp. 67–107.

[4] Ibid., p. 77.

[5] Sandra Postel, *The Last Oasis: Facing Water Scarcity*. London: Earthscan Publications, 1992, p. 29.

[6] Marq de Villiers, *The Fate of Our Most Precious Resource*. New York: Houghton Mifflin/Mariner, 2001, p. 190.

most of the River Jordan to supply its own needs through a large pipeline. Neighbouring Jordan, now faced with a seven-eighths reduction in the flow of that river, has had to institute occasional water rationing in Amman and pump increasing amounts of water from underlying aquifers. Water rationing is also practised in Lebanon, where the breakdown of civil authority between 1976 and 1990 left farmers chronically short of water despite the abundance of the Litani River.

Israel itself will face water rationing if future projections hold. Even the 2009/2010 rainy season, which brought normal levels of rainfall after several years of dry conditions, could not ease the water deficit in which Israel finds itself: every year, it consumes hundreds of millions of cubic metres more than is replenished. Such considerations are believed to be one of the reasons why Israel continues to occupy the Golan Heights, which it took from Syria in 1967. Its control of this territory not only has strategic value but also confers control of the water resources of the Dan and Banyias rivers, which flow into the Jordan above Lake Tiberias—an increasingly precious resource in this troubled region.

The political implications of how Canada handles its own water resources provide our final example, and they are the subject of an interesting chapter in the book by Marq de Villiers. He refers, as many do when consideration of this issue is raised, to the concern that Canada's water resources may become a tradeable commodity under the terms of Chapter 11 of the NAFTA agreement. Environmental activists (such as CELA, the Canadian Environmental Law Association) have expressed fears that if this happens, Canada will lose control over an important resource. Canadian nationalists (such as the Council for Canadians) have pointed to the problems for this country's sovereignty if the United States is able to gain access to Canadian water supplies.

Matters were brought to a head in 1998 when a company called the Nova Group received a permit to export 600 million litres of Great Lakes water to Asia. How they were to achieve this was never disclosed; the Ontario environment minister cancelled the permit after its issuance unleashed a storm of public protest. However, as de Villiers concludes, if we believe that this is the end of the issue, then we fundamentally misunderstand some important points: Canadians misuse their own water supplies through pollution and waste, and Canada already exports more water overseas (in the guise of beer and mineral water) than would ever be feasible by a tanker trade in fresh water. As an editorial in Toronto's *Globe and Mail* very forcefully commented, "We say that [water] is priceless, but act as if it were absurdly cheap."

Canada's most northern waters also look set to become the focus of renewed political debate over issues of Arctic sovereignty. One of the results of global warming will be to make the Northwest Passage (see Chapter 1) navigable for commercial shipping and, if that route is interpreted as an "international waterway" (as the United States insists), to become used freely by the world's fleets. Greater ease of access to the Arctic combined with growing interest in fossil fuel and other resources has also meant that almost all of the countries with Arctic coastlines (including Russia, Norway, the United States, and Denmark) now vie with Canada to stake out legal title to the Arctic seabed, thus making Arctic sovereignty a geopolitical issue that Canada is being forced to address. As recently as August 2008, the federal government announced that it was funding an initiative to find the remains of the Franklin expedition (see Chapter 1), an endeavour that, if it were to succeed, would establish a prior claim to those Arctic islands and waters. Certainly the example of the Northwest Passage shows how environmental change can force a reassessment of the geopolitical value of space.

CONCLUSION

The globalization of the economy has been largely facilitated by the actions of states extending their spheres of influence and paving the way for the smooth functioning of markets and industries. Political geography is as much about what happens at the global level as it is about what happens at other levels of spatial resolution, from the region to the neighbourhood to the household and the individual.

Theories of the state have been one of geography's most important contributions to understanding politics. Ratzel's emphasis on the relationship between power and territory and Mackinder's model of the geographical heartland remind us that space and territory shape the actions of states in both dramatic and mundane ways. Time as well as space shape politics, and events distant in time and space—such as colonialism—continue to have impacts long after decolonization.

Continuing strife is also the case with the enduring North–South divide that pits core countries against peripheral, mostly formerly colonial, countries. Perhaps the most surprising political geographical transformation of the twentieth century was the near dissolution of the East–West divide. Although it is too soon to tell whether communism has truly been superseded by capitalism, it is certainly the case that the distinctions between them are more blurred than clear (take the example of "Communist" China).

The pairing of the terms *politics* and *geography* serves to remind us that politics is clearly geographical at the same time that geography is unavoidably political. The simple divisions of area into states, counties, cities, and towns means that where we live shapes our politics, and vice versa. Geography is politics just as politics is geography. And geographical systems of representation, as well as identity politics based on regional histories, confirm these interactive relationships.

Today—and for the future—access to increasingly scarce resources, such as water, will require nations and states to negotiate conflicts and cooperate if they are to survive.

MAIN POINTS REVISITED

■ **A subfield of the discipline of geography, political geography examines complex relationships between politics and geography (both human and physical).**

As societies are organized around territorial units, geography and access to it are often at the centre of political conflicts and can also enable the resolution of conflicts.

■ **Political geographers recognize that the relationship between politics and geography is two-way: political geography can be seen both as the geography of politics and the politics of geography.**

The geography-of-politics approach recognizes that systems of political representation are geographically anchored and shape the opportunities of the people who live within them.

■ **The relationship between politics and geography is often driven by particular theories and practices of the world's states. Understanding nation-state, imperialism, colonialism, and geopolitical theory is key to comprehending how, within the context of the world-system, geography has influenced politics and how politics has influenced geography.**

At the present moment, theories about globalization and the interconnectedness of places are particularly important, whereas the domino theory and heartland theory have waned in their intellectual and popular appeal.

■ **Political geography deals with phenomena occurring at all scales from the global to the household. Important East–West and North–South divisions dominate international politics, whereas regionalism and similar divisions dominate intra-state politics.**

No one scale necessarily dominates any other, and changes emanating from a locality may have international impacts and vice versa.

■ **Political geography recognizes the importance of the environment. Global change and population growth both make it likely that increased competition for future resources will also involve political conflict.**

As limited resources, such as water, become much more scarce, issues of human security will require us to reframe traditional concepts of sovereignty to cooperate in the use of resources.

Key Terms

centrifugal forces (p. 405)
centripetal forces (p. 405)
confederation (p. 434)
decolonization (p. 415)
democratic rule (p. 434)
domino theory (p. 419)
East–West divide (p. 419)
Enlightenment (p. 405)
environmental scarcity (p. 436)

federal state (p. 435)
geopolitics (p. 396)
imagined community (p. 406)
international organization (p. 424)
nation (p. 403)
nationalism (p. 405)
nation-state (p. 403)
North–South divide (p. 414)
reapportionment (p. 435)

regionalism (p. 430)
self-determination (p. 430)
sovereignty (p. 403)
supranational
   organizations (p. 425)
territorial organization (p. 434)
territory (p. 397)
unitary state (p. 434)
zionism (p. 434)

Additional Reading

Alia, R., and L. Lifschultz. *Why Bosnia? Writings on the Balkan War*. Stony Creek, CT: The Pamphleteer's Press, Inc., 1993.

Anderson, B. *Imagined Communities: Reflections on the Origin and Spread of Nationalism*. London: Verso, 1983.

Anderson, J., C. Brook, and A. Cochrane (eds.). *A Global World? Re-ordering Political Space*. Oxford: Oxford University Press, 1995.

Bradshaw, Y.W., and M. Wallace. *Global Inequalities*. Thousand Oaks, CA: Pine Forge Press, 1996.

Brockway, L.H. *Science and Colonial Expansion: The Role of the British Royal Botanic Gardens*. New York: Academic Press, 1979.

Brodie, J. "Restructuring and the New Citizenship." In Isabella Bakker (ed.), *Rethinking Restructuring: Gender and Change in Canada*. Toronto: University of Toronto Press, 1996, 126–140.

De Leeuw, S. "Intimate Colonialisms: The Material and Experienced Places of British Columbia's Residential Schools," *Canadian Geographer* 3, 2007, 339–359.

Dodds, K. *Geopolitics: A Very Short Introduction*. New York: Oxford University Press, 2007.

Dodds, K. *Geopolitics in a Changing World*. Harlow, UK: Prentice Hall, 2000.

Dyer, G. *War: The New Edition*. Toronto: Random House of Canada, 2004.

Enloe, C. *Bananas, Beaches and Bases: Making Feminist Sense of International Politics*. Berkeley: University of California Press, 1989.

Gould, K.A., A. Schnaiberg, and A.S. Weinberg. *Local Environmental Struggles: Citizen Activism in the Treadmill of Production*. New York: Cambridge University Press, 1996.

Hampson, F. Osler, M. Hart, and M. Rudner (eds.). *A Big League Player? Canada among Nations 1999*. Don Mills, ON: Oxford University Press, 1999.

Hobsbawm, E., and T. Ranger (eds.). *The Invention of Tradition*. Cambridge: Cambridge University Press, 1983.

Juergensmeyer, M. *The New Cold War? Religious Nationalism Confronts the State*. Berkeley: University of California Press, 1993.

Knight, D.B. "People Together, Yet Apart: Rethinking Territory, Sovereignty, and Identities." In G.J. Demko and W.B. Wood, *Reordering the World: Geopolitical Perspectives on the 21st Century*. Boulder: Westview Press, 1994, 71–86.

McRae, D.M. "Arctic Sovereignty: Loss by Dereliction?" In W.C. Wonders (ed.), *Canada's Changing North*, 2nd ed. Montreal and Kingston: McGill-Queen's University Press, 2003, 427–440.

Nash, A. "The Handwriting Is on the Berlin Wall," *Policy Options* 11(5), 1990, 26–27.

Pratt, C. "The Impact of Ethical Issues on Canadian Foreign Aid Policy," *Canadian Foreign Policy* 9(1), 2001.

Riesebrodt, M. *Pious Passion: The Emergence of Modern Fundamentalism in the United States and Iran*. Translated from the German *Fundamentalismus als patriarchalische Protestbewegung* by Don Reneau. Berkeley: University of California Press, 1993.

Smith, S. "Immigration and Nation-Building in Canada and the United Kingdom." In Peter Jackson and Jan Penrose (eds.), *Constructions of Race, Place and Nation*. Minneapolis: University of Minnesota Press, 1994, 50–77.

Stoett, P. *Human and Global Security: An Exploration of Terms*. Toronto: University of Toronto Press, 1999.

Thurow, L. *The Future of Capitalism*. New York: Morrow, 1996.

Discussion Questions and Research Activities

1. International boundaries are a prominent feature of the political geography of the contemporary world. In this exercise, you are asked to explore the impact of a boundary on nationalist attitudes and behaviours. You will need to use your university or college library's collection of Canadian newspapers (such as the *Globe and Mail*) and magazines (such as *Maclean's*) to complete this assignment. Using the United States–Canada border as your theme, describe the range of issues that derive from this juxtaposition of two different countries. You should concentrate on a five-year period and explain the issues that grew in importance, the issues that declined, and the issues that continued to have a consistent news profile throughout the period.

2. Using two maps of Europe (up to but not including Russia and the former Soviet Union), one from 1930 and one from 2000, compare the differences in them and provide explanations for the changes. How do issues of ethnicity, religion, and political system help explain these changes? Identify any areas on the map that you feel may be the sites of future border changes, and explain why.

MyGeosciencePlace

Visit **www.mygeoscienceplace.ca** to find chapter review quizzes, videos, maps, and much more.

10

Urbanization

São Paulo, Brazil

Urbanization is one of the most dynamic geographic phenomena in today's world. The United Nations Center for Human Settlements (UNCHS)[1] notes that the growth of cities and the urbanization of rural areas are now irreversible because of the global shift to technological-, industrial-, and service-based economies. Already, half the global population lives in cities; with the world's urban population growing at twice the general population rate, that share is expected to reach 80 percent by 2050. Clearly, the world's economic, social, cultural, and political processes are increasingly being played out within and between the world's systems of towns and cities.

The UNCHS has concluded that few countries are able to handle the urban population crush, which is causing problems on an unprecedented scale with everything from clean water to disease prevention. Already 10 million people are dying annually in densely populated urban areas from conditions produced by substandard housing and poor sanitation. UNICEF[2] has blamed "uncontrollable urbanization" in less developed countries for the widespread creation of "danger zones" in which increasing numbers of children are forced to become beggars, prostitutes, and labourers before reaching their teens. For millions of street kids in less developed countries, "work" means anything that contributes to survival: shining shoes, guiding cars into parking spaces, chasing other street kids away from patrons at an outdoor café, working as domestic help, making fireworks, selling drugs. In Abidjan, in the Ivory Coast, 15-year-old Jean-Pierre Godia, who cannot read or write, spends his days trying to sell packets of toilet paper to motorists at a busy intersection. He buys the packets for about US$1.20 and sells them for US$2. Some days he doesn't sell any. In the same city, 7-year-old Giulio guides cars into parking spaces outside a chic pastry shop. He has been doing this since he was 5, to help his mother and four siblings, who beg on a nearby corner.

Yet the processes and challenges of urbanization are also well known in the developed countries of the core. For example, artist Stan Douglas's 2001 photomontage *Every Building on 100 West Hastings* shows a part of Vancouver's Downtown Eastside, an area that has a reputation across Canada as a "problem" inner-city neighbourhood, the haunt of drug dealers, prostitutes, and the down-and-out.[3] When it was first exhibited in the Contemporary Art Gallery in Vancouver, Reid Shier remarked that the picture,

> shows a row of buildings in evident disrepair. Many of them are boarded
> up and appear on the verge of demolition. Paradoxically, there's a stark

---

[1] United Nations Center for Human Settlements (Habitat), *Cities in a Globalizing World: Global Report on Human Settlements, 2001.* London: Earthscan Publications, 2001.

[2] *The Progress of Nations.* New York: United Nations International Children's Fund (UNICEF), 1995.

[3] In 2009, David Look created a virtual tour of the 100 Block with Google Street View. You can take the tour at **http://www.everybuildingon100westhastings.info/**.

contrast between the buildings in Douglas' panoramic image and ones directly around the corner and down the street. Save for an area to its east, the architecture of the 100 block stands yards from buildings that are, economically and socially, worlds apart. Three blocks west the heart of the downtown core begins, and with it the start of the most expensive commercial real estate in Vancouver. Two blocks north along Water Street in Gastown, buildings in every way similar to the dilapidated Edwardian structures of Hastings are renovated into loft apartments and tourist shops. To the south along False Creek, sparkling condominium towers rise in one of the most comprehensively planned inner city redevelopment schemes in North America. Within this enfolding sphere of civic entitlement and reimagination, the 100 block stands out in stunning relief.

As Shier remarks, "this conjunction of ruin and renovation isn't an oddity brought on by the vagaries of Vancouver's redevelopment." It marks, as he notes later in his essay on the picture, a "pattern of withdrawal from a city's problem area [that] is a common narrative, and is allusive of the familiar exodus from urban cores that has plagued many North American cities in the post-war years." One reason has been the movement of jobs by transnational industries to cheaper and less regulated countries in the periphery; another has been the process of gentrification, which has become "part of a meticulously planned global phenomenon.[4]

In this chapter, we describe the extent and pattern of urbanization across the world, explaining its causes and the resultant changes brought in people and places. The next chapter, Chapter 11, will then consider the processes responsible for the internal shaping of cities and urban areas.

MAIN POINTS

- The urban areas of the world are the linchpins of human geographies at the local, regional, and global scales.
- The earliest urbanization developed independently in the various hearth areas of the first agricultural revolution.
- The expansion of trade around the world, associated with colonialism and imperialism, established numerous gateway cities.
- The Industrial Revolution generated new kinds of cities and many more of them.
- Today, the single most important aspect of world urbanization from a geographical perspective is the striking difference in trends and projections between the core regions and the peripheral regions.
- Cities form linked networks, known as *urban systems*, which determine the importance of component cities of the system and organize these cities into their various functional niches within an economy.

---

[4] Ibid., p. 12. In their essays in this book, geographers Nick Blomley and Neil Smith expand on these wider processes of urban growth and change.

- Canada's urban system is a product of processes that operate in both core and peripheral regions.

- A small number of "world cities," most of them located within the core regions of the world-system, occupy key roles in the organization of global economics and culture.

- The populations of many of the largest cities in the periphery have a doubling time of only 10 to 15 years.

- Many of the megacities of the periphery are primate and exhibit a high degree of centrality within their urban systems.

URBAN GEOGRAPHY AND URBANIZATION

From small market towns and fishing ports to megacities with millions of people, the urban areas of the world are the linchpins of human geographies. They have always been a crucial element in spatial organization and the evolution of societies, but today they are more important than ever. In Canada, for example, urban centres have been the focus of the country's economic transformation since the beginning of European contact, and the great majority of Canadians now live in cities. Worldwide, the number of city dwellers rose by more than 1.5 billion between 1980 and 2010; as a consequence, more than half of the world's population now lives in cities. In fact, much of the developed world has become almost completely urbanized (**Figure 10.1**), whereas in many peripheral and semiperipheral regions the current *rate* of urbanization is without precedent (**Figure 10.2**). The United Nations Human Settlements Program (UN-Habitat) estimates that 60 percent of the world's population will live in cities by 2030, of which 80 percent will be in peripheral and semiperipheral countries. In absolute terms, that equals the addition of a city of 1 million residents every week! Urbanization on

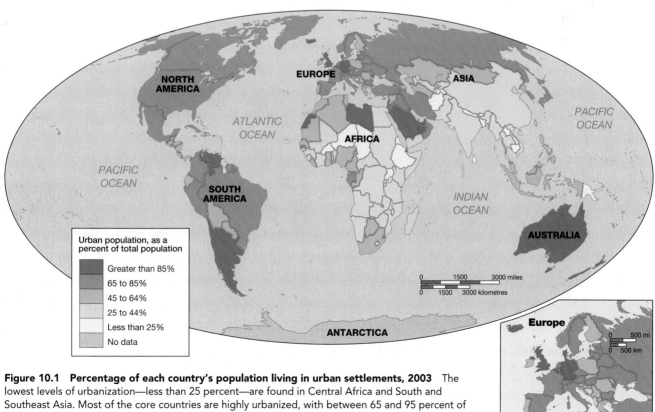

Figure 10.1 Percentage of each country's population living in urban settlements, 2003 The lowest levels of urbanization—less than 25 percent—are found in Central Africa and South and Southeast Asia. Most of the core countries are highly urbanized, with between 65 and 95 percent of their populations living in urban settlements. (*Source:* Data from United Nations Department of Economic and Social Affairs, Population Division, *World Urbanization Prospects: The 2003 Revision.*)

Even *within* the urban population, the process of concentration is accelerating: already, half of the urban population lives in one of 961 cities with more than half a million residents. According to a 2010 report by the U.N. Population Division of the U.N. Department of Economic and Social Affairs (DESA), there are now 54 cities of more than five million, and 21 cities with more than 10 million residents.

this scale is a remarkable and unprecedented geographical phenomenon—one of the most important processes shaping the world's landscapes today and in the future.

Cities are centres of cultural innovation, social transformation, and political change. They can also be engines of economic development: the gross product of large cities like London, Los Angeles, Mexico City, or Paris can exceed that of entire countries like Australia or Sweden. Although they often pose social and environmental problems, they clearly are essential elements in human economic and social organization. Experts on urbanization point to four fundamental aspects of the role of cities in human economic and social organization:

- The *mobilizing function* of urban settlement. Cities provide efficient and effective environments for organizing labour, capital, and raw materials and for distributing finished products.

- The *decision-making capacity* of urban settlement. Because urban settings bring together the decision-making machinery of public and private

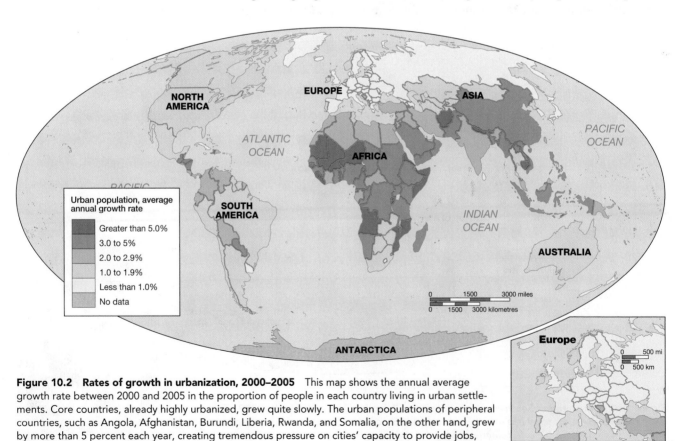

Figure 10.2 Rates of growth in urbanization, 2000–2005 This map shows the annual average growth rate between 2000 and 2005 in the proportion of people in each country living in urban settlements. Core countries, already highly urbanized, grew quite slowly. The urban populations of peripheral countries, such as Angola, Afghanistan, Burundi, Liberia, Rwanda, and Somalia, on the other hand, grew by more than 5 percent each year, creating tremendous pressure on cities' capacity to provide jobs, housing, and public services. (*Source:* Data from United Nations Department of Economic and Social Affairs, Population Division, *World Urbanization Prospects: The 2009 Revision.*)

institutions and organizations, they become concentrations of political and economic power.

- The *generative functions* of urban settlement. The concentration of people in urban settings makes for much greater interaction and competition, which facilitate the generation of innovation, knowledge, and information.

- The *transformative capacity* of urban settlement. The size, density, and variety of urban populations allow people to escape the rigidities of traditional rural society and to participate in a variety of lifestyles and behaviours.

Urban geographers are concerned with the development of towns and cities around the world, particularly with the similarities and differences both *within* and *between* urban places. For urban geographers, some of the most important questions include: What attributes make towns and cities distinctive? How did these distinctive identities evolve? What are the relationships and interdependencies between particular sets of towns, cities, and their surrounding territories? Do significant regularities exist in the spatial organization of land use within cities, in the patterning of neighbourhood populations, or in the layout and landscapes of particular kinds of cities?

Urban geographers also want to know about the causes of the patterns and regularities they find. How, for example, do specialized urban subdistricts evolve? Why did urban growth occur in a particular region at a particular time? Why did urban growth exhibit a distinctive physical form during a certain period? In pursuing such questions, urban geographers have learned that the answers can ultimately be found in the wider context of economic, social, cultural, and political life. In other words, towns and cities must be viewed as part of the economies and societies that maintain them.

Urbanization, therefore, is not simply a process of the demographic growth of towns and cities. It also involves many other changes, both quantitative and qualitative. From the geographer's perspective, these changes can be conceptualized in several different ways. One of the most important of these is by examining the attributes and dynamics of urban systems. An **urban system**, or city system, is any interdependent set of urban settlements within a given region. For example, we can speak of the Canadian urban system, the African urban system, or even the global urban system. As urbanization takes place, the attributes of urban systems will, of course, reflect the fact that increasing numbers of people are living in ever-larger towns and cities. They will also reflect other important changes, such as changes in the relative size of cities, in their functional relationships with one another, and in their employment base and population composition.

urban system: an interdependent set of urban settlements within a specified region

Another important aspect of change associated with urbanization processes concerns **urban form**—the physical structure and organization of cities in their land use, layout, and built environment. As urbanization takes place, not only do towns and cities grow bigger physically, extending upward and outward, but they also become reorganized, redeveloped, and redesigned in response to changing circumstances.

urban form: the physical structure and organization of cities

These changes, in turn, are closely related to a third aspect of change—transformations in patterns of **urban ecology**, the social and demographic composition of city districts and neighbourhoods. Urbanization not only brings more people to cities, but it also brings a greater variety of people. As different social, economic, demographic, and ethnic subgroups sort themselves into different territories, distinctive urban ecologies emerge. As new subgroups arrive or old ones leave, these ecologies change.

urban ecology: the social and demographic composition of city districts and neighbourhoods

A fourth aspect of change associated with urbanization concerns people's attitudes and behaviour. New forms of social interaction are brought about by the liberating and transformative effects of urban environments. These changes have given rise to the concept of urbanism, which refers to the distinctive nature of social and cultural organization in particular urban settings. **Urbanism** describes the way of life fostered by urban settings, in which the number, physical density, and variety of people often result in distinctive attitudes, values, and patterns of

urbanism: the way of life, attitudes, values, and patterns of behaviour fostered by urban settings

behaviour. Geographers are interested in urbanism because of the ways in which it varies both within and between cities.

URBAN ORIGINS

It is important to put the geographical study of towns and cities in historical context. After all, many of the world's cities are the product of a long period of development. We can understand a city, old or young, only if we know something about the reasons behind its growth, the rate at which it has grown, and the processes that have contributed to its growth.

In broad terms, the earliest urbanization developed independently in the various hearth areas of the first agricultural revolution. The very first region of independent urbanism was in the Middle East, in the valleys of the Tigris and Euphrates (in Mesopotamia) and in the Nile Valley from around 3500 B.C. (**Figure 10.3**). Together, these intensively cultivated river valleys formed the so-called Fertile Crescent. By 2500 B.C. cities had appeared in the Indus Valley, and by 1800 B.C. they were established in northern China. Other areas of independent urbanism include Mesoamerica (from around 100 B.C.) and Andean America (from around A.D. 800). Meanwhile, the original Middle Eastern urban hearth continued to produce successive generations of urbanized world-empires, including those of Greece (**Figure 10.4**), Rome, and Byzantium.

Experts differ in their explanations of these first transitions from subsistence mini-systems to city-based world-empires. The classical archaeological interpretation emphasizes the availability of an agricultural surplus large enough to allow the emergence of specialized, nonagricultural workers. An alternative explanation hypothesizes that urbanization may also have resulted from the pressure of population growth. This pressure, it is thought, disturbed the balance between population and resources, causing some people to move to marginal agricultural areas, where they either had to devise new techniques of food production and storage or establish a new form of economy based on services such as trade, religion, or defence. Any such economy would have required concentrations of people in urban settlements.

Figure 10.3 Erbil Erbil (Ancient Arbela) in northeast Iraq is located atop a *tell*, a mound representing the remains of generations of sun-dried mud-brick buildings, visible as a hill rising high above the surrounding plain. The 30-metre-high Erbil tell is believed to be the rubble of 6,000 years of continuous occupation. Other Mesopotamian cities on the rich alluvial soils of the river floodplains included Ur (in present-day Iraq), the capital from about 2300 to 2180 B.C., as well as Eridu and Uruk. These fortified city-states contained tens of thousands of inhabitants; social stratification, with religious, political, and military classes; innovative technologies, including massive irrigation projects; and extensive trade connections.

Corinth began to develop as a commercial centre in the eighth century B.C., though its site had been inhabited since before 3000 B.C. This photograph shows the ruins of the Temple of Apollo.

Ancient Athens was at its peak in the fifth century B.C., when, as the largest and wealthiest *polis* (city-state), it became the cultural and intellectual centre of the classical Greek world. The Parthenon, built on top of the Acropolis, dates from this time.

Figure 10.4 Greek colonization The Greeks traded and colonized throughout the Aegean from the eighth century B.C. onward. Later, they extended their activities to the central Mediterranean and Black Sea, where their settlements formed important nuclei for subsequent urbanization. The shaded area on the map shows the extent of the *polis*, the Greek ideal of a democratic city-state. Note the emphasis on coastal locations.   (*Source for map*: J. Rich and A. Wallace-Hadrill (eds.), *City and Country in the Ancient World*. London: Routledge, 1991, fig. 1b.)

Changes in social organization were an important precondition for urbanization. Specifically, urbanization required the emergence of groups that were able to exact tributes, impose taxes, and control labour power, usually through some form of religious persuasion or military coercion. Once established, this elite group provided the stimulus for urban development by using its wealth to build palaces, arenas, and monuments to show off its power and status. This activity not only created the basis for the physical core of ancient cities (**Figure 10.5**) but also required an increased degree of specialization in nonagricultural activities—construction, crafts, administration, the priesthood, soldiery, and so on—which could be organized effectively only in an urban setting. By A.D. 1000, city-based world-empires had emerged in Europe, the Middle East, and China, including a dozen major cities with populations of 100,000 or more (**Figure 10.6**).

The urbanized economies of world-empires were a precarious phenomenon, however, and many of them lapsed into ruralism before being revived or recolonized. In a number of cases, the decline of world-empires was a result of demographic setbacks associated with wars or epidemics. Such disasters left too few people to maintain the social and economic infrastructure necessary for urbanization. This lack of labour power seems to have been a major contributing factor to the eventual collapse of the Mesopotamian Empire. Similarly, the population of the Roman Empire began to decline in the second century A.D., giving

Figure 10.5 Ancient Troy Situated on the southern end of the Dardanelles, the ancient city of Troy could easily control all seaborne trade between the Aegean and the Black Sea. Declared a World Heritage site in 1998, and identified as the most likely site of the legendary Trojan War (which, if it actually took place, has been dated to approximately 1250 B.C.), these ruins have long attracted the attention of archaeologists eager to explore the city evoked in Homer's poem *The Iliad* (which itself dates from about 700 B.C.). New excavations suggest that the city's origins date back to almost 3000 B.C.

rise to labour shortages, abandoned fields, and depopulated towns and allowing the infiltration of "barbarian" settlers and tribes from the Germanic lands of east-central Europe. On the other hand, the abandonment of much of the Maya Empire more than 500 years before the arrival of the Spanish may be due to environmental change and social upheaval.

The Roots of European Urban Expansion

In Europe, the urban system introduced by the Greeks and re-established by the Romans almost collapsed during the Dark Ages of early medieval Europe (A.D. 476–1000). During this period, feudalism gave rise to a fragmented landscape of inflexible and inward-looking world-empires. *Feudalism* was a rigid, rurally oriented form of economic and social organization based on the communal chiefdoms of Germanic tribes who had invaded the disintegrating Roman Empire. Essentially, these rulers held all the land in a chiefdom but allowed it to be farmed by the local population of peasants in return for rents, taxes, and military services. From this unlikely beginning, an elaborate urban system developed, its largest centres eventually growing into what would become the nodal centres of a global world-system.

Figure 10.6 Kyoto The ancient city of Kyoto had a population of 180,000 in A.D. 1000.

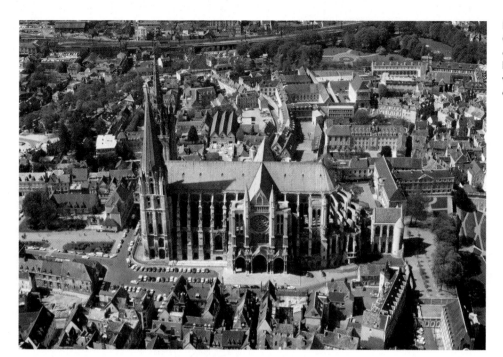

Figure 10.7 Chartres, France
Chartres was an important ecclesiastical centre. The cathedral, built in the thirteenth century, is widely considered the finest gothic cathedral in France.

Early medieval Europe, divided into a patchwork of feudal kingdoms and estates, was mostly rural. Each feudal estate was more or less self-sufficient regarding foodstuffs, and each kingdom or principality was more or less self-sufficient regarding the raw materials needed to craft simple products. Most regions, however, did support at least a few small towns. The existence of these towns depended mainly on their role:

- *Ecclesiastical or university centres*—Examples include Rheims and Chartres (**Figure 10.7**) in France, Bremen in Germany, and Lund in Sweden.

- *Defensive strongholds*—Examples include the hilltop towns of central Italy, such as Urbino (**Figure 10.8**), and the *bastide,* or fortress, towns of south-western France, such as Aigues-Mortes (**Figure 10.9**).

- *Administrative centres* for the upper tiers of the feudal hierarchy—Examples include Cologne (**Figure 10.10**), Mainz, and Magdeburg in Germany.

Figure 10.8 Urbino, Italy Built on a classic hilltop defensive site, Urbino had been settled by Etruscans and Romans before coming under church rule in the ninth century. It became an eminent artistic centre during the Renaissance.

Figure 10.9 Aigues-Mortes, France The walled medieval town of Aigues-Mortes in southern France is one of the best-preserved examples of thirteenth-century military architecture. The town of rectilinear streets is surrounded by a wall with 5 towers and 10 fortified gates.

From the eleventh century onward, however, the feudal system faltered and disintegrated in the face of successive demographic, economic, and political crises, which were caused by steady population growth in conjunction with only modest technological improvements and limited amounts of cultivable land. To bolster their incomes and raise armies against one another, the feudal nobility began to levy increasingly higher taxes. The rural peasants were consequently obliged to sell more of their produce for cash on the market. As a result, a more extensive money economy developed, along with the beginnings of a pattern of trade in basic agricultural produce and craft manufactures. Some long-distance trade even began in luxury goods, such as spices, furs, silks, fruit, and wine. Towns began to increase in size and vitality on the basis of this trade. Indeed, the role of such trade in rejuvenating Europe's cities cannot be overemphasized.

The regional specializations and trading patterns that emerged provided the foundations for a new phase of urbanization based on merchant capitalism (**Figure 10.11**). Beginning with networks established by the merchants of Venice, Pisa, Genoa, and Florence (in northern Italy) and the trading partners

Figure 10.10 Cologne In the late 1400s, when this woodcut was made, Cologne was an important commercial and manufacturing centre, with a university that was already more than 100 years old. The city was founded as the Roman settlement of *Colonia*—an early example of a world-empire colonizing external territory.

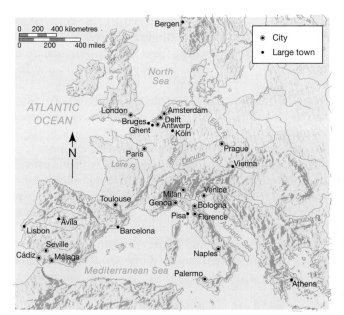

Bergen,
Norway

Avila,
Spain

Ghent,
Belgium

Florence,
Italy

Figure 10.11   The towns and cities of Europe, c. 1350   Cities with more than 10,000 residents were uncommon in medieval Europe except in northern Italy and Flanders, where the spread of cloth production and the growth of trade permitted relatively intense urbanization. Elsewhere, large size was associated with a complex of administrative, religious, educational, and economic functions. By 1350, many of the bigger towns (for example, Barcelona, Cologne, or Prague) supported universities as well as a variety of religious institutions. Most urban systems, reflecting the economic and political realities of the time, were relatively small in extent.   (*Source for map:* P.M. Hohenberg and L.H. Lees, *The Making of Urban Europe 1000–1950*. Cambridge, MA: Harvard University Press, 1985, fig. 2.1.)

of the Hanseatic League (a federation of city-states around the North Sea and Baltic coasts), a trading system of immense complexity soon came to span Europe from Bergen to Athens and from Lisbon to Vienna. By 1400, long-distance trading was well established, based not on the luxury goods of the pioneer merchants but on bulky staples, such as grains, wine, salt, wool, cloth, and metals. The populations of Milan, Genoa, Venice, and Bruges had all grown to 100,000 or more. Paris was the dominant European city, with a population of about 275,000. This was the Europe that stood poised to extend its grasp to a global scale.

Between the fifteenth and seventeenth centuries, a series of changes occurred that transformed not only the cities and city systems of Europe but also the entire world economy. Merchant capitalism increased in scale and sophistication; economic and social reorganization was stimulated by the Protestant Reformation and the scientific revolution. Meanwhile, aggressive overseas colonization made Europeans the leaders, persuaders, and shapers of the rest of the world's economies and societies. Spanish and Portuguese colonists were the first to extend the European urban system into the world's peripheral regions. They established the basis of a colonial Latin American urban system in just 60 years, between 1520 and 1580. Spanish colonists founded their cities on the sites of native American cities (Oaxaca and Mexico City in Mexico, Cajamarca and Cuzco in Peru, and Quito in Ecuador) or in regions of dense indigenous populations (Puebla and

Guadalajara in Mexico, and Arequipa and Lima in Peru). These colonial towns were established mainly as administrative and military centres from which the Spanish Crown could occupy and exploit the New World. Portuguese colonists, in contrast, situated their cities—Recife, Salvador, São Paulo, and Rio de Janeiro—with commercial rather than administrative considerations in mind. They, too, were motivated by exploitation, but their strategy was to establish colonial towns in locations best suited to organizing the collection and export of the products of their mines and plantations.

In Europe, Renaissance reorganization saw the centralization of political power and the formation of national states, the beginnings of industrialization, and the funnelling of plunder and produce from distant colonies. In this new context, the port cities of the North Sea and Atlantic coasts enjoyed a decisive locational advantage. By 1700, London's population had grown to 500,000, while Lisbon's and Amsterdam's populations had each grown to about 175,000. The cities of continental and Mediterranean Europe expanded at a more modest rate. By 1700, Venice had added only 30,000 inhabitants to its 1400 population of 110,000, and Milan's population did not grow at all between 1400 and 1700.

The most important aspect of urbanization during this period, however, was the establishment of gateway cities around the rest of the world (**Figure 10.12**). A **gateway city** is one that serves as a link between one country or region and others because of its physical situation. It is a control centre that commands entrance to and exit from its particular country or region. European powers founded or developed literally thousands of towns as they extended their trading networks and established their colonies. The great majority of them were ports. Protected by fortifications and European naval power, they began as trading posts and colonial administrative centres. Before long, they developed manufacturing of their own to supply the pioneers' needs, along with more extensive commercial and financial services.

As colonies were developed and trading networks expanded, some of these ports grew rapidly, acting as gateways for colonial expansion into continental interiors. Into their harbours came waves of European settlers; through their docks was funnelled the produce of continental interiors. Rio de Janeiro (Brazil) grew on the basis of gold mining; Accra (Ghana) on cocoa; Buenos Aires (Argentina) on mutton, wool, and cereals; Calcutta (now Kolkata, India) on jute, cotton, and textiles; São Paulo (Brazil) on coffee; and so on. As they grew into major population centres, these cities became important markets for imported European manufactured goods, adding even more to their functions as gateways for international transport and trade.

Throughout the nineteenth century, European imperialism gave a significant impetus to urbanization in the world's peripheral regions. New gateway cities were founded, and, as Europeans raced to establish economic and political control over continental interiors, colonial cities were established as centres of administration, political control, and commerce. **Colonial cities** are those that were deliberately established or developed as administrative or commercial centres by colonial or imperial powers. In these cities, the colonial imprint is still visible in and around the city centre in the formal squares and public spaces, the layout of avenues, and the presence of colonial architecture and monuments (**Figure 10.13**).

Industrialization and Urbanization

It was not until the late eighteenth century that urbanization became an important dimension of the world-system in its own right. In 1800, less than 5 percent of the world's 980 million people lived in towns and cities. By 1950, however, 16 percent of the world's population was urban, and more than 900 cities with 100,000 or more inhabitants existed around the world. The Industrial Revolution and European imperialism had created unprecedented

gateway city: a city that serves as a link between one country or region and others because of its physical situation

colonial cities: cities that were deliberately established or developed as administrative or commercial centres by colonial or imperial powers

New York, at first a modest Dutch fur-trading port, became the gateway for millions of European immigrants and for a large volume of U.S. agricultural and manufacturing exports.

Boston first flourished as the principal colony of the Massachusetts Bay Company, exporting furs and fish and importing slaves from West Africa, hardwoods from central America, molasses from the Caribbean, manufactured goods from Europe, and tea (via Europe) from South Asia.

Salvador, Brazil, was the landfall of the Portuguese in 1500. They established plantations that were worked by slave labour from West Africa. Salvador became the gateway for most of the 3.5 million slaves who were shipped to Brazil between 1526 and 1870.

Guangzhou was the first Chinese port to be in regular contact with European traders—first Portuguese in the sixteenth century and then British in the seventeenth century.

Nagasaki was the only port that feudal Japanese leaders allowed open to European traders, and for more than 200 years Dutch merchants held a monopoly of the import-export business through the city.

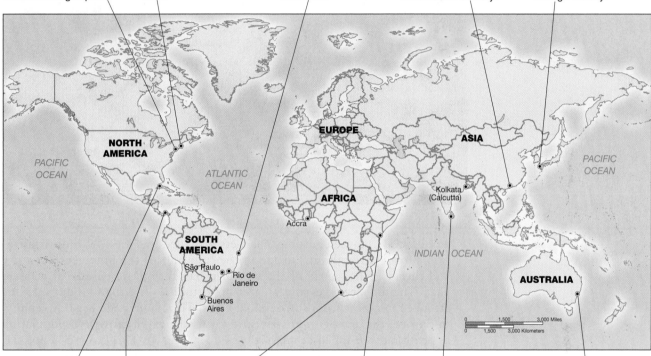

Havana was founded and developed by the Spanish in 1515 because of its excellent harbour. It was used as the assembly point for annual convoys returning to Spain.

Panama City, founded by the Spanish in 1519, became the gateway for gold and silver on its way by galleon to Spain.

Cape Town was founded in 1652 as a provisioning station for ships of the Dutch East India Company. Later, under British rule, it developed into an import-export gateway for South Africa.

Mombasa (in present-day Kenya) was already a significant Arab trading port when Vasco da Gama visited it in 1498 on his first voyage to India. The Portuguese used it as a trading station until it was recaptured by the Arabs in 1698. It did not become an important gateway port until it fell under British Imperial rule in the nineteenth century, when railroad development opened up the interior of Kenya, along with Rwanda, Uganda, and northern Tanzania.

Colombo's strategic situation on trade routes saw it occupied successively by the Portuguese, the Dutch, and the British. It became an important gateway after the British constructed an artificial harbour to handle the exports from tea plantations in Ceylon (now Sri Lanka).

Sydney, Australia, was not settled until the late eighteenth century, and even then many of the settlers were convicts who had been forcibly transported from Britain. It soon became the gateway for agricultural and mineral exports (mostly to Britain) and for imports of manufactured goods and European immigrants.

Figure 10.12 Gateway cities in the world-system periphery Gateway cities are control centres that command entrance to and exit from their particular country or region. Many of the world's most important cities grew to prominence as gateway cities because they commanded routes into and out of developing colonies.

concentrations of humanity that were intimately linked in networks and hierarchies of interdependence.

Cities were synonymous with industrialization. Industrial economies could be organized only through the large pools of labour; the transportation networks; the physical infrastructure of factories, warehouses, stores,

Figure 10.13 Colonial architecture and urban design Cities in the periphery of the world-system have grown very rapidly since the colonial era, but the legacy of the colonial period can still be seen in the architecture, monuments, and urban design of the period. This painting of the Indian Peninsular Terminus in Mumbai (Bombay) shows the influence of Victorian British architecture. The station is still in use today.

shock city: a city that is seen as the embodiment of surprising and disturbing changes in economic, social, and cultural lives

and offices; and the consumer markets provided by cities. As industrialization spread throughout Europe in the first half of the nineteenth century and then to other parts of the world, urbanization increased—at a faster pace. The higher wages and greater opportunities in urban labour markets attracted migrants from surrounding areas. The countryside began to empty. In Europe, the *demographic transition* caused a rapid growth in population as death rates dropped dramatically (see Chapter 3). This growth in population provided a massive increase in the labour supply throughout the nineteenth century, further boosting the rate of urbanization, not only within Europe itself but also in Australia, Canada, New Zealand, South Africa, and the United States, as emigration spread industrialization and urbanization to the frontiers of the world-system.

The shock city of nineteenth-century European industrialization was Manchester, England, which grew from a small town of 15,000 in 1750 to a city of 70,000 in 1801, a metropolis of 500,000 in 1861, and a world city of 2.3 million by 1911. A **shock city** is one that is seen at the time as the embodiment of surprising and disturbing changes in economic, social, and cultural lives. As industrialization took hold in North America, the shock city was Chicago, which grew from fewer than 30,000 in 1850 to 500,000 in 1880, 1.7 million in 1900, and 3.3 million in 1930. Both Manchester and Chicago were archetypal forms of an entirely new kind of city—the *industrial city*—whose fundamental reason for existence was not, as in earlier generations of cities, to fulfill military, political, ecclesiastical, or trading functions. Rather, it existed mainly to assemble raw materials and to fabricate, assemble, and distribute manufactured goods. Both Manchester and Chicago had to cope, however, with unprecedented rates of growth and the unprecedented economic, social, and political problems that were a consequence of their growth (see **Visualizing Geography 10.1—Shock Cities: Manchester and Chicago**). Both were also *world cities*, cities in which a disproportionate part of the world's most important business—economic, political, and cultural—is conducted. At the top of a global urban system, these cities experience growth largely as a result of their role as key nodes in the world economy.

Shock Cities: Manchester and Chicago

"One day I walked with one of these middle-class gentlemen into Manchester. I spoke to him about the disgraceful unhealthy slums and drew his attention to the disgusting condition of that part of the town in which the factory worker lived. I declared that I had never seen so badly built a town in my life. He listened patiently and at the corner of the street he remarked: 'And yet there is a great deal of money to be made here. Good morning, Sir!'"

Friedrich Engels,
*The Condition of the Working
Class in England in 1844*

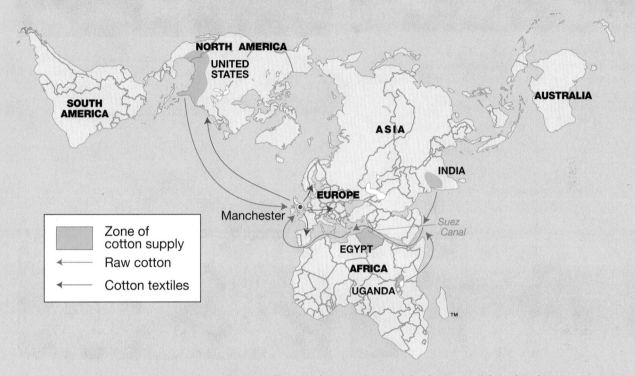

Zone of cotton supply

← Raw cotton

← Cotton textiles

The opening of the Suez Canal in 1869 halved the travelling time between Britain and India. It ruined the Indian domestic cotton textile industry, but it allowed India to export its raw cotton to Manchester. Around the same time, British colonialists established cotton plantations in Egypt and Uganda, providing another source of supply.

Manchester City Hall, a classic example of Victorian Gothic architecture, was built to show the world that the city had arrived. Manchester in the nineteenth century was a city of enormous vitality, not only in its economic life but also in its political, cultural, and intellectual lives.

In the mid-nineteenth century, the United States produced more than 80 percent of the world's raw cotton, much of it from plantations like this one in Georgia. Manchester was the chief consumer of this cotton, and it, in turn, became the world's chief exporter of cotton textiles.

Canals were at the heart of the development of industrial Manchester. They enabled coal and raw materials to be carried right to the heart of the city and finished goods to be transported away easily.

Part of the redeveloped Salford Quays, the Lowry Centre (named after L.S. Lowry, the Manchester artist famous for painting scenes of life in the industrial districts of northern England during the early twentieth century) is a combined theatre and gallery complex, illustrating the concept of *place marketing* (see Chapter 6).

In 1894 the Manchester Ship Canal was opened, allowing ocean-going vessels to reach docks close to the centre of Manchester. The canal revived the city's trade and made possible the development of a concentration of heavy industry.

Railway viaducts, like this one in Stockport, just outside Manchester, brought rail transportation to Manchester early in the nineteenth century and helped to make the city a major transportation hub.

With the development of deep-water container ports and roadways, the central docks of Manchester became obsolete. In the 1990s, some of them were redeveloped as Salford Quays, with upscale condominiums and stores.

Manchester's first cotton mill was built in the early 1780s, and by 1830 there were 99 cotton-spinning mills. As the city grew, it spilled out into the surrounding countryside, bringing its characteristic landscape of red-brick terrace (row) housing and "Dark Satanic Mills" with their tall brick chimneys.

In the late nineteenth century, working-class housing was built to conform with local building codes—but only just. Much of it has now been replaced, but a good deal still remains.

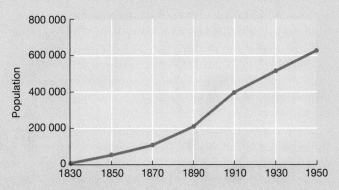

Migrants from Ireland and northern England contributed to Manchester's rapid growth from the mid-nineteenth century.

When Chicago was first incorporated as a city in 1837, its population was only 4,200. Its growth followed the arrival of the railroads, which made the city a major transportation hub. By the 1860s, lake vessels were carrying iron ore from the Upper Michigan ranges to the city's blast furnaces, and railroads were hauling cattle, hogs, and sheep to the city for slaughtering and packing. The city's prime geographical situation also made it the pre-eminent lumber-distributing centre by the 1880s.

Chicago's immigrant and African-American neighbourhoods were an entirely new urban phenomenon—highly segregated and with very distinctive social and cultural attributes. The 1880 and 1890 censuses showed that more than three-quarters of Chicago's population was made up of foreign-born immigrants and their children. These photographs of ethnic neighbourhoods in Chicago's Southside were taken in 1941.

Chicago announced its prosperity through elaborate skyscrapers and towers. The Tribune Tower, shown here, was built in Gothic Revival style and based on the winning entry in an international design competition organized by the *Chicago Tribune* in 1922. The city has regarded itself ever since as a sponsor of landmark architecture.

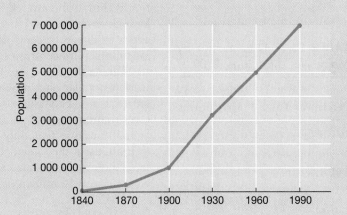

Immigrants from Europe fuelled Chicago's phenomenal growth.

Chicago

Hog-butcher for the World,
Tool Maker, Stacker of Wheat
Player with Railroads and the Nation's
    Freight Handler;
Stormy, husky, brawling,
City of the Big Shoulders. . . .
—*Carl Sandburg, 1916*

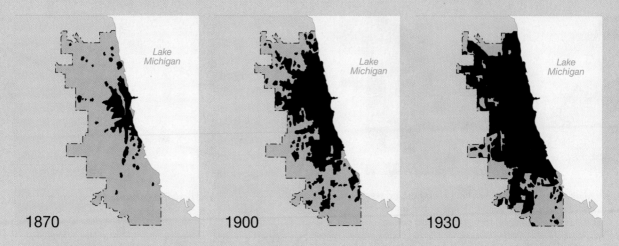

1870   1900   1930

In 1870, when Manchester was already a thriving metropolis, Chicago was at the beginning of a period of explosive growth. A year later, 9 square kilometres of the city, including the business district, were destroyed by fire. They were rebuilt rapidly, with prosperous industrialists taking the opportunity to build impressive new structures in the downtown area. The city's economic and social elite colonized the Lake Michigan shore, while heavy industry, warehouses, and railyards crowded the banks of the Chicago River, stretching northwestward from the city centre. To the south of the city centre were the Union Stockyards and a pocket of heavy industry where the Calumet River met Lake Michigan. All around were the homes of working families, in neighbourhoods that spread rapidly outward as wave after wave of immigrants arrived in the city.

WORLD URBANIZATION TODAY

It is difficult to say just how urbanized the world has become. In many parts of the world, urban growth is taking place at such a pace and under such chaotic conditions that it is impossible even for experts to do more than provide informed estimates. The most comprehensive source of statistics is the United Nations, whose data suggest that more than half of the world's population is now urban. These data incorporate the very different definitions of *urban* used by different countries. Some countries (Australia and Canada, for example) count any settlement of 1,000 people or more as urban; others (including Italy and Jordan) use 10,000 as the minimum for an urban settlement; and Japan uses 50,000 as the cut-off. This tells us something about the nature of urbanization itself: it is a *relative* phenomenon. In such countries as Peru, where population is thin and scattered, a settlement of 2,000 represents a significant centre. In such countries as Japan, however, with greater numbers, higher densities, and a tradition of centralized rather than scattered agricultural settlement, a much larger concentration of people is required to count as "urban."

Taking the definitions used in individual countries, more than one-half of the world's population is now urbanized. As **Table 10.1** shows, North America is the most urbanized continent in the world, with more than 80 percent of its population living in urban areas. In contrast, Africa is less than 40 percent urban. To put these figures in perspective, only 29.7 percent of the world's population was urbanized in 1950, using the same definitions of urban settlements. **Table 10.2** illustrates the rapid increase in urbanization since then. Today, 1 in 20 people worldwide lives in a megacity of 10 million or more; by 2025, that number will rise to 1 in 10.

Regional Trends and Projections

The single most important aspect of world urbanization, from a geographical perspective, is the striking difference in trends and projections between the core regions and the semiperipheral and peripheral regions. In 1950, two-thirds of the world's urban population was concentrated in the more developed countries of the core economies. Since then, the world's urban population has increased

TABLE 10.1 Urbanization by Major World Regions, 2009

Percent of Total	Population in Urban Areas
Africa	39.6
Asia	41.7
Latin America	79.3
North America	81.9
Europe	72.5
Oceania	70.2
World	50.2

Source: Data from United Nations, *World Urbanization Prospects: The 2009 Revision.*

TABLE 10.2 Percentage of Urbanized Population and Number of Large Cities, 1950, 2009, and 2025

	1950	2009	2025 (est.)
Urbanized population in percent	29.7	50.2	52
Number of cities over 1 million	83	374	475
Number of cities over 5 million	8	32	46
Number of cities over 10 million	2	21	29

Source: Data from United Nations, *World Urbanization Prospects: The 2009 Revision.*

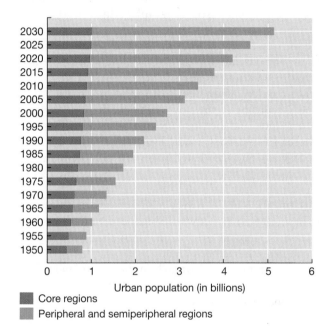

Core regions
Peripheral and semiperipheral regions

Figure 10.14 Urban population growth, 1950–2030 Although the metropolitan areas of the world's core countries have continued to grow, most of them have been overtaken by the startling growth of the "unintended" metropolises of peripheral and semi-peripheral countries.   (*Source:* Data from United Nations, *World Urbanization Prospects.* New York: UN Department of Economic and Social Affairs, 1998.)

TABLE 10.3 The World's 10 Largest Metropolitan Areas, Ranked by Population Size, 1950, 1980, and 2009 (in millions)

1950	Population	1980	Population	2009	Population
New York	12.3	Tokyo	28.5	Tokyo	36.5
London	8.7	New York	15.6	Delhi	21.7
Tokyo	6.9	Mexico City	13.0	São Paulo	20.0
Paris	5.4	São Paulo	12.1	Mumbai	19.7
Moscow	5.4	Shanghai	11.7	Mexico City	19.3
Shanghai	5.3	Osaka	10.0	New York	19.3
Essen	5.3	Buenos Aires	9.9	Shanghai	16.3
Buenos Aires	5.0	Los Angeles	9.5	Kolkata	15.3
Chicago	4.9	Kolkata	9.0	Dhaka	14.3
Kolkata	4.4	Beijing	9.0	Buenos Aires	13.0

Source: Data from United Nations, *World Urbanization Prospects: The 2009 Revision.*

threefold, the bulk of the growth having taken place in the less developed countries of the periphery (**Figure 10.14**). In 1950, seven of the world's largest 10 metropolitan areas were located in core countries; by 2009, only two core cities (Tokyo and New York) were left among the top 10 (**Table 10.3**).

Nowhere is the trend toward rapid urbanization more pronounced than in China, where for decades the communist government feared the transformative and liberating effects of cities and imposed strict controls on where people were allowed to live. By tying people's jobs, school admission, and even the right to buy food to the places where people were registered to live, the government made it almost impossible for rural residents to migrate to towns or cities. As a result, more than 80 percent of China's 1 billion people still lived in the countryside in 1980. In recent years, the Chinese government, having decided that towns and cities can be engines of economic growth, has not only relaxed residency laws but also drawn up plans to establish more than 430 new cities. As a result, between 1981 and 2009, the number of people living in cities in China almost quadrupled to more than 600 million, lifting the percentage of urban dwellers to almost 50 percent (see **Geography Matters 10.2—The Pearl River Delta: An Extended Metropolis**). Currently, one-quarter of the world's biggest 1,000 cities are located in China, and the growth seems far from over: according to the United Nations, the number of Chinese cities over 500,000 is set to rise to more than 350 within the next 25 years.

In the world's core countries, levels of urbanization are high and have been so for some time. According to their own national definitions, the populations of Belgium, the Netherlands, and the United Kingdom are more than 90 percent urbanized, whereas those of Australia, Canada, Denmark, France, Germany, Japan, New Zealand, Spain, Sweden, and the United States are all more than 75 percent urbanized. In these core countries, however, *rates* of urbanization are relatively low, just as their overall rate of population growth is slow (see Chapter 3).

Levels of urbanization are also very high in many of the world's semiperipheral countries. Brazil, Mexico, Taiwan, Singapore, and South Korea, for example, are all at least 75 percent urbanized. Unlike the core countries, however, their *rate* of urban growth has been high.

Whatever the current level of urbanization in peripheral countries, almost all are experiencing high rates of urbanization, with growth forecasts of unprecedented speed and unmatched size. Karachi, Pakistan, a metropolis of 1.03 million in 1950, had reached 8.5 million in 1995 and is expected to reach 16.2 million by 2015. Likewise, Cairo, Egypt, grew from 2.41 million to 9.7 million between 1950 and 1995 and is expected to reach 13 million by 2015. Mumbai (formerly Bombay, India), Jakarta (Indonesia), Lagos (Nigeria), São Paulo (Brazil), and Shanghai (China) are all projected to have populations in excess of 17 million by 2015.

The reasons for this urban growth vary. Wars in Liberia and Sierra Leone have pushed hundreds of thousands of people into their capitals, Monrovia and Freetown. In Mauritania, Niger, and other countries bordering the Sahara, deforestation and overgrazing have allowed the desert to expand and swallow up villages, forcing people toward cities. For the most part, though, urban growth in peripheral countries has resulted from the onset of the demographic transition (see Chapter 3), which has produced fast-growing rural populations in regions that face increasing problems of agricultural development (see Chapter 8). As a response, many people in these regions migrate to urban areas seeking a better life.

Many of the largest cities in the periphery are growing at annual rates of between 4 percent and 7 percent; at the higher rate the population will double in 10 years; at the lower rate, it will double in 17 years. The *doubling time* of a city's population is the time needed for it to double in size at current growth rates. Some metropolitan areas, such as Mexico City and São Paulo, are adding half a million people to their population each year—nearly 10,000 every week, even after accounting for deaths and out-migration. It took London 190 years to grow from half a million to 10 million; it took New York 140 years. By contrast, Mexico City, São Paulo, Buenos Aires, Kolkata (formerly Calcutta), Rio de Janeiro, Seoul, and Mumbai all took less than 75 years to grow from half a million to 10 million inhabitants.

The Pearl River Delta: An Extended Metropolis

The Pearl River Delta is one of the fastest-growing urban regions in the world. Anchored by the major metropolitan centres of Guangzhou, Hong Kong, Macao, Shenzhen, and Zhuhai, the Pearl River Delta is an extended metropolitan region of nearly 50 million people. It is one of three extended metropolitan regions—Beijing-Tianjin and Shanghai are the others—that have been fostered by the Chinese government as engines of capitalist growth since liberal economic reforms were introduced in the late 1970s.

Hong Kong (**Figure 10.2.1**), a British colony until 1997, is a metropolis of 6.9 million with a thriving industrial and commercial base that is recognized as a capitalist economic dynamo by the Chinese government, which has created a Special Administrative District for the metropolis. As a result, Hong Kong's citizens have retained their British-based legal system and its guaranteed rights of property ownership and democracy. Hong Kong is the world's largest container port, the third-largest centre for foreign-exchange trade, the seventh-largest stock market, and the tenth-largest trading economy.

Figure 10.2.1 City of Hong Kong Although most of its manufacturing has been transferred to neighbouring Guangdong Province, where wages are much lower, thousands of companies are located in Hong Kong simply for the purpose of doing business with China. As a result, Hong Kong remains a major world city—a major financial hub with a thriving commercial sector and a population of 6.9 million.

Hong Kong's success encouraged the Chinese government to establish two of its first Special Economic Zones (SEZs) in nearby Shenzhen and Zhuhai. Designed to attract foreign capital, technology, and management practices, these SEZs were established as export-processing zones that offered cheap labour and land, along with tax breaks, to transnational corporations. Investors from Hong Kong and Taiwan responded quickly and enthusiastically. By 1993, more than 15,000 manufacturers from Hong Kong alone had set up businesses in Guangdong Province, and a similar number had established subcontracting relationships, contracting out assembly-line work to Chinese companies in the Pearl River Delta. Meanwhile, the entire delta region was subsequently designated an Open Economic Region, where local governments, individual enterprises, and farm households could enjoy a high degree of autonomy in economic decision making.

The relaxation of state control over the regional economy allowed the region's dense and growing rural population to migrate to urban areas in search of assembly-line jobs or to stay in rural areas and diversify agricultural production from paddy-rice cultivation to more profitable activities such as market-farming activities, livestock husbandry, and fishery to supply the growing urban food demand. Economic freedom also facilitated rural industrialization—mostly low-tech, small-scale, labour-intensive, and widely scattered across the countryside. The result is a distinctive "extended metropolis" in which numerous small towns play an increasingly important role in fostering the process of urbanization, with an intense mixture of agricultural and nonagricultural activities and an intimate interaction between urban and rural areas.

The metropolitan cores of the region, aiming to increase their competitiveness and prominence in the globalizing world economy, have meanwhile invested heavily in infrastructure projects geared to the needs of local and international capital. These include major airports, high-speed toll highways, satellite ground stations, port installations, metro and light-rail networks, and new water-management systems. These, in turn, have attracted business and technology parks, financial centres, and resort complexes in a loose-knit sprawl of urban development.

Today the Pearl River Delta provides a thriving export-processing platform that has driven double-digit annual economic growth for much of the past two decades. The region's GDP grew from just over US$8 billion in 1980 to over US$200 billion in 2005. During that period, the average annual rate of GDP growth in the Pearl River Delta Economic Zone exceeded 16 percent, well above the People's Republic of China national figure of 9.8 percent. By 2005, and with only 3.5 percent of the country's population, the region was contributing 9.9 percent of the country's GDP and 28.9 percent of its total trade.

Guangzhou is a megacity with a population of 12.7 million in 2010 (**Figure 10.2.2**). Shenzhen has grown from a population of just 19,000 in 1975 to 8.9 million in 2010. The southern border of the Shenzhen SEZ adjoins Hong Kong, but the northern border is walled off from the rest of China by an electrified fence to prevent smuggling and to keep back the large number of people trying to migrate illegally into Shenzhen and Hong Kong.

Figure 10.2.2   Guangzhou, China

Urban Systems

Every town and city is part of one of the interlocking urban systems that link regional-, national-, and international-scale human geographies in a complex web of interdependence. These urban systems organize space through hierarchies of cities of different sizes and functions. Many of these hierarchical urban systems exhibit certain common attributes and features, particularly in the relative size and spacing of individual towns and cities.

Central Places   In the 1930s, the German geographer Walter Christaller recognized that towns and cities function as market centres and that this results in a hierarchical system of **central places**—settlements in which certain types of products and services are available to consumers. Christaller had noticed that southern Germany had quite a number of smaller places, each offering a limited assortment of stores, services, and amenities for its residents and the residents of nearby areas. He noticed that these places tended to be located at relatively short and consistent distances from one another. Large towns and cities, on the other hand, were fewer and farther between but offered a much greater variety of stores, services, and amenities, many of them catering to customers and clients from quite distant towns and intermediate rural areas.

His findings gave rise to **central place theory**, which seeks to explain the relative size and geographical spacing of towns and cities as a function of people's shopping behaviours. In the same way that Weber's theory of industrial location (Chapter 7), von Thünen's theory of agricultural location (Chapter 8), and Burgess's theory of urban residential patterns (Chapter 11) offered insight into the operation of a variety of geographic processes across space, so Christaller's work on the size and location of towns and cities offered an explanation for urban geographers that could be expressed in the almost geometric, abstract language of *locational analysis*.

To explain the observed hierarchy of central places, Christaller drew on principles concerning the range and threshold of central place functions. The **range** of a product or service is the maximum distance that consumers will normally travel to obtain it. "High-order" goods and services are those that are relatively costly and generally required infrequently (specialized equipment, professional sports, and specialized medical care, for example). They have the greatest range—100 or more kilometres is not unusual. At the other extreme, "low-order" goods and

central places: settlements in which certain products and services are available to consumers

central place theory: a theory that seeks to explain the relative size and spacing of towns and cities as a function of people's shopping behaviours

range: the maximum distance that consumers will normally travel to obtain a particular product or service

services are those that are relatively inexpensive and required at frequent intervals (baked goods, coffee, dairy products, and groceries, for example). They have a very short range, perhaps as low as 500 metres.

The **threshold** of a good or service can be thought of as the minimum market area with enough potential buyers to make the enterprise profitable. High-order services, such as hospitals, have thresholds in the tens of thousands of people. Low-order services, such as small grocery stores, can have thresholds of between 200 and 300 people.

It follows that, in any given region, a need will exist for only a limited number of large central places in which all the higher-order goods and services are provided. Similarly, the number and spacing of smaller central places will depend on the combination of different-sized ranges and thresholds. Christaller was able to demonstrate that, under ideal circumstances (on flat plains with good transportation in every direction), towns and cities tend to be arranged in clear hierarchies, with hexagonal-shaped market areas of different sizes (**Figure 10.15**). Although such circumstances are never found in real life, and although other, non-market functions of towns and cities are becoming increasingly important, the urban systems of most regions do exhibit a clear hierarchical structure. This is partly a legacy of past eras, when towns and cities did function mainly as market centres for surrounding agricultural areas. **Figure 10.16** shows a typical example: the Spanish urban system, with smaller towns and cities functioning interdependently with successively larger ones, the whole system dominated by one or two metropolitan areas whose linkages are national in scope.

Urban systems also exhibit clear *functional* differences within such hierarchies, yet another reflection of the interdependence of places. The geographical division of labour resulting from such processes of economic development (Chapter 7) means that many medium- and larger-sized cities perform quite specialized economic functions and so acquire quite distinctive characters. Thus, for example, there are steel towns (for example, Sydney, Nova Scotia; Sheffield, England), textile towns (for example, Lowell, Massachusetts; Manchester, England), and auto-manufacturing towns (for example, Windsor, Ontario; Oxford, England; Turin, Italy; Toyota City, Japan). Some towns and cities, of course, do evolve as general-purpose urban centres, providing an evenly balanced range of functions for their own particular sphere of influence.

threshold: the minimum market size required to make the sale of a particular product or service profitable

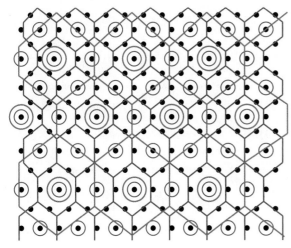

- ● A size: smallest

- ◯ B size: next largest

- ◯ C size: next size place

Figure 10.15 Central places and locational hierarchies This illustration shows Walter Christaller's basic concept of a hierarchy of settlements (central places) of different sizes, with successively larger settlements offering a greater variety of goods and services, thus commanding a broader market territory. The hexagonal market areas were hypothetical, allowing Christaller to avoid gaps or overlapping market areas.

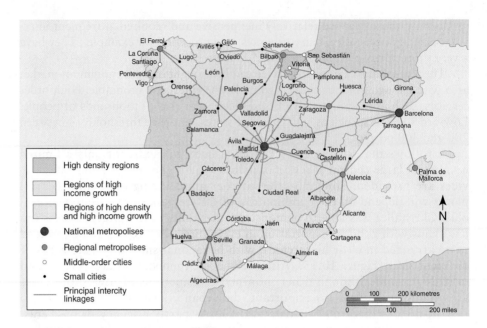

Figure 10.16   The Spanish urban system   Note how the smaller cities tend to be linked to middle-order cities, while these, in turn, are linked to regional metropolises, which are linked to the national metropolises, Madrid and Barcelona. These linkages represent the major flows of capital, information, and goods within the Spanish urban system.   (*Source:* L. Bourne, R. Sinclair, M. Ferrer, and A. d'Entremont (eds.), *The Changing Geography of Urban Systems.* Department of Human Geography. Navarra, Spain: Universidad de Navarra, 1989, fig. 2, p. 46.)

Canada's urban system provides an excellent example of the development of such a hierarchy (**Figure 10.17**). The top tier of cities consists of Toronto, Montreal, and Vancouver—cities that provide high-order functions to the national marketplace. Historically, Montreal was Canada's principal city, in terms of population size and economic importance, and served as the control point for European and U.S. investment in Canada. Over the last three decades, however, Toronto has eclipsed Montreal—not least because of investors' concerns about a possible separation of Quebec from Canada. Vancouver is the

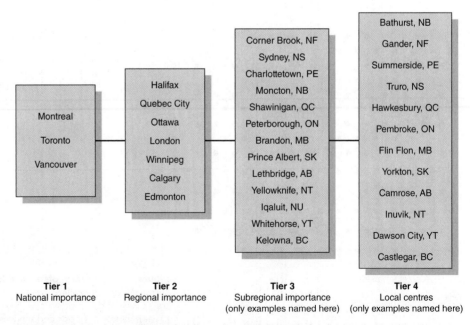

Figure 10.17   Canada's urban hierarchy   This illustration shows the structure and composition of the top levels of Canada's urban system.

most recent addition to the first tier of Canadian cities and has benefited from considerable immigration and investment from Hong Kong.

The second tier of Canadian cities consists of Halifax, Quebec City, Ottawa-Hull, London (Ontario), Winnipeg, Calgary, and Edmonton. These can be described as general-purpose cities with diverse functions but only regional importance.

The third tier is made up of more specialized centres of subregional importance. Smaller provincial capitals, such as Regina or Charlottetown; northern cities, such as Yellowknife, Whitehorse, and Iqaluit; important centres, such as the rapidly growing city of Kelowna, British Columbia; the university and agricultural service cities of Brandon, Manitoba, and Lethbridge, Alberta; and industrial centres such as Corner Brook, Newfoundland, all provide examples of third-order functions.

The fourth functional tier in the Canadian urban hierarchy comprises those centres that have only local importance—such towns as Castlegar, British Columbia, or Bathurst, New Brunswick, for example, which can provide their populations with little more than a basic range of shopping and services.

In total, the Canadian urban system consists of only approximately 750 communities, of which approximately 140 are cities with more than 10,000 people. As a number of Canadian geographers have observed, this urban system, for most practical purposes, *is* Canada. The relationships between the cities of this system define the major geographical regions of our country. Certainly, the present urban hierarchy, dominated by the cities of the Quebec City–Windsor "corridor," embodies the dichotomy between core and periphery, heartland and hinterland, that lies at the root of so much of our country's geographical patterns.

City-Size Distributions, Primacy, and Centrality   The functional interdependency between places within urban systems tends to result in a distinctive relationship between the population size of cities and their rank within the overall hierarchy. This relationship is known as the **rank-size rule,** which describes a certain statistical regularity in the city-size distributions of countries and regions. The relationship is such that the *n*th largest city in a country or region is $1/n$ the size of the largest city in that country or region. If the largest city in a particular system has a population of 1 million, the fifth-largest city should have a population one-fifth as big (that is, 200,000); the hundredth-ranked city should have a population one-hundredth as big (that is, 10,000); and so on. Plotting this relationship on a graph with a logarithmic scale for population sizes would produce a perfectly straight line. The actual rank-size relationship for the U.S. urban system has always come close to this (**Figure 10.18**). Over time, the slope has moved to the right on the graph, reflecting the growth of towns and cities at every level in the urban hierarchy.

In some urban systems, the top of the rank-size distribution is distorted as a result of the disproportionate size of the largest (and sometimes also the second-largest) city. Geographers call this **primacy,** a condition occurring when the population of the largest city in an urban system is disproportionately large in relation to the second- and third-largest cities in that system. Such cities are called *primate cities*. In Argentina, for example, Buenos Aires is more than 10 times the size of Rosario, the second-largest city. (According to the rank-size rule, the largest city should be just twice the size of the second-largest city.) In the United Kingdom, London is more than 9 times the size of Birmingham, the second-largest city. In France, Paris is more than 8 times the size of Marseilles, France's second-largest city.

Primacy is not simply a matter of sheer size. Some of the largest metropolitan areas in the world—Karachi, New York, and Mumbai—are not primate. Further, primacy is a condition that is found in both the core and the periphery

rank-size rule: a statistical regularity in city-size distributions of countries and regions

primacy: a condition in which the population of the largest city in an urban system is disproportionately large in relation to the second- and third-largest cities in that system

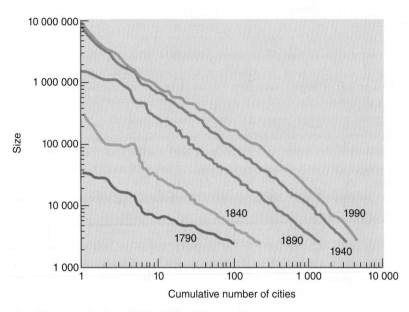

Figure 10.18 The rank-size distribution of cities in the U.S. urban system, 1790–1990 This graph shows that the U.S. urban system has conformed fairly consistently to the rank-size rule. As urbanization brought increased populations to cities at every level in the urban hierarchy, the rank-size graph has moved to the right. (*Source:* Reprinted with permission of Prentice Hall from P.L. Knox, *Urbanization,* © 1994, p. 32.)

of the world-system. This suggests that primacy is a result of the roles played by particular cities within their own national urban systems. A relationship does exist to the world economy, however. Primacy in peripheral countries is usually a consequence of primate cities' early roles as gateway cities. In core countries, it is usually a consequence of primate cities' roles as imperial capitals and centres of administration, politics, and trade for a much wider urban system than their own domestic system.

When cities' economic, political, and cultural functions are disproportionate to their population, the condition is known as **centrality**, or the functional dominance of cities within an urban system. Cities that account for a disproportionately high share of economic, political, and cultural activities have a high degree of centrality within their urban system. Very often, primate cities exhibit this characteristic, but cities do not necessarily have to be primate to be functionally dominant within their urban system. Extreme examples of centrality are found in the world-system periphery. Bangkok, for instance, with around 10 percent of the Thai population, accounts for approximately 38 percent of the country's overall GDP; over 85 percent of the country's GDP in banking, insurance, and real estate; and 75 percent of its manufacturing. Similarly, Shanghai, with only 2 percent of China's population, generates 15 percent of the country's GDP; and in Peru, we find 90 percent of the country's banking facilities located in Lima.

World Cities Ever since the evolution of a world-system in the sixteenth century, certain cities known as *world cities* (sometimes referred to as *global cities*) have played key roles in organizing space beyond their own national boundaries. In the first stages of world-system growth, these key roles involved the organization of trade and the execution of colonial, imperial, and geopolitical strategies. The world cities of the seventeenth century were London, Amsterdam, Antwerp, Genoa, Lisbon, and Venice. In the eighteenth century, Paris, Rome, and Vienna also became world cities, whereas Antwerp and Genoa became less influential. In the nineteenth century, Berlin, Chicago,

centrality: the functional dominance of cities within an urban system

Manchester, New York, and St. Petersburg became world cities, whereas Venice became less influential.

Today, with the globalization of the economy, the key roles of world cities are concerned less with the deployment of imperial power and the orchestration of trade and more with transnational corporate organization, international banking and finance, supranational government, and the work of international agencies. World cities have become the control centres for the flows of information, cultural products, and finance that collectively sustain the economic and cultural globalization of the world (**Figure 10.19**).

World cities also provide an interface between the global and the local. They contain the economic, cultural, and institutional apparatuses that channel national and provincial or territorial resources into the global economy and that transmit the impulses of globalization back to national and provincial centres. As such, world cities possess several functional characteristics:

- They are the sites of most of the leading global markets for commodities, commodity futures, investment capital, foreign exchange, equities, and bonds.

- They are the sites of clusters of specialized, high-order business services, especially those that are international in scope and attached to finance, accounting, advertising, property development, and law.

- They are the sites of concentrations of corporate headquarters—not just of transnational corporations but also of major national firms and large foreign firms.

- They are the sites of concentrations of national and international headquarters of trade and professional associations.

- They are the sites of most of the leading non-governmental organizations (NGOs) and intergovernmental organizations (IGOs) that are international in scope.

- They are the sites of the most powerful and internationally influential media organizations and culture industries.

A great deal of synergy exists among these various functional components. A city, for example New York, attracts transnational corporations because it is a centre of culture and communications. It attracts specialized business services because it is a centre of corporate headquarters and of global markets, and so on. These interdependencies represent a special case of the geographical *agglomeration effects* we discussed in Chapter 7. Agglomeration is the clustering of functionally related activities. In the case of New York City, corporate headquarters and specialized legal, financial, and business services cluster together because of the mutual cost savings and advantages of being close to one another.

At the same time, different world cities fulfill different roles within the world-system. For example, Brussels is relatively unimportant as a corporate headquarters location but qualifies as a world city because it is the administrative centre of the European Union. Similarly, Milan has global status in terms of cultural influence (especially fashion and design).

Today, the global urban system is dominated by three world cities whose influence is truly global: London, New York, and Tokyo. The second tier of the system consists of world cities with influence over large regions of the world-system. These include, for example, Brussels, Frankfurt, Los Angeles, Paris, Singapore, and Zürich. A third tier consists of important international cities with more limited or more specialized international functions (including Amsterdam, Madrid, Miami, Mexico City, Seoul, Sydney, Toronto, and Vancouver). A fourth tier exists of cities of national importance and with some transnational functions (including Barcelona, Dallas, Manchester, Munich, Melbourne, and Philadelphia).

Top-Tier World Cities
London
New York
Tokyo

2nd-Tier World Cities
Brussels   São Paulo
Chicago   Singapore
Frankfurt   Washington, DC
Los Angeles   Zürich
Paris

3rd-Tier World Cities
Amsterdam   Johannesburg   Milan   Seoul
Bangkok   Madrid   Mumbai (Bombay) Sydney
Berlin   Manila   Osaka   Taipei
Buenos Aires   Mexico City   Rio de Janeiro   Toronto
Hong Kong   Miami   San Francisco   Vancouver
Houston

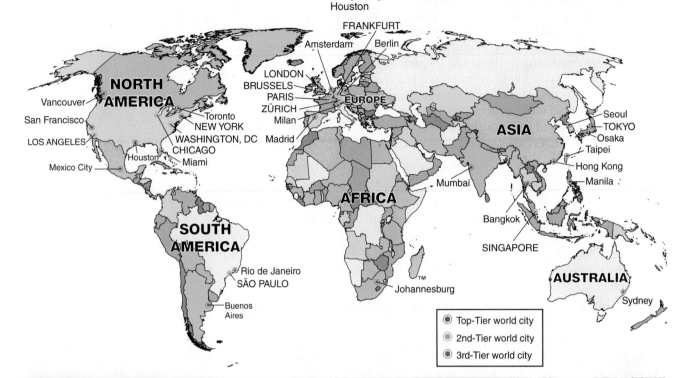

◉ Top-Tier world city
◉ 2nd-Tier world city
◉ 3rd-Tier world city

London

New York

London, New York, and Tokyo are major world cities because of their major financial markets, their transnational corporate headquarters, and their concentrations of financial services. Because of their geographical locations in different time zones, office hours in each city overlap just enough to allow 24-hour trading and decision making.

Tokyo

Brussels qualifies as a world city because it is the administrative centre of the European Union and because it has attracted a large number of non-governmental organizations that are transnational in scope.

Milan has global status in terms of cultural influence (especially fashion and design) and is an important regional financial centre, but it is relatively dependent in terms of corporate control and information-processing activities.

Figure 10.19   World cities   World cities are not simply the world's largest and economically most important cities. Rather, they are the control centres of the world economy, places where critical decision making and interaction take place with regard to global economic, cultural, and political issues.   Among Canadian cities, only Toronto and Vancouver qualify.   (*Source:* Map projection, Buckminster Fuller Institute and Dymaxion Map Design, Santa Barbara, CA. The word *Dymaxion* and the Fuller Projection Dymaxion™ Map design are trademarks of the Buckminster Fuller Institute, Santa Barbara, California, © 1938, 1967, & 1992. All rights reserved.)

Figure 10.20 Mexico City   Every year another half million or more people are added to the city. In 2011, the population of the agglomeration had reached almost 20 million, making it the second-largest city in the Western Hemisphere (after São Paulo).

Figure 10.21   Shanghai   Shanghai is China's most populous city, with 23 million people in the greater metropolitan area.

Megacities   Megacities are not necessarily world cities, though some of them are (London and Tokyo, for example). **Megacities** are very large cities characterized by a high degree of centrality within their national economy. Their most important common denominator is their sheer size—most of them number 10 million or more in population. This, together with their functional centrality, means that in many ways they have more in common with one another than with the smaller metropolitan areas and cities within their own countries.

Examples of such megacities include Bangkok, Beijing, Cairo, Dhaka, Jakarta, Lagos, Manila, Mexico City (**Figure 10.20**), New Delhi, São Paulo, Shanghai (**Figure 10.21**), and Tehran. Each one of these has more inhabitants than 100 of the member countries of the United Nations. Although most of them do not function as world cities, they do provide important intermediate roles between the upper tiers of the system of world cities and the provincial towns and villages of large regions of the world. They not only link local and provincial economies with the global economy but also provide a point of contact between the traditional and the modern, and between formal and informal economic sectors. The **informal sector** of an economy involves a wide variety of economic activities that take place beyond official record and are not subject to formalized systems of regulation or remuneration.

megacities: very large cities characterized by high centrality within their national economy

informal sector: economic activities that take place beyond official record and are not subject to formalized systems of regulation and remuneration

URBAN GROWTH PROCESSES

The large-scale urbanization triggered in the world's core countries by the evolution of a world-system, and later reinforced by the Industrial Revolution, was based on growth processes that were self-sustaining. Cities themselves were the engines of economic growth, and this growth, in turn, attracted the migrants, settlers, and immigrants that made for rapid population growth. In this urbanization process, a close and positive relationship existed between rural and urban development. The appropriation of new land for agriculture, together with mechanization and the innovative techniques that urbanization allowed, resulted in increased agricultural productivity. This extra productivity released rural labour to work in the growing manufacturing sector in towns and cities. At the same time, it provided the additional produce needed to feed growing urban populations. The whole process was further reinforced by the capacity of urban labour forces to produce agricultural tools, machinery, fertilizer, and other products that made for still greater increases in agricultural productivity.

Urbanization and Economic Development

economic base: set of manufacturing, processing, trading, or service activities that serve markets beyond the city

basic functions: economic activities that provide income from sales to customers beyond city limits

nonbasic functions: economic activities that serve a city's own population

In this self-sustaining process of urbanization, the actual rate and amount of a city's growth depends on the size of its economic base. A city's **economic base** consists of those economic functions that involve the manufacturing, processing, or trading of goods or the provision of services for markets *beyond the city itself*. Activities that provide income-generating "exports" for a city are termed **basic functions**. In contrast, **nonbasic functions** are those that cater to the city's own population and so do not generate profit from "outside" customers. Examples of nonbasic activities include local newspapers, local bakeries and restaurants, schools, and local government.

The fundamental determinant of cities' growth in population, employment, and income in the world's core countries is the percentage of their economies that is devoted to basic activities. The prosperity generated by basic economic activities leads to increased employment in nonbasic activities to satisfy the demand for housing, utilities, retailing, personal services, and other services *in the city itself*. The incomes generated by the combination of basic and nonbasic economic activities allow for higher potential tax yields, which can be used to improve public utilities, roads, schools, health services, recreational amenities, and other infrastructure. These activities are also nonbasic, but they all serve to improve the efficiency and attractiveness of the city for further rounds of investment in basic economic activities. The whole process is one of cumulative causation (Chapter 7), in which a spiral buildup of advantages is enjoyed by a particular place as a result of the development of external economies, agglomeration effects, and localization economies.

metropolitanism: the process by which the economic growth of a city enables it to attain a position of national dominance and, in so doing, creates the geographical structure of a metropolis and hinterland

This process is by no means uniform across space, even in the core countries. Canada, with an urban system that has developed according to a process called **metropolitanism**, provides an interesting illustration of this. According to this explanation, the cities that have been able to dominate the Canadian urban hierarchy have done so because of their ability to control the economy of the heartland. Cities in this favoured position, such as Toronto, have been able to develop into manufacturing and service centres of national dominance through the upward spiral of cumulative forces. Meanwhile, the peripheral centres of the hinterland may never be able to develop beyond their initial function as resource centres designed to exploit the staples of this country's hinterland (**Figure 10.22**).

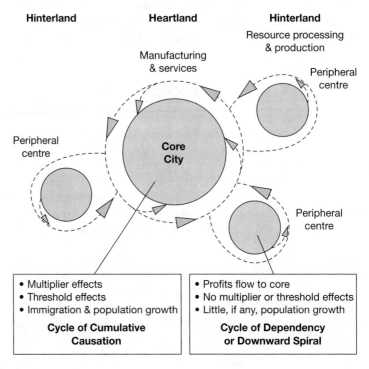

Figure 10.22 Metropolitanism
Urban growth in Canada's heartland cities has occurred through a process of upward cumulative causation. It has also benefited from the resources of the hinterland. In fact, as this illustration shows, the ability of the heartland cities to profit from the economic surpluses of the hinterland centres has prevented the latter from ever reaching self-sustained growth.

This is because the economic investment that they would need to do this is chan-nelled to the metropolitan centres of the heartland instead.

Certainly, cities in the periphery have responded to the pulse of global demand for their resources and have been the focus of inward investment to exploit such materials. However, the profits of those investments have seldom remained in the periphery, and population—unless directly work-ing in resource extraction—is not attracted to the limited economic potential of single-industry towns. In this manner, the spiral of cumulative causation rarely begins, and Canada's resource towns of the hinterland remain tribu-tary to the metropolitan heartland. Therefore, the core continually creates the peripheral spaces of Canada and maintains the relative size and function of Canada's urban places.

Of course, this model is too simple to be an entirely adequate explanation of the differential growth of Canadian cities and their economies. The growth of Vancouver, a peripheral resource town in its early years, attests to the ability of some peripheral centres to take off economically.

Deindustrialization and Decentralization

The logic of economic development does not always work uniformly in the direction of population concentration and urban growth. The forces of cumulative causation are refocused from time to time as new technolo-gies, new resources, and new opportunities alter the balance of compara-tive advantages enjoyed by particular places within the world's core and semiperipheral countries. New rounds of urbanization are initiated in the places most suited to the new circumstances, whereas those least suited are likely to suffer a spiral of *deindustrialization* and urban decline. Deindus-trialization involves a decline in industrial employment in core regions as firms scale back their activities in response to lower levels of profitability (see Chapter 7). Such adversity particularly affected such cities as Pittsburgh and Cleveland (United States), Sheffield and Liverpool (United Kingdom), Lille (France), and Liège (Belgium)—places where heavy manufacturing con-stituted a key economic sector. Cities like these suffered substantial reduc-tions in employment throughout the 1970s and 1980s.

During the same period, better and more flexible transport and communi-cations networks allowed many industries to choose from a broader range of potential locations. The result has been a *decentralization* of jobs and people from larger to smaller cities within the urban systems of core countries. In some cases, routine production activities relocated to smaller metropolitan areas or to rural areas with cheaper land and real estate, lower labour costs, or more hospitable business climates. In other cases, these activities moved overseas—as part of the new international division of labour (see Chapters 2 and 7)—or were eliminated entirely.

These trends toward deindustrialization and decentralization have been inten-sified by the dampening effects of *agglomeration diseconomies* (see Chapter 7) on the growth of larger metropolitan areas. Agglomeration diseconomies are the neg-ative effects of urban size and density: noise, air pollution, increased crime, com-muting costs, the costs of inflated land and housing prices, traffic congestion, and crowded port and railroad facilities.

Counterurbanization, Reurbanization, and Splintering Urbanization

The combination of deindustrialization in core manufacturing regions, agglomeration diseconomies in major metropolitan areas, and the improved accessibility of smaller towns and rural areas (both in terms of traffic and

counterurbanization: the net loss of population from cities to smaller towns and rural areas

communications) can give rise to the phenomenon of counterurbanization. **Counterurbanization** occurs when cities experience a net loss of population to smaller towns and rural areas. This process results in the deconcentration of population within an urban system. This is, in fact, what happened in Canada, the United States, Britain, Japan, and many other developed countries in the 1970s and early 1980s. Metropolitan growth slowed dramatically, whereas the growth rates of small- and medium-sized towns and of some rural areas increased.

Counterurbanization was a major reversal of long-standing trends, but it seems to have been a temporary adjustment rather than a permanent change. The globalization of the economy and the growth of postindustrial activities in revamped and expanded metropolitan settings have restored the trend toward the concentration of population within urban systems. Increasingly, this *reurbanization* trend is also driven by retiring baby boomers and young professionals moving to new condo developments in the central districts of metropolitan areas to live close to restaurants, theatres, and other cultural amenities.

Finally, we must acknowledge that the processes underlying globalization are changing the global geography of urbanization in entirely new ways (see **Geography Matters 10.3—Globalization and Splintering Urbanism**).

The Unintended Metropolis

Urban growth processes in the world's peripheral regions have been substantially different from those in core regions. In contrast to the self-sustaining urban growth of the world's core regions, the urbanization of peripheral regions has been a consequence of demographic growth that has *preceded* economic development. Although the demographic transition is a fairly recent phenomenon in the peripheral regions of the world (see Chapter 3), it generated large increases in population well in advance of any significant levels of industrialization or of rural economic development.

For the mainly rural populations of peripheral countries, the result was more and more of worse and worse. Problems of agricultural development (see Chapter 8) meant that fast-growing rural populations faced an apparently hopeless future of drudgery and poverty. Emigration provided one potential safety valve, but as the frontiers of the world-system closed out, the more affluent core countries put up barriers to immigration. The only option for the growing numbers of impoverished rural residents was—and still is—to move to the larger towns and cities, where at least there is the hope of employment and the prospect of access to schools, health clinics, piped water, and the kinds of public facilities and services that are often unavailable in rural regions. Cities also have the lure of modernization and the appeal of consumer goods. Overall, the metropolises of the periphery have absorbed four out of five of the 1.5 billion city dwellers added to the world's population since 1980.

Rural migrants have poured into cities out of desperation and hope, rather than being drawn by jobs and opportunities. Because these migration streams have consisted disproportionately of teenagers and young adults, an important additional component of urban growth has followed: exceptionally high rates of natural population increase. In most peripheral countries, the rate of natural increase of the population in cities exceeds that of net in-migration. On average, about 60 percent of urban population growth in peripheral countries is attributable to natural increase.

The consequence of all this urban population growth has been described as **overurbanization,** which occurs when cities grow more rapidly than the jobs and

overurbanization: a condition in which cities grow more rapidly than the jobs and housing they can sustain

Globalization and Splintering Urbanism

The major cities and metropolitan regions of the world are pivotal settings for the processes involved in economic and cultural globalization. As a result, they also reflect these processes in their own patterns of growth and change. Central to this close relationship between urbanization and globalization are networked infrastructures of transportation, information, and communications technologies.

According to the United Nations Center for Human Settlements (UNCHS),[5] information and communications technologies are intensifying global urbanization in three main ways. First, they allow specialist urban centres, with their high value-added services and manufacturing, to extend their powers, markets, and control to ever more distant spheres of influence. Second, the growing speed, complexity, and riskiness of innovation in a global economy require a concentration of technological infrastructure and an associated, knowledgeable, technology-oriented culture in order to sustain competitiveness. Third, demand for information and communications technologies is overwhelmingly driven by the growth of metropolitan markets. World cities especially are of disproportionate importance in driving innovation and investment in networked infrastructures of information and communications technologies. This is because of their cultures of modernization, concentrations of capital, relatively high average disposable personal incomes, and concentrations of internationally oriented firms and institutions.

In contrast to the infrastructure networks of earlier technology systems that underpinned previous phases of urbanization, these information and communications technologies are not locally owned, operated, and regulated. Rather, they are designed, financed, and operated by transnational corporations to global market standards. Detached from local processes of urban development, these critical networked infrastructures are highly uneven in their impact, selectively serving only certain neighbourhoods, certain cities, and certain kinds of metropolitan settings. This important new tendency has been called *splintering urbanism* by geographers Stephen Graham and Simon Marvin.

Splintering urbanism is characterized by an intense geographical differentiation, with individual cities and parts of cities engaged in different—and rapidly changing—ways in ever broadening and increasingly complex circuits of economic and technological exchange. The uneven evolution of networks of information and communications technologies is forging new landscapes of innovation, economic development, and cultural transformation, and at the same time intensifying social and economic inequalities between the fast world and the slow world. The conclusion of the 2001 UNCHS report "Cities in a Globalizing World" is that traditional patterns of urbanization are rapidly giving way across the globe to a very new dynamic, one that is dominated by "enclaves of superconnected people, firms, and institutions, with their increasingly broadband connections to elsewhere via the Internet, mobile phones and satellite TVs and their easy access to information services, often exist[ing] cheek-by-jowl with much larger numbers of people with at most rudimentary access to modern communications technologies and electronic information."[6]

The chief beneficiaries of splintering urbanism are world cities and major regional metropolitan centres, particularly in core countries where large corporations are able to undertake the necessary capital investments in new networked infrastructures and where national governments and entrepreneurial urban agencies are able to subsidize and facilitate them. We can identify several specific kinds of urban settings that are most directly involved in this dimension of globalization:

- Enclaves of Internet and digital multimedia technology development, mostly in core-country world cities. Examples include "Multimedia Gulch" in the SOMA (South of Market Street) district of downtown San Francisco and New York's "Silicon Alley" (just south of 41st Street in Manhattan).

- Technopoles and clusters of high-tech industrial innovation. These have emerged in campus-like suburban and ex-urban settings around core-country world cities (as in London, Paris, and Berlin); in new and renewed industrial regions within core countries (as in Southern California, Baden-Württemberg in Germany, and Rhône-Alpes in France); and in emerging high-tech production and innovation spaces in semiperipheral countries (as in Bangalore, India, and the Multimedia Super Corridor south of Kuala Lumpur, Malaysia).

- Places configured for foreign direct investment in manufacturing, with customized infrastructure, expedited development approval processes, tax concessions, and in some cases exceptions to labour and environmental regulations. Such places have emerged in economically depressed regions of core countries (including northern England and parts of the U.S. Manufacturing Belt), but are mostly found in or near major cities in peripheral and semiperipheral countries (as in the Brazilian cities of Porto Alegre and Paranà, which have attracted foreign-owned automobile plants).

---

[5] United Nations Center for Human Settlements (Habitat), *Cities in a Globalizing World: Global Report on Human Settlements, 2001.* London: Earthscan Publications, 2001, p. 6.

[6] Ibid.

Figure 10.3.1   London's financial core   London's status as a world city rests heavily on the "square mile" of the City of London, with its concentration of banking, insurance, and other advanced business services.

- Enclaves of international banking, finance, and business services in world cities and major regional centres. Examples include the business districts in Lower Manhattan, the City of London (**Figure 10.3.1**), Frankfurt, Hong Kong, and Kuala Lumpur.

- Enclaves of modernization in the megacities and major regional centres of peripheral countries. This modernization typically includes advanced telecommunications and satellite complexes, trade centres, retail and commercial centres, and new university precincts. Examples include the Pudong development zone in Shanghai (**Figure 10.3.2**) and "growth corridors" and "new towns in town" in Bangkok, Thailand.

- Enclaves of back-office spaces, data-processing, e-commerce, and call centres. These have emerged in older industrial cities within core countries (for example, Roanoke, Virginia, and Sunderland, England) and in many cities within semiperipheral countries, most notably in the Caribbean, the Philippines, and India.

Figure 10.3.2   Pudong, Shanghai   One of the most spectacular development zones in the world, Pudong (foreground) was a 556-square-kilometre area of farmland until the 1990s. It has been developed around a new deep-water port, a new airport, and a new infoport, with massive investments in the rail network, highway network, and cross-river transportation network, and has become symbolic of China's economic reform and growth.

- Spaces customized as "logistics zones." Airports, ports, export-processing zones—enclaves in major cities around the world within which the precise and rapid movement of goods, freight, and people are coordinated, managed, and synchronized among various transport modes.

Connected to one another through a complex dynamic of flows, these urban spaces and settings represent the spatial framework for the fast world. They are embedded within regions and metropolitan areas whose economic foundations derive from earlier technology systems and whose social and cultural fabric derives from more traditional bases. The result, as we shall see in Chapter 11, is that traditional patterns of land use and spatial organization in many parts of the world are being transformed by the local effects of splintering urbanism.

squatter settlements: residential developments on land that is neither owned nor rented by its occupants

housing they can sustain. In such circumstances, urban growth produces instant slums—shacks set on unpaved streets, often with open sewers and no basic utilities. The shacks are constructed out of any material that comes to hand, such as planks, cardboard, tarpaper, thatch, mud, and corrugated iron. Such is the pressure of in-migration that many of these instant slums are squatter settlements, built illegally by families who are desperate for shelter. **Squatter settlements** are residential developments on land that is neither owned nor rented by its occupants. Collectively, these slums and squatter settlements account for well over one-third and sometimes up to three-quarters of the population of the megacities of the periphery (**Figure 10.23**). As we shall see in the next chapter, this often leads to severe problems of social disorganization and environmental degradation. Nevertheless, many neighbourhoods are able to develop self-help networks and organizations that form the basis of community amid dauntingly poor and crowded cities.

Figure 10.23 Slum housing in peripheral cities Throughout much of the world, the scale and speed of urbanization, combined with the scarcity of formal employment, have resulted in very high proportions of slum housing, much of it erected by squatters. In Nairobi, Kenya, 40 percent of the city's population lives in unauthorized settlements. The most extensive slums, according to U.N. statistics, are in the cities of sub-Saharan Africa, where over 70 percent of the population live in unfit accommodations.

CONCLUSION

Urbanization is one of the most important geographical phenomena. Cities can be seedbeds of economic development and cultural innovation. Cities and groups of cities also organize space—not just the territory immediately around them but, in some cases, national and even international spaces. The causes and consequences of urbanization are very different in different parts of the world. For example, the urban experience of the world's peripheral regions stands in sharp contrast to that of the developed core regions. This contrast is a reflection of some of the demographic, economic, and political factors that we have explored in previous chapters.

Much of the developed world has become almost completely urbanized, with highly organized systems of cities. Today, levels of urbanization are high throughout the world's core countries, whereas rates of urbanization are relatively low. At the top of the urban hierarchies of the world's core regions are world cities, such as London, New York, Tokyo, Paris, and Zurich, which have become control centres for the flows of information, cultural products, and finance that collectively sustain the economic and cultural globalization of the world. In doing so, they help to consolidate the hegemony of the world's core regions.

Few of the metropolises of the periphery, however, are world cities that occupy key roles in the organization of global economics and culture. Rather, they operate as connecting links between provincial towns and villages and the world economy. They have innumerable economic, social, and cultural linkages to their provinces on one side and to major world cities on the other. Almost all peripheral countries, meanwhile, are experiencing high rates of urbanization, with forecast growth of unprecedented speed and unmatched size. In many peripheral and semiperipheral regions, current rates of urbanization have given rise to unintended metropolises and fears of "uncontrollable urbanization," with urban "danger zones" where "work" means anything that contributes to survival. The result, as we shall see in Chapter 11, is that these unintended metropolises are quite different from the cities of the core as places in which to live and work.

MAIN POINTS REVISITED

- **The urban areas of the world are the linchpins of human geographies at the local, regional, and global scales.**

  Towns and cities are engines of economic development and centres of cultural innovation, social transformation, and political change. They now account for more than half of the world's population.

- **The earliest urbanization developed independently in the various hearth areas of the first agricultural revolution.**

  The very first region of independent urbanism, in the Middle East, produced successive generations of urbanized world-empires, including Greece, Rome, and Byzantium.

- **The expansion of trade around the world, associated with colonialism and imperialism, established numerous gateway cities.**

  European powers founded or developed literally thousands of towns as they extended their trading networks and established their colonies. The great majority of the towns were ports that served as control centres commanding entrance to, and exit from, their particular country or region.

- **The Industrial Revolution generated new kinds of cities and many more of them.**

  Industrial economies could be organized only with the large pools of labour; the transportation networks; the physical infrastructure of factories, warehouses, stores, and offices; and the consumer markets provided by cities. As industrialization spread throughout Europe in the first half of the nineteenth century and then to other parts of the world, urbanization increased at a faster pace.

- **Today, the single most important aspect of world urbanization from a geographical perspective is the striking difference in trends and projections between the core regions and the peripheral regions.**

  In 1950, two-thirds of the world's urban population was concentrated in the more developed countries of the core economies. Since then, the world's urban population has increased threefold, the bulk of the growth having taken place in the less developed countries of the periphery.

- **Cities form linked networks, known as *urban systems*, which determine the importance of component cities of the system and organize these cities into their various functional niches within an economy.**

  A hallmark of the integrated spatial economies found in the developed countries of the core, an urban system is a network of cities in which each city serves the needs of its immediate region and larger cities (defined in terms of their functions) also meet the more specialized demands of a wider area.

- **Canada's urban system is the product of processes that operate in both core and peripheral regions.**

  The development of this country's urban system is the result of metropolitanism, a process in which the cities of Canada's heartland have been able to grow at the expense of cities in the hinterland.

- **A small number of "world cities," most of them located within the core regions of the world-system, occupy key roles in the organization of global economics and culture.**

  At the top of a global urban system, these cities experience growth largely as a result of their role as key nodes in the world economy. World cities have become the control centres for the flows of information, cultural products, and finance that collectively sustain the economic and cultural globalization of the world.

- **The populations of many of the largest cities in the periphery have a doubling time of only 10 to 15 years.**

  The doubling time of a city's population is the time needed for it to double in size at current growth rates.

- **Many of the megacities of the periphery are primate and exhibit a high degree of centrality within their urban systems.**

  Primacy occurs when the population of the largest city in an urban system is disproportionately large in relation to the second- and third-largest cities in that system. *Centrality* refers to the functional dominance of cities within an urban system. Cities that account for a disproportionately high share of economic, political, and cultural activities have a high degree of centrality within their urban system.

Key Terms

basic functions (p. 472)
centrality (p. 468)
central place theory (p. 464)
central places (p. 464)
colonial cities (p. 454)
counterurbanization (p. 474)
economic base (p. 472)
gateway city (p. 454)

informal sector (p. 471)
megacities (p. 471)
metropolitanism (p. 472)
nonbasic functions (p. 472)
overurbanization (p. 474)
primacy (p. 467)
range (p. 464)
rank-size rule (p. 467)

shock city (p. 456)
squatter settlements (p. 476)
threshold (p. 465)
urban ecology (p. 447)
urban form (p. 447)
urbanism (p. 447)
urban system (p. 447)

Additional Reading

Abrahamsun, M. *Global Cities*. New York: Oxford University Press, 2004.

Angotti, T. *Metropolis 2000*. New York: Routledge, 1993.

Bourne, L.S., and D.F. Ley (eds.). *The Changing Social Geography of Canadian Cities*. Montreal and Kingston: McGill-Queen's University Press, 1993.

Brunn, S., and J.F. Williams (eds.). *Cities of the World*, 2nd ed. New York: HarperCollins, 1993.

Bunting, T., and P. Filion (eds.). *Canadian Cities in Transition: The Twenty-First Century*, 2nd ed. Toronto: Oxford University Press, 2000.

Chandler, T. *Four Thousand Years of Urban Growth: An Historical Census*. Washington, DC: Worldwatch Institute, 1987.

Gugler, J. (ed.). *Cities in the Developing World: Issues, Theory, and Policy*. Oxford: Oxford University Press, 1997.

Hall, P. *Cities of Tomorrow*. New York: Blackwell, 1988.

King, A.D. *Urbanism, Colonialism, and the World Economy: Cultural and Spatial Foundations of the World Urban System*. New York: Routledge, 1991.

Knox, P.L. *Urbanization: An Introduction to Urban Geography*. Englewood Cliffs, NJ: Prentice Hall, 1994.

Knox, P.L., and P.J. Taylor (eds.). *World Cities in a World-System*. Cambridge: Cambridge University Press, 1995.

Merrifield, A. *Metromarxism*. London: Routledge, 2002.

Potter, R.B., and S. Lloyd-Evans. *The City in the Developing World*. Harlow, UK: Addison Wesley Longman, 1998.

Sassen, S. *Cities in a World Economy*. Thousand Oaks, CA: Pine Forge Press, 2000.

Short, J.R., and Y.H. Kim. *Globalization and the City*. New York: Addison Wesley Longman, 1999.

United Nations Centre for Human Settlements (HABITAT). *An Urbanizing World: Global Report on Human Settlements, 1996*. Oxford: Oxford University Press, 1996.

World Resources Institute. *World Resources 1996–97: The Urban Environment*. New York: Oxford University Press, 1996.

Discussion Questions and Research Activities

1. Canada, like most core countries, is already highly urbanized and has a relatively low rate of urbanization. Nevertheless, some Canadian cities have been growing much faster than others. Which have been the fastest-growing Canadian cities in recent times, and what reasons can you suggest for their relatively rapid growth? You can find the data on the Statistics Canada website (**www.statcan.ca**).

2. Using the census data published by Statistics Canada, find out the population of the town or city you know best. Do the same for every census year, going back from 1991 to 1981, 1971, and so on, all the way back to 1851. Then, plot these populations on a simple graph. What explanations can you offer for the pattern that the graph reveals? Now, draw a larger version of the same graph, annotating it to show the landmark events that might have influenced the city's growth (or decline).

3. The following cities all have populations in excess of 2 million. How many of them could you locate on a world map? Their size reflects a certain degree of importance, at least within their regional economy. What can you find out about each? Compile for each a 50-word description that explains its chief industries and a little of its history.

Poona	Ibadan	Recife
Bangalore	Turin	Ankara

4. "Were you ever in Quebec, Stowing timber on the deck. . . ." So run the lines of an old sea shanty, referring, in this verse, to Quebec City, a colonial gateway city on the St. Lawrence. Find out about the commodities and manufactured goods that it imported and exported in the nineteenth century and about the origin and destination of these imports and exports. Which geographical concepts do you consider to be useful in explaining these facts?

My GeosciencePlace

Visit **www.mygeoscienceplace.ca** to find chapter review quizzes, videos, maps, and much more.

Urban sprawl in Winnipeg, Manitoba

The neighborhood shopping street is at the end of the block. It is a narrow lane, barely wide enough for one car to pass, and is lined on both sides with small shops whose fronts open widely to the street . . . and invite customers in. There are more and more boutiques and other new arrivals on the street, including an extremely busy supermarket, but there are still quite a few of the older establishments left as well: fishmongers, rice sellers, a noodle maker, a cracker bakery, a cubby-hole that sells only buttons, a glazier's shop, and countless other, small places for the local market. Tucked away to the side is the neighborhood's Buddhist temple. It is a new building but designed in a traditional style, and has a welcome open space for community fairs and other gatherings in front, and a lovely Japanese garden at the back. The garden is such a contrast to the harsh lines and bustling activity of the surrounding city that at times it seems to me to be the most secluded and contemplative place in the world.[1]

We can recognize in this description of a Tokyo neighbourhood several elements that are fairly common in central cities throughout the world's core regions: the mixture of old stores, new boutiques, and local supermarkets, for example. However, some elements are unique: the noodle maker and the Buddhist temple with its Japanese garden. In this chapter, we turn our attention to the internal dynamics of cities, looking at the ways in which patterns and processes tend to vary according to the type of city and its history. In many ways, the most striking contrasts are found between the cities of the core regions and those of the periphery. The evolution of the unintended metropolis of the periphery has been very different from the evolution of metropolitan areas in the world's core regions. The problems they face are also very different.

MAIN POINTS

- The typical North American city is structured around a central business district (CBD); a transitional zone; suburbs; secondary business districts and commercial strips; industrial districts; and, in larger metropolitan areas, edge cities.
- The overall structure of North American cities is shaped primarily by competition for territory and location. In general, all categories of land users—commercial and industrial, as well as residential—compete for the most convenient and accessible locations within the city.
- Cities experiencing high rates of in-migration tend to become structured into a series of concentric zones of neighbourhoods of different ethnicity, demographic composition, and social status through processes of invasion and succession.

---

[1] Roman Cybriwsky, *Tokyo*. London: Belhaven Press, 1991, p. 3.

- In cities where growth has been less dominated by successive waves of immigrant ethnic groups, neighbourhood patterns tend to be structured around the development of industrial corridors and high-class residential corridors.

- Urban structure varies a good deal from one region of the world to another because of the influence of history, culture, and the different roles that cities have played within the world-system.

- Geographers are interested in the distinctive physical features of urban landscapes because they can be read as multi-layered texts that show how cities have developed, how they are changing, and how people's values and intentions take expression in urban form.

- The most acute problems of the postindustrial cities of the world's core regions are localized in the central city areas, which have borne the brunt of restructuring from an industrial to a postindustrial economy.

- Canadian cities are different from U.S. cities.

- The problems of the cities of the periphery stem from the way in which their demographic growth has outstripped their economic growth.

- Cities are created as "places" and can become "place makers."

URBAN STRUCTURE AND LAND USE

The internal organization of cities reflects the way that they function, both to bring people and activities together and to sort them out into neighbourhoods and functional subareas. The simple stereotype of the North American city, for example, is based on several main land uses. Traditionally, the very centre of the city has been the principal hub of shops and offices, together with some of the major civic and institutional land uses, such as the city hall, libraries, and museums. This centre, known as the central business district, or **CBD** (**Figure 11.1**), is a city's nucleus of commercial land uses. It contains the densest concentration of shops and offices and the tallest group of nonresidential buildings in the city. It usually develops at the nodal point of transportation routes so that it also contains bus stations, railway terminals, and hotels. The CBD typically is surrounded by a zone of mixed land uses: warehouses, small factories and workshops, specialized stores, apartment buildings, and older residential neighbourhoods (**Figure 11.2**). This zone is often referred to as the **zone in transition** because of its mixture of growth, change, and decline. Beyond this zone are residential neighbourhoods, suburbs of various ages and different social and ethnic compositions.

central business district (CBD): the central nucleus of commercial land uses in a city

zone in transition: area of mixed commercial and residential land uses surrounding the CBD

Figure 11.1 Downtown Edmonton from the air This photograph of Edmonton's CBD shows the concentration of high-rise buildings that is typical of CBDs in North America. In Edmonton, as in other major cities, the CBD originally grew around the point of maximum accessibility: near railway stations and the intersection of the city's principal road and water transportation routes. Particularly in the western parts of North America, the location of the city itself is often the result of transportation factors: cities sprang up where the railroad crossed the river.

Figure 11.2   The zone in transition
This photograph of stores along the western end of Queen Street in Toronto shows part of the zone in transition. In many North American cities, the CBD is surrounded by such a zone, which consists of older neighbourhoods with mixed land uses, some of which are in long-term decline, whereas others are undergoing redevelopment.

As cities grew larger and more complex, the simple stereotype was enlarged by several additional elements. *Secondary business districts* and *commercial strips* have emerged in the suburbs to cater to local neighbourhood shopping and service needs. *Industrial districts* have developed around large factories and airports, and in larger metropolitan areas, edge cities have emerged as new suburban hubs of shops and offices that overshadow the old CBD. **Edge cities** are nodal concentrations of shopping and office space that are situated on the outer fringes of metropolitan areas, typically near major highway intersections. Meanwhile, other changes have occurred in more central locations as older buildings and neighbourhoods have been restructured to meet new needs. One of the most striking of these changes has been the gentrification of older, centrally located, working-class communities (**Figure 11.3**).

Gentrification occurs when higher-income households, seeking the character and convenience of less expensive and centrally located residences, move into neighbourhoods previously occupied by working-class, lower-income

edge cities: nodal concentrations of shopping and office space that are situated on the outer fringes of metropolitan areas, typically near major highway intersections

gentrification: the movement into older, centrally located working-class neighbourhoods by higher-income households seeking the character and convenience of less-expensive and well-located residences

Figure 11.3   Gentrification   A newly renovated row of townhouses in Halifax, Nova Scotia, where the process of gentrification has redeveloped an older neighbourhood that had previously been occupied by lower-income households.

households. Although gentrification can displace original occupants, it can also result in the physical renovation and upgrading of housing.

Territoriality, Congregation, and Segregation

In cities, as at other geographical scales, territoriality provides a means of establishing and preserving group membership and identity. **Congregation**—the territorial and residential clustering of specific groups or subgroups of people—enables group identity to be consolidated in relation to people and places outside the group. Congregation is thus a place-making activity and an important basis for urban structure and land use. It is particularly important in situations in which there are distinctive minority groups. Defined in relation to a general population or host community, **minority groups** are population subgroups that are seen—or that see themselves—as somehow different from the general population. Their defining characteristics can be based on ethnicity, language, religion, nationality, caste, sexual orientation, or lifestyle.

Congregation offers several specific advantages for minority groups:

- Congregation provides a means of cultural preservation. It allows religious and cultural practices to be maintained and strengthens group identity through daily involvement in particular routines and ways of life. In particular, clustering can foster within-group marriage and kinship networks.

- Congregation helps minimize conflict and provides defence against "outsiders."

- Congregation provides a place where mutual support can be established through minority institutions, businesses, social networks, and welfare organizations.

- Congregation helps establish a power base in relation to the host society. This power base can be democratic (e.g., by electing a minority candidate in the local riding), or it can take the form of a territorial heartland for insurrectionary groups.

Congregation is not always voluntary, of course, but can also be a response to *discrimination* (**Figure 11.4**). Spatial discrimination effects include exclusion and prejudice in local labour markets, the manipulation of private land and housing markets (for example, when banks reject mortgage applications from certain neighbourhoods), the steering of capital investment away from minority areas, and the institutionalization of discrimination through the practices and spatial policies of public agencies (for example, when bus routes "skip" certain areas).

congregation: the territorial and residential clustering of specific groups or subgroups of people

minority groups: population subgroups that are seen—or that see themselves—as somehow different from the general population

Figure 11.4 Congregation and segregation—Chinatown, Montreal In most larger cities, there is a patchwork of distinctive neighbourhoods that results from processes of congregation and segregation. Most distinctive of all are neighbourhoods of ethnic minorities, such as the Chinatowns and Little Italys found in a number of Canadian cities.

11.1 Geography in the Information Age

The uneven distribution of supermarkets in U.S. cities can serve as an example of how capital investment can be steered away from minority areas or poor neighbourhoods—and how geographers can help in rectifying that situation. You will remember from previous discussions (in Chapters 1, 2, and 7, for example) that geographers are involved in finding the most profitable or accessible location for a business. In this video case study produced by Penn State University, you can see how geographers also help to even out the spatial inequalities created by such purely profit-oriented locational decisions. In this three-minute video you can learn how geographers employ GIS and other methods to identify areas that are underserved by supermarkets (**http://geospatialrevolution.psu.edu/episode2/chapter3**).

The combined result of congregation and discrimination is **segregation**, the spatial separation of specific subgroups within a wider population. Segregation varies a great deal, both in intensity and in form, depending on the relative degree and combination of congregation and discrimination (**Figure 11.5**). Geographers and demographers have developed indexes of segregation that measure the relative spatial concentration of population subgroups. Comparisons are often problematic, however, because of the influence of spatial scale on the computation and construction of such indexes. In terms of *form*, geographers have identified three principal situations:

- *Enclaves,* in which tendencies toward congregation and discrimination are long-standing but dominated by internal cohesion and identity. The Jewish districts of many of today's cities in Europe and the eastern United States are examples of enclaves.

- *Ghettos,* which are also long-standing but are more the product of discrimination than of congregation. Examples are the segregation of African Americans and Hispanics in U.S. cities.

- *Colonies,* which may result from congregation, discrimination, or both, but in relatively weak and short-lasting ways. Their persistence over time therefore depends on the continuing arrival of new minority-group members. For example, in the nineteenth century, Canadian cities contained distinctive colonies of Irish immigrants, which have now all but disappeared.

segregation: the spatial separation of specific population subgroups within a wider population

Figure 11.5 Segregation and congregation—Loyalist neighbourhood in Belfast, Northern Ireland Congregation is an important place-making activity. It enables group identity to be established and preserved in relation to "other" people and places.

Competing for Space in North American Cities

The overall structure of North American cities is shaped primarily by competition for territory and location. Individual households and population groups compete for the most socially desirable residences and neighbourhoods, whereas all categories of land users—commercial and industrial, as well as residential—compete for the most convenient and accessible locations within the city. Geographers draw on several different perspectives when examining competition between urban land users:

- an economic perspective based on the concept of accessibility

- an economic perspective that emphasizes the functional links between types of land uses

- a sociocultural perspective that examines the congregation and segregation of groups of people

- a historical perspective that emphasizes the influence of transport corridors

We will now consider each of these four perspectives in turn, but before we do, it is worth noting that they all share an approach to geographical study known as *locational analysis* (sometimes also known as *spatial analysis*) that flourished in the 1960s as part of the so-called New Geography (see Chapter 1). Just like industrial location (Chapter 7) and agricultural land use (Chapter 8), urban structure and land use can be examined using locational theories that assume that the use of space is shaped by rational—and thus predictable—economic decision making.

What this also means, of course, is that when the economy or society changes, then the rationale for a particular use of space changes. In other words, urban structure provides another example of our finding that our economies and societies *create* space (see Chapter 1). Certainly, these four perspectives, as we shall see, provide important illustrations of how changes in the relative importance of various activities can affect urban structures.

Accessibility and Land Use   Most urban land users want to maximize the *utility* that they derive from a particular location. The utility of a specific place or location refers to its usefulness to particular persons or groups. The price they are

isotropic surface: a hypothetical, uniform plane—flat and with no variations in its physical attributes

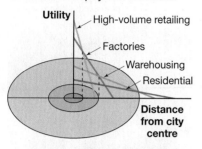

Figure 11.6   Accessibility, bid-rent, and urban structure   Competition for accessible sites near the city centre is an important determinant of land-use patterns. Different land users are prepared (or able) to pay different amounts—the bid-rent—for locations at various distances from the city centre. The result is a tendency for a concentric pattern of land uses.   (*Source:* Reprinted with permission of Prentice Hall, from P. Knox, *Urbanization*, © 1994, p. 99.)

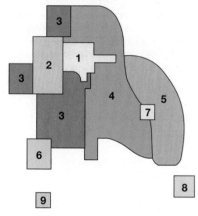

1. Central business district
2. Wholesale light manufacturing
3. Low-income residential
4. Medium-income residential
5. High-income residential
6. Heavy manufacturing
7. Outlying business district
8. Residential suburb
9. Industrial suburb

Figure 11.7   Multiple-nuclei model of urban land use   When cities reach a certain size, the traditional downtown (1) is no longer sufficient to serve the commercial needs of the whole city, and so additional nodes of shops and offices emerge in outlying districts (7). Functional groupings of related activities of other kinds—manufacturing (2, 6), wholesaling (2), and so on—also tend to develop, creating multiple nuclei of economic activities around which the city is organized.   (*Source:* C.D. Harris and E.L. Ullman, "The Nature of Cities." *Annals of the American Academy of Political and Social Science* 242(1), 1945, fig. 5.)

prepared to pay for different locations—the bid-rent—will be a reflection of this utility. In general, utility will be a function of *accessibility*. Commercial land users want to be accessible to one another, to markets, and to workers; private residents want easy access to jobs, amenities, and friends; public institutions want to be accessible to their clients. In an idealized city built on an isotropic surface, the point of maximum accessibility is the city centre. An **isotropic surface** is a hypothetical, uniform area—flat and with no variations in its physical attributes. Under these conditions, accessibility falls off steadily with distance from the city centre. Likewise, utility falls off, but at different rates for different land users. The result is a tendency for concentric zones of different mixes of land use (**Figure 11.6**).

According to this concentric model, the poorest households would end up occupying the periphery of the city, where we would expect land to be cheap. In core countries, however, the farthest suburbs are the domain of wealthier households, whereas the poor occupy more accessible locations closer to city centres. Clearly, we must modify some of our assumptions. In this case, we must assume that wealthier households trade off the convenience of accessibility for the greater utility of the privacy provided by larger suburban lots. Poorer households, unable to afford the recurrent costs of commuting, must trade off living space for accessibility to jobs so that they locate in high-density areas near their low-wage jobs. Because of the presumed trade-off between accessibility and living space, this urban land-use model is often referred to as a *trade-off model*.

Functional Clustering: Multiple Nuclei   The multiple-nuclei model of urban land use is based on the observation that some activities attract one another, and others repel one another. Without denying the concentric patterns that result from principles of distance, accessibility, and utility, geographers recognize that certain categories of land use are drawn together into functional clusters, or nuclei, whereas others tend to repel one another. At the broadest scale, economic relationships draw manufacturing, transportation, and warehousing together. These activities need to be in proximity to one another so that each can function as effectively and efficiently as possible. Similarly, functional relationships exist between these land uses and blue-collar housing, which tends to result in their mutual attraction. Conversely, upper-middle-class housing is repelled by industrial and working-class districts. The result is that urban land use becomes spatially segregated, with nodes or nuclei of different groupings of land users (**Figure 11.7**).

Social and Ethnic Clustering: Social Ecology   Just as different categories of land use attract and repel one another, so do different social and ethnic groups. The third model of land use is based on an ecological perspective developed by Chicago School sociologists Park and Burgess to explain this phenomenon, with special reference to cities in the United States whose rapid growth has been fuelled by streams of migrants and immigrants with very different backgrounds. It is based on the idea of city neighbourhoods being structured by the "invasion" of successive waves of migrants and immigrants.

When immigrants first arrive in the city looking for work and a place to live, they have little choice but to cluster in the cheapest accommodation, typically found in the zone in transition around the CBD. The classic example is provided by Chicago in the 1920s and 1930s. Immigrants from Scandinavia, Germany, Italy, Ireland, Poland, and Lithuania established themselves in Chicago's low-rent areas, the only places they could afford. By congregating together in these areas, immigrants accomplished several things: they were able to establish a sense of security; speak their native language; have familiar churches or synagogues, restaurants, bakeries, butcher shops, and taverns; and support their own community organizations. These immigrants were joined in the city's zone in transition by African-American migrants from the South, who also established their own neighbourhoods and communities. In Chicago, as in other U.S. cities of the period, the various ethnic groups formed a patchwork or mosaic of communities encircling the CBD.

These ethnic communities lasted from one to three generations, after which they started to break up. Many of the younger, city-born individuals did not feel the need for the security and familiarity of ethnic neighbourhoods. Gradually, increasing numbers of them were able to establish themselves in better jobs and move out into newer, better housing. As the original immigrants and their families moved out, their place in the transitional zone was taken by a new wave of migrants and immigrants. In this way, Chicago became structured into a series of *concentric zones* of neighbourhoods of varying ethnicity and status (**Figure 11.8**).

Throughout this process of invasion and succession, people of the same background tend to stick together—partly because of the advantages of residential clustering and partly because of discrimination. **Invasion and succession** is a process of neighbourhood change whereby one social or ethnic group succeeds another in a residential area. The displaced group, in turn, invades other areas, creating over time a rippling process of change throughout the city. The result is that within each concentric zone, there exists a mosaic of distinctive neighbourhoods, which can be thought of as *ecological niches* within the overall metropolis—settings where a particular mix of people have come to dominate a particular territory and a particular physical environment, or habitat.

invasion and succession: a process of neighbourhood change whereby one social or ethnic group succeeds another

Corridors and Sectors   The fourth model of land use is a historical one. It is generally known as the Hoyt "sector" model. In cities where growth has been less dominated by successive waves of different immigrant ethnic groups, neighbourhood patterns are often structured around the development of two different types of district: industrial districts and high-class residential districts. Over time, both tend to grow outward from the centre of the city, but for different reasons and in different directions. Industry tends to follow transportation corridors along low-lying, flat land where space exists for large factories, warehouses, and railway marshalling

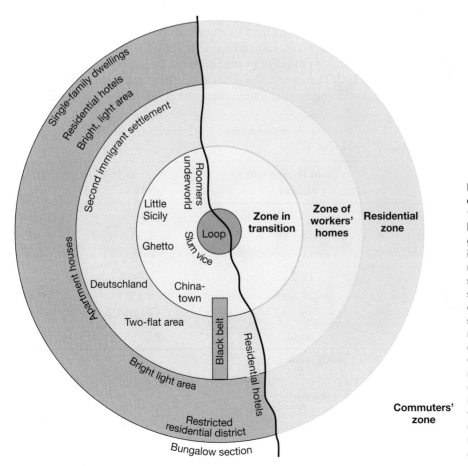

Figure 11.8   The ecological model of urban land use: Chicago in the 1920s   Competition between members of different migrant and immigrant groups for residential space in the city often results in distinctive neighbourhoods that have their own social "ecology." The classic example, shown in this illustration, is Chicago of the 1920s, which had developed a series of concentric zones of distinctive neighbourhoods as successive waves of immigrants established themselves. Over time, most immigrant groups made their way from low-rent, inner-city districts surrounding the CBD (known in Chicago as the Loop) to more attractive and expensive districts farther out. (*Source:* R.E. Park, E.W. Burgess, and R.D. McKenzie, *The City.* Chicago: University of Chicago Press, 1925, p. 53.)

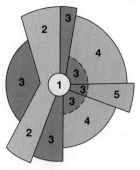

1. Central business district
2. Industrial area
3. Working-class residential district
4. Middle-class development
5. High-income residential district

Figure 11.9 Corridors and sectors
Cities that have not been dominated by successive waves of migrant or immigrant ethnic groups tend to be organized around the linear development of two main features that grow outward from the CBD (1): corridors of industrial development (2) and sectors of high-status residential development (5). Sectors of working-class residential districts (3) surround the industrial corridors, whereas sectors of middle-class residential districts (4) surround the high-status developments. (*Source*: C.D. Harris and E.L. Ullman, "The Nature of Cities," *Annals of the American Academy of Political and Social Science* 242(1), 1945, fig. 5.)

yards. Working-class residential areas grow up around these corridors, following them out in sector-shaped neighbourhoods as they grow (**Figure 11.9**).

High-status residential districts, conversely, tend to grow outward from a different side of town, often following a ridge of high ground (free from flooding and with panoramic views and better air quality). This outward growth creates another sectoral component of urban structure. The social status of this sector attracts middle-class housing, which, in turn, creates additional sectors of growth, thus completing the city's overall structure.

Canadian Cities

Difference Originally, the patterns and processes outlined in the previous section were believed to apply equally across North America (a region that, in urban geography, traditionally excludes Mexico). Beginning with the publication in 1986 of Goldberg and Mercer's *The Myth of the North American City*,[2] however, scholars have highlighted important differences between Canadian and U.S. cities. When compared with the average American city, for example, Canadian cities

- are more compact in size
- have a higher density of population
- have far fewer inner-city zones of poverty ("urban blight") and contain far lower levels of poverty overall
- have greater levels of public transit provision and use
- have greater levels of public investment in infrastructure and facilities
- have more dispersed immigrant populations
- have more powerful and less fragmented municipal governments
- in total, represent an even larger share of the country's population than that found in the United States

History and politics contribute significantly to these differences. Historically, the Canadian city developed as part of a colonial economy that was dependent and export-driven. As a result, Canada required only a handful of administrative and port centres, which continue to predominate in our country and its urban systems (**Table 11.1**). In contrast, the American urban system grew from a locally run economy, producing food and manufactured goods for its own needs.

TABLE 11.1 The Urban Transformation of Canada: Urban Population Distributions, 1901–2001

Year	Total Population (000s)	Urban* Population (000s)	Urban* Population (%)
1901	5,371	2,014	37.5
1921	8,788	4,352	49.5
1941	11,507	6,271	54.5
1961	18,232	12,700	69.6
1981	24,343	18,436	75.7
1991	27,296	21,008	77.0
2001	30,007	23,908	79.7

Sources: Census of Canada, various years.

*Definitions of urban populations from 1901 to 1941 were not the same as those from the 1951 census to the present.

[2] M.A. Goldberg and J. Mercer, *The Myth of the North American City: Continentalism Challenged*. Vancouver: University of British Columbia Press, 1986.

Political differences contribute most significantly to the differences between urban settlements in the two countries. In Canada, the government and public sector have always been deeply involved in urban affairs. In contrast, the United States favours fragmented and less powerful municipal administrations because Americans place a high value on individual rights and freedoms and local autonomy.

Canada's more expansive social welfare net has meant that far fewer people experience poverty and homelessness than in the United States. This is reflected in the relative lack of inner-city "urban blight" areas in this country, an unfortunate hallmark of American cities and one that is partly responsible for what has been called the "white flight" to the suburbs. The existence of fewer and less fragmented municipalities in this country makes local government much more effective, not least because inner cities and suburbs are part of the same tax base. Canada's universal health care system and provincial and territorial commitments to education also result in more equitable distributions of institutions and schools throughout our cities.

The provision of government-subsidized public transit systems, coupled with the more extensive zoning and land-use controls in this country, has meant that Canadian cities are generally more dense and compact than their American counterparts, where controls are seen as restrictions on individual property rights and public spending as inhibiting free competition.

The net result, according to many commentators, is that when compared with the United States, Canada has been able to create far more "liveable" cities. In its approach to urban life, Canada is in many ways much closer to Europe than to the United States, which is why Canadian cities are often described as representing an "intermediate" urban form.

Ironically, just as Canadian urban geographers are beginning to document the distinct qualities of the Canadian city, they are also beginning to see signs of its disappearance. This is because the increasing cutbacks in government spending that occurred in Canada in the 1980s and 1990s and the growing implications of NAFTA have begun to remove the causes of the differences between Canadian and U.S. cities. Troubling trends, such as the increasing incidence of poverty, homelessness, and food bank use across Canadian cities, suggest that in the future, our cities may more closely resemble those of the United States.

Change   We can now turn our attention to the Canadian city in its own right and examine the changes it has experienced in recent years, changes wrought by economic, demographic, social, and cultural forces.

The twin forces of the baby boom (which lasted in Canada from 1947 to 1966) and the post–World War II economic boom spurred the development of the Canadian suburb to its present position as the place where the majority of Canadians live. The growth in both the number of households and the size of homes, easy credit, and the desire for a modern and healthy lifestyle have fuelled the continuous expansion of this urban form since the 1950s. Recent developments have included the creation of "suburban downtowns," such as in

11.2   Geography in the Information Age

Certainly, we need to be careful not to glorify the Canadian city or overlook the possibility that American cities can offer useful and inspiring examples for urban development. The city of Portland (Oregon) provides a compelling case study of how a forward-looking municipal administration can use geographical tools such as GIS and LIDAR (Laser Radar) to create a more walkable, accessible, and ultimately more liveable city. You can watch a six-minute video by Penn State University on "creating the interactive city" here: **http://geospatialrevolution .psu.edu/episode2/chapter1.**

Scarborough (a borough of Toronto featured in **Visualizing Geography 11.1— The Development of Urban Planning in Canada**). Meanwhile, at the advancing front of suburban sprawl, we find ever-larger shopping malls and stand-alone "big-box stores" (exemplified by Walmart) set within their own giant parking lots (see Geography Matters 7.5—Walmart's Economic Landscape on p. 343).

Increasing suburban sprawl has created its own set of problems. For example, environmentalists decry the loss of agricultural land and the wasteful use of energy for commuting (mostly individually in cars). Social critics have noted that the physical separation of work (city) and home (suburb), often enforced by zoning regulations, was based on a 1950s concept of social relations that saw "work" as a man's space—a public domain—and "home" as a woman's place—a domestic, private space. This literal concretizing of gender relations in space has made it far harder, these critics argue, for the city to accommodate current social changes.

More recent economic and demographic change has had its own profound effects on the Canadian inner city. The massive loss of manufacturing jobs that occurred as part of the economic restructuring of the 1980s and 1990s might have led to an abandonment of the inner city, had it not been for the almost simultaneous development there of quaternary industry (that is, the professional and information sector) and the easing of municipal restrictions on condominium development and loft conversions. Significantly, a large number of the people employed in these new occupations also chose to live in the inner city and so initiated a considerable degree of gentrification in these areas.

Research by Professor David Ley of the University of British Columbia into the processes of change in Canadian inner cities has examined the six metropolitan areas of Toronto, Montreal, Vancouver, Ottawa-Hull, Edmonton, and Halifax over the period from 1971 to 1991.[3] Over those 20 years, the inner-city areas lost almost 230,000 nonquaternary jobs but gained 160,000 new quaternary sector jobs.

This gain has been aided by a number of factors, such as city authorities encouraging the conversion of rental properties and vacant lots to condominiums geared toward single households, and the trendiness of inner-city living resulting from postmodernism's emphasis on heritage and a carnival-like atmosphere. In effect, an upward spiral has been created in which a number of factors mutually reinforce one another and ensure the continued viability of these areas as desirable places in which to live.

An important illustration of this is that until very recently, average household income levels in Canadian inner-city areas have seen very little decline when compared with equivalent U.S. statistics. Also, the problem of displaced poorer families is not as evident. With respect to the 460 census tracts included in his study of the six inner cities, Ley concludes that "while the social status of a few tracts declined over the twenty-year period, the dominant movement was upwards, and some tracts rose markedly."[4] In other words, Canadian inner cities have fared relatively well.

Of course, this very broad description cannot hope to capture all of the differences and complexities of Canadian urban life. In the final analysis, Canada's cities are dynamic and vibrant entities, each city a unique place with its own character. And even within each of the urban zones we discussed earlier, there is considerable variety. For example, Ley points to the range of types within the inner city: the pockets of poverty, the areas of affluence, the heritage zones, and the "ethnic" villages.

Finally, no examination of urban geography should overlook Canada's small towns. Defined as having fewer than 10,000 people, these communities lie beyond the spheres of Canada's urban centres and comprise a very small percentage of Canada's total population. Nevertheless, their place in the Canadian imagination

---

[3] David Ley, "The New Middle Class in Canadian Central Cities." In J. Caulfield and L. Peake (eds.), *City Lives and City Forms: Critical Research and Canadian Urbanism*. Toronto: University of Toronto Press, 1996, pp. 15–32.

[4] Ibid., p. 19.

Visualizing Geography

The Development of Urban Planning in Canada

Although obviously the result of deliberate intent, the small urban settlements developed by the European colonial powers in Canada were not the first settlements in this country, nor were their layouts planned. For instance, the winding streets of Quebec City, founded by the French in 1608, continue European traditions of the medieval city, in which streets follow the topography (**Figure 11.1.1**).

In eighteenth-century Canada, the Enlightenment's emphasis on rationality and scientific thought can be seen in the design of the massive fortress of Louisbourg (Nova Scotia) and the streets of Charlottetown (Prince Edward Island) (**Figure 11.1.2**), which were deliberately laid out to conform to the aesthetics of geometry, not to the lay of the land or the desires of the locals.

This approach continued into the nineteenth century (**Figure 11.1.3**). Indeed, the efficient grid plan became the preferred design for the thousands of settlements founded in the Canadian Prairies by European immigrants. Because its layout imposed a very visible order and authority across the landscape, the grid plan itself expressed a worldview that celebrated progress, economic growth, and the taming of a disorderly nature in the creation of urban places.

By the late nineteenth century, Canadian cities became victims of their own success. Urbanization in Canada was proceeding swiftly and beginning to cause problems of overcrowding and poor sanitation, especially in the larger cities. In an attempt to reduce urban disease, municipal authorities began to build water and sewer lines and introduced planning controls.

On a more general level, urban problems triggered an urban reform movement that spread across North America in the early twentieth century. One reform approach to city planning followed the American **City Beautiful movement**, which was a Progressive Era (c. 1890–1920) attempt to remake cities in ways that would reflect the higher values of society, using neo-classical architecture, grandiose street plans, parks (see Chapter 6), and inspirational monuments and statues.

Planners work on the design of Ottawa. These assistants were photographed in 1949 as they prepared a model of Jacques Greber's 1937 plan for the National Capital Region. The plan guided federal development for the capital for more than a generation. The section in the foreground contains the Parliament Hill area; Hull is at the lower left.

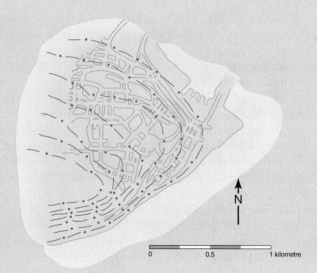

Figure 11.1.1 Quebec City Founded by the French in 1608, this city illustrates an organic street layout that connected places of industry and trade with places people lived, and reflected the city's topography. (*Source:* J. Grant, "Planning Canadian Cities: Context, Continuity, and Change." In T. Bunting and P. Filion [eds.], *Canadian Cities in Transition: The Twenty-First Century*, 2nd ed. Toronto: Oxford University Press, 2000, pp. 443–461, fig. 19.1, p. 443.)

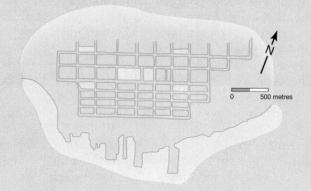

Figure 11.1.2 Charlottetown Laid out by British soldiers in 1768, the design for this town shows the simplicity of geometry, narrow blocks, and a central square. (*Source:* J. Grant, "Planning Canadian Cities: Context, Continuity, and Change." In T. Bunting and P. Filion [eds.], *Canadian Cities in Transition: The Twenty-First Century*, 2nd ed. Toronto: Oxford University Press, 2000, pp. 443–461, Figure 19.2, p. 444.)

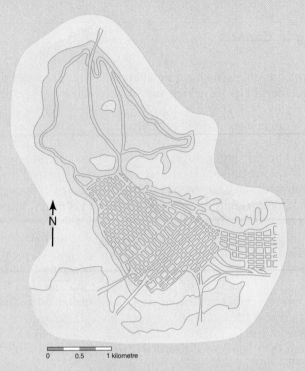

0   0.5   1 kilometre

Figure 11.1.3 Vancouver The rigidity of the survey grid is evident in the design of this city, which was first settled in 1862. *(Source:* J. Grant, "Planning Canadian Cities: Context, Continuity, and Change." In T. Bunting and P. Filion [eds.], *Canadian Cities in Transition: The Twenty-First Century,* 2nd ed. Toronto: Oxford University Press, 2000, pp. 443–461, fig. 19.3, p. 444.)

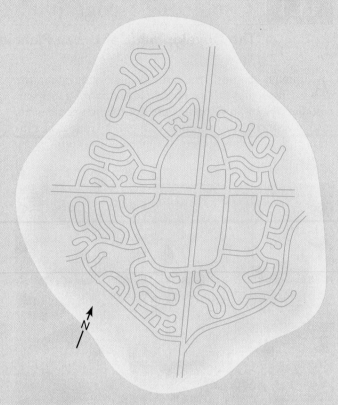

Figure 11.1.4 Don Mills Based on garden city precepts and the neighbourhood unit, this Toronto suburb was developed by Macklin Hancock in the 1950s. Stripped down to its fundamentals (wide lots, winding streets, and retail strips), the form was repeated across Canada and came to represent suburbia. *(Source:* J. Grant, "Planning Canadian Cities: Context, Continuity, and Change." In T. Bunting and P. Filion [eds.], *Canadian Cities in Transition: The Twenty-First Century,* 2nd ed. Toronto: Oxford University Press, 2000, pp. 443–461, Figure 19.3, p. 444.)

Another, even more profound reform vision arose from the **Garden City movement,** established in England in 1899 by Sir Ebenezer Howard, who believed that people should be able to combine the benefits of urban living with a more healthy rural way of life. To achieve this, he stressed the importance of overall planning and particularly emphasized the need for spaciousness and environmental quality in the urban context.

The ideal "garden city," Howard believed, should be built on land that was owned by the community to prevent land speculation and enable efficient planning. It should be relatively small (about 30,000 people) and should contain separate residential and industrial areas. Its design should feature wide boulevards (often curvilinear, or "organic" in plan), low-density housing of high quality, and public parks, all surrounded by a greenbelt. The success of the garden cities Letchworth and Welwyn, both built near London, England, helped transfer Howard's ideas to Canada: between 1914 and 1923, Howard's talented assistant Thomas Adams was Town Planning Advisor to the Commission of Conservation, developing plans for parts of Halifax and Ottawa, and for the cities of Prince Rupert and Corner Brook, for example.

Unfortunately, the Depression and World War II virtually eliminated any energy or funds for urban planning. By the 1950s, however, the pent-up demand for housing and the desire to create truly modern urban forms led to the development of what was to become the classic form of the modern Canadian suburb, best shown by the example of Don Mills, Ontario (**Figure 11.1.4**). Its design merged garden city principles with the "neighbourhood concept" to create a layout that was both adapted to the increasing use of the automobile and the desire of people for a healthier, more spacious lifestyle.

Desire for improvement also led to the urban renewal movements of the 1960s and 1970s in which large tracts of poor quality inner-city housing were demolished and, in their place, large social housing projects created. Examples include La Cité development in Montreal (**Figure 11.1.5**) and the Regent Park project in Toronto. Initially, these examples of modern planning, with their emphasis on efficiency, order, and equality, were praised by residents and planners alike. However, the appetite for such grandiose attempts at social engineering soured by the mid-1970s as it became obvious that such developments had no "soul" and lacked the character and social cohesion of the communities that had been bulldozed. At the same time, noted commentators on urban life, such as Jane Jacobs, began to promote older forms of urban existence, such as had been found in the inner city, as more conducive to successful and safe urban living.

Figure 11.1.5 La Cité development, Montreal The original late-1960s plan for this development called for the demolition of 255 houses as part of a slum clearance program. However, the project was greatly amended by community action. Only one-third of the houses were demolished and a greatly scaled down complex (consisting of 1,350 apartments in three towers) was constructed in the late 1970s. The remaining homes (some 600 housing units) became integrated into cooperative and non-profit housing associations.

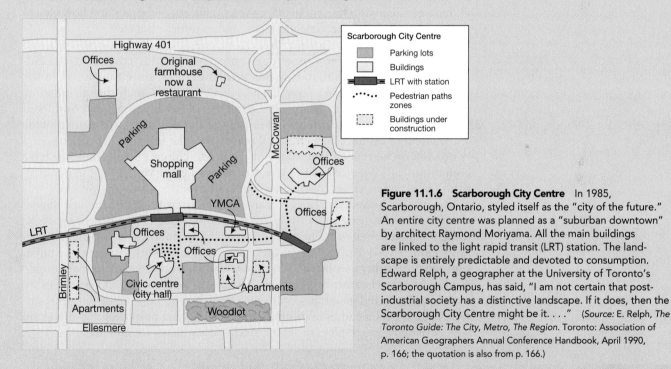

Figure 11.1.6 Scarborough City Centre In 1985, Scarborough, Ontario, styled itself as the "city of the future." An entire city centre was planned as a "suburban downtown" by architect Raymond Moriyama. All the main buildings are linked to the light rapid transit (LRT) station. The landscape is entirely predictable and devoted to consumption. Edward Relph, a geographer at the University of Toronto's Scarborough Campus, has said, "I am not certain that post-industrial society has a distinctive landscape. If it does, then the Scarborough City Centre might be it. . . ." (*Source:* E. Relph, *The Toronto Guide: The City, Metro, The Region.* Toronto: Association of American Geographers Annual Conference Handbook, April 1990, p. 166; the quotation is also from p. 166.)

The conjunction of these ideas with the growing trend toward gentrification in Canadian cities during the late 1980s and 1990s has led to a rediscovery of older urban forms as a postmodern expression of the differences of urban living (**Figure 11.1.6**).

City Beautiful movement: an attempt to remake cities in ways that would reflect the higher values of society, using neo-classical architecture, grandiose street plans, parks, and inspirational monuments and statues

Garden City movement: an attempt to plan cities in ways that combined the benefits of urban living with the spaciousness and environmental quality of rural life

is secure, for they (just like the rural Canada we discussed in Chapter 8) are seen as repositories of old-fashioned values and neighbourliness—even if most people only experience them (or, more precisely, consume them) on weekend visits, for example, when buying antiques in St. Jacob's, Ontario, or jam in Knowlton, Quebec.

In reality, of course, these small centres face an array of problems—including the loss of their business to larger centres, the collapse of resource industries, and the decline of Canadian agriculture (see Chapter 8). Such problems of decline are sometimes met with imaginative local responses that attempt to find other activities to support the economy. Examples include tourism development based on heritage (Lunenburg, Nova Scotia), dinosaurs (Drumheller, Alberta), and murals (Chemainus, British Columbia); the creation of ski resorts (Mont Tremblant, Quebec); and more specialized activities, such as documentary film festivals (Yorkton, Saskatchewan).

Reflecting on the City

As we have already seen in Chapter 5, there are many different ways of viewing space, and in that chapter we examined the processes by which space can be differently structured depending on factors such as ethnicity (for example, the Chinatowns found in many Canadian cities) or gender (for example, downtown Montreal's Gay Village). For a moment, we should also remember that there is more to cities than the objective, quantifiable, and often economically driven aspects of city life that we have considered so far. These other aspects concern our senses and how we use them to construct and negotiate our places and identities in city life.

For instance, we have seen already (in our discussions of aesthetics and garden design in Chapter 6) how our appreciation of the senses is itself a cultural construction. It is therefore not surprising that, since the period of the Enlightenment, our senses have been tacitly "ranked" such that those most associated with physical labour and proximity (smell, touch) are considered "inferior" to sight and hearing—senses that are more associated with aesthetic sensibility and distance (which is still reflected in the fact that art galleries and symphony orchestras are mainstays of the urban cultural elite). Thus, we have been historically conditioned to place the strongest emphasis on sight in our evaluation of experience: we "read" an urban landscape.

Gradually, however, urban geographers have come to appreciate how important the sensual experience of the city is for people's sense of place. For example, the gentleman *flaneur* who had the time to simply walk and observe crowds in nineteenth-century Paris while leisurely using all of his senses has many equivalents today, whether they be peoplewatchers in a Starbucks in Hamilton or domino players on a street corner in Jerusalem. The city is much richer as a place than we have imagined, and geographers are realizing that we need all of our senses to experience the full nuances of its urban structure. To that purpose, geographers are now developing geographies of sound, smell, or blindness, for instance.

11.3   Geography in the Information Age

In an age where continuous connectedness and accessibility are expected as a matter of course, it is worth reminding ourselves that these are very recent phenomena. Even as late as the 1950s, many Canadians put their cars away for the winter and accepted the limitations of the season. We now, however, expect to be able to continue to drive throughout the winter, and expect to have the streets plowed to enable us to do so. Perhaps there is no better example of how we have allowed modern urban life almost completely to erase our experiences, and thereby to dull our senses! On second thought, however, we should not be surprised: wasn't the original idea of the city to overcome the limitations of nature?

Comparative Urban Structure

Certain fundamental forces—economic competition for space and accessibility, social and ethnic discrimination and congregation, functional agglomeration, and residential search behaviour—can be traced in many of the world's cities, particularly in affluent core regions where economic, social, and cultural forces are broadly similar. Nevertheless, urban structure varies considerably because of the influence of history, culture, and the different roles that cities have played within the world-system, as we will see in the following examples.

European Cities What distinguishes most European cities from North American cities is that they are the product of several major epochs of urban development. Among their distinctive historical features are the narrow and complex streets and the compact, dense form that are the product of the long, slow growth of European cities in the pre-automobile era. At the same time, the constraints of peripheral defensive walls made urban land expensive and encouraged a tradition of high-density living in tenements and apartment houses (**Figure 11.10**).

Another important historical legacy in many European cities are the plazas, squares, and marketplaces that are still important nodes of urban activity (**Figure 11.11**). European history also means that its cities bear the accessories and scars of war. The legacy of defensive hilltop and clifftop sites and city walls has limited and shaped the growth of modern cities, while in more recent times the bombings and shellings of World War II destroyed many buildings in a large number of cities (**Figure 11.12**).

From a more contemporary perspective, we can note the following distinctive features of European cities:

- *Low skylines* Although the larger European cities have a fair number of high-rise apartment buildings and a sprinkling of office skyscrapers, they all offer a predominantly low skyline. This is partly because much of their growth came before the invention of the elevator and the development of steel-reinforced, concrete building techniques; and partly because of master plans and building codes (some written as long ago as the sixteenth century) seeking to preserve the dominance of monumental buildings like palaces and cathedrals. (Kingston, Ontario, is one of the rare cities in Canada to have such a restriction.)

- *Lively downtowns* The CBDs of European cities have retained their focal position in residents' shopping and social lives because of the relatively late arrival of the suburbanizing influence of the automobile and strong planning controls directed against urban sprawl.

- *Neighbourhood stability* On average, Europeans change residence every 10 years, about half as often as Canadians. In addition, the physical life cycle

11.4 Geography in the Information Age

Cities reflect place-making influences in their buildings and layouts, and these "built forms" can become potent place-making factors in their own right as they, in turn, shape our behaviour and our memories as urban dwellers. In this sense, just as our cultures create cities, so do those cities create their own culture, or "place." Thus, world cities, such as Paris, New York, and Berlin, have a unique and defining sense of place that is immediately recognizable. That is why movie producers and novelists turn to that sense of place as shorthand to set the scene, whether it is romance in Paris or intrigue in Berlin, trapping the real city in our own images of it. The circle closes when we, as tourists, then visit those cities to experience this sense of place we "already know" from movies and novels.

Figure 11.10 Distinctive historical characteristics of European cities This photograph of Florence, Italy, shows the city's narrow and complex streets, compact form, and high density that are a legacy of pre-automobile urban development.

Figure 11.11 Vigevano, Italy Widely considered one of the finest piazzas in Italy, the Piazza Ducale in Vigevano was designed in 1492. Completely surrounded by arcades, the piazza still provides an important social space for the citizens of the town.

Figure 11.12 Cologne, Germany, 1945 About 90 percent of Cologne's central area was destroyed or severely damaged by Allied bombing during World War II. One of the few structures to survive intact was the cathedral, built between the thirteenth and nineteenth centuries: because its Gothic design featured vast areas of stained glass windows rather than solid walls, the shock waves could blow right through the building without doing too much structural damage.

of city neighbourhoods tends to be longer because residences are built of solid brick and stone. As a result, European cities provide relatively stable socio-economic environments.

■ *Municipal services* For decades, European welfare states have provided a broad range of municipal services and amenities, from clinics to public transit systems. Perhaps the most important to urban structure is social housing (public housing), which accounts for 20 to 40 percent of all housing in most larger English, French, and German cities. In recent years, neoliberal policies have resulted in a reduction in public service provision and privatization of social housing stock.

Putting all this together, we can produce a composite model of the Western European city (**Figure 11.13**). We should note, however, that the richness of European history and the diversity of its geography mean that there are important regional variations: The industrial cities of northern England, northeastern France, and the Ruhr district of Germany, for example, are quite different in character from the cities of Mediterranean Europe.

One of the most interesting regional variations is the Eastern European city, in which 44 years of socialist urbanism (1945–1989) were grafted onto cities that had already developed mature patterns of land use and social differentiation. Major examples include Belgrade, Budapest, Katowice, Kraków, Leipzig, Prague, and

CBD, Vienna

Low-density Villa Belt, Vienna

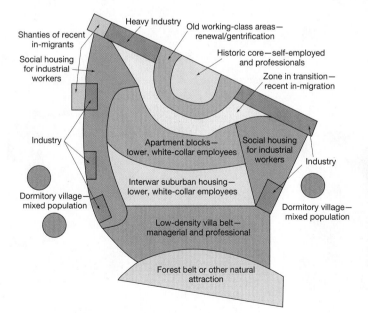

Alt-Erlaa Complex of Social Housing, Vienna

Figure 11.13 Urban structure in continental Western Europe In the typical continental Western European city, the historic core has retained a much more dominant role in commercial and social life than in North American cities. This illustration depicts land-use patterns in the generic Western European city. The density of residential development is high, with large areas of nineteenth-century housing—including stable, high-status neighbourhoods close to the city centre—and significant tracts of social housing. (*Source:* P. White, *The West European City.* London: Longman, 1984, fig. 7.6, p. 188. Reprinted by permission of Addison Wesley Longman Ltd.)

Warsaw. Public ownership of land meant that the economics of land-use competition (see Figure 11.6) could be ignored, and cities could therefore be planned on a more centralized basis, resulting in huge public housing estates and industrial zones in outlying districts. The structure of the older city was little altered, however, apart from the addition of socialist monuments and the renaming of streets. In fact, inner cities were often purposefully neglected because of their "bourgeois" legacy.

Colonial Cities   Colonial cities are those that were deliberately established or developed as administrative or commercial centres by colonial or imperial powers. Examples are Accra (Ghana), Hanoi (Vietnam), Macau (China), Nairobi (Kenya), and New Delhi (India). The stereotypical colonial city reflects a fundamental division among three original functional components: colonial administration and commerce, military security, and indigenous commerce and residence. Usually located on a coastal site or navigable river, the form and structure of colonial cities were dictated by European models of urban design, with a gridiron pattern of town planning and deliberate racial segregation (**Figure 11.14**).

Fort

European quarter bungalow

Bazaar-based, high-intensity commercial and residential land uses

Native or black town

Administrative quarters

Mixed-race residences

Port extension

Central business district

Original port

Fort

Open space

European town

Figure 11.14 Urban structure in colonial cities   The typical colonial city was developed around a port facility and often protected by a fort (with an open space around it to provide a field of fire). Colonial administrative offices were nearby, with military barracks and European civilian residences set apart from "native" residential areas.   (*Source:* S. Brunn and J. Williams [eds.], *Cities of the World*, 2nd ed. New York: HarperCollins, 1993, fig. 9.7, p. 360. © 1993. Reprinted by permission of Addison-Wesley Educational Publishers Inc. Top left photo © John Elk/Stock Boston/PNI.)

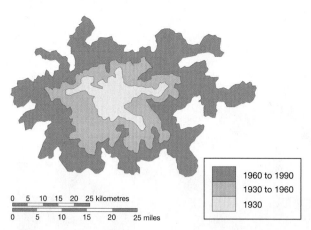

Figure 11.15 The growth of São Paulo Since 1930, the city has grown 16-fold in extent. (*Source: Urban Transport.* Washington, DC: The World Bank, 1986, fig. 3, p. 5.)

1960 to 1990
1930 to 1960
1930

0 5 10 15 20 25 kilometres

0 5 10 15 20 25 miles

Cities of the Periphery   The cities of the world-system periphery, often still referred to as Third World cities, are numerous and varied. What they have in common is the experience of unprecedented rates of growth driven by rural "push"—overpopulation and the lack of employment opportunities in rural areas—rather than the "pull" of prospective jobs in towns and cities. Most of them have also grown a great deal in a relatively short period of time. São Paulo, Brazil, provides an eloquent example (**Figure 11.15**). In 1930, the urban area of São Paulo was approximately 150 square kilometres, and the population was 1 million. By 1995, the city covered 2,400 square kilometres with a population of 15 million. In 2010, São Paulo's population topped 20 million—a number that, according to UN projections made in 2007, should not have been reached until 2015.[5]

To the extent that it is possible to generalize about the urban structure of the cities of the periphery, we can say that it varies according to four factors:

- relative levels of economic development, and the degree to which the cities have become industrialized and modernized

- regional cultural values as, for example, in the traditional layout and design of Islamic cities (see **Visualizing Geography 11.2—Islamic Cities**)

- whether society is organized more strongly along class or ethnic divisions

- how extensively slums or squatter neighbourhoods contribute to uncontrolled growth

Later in this chapter, we will see how prominent this last element has come to be in the unintended metropolises of the periphery where once-distinctive patterns of spatial organization and land use have been erased by the congestion and overcrowding of overurbanization.

Planned Urban Design

City planning and design have a long history. As we have seen, many ancient Greek and Roman settlements were deliberately laid out on grid systems, within which the location of key buildings and the relationship of neighbourhoods to one another were carefully thought out. In ancient China, cities were laid out with strict regard to Taoist ideas about the natural order of the universe, with the placement of major streets and the interior layout of buildings designed to be in harmony with cosmic energy. This kind of mystical interpretation of nature is known as *geomancy*, and its application to design is known as *feng shui*. It continues to influence many aspects of urban planning and design in the Far East

---

[5] United Nations Department of Economic and Social Affairs, Population Division, *World Urbanization Prospects: The 2009 Revision*. New York: United Nations Department of Economic and Social Affairs, Population Division, 2010. Available at **www.un.org/esa/population/unpop.htm**.

Islamic Cities

Islamic cities provide good examples of how social and cultural values and people's responses to their environment are translated into spatial terms through urban form and the design of the built environment. Indeed, it is precisely because of similarities in cityscapes, layout, and design that geographers are able to talk about the Islamic city as a meaningful category. Most cities in North Africa and South-Central Asia are Islamic, and many elements of the classic Islamic city can be found in towns and cities as far away as Seville, Granada, and Córdoba in southern Spain (the western extent of Islam), Kano in northern Nigeria and Dares-Salaam in Tanzania (the southern extent), and Davao in the Philippines (the eastern extent).

The fundamentals of the layout and design of the traditional Islamic city are so closely attached to Islamic cultural values that they are found in the Qur'an, the holy book of Islam. Although urban growth does not have to conform to any overall master plan or layout, certain basic regulations and principles are intended to ensure Islam's emphasis on personal privacy and virtue, on communal well-being, and on the inner essence of things rather than on their outward appearance.

The most dominant feature of the traditional Islamic city is the *Jami*—the city's principal mosque (**Figure 11.2.1**). Located centrally, the mosque complex is a centre not only

Figure 11.2.2 The suq The *suq*, a covered bazaar or open street market, is one of the most important distinguishing features of a traditional Islamic city. Typically, a suq consists of small stalls located in numerous passageways. Many important suqs are covered with vaults or domes. Within them is typically a marked spatial organization, with stalls that sell similar products clustered tightly together. This photograph shows the Grand Bazaar in Istanbul, Turkey, one of the oldest and largest covered markets in the world. Every day, up to half a million visitors roam through its 4,000 shops on more than 50 streets.

of worship but also of education and the hub of a broad range of welfare functions. As cities grow, new, smaller mosques are built toward the edge of the city, each out of earshot from the call to prayer from the Jami and from one another. The traditional Islamic city was walled for defence, with several lookout towers and a *Kasbah*, or citadel (fortress) containing palace buildings, baths, barracks, and its own small mosque and shops.

Traditionally, gates controlled access to the city, allowing careful scrutiny of strangers and permitting the imposition of taxes on merchants. The major streets led from these gates to the main covered bazaars or street markets (*suqs*) (**Figure 11.2.2**). The suqs nearest the Jami typically specialize in the cleanest and most prestigious goods, such as books, perfumes, prayer mats, and modern consumer goods. Those nearer the gates typically specialize in bulkier and less valuable goods such as basic foodstuffs, building materials, textiles, leather goods, and pots and pans. Within the suqs, every profession and line of business had its own alley, and the residential districts around the suqs were organized into distinctive quarters, or *ahya'*, according to occupation (or sometimes ethnicity, tribal affiliation, or religious sect).

Privacy is central to the construction of the Islamic city. Above all, women must be protected, according to Islamic values, from the gaze of unrelated men. Traditionally, doors must not face each other across a minor street, and windows must be small, narrow, and above normal eye level (**Figure 11.2.3**). Cul-de-sacs (dead-end streets) are used where possible to restrict the number

Figure 11.2.1 Central Mosque, Hurghada, Egypt The dominant feature of traditional Islamic cities is the *Jami*, or main mosque.

Figure 11.2.3 Islamic architecture In Islamic societies, the privacy of individual residences is paramount, and elaborate precautions are taken through architecture and urban design to ensure the privacy of women. Entrances are L-shaped and staggered across the street from one another. Windows are screened and often placed high above pedestrian access, as in this example in Jeddah, Saudi Arabia. Architectural details also reflect climatic influences: Window screens and narrow, twisting streets help to maximize shade, while air ducts and roof funnels help create dust-free drafts.

of persons needing to approach the home, and angled entrances are used to prevent intrusive glances. Larger homes are built around courtyards, which provide an interior and private focus for domestic life.

The rights of others are also given strong emphasis, the Qur'an specifying an obligation to neighbourly cooperation and consideration—traditionally interpreted as applying to a minimum radius of 40 houses. Roofs, in traditional designs, are surrounded by parapets to preclude views of neighbours' homes, and drainage channels are directed away from neighbours' houses. Refuse and wastewater are carefully recycled.

Because most Islamic cities are located in hot, dry climates, these basic principles of urban design have evolved in conjunction with certain practical responses to intense heat and sunlight. Twisting streets, as narrow as permissible, help to maximize shade, as do latticework on windows and the cellular, courtyard design of residential areas. In some regions, local architectural styles include air ducts and roof funnels with adjustable shutters that can be used to create dust-free drafts. The overall effect is to produce a compact, cellular urban structure within which it is possible to maintain a high degree of privacy (**Figure 11.2.4**).

All these features are still characteristic of Islamic cities, though they are especially clear in their old cores, or *medinas*. Like cities everywhere, however, Islamic cities also bear the imprint of globalization. Although Islamic culture is self-consciously resistant to many aspects of globalization, it has been unable to resist altogether the penetration of the world economy and the infusion of the Western-based culture of global metropolitanism. The result is seen in international hotels, skyscrapers and office blocks, modern factories, highways, airports, and stores. Indeed, the leading cities of some oil-rich Islamic states have become the "shock cities" of the early twenty-first century, with phenomenal rates of growth characterized by breathtakingly ambitious architectural and urban design projects

(see **Visualizing Geography 11.3—"Shock City" of the Semiperiphery: Dubai, United Arab Emirates** on p. 505). Meanwhile, Islamic culture and urban design principles have not always been able to cope with the pressures of contemporary rates of urbanization, so the larger Islamic cities in less affluent states—cities such as Algiers, Cairo, Karachi, and Teheran—now share with other peripheral cities the common denominators of unmanageable size, shanty and squatter development, and low-income mass housing (see **Visualizing Geography 11.4—"Shock City" of the Periphery: Lagos, Nigeria** on p. 509).

Figure 11.2.4 Housing in Kalaa Sghira, Tunisia Seen from above, the traditional Islamic city is a compact mass of residences with walled courtyards—a cellular urban structure within which it is possible to maintain a high degree of privacy.

11.5   Geography in the Information Age

In Hong Kong, the GIS database for the 1990 Land Information System included a *feng shui* layer that recorded areas subject to development restrictions based on *feng shui* principles. Meanwhile, globalization has brought *feng shui* to the rest of the world, prompting developers, architects, and interior designers to use *feng shui* principles in the construction of new suburbs (in Vancouver) and in the design of skyscrapers and commercial developments (in London and New York).

because many people believe that creating a positive energy flow through a home or place of business brings good luck and fortune.

The roots of modern Western urban planning and design can be traced to the Renaissance and Baroque periods (between the fifteenth and seventeenth centuries) in Europe, when rich and powerful regimes used urban design to produce extravagant symbolizations of wealth, power, and destiny. As societies and economies became more complex with the transition to industrial capitalism, national rulers and city leaders looked to urban design to impose order, safety, and efficiency, as well as to symbolize the new seats of power and authority. One of the most important early precedents was set in Paris by Napoleon III, who presided over a comprehensive program of urban redevelopment and monumental urban design. The work was carried out by Baron Georges Haussmann between 1853 and 1870. Haussmann demolished large sections of old Paris to make way for broad, new, tree-lined avenues, with numerous public open spaces and monuments. In doing so, he not only made the city more efficient (wide boulevards meant better flows of traffic) and a better place to live (parks and gardens allowed more fresh air and sunlight in a crowded city and were held to be a "civilizing" influence), but he also made it safer from revolutionary politics (wide boulevards were hard to barricade but easy to use artillery on; monuments and statues helped to instill a sense of pride and identity).

At the same time, planning restrictions ensured that the new buildings along the avenues presented a unified front, giving Paris its unmistakable architectural "face" (**Figure 11.16**). The preferred architectural style for these new designs was the **Beaux Arts** style, which takes its name from the École des Beaux Arts in Paris. In this school, architects were trained to draw on Classical, Renaissance, and Baroque styles, synthesizing them in designs for new buildings for the industrial

Beaux Arts: a style of urban design that sought to combine the best elements of all of the classic architectural styles

Figure 11.16   Boulevard Montmartre, Paris   Central Paris owes much of its character to the *grandes boulevards* that were key to the urban renewal schemes of Baron Georges-Eugène Haussmann.   (*Source:* From *The Boulevard Montmartre, Paris*, by Camille Pisarro, 1830–1903.)

Figure 11.17   The Chicago Plan, 1909   Daniel Burnham's Chicago Plan of 1909 was based on aesthetic means toward social objectives. By giving the city a strong visual and aesthetic order, Burnham wanted to create the physical preconditions for the emergence of a harmonious social climate and strong moral order. These were popular sentiments in the Progressive Era, and much of Burnham's ambitious plan was actually carried out.   (*Source:* R. Burnham and E. Bennett, *Plan of Chicago.* New York: Princeton Architectural Press, 1993, plate CXXXII, p. 112. Jules Guerin [American, 1866–1946], pencil and watercolour on paper, 1908, 75.5 cm × 105.5 cm. On permanent loan to The Art Institute of Chicago, 28.148.1966.)

age. The idea was that the new buildings would blend artfully with the older palaces, cathedrals, and civic buildings that dominated European city centres. Haussmann's ideas were widely influential and extensively copied.

In North America, the City Beautiful movement, which began in the late nineteenth century, drew heavily on Haussmann's ideas and Beaux Arts designs. This movement was an attempt to remake cities in ways that would reflect the higher values of society, using neo-classical architecture, grandiose street plans, parks (see Chapter 6), and inspirational monuments and statues. The idea, again, was to deliberately exploit urban design as an uplifting and civilizing influence while emphasizing civic pride and power. Daniel Burnham's 1909 Chicago Plan (**Figure 11.17**) provides a good example. During the same period, European imperial powers imposed similar designs on their colonial capitals and administrative centres, for example in New Delhi (India), Rangoon (Burma, now Myanmar), Saigon (Vietnam), and Windhoek (Namibia).

Early in the twentieth century, a different intellectual and artistic reaction emerged in response to the pressures of industrialization and urbanization. This was the **modern movement**, which was based on the idea that buildings and cities should be designed and run like machines. Equally important to the modernists was that urban design, rather than merely reflecting dominant social and cultural values, should actually help *create* a *new* moral and social order. The movement's best-known advocate was Le Corbusier, a Swiss architect who provided the inspiration for technocratic urban design. Modernist buildings sought to dramatize technology, exploit industrial production techniques, and use modern materials and unembellished, functional design. Le Corbusier's ideal city (*La Ville Radieuse*—**Figure 11.18**) featured linear clusters of high-density, medium-rise apartment blocks, elevated on stilts and segregated from industrial districts; high-rise tower office blocks; and transportation routes—all separated by broad expanses of public open space.

After World War II, this concept of urban design became pervasive, part of what became known as the International Style: boxlike steel-frame buildings with concrete and glass façades that were avant-garde yet respectable and, above all, comparatively inexpensive to build. As a result, the design was used in many of the social housing projects of the post–World War II era (see Figures 11.1.5 on p. 493 and 11.13 on p. 497), but also in many downtown office towers (Toronto's TD Bank towers, designed by Mies van der Rohe, are one well-known early example—see Figure 6.29 on p. 284). Globalization has made the International Style part of the design of big cities in every part of the world. Furthermore, the International Style has often been the preferred basis for large-scale urban design projects around the world. One of the best examples of this is Brasilia, the capital of Brazil, founded in 1956 (see Chapter 6).

modern movement: the idea that buildings and cities should be designed and run like machines

Figure 11.18 *La Ville Radieuse* The modern era and the advent of new transportation and construction technologies encouraged the Utopian idea that cities could be built as efficient and equitable "machines" for industrial production and progressive lifestyles. One of the most famous and influential examples was *La Ville Radieuse* (1933), a visionary design by Swiss architect Le Corbusier. His vision was for the creation of open spaces through collectivized, high-density residential areas, strictly segregated from industrial areas and highways through a geometric physical plan. (*Source:* Le Corbusier, *La Ville Radieuse*. Paris: Éditions de l'Architecture d'Aujourd'hui, p. 170.)

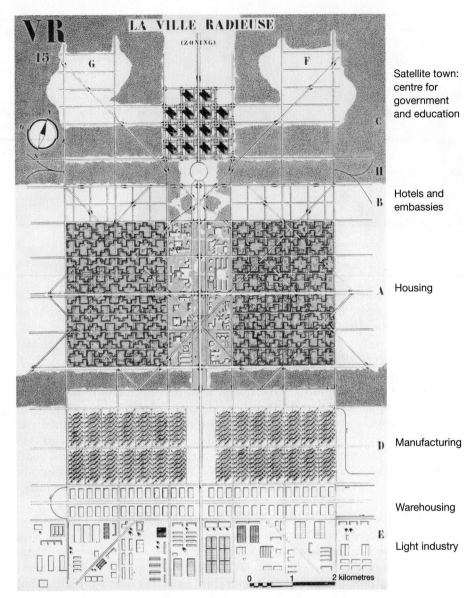

Satellite town: centre for government and education

Hotels and embassies

Housing

Manufacturing

Warehousing

Light industry

postmodern urban design: a style characterized by a diversity of architectural styles and elements, often combined in the same building or project

In fact, we could argue that the International Style has been one of the first visible instances of globalization.

Modern urban design has had many critics, mainly on the grounds that it tends to take away the natural life and vitality of cities, replacing varied and human-scale environments with monotonous and austere settings. In response to this, historic preservation has become an important element of urban planning in every city that can afford it. In addition, postmodern urban design has brought a return to traditional and decorative motifs and introduced a variety of deliberately "playful" and "interesting" architectural styles in place of the functional designs of modernism (**Figure 11.19** on p. 507). **Postmodern urban design** is characterized by a diversity of architectural styles and elements, often combined in the same building or project. It makes heavy use of symbolism, colour, and decoration. It is no coincidence that postmodern design has flourished in the most recent phase of globalization. Having emerged as a deliberate reaction to the perceived shortcomings of modern design, its emphasis on decoration and self-conscious stylishness has made it a very convenient form of packaging for the new global consumer culture. It is geared to a cosmopolitan market, and it draws quite deliberately on a mixture of elements from different places and times (see Figure 6.31 on p. 285). In many ways, it has become the new transnational style for the more affluent communities of the world's cities.

"Shock City" of the Semiperiphery: Dubai, United Arab Emirates

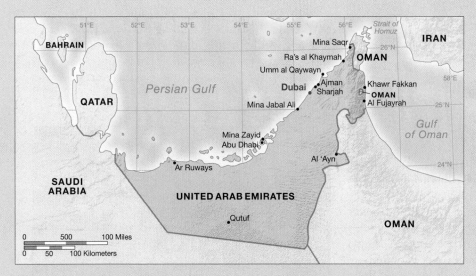

Dubai is one of seven emirates that constitute the United Arab Emirates (UAE). Since the discovery of oil in the UAE in the 1950s, the country has undergone a profound transformation and modernization, resulting in a high standard of living. Because oil reserves will only last another 20 years, the government has been pursuing a major diversification program with investment in national infrastructure, health care, education, and tourism. As a result, Dubai has become a major financial and trading centre and an important tourist destination for the wealthy: only 5 percent of its revenues still come from oil and gas.

The city of Dubai has grown exponentially: the first census in 1968 (three years before independence from Great Britain) counted barely 60,000 residents. By 1995, that number had increased tenfold to more than 600,000, only to double again by 2010. Growth rates exceed 10 percent a year, fuelling a phenomenal construction boom that depends on immigrant labour from Iran, Bangladesh, Pakistan, India, the Philippines, and other Asian nations. Although the 2008 financial crisis put a temporary damper on this development, Dubai has now resumed its growth trajectory.

Dubai's population of 1.3 million is dominated by immigrants from Asia and the Middle East, who account for over 70 percent of the city's residents. The construction boom is sustained by more than 500,000 low-skilled, poorly paid South Asian migrant workers who live in substandard conditions with few rights. Because they are mostly male, the ratio between males and females in Dubai is 3:1, which presents its own suite of social problems. The UAE has a minimum legal wage, but it is rarely enforced, so that migrant construction workers receive, on average, the equivalent of US$175 a month.

from what had hitherto been an impoverished setting. Along with the Burj Khalifa and the Burj Al Arab hotel, the Jumeirah Palm is emblematic of the aggressive growth agenda of Dubai. The Jumeirah Palm is one of two artificial islands extending from the Dubai city waterfront. Built in the shape of date palm trees with a surrounding breakwater, the islands support more than 60 luxury hotels and 10,000 exclusive residences, as

Awash—for a while—with petrodollars, Dubai has been able to offer generous tax breaks to companies willing to relocate their activities to the city, creating a major business hub that will provide an economic base when the oil and gas run out. The city's skyline reflects its emerging role as a globally important business hub: the Burj Khalifa tower, at 818 metres, now claims the title of the tallest building in the world—nearly 40 percent taller than the second-highest building, the Taipei 101, in Taipei, Taiwan.

Dubai's "shock city" status derives as much from its spectacular affluence as its phenomenal rate of growth

well as marinas, water theme parks, restaurants, shopping malls, sports facilities, health spas, cinemas, etc.

The Burj Al Arab hotel overlooking the Jumeira beach is the world's most expensive hotel and the only seven-star hotel in the world.

Dubai built its reputation for luxury shopping with the duty-free stores at Dubai airport, exploiting the city's role as a stopover point for travellers between Europe and Asia. Increasingly, however, Dubai has become a destination for shopping trips with more than 70 malls and more than 15 million visitors annually.

The luxury orientation of Dubai's development not only strains the environment but also puts in question the sustainability of this shock city. Energy demand for air conditioning and water use for golf courses in the desert environment are just two examples of the resource demands.

Ski Dubai, part of an enormous complex at the Mall of the Emirates, provides five different runs with fresh

snow for skiing, snowboarding, and tobogganing. Dubai is among the 10 most visited cities in the world, frequently for the purposes of shopping and luxury tourism.

Figure 11.19 Postmodern architecture: Park Place mall, Lethbridge Postmodern architecture is characterized by an almost playful diversity of different architectural styles from previous times, often combined in the same building. This example from Lethbridge, Alberta, shows a recently completed mall that is designed to be reminiscent of a nineteenth-century downtown, complete with its clock tower and use of patterned brick. The mall's name and interior use of park benches make reference to Galt Gardens, which is immediately adjacent.

URBAN TRENDS AND PROBLEMS

In the last section, we saw that urban *growth* processes are different in the world's core regions and in the underdeveloped periphery; in this section, we will see that the patterns and processes of urban *change* differ, too. In the core regions, urban change is dominated by the consequences of the transformation to a postindustrial economy. Together with the continuing revolution in communications and information-processing technologies and the increasing dominance of transnational corporate organizations, this transformation has made for a fundamental restructuring of metropolitan areas. Traditional manufacturing and related activities have been moved out of inner-city areas, leaving deteriorating neighbourhoods and a population of elderly and socially and economically marginalized people. New commercial activities have meanwhile begun to cluster in redeveloped (and gentrified) sections of the CBD and in edge cities around metropolitan fringes. The logic of agglomeration economies

Figure 11.20 Rio de Janeiro This photograph, looking toward Rio de Janeiro's famous Ipanema Beach, shows very clearly the dualism of peripheral metropolises, with shanty housing (*favelas*) in the foreground next to luxury apartments near the beach.

dualism: the juxtaposition in geographical space of the formal and informal sectors of the economy

has created *100-mile cities*—metropolitan areas that are literally 100 miles (160 kilometres) or so across—consisting of a series of cities and urban districts that are bound together through urban freeways. One example is the area around Chicago. In Canada, economic change has been less aggressive than in the United States, but agglomeration effects can be seen in the "corridor" between Quebec City and Windsor, in particular on the stretch from Kitchener-Waterloo to Oshawa.

In contrast, the basic trend affecting the cities of the world's periphery is demographic—the phenomenal rates of natural increase and in-migration that have given rise to overurbanization. This trend is reflected in an ever-growing informal sector of the economy in which people seek economic survival.

At the same time, however, these cities under stress represent local and regional concentrations of investment, manufacturing, modernization, and political power. As we have seen, the typical peripheral metropolis plays a key role in international economic flows, linking provincial regions with the hierarchy of world cities and, thus, with the global economy. Within peripheral metropolises, this role results in a pronounced **dualism**, or juxtaposition in geographical space of the formal and informal sectors of the economy (**Figure 11.20**). It is among these peripheral metropolises—Mexico City (Mexico), Lagos (Nigeria), and Manila (the Philippines) are examples—that we can find contenders for the title of the peripheral shock city of the early twenty-first century—the city that is the embodiment of the most remarkable and disturbing changes in economic, social, and cultural life (see Visualizing Geography 11.4—"Shock City" of the Periphery: Lagos, Nigeria).

Problems of Postindustrial Cities

For all their relative prosperity, the postindustrial cities of the world's core regions have their share of problems. The most acute are localized in the central city areas that have borne the brunt of restructuring from an industrial to a postindustrial economy. These areas are experiencing several interrelated problems: fiscal problems; infrastructure problems; and localized spirals of neighbourhood decay, cycles of poverty, and homelessness. A discussion of each condition follows.

Fiscal Problems Economic restructuring and metropolitan decentralization have meant that central cities have been left since the mid-1970s with a chronic problem that geographers call "fiscal squeeze." The squeeze comes from increasing limitations on revenues and increasing demands for expenditure. The revenue-generating potential of central cities has steadily fallen as metropolitan areas have decentralized, losing both residential and commercial taxpayers to newly

"Shock City" of the Periphery: Lagos, Nigeria

A Day in the Life of Kate Adikiwe

Kate Adikiwe lives in the suburban district of Olaleye, Lagos (**Figure 11.4.1**), once a small village whose residents grew herbs, fruits, and vegetables; fished; trapped; made palm wine; and processed palm oil. The village grew rapidly when a railway line was constructed through it and as Lagos grew outward after independence. In the mid-1960s, Olaleye had about 2,500 residents; today, there are about 25,000. Within its small site of some 35 hectares is an enormous range of economic activities—a large market, beer parlours, nightclubs, brothels, a makeshift movie theatre, tailors, shoemakers, blacksmiths, tinkers, watch repairers, knife sharpeners, mechanics, battery chargers, and itinerant barbers and beauticians. Many of the women produce and sell a great variety of cooked foodstuffs, whereas many of the men work outside the district in factories or offices.

Kate is one of six children. Her father is a clerical worker in one of the city's department stores. Her mother is a seamstress, working from the house. The house itself shelters 12 families, each occupying a single room and sharing the one kitchen, toilet, and bathroom in the building. One of Kate's jobs is to draw water from the nearby well each morning before school. The water is stored in plastic buckets in the living room until needed. After school, Kate has to complete her homework and help her

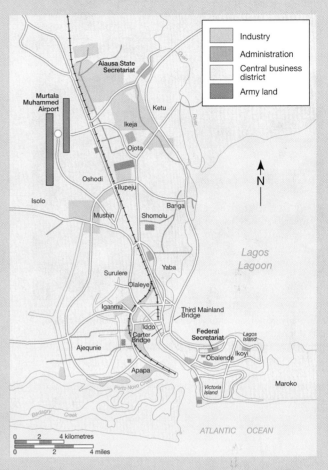

Figure 11.4.1 Layout of Lagos Lagos developed from an initial settlement at Iddo on the northern shore of Lagos Island. Ikoyi, on Lagos Island, was laid out in 1918 as a government residential estate to house colonial officials. Most of the city's growth, however, has been unplanned and irregular, with swamps, coves, and canals impeding efficient development. (*Source:* M. Peil, *Lagos.* London: Belhaven Press, 1991, p. 23.)

Lagos, like most metropolises in the world's periphery, has grown exponentially in recent decades. The combination of the demographic transition, political independence, and an economic boom stimulated by the discovery of oil reserves in southeastern Nigeria triggered an explosive growth in population. Because of its difficult site on sand spits and lagoons, this growth has resulted in an irregular sprawl and, in the central area, a density of population higher than that of Manhattan Island in New York.

The dualistic cityscape on Lagos Island reflects both residential congestion and the postcolonial development of the city as a peripheral metropolis with important corporate functions.

For many people, economic survival in the unintended metropolis depends on a tremendous variety of informal economic activities, from street vending to selling home-brewed beer, and from prostitution to drug peddling. The photograph on the left shows the most common form of informal activity: street trading, which takes place on almost every unoccupied sidewalk, street, or unclaimed space.

mother prepare food for the family. Most of the cooking is done on kerosene stoves in the passageway. After the meal, Kate and her older sister help their mother with sewing. They do not expect to be able to get jobs after school, and so they are learning to sew to become seamstresses.

Kate's story is typical of many of the residents of Lagos, a city that already ranks among the 20 largest cities of the world (see Chapter 10), but continues to grow at a phenomenal rate. Owing its origins to the Portuguese, who from 1472 onwards traded with what was once a small coastal Yoruba village, the settlement became known from the lakes (or *lagos* in Portuguese) that surrounded it, and developed as a centre for the slave trade until 1861 when Britain captured the city and abolished the activity. From 1914, Lagos served as the capital of Nigeria and grew at a sedate pace. In 1950, for example, it contained no more than 300,000 people, a total that rose to 5.09 million by 1976, the year when the purpose-built city of Abuja replaced it as the national capital (see Chapter 6).

By 1980, the city's population had at least doubled and was beginning to show the problems of unplanned growth: 42 slums (covering 1,622 hectares) were officially acknowledged to exist—a total that has risen to 62 in 1995, and 100 in 2003. With an estimated 600,000 people a year migrating from rural west Africa into Lagos each year, the growing size of the city demonstrates the "urbanisation of poverty," to use the words of a city official quoted by UN-HABITAT.[6]

Getting work in such a city of slums and deprivation becomes increasingly difficult, and its residents are driven to whatever means they can to survive. Consider, for example, George Packer's account of a visit he took to the city's main garbage dump in 2006:

Hundreds of pickers were trudging across an undulating landscape of garbage. Every minute, another dump truck backed and released its load . . . the pickers rushed over it, swarming dangerously close to the vehicles. Bent under their sacks, they worked quickly and with focus, knowing what they were looking for. Some pickers wanted only copper; others specialized in printer cartridges. . . .

Overwhelmed by an unprecedented rate of urbanization, an economy that cannot provide regularly paid employment for a significant proportion of its residents, and a municipal government that has neither the financial resources nor the personnel to deal with the problems, Lagos has become emblematic of the problems of overurbanization. Shanty housing is a direct consequence of widespread poverty; open sewers are a consequence of limited or nonexistent municipal resources.

For many of the pickers, the dump not only provided their livelihood, but also their home. "Across the floor of the pit," Packer writes, "are hundreds of hovels, a sizable shantytown of dwellings made of plastic sheeting and scrap metal bound together

[6] "A Tale of Two Cities: Lagos and Rio de Janeiro." *UN-Habitat Feature/Backgrounder*. World Urban Forum III: An International UN-Habitat Event on Sustainability, Vancouver 2006, available at www.unhabitat.org.

with baling wire." They have, he adds, even built a mosque and a church, which they decorate at Christmas.[7]

The image of this garbage pit may be emblematic of the present situation of Lagos, but it is also seen by a number of urban theorists as key to the city's role as a "shock city" and to the role of similar cities now and in the future. The garbage pickers may be part of the extreme poverty of Lagos, but according to this interpretation, their ability to make a living out of almost nothing, and the ingenuity they show in doing it, represents opportunities. Rem Koolhaas, a professor at the Harvard Graduate School of Design, observes how there is almost a mutual dependency between the areas of extreme deprivation and those of development within the city, and describes how the interplay between them creates continual opportunities for improvising employment. The garbage pit pickers are but one example of this process. Another is the way in which massive traffic jams instantly become the site of informal markets as traders seize an opportunity to sell to a suddenly immobile population. Lagos is not "a kind of backward situation," Koolhaas notes, but "an announcement of the future."[8]

Certainly, to make a go of it in such an environment requires constant work. As one person told George Packer, "If you sit down, you will die of hunger." And what happens when you get sick—or old? Others have seen such megacities as simply too big to provide the necessary economic niches for everyone—however creative they may be. "The really disturbing thing about Lagos's pickers and vendors," Packer concludes, "is that their lives have essentially nothing to do with ours. They scavenge an existence beyond the margins of macroeconomics. They are, in the harsh terms of globalization, superfluous."

[7] George Packer, "The Megacity: Decoding the Chaos of Lagos," *New Yorker*, 13 November 2006, pp. 62–75; the quotations are from pp. 64–65.

[8] Rem Koolhaas, *Lagos: How It Works*. Baden, Switzerland: Lars Müller Publishing, 2007.

established suburban jurisdictions. However, central city governments are still responsible for services and amenities used by the entire metropolitan population: municipal galleries and museums, sports facilities, parks, traffic police, and public transport, for example. As a result, cities are in a constant competition with each other, trying to finance and attract revenue-generating tourism developments such as museums, sports franchises, and business and conference centres (see Figure 6.19 on p. 273).

In Canada, these problems are far less acute than in many U.S. cities. This is because our central cities have lost far less revenues, our cities are more compact, and our municipal governments cover much wider areas than do cities in the United States. The reorganizations of Toronto, Montreal, Ottawa, Hull, Hamilton, Winnipeg, Quebec City, and Halifax are as much an attempt by the provinces to win greater efficiencies from local government as they are responses to the growing status of Canadian suburbs.

These recent municipal mergers have sparked great debate. Critics mourn the loss of local identity and control over their own affairs. Proponents argue that the advantages of merger include a greater municipal tax base and the end to fragmented local planning jurisdictions that make integrated city planning impossible.

Infrastructure Problems   The continued growth of cities in the core countries has often ignored the need to renew original infrastructure built many years ago, in some cases even a century ago. Many roads, bridges, and buildings need upgrading or replacing, but the most problematic infrastructure backlog concerns the treatment facilities for water and sewage and the pipe infrastructure. Many cities still use water-cleaning technology dating from World War I, and a number of coastal cities in Canada still discharge untreated sewage into the sea and therefore need to invest in expensive treatment systems. In addition, many water and sewage pipes have deteriorated to the point where the leakage has reached critical proportions. The City of Toronto, for example, has almost 6,000 kilometres of water mains with an average age of 55 years (17 percent are over 80 years old, and 6.5 percent are even more than 100 years old!). Every day, three or four water mains break and need to be dug up for repair. Despite spending between $120 and $160 million a year on its water mains, the city can replace only 100 kilometres of pipes annually.[9]

Poverty and Neighbourhood Decay As we have seen, the relative lack of urban decay in Canadian cities has been one of the major differences between our urban geography and that of the United States. In U.S. cities, inner-city poverty and neighbourhood decay have become increasingly pronounced since the 1960s, as manufacturing, warehousing, and retailing jobs have moved out to suburban and edge-city locations and as many of the more prosperous households have moved out to the suburbs. The spiral of neighbourhood decay begins with substandard housing occupied by low-income households that can afford to rent only a minimal amount of space. The consequent overcrowding not only causes greater wear and tear on the housing itself but also puts pressure on the neighbourhood infrastructure of streets, parks, schools, and playgrounds. The need for maintenance and repair increases quickly but is rarely met. Individual households cannot afford it, and landlords have no incentive to do so because they have a captive market. Public authorities face a fiscal squeeze and are, in any case, often indifferent to the needs of such neighbourhoods that have a relative lack of political power (**Figure 11.21**).

There is, meanwhile, a dismal cycle of poverty that intersects with these localized spirals of decay. The **cycle of poverty** involves the transmission of poverty and deprivation from one generation to another through a combination of domestic circumstances and local neighbourhood conditions. This cycle begins with a local absence of employment opportunities and, in turn, a concentration of low incomes, poor housing, and overcrowded conditions. Such conditions are unhealthy. Overcrowding makes people vulnerable to poor health, which is compounded by poor diets. This, in turn, contributes to absenteeism from work,

cycle of poverty: transmission of poverty and deprivation from one generation to another through a combination of domestic circumstances and local neighbourhood conditions

Figure 11.21 Urban decay Concentrations of poverty are found in many American inner-city areas, as in this example in Washington, DC, a short distance from the Capitol.

[9] The *Toronto Water* website of the City of Toronto: **www.toronto.ca/water/index.htm**.

which results in decreased income. Similarly, absenteeism from school through illness contributes to the cycle of poverty by constraining educational achievement and occupational skills, thus leading to low wages. Crowding also produces psychological stress, which contributes to social disorganization and a variety of pathological behaviours, including crime and vandalism. Such conditions not only affect people's educational achievement and employment opportunities but can also lead to the *labelling* of the neighbourhood, whereby all residents may find their employment opportunities affected by the poor image of their neighbourhood.

Social trends have compounded the problems of these areas in many instances. Increased divorce rates and a high incidence of teen pregnancy have led to far greater numbers of single-parent families and a feminization of poverty. These families have been portrayed in much American writing on this topic as the core of a geographically, socially, and economically isolated underclass. The idea of an **underclass** refers to a group of individuals who experience a form of poverty from which it is very difficult to escape because of their isolation from mainstream values and the formal labour market. Isolated from the formal labour force and the social values and behavioural patterns of the rest of society, the underclass has been perceived as being subject to an increase in social disorganization and deviant behaviour. In U.S. cities, localized inner-city poverty is now characterized by senseless and unprovoked violence, premeditated and predatory violence, domestic violence, the organized violence of street gangs, and epidemic levels of AIDS and other communicable diseases—all closely associated with drug use and drug dealing.

underclass: a subset of the poor, isolated from mainstream values and the formal labour market

Homelessness   One consequence of extreme poverty is *homelessness*. Chronic, long-term homelessness means not having customary and regular access to a conventional dwelling. This includes people who have to sleep in shelters, flophouse cubicles, and emergency dormitories and missions, as well as those sleeping in doorways, bus stations, cars, tents, temporary shacks, and cardboard boxes and on park benches and steam grates.

The number of homeless persons in the world's more affluent cities rose sharply in the 1980s. This was mainly a consequence of the increased poverty and the economic and social dislocation caused by economic restructuring and the transition to a globalized, postindustrial economy. Homelessness was intensified by the fiscal squeeze confronting central cities and by the trend for governments to cut back on welfare programs to balance their budgets. It was also intensified by the adoption of revolving-door policies of mental-health hospitals, which released large numbers of patients who had formerly been institutionalized. As a result, the homeless are now very visible throughout the major cities of the developed world. In Canada, the homeless have now become an enduring feature of many Canadian towns and cities.

Canada has no official statistics on the homeless, and semi-official estimates vary between 150,000 and 300,000 homeless people in Canada.[10] Estimates in other countries are equally varied, but they all seem to range between 0.5 and 1 percent of the population. Even in former communist countries, where homelessness was virtually unknown, homelessness has become a grave problem: in Moscow alone, almost 100,000 people became homeless during the 1990s.

---

[10] This topic is the focus of continued debate. The Homelessness Partnership Strategy, a federal government initiative set up in 2006 to research and propose solutions to the problems of homelessness, discusses the difficulties of gathering data in its background document "Understanding Homelessness." Human Resources and Social Development Canada, Homelessness Partnership Strategy, 2008, available at **www.hrsdc.gc.ca/en/homelessness/general_information/understanding_homelessness .shtml**. In terms of individual cities, very useful material and statistics for Toronto can be found in the City of Toronto's *Housing and Homelessness Report Card, 2003*. Toronto: City of Toronto, 2003, at **www.toronto.ca/homelessness/** (regretably, there hasn't been a more recent report card). The situation in Ottawa has been the subject of considerable work by a research team led by Carleton University geographer Fran Klodawsky; see, for example, her study "Landscapes on the Margins: Gender and Homelessness," *Gender, Place and Culture* 13(4), 2006, pp. 365–388.

What makes contemporary homelessness such a striking problem is not just the scale of the problem but also the nature of it. Whereas homelessness had previously involved white, adult males, relatively few of whom actually had to sleep outdoors, the new homeless are from all ethnic groups (sadly, First Nations are greatly overrepresented) and include significant numbers of women, children, and the elderly. The new homeless are also much less likely to find shelter indoors and so have become much more visible in the public spaces of many cities.

Problems of Unintended Metropolises

The Informal Sector   The problems of the cities of the periphery stem mainly from the way in which their demographic growth has outstripped their economic growth. According to the Worldwatch Institute, between half and three-quarters of the population of peripheral cities is forced to seek survival through the informal sector, which means that more than 1 billion people around the world must feed, clothe, and house themselves entirely through informal activities (**Figure 11.22**). Across Africa, the International Labour Organization estimates that informal-sector activities are growing 10 times faster than formal-sector employment.

The low and unreliable income from informal-sector activities leads directly to further problems—chronic poverty and slum housing. On top of all this, the combination of rapid population growth and economic underdevelopment gives rise to transport and infrastructure problems and to problems of environmental degradation. Finally, the informal sector pays no taxes, thus depriving governments of badly needed revenues to deliver services to the population. Together, these problems are so severe that they pose almost impossible tasks for metropolitan governance and management in peripheral metropolises.

Some commentators have argued that, despite this grim picture, the informal sector also has a few positive aspects. Pedicabs, for example, provide an affordable, nonpolluting means of transportation in crowded metropolitan settings. Garbage picking, although it may seem desperate and degrading in Western eyes, provides an important means of recycling paper, steel, glass, and plastic: one study of Mexico City estimated that as much as 25 percent of the municipal waste ends up being recycled by the 15,000 or so scavengers who work over the city's official dump sites. This positive contribution to the economy, though, scarcely balances the lives of poverty and degradation experienced by the scavengers.

Urban geographers also recognize that the informal sector represents an important resource to the formal sector of peripheral economies. The informal sector provides a vast range of cheap goods and services that reduce the cost of living for employees in the formal sector, thus enabling employers to keep wages low. Although this network does not contribute to urban economic growth or help alleviate poverty, it does keep companies competitive within the context of the global

Figure 11.22 Informal economic activities   In cities where jobs are scarce, people have to cope through the informal sector of the economy, which includes a very broad variety of activities.

Street market, Surabaja, Indonesia

economic system. For export-oriented companies, in particular, the informal sector provides a considerable indirect subsidy to production. We must recognize, too, that this subsidy is often passed on to consumers in the core regions in the form of lower prices for goods and consumer products made in the periphery.

Consider, for example, the paper industry in Cali, Colombia. This industry is dominated by one company, Cartón de Colombia, which was established in 1944 with North American capital and subsequently acquired by the Mobil Oil Company. Most of the company's lower-quality paper products are made from recycled waste paper, and 60 percent of this waste paper is gathered by local garbage pickers. Cali has 1,200 to 1,500 garbage pickers. Some work the city's municipal waste dump, some work the alleys and yards of shopping and industrial areas, and some work the routes of municipal garbage trucks, intercepting trash cans before the truck arrives. They are part of Cali's informal economy, for they are not employed by Cartón de Colombia nor do they have any sort of contract with the company or its representatives. They simply show up each day to sell their pickings. This way the company can avoid paying both wages and benefits, while dictating the price it will pay for various grades of waste paper. The company can operate profitably while keeping the price of its products down—the arrangement is a microcosm of core–periphery relationships.

Another example is the recycling of electronic waste in China, illustrated on film by a documentary on the work of eminent Canadian photographer Edward Burtynsky. Entitled *Manufactured Landscapes*, this 2006 film shows the often literally breathtaking scenes of garbage pickers collecting recyclable metals from the still-burning plastic shells of huge piles of obsolete computer equipment, discarded in countries such as Canada and shipped to China where labour costs are much cheaper and health standards are low enough to allow such work to continue.

Slums of Hope, Slums of Despair   The informal labour market is directly paralleled in informal shantytowns and squatter housing: because so few jobs with regular wages exist, few families can afford rent or house payments for sound housing. In situations where urban growth has swamped the available stock of cheap housing and outstripped the capacity of builders to create affordable new housing, the inevitable outcome is makeshift, shanty housing that offers, at best, precarious shelter. Such housing has to be constructed on the cheapest and least desirable sites.

Often, this means building on bare rock, over ravines, on derelict land, on swamps, or on steep slopes. Nearly always, it means building without any basic infrastructure of streets or utilities. Sometimes, it means adapting to the most extreme ecological niches, as in Cairo, where for generations the poor have transformed catacombs and cemeteries into living spaces. In many cities, more than half of the housing is substandard. The United Nations estimated in 2005 that more than 1.6 billion people worldwide live in inadequate housing in urban areas.

11.6   Geography in the Information Age

Arrangements such as these illustrate how abstract notions of core–periphery relations really affect individuals and places: it may well be my computer that is being recycled in such a noxious way, and the rare earths reclaimed from it may return as part of your next smartphone. Along the way, informal livelihoods will be earned, bodies contaminated, profits made, environments degraded, economies fostered, consumption enabled, garbage produced, and lives ruined or made more convenient—we are all interconnected through these flows, and more than anything else the roles we play are determined by where we are born—in other words, the sheer luck of the draw.

11.7   Geography in the Information Age

Globalization and the accompanying trend toward neoliberal economic policies have intensified problems of poverty and slum housing in many cities. The United Nations Human Settlement Programme reported in 2004 that

> The reduction of fiscal deficits has partly entailed reduction of public expenditure through downsizing of the civil service and privatization of state enterprises, resulting in the laying-off of large numbers of public-sector employees in many countries. Trade liberalization has often resulted in the closure of some industries that have been unable to compete against cheap imports, again leading to massive retrenchment and higher unemployment levels. Rising urban unemployment and increasing poverty have forced large numbers of the urban poor into the informal sector. Underpaid formal-sector employees have also entered the informal sector as a survival strategy. This, in turn, leads to the erosion of the tax base and decreasing ability of national and local governments to assist the poor through social and basic services. The removal of price controls on subsistence goods, and increased utility charges through privatization . . . have resulted in rising inequalities and increasing poverty.[11]

[11] United Nations Human Settlements Programme, *The State of the World's Cities 2004/2005. Globalization and Urban Culture.* Sterling, VA: Earthscan, 2004, p. 102.

Faced with the growth of these slums, the first response of many governments has been to eradicate them. However, the thinking now is that informal-sector housing should be seen as a rational response to poverty. Shanty and squatter neighbourhoods provide affordable shelter and function as important reception areas for migrants to the city, with supportive communal organizations and informal employment opportunities that help them to adjust to city life. They can, in other words, be "slums of hope." City authorities, recognizing the positive functions of informal housing and self-help improvements, are now increasingly disposed to be tolerant and even helpful toward squatters rather than sending in police and municipal workers with bulldozers (**Figure 11.23**).

Nevertheless, there are many shanty and squatter neighbourhoods where self-help and community organization do not emerge. Instead, grim and desperately miserable conditions prevail. These are "slums of despair." Consider, for example,

Self-help housing, Ndola, Zambia

Sites-and-services housing, Lusaka, Zambia

Figure 11.23   Self-help as a solution to housing problems   Self-help is often the only solution to housing problems because migrants' wages are so low. One of the most successful ways of encouraging self-help housing is for municipal authorities to prepare the site, put in the footings for small dwellings, and install a basic framework of water and sewage utilities. This "sites-and-services" approach has become the mainstay of urban housing policies in many peripheral countries.

Life in a Mega-Slum

"I came to stay with relatives in Dharavi when I was six, got married when I was 16 and gave birth to my first daughter soon after. She is now 11 years old. I have two more daughters, aged nine and five.

"Both my husband and I work and we try to share our responsibilities equally. I work as a domestic maid and he works in an aluminium vessel manufacturing company.

"Every day I wake up at 6 AM and finish off the household work such as getting my children ready for school, cooking food and preparing a lunchbox for my husband.

"I work for about three-and-a-half hours in a home nearby, where I clean and dust and wash vessels and clothes.

"I return home by about 1.30 PM. Then I make flower bands to earn some extra money. I cook dinner and supervise my children's studies.

"My husband returns home around 8 PM and then we walk for about 10 minutes to get water for our use the next day.

"I don't have a direct water supply in my house—none of the houses in my area have a tap with running water. All of us must cross the railway tracks to get it.

"We don't earn enough money for our expenses and often end up borrowing. Right now, I owe a lender 15,000 rupees (US$327). I pay 1,500 rupees (US$33) as interest and he hasn't even started deducting anything from my loan amount yet.

"Most of the money is spent on medicines for my girls because I want to give them the best possible treatment. That sometimes means I have to take to them to a private doctor.

"I am constantly concerned for the safety of my children and I practically lock them in the house after 6 P.M. Not only is it unsafe to play near the tracks but also the possibility of them being kidnapped or assaulted petrifies me."

Source: BBC News, "Life in a Slum: Domestic Maid," http://news.bbc .co.uk/1/shared/spl/hi/world/06/dharavi_slum/html/dharavi_slum_1 .stm.

Name: Vimla

Age: 27 years old

Occupation: Domestic maid and flower band maker

Earns: About US$22 per month—husband earns US$54

Home: Hut by railway tracks, with no toilet or water

Time in slum: 16 years—hopes for relocation in Dharavi

---

the "mega-slum" of Dharavi in Mumbai, India.[12] Dharavi is about 2.5 square kilometres in size and home to over a million people. This means that as many as 30,000 people crowd into a single hectare of land (roughly two football fields). Rents can be as low as 185 rupees (US$4) per month. Recycling is one of the slum's biggest industries: thousands of tons of scrap plastic, metals, paper, cotton, soap, and glass revolve through Dharavi each day. Ruined plastic toys are tossed into massive grinders, chopped into tiny pieces, and melted down into multicoloured pellets, ready to be refashioned into knockoff Barbie dolls. Dharavi also houses about 15,000 hutment factories, each typically stuffed with children as well as adults sewing cotton, melting plastic, hammering iron, and moulding clay, as well as producing embroidered garments, export-quality leather goods, pottery, and plastic.

The aggregate annual turnover of these businesses is estimated to be more than US$650 million a year, yet conditions for its residents are miserable (see **Geography Matters 11.5—Life in a Mega-Slum**). In Dharavi, there is only one toilet per 1,440 people—and during the monsoon rains, flooded lanes run with human excrement. Nine out of ten children under 4 have less than the minimum calories needed for a healthy diet. Infant and child mortality is high—though nobody knows just how high—with malaria, tetanus, diarrhea, dysentery, and cholera as the principal causes of death among under-fives.

---

[12] See *The Economist*, 2007, "A Flourishing Slum," www.economist.com/world/asia/displaystory .cfm?story_id=10311293; M. Jacobson, "Mumbai Slum," *National Geographic, 2007,* http://ngm .nationalgeographic.com/ngm/0705/feature3/index.html; C.W. Dugger, "Toilets Underused to Fight Disease, U.N. Study Finds," *New York Times*, 2006, www.nytimes.com/2006/11/10/world/10toilet .html?_r=1&ex=1189828800&en=905358c57769b677&ei=5070&oref=slogin.

Figure 11.24 **Urban transportation** Creative responses to the problem of transportation come in many forms, but their success is limited by the sheer congestion of overurbanization.

Transport and Infrastructure Problems In many peripheral cities, road traffic is breaking down, with poorly maintained roads, traffic jams, long delays at intersections, and frequent accidents. Many governments have invested in expensive new freeways and street-widening schemes, but because they tend to focus on city centres (which are still the settings for most jobs and most services and amenities), they ultimately empty vehicles into a congested and chaotic mixture of motorized traffic, bicycles, animal-drawn vehicles, and hand-drawn carts (**Figure 11.24**). Some of the worst traffic tales come from Mexico City—where traffic backups total 100 kilometres each day, on average—and São Paulo, where gridlock can span 160 kilometres and traffic jams can last 15 hours. In Bangkok, the 24-kilometre trip into town from Don Muang Airport can take three hours, contributing to an estimated 1 percent drain on the gross national product.

Water supplies and sewerage also present acute problems for many cities. The World Bank estimates that worldwide, only about 70 percent of urban residents in less developed countries have access to a satisfactory water source, and only about 40 percent are connected to sewers (90 percent of which discharge their waste untreated into a river, lake, or sea). Hundreds of millions of urban dwellers have no alternative but to use contaminated water—or at least water whose quality is not guaranteed (**Figure 11.25**). São Paulo, for instance, has more than 1,600 kilometres of open sewers, and raw sewage from the city's slums drains into the Billings Reservoir, a major source of the city's drinking water.

Environmental Degradation With pressing problems of poverty, slum housing, and inadequate infrastructure, it is not surprising that peripheral cities are unable to devote many resources to environmental problems. Because of the speed of population growth, these problems are escalating rapidly. Industrial and human wastes pile up in lakes and lagoons, polluting long stretches of rivers, estuaries, and coastal zones. Groundwater is polluted through the leaching of chemicals from uncontrolled dumping sites, and the forests around many cities are being denuded by the demand of cities for timber and domestic fuels. This environmental degradation is, of course, directly linked to human health. People living in such environments have much higher rates of respiratory infections, tuberculosis, and diarrhea and much shorter life expectancies than people living in surrounding rural communities (**Figure 11.26**).

Governance and Management The governments of towns and cities in the world's periphery are faced with tremendous problems. Just keeping up with the rate of physical and demographic growth presents an enormous challenge. Typical growth rates mean that cities' physical infrastructure of roads, bridges, and

Outdoor standpipe, Ankara, Turkey   Street water pump, Raipur, India

Figure 11.25   Water supply problems
Many peripheral cities have grown so quickly, and under such difficult conditions, that large sections of the population do not have access to clean water. Where a public supply exists—a well or an outdoor standpipe—water consumption is limited by the time and energy required to collect water and carry it home. It is not rare for 1,000 or more people to have to share a single tap. Because low-income people work very long hours, the time spent waiting in line for water and then transporting buckets to homes is time that could have been used in earning an income. Limited quantities of water mean inadequate supplies for personal hygiene and for washing food, cooking utensils, and clothes. Where public agencies provide no water supply—as is common in squatter settlements—the poor often obtain water from private vendors and can pay 20 to 30 times the cost per litre paid by households with piped supplies. Water vendors probably supply about one-quarter of the population of peripheral metropolises.

Figure 11.26   Cubatao, Brazil   Most of the city's housing is of extremely poor quality, with many industrial workers living in shantytowns built on stilts above swamps. Toxic industrial wastes have been dumped in the surrounding forests and are contaminating the city's water supplies. In 1984, hundreds of inhabitants were killed after a gasoline pipeline leaked into a swamp under one shanty and caught fire. Vegetation in and around the city has suffered substantially from air pollution, and because dying vegetation can no longer retain the soil on steeper slopes, landslides have become a danger to shanty dwellers.

utilities needs to be tripled every 10 years. Meanwhile, most city governments find it nearly impossible to take care of the daily upkeep of their existing infrastructure because of the wear and tear that is caused by overurbanization. Somehow, basic services have to be provided to populations that cannot afford to pay more than a fraction of their costs.

The governance of most peripheral countries tends to be highly centralized, with relatively little political power allocated to city or metropolitan governments. In addition, city and metropolitan governments are typically fragmented—both geographically and functionally—as well as being understaffed and underfinanced.

Although many of the individuals involved do the best they can, metropolitan governance and management seem doomed to be ineffective and inefficient until some way can be devised to improve the institutional framework (in both geographical and democratic terms) and reduce the financial constraints faced by municipal governments. This last point, regarding financial constraints, brings us back to local–global interdependencies once again, for the financial predicament of peripheral cities is ultimately tied to their dependent role in the global economic system.

CONCLUSION

Patterns of land use and the functional organization of economic and social subareas in cities are partly a product of the economic, political, and technological conditions at the time of the city's growth and partly a product of regional cultural values. Geographers can draw on four particularly useful perspectives in looking at patterns of land use within North American cities: an economic perspective that emphasizes competition for space, an economic perspective that emphasizes functional linkages between land uses, a sociocultural perspective that emphasizes ethnic congregation and segregation, and a historical perspective that emphasizes the influence of transportation technology and infrastructure investment.

In many ways, the most striking contrasts in urban structure are found between the cities of the core regions and those of the periphery. The evolution of the unintended metropolis of the periphery has been very different from the evolution of metropolitan areas in the world's core regions. Similarly, the problems they face are very different. In the core regions, urban change is dominated by the consequences of an economic transformation to a postindustrial economy. Traditional manufacturing and related activities have been moved out of central cities. New postindustrial activities have begun to cluster in redeveloped CBDs and in edge cities around metropolitan fringes.

In other parts of the world, patterns of land use and the functional organization of economic and social subareas are quite different, reflecting different historical legacies and different environmental and cultural influences. The basic trend affecting the cities of the world's periphery is demographic—the phenomenal rates of natural increase and in-migration that have given rise to overurbanization. The example of Lagos provides some sobering insights into the human consequences of overurbanization. An ever-growing informal sector of the economy, in which people seek economic survival, is reflected in extensive areas of shanty housing. High rates of unemployment, underemployment, and poverty generate acute social problems, which are overwhelming for city governments that are understaffed and underfunded. If present trends continue, such problems are likely to characterize increasing numbers of the world's largest settlements. In the next chapter, we consider this question as part of a broader discussion of future geographies.

MAIN POINTS REVISITED

- The typical North American city is structured around a central business district (CBD); a transitional zone; suburbs; secondary business districts and commercial strips; industrial districts; and, in larger metropolitan areas, edge cities.

  This internal organization of cities reflects the way that they function, both to bring certain people and activities together and to sort them out into neighbourhoods and functional sub-areas.

- The overall structure of North American cities is shaped primarily by competition for territory and location. In general, all categories of land users—commercial and industrial, as well as residential—compete for the most convenient and accessible locations within the city.

  An important exception is that wealthier households tend to trade off the convenience of accessibility for larger amounts of (relatively cheaper) suburban space. Poorer households, unable to afford the recurrent costs of commuting, are forced to trade off living space for accessibility to jobs so that they end up in high-density areas at expensive locations near their low-wage jobs.

- Cities experiencing high rates of in-migration tend to become structured into a series of concentric zones of neighbourhoods of different ethnicity, demographic composition, and social status through processes of invasion and succession.

  Within each concentric zone, a mosaic of distinctive neighbourhoods tends to develop—ecological niches where particular mixes of people have come to dominate a particular territory or geographical setting.

- In cities where growth has been less dominated by successive waves of immigrant ethnic groups, neighbourhood patterns tend to be structured around the development of industrial corridors and high-class residential corridors.

  Industry tends to follow transportation corridors along low-lying, flat land where space exists for large factories, warehouses, and railway marshalling yards. Working-class residential areas grow up around these corridors, following them out in sector-shaped neighbourhoods as they grow. High-status residential districts, in contrast, tend to grow outward from a different side of town, often following a ridge of high ground (free from flooding and with panoramic views).

- Urban structure varies a good deal from one region of the world to another because of the influence of history, culture, and the different roles that cities have played within the world-system.

- European cities have evolved under circumstances very different from those faced by North American cities; consequently, European cities exhibit some distinctive characteristics in urban form. European urban ideals have influenced many colonial cities, while the new cities of the world's peripheral regions are distinctive because of their explosive growth.

- Geographers are interested in the distinctive physical features of urban landscapes because they can be read as multi-layered texts that show how cities have developed, how they are changing, and how people's values and intentions take expression in the urban form.

  The built environment is what gives expression, meaning, and identity to the various forces involved in urbanization. It becomes a biography of urban change, offering people cues and contexts for behaviour, landmarks for orientation, and symbols that reinforce collective values.

- The most acute problems of the postindustrial cities of the world's core regions are localized in the central city areas, which have borne the brunt of restructuring from an industrial to a postindustrial economy.

  In these areas, there are several interrelated problems: fiscal problems, infrastructure problems, and localized spirals of neighbourhood decay, cycles of poverty, and homelessness.

- Canadian cities are different from U.S. cities.

  Unlike U.S. cities, Canadian cities have avoided inner-city decline, have experienced far greater levels of gentrification, are more compact in form, and have experienced greater government involvement in their management and planning.

- The problems of the cities of the periphery stem from the way in which their demographic growth has outstripped their economic growth.

  The result is high rates of long-term unemployment and underemployment; low and unreliable wages of informal-sector jobs; chronic poverty; and slum housing. The low rates of economic growth of these peripheral cities reflect their dependent position in the global economy.

- Cities are created as "places" and can become "place makers."

  The physical form of a city (its buildings and layout) reflects the culture that built it. In turn, that form comes to shape our image of the city.

Key Terms

Beaux Arts (p. 502)
central business district (CBD) (p. 482)
City Beautiful movement (p. 493)
congregation (p. 484)
cycle of poverty (p. 512)

dualism (p. 508)
edge cities (p. 483)
Garden City movement (p. 493)
gentrification (p. 483)
invasion and succession (p. 487)
isotropic surface (p. 486)

minority groups (p. 484)
modern movement (p. 503)
postmodern urban design (p. 504)
segregation (p. 485)
underclass (p. 513)
zone in transition (p. 482)

Additional Reading

Angotti, T. *Metropolis 2000*. New York: Routledge, 1993.

Artibise, A.F.J., and G.A. Stetler (eds.). *The Usable Past: Planning and Politics in the Modern Canadian City*. Toronto: Macmillan, 1979.

Bourne, L.S., and D.F. Ley (eds.). *The Changing Social Geography of Canadian Cities*. Montreal and Kingston: McGill-Queen's University Press, 1993.

Bradbury, B., and T. Myers (eds.). *Negotiating Identities in 19th- and 20th-Century Montreal*. Vancouver: UBC Press, 2005.

Brunn, S., and J.F. Williams (eds.). *Cities of the World*, 2nd ed. New York: HarperCollins, 1993.

Bunting, T., and P. Filion (eds.). *Canadian Cities in Transition: The Twenty-First Century*, 2nd ed. Toronto: Oxford University Press, 2000.

Caulfield, J., and L. Peake (eds.). *City Lives and City Forms: Critical Research and Canadian Urbanism*. Toronto: University of Toronto Press, 1996.

Florida, R. *Cities and the Creative Class*. New York: Routledge, 2005.

Florida, R. *Who's Your City? How the Creative Economy Is Making Where You Live the Most Important Decision of Your Life*. Toronto: Random House of Canada, 2008.

Germain, A., and D. Rose. *Montreal: The Quest for a Metropolis*. Chichester: John Wiley, 2000.

Goldberg, M.A., and J. Mercer. *The Myth of the North American City: Continentalism Challenged*. Vancouver: University of British Columbia Press, 1986.

Gugler, J. (ed.). *Cities in the Developing World: Issues, Theory, and Policy*. New York: Oxford University Press, 1997.

Hall, P. *Cities in Civilization*. New York: Pantheon, 1998.

Hall, P. *Cities of Tomorrow*. New York: Blackwell, 1988.

Knox, P.L. *Urbanization: An Introduction to Urban Geography*. Englewood Cliffs, NJ: Prentice Hall, 1994.

Knox, P.L., and S. Pinch. *Urban Social Geography*, 4th ed. London: Longman Scientific, 2000.

Lemon, J. *Toronto Since 1918: An Illustrated History*. Toronto: James Lorimer; Ottawa: National Museum of Civilization, 1985.

Musterd, S., W. Ostendorf, and M. Breebaart. *Multi-Ethnic Metropolis: Patterns and Policies*. Boston: Kluwer Academic, 1998.

Potter, R.B., and S. Lloyd-Evans. *The City in the Developing World*. Harlow, UK: Addison Wesley Longman, 1998.

Simpson, M. *Thomas Adams and the Modern Planning Movement: Britain, Canada and the United States, 1900–1940*. London: Mansell, 1984.

Sloan, J. (ed.). *Urban Enigmas: Montreal, Toronto, and the Problem of Comparing Cities*. Montreal and Kingston: McGill-Queen's University Press, 2007.

Smith, D.A. *Third World Cities in Global Perspective*. Boulder, CO: Westview Press, 1996.

Taylor, J.H. *Ottawa: An Illustrated History*. Toronto: James Lorimer; Ottawa: National Museum of Civilization, 1986.

Taylor, Z., and J. van Nostrand. *Shaping the Toronto Region, Past, Present and Future*. Toronto: The Neptis Foundation, 2008.

U.S. Congress, Office of Technology Assessment. *The Technological Reshaping of Metropolitan America*. OTA-ETI-643. Washington, DC: U.S. Government Printing Office, 1995.

U.S. Department of Housing and Urban Development. *The State of the Cities 1999*. Washington, DC: U.S. Department of Housing and Urban Development, 1999.

Vance, J.E. Jr. *The Continuing City: Urban Morphology in Western Civilization*. Baltimore: Johns Hopkins University Press, 1990.

Wynn, G., and T. Oke (eds.). *Vancouver and Its Region*. Vancouver: University of British Columbia Press, 1992.

Discussion Questions and Research Activities

1. Collect a week's worth of local newspapers, and review the coverage of urban problems. What kinds of problems are covered and for what kinds of cities? Compile a list of such categories, and then carefully analyze the content of the week's coverage, calculating the amount of space devoted to each category of problems. What are the problems? Are they grave or relatively superficial? Would you agree that those are the most pressing problems for the city in question? Why do you think these problems made the news (or were selected to make the news)?

2. Use your local newspaper or free real estate publications to obtain information about the distribution of houses and apartments for sale or rent in different cost brackets in your city. Plot the information on a city map. What can you say about the spatial distribution that is revealed? What does the spatial distribution of house prices reveal about the structure of the city? Can you relate it in some way to the problems identified in Exercise 1?

3. Select three cities each in the core, semiperiphery, and periphery and research what famous buildings, landmarks, or cityscapes are associated with them. What is the significance for these cities of having such symbolic locales? Were they created intentionally? Who commissioned or paid for them, and what purpose do they serve? Has that purpose changed over time?

4. Most cities consist of "ordinary" cityscapes that are strongly evocative because they are widely understood as being a particular kind of place. Write a brief essay (500 words, or two double-spaced, typed pages) describing an "ordinary" cityscape with which you are familiar. What are its principal features, and why might it be considered typical of a particular kind of place?

MyGeosciencePlace

Visit **www.mygeoscienceplace.ca** to find chapter review quizzes, videos, maps, and much more.

12

Future Geographies

The Sharp Centre for Design at Ontario's College of Art and Design. Instead of building on land next to the existing college, architect Will Alsop's 2004 two-storey extension stands 26 metres on 12 legs above the existing buildings of the college. The design conserves urban space and represents a type of thinking "outside the box" that may be a hallmark of the future.

Jane Jacobs, a passionate advocate of cities and urban life and one of the most influential public intellectuals in North America in the last century, argues that the United States is slipping toward the beginnings of a new "Dark Age" as the five pillars of modern society crumble: community and family, higher education, the application of science and technology, the integrity of the professions, and the role of government in relation to society's needs and potential. "A culture is unsalvageable," writes Jacobs, "if stabilizing forces themselves become ruined."[1]

This is what she has to say about universities: They have become credential factories, stripping the arts, poetry, ethics, idealism, and the notion of the public good out of education. They are complicit in allowing scientific research to be controlled by corporations and directed—and sometimes suppressed—by governments (as has been done, for instance, with "inopportune" results of climate change research). Rather than serving as one of the cultural pillars of society, universities now serve employers and act as "colleges of heraldry," awarding graduates a "coat of arms" (i.e., university degree) to distinguish them from those without marketable credentials.

She is equally direct about the professions. This time it is not city planners and urban design professionals that are the focus of her concern, but accountants, bankers, lawyers, and other financial professions whose ethics and practices have repeatedly been called into question in the vast corporate scandals of the past two decades, culminating in the 2008 financial crisis. Nevertheless, the design and public policy professions are implicated in her critique of urban trends. Cities—vital economic engines and crucibles of cultural change and innovation—are being starved of the money they need by national, regional, and local governments. Neoliberal policies are responsible for sagging public transit and public education systems, increasing pollution, increasing social polarization, the erosion of community, and the burgeoning sullenness of citizens. Families, she argues, are rigged to fail by public policies that, unintentionally, force both parents to work to meet financial needs. Communities are rigged to fail by public policies that foster sprawling, placeless, and automobile-dependent suburbs—a reprise of her earlier critique in *The Death and Life of Great American Cities*.

Jacobs' critique casts a cautionary light on the future we have imagined in this book: we saw that more and more Canadians are living in cities, that the social fabric of Canadian cities is changing and becoming more like that of American cities, and that the urban structure of Canadian cities is changing

---

[1] J. Jacobs, *Dark Age Ahead: Caution*. New York: Random House, 2004.

in response to economic, demographic, and political forces that often originate in the various processes of globalization—some of which we can influence; others we have no control over. Clearly, Jacobs thinks that (notwithstanding "beacon" projects like the Sharp Centre for Design) we are heading in the wrong direction—that even we, the people living in the core, with the best education and the most resources at our disposal, are not creating a safe, equitable, and sustainable future for ourselves. How much harder still would it be for the majority of the world's people living in the periphery to do so? These are difficult questions to contemplate, let alone answer.

Jacobs confides that "I have written this cautionary book in hopeful expectations that time remains for corrective actions." Your generation will be called upon to make those corrections. To evaluate and implement the corrections you deem necessary, you could do no better than rely on the foundation of geographic knowledge that you have acquired throughout this book and the course in which you are registered. So let's put this knowledge to work in this final chapter and think about what kind of "Future Geographies" are possible—and desirable.

MAIN POINTS

- In some ways, the future is already here, embedded in the world's institutional structures and in the dynamics of its populations.
- New and emerging technologies that are likely to have the most impact in reshaping human geographies include advanced transportation technologies, biotechnology, materials technologies, and information technologies.
- We must not underestimate the scope and impact of future environmental change in shaping future geographies.
- The changes involved in shaping future geographies will inevitably bring some critical issues, conflicts, and threats, including important geographical issues that centre on scale, boundaries, and territories; on cultural dissonance; on security; and on the sustainability of development.

MAPPING OUR FUTURE

Will the Internet bring about new patterns of human interaction? Will the rapid development of communication technologies really diminish the importance of distance and space? Will globalization bring an end to distinctive regional cultures? Will we be able to cope with the environmental stresses that increasing industrialization and rapid population growth will inevitably create? Which nation will succeed the United States as the world's most powerful and influential nation? Will more countries move up from peripheral status to join the semiperiphery and core of the future world-system? What kind of problems will the future bring for local, regional, and international development? Will new regions emerge based on new types of connectivity such as trade, the Internet, or any number of political movements such as mobilizations against globalization or the human rights movement? What new technologies are likely to have the most impact in reshaping human geographies?

We can tackle these questions by first getting a sense of how different aspects of globalization are changing the world and how they might continue to do so. As we discussed in Chapter 2, the globalization of the capitalist world-system involves processes that have been occurring for at least 500 years. But since World War II, world integration and transformation have dramatically accelerated. Among the forces driving integration and transformation are the strengthening of regional alliances such as the European Union, the meteoric rise of China and India, the increasing connectedness of even the most remote regions of the world through telecommunications and transportation linkages, the emergence of the New Economy in the core countries, and the rise of global institutions like the World Trade Organization.

Experts try to extrapolate the future from the past effects of these forces (**Figure 12.1**). Broadly speaking, there are two sorts of scenarios—optimistic and pessimistic. Optimistic futurists stress the potential for technological innovations to discover and harness new resources, to provide faster and more effective means of transportation and communication, and to enable new ways of living. This sort of futurism is often characterized by science-fiction cities with towering skyscrapers and spaceship-style living pods, by ecological harmony, and by unprecedented social and cultural progress fostered through universal access to information via the Internet. It projects a world that will be stabilized and homogenized by supranational or even "world" governments. The sort of geography implied by such scenarios is rarely spelled out. Space and place, we are led to believe, will become inconsequential, transcended by technological fixes.

To pessimistic futurists, however, this is just "globaloney." They point out the finite nature of Earth's resources, the fragility of its environment, and population growth rates that exceed the capacity of the peripheral regions to sustain them. Such doomsday forecasting is characterized by scenarios that include irreversible environmental degradation, increasing social and economic polarization, and the breakdown of law and order. Again, the geography associated with these scenarios is rarely made explicit, but it usually involves the probability of a sharp polarization between the haves and have-nots at every geographical scale.

Fortunately, we don't have to choose between these two visions of utopia and dystopia. Using what we have learned from the study of human geography, we can suggest a more grounded outline of future geographies. To do so, we must first glance back at the past. Then, looking at present trends and using what we know about processes of geographical change and principles of spatial organization, we can begin to map out the kinds of geographies that the future most probably holds.

Looking back at the way that the geography of the world-system has unfolded, we can see now that a fairly coherent period of economic and geopolitical development occurred between the outbreak of World War I (in 1914) and the collapse of the Soviet Union (in 1989). Some historians refer to this period as the "short twentieth century." It was a period when the modern world-system developed its triadic core of the United States, Western Europe, and Japan; when geopolitics was based on an East–West divide; and when geoeconomics was based on a North–South divide. This was a time when the geographies of specific places and regions within these larger frameworks were shaped by the needs and opportunities of technology systems that were based on the internal combustion engine, oil and plastics, electrical engineering, aerospace industries, and electronics (see Chapter 2). In this short century, the modern world was established, along with its familiar landscapes and spatial structures—from the industrial landscapes of the core to the unintended

Scenario 1—The world becomes populated by consumers rather than citizens. Technology breeds unlimited, customized choices. Computers do increasing amounts of white-collar work. Real leisure increases. Governments become virtual corporations and come to rely on electronic voting. Southeast Asia and the coast of China manufacture most of the world's goods and consume almost half themselves. Latin America is their branch office. Japan gets richer and unhappier. Russia exports trouble in the form of neo-religious cultists and mafioso. The United States and Europe become large theme parks.

Scenario 2—The world becomes dominated by a new international division of labour, based on an intensive use of networked communications. Technology dominates global culture, which turns inward toward personal spaces. Old public spaces crumble, and ethnic subcultures give way to a patchwork of unbridled individual variety. Europe is wracked by civil strife as its collectively oriented civilization unravels. Russia rebounds, while Japan lags. China and the developing countries become huge flea markets where anything goes.

Scenario 3—Economic development is slowed in reaction to earlier decades of high crime and chaos. Europe experiences a second renaissance, becoming a moral beacon. Communitarian values become stronger, and governments undertake large-scale public works directed at environmental improvement. Dirty technologies are tightly regulated, and this increases the income gap between the core and peripheral regions. Asia and Latin America become refuges for the young and restless of the core regions who find environmentalism and communitarianism too dogmatic; they settle in "free economic zones" where their education and their energy help stimulate economic growth.

Scenario 4—The world is divided into three rigid and distinct trading blocs, but political boundaries are more fragmented than ever. The European Union, including most of Europe and Russia, has a common currency and tight border controls. The Asia–Pacific region evolves into a trading bloc in response to the European Union, but it is weakened by internal political and economic differences. Mexico collapses under civil war. Canada breaks up after Quebec's withdrawal. The third trading bloc is centred on the Indian Ocean, with India, South Africa, Saudi Arabia, and Iran as the key members. Throughout the world, political conflicts and weaknesses allow widespread terrorism, organized crime, and environmental degradation.

Scenario 5—The world settles into small, powerful city-states. Civic pride blossoms, and governments use advanced technologies to create public works of an unprecedented scale and scope. Rural areas of the world are second class but have widespread virtual hookups. Europe fractionalizes into more than 50 countries; China, Russia, Brazil, and India devolve into black-market ethnic states. Gangs and militia in peripheral countries and old inner-city areas transform into political law-and-order machines.

Figure 12.1 Future scenarios In some ways, the future is already here, embedded in the world's institutional structures and the dynamics of its populations. However, there are some aspects of the future that we can only guess at. Given the impossibility of knowing precisely how the future will unfold, business strategists attempt to make decisions that play out well across several possible futures. To find the most robust strategy, several different scenarios are created, each representing a plausible outcome. (*Sources:* L. Beach, "How to Build Scenarios," *Wired Scenarios* 1.01, October 1995, pp. 74–81; P. Schwartz, "The New World Disorder," *Wired Scenarios* 1.01, October 1995, pp. 104–106.)

metropolises of the periphery, from the voting blocs of the West to the newly independent nation-states of the South.

Looking around now, much of the familiarity of the modern world and its geographies seems to be disappearing as we stumble through a period of transition, triggered by the end of the cold war in 1989 and rendered more complex by the geopolitical and cultural repercussions of the terrorist attacks of September 11, 2001, and the global financial meltdown of 2008. The result is a series of unexpected developments and unsettling juxtapositions: the United States has given economic aid to Russia while Eastern European countries want to join NATO and the European Union; Germany has unified, but Czechoslovakia and Yugoslavia have disintegrated; Israel has established a fragile peace with Egypt and Jordan but is unable to find an arrangement with the Palestinians; South Africa has been transformed, through an unexpectedly peaceful revolution, to black majority rule. Meanwhile, Islamist terrorists shoot up tourist buses, bomb office buildings, and sabotage aircraft; former communist Russian ultranationalists have become comradely with German neo-Nazis; Hindus, Sikhs, and Muslims are in open warfare in South Asia; the United States has invaded Iraq; and Somali pirates seize ships in the waters of the Arabian Sea and Indian Ocean. Finally, within Western countries, the cultural shifts and neoliberal political climate that have emerged over the same transitional period have weakened the fundamental pillars of civil society as Jane Jacobs expressed at the beginning of this chapter.

These examples show that we cannot simply project our future geographies from the landscapes and spatial structures of the past. Rather, we must map them out from a combination of existing structures and budding trends. Although this is certainly a speculative and tricky undertaking, we can draw with a good deal of confidence on what we know about processes of geographical change and principles of spatial organization. The study of human geography has taught us to understand spatial change as a composite of local place-making processes (see Chapter 6) that are subject to certain principles of spatial organization and that operate within the dynamic framework of the world-system (Chapter 2). It has also taught us that many important dimensions exist to spatial organization and spatial change, from the demographic dimension (Chapter 3) to the urban (Chapters 10 and 11) and the cultural (Chapters 5 and 6).

As we look ahead to the future, we can appreciate that some dimensions of human geography are more certain than others. In some ways, the future is already here, embedded in the world's institutional structures and the dynamics of its populations (**Table 12.1**). We know, for example, a good deal about the demographic trends of the next quarter-century, given present populations, birth and death rates, and so on (see Chapter 3 and **Figure 12.2**). We also know a good deal about the distribution of environmental resources and constraints (Chapters 4 and 8), about the characteristics of local and regional economies (Chapter 7), and about the legal and political frameworks (Chapter 9) within which geographical change will probably take place.

On the other hand, we can only guess at some aspects of the future. Two of the most speculative realms are those of politics and technology. Although we can foresee some of the possibilities (maybe a spread and intensification of ethno-nationalism, perhaps a new railway era based on high-speed trains?), politics and technology are both likely to spring surprises at any time. The events of September 11, 2001, have shown how geographies can be rewritten suddenly and dramatically, not only in those countries gripped by the "War on Terrorism," but also in the Western nations as they reorient their legal, financial, economic, and political geographies to the ever more elusive goal of "security." In fact, the lasting lesson of the last decade may well be that "security" is no longer achievable: the *risk society* we discussed in Chapter 1 has become the norm (**Figure 12.3**). As we review the prospects for geographical change, therefore, we must always be mindful that our prognoses are all open to the unexpected. As we shall see, this is perhaps also our biggest cause for optimism.

TABLE 12.1 The 2020 Global Landscape

Relative Certainties	Key Uncertainties
A global multipolar system is emerging with the rise of China, India, and others.	Whether an energy transition away from oil and gas—supported by improved energy storage, biofuels, and clean coal—is completed during the 2025 time frame.
The relative power of nonstate actors—businesses, tribes, religious organizations, and even criminal networks—also will increase.	How quickly climate change occurs and the locations where its impact is most pronounced.
The unprecedented shift in relative wealth and economic power roughly from West to East now underway will continue.	Whether mercantilism stages a comeback and global markets recede.
The United States will remain the single most powerful country but will be less dominant.	Whether advances toward democracy occur in China and Russia.
Continued economic growth—coupled with 1.2 billion more people by 2025—will put pressure on energy, food, and water resources.	Whether regional fears about a nuclear-armed Iran trigger an arms race and greater militarization.
The number of countries with youthful populations in the "arc of instability" will decrease, but the populations of several youth-bulge states are projected to remain on rapid growth trajectories.	Whether the greater Middle East becomes more stable, especially whether Iraq stabilizes, and whether the Arab–Israeli conflict is resolved peacefully.
The potential for conflict will increase owing to rapid changes in parts of the greater Middle East and the spread of lethal capabilities.	Whether Europe and Japan overcome economic and social challenges caused or compounded by demography.
Terrorism is unlikely to disappear by 2025, but its appeal could lessen if economic growth continues in the Middle East and youth unemployment is reduced. For those terrorists that are active the diffusion of technologies will put dangerous capabilities within their reach.	Whether global powers work with multilateral institutions to adapt their structure and performance to the transformed geopolitical landscape.

Source: National Intelligence Council, *Global Trends 2025: A Transformed World*. Washington, DC: U.S. Government Printing Office, 2008, pp. iv–v.

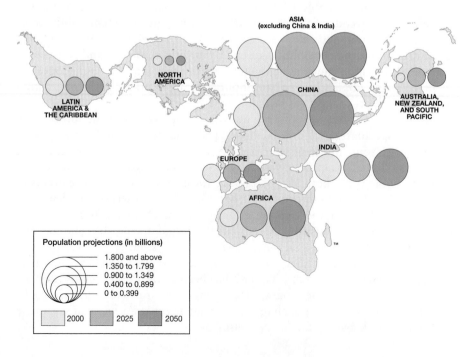

Figure 12.2 Population geography of the future Population projections show a very marked disparity between world regions, with core countries and core regions growing very little in comparison with the periphery. (*Source:* Map projection, Buckminster Fuller Institute and Dymaxion Map Design, Santa Barbara, CA. The word *Dymaxion* and the Fuller Projection Dymaxion™ Map design are trademarks of the Buckminster Fuller Institute, Santa Barbara, California, © 1938, 1967, & 1992. All rights reserved. Data from United Nations Population Division, *Long-Range World Population Projections, 1999 Revision*. New York: Population Division of the UN Department of Economic and Social Affairs, 1999.)

Figure 12.3   International terrorism
Floral tributes lie outside Edgware Road underground station in London, England, after al-Qaeda bombers killed 49 people and injured 700 during morning rush hour terrorist attacks on London buses and subways on July 7, 2005.

GLOBAL OUTLOOK, REGIONAL PROSPECTS

For many years now, such organizations as the United Nations and the World Bank have prepared forecasts of the world economy. These forecasts are based on economic models that take data on macroeconomic variables (for example, trends in countries' gross domestic product, their imports and exports, their economic structure, their investment and savings performance, and their demographic dynamism) and use known relationships between these variables to predict future outcomes. The problem is that economic projection is an inexact science. Economic models are not able to take into account the changes brought about by major technological innovations, significant geopolitical shifts, governments' willingness and ability to develop strong economic policies, or the rather mysterious longer-term ups and downs that characterize the world economy. What is clear is that in *overall* terms the global economy is vastly richer, more productive, and more dynamic than it was just 15 or 20 years ago, and there is every possibility that, in the longer term, the world economy will continue to expand, in spite of the instability and recession triggered by the 2008 global financial crisis. As we will see later in this chapter, the limited availability of energy and resources is both a constraint and a driver (through innovation) for this expansion.

Uneven Development

When we leave the global level and focus on the prospects of particular regions and places, projections are even harder to make because we often cannot predict how those places will experience global change. Some places will be able to benefit from future changes in ways we cannot imagine at present; other areas will find that certain changes spell the end for a particular way of life. We cannot tell. But, as geographers, we understand the importance of place and thus know that any expansion will be uneven as place mediates the processes of change. The world in 2020 will have changed radically as it recovers from the current recession. Emerging powers—such as the BRICS countries Brazil, Russia, India, China, South Africa (see Chapter 2), and possibly also Indonesia—have the potential to render obsolete the old categories of East and West, North and South, aligned and nonaligned, developed and developing. Traditional geographic groupings will increasingly lose salience in international relations. A state-bound world and a world of megacities, linked by flows of telecommunications, trade, and finance, will coexist. Competition for allegiances will be more open, less fixed than in the past.

In parallel with the world-system categorization of core, semiperipheral, and peripheral regions, we can think of large sectors of the world's population as being in one of three categories: the elite, the embattled, and the marginalized. The elite are participants in—and beneficiaries of—the fast world of new transport and communications technologies, globalized production networks, and global consumer culture (see Chapter 2). The embattled are also participants, but in dependent roles, with fewer benefits and limited opportunities: assembly-line workers, for example, in offshore commodity chains (see Chapter 7). The marginalized have to survive within the slow world, largely disconnected from formal economies (see Chapter 11) and buffeted by the dynamics of globalization.

The most significant point to keep in mind about the stratification of the world economy through contemporary globalization is that the elite, the marginalized, and the embattled are likely to be less concentrated than they once were in particular regions. It is no longer accurate to see Nigeria, for instance, as a wholly embattled region or its population as exclusively embattled. Instead, Nigeria, like Canada and most other countries, contains a range of stratified regions and groups within its national boundaries such that elite, embattled, and marginalized social groups are all part of the larger whole (**Figure 12.4**). Moreover, the elite regions and social groups have more in common with elite regions and groups in other parts of the world than they do with the embattled and marginalized groups within their own national boundaries (**Figure 12.5**).

Nevertheless, an even greater gap between the haves and have-nots of the world seems likely to structure future geographies at all scales. At the global level, the gulf between the world's core areas and the periphery has already begun to widen significantly: the United Nations has calculated that the ratio of GDP per capita (measured at constant prices and exchange rates) between the developed and developing areas of the world increased from 10:1 in 1970 to 13:1 in 2005. Little hope exists that any future boom in the overall world economy will reverse this trend.

At the same time, the degree of income inequality *within* core countries is the same as in China, Bolivia, Malaysia, Senegal, and Russia (**Figure 12.6**). Because the existence of cores and peripheries at all scales is an integral aspect of the world-system model (see Chapter 2), we should not be surprised that Canada, too, is a stratified society with marked spatial inequalities (remember the plight of many of Canada's Aboriginal peoples we discussed in Chapter 3).

Returning to the global level, let us consider for a moment the ways in which globalization has contributed to the widening disparities. For many peripheral countries, participation in global trade at disadvantageous conditions dictated by the core meant that they did not receive enough revenues to balance their expenditures: they had to take on debt. Because the terms of trade for many peripheral countries have worsened still over the last few decades (because of dropping commodity prices, increasing cost of energy imports, devaluation of their currencies, etc.), many peripheral countries could not repay their loans and had to take on even more debt. In many peripheral countries, one-quarter or more of all export earnings are now swallowed up by debt service—the annual interest on international debts (**Figure 12.7** on p. 535). Practically none of the actual loan is ever likely to be repaid, but so long as banks in the core countries continue to receive interest on their loans, they will be satisfied. Indeed, they are doing extremely well from this aspect of international finance, taking in several times more money in debt servicing than they pay out in new loans. Thus, in spite of the globalization of the world-system (or in many ways *because* of it), much of the world has been all but written off by the bankers and corporate executives of the core.

At the Margins

As for the countries being "written off," their future looks bleak, indeed. It is not just that they have already been dismissed by investors in the core or that their domestic economies are simply threadbare (see Chapter 11)—they also face unprecedented

Figure 12.4 Global social hierarchy These photographs underscore the new social hierarchy that has emerged around globalization. Pictured here are (top) members of the marginalized lower stratum in Haiti; (middle) members of the embattled middle stratum in Mexico; and (bottom) members of the elite higher stratum in the United Kingdom.

levels of demographic, environmental, economic, and societal stresses. In the worst-off regions—including much of West and Central Africa, for example—the events of the next 50 years are going to play out from a starting point of scarce basic resources and infrastructure, serious environmental degradation, overpopulation, disease, refugee migrations, and criminal anarchy. African countries will be further disadvantaged because the prices of commodities produced there and in other peripheral locations have been dropping, while imported goods from the core have become more expensive. Continuing to disable the periphery's full participation in the global economy are

Figure 12.5 The global elite Where was this picture taken? The point is that it could have been taken anywhere in the world as there are "lifestyle niches" in almost every city in the world where the global elite can enjoy the same amenities.

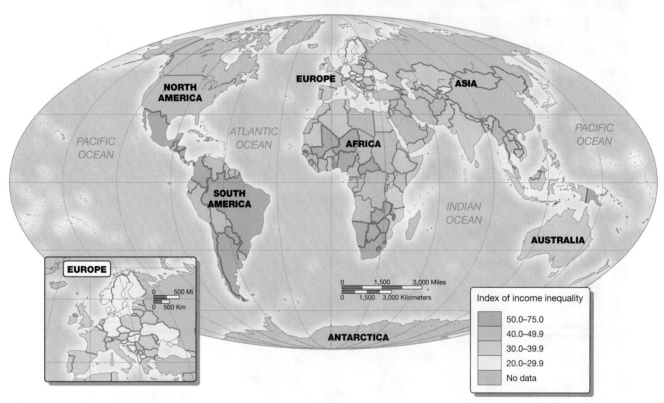

Figure 12.6 Index of income inequality This map shows the degree of inequality of income distributions within countries using the Gini coefficient, a commonly used indicator that compares actual income distributions to a hypothetical distribution of perfect equality. The higher the index score, the greater the degree of inequality within a country. (*Source:* United Nations Development Programme, *Cities in a Globalizing World.* Sterling, VA: Earthscan Publications, 2001, p. 18.)

the combined effects of the debt crisis, dwindling amounts of foreign aid, and insufficient resources to purchase technology or develop domestic technological innovations.

The U.S. State Department has estimated that during the 1990s, wars in Africa produced more than 8 million refugees and claimed more than 7 million lives, including about 2 million children. Many of these wars are the result of the artificial boundaries created by the colonial powers (see Chapter 9) or the legacy of the political dependency Europe imposed on Africa as part of the emergence of the modern world-system (see Chapter 2). Most conflicts in Africa, however,

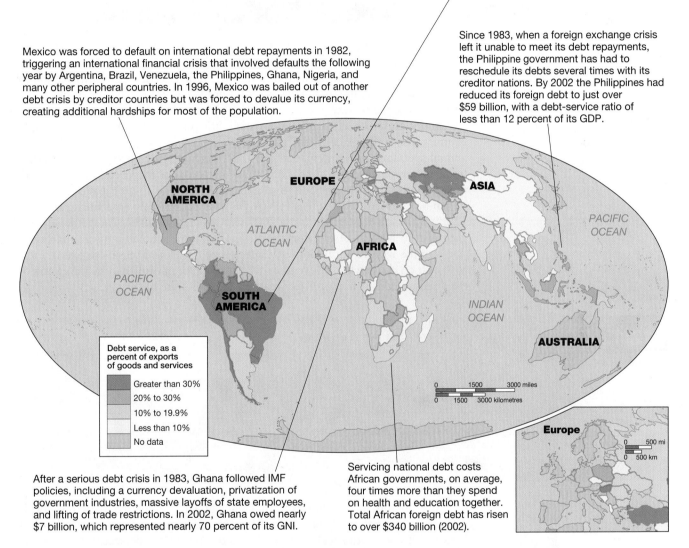

Brazil borrowed so much money in the 1970s and 1980s that it could no longer meet the interest payments. Between 1983 and 1989 the International Monetary Fund (IMF) bailed the country out but imposed austerity measures that were designed to curb imports. These included a 60 percent increase in gasoline prices and a reduction of the minimum wage to $50 a month, which gave workers half the purchasing power they had in 1940. Nevertheless, by 2002, the country's debt had reached nearly $228 billion, annual inflation rates in the 1990s having ranged between 500 percent and 2000 percent.

Since 1983, when a foreign exchange crisis left it unable to meet its debt repayments, the Philippine government has had to reschedule its debts several times with its creditor nations. By 2002 the Philippines had reduced its foreign debt to just over $59 billion, with a debt-service ratio of less than 12 percent of its GDP.

Mexico was forced to default on international debt repayments in 1982, triggering an international financial crisis that involved defaults the following year by Argentina, Brazil, Venezuela, the Philippines, Ghana, Nigeria, and many other peripheral countries. In 1996, Mexico was bailed out of another debt crisis by creditor countries but was forced to devalue its currency, creating additional hardships for most of the population.

Debt service, as a percent of exports of goods and services

- Greater than 30%
- 20% to 30%
- 10% to 19.9%
- Less than 10%
- No data

After a serious debt crisis in 1983, Ghana followed IMF policies, including a currency devaluation, privatization of government industries, massive layoffs of state employees, and lifting of trade restrictions. In 2002, Ghana owed nearly $7 billion, which represented nearly 70 percent of its GNI.

Servicing national debt costs African governments, on average, four times more than they spend on health and education together. Total African foreign debt has risen to over $340 billion (2002).

Figure 12.7 The debt crisis In some countries the annual interest on international debts (their "debt service") accounts for more than 20 percent of the annual value of their exports of goods and services. Many countries first got into debt trouble in the mid-1970s, when Western banks, faced with recession at home, offered low-interest loans to the governments of peripheral countries rather than being stuck with idle capital. When the world economy heated up again, interest rates rose and many countries found themselves facing a debt crisis. The World Bank and the IMF, in tandem with Western governments, worked to prevent a global financial crisis by organizing and guaranteeing programs that eased poor countries' debt burdens. Western banks were encouraged to swap debt for equity stakes in nationalized industries, while debtor governments were persuaded to impose austere economic policies. These policies have helped ease the debt crisis, but often at the expense of severe hardship for ordinary people—the reason why the IMF has become known among radical development theorists as "imposing misery and famine."

Figure 12.8 Darfur In Sudan, the brutal oppression, ethnic cleansing, and genocide sponsored by the central government allowed Arab rebels known as the *Janjaweed* to slaughter thousands of people in the Darfur region, causing the mass displacement of an estimated 1 million refugees. The people of the Darfur region organized popular political and military resistance, forming a political movement known as the Sudan Liberation Movement. Five members of its military wing, the Sudan Liberation Army (SLA), stand in front of their transport in 2004.

are civil wars. Some governments, for example in Sudan (**Figure 12.8**), have lost control of large parts of their territories: groups of unemployed youths plunder travellers; tribal groups war with one another; refugees trudge from war zones to camps and back again; and environmental degradation proceeds unchecked and is even worsened by war.

Amid this chaos, disease has flourished. It is possible that parts of Africa may be more unhealthy places today than they were a century ago. In Uganda, where annual spending on health is less than US$5 per person (compared with international debt repayments of almost US$20 per person), one in five children die before their fifth birthday. Malaria and tuberculosis are now a serious problem over much of sub-Saharan Africa, whereas HIV/AIDS has become truly epidemic: 1 in every 12 people in sub-Saharan Africa in 2007 was infected with HIV. Altogether, Africa, with just 10 percent of the world's total population, is home to more than two-thirds of the world's 33 million HIV-infected people. The disease also exerts a terrible cost on those who survive: the number of children orphaned by the effects of the disease in this region of Africa reached 12 million in 2007.[2]

12.1 Geography in the Information Age

Post-independence ideals of modernization and democracy now seem more remote than ever in these regions as corrupt dictators have created "kleptocracies" (as in *kleptomania*: an irresistible desire to steal) in place of democracies. Of the estimated US$12.42 billion in oil revenues that came to Nigeria as a result of the Persian Gulf crisis of 1990 to 1991, for example, US$12.2 billion seems to have been clandestinely disbursed.

Given all this, it is not surprising that much of Africa is unattractive to the globalizing world economy, and indeed it appears that many core countries have abandoned Africa as it does not provide the conditions for profitable and secure investments. China, however, has dramatically increased its engagement in Africa as it is looking to secure resources and particularly energy sources to supply its burgeoning economy: China gives generous loans to African countries, which repay the loans in oil, timber, cocoa, or other resources. China also buys up millions of hectares of land.

A New World Order?

At the other end of the spectrum, the prospects for the core economies are bright, especially for large, core-based transnational corporations. With the end of

---

[2] Joint United Nations Programme on HIV/AIDS (UNAIDS), *2008 Report on the Global AIDS Epidemic*. Geneva: UNAIDS, 2008, pp. 5, 21 (available at **www.unaids.org**).

the cold war, new markets in east-central Europe have opened up to capitalist industry, along with more resources and a skilled labour force. New transport and communications technologies have already facilitated the beginnings of the globalization of production and the emergence of a global consumer culture. Top companies have reorganized themselves to take full advantage of this globalization. Reforms to the ground rules of international trade have removed many of the impediments to free-market growth, and a new, global financial system is now in place, ready to service the new global economy (see Chapter 7 for a full review of these developments).

For the world-system core, therefore, the long-term question is not so much one of economic prosperity but of relative power and dominance. The same factors that will consolidate the advantages of the core as a whole—the end of the cold war, the availability of advanced telecommunications, the transnational reorganization of industry and finance, the liberalization of trade, and the emergence of a global culture—will also open the way for a new geopolitical and geoeconomic order. This is likely to generate some new relationships between places, regions, and countries.

As we have suggested, the old order of the "short" twentieth century (1914–1989), dominated both economically and politically by the United States, is rapidly disintegrating. In our present transitional phase, the new world order is up for grabs: we are coming to the end of a leadership cycle (see **Geography Matters 12.1—The Contenders**). This does not necessarily mean, however, that the United States will be unable to renew its position as the world's dominant power. As we saw in Chapter 2, Britain had two consecutive stints as the hegemon and was able to impose its political view on the world and set the terms for a wide variety of economic and cultural practices.

Alternatively, we may not see the same kind of hegemonic power in the new world order of the twenty-first century; there may not be a new hegemony at all. Instead, the globalization of economics and culture may result in a polycentric network of nations, regions, and world cities bound together by flows of goods and capital. Order may come not from military strength rooted in national economic muscle but from a mutual dependence on transnational production and marketing, with stability and regulation provided by powerful international institutions (such as the World Bank, the IMF, the WTO, the EU, NATO, and the UN).

12.2 Geography in the Information Age

An example of this is the supranational World Trade Organization. The WTO has begun to provide a system of regulations that supersedes national-level regulations and laws. In practice, this seems to mean that national restrictions over foreign corporations are increasingly subordinated to the new rules of the WTO. Proponents of the WTO argue that without such an organization, the terms of international trade are more likely to be set by powerful countries and transnational corporations at the expense of the weak. Subordinating powerful national interests to WTO-enforced free trade, they argue, will benefit less affluent countries by giving them free access to core-country markets and by requiring core countries to stop dumping the products of their subsidized agricultural sectors in peripheral markets. Critics of the WTO argue that the aims of the WTO have been shaped by international business and that the way that WTO negotiations take place—with dispute resolution panels made up of unelected bureaucrats rendering decisions behind closed doors—advances the interests of business, in general, and transnational corporations, in particular.

The Contenders

Because of the globalization of industry, finance, and culture and the dissolution of the Soviet Union—one of the cornerstones of the old world order—the world is currently in a state of transition. Looking ahead 25 to 50 years, several contenders exist for economic and political leadership.

China and India

According to the U.S. National Intelligence Council (NIC), the greatest benefits of globalization will accrue to countries and groups that can access and adopt new technologies. The council's report on *Mapping the Global Future* concludes that China and India are well positioned to become technology leaders and that the expected next revolution in high technology—involving the convergence of nano-, bio-, information, and materials technology—could further boost China and India's prospects. Both countries are investing in basic research in these fields and are well placed to be leaders in a number of key fields. As the NIC report puts it:

> The likely emergence of China and India, as well as others, as new major global players—similar to the advent of a united Germany in the 19th century and a powerful United States in the early 20th century—will transform the geopolitical landscape, with impacts potentially as dramatic as those in the previous two centuries. In the same way that commentators refer to the 1900s as the "American Century," the 21st century may be seen as the time when Asia, led by China and India, comes into its own. A combination of sustained high economic growth, expanding military capabilities, and large

populations will be at the root of the expected rapid rise in economic and political power for both countries. . . . Barring an abrupt reversal of the process of globalization or any major upheavals in these countries, the rise of these new powers is a virtual certainty.[3]

Most forecasts indicate that sometime after 2020 China's GNI will exceed that of the United States, whereas India will overtake the larger European economies. Because of the sheer size of China's and India's populations—projected to be 1.5 billion and almost 1.4 billion, respectively, by 2025—their standard of living need not approach Western levels for these countries to become important economic powers. How China and India exercise their growing power and whether they relate cooperatively or competitively to each other and to other powers in the international system, however, are key uncertainties.

Many observers predict a "Pacific Destiny" for the twenty-first century, in which China in particular will be the hub of a world economy whose centre of gravity is around the rim of the Pacific rather than the North Atlantic. China certainly has the potential to be a contender. It has a vast territory with a comprehensive resource base and a long history of political, cultural, and economic integration. It has the largest population of any country in the world and an economy that has been doubling in size about every 10 years. China's increased participation in the world economy has created an entirely new situation, causing a deflationary trend in world prices for manufactured goods (**Figure 12.1.1**). Not only does the Chinese economy's

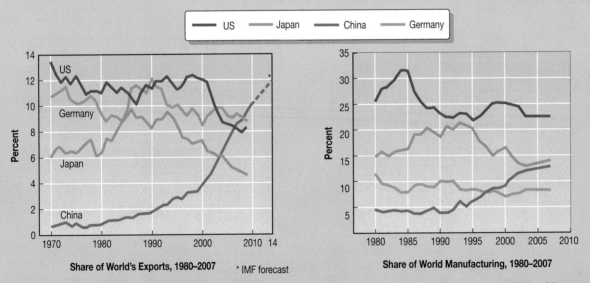

Figure 12.1.1 China's changing role in the world economy China's emergence as a significant player in the world economy is reflected in trends of manufacturing output and exports.

[3] National Intelligence Council, *Mapping the Global Future: Report of the National Intelligence Council's 2020 Project.* Washington, DC: U.S. Government Printing Office, 2004, p. 11.

12.3 Geography in the Information Age

In 2007, China displaced Germany as the third largest economy in the world; only four years later, it bumped Japan from second spot. Sometime after 2020, China is set to overtake the United States as the largest economy (it already is the largest car market, energy consumer, steel producer, and emitter of carbon dioxide). At that point, China would return to its traditional position as the world's leading economy, a position it held for 9 out of the last 10 centuries. In other words, China's relative weakness during the twentieth century was an exception, rather than the rule.

12.4 Geography in the Information Age

China's rapid rise also raises issues in other countries. As we saw earlier, China invests heavily in overseas resources (including a number of Canadian mining and energy corporations). But China's development also has fuelled a demand for food imports, and this is having an effect as far afield as the Brazilian Amazon, where substantial acreages of soya beans are now planted under contract for the Chinese market.[4] Other examples include the Chinese government's support for countries with a record of human rights abuse because they offer to supply China with oil (such as Sudan), and, critics argue, the continued occupation of areas such as Tibet because this enables the Chinese to control that country's abundant water supplies[5] (**Figure 12.1.2**).

size make it a major producer, but its huge labour force ensures that its wage levels will not approach Western levels for a long time, thus guaranteeing a key competitive advantage.

Nevertheless, China's economy will remain largely agrarian for some time yet. The task of feeding, clothing, and housing its enormous population will also constrain its ability to modernize its economy to the point where it can dominate the world economy. Meanwhile, a great deal of social and political reforms remain to be accomplished before free enterprise can really flourish. Finally, before China can emerge as a hegemonic power it must resolve a major contradiction of its contemporary human geography: the dramatically uneven development that has been a consequence of its economic reforms. The positive spiral of cumulative causation has affected only the larger cities and coastal regions (see Chapter 7), whereas the vast interior regions of the country remain impoverished. This, ironically, is the very geographical pattern of spatial inequality and social polarization that led to the communist revolution in the 1940s. Today, it is once again a source of potential instability and unrest.

[4] Jonathan Watts, "A Hunger Eating Up the World," *Guardian Weekly*, 20–26 January 2006, p. 31.

[5] China's extensive economic involvement with Africa now includes ties with, among others, Angola, Nigeria, Somalia, Mozambique, Zambia, Ghana, Sudan, the DRC and the People's Republic of the Congo, and Equatorial Guinea; it imports substantial supplies of timber, copper, minerals, and oil, respectively, from these countries (see Richard Behar, "Special Report: China Storms Africa," *Fast Company*, June 2008, available at **www.fastcompany.com/magazine/126/special-report-china-in-africa.html**).

Russia

In terms of geography, Russia should be a strong contender for hegemony: it is the world's largest state by land area, possesses the world's largest oil and gas reserves as well as major reserves of important industrial raw materials, and occupies a pivotal strategic location in the centre of the Eurasian land mass (see Chapter 9). Now freed from the economic constraints of state socialism, Russia stands to benefit greatly by establishing economic linkages with the expanding world economy (**Figure 12.1.3**). With a population of 144 million in 2004, the Russian economy also has an ample labour force and a domestic market large enough to form the basis of a formidable economy.

Nevertheless, Russia has to be a long-odds contender. At present, the Russian economy is shrinking as it withdraws from the centrally planned model and battles widespread corruption, tax evasion, and organized crime. Technologically, the latter years of the Soviet system left Russian industry with obsolete technology and low-grade product lines. As a result, the Russian economy now faces a massive task of modernization before it can approach its full potential. At the same time, there looms the equally massive task of renewing civil society and the institutions of law, business, and democracy after 70 years of state socialism. Russia has been unable to create some of the essential pillars of a market economy. The institutional framework for the legal enforcement of private contracts and effective competition is still rudimentary.

Another major weakness has been public finances. A system of fair and efficient tax collection has yet to

Figure 12.1.2 Tibetan monks protest in Nepal China's refusal to acknowledge an independent Tibet has sent the Dalai Lama on numerous international tours to broadcast the plight of Tibetans, who are experiencing extreme persecution. Pictured here are Tibetan monks in exile in Nepal who are protesting ouside the Chinese embassy there marking the anniversary of the failed 1959 uprising against China and demanding that China grant sovereignty to Tibet.

Figure 12.1.3 Post–cold war Russia In the new Russia, economic polarization and cultural tensions have resulted from the "shock therapy" of competitive capitalist markets. These contrasts have become symbols for Russia's polarized politics, breeding a resentment among workers and pensioners that is exploited by nationalist politicians who want to restore Russia's superpower status through a self-reliant economy and renewed military strength. (*Source:* Les Stone/Corbis Sygma.)

be put in place, while the relationship between federal and state taxes and spending has remained obscure. Meanwhile, real wages for most people have already dropped to 1950s levels, and life expectancies are falling, the result of alcoholism and malnutrition. These problems have serious implications for the future world order: a weak Russia is a geopolitical temptation in Europe and throughout all of Eurasia: it tempts both the Americans and Europeans to overextend themselves geopolitically as the recent expansion of NATO eastwards illustrates.

The European Union

In geopolitical terms, the collapse of the Soviet Union has advanced the prospects of the European Union to become a strong contender for world leadership. The European Union (EU) is an *economic* union (with *integrated* economic and social policies among member states) and is moving toward becoming a *supranational political union* (with a single set of institutions and policies).[6] The 27-member EU now has a total population of 491 million (the combined population of Canada and the United States is 340 million) and an overall economy in 2010 of US$16.2 trillion (the combined GDP of Canada and the United States in 2009 was US$15.5 trillion). If and when it achieves full political union, its size will enable it to outvote the United States in the IMF and the World Bank.

The EU has evolved dramatically since its start with six member nations in 1952. Now there is a common EU passport, and a single currency, the euro, is used by many of its members. The EU regulates trade and coordinates energy distribution, communications, and transportation.

It has a governing body (**Figure 12.1.4**), a parliament, foreign policy powers, and a court whose decisions are binding on member countries and individuals. The EU is the world's largest internal market and largest exporting power. Of the world's 20 largest commercial banks, 10 are European (the others are 6 American, 3 Chinese, and 1 Japanese). The EU also has one of the world's most vibrant and sophisticated industrial core regions that stretches from southeast England to northern Italy; its economic policies and infrastructure investments have fostered emerging axes of economic growth that stretch east–west and north–south (see Figure 12.11 on p. 546); and European industries are world leaders in chemicals, insurance, engineering, construction, and aerospace industries. The EU also offers a distinctive message. In contrast to the American Dream,

> The European Dream emphasizes community relationships over individual autonomy, cultural diversity over assimilation, quality of life over the accumulation of wealth, sustainable development over unlimited material growth, deep play over unrelenting toil, universal human rights and the rights of nature over property rights, and global cooperation over the unilateral exercise of power.[7]

Europe is poised either to challenge U.S. hegemony or to become a senior partner among superpowers. EU citizens, however, have expressed reservations about establishing a constitution to underpin a supranational political union for fear of losing their national autonomy. There are also concerns that further extension of the EU would risk destroying its own internal balance and cohesion. Europe's future international role also depends greatly on whether it undertakes major structural

[6] Information about the European Union is readily available from its statistical arm, *Eurostat*, and via its website, *Europa* (**http://europa.eu/index_en.htm**).

[7] J. Rifkin, *The European Dream*. Los Angeles: J.P. Tarcher, 2004, p. 3.

Figure 12.1.4 Headquarters of the European Union in Brussels
The European Union had its origins as an amalgamation in 1967 of three institutions—Euratom, the European Coal and Steel Community, and the European Economic Community—which had been set up in the 1950s to promote European economic integration. The six original members—Belgium, France, Italy, Luxembourg, the Netherlands, and West Germany—were joined in 1973 by Denmark, the Republic of Ireland, and the United Kingdom. With the addition of Greece in 1981, Portugal and Spain in 1986, Austria, Sweden, and Finland in 1995, a further 10 countries in 2004, and Bulgaria and Romania in 2007, the 27-member EU now has a population and an economy larger than those of North America. In 2011, Croatia completed accession talks to become the 28th member.

economic and social reforms to deal with the problem of its aging workforce. This will demand more immigration and better integration of workers, most of whom will likely come from North Africa and the Middle East. Even if more migrant workers are not allowed in, Western Europe will have to integrate a growing Muslim population. Barring increased legal entry may only lead to more illegal migrants who will be harder to integrate, posing a long-term problem.

Japan

In the few decades between the end of World War II and the 1970s, Japan rose to become the second-largest national economy in the world. Despite its limited resources and the literal ruins of military defeat in 1945, Japan quickly gained competitive advantages in a wide range of industrial and financial activities that served global markets and established itself as the leader in optics, electronics, and automotive technologies. For Japan's citizens, this sustained export boom brought some of the highest incomes and standards of living in the world: the average annual income per household was US$65,560 in 2007, the highest of all the major core countries.[8] Japan is also the world's major creditor (followed by China).

Often attributed to a system of informal alliances among politics, business, and bureaucracy, the "Japanese miracle" includes the key elements of the Ministry of Finance, the Ministry of International Trade and Industry (MITI), and Nikkeiren, the national business association. This system, sometimes known as "Japan, Inc.," has systematically identified leading economic sectors and planned their success, first in Japan and then at a global scale. The system is still in place, and its success invites speculation that Japan will be the nation-state best equipped to cope with a globalized world economy and thus be a contender for world leadership.

Nevertheless, Japan faces several important handicaps as a contender. First, it is heavily dependent on external sources of raw materials. Japan is the number one importer not only of basic raw materials (petroleum, iron ore, and copper ore, for example) but also of agricultural goods. Second, Japan is geographically isolated from its major industrial markets and trading partners. Although the Asian side of the Pacific Rim has great potential for growth, Japan's investments and partnerships are oriented overwhelmingly toward Europe and North America. Third, Japan faces a demographic trap. With an aging population, a declining birth rate, and a resolute unwillingness to allow large-scale immigration, Japan will face a serious labour shortage that can only be overcome by channelling more and more investment overseas. Fourth, Japan's self-imposed military restraint means that it is dependent on the United States as the guarantor of its autonomy vis-à-vis its mighty neighbours Russia and China.

Moreover, throughout the 1990s, Japan's economy experienced a prolonged recession, now called the "lost decade." The effects of this crisis were still lingering when the April 2011 earthquake and tsunami destroyed the Fukushima nuclear reactors and severely curtailed Japan's power generating capacity. The effects of this catastrophe will hamper the Japanese economy for several years to come. Taking all of these handicaps together, Japan can no longer be regarded as a serious contender for world leadership.

In the future, Japan may have to choose between dealing with neighbouring China either as a possible military threat or as a colossal market to help sustain its own economy. In the former case, Japan's role could well become that of an "Asian Germany," an advanced strategic base for American forces in a new, Eastern cold war with China. In the latter case, commercial alliances with China would likely strengthen the Asia–Pacific region as a joint contender for geopolitical hegemony.

---

[8] Statistics Bureau, *Statistical Handbook of Japan*. Tokyo: Ministry of Internal Affairs and Communication, 2007, available at **www.stat .go.jp/english/data/index.htm**. This is a very useful set of data and graphics on Japanese family budgets.

The United States

The United States is the reigning hegemon—at least for the time being. The U.S. economy is still the largest in the world (likely until the end of this decade), with a broad resource base; a large, well-trained, and sophisticated workforce; a domestic market that has greater purchasing power than any other single country; and a high level of technological sophistication. The United States also has the most powerful and technologically sophisticated military apparatus, which gives it the dominant voice and last word in international economic and political affairs. It is at least as well placed as its rivals to exploit the new technologies and new industries of a globalizing economy. It is also the only major contender for future world leadership with a global message: free markets, personal liberty, private property, electoral democracy, and mass consumption.

At the same time, the United States is a declining hegemon, at least in relative terms (in the sense that others are catching up). Its economic dominance is no longer unquestioned in the way it was in the 1950s, 1960s, and 1970s. Following the 2008 financial crisis, the United States entered a stubborn recession that still continues and further weakens its position vis-à-vis its greatest rival, China. On some measures of economic development, the European Union has already overtaken the United States. More importantly, the globalization of the economy has severely constrained the ability of the United States to translate its economic might into the firm control of international financial markets that it used to enjoy.

From 1989 to the events of September 11, 2001, when a new external threat galvanized the Americans into a self-declared war against terrorism, the United States faced a curious paradox: America had "won" the cold war, but it had lost its identity as Defender of the Free World and legitimacy as global police officer. The absence of a cold war enemy and the globalization of economic affairs also made it much more difficult for the United States to identify and define the national interest. The hesitancy in U.S. policies toward Kosovo, East Timor, Somalia, Sudan, Bosnia, and Haiti in the 1990s was symptomatic of such problems. Since the events of 11 September 2001, the United States has turned to a more forward and aggressive policy, but as its invasions of Afghanistan in 2002 and Iraq in 2003 have shown, these actions have cost it support around the world.

In summary, although the United States must be considered the strongest contender for the time being, it is by no means a foregone conclusion that it will, in fact, become the leader for the next cycle of economic and political leadership. The United States has choices not unlike those faced by the British at the end of the nineteenth century: it can either oppose its rivals or accommodate them. It can oppose by pressing for a seamless global system that remains under its own hegemony, or it can try to accommodate by coaxing the others into a global sharing of power, with some mix of regional spheres of interest and collective world responsibilities.

RESOURCES, TECHNOLOGY, AND SPATIAL CHANGE

As we saw in Chapter 2, technological breakthroughs and the availability of resources have had a profound influence on past patterns of development, and the same factors will certainly be a strong influence on future geographies. The expansion of the world economy and the globalization of industry will undoubtedly boost the overall demand for raw materials of various kinds, and this will spur the development of some previously underexploited but resource-rich regions in Africa, Eurasia, and East Asia. (Canada, too, stands to benefit from its resource endowment!)

Resources and Development

Raw materials, however, will be only a fraction of future resource needs. The main issue, by far, will be energy resources. World energy consumption has been increasing steadily over the recent past. As the periphery is being industrialized and its population increases further, the global demand for energy will expand rapidly. The International Energy Agency, assuming (fairly optimistically) that energy in peripheral countries will be generated in the future as efficiently as it is today in core countries, estimates that developing-country energy consumption will more than double by 2015, lifting total world energy demand by almost 50 percent. By 2020, peripheral and semiperipheral countries will account for

Figure 12.9 The changing face of China In a dramatic break with the past, many Chinese cities now bristle with high-rise towers and construction cranes as an unprecedented building boom is rapidly urbanizing the country. With urbanization and industrialization comes drastically increased energy consumption.

more than half of world energy consumption. Much of this will be driven by industrialization geared to meet the growing worldwide market for consumer goods, such as private automobiles, air conditioners, refrigerators, televisions, and household appliances, with China alone accounting for a third of the increase (**Figure 12.9**).

12.5 Geography in the Information Age

The global energy situation shows once again how global statistics can mask grave inequalities at smaller scales. Despite the rapid increases in global energy consumption over the last few decades, almost 2 billion people still do not have access to commercial forms of energy and a further billion only have access to periodic and unreliable forms of supply. "If about half of the world's population," a 2007 report by the World Energy Council cautions, "continues in this condition, the world as a whole faces a significant threat to stability and the quality of life everywhere."[9]

Certainly, without higher rates of investment in exploration and extraction than at present, production will be slow to meet the escalating demand. Even worse, many experts believe that current levels of production may in fact represent "peak oil" (i.e., the highest level of production we will ever see) and that by 2020 global oil production may be only 90 percent of its current level. The result might well be a significant increase in energy prices. This would have important geographical ramifications: companies would be forced to reconsider their operations, core households would be forced to re-evaluate their residential preferences and commuting behaviours, and peripheral households would be pushed further into poverty.

[9] World Energy Council, *Energy Policy Scenarios to 2050*. London: World Energy Council, November 2007, pp. 67 and 72, available at **www.worldenergy.org/publications/energy_policy_scenarios_to_2050/default.asp**.

If the oil-price crisis of 1973 (when crude oil prices were quadrupled by the OPEC cartel) is anything to go by, the outcome (apart from a global economic depression) could be a significant revision of the patterns of industrial location and a substantial reorganization of the metropolitan form. Significantly higher energy costs may change the optimal location (see Chapter 7) for many manufacturers, leading to deindustrialization in some regions and to new spirals of cumulative causation in others. It is also relevant to note that almost all of the increase in oil production over the next 15 or 20 years is likely to come from outside the core economies. This means that the world economy will become increasingly dependent on OPEC governments, which control over 70 percent of all proven oil reserves, most of them in the Middle East.

In countries that can afford the costs of research and development, new materials will reduce the growth of demand both for energy and traditional raw materials, such as aluminium, copper, and tin. For example, North American cars now are one-quarter lighter than their 1974 predecessors and thus require less gasoline. Japan is trying to further reduce motor vehicle fuel consumption by 15 percent (and thereby reduce its total fuel oil consumption) by using ceramics for major parts of engines. Other technological developments may make renewable energy sources (such as wind, tidal, and solar power) commercially more viable. As with earlier breakthroughs that produced steam energy, electricity, gasoline engines, and nuclear power, such advances would provide the catalyst for a major reorganization of the world's economic geographies.

12.6   Geography in the Information Age

How dramatic such a reorganization can be is well illustrated by China's explosive rise to the world's top producer of solar panels. Installation of solar energy panels currently is growing by 50 percent annually—and almost all of this additional capacity is manufactured in China, which is aggressively expanding its production lines. Even in Germany—as recently as 2005 the world leader in solar power technology—almost half of all installed photovoltaic panels now are Chinese-made. In less than a decade, China has almost completely displaced Germany as the industry leader.

New Technologies and Spatial Change

Just what new technologies are likely to have the most impact in reshaping human geographies? Given what we know about past processes of geographical change and principles of spatial organization, it is clear that changes in transportation technology are of fundamental importance (remember from Chapter 2 the impact of ocean-going steamers and railroads on the changing geographies of the nineteenth century, and the impact of automobiles and trucks on the changing geographies of the twentieth century). Among the most important of the next generation of transportation technologies that will influence future geographies are high-speed rail systems, smart roads, and smart cars. Several emerging industrial technologies also exist whose economic impact is likely to be so great that they will influence patterns of international, regional, and local development. Studies by the Organisation for Economic Co-operation and Development (OECD) and the United Nations have all identified biotechnology, materials technology, and information technology as the most critical areas for future economic development. We will look at them in sequence.

Transportation Technologies   New high-speed rail systems with improved locomotive technologies and specially engineered tracks and rolling stock have made it possible to travel at speeds of 275 to 370 kilometres per hour. With shorter check-in times and in-town rail terminals, door-to-door travel times between certain European cities are now shorter by rail than by air. In 2005, the EU announced plans for the development of 20,000 kilometres of high-speed rail track as part of the Trans-European Network (or TEN-T), designed to meet a predicted doubling of Europe's transport needs between 2005 and 2020 (**Figure 12.10**). The TEN-T represents an ambitious infrastructure investment of almost $400 billion. Just to complete the line between Lyon and Turin, for example, requires 10 years of boring a 53-kilometre tunnel under the Alps.[10] Once completed, however, the geographical implications of these

The Eurostar at Waterloo International Station, London.

Figure 12.10 High-speed rail in Europe European geography, with its relatively short distances between major cities, is ideally suited to rail travel and less suited, because of population densities and traffic congestion around airports, to air traffic. Allowing for check-in times and accessibility to terminals, it is already quicker to travel between many major European cities by rail than by air. High-speed rail routes have only a few scheduled stops because the time penalties resulting from deceleration and acceleration undermine the advantages of high-speed travel. Places with no scheduled stops will be less accessible and so less attractive for economic development (see Figure 12.11).

---

[10] Directorate-General for Energy and Transportation, "Trans-European Transport Network: TEN-T Priority Axes and Projects 2005." European Commission 2005, pp. 2 and 6 (available at **http://ec.europa.eu/ten/transport/projects/doc/2005_ten_t_en.pdf**). Regarding the Alpine tunnel, see Le Monde-Diplomatique, "Lyon-Turin, un projet de ferroutage controversé." *L'Atlas environment: analyses et solutions.* Paris: Le Monde diplomatique, 2008, pp. 80–81.

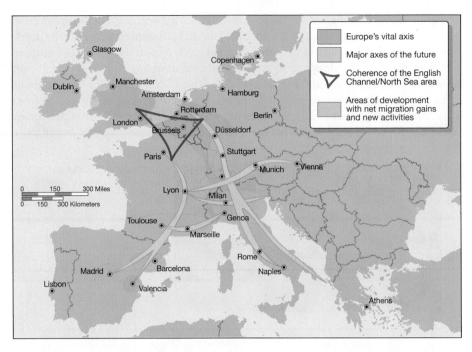

Figure 12.11   European growth axes   Most of Europe's major cities and advanced manufacturing regions lie along a crescent-shaped axis that runs from southeast England through southwest Germany to northern Italy and along emerging axes that extend to southern France, Spain, eastern Austria, and southern Italy. Note how the growth axes essentially reflect (and are reflected in) the extent of the high-speed rail system shown in Figure 12.10.

systems are significant: places that are linked to them will be well situated to grow in future rounds of economic development; places that are not will probably be left behind (**Figure 12.11**).

The same significance will attach to *intelligent transportation systems (ITS)*, should they be developed from their current prototypes to become commercially viable. An ITS is a combination of so-called smart highways and smart cars. The basic ITS target concept is an interactive link of vehicle electronic systems with roadside sensors, satellites, and centralized traffic management systems. This linkage allows for real-time monitoring of traffic conditions and allows drivers to receive alternative route information via two-way communications, on-board video screens, and mapping systems. With fewer gridlocked roads, driving would be safer, less polluting, and more efficient. Geographically, metropolitan areas and highway corridors that have the infrastructure of ITS technology will be at a significant advantage in attracting new industries and their workers.

12.7   Geography in the Information Age

The first generation of smart cars, buses, and trucks, with on-board, microprocessor-based electronics, is already on the road, using route-planning software, GPS, fleet management system software, and wireless communications. For example, GPS-guided navigation systems in German cars already receive coded traffic information from regional transmitters, which allows them to map out alternate routes that guide the driver past the traffic backup. The next step is completely automated highway systems, on which groups of vehicles would be guided automatically, in closely packed convoys, with virtually no active driver control.

Figure 12.12 Dangers of biotechnology In June 2000, biotechnology giant Monsanto took a 69-year-old farmer, Percy Schmeiser, to federal court. Some genetically modified canola had been found on Schmeiser's fields in Bruno, Saskatchewan. Monsanto argued that he had not paid them for a licence to grow their herbicide-resistant variety. Schmeiser claimed windblown seeds from nearby farms where the genetically modified canola was growing had contaminated his crop. However, experts for Monsanto argued that this was not possible, and Schmeiser lost the case. In a 2008 judgment in a civil suit, Monsanto did agree to pay for the costs of removing genetically modified canola from Percy Schmeiser's fields.

Biotechnology Although biotechnology is widely known for its use in the genetic engineering of crops (see Chapter 8) and the production of pharmaceuticals, it is also employed in the areas of animal husbandry, industrial production, renewable energy, waste recycling, and pollution control. The prospect, viewed optimistically, is that we can feed a hungry world efficiently. For instance, plants may be biogenetically engineered to be more salt-resistant than our current food crops. In this way, the increasing salinity of much of the world's irrigated lands (a major problem identified in Chapter 8 because it threatens to substantially reduce food production over large areas) could be rendered less problematic. Similarly, genetically modified crops can be engineered to be pest-resistant, thus saving both the dollar cost and the environmental cost of pesticides (conventional farming uses five or more broad-spectrum pesticide applications on crops each year).

Evidently, the implications for agricultural productivity are profound, as are the implications for the geography of agriculture. If crops can be genetically engineered to withstand pests, cold climates, and other adverse conditions, the whole geography of production may change, bringing the prospect of orange groves and avocado orchards in temperate climates, among other strange scenarios. In this way, the core may gain control over crops that are currently exclusively produced in the periphery and thereby continue to dominate world agriculture. Efforts to genetically engineer North American plant species to produce palm oil are underway and carry with them the potential to rob many tropical producers of their monopoly of this crop. This is, of course, nothing more than a continuation of ecological imperialism (see Chapter 4) in another guise, in this case using science to overcome biological barriers.

As it stands now, the future growth in the production of genetically modified food is by no means certain, as many studies point out its detrimental health and environmental consequences. In Europe and Japan, where consumers and their governments were already highly skeptical of genetically engineered foods ("frankenfoods"), the environmental lobby made genetically modified food a central issue in what promises to be one of the most critical cultural struggles of the early twenty-first century: local mobilization against transnational business.

It now seems likely that, in the near future at least, the commercial exploitation of genetic engineering will be slowed considerably by consumer resistance in the more affluent countries of the world. Meanwhile, more growth can be expected in industrial applications of biotechnology—enzymes, for example, that will be used as industrial catalysts in the microbial recovery of metals, in waste degradation, and in biomass fuels.

Materials Technologies   Materials technologies include new metal alloys, specialty polymers, plastic-coated metals, elastothermoplastics, laminated glass, and fibre-reinforced ceramics. They are important because they can replace scarce natural resources, reduce the quantity of raw materials used in many industrial processes, reduce the weight and size of many finished products, increase the performance of many products, produce less waste, and allow for the commercial development of entirely new products.

Unlike biotechnology, applications of materials technologies will require a fairly close association with an expensive infrastructure of high-tech industry. As a result, their immediate geographical impact is likely to be much more localized within the core regions of the world-system. On the other hand, peripheral regions and countries that are currently heavily dependent on the production and export of traditional raw materials—such as Guinea and Jamaica (bauxite), Zambia and the Democratic Republic of Congo (copper), Bolivia (tin), and Peru (zinc)—will probably be at the wrong end of the creative destruction process prompted by these new technologies. In other words, as new materials technologies reduce the demand for traditional raw materials, production and employment in the latter will decline, and investors will probably withdraw from producer regions to reinvest their capital in more profitable ventures elsewhere. In contrast, some peripheral regions and countries will benefit from the increasing demand for rare earth metals. Brazil, Nigeria, and the Democratic Republic of the Congo, for example, together account for almost 90 percent of the world's production of niobium (used with titanium in making superconductive materials); Brazil, Malaysia, Thailand, Mozambique, and Nigeria together account for about 75 percent of the world's production of tantalum (used in making capacitors that store and regulate the flow of electricity in electronic components). As one of the developed nations that most depends on the exploitation of raw materials, Canada must watch these new developments carefully. As was the case with the development of uranium and asbestos, the chances are that Canada will possess reserves of many materials required by new technology, but it would be wise to investigate the potential side effects of their use before proceeding with development.

Information Technologies   Information technologies comprise information-based, computer-driven, and communications-related activities—a wide array of technologies that includes both hardware (silicon chips, microelectronics, computers, satellites, and so on) and software. In addition to telematics—the automation of telecommunications and the linkage of computers by data transmission—information technologies include developments as diverse as real-time monitoring of traffic bottlenecks, computer-controlled manufacturing, chemical and biological sensors of effluent streams, 24-hour data-retrieval systems, bar-coded retail inventory control, telemetry systems for tracking parcels and packages, and geographic information systems. Information technologies have already found widespread applications in retailing, finance, banking, business management, and public administration; yet it is estimated that even in the more developed countries, only about one-third of the benefits to be derived from information-technology-based innovations have so far been realized.

As we have seen in earlier chapters, information technologies have already transformed certain aspects of economic geography: employment and production are geographically concentrated in highly localized agglomerations of activity, mainly in core countries. Examples include "Silicon Valley" (Santa Clara County) in California, the "high-tech" areas of Kitchener-Waterloo and Ottawa, and the "technopolis" (or science city) around the edges of the Osaka and Tokyo

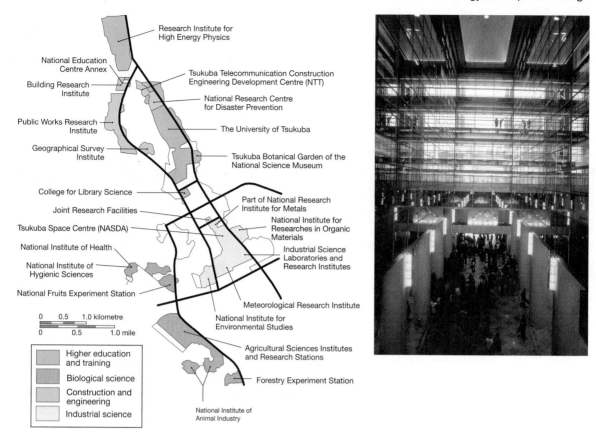

Figure 12.13 Technopolis Tsukuba Science City, about 65 kilometres northeast of Tokyo, has served as a model for the Japanese "Technopolis" program, which is a government-sponsored attempt to create a series of high-tech complexes to serve Japanese industry. Tsukuba was part of a strategic urban plan for the Tokyo metropolitan area, designed to exploit geographical principles of localization and agglomeration to foster Japanese high-tech industry. Although construction began only in the early 1970s, Tsukuba now has a population of over 180,000, of whom more than 12,000 are scientific researchers. The Technopolis program was master-planned by the Japanese Ministry of International Trade and Industry (MITI), and its 26 high-tech complexes will be the cornerstone of future high-tech development in Japan. Each technopolis, or high-tech growth-pole settlement, is designed as a garden-city-type setting for research universities, science centres, industrial research parks, joint research and development consortia, venture capital foundations, office complexes, international convention centres, and residential new towns. (*Source:* Map redrawn with permission from J.L. Bloom and S. Asano, "Tsukuba Science City," *Science,* 212. Copyright © 1981, American Association for the Advancement of Science.)

metropolitan areas in Japan (**Figure 12.13**). By contrast, routine production, testing, and assembly functions have been decentralized to semiperipheral countries—China, Singapore, Taiwan, and South Korea, in particular.

Although future geographies of production and employment will likely follow the same core–periphery pattern, there will also emerge new divisions of labour. India, for instance, has begun to carve a successful niche in software development, mainly because the Indian government invests heavily in engineering education and provides generous tax breaks and liberal foreign-exchange regulations for the industry. "Silicon Plateau" around Bangalore has more than 100 export-oriented software companies that are able to draw on a relatively cheap but highly educated labour pool. Meanwhile, "Multimedia Super Corridor" outside Kuala Lumpur, Malaysia, is emerging as a result of tax breaks that have attracted key investments from Microsoft, Sun Microsystems, Nippon Telegraph, and IBM.

Of most interest to geographers are the spatial effects of information technologies' *applications.* As we have seen in previous chapters, information technologies have already had an enormous impact in facilitating the globalization of industry, finance, and culture. At local and regional scales, although they have been instrumental in decentralizing jobs and residences, their impact has been very uneven across the world. In peripheral countries, for example, computers are mainly used for standard functions of inventory control, accounting, and payroll; but they remain much too expensive for widespread use in homes, small businesses, and local governments. We can expect future impacts of information technologies to exhibit the same unevenness: a marked lag will occur in the diffusion of information technologies to many peripheral regions, thus perpetuating and even accentuating the digital divide between the "fast world" and the "slow world."

12.8 | Geography in the Information Age

The rapid spread of smartphones and cloud computing may enable some "leap-frogging" to occur as it allows peripheral countries to skip some expensive infrastructure requirements, such as copper or fibre-optic cables or a reliable power supply network.

Cyberspace and Virtual Geography   For fast-world countries, such as Canada, the Internet poses very real challenges. On the one hand, there is the obvious potential for Canadian business to defeat the "friction of distance" in cyberspace and so compete on level terms in the global marketplace. On the other hand, because Canadian consumers are able to participate in e-commerce, much business that would have originally been done with local stores now takes place in cyberspace, often with American businesses. In this way, the virtual geography of this country has been fundamentally reconfigured. The way in which Amazon.com has affected the business of many local bookstores across this country is but one example of this process: we are now much "nearer" to book warehouses in the virtual world than we are to bookstores physically down the street—and able to access a far greater inventory.

In effect, e-commerce is not supplementing but competing with Canadian business. As geographer Donald Janelle has recently noted, "even within a country such as Canada, both peripheral and central regions could be impacted adversely. . . . The global centralization of internet technology may favour accumulation of capital at the upper levels in the global urban hierarchy and drain the time and income resources from local regions."[11] Ironically, we may find that the Internet is a technology that is unable to liberate Canada's peripheries and only serves to maintain this country's dependent position vis-à-vis the United States in the world-system.

As we saw throughout this book, cyberspace has its own geography, its "core" and its "periphery" of user access (the "fast" and "slow" worlds), its central nodes and its principal routes. Beyond this, whole imaginary worlds have been created that exist only in a virtual "reality," with their own geographies, and these may be visited at will. Increasingly, access to 3G/4G networks and WiFi links enables us to constantly live on the interface between that virtual reality and the physical reality—with all the implications our retreat from the real world has, particularly on communal life in the city, as Jane Jacobs criticized at the beginning of the chapter.

Cyberspace, of course, intersects with other spaces, and if we now turn our attention to its impact on economic space, we can consider the influence of computer gaming giant Ubisoft and its role as an economic rejuvenator in Montreal (**Figure 12.14**). Founded as a subsidiary of the French parent firm,

---

[11] Donald Janelle, "Globalization, the Internet Economy, and Canada," *Canadian Geographer* 45, 2001, p. 52.

Figure 12.14 Ubisoft Montreal The computer game business has expanded enormously in recent years. Ubisoft, a leading player in this new industry, has rejuvenated old industrial buildings and created thousands of high-tech jobs in Montreal.

Ubisoft Montreal established itself in that city in 1997, with the financial backing of the Quebec provincial government. Located in obsolete factory buildings toward the northern parts of Montreal, Ubisoft now has its own "campus" on St. Laurent Boulevard and has been responsible for the rejuvenation of much of the surrounding area. In an almost textbook-worthy example of Richard Florida's "creative city," Ubisoft's 3,000 highly paid and highly skilled computer programmers and game testers have bought up lofts and condominiums in the immediate vicinity and have also encouraged a resurgence of nearby stores and restaurants.

Further advances in computational capacity, telematics, GIS, smartphones, and computer-driven surveillance will mean that many of the complex, hard-to-manage aspects of society, such as street crime and traffic, will increasingly be subject to automated surveillance and management systems. These developments will bring new ethical challenges. The RCMP's desire to install video surveillance cameras on Kelowna's main street has prompted Canada's privacy commissioner to use a court injunction to prevent public space from being monitored in this way. The commissioner has argued that in this case, the profound challenge to the control of public space outweighs any crime-prevention goal.

New buildings, from individual houses to mega-developments, will be designed and tested in virtual space, and more environments will be "smart." These same technologies will also likely increase the gap between the haves and the have-nots within the fast world. Robotics and computers have already displaced millions of workers in the fast world. As the Information Revolution unfolds and matures, further changes in labour markets can be expected, creating high-wage jobs for those equipped to participate in new, knowledge-based industries. On the other hand, there is no reason to expect any expansion in jobs for unskilled or poorly educated workers. The net result is likely to be an increase in socioeconomic polarization.

WHAT KIND OF FUTURE?

Our review of future geographies and spatial change ends with a look at the interdependent and less-than-predictable dynamics of politics, culture, society, and environment. From what we have discussed already, it seems clear that the immediate future will be characterized by a phase of geopolitical and geoeconomic transition; by the continued overall expansion of the world economy; and by the continued globalization of industry, finance, and culture. In this future, new technologies—various transport technologies, biotechnology, materials technology, and especially information technologies—will be influential in shaping the opportunities and constraints for local, regional, and international development. The processes of change involved in shaping this kind of future will inevitably bring critical issues, conflicts, and threats. We can already identify what several of these might involve: dilemmas of scale, boundaries, and territories; fault lines of cultural dissonance; security concerns; and the sustainability of development.

Scale and Territory

The globalization of the economy is undermining the status of the territorial nation-state as the chief regulating mechanism of both the global and local dimensions of the world-system. This is not to say that nation-states are about to become outmoded. In the future, a strong logic will continue to exist for the territorial powers of nation-states as we discussed in Chapter 9, but the states themselves will become increasingly permeable to flows of capital and information. An awkward situation will arise in which capital, knowledge, entrepreneurship, management, and consumer tastes will continue to globalize, while governments remain locked into their nineteenth-century mould of national territories and institutions.

Without strong nation-states—or some alternative—some important aspects of geographical change will escape the authority of national governments. Consider three examples:

- Commercial information, patents, stocks, bonds, electronic cash transfers, and property deeds will flow in increasing volume across national boundaries, virtually unchecked and possibly untaxed by national governments and their agencies.

- Localities will be drawn more and more into dealing directly with overseas investors in their attempts to promote local development through their own "municipal foreign policy."

- Stealthy, temporary, "virtual states" will emerge illegally from clandestine alliances of political and military leaders and senior government officers to take advantage of the paralysis of national sovereignty.

These are prospective changes at a time when the end of the cold war has left an enormous zone of geopolitical uncertainty. The balance of power that stabilized international politics for 40 years has gone, and its sudden disappearance has revealed the precariousness of many domestic political systems. Previously held together by a common enemy, they are now especially vulnerable to internal economic, ethnic, and cultural divisions.

Some of the consequences are fairly predictable. The nation-states of the world-system core, unable to manage national economies and protect their populations from the winds of global change, will have to cope with severe economic recessions and persistent problems of poverty, unemployment, and homelessness. Mainstream parties of the political centre will become increasingly indistinguishable, leaving electorates to fragment and polarize around "issues" such as xenophobia, racism, family values, personal freedoms, and green politics. Because nation-building had always promoted the idea of a national society and a "national culture," the permeability of nation-states also raises the prospect of national identities leaking away into local "tribes" and lifestyle communities: software clubs, multi-user dungeons, ecologists, hockey fans, fundamentalists, neo-Nazis, and so on. As more and more of our life moves online, these communities also become transnational, eroding the importance of where one physically is or what jurisdiction one is in.

Some of the consequences of weak nation-states are, in fact, already beginning to appear. To stem economic leaks and gain some control over the globalizing economy, these nation-states are forming economic blocs, such as the North American Free Trade Agreement (NAFTA) and the European Union. Meanwhile, as we saw in Chapter 9, many of the same nation-states are accommodating internal cultural cleavages by decentralizing their governmental structures. In other cases, governments are dismantling expensive social welfare programs and opening up previously publicly operated industries (e.g., prisons) to the private sector—often to transnational corporations. For example, Canada's federal and provincial or territorial governments may have to rethink social programs in the name of global economic competition.

Often regarded as a public-sector success story, Canada's social welfare system is now under threat from powerful corporate interests, in the form of the Business Council on National Issues (now known as the Canadian Council of Chief Executives), who have campaigned to privatize and deregulate the government sector. Deregulation would mean the loss or reduction of public control over the environment, transportation, and energy resources, as well as the dismantling of universal social programs, including unemployment insurance, social assistance, health care, and pensions. Canadians have begun to counter-organize through coalitions of volunteer and nonprofit groups, such as the Council of Canadians. This alliance, which has few funds and no official standing, has managed, by an adroit use of the Internet and political theatre, to stir up latent public concern that privatization, deregulation, and trade liberalization could reduce nation-state governments to branch plants of transnational corporations.

The consequences of globalization will be much more dramatic in the world's peripheral regions. However strong governments may be in their apparatus of domestic power, they will be next to helpless in the face of acute environmental stress, increased cultural friction, escalating poverty and disease, and growing migrations of refugees. In these situations, it is possible that people will seek liberation through violence (**Figure 12.15**). The question may be not so much whether war and violence will exist within the periphery, but who will fight whom and for what purpose.

This is how one commentator sees the probable outcome:

> Future wars will be those of communal survival, aggravated or, in many cases, caused by environmental scarcity. These wars will be subnational, meaning that it will be hard for states and local governments to protect their own citizens physically. This is how many states will ultimately die. As state power fades—and with it the state's ability to help weaker groups within society, not to mention other states—peoples and cultures around the world will be thrown back upon their own strengths and weaknesses, with fewer equalizing mechanisms to protect them.[12]

With nation-states weakened through the transnational flow of capital, goods, and services, and the distinction between criminal violence and "legitimate" war blurred, the power of international drug cartels, local mafias, road-warrior platoons, popular militias, guerrilla factions, and private local armies will create the possibility of borderless territories that wax and wane in an ever-mutating space of chaos. Future maps of parts of the world periphery may have to be drawn without clear boundaries, just as medieval maps and the maps of European explorers were.

If this sounds far-fetched, consider some examples from the last decade: in such countries as Afghanistan, Colombia, the DRC, Lebanon, Liberia, Peru, Rwanda, Sri Lanka, Somalia, Sudan, and Uganda, civil wars, armed insurrections, and criminal violence made it difficult to be certain of which group or government controlled what territory. In a few places, the clearly defined *de jure* boundaries of international treaties and school atlases have been rendered

Figure 12.15 Militia factions and road warriors In some parts of Africa, civil war and the breakdown of law and order leave some areas under the control of various private armies, armed gangs, and militarized factions. Some of this conflict is a direct legacy of inter-ethnic tensions created under nineteenth- and early twentieth-century colonialism. This photograph shows Ethiopian militia in position opposite the Eritrean army. (*Source:* Patrick Robert/Corbis Sygma.)

---

[12] R.D. Kaplan, "The Coming Anarchy," *Atlantic Monthly*, February 1994, p. 74.

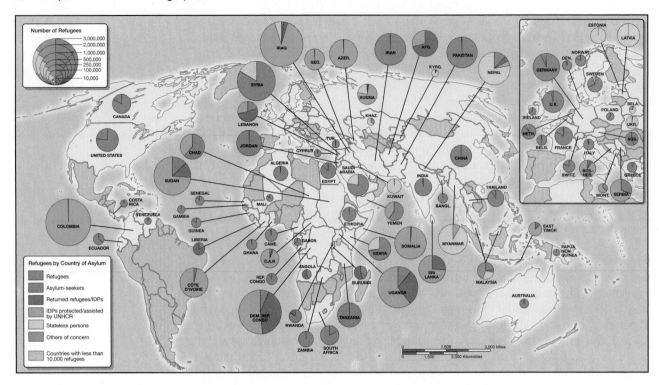

Figure 12.16 Wild zones Parts of Africa, the Middle East, and South Asia have become "wild zones," places where national governments have lost control over economic development, ethnic conflict, and environmental degradation. In 2007, according to estimates supplied by the United Nations High Commissioner for Refugees, there were more than 25 million refugees, asylum seekers, and displaced persons in the world. The map shows the areas of concern listed by the UNHCR in its report for 2007. (*Source:* United Nations High Commissioner for Refugees, *2007 Global Trends: Refugees, Asylum-seekers, Returnees, Internally Displaced and Stateless Persons.* UNHCR, 2008. See **www.unhcr .org/statistics/2007Global-Trends.zip**.)

fictional by *de facto* buffer zones: the Kurdish and Azeri buffer "states" between Turkey and Iran, for example, and the Turkic Uighur buffer territory between Central Asia and China. In the final analysis, most of these failures of the nation-state will bring human suffering and the displacement of large segments of the population as they try to flee the violence (**Figure 12.16**).

Cultural Dissonance

In the realm of culture, globalization has brought a homogenization through the language of consumer goods. The result is a ubiquitous "consumer culture," a "Planet Reebok" that is interlinked by Airbus jets, CNN, music video channels, smartphones, and the Internet; and swamped by Coca-Cola, Budweiser, Subway, iPods, PlayStations, Disney franchising, and formula-driven Hollywood movies. Furthermore, sociologists have recognized that a distinctive culture of "global metropolitanism" is emerging among the self-consciously transnational upper- and middle classes. This is simply homogenized culture at a higher plane of consumption (French wines instead of Budweiser, BMWs instead of Hondas, and so on). The members of this new culture are people who hold international conference calls, make decisions and transact investments that are transnational in scope, edit the news, design and market international products, and travel the world for business and pleasure.

These trends are transcending some of the traditional cultural differences around the world. We can, perhaps, more easily identify with people who use the same products, listen to the same music, and appreciate the same sports stars that we do. In the process, however, sociocultural cleavages are opening up between the haves of the fast world (the elites) and the have-nots of the slow world (the marginalized). By focusing people's attention on material consumption, these trends are also obscuring the emergence of new fault lines—between previously compatible cultural groups and between ideologically divergent civilizations.

Several reasons account for the appearance of these new fault lines. One is the release of pressure brought about by the end of the cold war. The evaporation of external threats has allowed people to focus on other perceived threats and intrusions. Another is the globalization of culture itself. As people's lives are homogenized through their jobs and material culture, many of them want to revive subjectivity, reconstruct we/us feelings, and re-establish a distinctive cultural identity. In the slow world of the have-nots, a different set of processes is at work, however. The juxtaposition of poverty, environmental stress, and crowded living conditions alongside the materialism of Planet Reebok creates a fertile climate for gangsterism. The same juxtaposition also provides the ideal circumstance for the spread and intensification of religious fundamentalism. This, perhaps more than anything else, represents a source of serious potential cultural dissonance.

The overall result is that cultural fault lines are opening up at every geographical scale. This poses the prospect of some very problematic dimensions of future geographies at every scale. The prospect at the metropolitan scale is one of fragmented and polarized communities, with outright cultural conflict suppressed only through electronic surveillance (**Figure 12.17**) and the "militarization" of urban space via security posts and "hardened" urban design using fences and gated communities (**Figure 12.18**). This, of course, presupposes a certain level of affluence to meet the costs of keeping the peace across economic and cultural fault lines. In the unintended metropolises of the periphery, where unprecedented numbers of migrants and refugees will be thrown together, there is the genuine possibility of anarchy and intercommunal violence—unless intergroup differences can be submerged in a common cause, such as religious fundamentalism.

At the regional scale, the prospect is one of increasing ethnic rivalry, parochialism, and insularity. Examples of these phenomena can be found throughout the world. In Europe, they include the secessionism (from Spain) of the Basques and the separatist movement of the Catalans (also in Spain), as well as the regional elitism of Northern Italy, not to mention the outright war between Serbs, Croats, and Bosnians in the 1990s. In South Asia, examples are provided by the recurring hostility between Hindus and Muslims throughout the Indian subcontinent and between the Hindu Tamils and Buddhist Sinhalese of Sri Lanka. In Africa, we can point to the continuing conflict between the Muslim majority in northern

Figure 12.17 Surveillance societies
Social, economic, and ethnic polarization in the cities of the world's core countries has led to an increase in the electronic surveillance of both public and private spaces. Another significant change has been the increased presence of private security personnel in upscale settings: private security officers now outnumber police officers in the United States. This photo shows the interior of Chicago's Office of Emergency Management.

Figure 12.18 The shape of things to come? Economic and social polarizations in the cities of the world's core can lead to significant change in the urban landscape. Increased electronic surveillance is now a feature of many public and private spaces, and the use of private security personnel has become an aspect of urban living in some wealthy neighbourhoods. "Gated communities," such as the one shown in this photograph, may protect their inhabitants, but they do so by excluding other residents of the city, and they create clearly visible physical barriers in the urban fabric.

Sudan and the Christian minority in the south, or the widespread unrest in Central Africa. Where the future brings prosperity, tensions and hostilities such as these will probably abate; where it brings economic hardship or decline, they will undoubtedly intensify.

At the global scale, people might increasingly define their identities in terms of their broader historical, geographical, and racial "civilizations": Western, Latin American, Confucian, Japanese, Islamic, Hindu, and Slavic-Orthodox. According to some observers, deepening cleavages of this sort could replace the ideological differences of the cold war era as the major source of tension and potential conflict in the world, epitomized by the current conflict between Islamism (not Islam!) and the West. But, as some globalization experts have observed, they may also point the way toward new foundations for cooperation and unity as people see themselves less as citizens of a particular nation or state and more as world citizens sharing a common regional cause (see Chapter 9). However, given the steep economic differences that will almost certainly persist between the world's core regions and the periphery, the prospect of an overt "West (and Japan) versus the Rest" scenario for international relations remains at least as likely.

Security

Globalization will inevitably generate enormous economic and, consequently, political upheavals that will translate into a complex set of security issues. With the gradual integration of China, India, and other emerging countries into the global economy, hundreds of millions of working-age adults will become available for employment in a more integrated world labour market. This enormous workforce—a growing portion of which will be well educated—will be a competitive source of low-cost labour at the same time that technological innovation is expanding the range of globally mobile occupations. The transition will hit the middle classes of the core regions in particular, bringing more rapid job turnover and requiring professional retooling, while outsourcing on an increasing scale will intensify the anti-globalization movement.

Where these pressures lead will depend on how political leaders respond, how flexible labour markets become, and whether overall economic growth is sufficiently robust to absorb a growing number of displaced workers. In some regions, it is quite possible that weak governments, lagging economies, religious extremism, and youth bulges will align to create a perfect storm for internal conflict, with far-reaching repercussions for security elsewhere. Such internal conflicts, particularly those that involve ethnic groups straddling national boundaries, risk escalating into regional conflicts and the failure of states, with expanses of territory and populations devoid of effective governmental control. These territories can become sanctuaries for transnational terrorists (such as al-Qaeda in Afghanistan and Yemen) or for criminals and drug cartels (such as in Mexico).

Economic and political turbulence and instability will also be conducive to transnational crime. Transnational crime syndicates pose a considerable threat to global security. They distribute harmful materials, weapons, and drugs; exploit local communities; disrupt fragile ecosystems; and control significant economic resources. In 2007, transnational crime syndicates may have grossed up to US$2 trillion—more than any national economy with the exception of the United States, Japan, or Germany. More than US$520 billion of this comes from counterfeiting and piracy. The drug trade is the second-biggest earner, with an estimated US$320 billion in takings. Trafficking in humans—for labour, sex work, and even for the removal of organs for transplanting—is another aspect of transnational crime. It is a small industry in comparison to drugs, worth under US$44 billion, but arguably the most pernicious aspect of organized crime. The U.S. State Department estimates that at least 600,000 to 800,000 people are sold internationally each year. According to the United Nations, up to 27 million people are now held in slavery, far more than at the peak of the African slave trade. The majority of the victims this time are Asian women. Surprisingly, weapons trafficking earns the syndicates comparatively little—estimated at less than US$1 billion annually—but it contributes significantly to the complex security issues facing most countries.

Sustainability

As we saw in Chapter 4, the world currently faces a daunting list of environmental threats: the destruction of tropical rain forests and the consequent loss of biodiversity; widespread, health-threatening pollution; the degradation of soil, water, and marine resources essential to food production; stratospheric ozone depletion; acid rain; and the list goes on. Most of these threats are greatest in the world's periphery, where daily environmental pollution and degradation amount to a catastrophe that will continue to unfold, slow-motion, as the periphery industrializes—but the effects will be felt worldwide (see **Geography Matters 12.2— The Asian Brown Cloud**).

Global climate change in particular seems to pose its greatest threats to poorer, peripheral countries, as we saw in Chapter 4. If current trends continue, by 2050 the Maldives will be permanently flooded. The fate of these islands in the Indian Ocean is an indicator of what could happen elsewhere. About 70 percent of Bangladesh, for example, is at sea level, while much of Egypt's most fertile land, in the Nile delta, is also at sea level. Meanwhile, extensive regions of Africa, Asia, and Latin America are so marginal for agriculture that further drought could prove disastrous. In contrast, farmers in many core countries in Europe and North America would welcome a local rise in mean temperatures because it would extend their options for the kinds of crops that they could profitably grow. However, we have seen how a rise in temperature in the Canadian Prairies has also increased the number of pests present. Concerns such as these have led many Canadians to take active steps to reduce their own impact on climate change by a variety of initiatives, including recycling and energy conservation schemes, as discussed in more detail in **Human Geography and Climate Change 12.3—Climate Change and Social Action** on p. 560.

Overall, it is likely that future trends will only intensify the contrasts between the rich and poor regions. We know enough about the growth of population and the changing geography of economic development to be able to calculate with some confidence that the air and water pollution generated by semiperipheral and

The Asian Brown Cloud

At the heart of the World Summit on Sustainable Development in Johannesburg in September 2002 was the following question: How can developing nations grow economically without overburdening Earth's environment and creating an uninhabitable planet for future generations? Emblematic of this issue is the Asian Brown Cloud, a blanket of air pollution 3 kilometres thick that hovers over most of the tropical Indian Ocean and South, Southeast, and East Asia, stretching from the Arabian Peninsula across India, Southeast Asia, and China almost to Korea. The brown haze is clearly visible in satellite photographs and from the Himalayas (**Figure 12.2.1**).

The Asian Brown Cloud consists of sulfates, nitrates, organic substances, black carbon, and fly ash, along with several other pollutants. It is an accumulated cocktail of contamination resulting from a dramatic increase in the burning of fossil fuels in vehicles, industries, and power stations in Asia's megacities, from forest fires used to clear land, and from the emissions from millions of inefficient cookers burning wood or cow dung. A study of the Asian Brown Cloud sponsored by the U.N. Environment Program and involving more than 200 scientists suggests that the Asian Brown Cloud not only influences local weather but also may have worldwide consequences.

The smog of the Asian Brown Cloud reduces the amount of solar radiation reaching the Earth's surface by 10 to 15 percent, with a consequent decline in the productivity of crops. But it can also trap heat, leading to warming of the lower atmosphere. It suppresses rainfall in some areas and increases it in others, while damaging forests and crops because of acid rain. The haze is also believed to be responsible for hundreds of thousands of premature deaths from respiratory diseases.

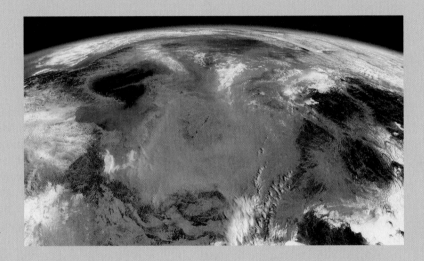

Figure 12.2.1 The Asian Brown Cloud This view shows a dense haze over eastern China, looking eastward across the Yellow Sea toward Korea.

peripheral countries will more than double in the next 15 years. We know, in short, that environmental problems will be inseparable from processes of demographic change, economic development, and human welfare. In addition, it is becoming clear that environmental problems are going to be increasingly enmeshed in matters of national security and regional conflict. For this reason, the Canadian government increasingly talks in terms of **human security**, a concept that encompasses environmental sustainability and population-carrying capacity.

The *spatial interdependence* of economic, environmental, and social problems means that some parts of the world are ecological time bombs. The prospect of civil unrest and mass migrations resulting from the pressures of rapidly growing populations, deforestation, soil erosion, water depletion, air pollution, disease epidemics, and intractable poverty is real. These spectres are alarming not only for the peoples of the affected regions but also for their neighbours and for the peoples of rich and far-away countries, whose continued prosperity will depend on processes of globalization that are not disrupted by large-scale

human security: a concept that includes environmental sustainability and population-carrying capacity in the measure of a country's ability to promote and defend its citizens' interests

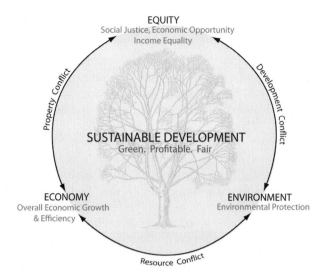

EQUITY
Social Justice, Economic Opportunity
Income Equality

Property Conflict

Development Conflict

SUSTAINABLE DEVELOPMENT
Green. Profitable. Fair

ECONOMY
Overall Economic Growth
& Efficiency

ENVIRONMENT
Environmental Protection

Resource Conflict

Figure 12.19 Sustainability In the long run, there are three key aspects of sustainability—the physical environment, equity, and efficiency—but there are also tensions between each of these.

environmental disasters, unmanageable mass migrations, or the breakdown of stability in the world-system as a whole.

How can we move forward from this seemingly intractable situation? One perspective that has received much attention is the concept of sustainable development. **Sustainable development** is a vision of development that seeks a balance between economic growth, environmental impacts, and social equity (**Figure 12.19**). In practice, sustainable development means that economic growth and change should occur only when the impacts on the environment are benign or manageable and when the impacts (both costs and benefits) on society are fairly distributed across classes and regions. Sustainable development is geared to meeting the needs of the present without compromising the ability of future generations to meet their needs. It envisages a future when improvements to the quality of human life are achieved within the carrying capacity of local and regional ecosystems. **Carrying capacity** is the maximum number of users that can be sustained over the long term by a given set of natural resources.

Sustainable development means using renewable natural resources in a manner that does not eliminate or degrade them—by making greater use, for example, of solar and geothermal energy and by greater use of recycled materials. It means managing economic systems so that all resources—physical and human—are used optimally. It means regulating economic systems so that the benefits of development are distributed more equitably (if only to prevent poverty from causing environmental degradation). It also means organizing societies so that improved education, health care, and social welfare can contribute to environmental awareness and sensitivity and an improved quality of life.

A final and more radical aspect of sustainable development is—as we saw in Chapter 8 with the concepts of locavores and Community Supported Agriculture—a move away from wholesale globalization toward increased "localization": a desire to return to a more locally based economy where production, consumption, and decision making can be oriented to local needs and conditions. Thus, peripheral countries, as well as workers and citizens throughout many parts of the core, are demanding a reinstatement of control over the economic events and institutions that directly shape their lives.

Put this way, sustainable development sounds eminently sensible yet impossibly utopian. The first widespread discussion of sustainability took place in the early 1990s and culminated in the "Earth Summit" (the United Nations Conference on Environment and Development) in Rio de Janeiro in 1992. Attended by 128 heads of state, it attracted intense media attention. At the conference, many examples were described of successful sustainable development programs at the local level. Some of these examples centred on the use of renewable sources of energy, as in the creation of small hydroelectric power stations

sustainable development: a vision of development that seeks a balance among economic growth, environmental impacts, and social equity

carrying capacity: the maximum number of users that can be sustained over the long term by a given set of natural resources

Climate Change and Social Action

Every day, Canadians engage in activities that place pressure on the environment. Once a relatively low priority, attitudes toward climate change have shifted dramatically since the millennium. A 2010 Angus Reid poll,[13] which questioned Canadians from across the country about the environment, found that approximately 60 percent felt that climate change is a fact and is caused by emissions from industry and vehicles. Nearly 40 percent believe that climate change will affect their lives and the lives of future generations. In comparison, only 41 percent of Americans and 38 percent of Britons see climate change as a fact. However, Canadians are even more concerned with broader environmental issues such as air and water pollution and that the federal government has not responded sufficiently to environmental issues.

Canadians have responded to climate change by increasingly purchasing such things as compact fluorescent light bulbs or programmable thermostats. Similarly, the residential recycling rate, or the amount diverted from landfills as a proportion of waste generated, has increased from 19 percent in 2000 to 29 percent in 2006[14] (**Figure 12.3.1**). Increased awareness, access to recycling programs, and an increased range of recyclable products has likely helped this change. Although waste production is a small part of global greenhouse gas emissions, landfill sites produce methane, a greenhouse gas. Recycling also reduces environmental pollution, reduces energy consumption, and conserves materials.[15]

Figure 12.3.1 Recycling Municipalities have increasingly promoted recycling initiatives. In addition to saving landfill space, recycling reduces greenhouse gas production by reducing demand for new products.

Despite our concern with climate change and its effects, the Canadian consumer remains guarded in their response to green products and technology, and most Canadians continue to commute to work alone in a car or truck.[16] Moreover, although public opinion polls such as the Angus Reid poll have consistently shown that a significant percentage of consumers favour environmentally conscious products and companies, consumers' efforts to do so in real life have remained limited. In part, worsening economic conditions since 2008 have meant that consumers tend to be more concerned with economic growth, including job security, as compared to environmental concerns.[17] Reduced spending power has also cut into the purchase of green products. For example, although most major automotive manufacturers are actively selling or developing hybrid vehicles, and Canadians would rather buy an environmentally friendly car than their dream car,[18] sales of hybrid cars still represent only a small portion of the total market share and have in fact fallen with the recession, owing to the premium cost for hybrid vehicles and temporarily lower fuel prices.[19] Green marketing is also increasingly visible in sales promotions, as manufacturers emphasize fuel efficiency and their drive to go green. Interestingly, the "green" incentive is more often economic than ethical, with the uptake of green products encouraging savings or economic benefits.

This underscores a larger problem—despite the desire for green products, interest has not yet translated into large-scale shifts in consumer preferences and purchases. For instance, **green marketing**, or the marketing and sale of products that are presumed to be environmentally safe, still represents a niche market. Barriers to the broader adoption of green products and services include premium prices, low familiarity or lack of knowledge of green products, limited selection, and issues of product standards (i.e., "How green is green?"). Many consumers are fearful of **greenwashing**, a term used to describe the act of misleading consumers regarding the environmental benefits of a product or service or the environmental practices of a company. At the same time, Canadians typically don't want to pay more for green products or other solutions.[20]

[13] Angus Reid Polling Strategies. 2010. *Views on Global Warming Vary in Three Countries*. www.angusreidstrategies.com.

[14] Statistics Canada. 2010. *Envirostats*, 4(4). Ottawa: Government of Canada.

[15] IPCC 4th Assessment Report, 2007, www.ipcc.ch/index.htm.

[16] Statistics Canada. 2007. *Envirostats*, 1(1). Ottawa: Government of Canada.

[17] Angus Reid Polling Strategies. 2009. *Economy Trumps Environment for Americans*. www.angusreidstrategies.com.

[18] Angus Reid Polling Strategies. 2010. *North Americans, Britons, Would Pick a Green Car*. www.angusreidstrategies.com.

[19] Marc-André Hallé, "US Government Artificially Boosts Hybrid Sales," www.Auto123.com.

[20] Martin Mittelstaedt, "Taking the Blame for Eco-Woes," *The Globe and Mail*, 24 April 2008, A5.

Despite problems, green products are gaining increased attention, provided they achieve the same outcome as traditional products. Attempts to encourage green consumers reflect marketing techniques that aim to make consumers aware of options. The Energy Star label, for example, promotes energy-efficient consumer products and is quickly identifiable. More broadly, campaigns have targeted changing social attitudes toward climate change. The rather provocative title of Canada's "Flick Off" campaign (**www.flickoff.org**) has taken the message of climate change and action steps aimed at reducing energy use to Canadian youth. Marketers have increasingly turned to online social networks to pitch their sales, with different networks providing opportunities for users to connect and share. For example, interactive websites may allow people to link and arrange carpools or for reusing of goods. Likewise, shopping sites may allow people to connect and share green products and their reviews. At the same time, marketers are able to directly target and engage consumers by placing advertisements in social networks. Facebook, for instance, allows marketers to directly target members with advertisements based on the member's profile, social connections, and recent online activities.

The greening of the Canadian consumer is a slow and ongoing process, but one that is likely to gather momentum in coming years as consumers are presented with new products and options and consumers increasingly demand greener products. Concurrently, use of recycling and reusing options, along with the incorporation of other green practices, will facilitate a greener society. Overriding this, economic incentives will likely be important in driving change. However, as the IPCC notes, governments will need to be more involved in the mitigation of climate change to ensure that longer-term benefits are realized.[21]

green marketing: the marketing and sale of products that are presumed to be environmentally safe

greenwashing: a term used to describe the act of misleading consumers regarding the environmental benefits of a product or service or the environmental practices of a company

[21] IPCC 4th Assessment Report, 2007, **www.ipcc.ch/index.htm**.

to modernize Nepalese villages. Most examples, however, centred on sustainable agricultural practices for peripheral countries, including the use of intensive agricultural features, such as raised fields and terraces in Peru's Titicaca Basin, techniques that had been successfully used in this difficult agricultural environment for centuries, before European colonization. After the conference, however, many observers commented bitterly on the starkly diverging interests of core countries and peripheral countries that were exposed by the summit. Without radical and widespread changes in value systems and unprecedented changes in political will, "sustainable development" will remain an embarrassing contradiction in terms. Certainly, until the core countries radically cut back their levels of consumption, we will not have seriously met the needs of a sustainable future.

We cannot just wait to see what the future will hold. If we are to have a better future (and if we are to *deserve* a better future), we must use our understanding of the world—and of geographical patterns and processes—to work toward more desirable outcomes. No discipline is more relevant to the ideal of sustainable development than geography. Where else, as British geographer W.M. Adams has observed, can the science of the environment (physical geography) be combined with an understanding of economic, technological, social, political, and cultural change (human geography)? What other discipline offers insights into environmental change, and who but geographers can cope with the diversity of environments and the sheer range of scales at which it is necessary to manage global change?

Those of us in the richer countries of the world have a special responsibility for leadership in sustainable development because our present affluence is based on a cumulative past (and present) exploitation of the world's resources that is disproportionate to our numbers. We also happen to have the financial, technical, and human resources to enable us to take the lead in developing cleaner, less resource-intensive technologies in transforming our economies to protect and work with natural systems, in providing more equitable access to economic opportunities and social services, and in supporting the technological and political frameworks necessary for sustainable development in poor countries. We cannot do it all at once, but we will certainly deserve the scorn of future generations if we do not try.

CONCLUSION

It is clear that the beginning of the twenty-first century is going to be a period of fluid and transitional relationships among and between places, regions, and nations. Nevertheless, we know enough about contemporary patterns and trends, as well as geographical processes, to be able to map out some plausible scenarios for the future. However, we can only guess at some aspects of the future. Two of the most speculative realms are those of politics and technology.

The future of the worst-off peripheral regions could be very bad, indeed. They face unprecedented levels of demographic, environmental, and societal stress, with the events of the next 50 years being played out from a starting point of scarce basic resources, serious environmental degradation, overpopulation, disease, unprovoked crime, refugee migrations, and criminal anarchy.

For the world-system core, however, the long-term question is one of relative power and dominance. The same factors that consolidate the advantages of the core as a whole—the end of the cold war, the availability of advanced telecommunications, the transnational reorganization of industry and finance, the liberalization of trade, and the emergence of a global culture—will also open the possibility of a new geopolitical and geoeconomic order, within which the economic and political relationships among core countries might change substantially.

Many aspects of future geographies will depend on trends in demand for resources and on the exploitation of new technologies. The expansion of the world economy and the globalization of industry will undoubtedly boost the overall demand for raw materials of various kinds, and this will spur the development of previously underexploited but resource-rich regions in Africa, Eurasia, and East Asia (as well as Canada). Raw materials will be only a fraction of future resource needs, however; the main issue, by far, will be energy resources (again, Canada is well positioned).

It also appears that the present phase of globalization has the potential to create such disparities between the haves and the have-nots (as well as between the core and the periphery) that social unrest will ensue. The evidence of increasing dissatisfaction with the contemporary distribution of wealth both within and between the core and the periphery is widespread. In Russia, where public demonstrations against the government have been outlawed for decades, the new Russians are taking to the streets to protest government policies that favour transnational economic development at the expense of workers' minimum wages. In India, farmers damaged a KFC restaurant for its role in dislocating the domestic poultry industry. In Mexico, industrial workers in transnational plants are challenging the absence of health and safety regulations that leave some exposed to harmful chemicals.

At the same time that protests against globalization and new geographies are being waged, the products of a global economy and culture are being widely embraced. The market for blue contact lenses is growing in such unlikely places as Bangkok and Nairobi; plastic surgery to reshape eyes is increasing in many Asian countries. Highway systems, airports, and container facilities are springing up throughout the periphery.

In short, future geographies are being negotiated at this very moment—from the boardrooms of transnational corporations to the huts of remote villagers. The outcomes of these negotiations are still in the making as we, in our daily lives, make seemingly insignificant decisions about what to wear, what to eat, where to work, how to travel, and how to entertain ourselves. These decisions help to either support or undermine the larger forces at work in the global economy, such as where to build factories, what products to make, or how to package and deliver them to the consumer. In short, future geographies can be shaped by us through our understanding of the relatedness of people, places, and regions in a globalized economy.

MAIN POINTS REVISITED

■ **In some ways, the future is already here, embedded in the world's institutional structures and in the dynamics of its populations.**

We know, for example, a good deal about the demographic trends of the next quarter-century, given present populations and birth and death rates. We also know a good deal about the distribution of environmental resources and constraints, the characteristics of local and regional economies, and the legal and political frameworks within which geographical change will probably take place.

■ **New and emerging technologies that are likely to have the most impact in reshaping human geographies include advanced transportation technologies, biotechnology, materials technologies, and information technologies.**

The evolution of the world's geographies has always been shaped by the opportunities and constraints presented to different places and regions by successive technology systems. Many aspects of future geographies will depend on trends in the demand for particular resources and on the exploitation of these new technologies.

■ **We must not underestimate the scope and impact of future environmental change in shaping future geographies.**

Future environmental changes are very hard to predict. However, it is becoming clear that we should—at the very least—consider the possibility of such changes when discussing future geographies and expect some of these changes (such as climate change) to be extremely unpredictable in terms of their local impacts.

■ **The changes involved in shaping future geographies will inevitably bring some critical issues, conflicts, and threats, including important geographical issues that centre on scale, boundaries, and territories; on cultural dissonance; on security; and on the sustainability of development.**

Many of these issues stem from the globalization of the economy, which is undermining the status of the territorial nation-state as the chief regulating mechanism of both global and local dimensions of the world-system. The implications for peripheral places and regions are dismal: no matter how strong governments may be in their apparatus of domestic power, they will be next to helpless in the face of acute environmental stress, increased cultural friction, escalating poverty and disease, and growing migrations of refugees.

Key Terms

carrying capacity (p. 559) **greenwashing** (p. 561) **sustainable development** (p. 559)
green marketing (p. 561) **human security** (p. 558)

Additional Reading

Agnew, J., and S. Corbridge. *Mastering Space: Hegemony, Territory, and International Political Economy.* New York: Routledge, 1995.

Atkinson, R.D. "Technological Change and Cities," *Cityscape: A Journal of Policy Development and Research* 3(3), 1998, 129–170.

Berry, B.J.L. *Long-Wave Rhythms in Economic Development and Political Behavior.* Baltimore: Johns Hopkins University Press, 1991.

Castells, M. *End of Millennium. Vol. 3. The Information Age: Economy, Society and Culture.* Oxford: Blackwell, 1998.

Coates, J.F., J.B. Mahaffie, and A. Hines. *2025: Scenarios of U.S. and Global Society Reshaped by Science and Technology.* Greensboro, NC: Oakhill Press, 1997.

De Alcantara, C.H. (ed.). *Social Futures, Global Visions.* Oxford: Blackwell, 1996.

Diamond, J. *Collapse: How Societies Choose to Fail or Succeed.* New York: Viking Penguin, 2005.

Hammond, A. *Which World? Scenarios for the 21st Century.* Washington, DC: Island Press, 1998.

Huntington, S. "The Clash of Civilizations?" *Foreign Affairs* 72, 1993, 22–49.

Janelle, D. "Globalization, the Internet Economy and Canada," *Canadian Geographer* 45, 2001, 48–53.

Johnston, R.J., P.J. Taylor, and M. Watts (eds.). *Geographies of Global Change.* Cambridge, MA: Blackwell, 1995.

Kaplan, R.D. "The Coming Anarchy," *Atlantic Monthly*, February 1994, 44–76.

Leamer, E.E., and M. Storpes. "The Economic Geography of the Internet Age," *Journal of International Business Studies* 32(4), 2001, 641–665.

Lemmen, D., F. Warren, E. Bush, and J. Lacroix (eds.). *From Impacts to Adaptation: Canada in a Changing Climate 2007.* Ottawa: Natural Resources Canada, 2007, available at http://adaptation.nrcan.gc.ca/.

Nash, A. "Environmental Refugees: Consequences and Policies from a Western Perspective," *Discrete Dynamics in Nature and Society* 3, 1999, 227–238.

O'Tuathail, G., and T. Luke. "Present at the (Dis)integration: Deterritorialization and Reterritorialization in the New Wor(l)d Order," *Annals of the Association of American Geographers* 84, 1994, 381–398.

Sassen, S. *Globalization and Its Discontents.* New York: New Press, 1998.

Slaymaker, O. "Why So Much Concern about Climate Change and So Little Attention to Land Use Change?" *Canadian Geographer* 45, 2001, 71–78.

Thurow, L. *Head to Head: The Coming Economic Battle among Japan, Europe, and America.* New York: William Morrow, 1992.

United Nations. *Global Outlook 2000: An Economic, Social, and Environmental Perspective.* New York: United Nations Publications, 1990.

United Nations Development Programme (UNDP). *UNDP Report 2004.* New York: UNDP, 2004.

Wallace, I. "Sustaining Geography; Sustainable Geographies: The Linked Challenge," *Canadian Geographer* 46, 2002, 98–107.

World Commission on Environment and Development. *Our Common Future.* New York: Oxford University Press, 1987.

Discussion Questions and Research Activities

1. Using census data, construct a population pyramid (see Chapter 3) for any county or city with which you are familiar. What does this tell you about the future population of the locality?

2. Drawing on what you know about the geography of this locality and its regional, national, and global contexts, construct two scenarios of about 200 words each (see Figure 12.1 on p. 528 for brief examples) for the future, each based on different assumptions about resources and technology.

3. Write a short essay (500 words, or two double-spaced, typed pages) in which you outline the possible effects of economic globalization on a particular place or region with which you are familiar.

4. What kind of world would you like to see 20 years from now? What changes would be necessary to make this future possible? What sort of personal sacrifices would you have to make to make it possible? In your answer, draw on the concepts you encountered in this book.

MyGeosciencePlace

Visit **www.mygeoscienceplace.ca** to find chapter review quizzes, videos, maps, and much more.

Glossary

accessibility: the opportunity for contact or interaction from a given point or location in relation to other locations.

acid rain: the wet deposition of acids on Earth created by the natural cleansing properties of the atmosphere.

administrative record linkage: the linking together of a number of different government databases to build one database with much more detailed information on each individual.

adaptability: a broad-based term which encompasses all actions taken to address the changes that climate change produces.

aesthetic: culturally determined standard of beauty and good taste.

age–sex pyramid: a representation of the population based on its composition according to age and sex.

agglomeration diseconomies: the negative economic effects of urbanization and the local concentration of industry.

agglomeration effects: cost advantages that accrue to individual firms because of their location among functionally related activities.

aging: a term used to describe the effects of an increasing proportion of older age groups on the population.

agrarian: referring to the culture of agricultural communities and the type of tenure system that determines access to land and the kind of cultivation practices employed there.

agribusiness: a set of economic and political relationships that organizes agro-food production from the development of seeds to the retailing and consumption of the agricultural product.

agricultural industrialization: the process whereby the farm has moved from being the centerpiece of agricultural production to becoming one part of an integrated string of vertically organized industrial processes including production, storage, processing, distribution, marketing, and retailing.

agriculture: a science, an art, and a business directed at the cultivation of crops and the raising of livestock for sustenance and profit.

allophone: a person whose mother tongue is neither English nor French.

ancillary activities: such activities as maintenance, repair, security, and haulage services that serve a variety of industries.

anglophone: a person whose mother tongue is English.

animistic perspective on nature: the view that natural phenomena—both animate and inanimate—possess an indwelling spirit or consciousness.

areal units: spatial units of measurement, such as a city block or province, used for recording statistics.

baby boom: the increased number of births in the two decades following World War II.

backwash effects: the negative impacts on a region of the economic growth of some other region.

basic functions: economic activities that provide income from sales to customers beyond city limits.

Beaux Arts: a style of urban design that sought to combine the best elements of all of the classic architectural styles.

biofuels: fuels made from plant material including corn, soy, and sugar cane.

biotechnology: any technique that uses living organisms (or parts of organisms) to improve, make, or modify plants and animals or to develop microorganisms for specific uses.

brownfield site: abandoned, idle, or underused industrial and commercial land on which redevelopment is hindered by the effects of contamination.

Buddhist perspective on nature: the view that nothing exists in and of itself and everything is part of a natural, complex, and dynamic totality of mutuality and interdependence.

carbon benefit: the reduction in carbon dioxide emissions for the same quantity of fuel.

carbon neutral: any carbon released upon burning is equivalent to the carbon absorbed when the plants grew.

carbon tax: a tax on emissions of CO_2 and other greenhouse gases.

carrying capacity: the maximum number of users that can be sustained over the long term by a given set of natural resources.

census: the count of the number of people in a country, region, or city.

centrality: the functional dominance of cities within an urban system.

central business district (CBD): the central nucleus of commercial land uses in a city.

central places: settlements in which certain products and services are available to consumers.

central place theory: a theory that seeks to explain the relative size and spacing of towns and cities as a function of people's shopping behaviours.

centrifugal forces: forces that can lead to the disintegration of the state.

centripetal forces: forces that integrate the state.

chemical farming: the application of synthetic fertilizers to the soil and herbicides, fungicides, and pesticides to crops to enhance yields.

City Beautiful movement: an attempt to remake cities in ways that would reflect the higher values of society, using neo-classical architecture, grandiose street plans, parks, and inspirational monuments and statues.

cognitive distance: the distance that people perceive to exist in a given situation.

cognitive images (mental maps): psychological representations of locations that are created from people's individual ideas and impressions of these locations.

cognitive space: space defined and measured in terms of the nature and degree of people's values, feelings, beliefs, and perceptions about locations, districts, and regions.

cohort: a group of individuals who share a common temporal demographic experience.

colonial cities: cities that were deliberately established or developed as administrative or commercial centres by colonial or imperial powers.

colonialism: the establishment and maintenance of political and legal domination by a state over a separate society.

commercial agriculture: farming primarily for sale, not for direct consumption.

commodity chains: networks of labour and production processes beginning with the extraction or production of raw materials and ending with the delivery of a finished commodity.

confederation: a grouping of independent jurisdictions, such as provinces, into a larger unit that is given separate powers.

conformal projections: map projections on which compass bearings are rendered accurately.

congregation: the territorial and residential clustering of specific groups or subgroups of people.

conservation: the view that natural resources should be used wisely and that society's effects on the natural world should represent stewardship, not exploitation.

core regions: regions that dominate trade, control the most advanced technologies, and have high levels of productivity within diversified economies.

cosmopolitanism: an intellectual and aesthetic openness toward divergent experiences, images, and products from different cultures.

counterurbanization: the net loss of population from cities to smaller towns and rural areas.

creative destruction: the withdrawal of investments from activities (and regions) that yield low rates of profit to reinvest in new activities (and new places).

crude birth rate (CBR): the ratio of the number of live births in a single year for every thousand people in the population.

crude death rate (CDR): the number of deaths in a single year for every thousand people in the population.

crude density (arithmetic density): the total number of people divided by the total land area.

cultural adaptation: the use of complex strategies by human groups to live successfully as part of a natural system.

cultural ecology: the study of the relationship between a cultural group and its natural environment.

cultural geography: study of the ways in which space, place, and landscape shape culture at the same time that culture shapes space, place, and landscape.

cultural hearth: the geographical origin or source of innovations, ideas, or ideologies (term coined by geographer Carl Sauer).

cultural landscape: a characteristic and tangible outcome of the complex interactions between a human group and a natural environment.

cultural nationalism: an effort to protect regional and national cultures from the homogenizing impacts of globalization.

cultural region: the area within which a particular cultural system prevails.

cultural system: a collection of interacting elements that, taken together, shape a group's collective identity.

cultural trait: a single aspect of the complex of routine practices that constitute a particular cultural group.

culture: a shared set of meanings that are lived through the material and symbolic practices of everyday life.

cumulative causation: a spiral buildup of advantages that occurs in specific geographical settings as a result of the development of external economies, agglomeration effects, and localization economies.

cycle of poverty: transmission of poverty and deprivation from one generation to another through a combination of domestic circumstances and local neighbourhood conditions.

D

decolonization: the re-acquisition of control by colonized peoples over their own territory.

deep ecology: an approach to nature revolving around two key ideas: self-realization and biospherical egalitarianism.

deforestation: the removal of trees from a forested area without adequate replanting.

deindustrialization: a relative decline in industrial employment in core regions.

democratic rule: a system in which public policies and officials are directly chosen by popular vote.

demographic collapse: phenomenon of near genocide of indigenous populations.

demographic transition: the replacement of high birth and death rates by low birth and death rates.

demography: the study of the characteristics of human populations.

dependency ratio: the measure of the economic impact of the young and old on the more economically productive members of the population.

derelict landscapes: landscapes that have experienced abandonment, misuse, disinvestment, or vandalism.

desertification: the degradation of land cover and damage to the soil and water in grasslands and arid and semi-arid lands.

dialects: regional variations from standard language, in terms of accent, vocabulary, and grammar.

diaspora: a spatial dispersion of a previously homogeneous group.

digital divide: inequality of access to telecommunications and information technology, particularly the Internet.

distance-decay function: the rate at which a particular activity or process diminishes with increasing distance.

division of labour: the specialization of different people, regions, or countries in particular kinds of economic activities.

domino theory: the belief that if one country in a region chose or was forced to accept a communist political and economic system, then neighbouring countries would fall to communism as well.

doubling time: the measure of how long it will take the population of an area to grow to twice its current size.

dualism: the juxtaposition in geographical space of the formal and informal sectors of the economy.

E

East–West divide: communist and noncommunist countries, respectively.

ecofeminism: the view that patriarchal ideology is at the centre of our present environmental malaise.

ecological footprint: a measure of the biologically productive land area needed to support a population by providing for its needs and absorbing its wastes.

ecological imperialism: introduction of exotic plants and animals into new ecosystems.

eco-migration: a population movement caused by the degradation of land and essential natural resources.

economic base: set of manufacturing, processing, trading, or service activities that serve markets beyond the city.

economies of scale: cost advantages to manufacturers that accrue from high-volume production, since the average cost of production falls with increasing output.

ecosystem: a community of different species interacting with one another and with the larger physical environment that surrounds them.

ecotourism: an activity which, in addition to following the goals of "sustainable tourism," also (1) contributes to the conservation of an area's natural and cultural heritage; (2) includes local indigenous communities in its planning; (3) interprets the natural and cultural heritage of the destination to the visitor; and (4) is aimed at smallsized groups.

ecumene: the total habitable area of a country. Because it depends on the prevailing technology, the available ecumene varies over time. It is an important concept in Canada's case, because the ecumene is so much smaller than the country's total area.

edge cities: nodal concentrations of shopping and office space that are situated on the outer fringes of metropolitan areas, typically near major highway intersections.

emigration: a movement in which a person *leaves* a country.

Enlightenment: an eighteenthcentury European movement that sought to replace ideas of authority or explanation drawn from God with those that individual humans could establish through their own reason.

environmental determinism: a doctrine holding that human activities are controlled by the environment.

environmental ethics: a philosophical perspective that prescribes moral principles as guidance for our treatment of nature.

environmental justice: movement reflecting a growing political consciousness, largely among the world's poor, that their immediate environs are far more toxic than those in wealthier neighbourhoods.

environmental refugees: people who have been physically displaced from their homes and livelihoods by the deterioration of the local environment.

environmental scarcity: a scarcity of renewable natural resources that, if not addressed by technological, social, or economic means, may cause social disruption or violent conflict.

epidemiological transition: a theory stating that the prevailing forms of illness changed from infectious to degenerative types as the demographic transition occurred.

equal-area (equivalent) projections: map projections that portray areas on Earth's surface in their true proportions.

ethnicity: a socially created system of rules about who belongs and who does not belong to a particular group based on actual or perceived commonality.

ethnocentrism: the attitude that a person's own race and culture are superior to those of others.

ethology: the scientific study of the formation and evolution of human customs and beliefs.

external arenas: regions of the world not yet absorbed into the modern world-system.

external economies: cost savings that result from circumstances beyond a firm's own organization and methods of production.

export-processing zones (EPZs): small areas within which especially favourable investment and trading conditions are created by governments to attract exportoriented industries.

F

family reconstitution: the process of reconstructing individual and family life histories by linking together separately recorded birth, marriage, and death data.

fast world: people, places, and regions directly involved, as producers and consumers, in transnational industry, modern telecommunications, materialistic consumption, and international news and entertainment.

federal state: a form of government in which powers are divided between the federal government and smaller units of government (such as provinces) within the country.

feminist geography: a field that examines the extent to which women and men experience spaces and places differently and how these differences themselves are part of the social construction of gender as well as that of place.

fertility: the childbearing performance of individuals, couples, groups, or populations.

fishing capacity: the ability of a fleet to catch fish, most easily measured by counting the number of boats in a fishing fleet.

food chain: five central and connected sectors (inputs, production, product processing, distribution, and consumption) with four contextual elements acting as external mediating forces (the state, international trade, the physical environment, and credit and finance).

food manufacturing: adding value to agricultural products through a range of treatments—such as processing, canning, refining, packing, and packaging—that occur off the farm and before they reach the market.

food regime: the specific set of links that exist between food production and consumption, as well as capital investment and accumulation opportunities.

forced migration: the movement by an individual against his or her will.

foreign direct investment: overseas business investments made by private companies.

francophone: a person whose mother tongue is French.

friction of distance: the deterrent or inhibiting effect of distance on human activity.

G

Garden City movement: an attempt to plan cities in ways that combined the benefits of urban living with the spaciousness and environmental quality of rural life.

gateway city: a city that serves as a link between one country or region and others because of its physical situation.

gender: category reflecting the social differences between men and women rather than the anatomical differences that are related to sex.

genre de vie: a functionally organized way of life that is characteristic of a particular cultural group.

gentrification: the movement into older, centrally located workingclass neighbourhoods by higher-income households seeking the character and convenience of less-expensive and well-located residences.

geodemographic analysis: the practice of assessing the location and composition of particular populations.

Geodemographic research: investigation using census data and commercial data (such as sales data and property records) about the populations of small districts to create profiles of those populations for market research.

geographical path dependence: the historical relationship between the present activities associated with a place and the past experiences of that place.

geographic information system (GIS): an organized collection of computer hardware, software, and geographical data that is designed to capture, store, update, manipulate, and display spatially referenced information.

geopolitics: the state's power to control space or territory and shape the foreign policy of individual states and international political relations.

global change: combination of political, economic, social, historical, and environmental problems at the world scale.

globalization: the increasing interconnectedness of different parts of the world through common processes of economic, environmental, political, and cultural change.

globalized agriculture: a system of food production increasingly dependent on an economy and a set of regulatory practices that are global in scope and organization.

Global Positioning System (GPS): a system of satellites that orbit Earth on precisely predictable paths, broadcasting highly accurate time and locational information.

green marketing: the marketing and sale of products that are presumed to be environmentally safe.

Green Revolution: the export of a technological package of fertilizers and high-yielding seeds, from the core to the periphery, to increase global agricultural productivity.

greenwashing: a term used to describe the act of misleading consumers regarding the environmental benefits of a product or service or the environmental practices of a company.

gross domestic product (GDP): an estimate of the total value of all materials, foodstuffs, goods, and services produced by a country in a particular year.

gross migration: the total number of migrants moving into and out of a place, region, or country.

gross national income (GNI): similar to GDP, but also includes the value of income from abroad and excludes the taxes and wages a country pays to outside interests.

gross national product (GNP): similar to GDP, but also includes the value of income from abroad.

growth poles: economic activities that are deliberately organized around one or more high-growth industries.

guest workers: individuals who migrate temporarily to take jobs in other countries.

H

hegemony: domination over the world economy exercised by one national state in a particular historical epoch through a combination of economic, military, financial, and cultural means.

hinterland: the sphere of economic influence of a town or city.

historical geography: the study of the geography of the past.

home language: the language most often spoken at home by an individual (as defined by Statistics Canada).

human geography: the study of the spatial organization of human activity and of people's relationships with their environments.

human security: a concept that includes environmental sustainability and population-carrying capacity in the measure of a country's ability to promote and defend its citizens' interests.

humanistic approach: places the individual—especially individual values, meaning systems, intentions, and conscious acts—at the centre of analysis.

hunting and gathering: activities whereby people feed themselves through killing wild animals and fish and gathering fruits, roots, nuts, and other edible plants.

I

imagined community: a group of people who believe that they share a common bond and thus are part of the same nation.

immigration: a movement in which a person *arrives in* another country.

imperialism: the extension of the power of a nation through direct or indirect control of the economic and political life of other territories.

import substitution: the process by which domestic producers provide goods or services that formerly were bought from foreign producers.

infant mortality rate: the annual number of deaths of infants under one year of age compared with the total number of live births for that same year.

informal sector: economic activities that take place beyond official record and are not subject to formalized systems of regulation and remuneration.

infrastructure (fixed social capital): the underlying framework of services and amenities needed to facilitate productive activity.

initial advantage: the critical importance of an early start in economic development; a special case of external economies.

intensive subsistence agriculture: practice that involves the effective and efficient use—usually through a considerable expenditure of human labour and application of fertilizer—of a small parcel of land to maximize crop yield.

internal migration: a move within a particular country or region.

international migration: a move from one country to another.

international organization: a group that includes two or more states seeking political or economic cooperation with each other.

invasion and succession: a process of neighbourhood change whereby one social or ethnic group succeeds another.

Islamic perspective on nature: the view that the heavens and Earth were made for human purposes.

isolate: a language that has no known relationship with any other and cannot be assigned to a language family.

isotropic surface: a hypothetical, uniform plane—flat and with no variations in its physical attributes.

J

Judeo-Christian perspective on nature: the view that nature was created by God and is subject to God in the same way that a child is subject to parents.

L

landscape as text: the idea that landscapes can be read and written by groups and individuals.

language: a means of communicating ideas or feelings by means of a conventionalized system of signs, gestures, marks, or articulate vocal sounds.

language branch: a collection of languages that possess a definite common origin but have split into individual languages.

language family: a collection of individual languages believed to be related in their prehistoric origin.

language group: a collection of several individual languages that are part of a language branch, share a common origin, and have similar grammar and vocabulary.

language shift: an indicator of the number of people who adopt a new language, usually measured by the difference between mother tongue and home language populations.

latitude: the angular distance of a point on Earth's surface, *measured north or south* from the equator, which is 0°.

law of diminishing returns: the tendency for productivity to decline, after a certain point, with the continued application of capital or labour or both to a given resource base.

leadership cycles: periods of international power established by individual states through economic, political, and military competition.

life expectancy: the average number of years an individual can expect to live.

localization economies: cost savings that accrue to particular industries as a result of clustering together at a specific location.

longitude: the angular distance of a point on Earth's surface, *measured east or west* from the prime meridian (the line that passes through both poles and through Greenwich, England, and that has the value of 0°).

M

map projection: a systematic rendering on a flat surface of the geographic coordinates of the features found on Earth's surface.

masculinism: the assumption that the world is, and should be, shaped mainly by men for men.

maximum sustainable yield (MSY): the equilibrium between a fish population's biological productivity and the level of fishing effort; theoretically, the MSY for a fish stock is the largest number that can be caught while ensuring that enough remain for a productive fishery next year.

mechanization: the replacement of human farm labour with machines.

medical geography: a subdiscipline of geography that studies the interconnections between population, health, and the environment.

megacities: very large cities characterized by high centrality within their national economy.

metropolitanism: the process by which the economic growth of a city enables it to attain a position of national dominance and, in so doing, creates the geographical structure of a metropolis and hinterland.

middle cohort: members of the population 15 to 64 years of age who are considered economically active and productive.

migration: a long-distance move to a new location.

mini-system: a society with a single cultural base and a reciprocal social economy.

minority groups: population subgroups that are seen—or that see themselves—as somehow different from the general population.

mobility: the ability to move, either permanently or temporarily.

model: often described as a theory or concept, a model is best thought of as "a simplification of reality" designed to help generalize our understanding of a particular process or set of phenomena; it can take the form of a diagram, equation, or simple verbal statement (such as a law) and may be used as a summary of past and present behaviour or to predict future events.

modern movement: the idea that buildings and cities should be designed and run like machines.

modernism: a forward-looking view of the world that emphasizes reason, scientific rationality, creativity, novelty, and progress.

mother tongue: the first language learned at home in childhood and still understood by the individual at the time of the census (as defined by Statistics Canada).

N

nation: a group of people often sharing common elements of culture, such as religion or language, or a history or political identity.

nationalism: the feeling of belonging to a nation as well as the belief that a nation has a natural right to determine its own affairs.

nation-state: an ideal form consisting of a homogeneous group of people governed by their own state.

natural decrease: the difference between the CDR and the CBR, which is the deficit of births relative to deaths.

natural increase: the difference between the CBR and the CDR, which is the surplus of births over deaths.

nature: a social creation as well as the physical universe that includes human beings.

neo-colonialism: economic and political strategies by which powerful states in core economies indirectly maintain or extend their influence over other areas or people.

net migration: the gain or loss in the total population of a particular area as a result of migration.

nonbasic functions: economic activities that serve a city's own population.

North–South divide: the differentiation made between the colonizing states of the Northern Hemisphere and the formerly colonized states of the Southern Hemisphere.

O

official languages: languages (in Canada, English and French) in which the government has a legal obligation to conduct its affairs, and in which the public has the right to receive federal services.

offshore financial centres: islands or microstates that have become specialized nodes in the geography of worldwide financial flows.

oil sands: a mixture of bitumen (a type of oil), sand, clay, and water.

old-age cohort: members of the population 65 years of age and older who are considered beyond their economically active and productive years.

ordinary landscapes (vernacular landscapes): the everyday landscapes that people create in the course of their lives.

overurbanization: a condition in which cities grow more rapidly than the jobs and housing they can sustain.

P

Paleolithic period: the period when chipped-stone tools first began to be used.

participation rate: the proportion of a cohort or group that becomes involved in a specific activity, such as attending an educational institution.

pastoralism: subsistence activity that involves the breeding and herding of animals to satisfy the human needs of food, shelter, and clothing.

peripheral regions: regions with dependent and disadvantageous trading relationships, obsolete technologies, and undeveloped or narrowly specialized economies with low levels of productivity.

picturesque: a landscape design inspired by eighteenth-century landscape painters in the Romantic tradition.

place: a concept with two levels of meaning: (1) an objective location that has both uniqueness and interdependence with other places; (2) a subjective social and cultural construct—somewhere that has personal meaning for individuals or groups.

place making: any activity, deliberate or unintentional, that enables space to acquire meaning.

plantations: large landholdings that usually specialize in the production of one particular crop for market.

political ecology: an approach to cultural geography that studies human–environment relationships through the relationships of patterns of resource use to political and economic forces.

postmodernism: a view of the world that emphasizes an openness to a range of perspectives in social inquiry, artistic expression, and political empowerment.

postmodern urban design: a style characterized by a diversity of architectural styles and elements, often combined in the same building or project.

preservation: an approach to nature advocating that certain habitats, species, and resources should remain off-limits to human use, regardless of whether the use maintains or depletes the resource in question.

primacy: a condition in which the population of the largest city in an urban system is disproportionately large in relation to the second- and third-largest cities in that system.

primary activities: economic activities that are concerned directly with natural resources of any kind.

producer services: services that enhance the productivity or efficiency of other firms' activities or that enable them to maintain specialized roles.

proxemics: the study of the social and cultural meanings that people give to personal space.

pull factors: forces of attraction that influence migrants to move to a particular location.

push factors: events and conditions that impel an individual to move away from a location.

Q

quaternary activities: economic activities that deal with the handling and processing of knowledge and information.

R

race: a problematic classification of human beings based on skin colour and other physical characteristics.

range: the maximum distance that consumers will normally travel to obtain a particular product or service.

rank-size rule: a statistical regularity in city-size distributions of countries and regions.

reapportionment: the process of allocating electoral seats to geographical areas.

region: a larger-sized territory that encompasses many places, all or most of which share similar attributes that are distinct from the attributes of places elsewhere.

regional geography: the study of the ways in which unique combinations of environmental and human factors produce territories with distinctive landscapes and cultural attributes.

regionalism: a feeling of collective identity based on a population's politico-territorial identification within a state or across state boundaries.

religion: belief system and a set of practices that recognize the existence of a power higher than humans.

remote sensing: the collection of information about parts of Earth's surface by means of aerial photography or satellite imagery designed to record data on visible, infrared, and microwave sensor systems.

resiliency: a measure of how damaging an event will be and how quickly and efficiently an area or group of vulnerable people within an area will recover from such an event.

romanticism: the philosophy that emphasizes interdependence and relatedness between humans and nature.

S

sacred space: an area recognized by individuals or groups as worthy of special attention as a site of special religious experiences or events.

scale: the general concept that there are various scales or levels of analysis (local, regional, national, global), that they are linked, and that processes operating at one scale can have significance at other.

secondary activities: economic activities that process, transform, fabricate, or assemble the raw materials derived from primary activities, or that reassemble, refinish, or package manufactured goods.

segregation: the spatial separation of specific population subgroups within a wider population.

self-determination: the right of a group with a distinctive politicoterritorial identity to determine its own destiny, at least in part, through the control of its own territory.

semiotics: the practice of writing and reading signs.

semiperipheral regions: regions that are able to exploit peripheral regions but are themselves exploited and dominated by core regions.

sense of place: feelings evoked among people as a result of the experiences and memories that they associate with a place and the symbolism they attach to it.

shifting cultivation: a system in which farmers aim to maintain soil fertility by rotating the fields within which cultivation occurs.

shock city: a city that is seen as the embodiment of surprising and disturbing changes in economic, social, and cultural lives.

siltation: the buildup of sand and clay in a natural or artificial waterway.

site: the physical attributes of a location—its terrain, soil, vegetation, and water sources, for example.

situation: the location of a place relative to other places and human activities.

slow world: people, places, and regions whose participation in transnational industry, modern telecommunications, materialistic consumption, and international news and entertainment is limited.

society: sum of the inventions, institutions, and relationships created and reproduced by human beings across particular places and times.

sovereignty: the exercise of state power over people and territory, recognized by other states and codified by international law.

spatial diffusion: the way in which things spread through space and over time.

spatial justice: the fairness of the distribution of society's burdens and benefits, taking into account spatial variations in people's needs and in their contributions to the production of wealth and social well-being.

spread effects: the positive impacts on a region of the economic growth of some other region.

squatter settlements: residential developments on land that is neither owned nor rented by its occupants.

staples thesis: a proposition arguing that the export of Canada's natural resources, or staples, locked this country into dependency as a resource hinterland for more advanced economies and so delayed the maturing of its own economy.

staples trap: an over-reliance on the export of staples makes an economy (national or regional) vulnerable to fluctuations in world prices and without alternatives when resource depletion occurs.

sublime: a landscape so impressive that it inspires awe or wonder.

subsistence agriculture: farming for direct consumption by the producers, not for sale.

supranational organizations: collections of individual states with a common goal that may be economic and/or political in nature; such organizations diminish, to some extent, individual state sovereignty in favour of the group interests of the membership.

sustainable development: a vision of development that seeks a balance among economic growth, environmental impacts, and social equity.

swidden: land that is cleared using the slash-and-burn process and is ready for cultivation.

symbolic landscapes: representations of particular values or aspirations that the builders and financiers of those landscapes want to impart to a larger public.

T

Taoist perspective on nature: the view that nature should be valued for its own sake, not for how it might be exploited.

technology: physical objects or artifacts, activities or processes, and knowledge or know-how.

technology systems: clusters of interrelated energy, transportation, and production technologies that dominate economic activity for several decades at a time.

territoriality: the persistent attachment of individuals or peoples to a specific location or territory.

territorial organization: a system of government formally structured by area, not by social groups.

territory: the delimited area over which a state exercises control and that is recognized by other states.

tertiary activities: economic activities involving the sale and exchange of goods and services.

threshold: the minimum market size required to make the sale of a particular product or service profitable.

topological space: the connections between, or connectivity of, particular points in space.

topophilia: the emotions and meanings associated with particular places that have become significant to individuals.

total fertility rate (TFR): the average number of children a woman will have throughout the years that demographers have identified as her childbearing years, approximately ages 15 through 49.

transhumance: the movement of herds according to seasonal rhythms: warmer, lowland areas in the winter and cooler, highland areas in the summer.

transnational corporations: companies with investments and activities that span international boundaries and with subsidiary companies, factories, offices, or facilities in several countries.

U

underclass: a subset of the poor, isolated from mainstream values and the formal labour market.

unitary state: a form of government in which power is concentrated in the central government.

urban ecology: the social and demographic composition of city districts and neighbourhoods.

urban form: the physical structure and organization of cities.

urban system: an interdependent set of urban settlements within a specified region.

urbanism: the way of life, attitudes, values, and patterns of behaviour fostered by urban settings.

urbanization economies: external economies that accrue to producers because of the package of infrastructure, ancillary activities, labour, and markets typically associated with urban settings.

utility: the usefulness of a specific place or location to a particular person or group.

V

visualization: a computer-assisted representation of spatial data, often involving three-dimensional images and innovative perspectives, that reveals spatial patterns and relationships more effectively.

vital records: information about births, deaths, marriages, divorces, and the incidences of certain infectious diseases.

voluntary migration: the movement by an individual based on choice.

vulnerability: a concept relating to the total exposure to risk brought on by climate change.

vulnerable populations: populations that include common characteristics making them more susceptible to "fall through the cracks," including the very young, the old, and those with existing health conditions.

W

world-empire: mini-systems that have been absorbed into a common political system while retaining their fundamental cultural differences.

world-system: an interdependent system of countries linked by economic and political competition.

Y

youth cohort: members of the population who are less than 15 years of age and generally considered too young to be fully active in the labour force.

Z

zionism: a late nineteenth-century European movement to establish a legally recognized home in Palestine for the Jewish people.

zone in transition: area of mixed commercial and residential land uses surrounding the CBD.

Photo Credits

Index